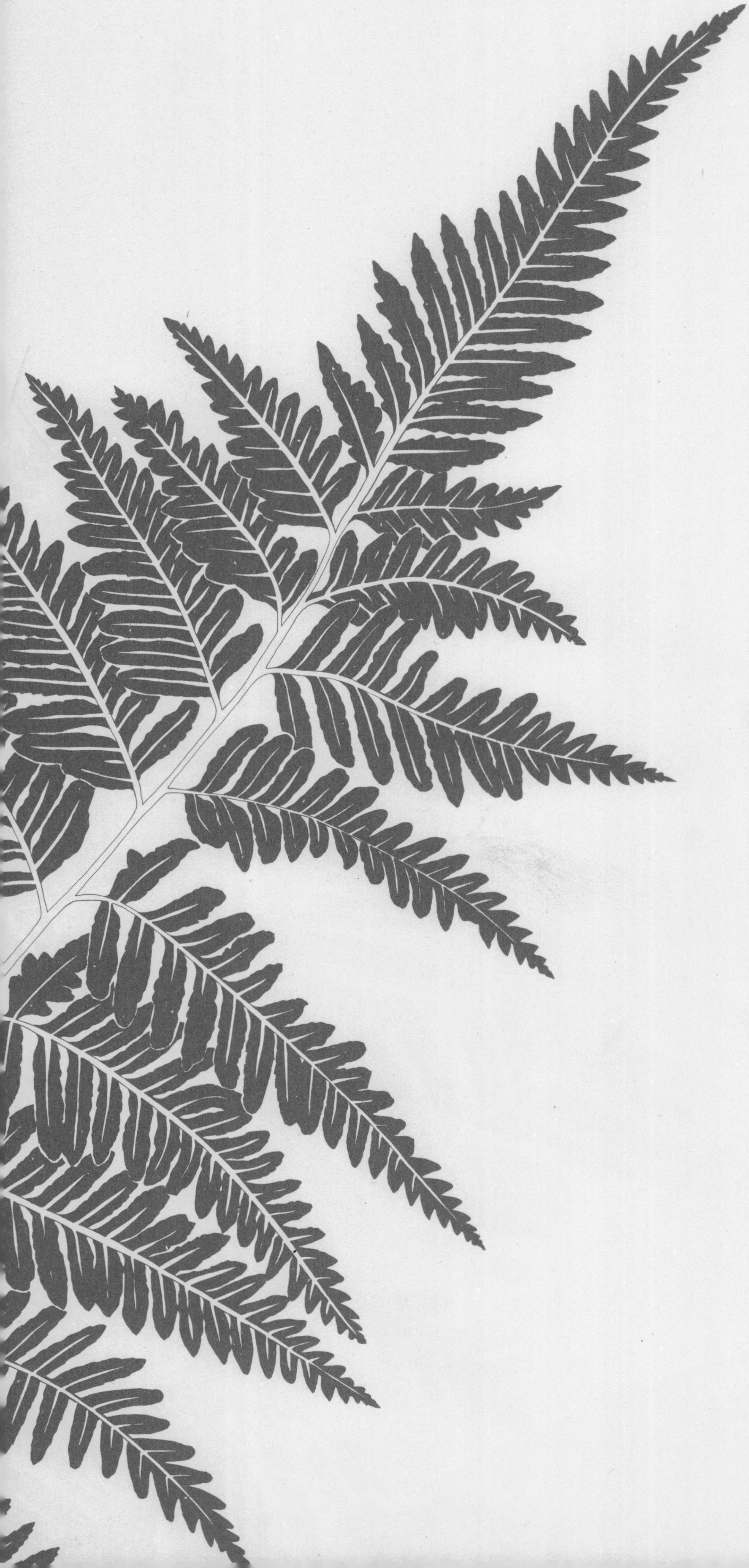

Salute to NEW ZEALAND

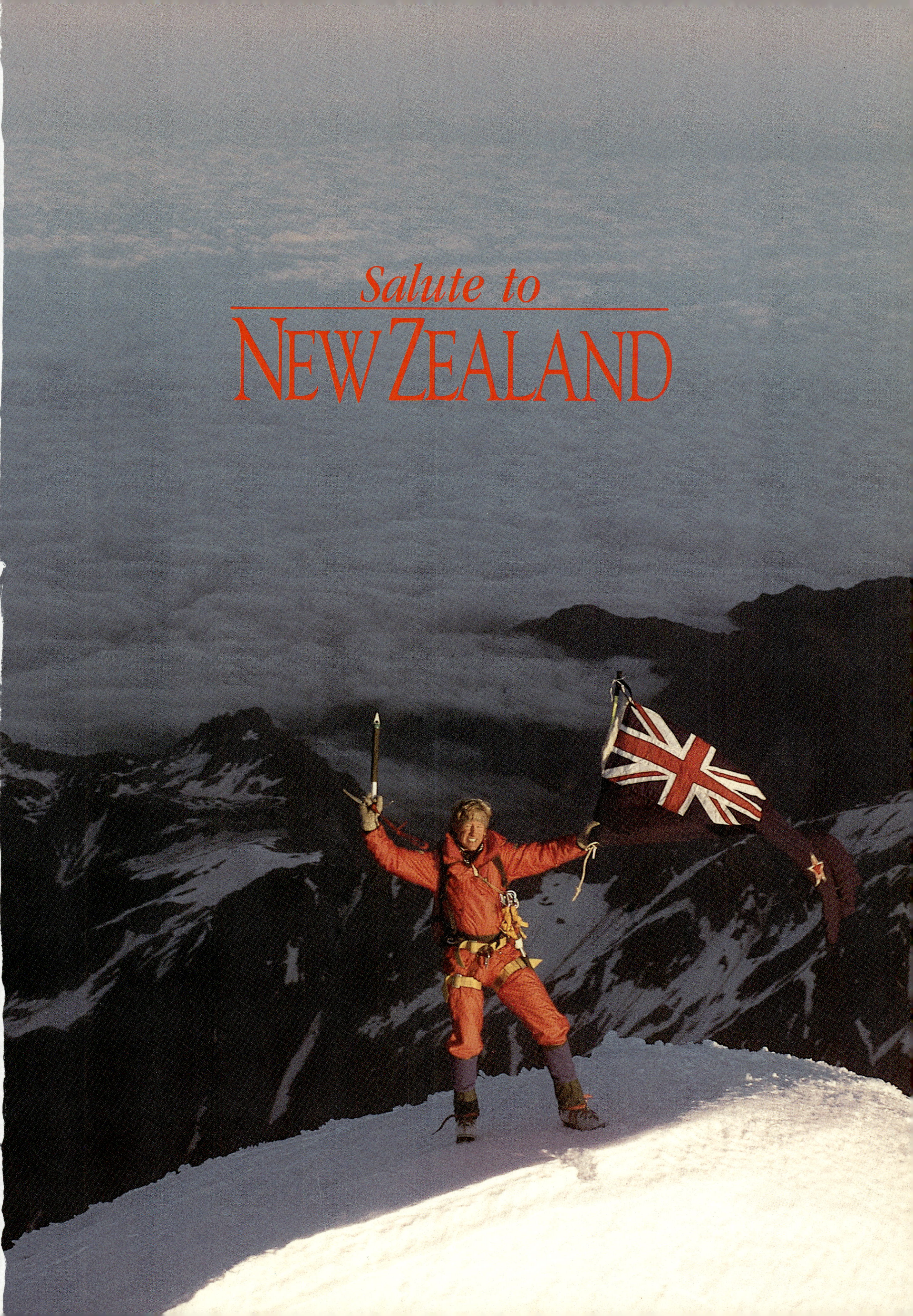

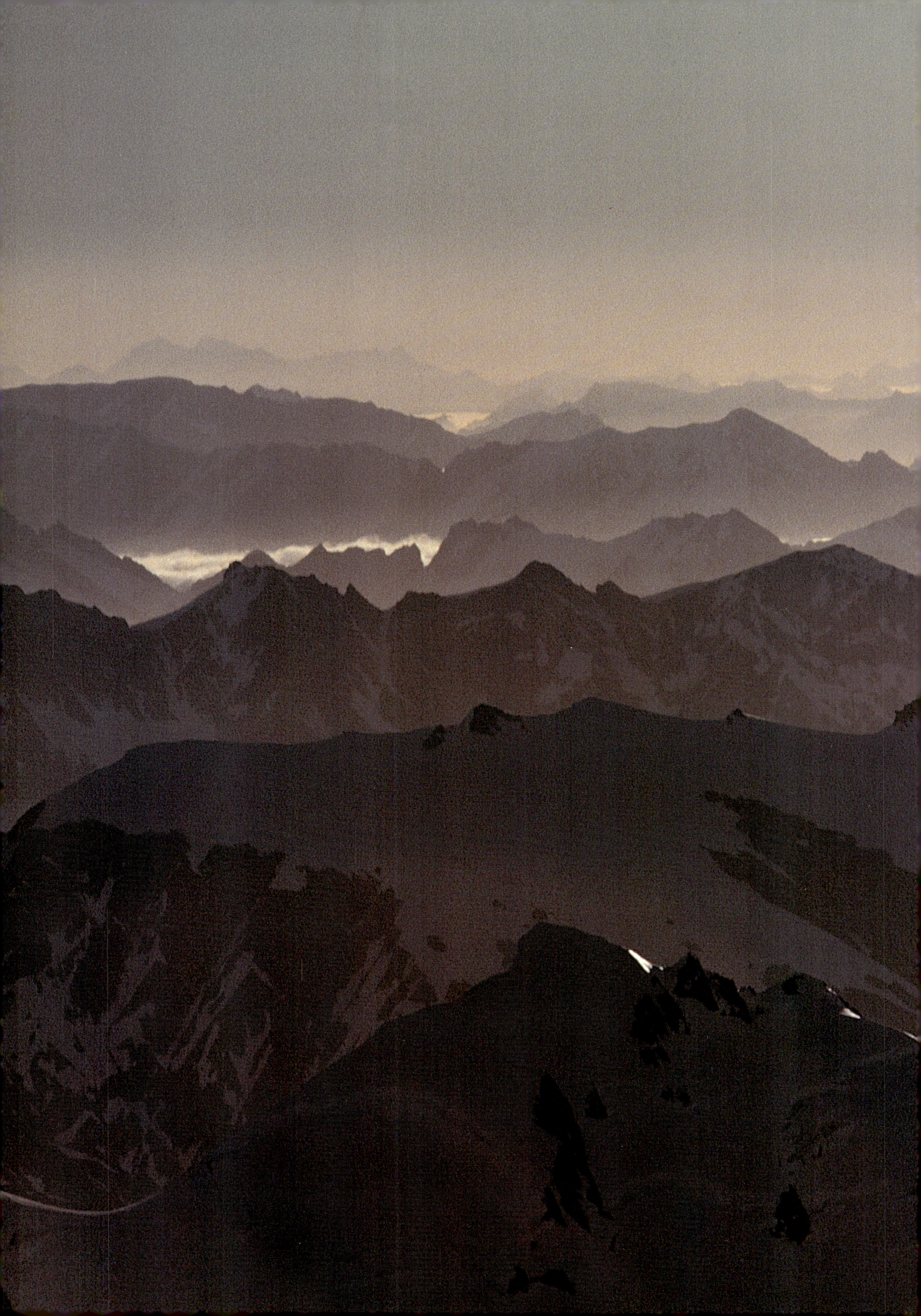

Salute to NEW ZEALAND

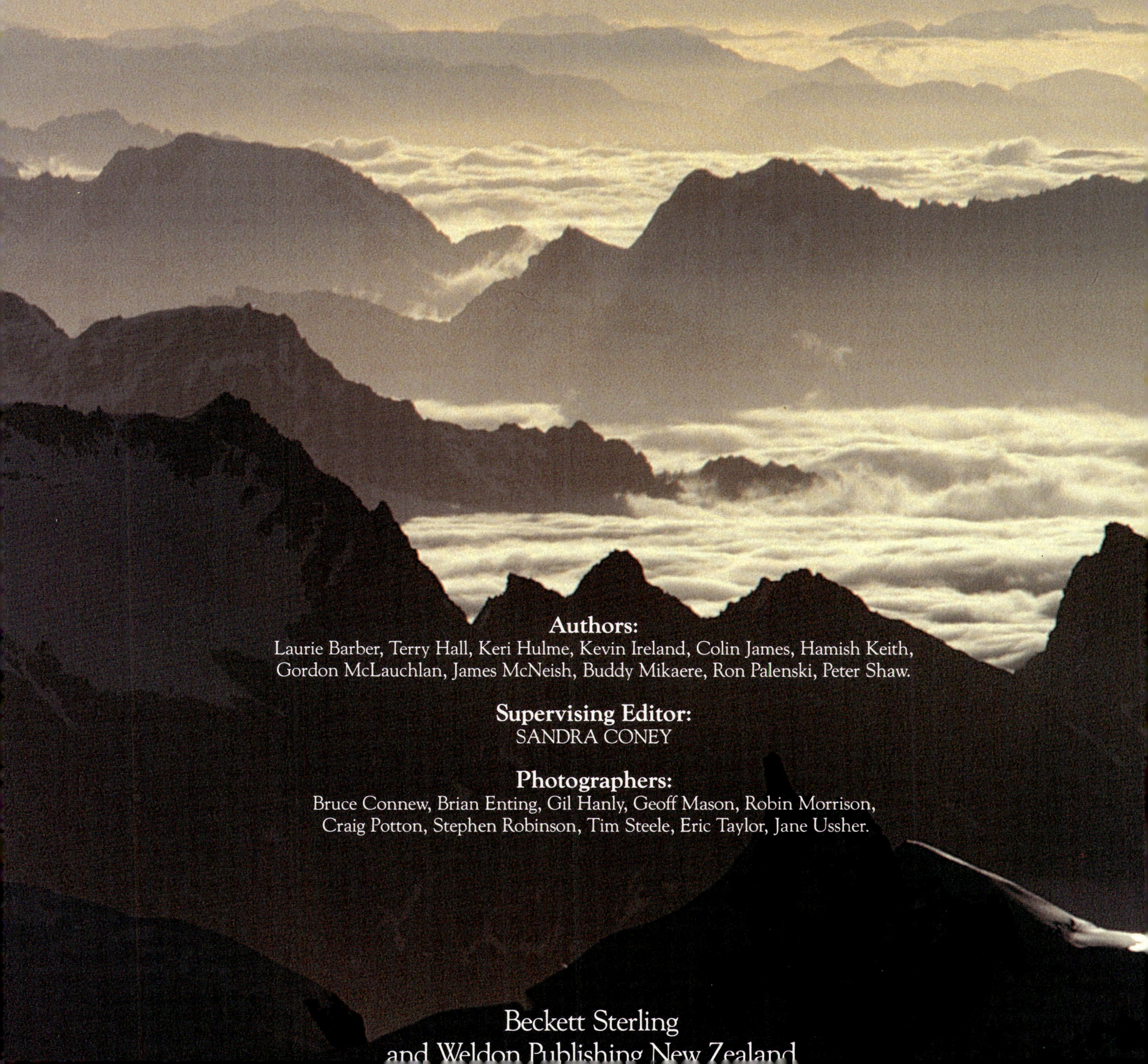

Authors:
Laurie Barber, Terry Hall, Keri Hulme, Kevin Ireland, Colin James, Hamish Keith, Gordon McLauchlan, James McNeish, Buddy Mikaere, Ron Palenski, Peter Shaw.

Supervising Editor:
SANDRA CONEY

Photographers:
Bruce Connew, Brian Enting, Gil Hanly, Geoff Mason, Robin Morrison, Craig Potton, Stephen Robinson, Tim Steele, Eric Taylor, Jane Ussher.

Beckett Sterling
and Weldon Publishing New Zealand

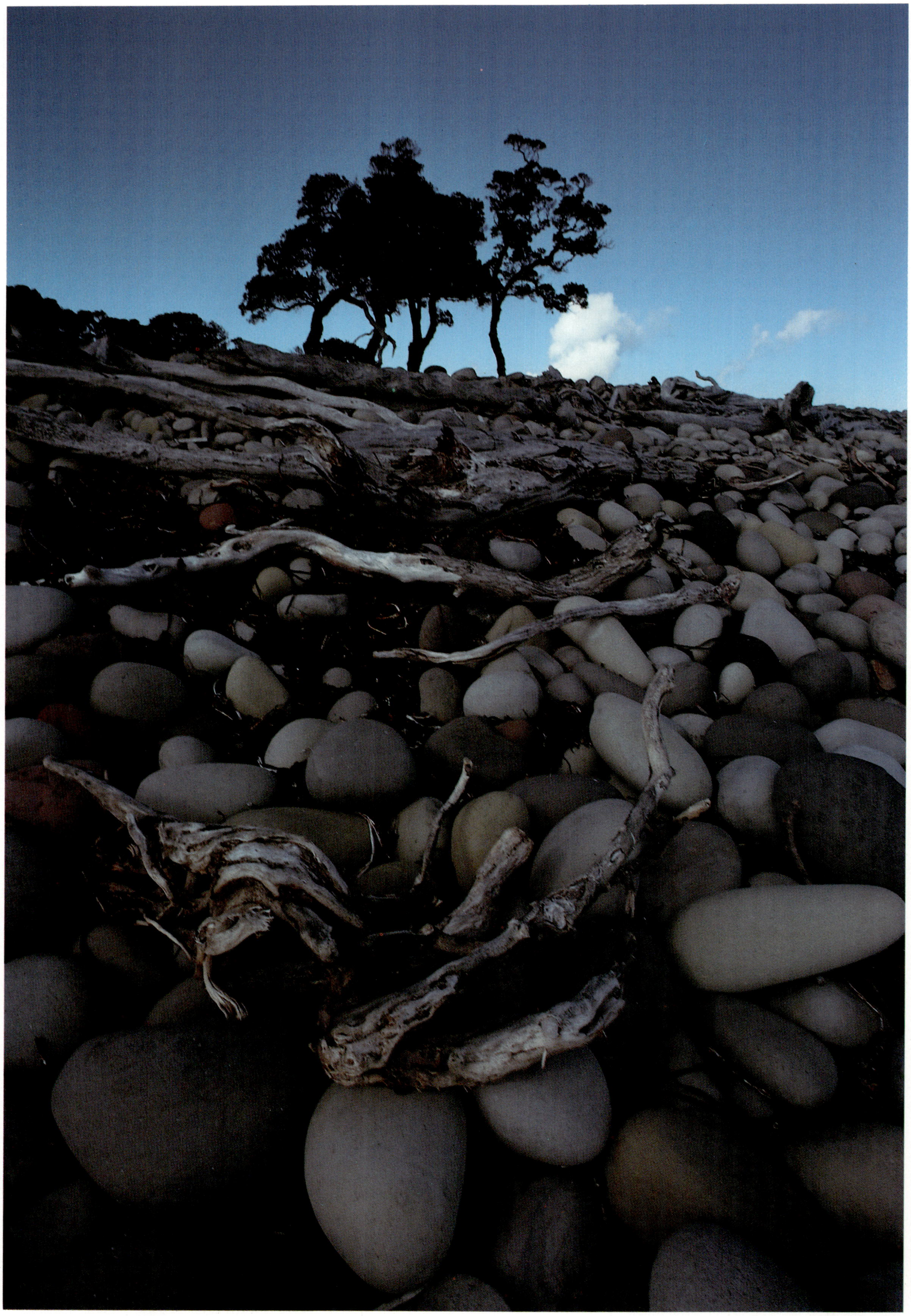

Little Barrier Island

ERIC TAYLOR

TRUST BANK

It was absolutely appropriate that Trust Bank should support *Salute to New Zealand*. This book looks back in time to explore the development of a nation and to celebrate its considerable achievements. It looks forward too, pointing to strengths, such as adaptability and vision, which will serve us well in the future.

Some of the banks that make up the Trust Bank Group have lived through the history discussed in this book, for the group's origins go back to the earliest pioneering days. The Otago and Southland members of the Trust Bank Group were founded in 1864, and, with other banks established in the following years, nurtured the beginnings and early growth of New Zealand communities.

When the banking industry was deregulated in the 1980s, nine of the original twelve trustee savings banks responded to the challenge by moving together in 1986 and forming the Trust Bank Group. While the traditional philosophy of service to local communities still remained central, this amalgamation enabled economies of scale to be made, leading to better services for customers.

Salute to New Zealand celebrates such innovation in many fields, recalling high points of New Zealand history, some of the people who have helped shape New Zealand, and describing the characteristics which have made us a strong South Pacific nation.

The book is in itself innovative, bringing together work by the country's foremost photographers with thought-provoking essays by some of the country's best writers.

Trust Bank is proud to be associated with such a unique project.

This book is dedicated to
Brian Brake
1927–1988

Brian Brake was a photographer whose contribution to New Zealand photography was not just in the legacy of superlative images he created over a lifetime's work. He fostered the publication of photographic work by and about New Zealand and he nurtured the development of many local photographers by willingly sharing the knowledge and skills he had gained through his overseas experience.

First published 1989 by BECKETT STERLING LTD,
28 Poland Road, Auckland, New Zealand
and WELDON PUBLISHING NEW ZEALAND
a division of Weldon International Pty Ltd

ISBN 0-908676-43-3

Project Manager: Robin Burgess
Project Coordinator: Donna Hoyle
Supervising Editor: Sandra Coney
Photographic selection: Donna Hoyle
Illustrations research for essays: Sandra Coney
Design: Donna Hoyle
Typesetting: Linda M. J. Smith, Auckland
Comset, Auckland
Finished artwork: P. R. Graphics, Auckland
Printing: Griffin Press Ltd, Australia

The initial selection of essays was made by the publishers and editorial consultants. Subsequent editorial supervision was undertaken by Sandra Coney who also wrote the photo captions in the essays.

The publishers of *Salute to New Zealand* wish to thank the advisory board members, the chairman of the board, Sir Leonard Thornton, and the sponsors for their assistance.

They also wish to thank Joan McCracken and Anne Upton at the Alexander Turnbull Library, John Timmins at the Otago Early Settlers Museum, Roger Blackley at the Auckland City Art Gallery, Gordon Maitland at the Auckland Institute and Museum, Joan Woodward at the Canterbury Museum, Joanne Buchanan at the *NZ Herald*, Mark Strange at the National Museum, Gerald Barnett at the National Art Gallery, Tim Garrity at the Hocken Library, Peter Webb Galleries, and the other individuals, living artists and estates of artists, who assisted by providing illustrative material.

PEEK DISPLAY CORPORATION
PHOTOGRAPHIC WHOLESALERS for the use of CANON photographic equipment
H. E. PERRY LIMITED

Budget rent a car

Kodak

air new zealand

Tourist Hotel Corporation of New Zealand
Resort and City Hotels
Proudly New Zealand owned and operated

FOREWORD

It may seem perverse to preface a book with a statement of what it isn't; but there will be apprehensions that this is just another coffee table luxuriant, or a dull historical chronology, or an autopsy, even an outpouring of national euphoria and self-congratulation.

It is none of these things. This book is a patchwork, a sampling, a celebration, and a remembrancer. It is the work of a selection of our outstanding writers and photographers, each working independently within the broad theme of New Zealand history. Each has sought to present, with pen or lens, those aspects of our past or visible present which seem to them the most notable or influential or most typical of the places, people and events which have brought us to the environment of today.

Inevitably the last fifty years command more attention than the preceding century, for much of this is personal reminiscence, to be valued as such. There is no sugary sentiment here in prose or picture, and no single interpretation will satisfy all comers. That is as it should be. But whether the thousand glimpses are in the fields of lifestyle or trade, personalities or processes, the arts or race relations, or sport, or any other contribution to human experience, there is honesty of purpose here, and keen insight. May it inspire discussion and individual search for some of the detail that must be omitted from a constricted study of this kind.

The contributors have woven a coat of many colours, dark as well as light. I hope that it will enable us all—and perhaps our friends abroad—to have a better understanding of some of the influences which have made us what we are. I hope too that we New Zealanders can find enough shared fortune and sentiment in these pages to face with greater confidence whatever may lie ahead of us as we move on through our second century together.

Sir Leonard Thornton KCB, CBE.

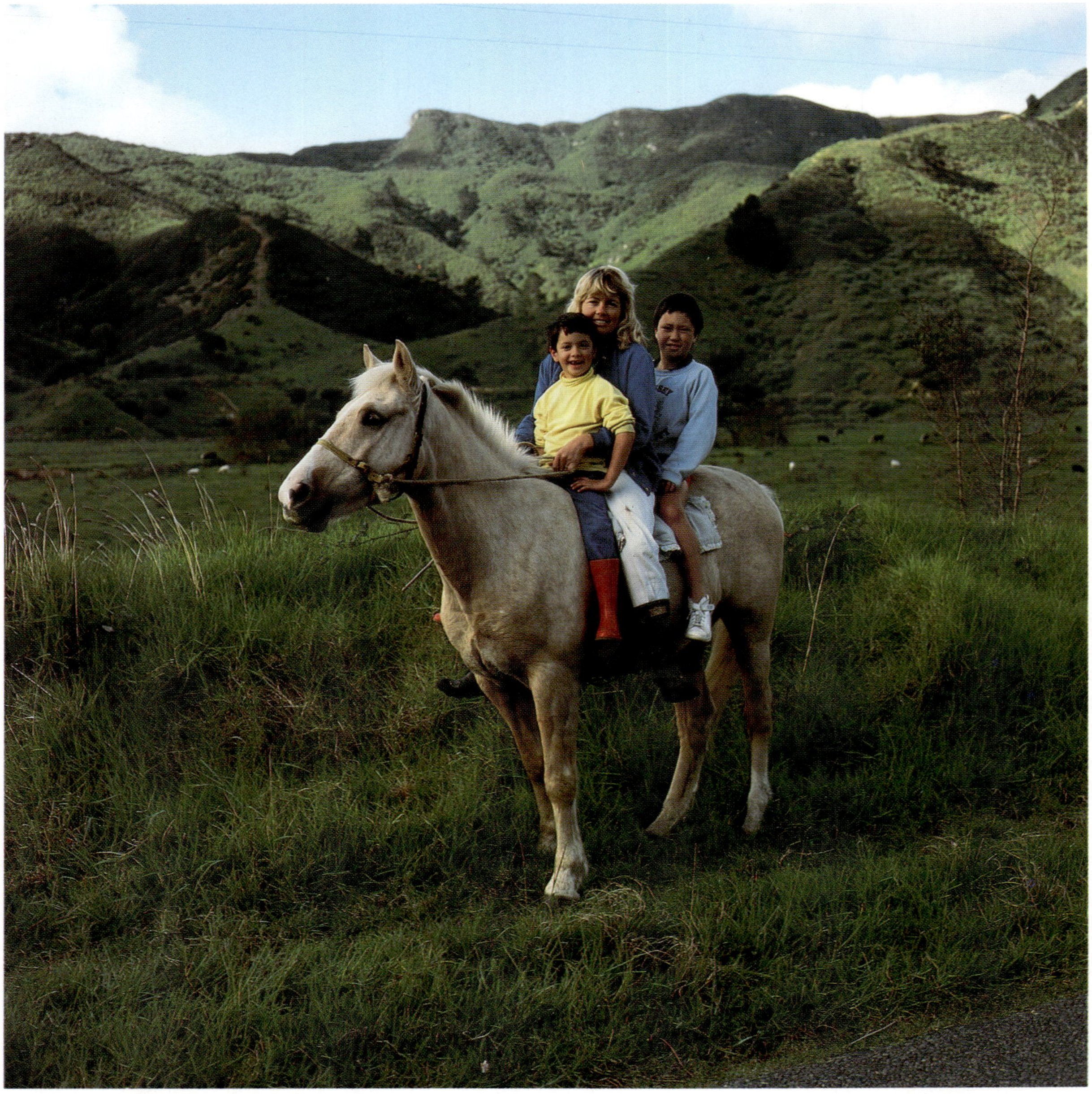

Family on horseback, Colville, Coromandel Peninsula ERIC TAYLOR

Pages 1 and 2 Mt Cook GEOFF MASON

Pages 3 and 4 The Southern Alps stretch endlessly south from Mt Cook GEOFF MASON

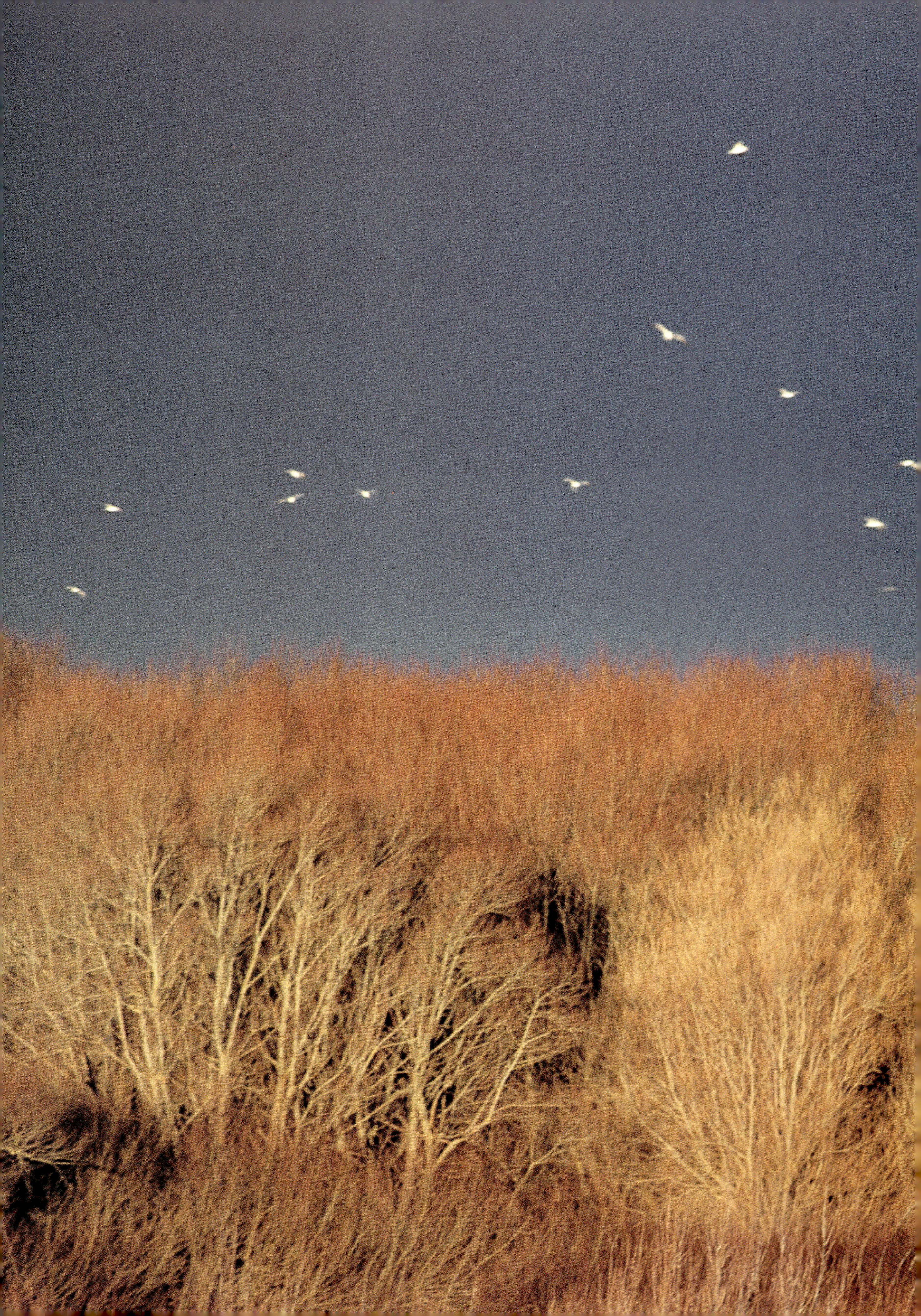

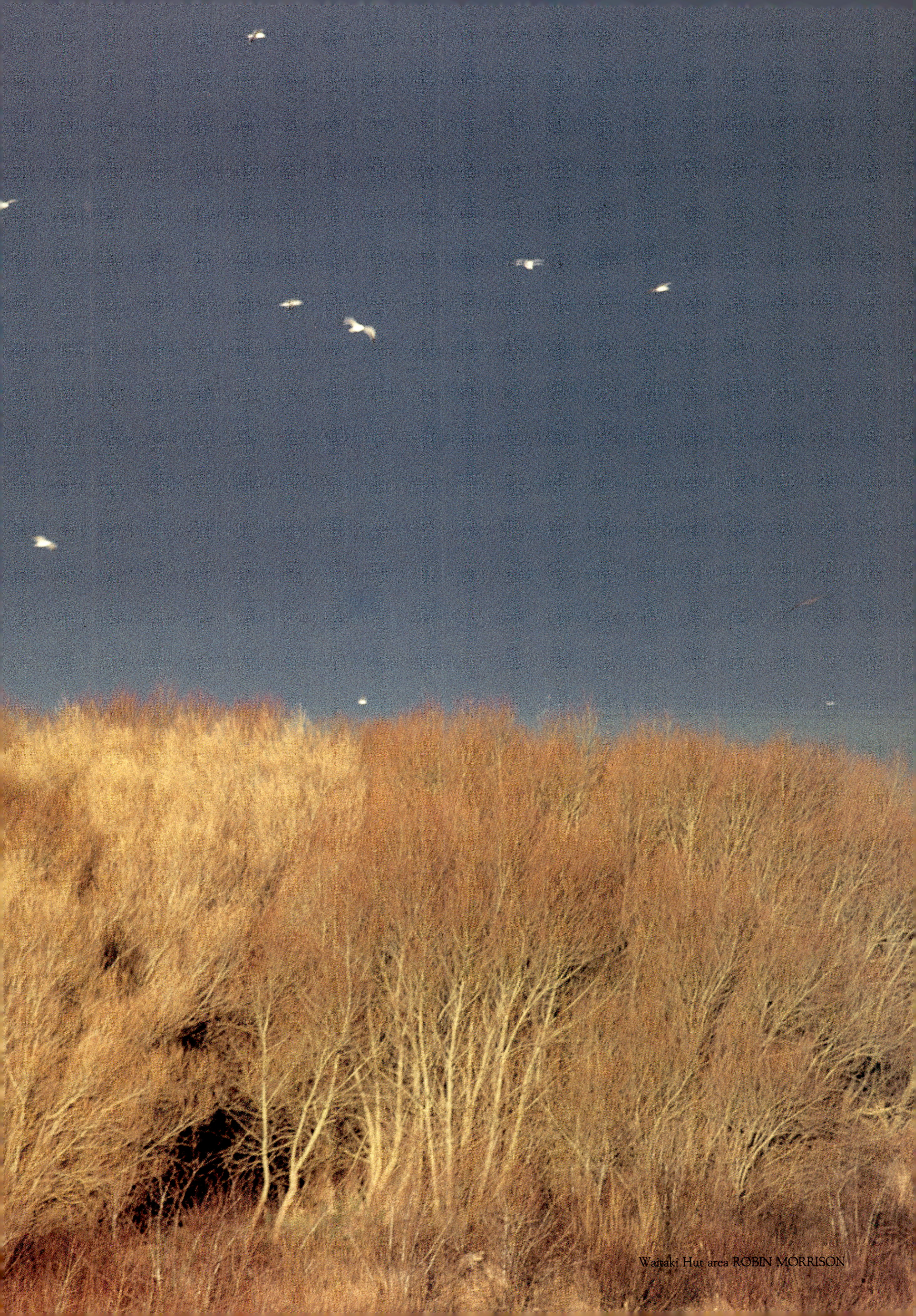

Waitaki Hut area ROBIN MORRISON

PRIVATE LANDSCAPES

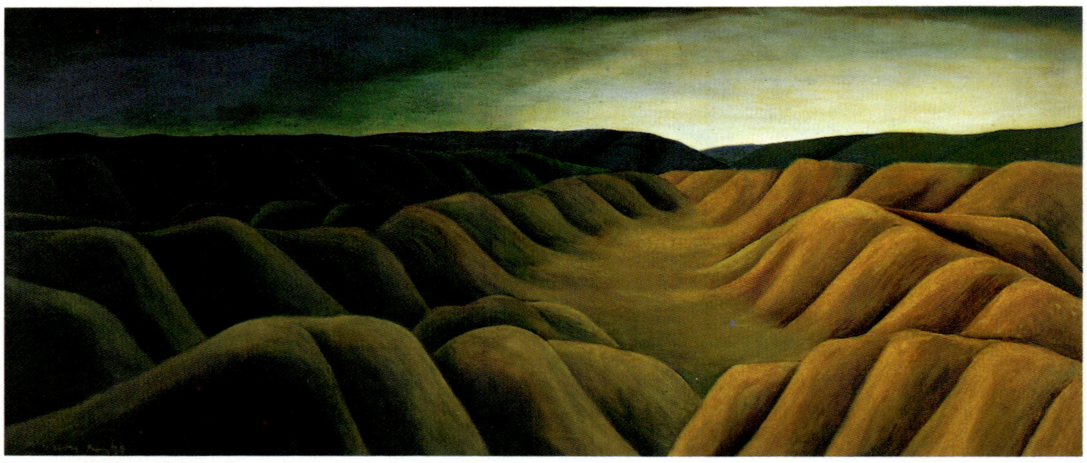

AUCKLAND CITY ART GALLERY

Takaka—Night and Day, 1948, oil by Colin McCahon.

Kevin Ireland

MY MOTHER WAS BORN in Feilding in 1907, but her own mother's family came from the lowland strip of the West Coast, in and about Hokitika, which owns the most dramatic long-distance views of landscape in New Zealand – high into walls of bush on one side and, on the other, past the desolate stumps of the old harbour works to the endless silver beaches stacked with the skeletons of trees, out across the raving salt-maddened Tasman Sea, and 100 km down the great spine of the Southern Alps to Mt Tasman and Mt Cook. The West Coast's reputation for foul weather is a myth and a libel. Every time I have been there I have stood in Hokitika and seen the mountains.

My mother's grandfather had prospered on the Coast. His experience of the Otago goldfields had taught him where money was reliably to be made – he supplied fine working boots to the hordes who joined the rush to the area around Kumara. Earlier in the nineteenth century, inter-tribal war had reduced the Maori population to possibly less than 100, and in the mid-1860s Europeans poured in their tens of thousands over the few tiny settlements. When the gold fever was over, most of these new arrivals melted away in their turn, but my maternal ancestors remained and made the Coast their heartland. The gorgeous glossy brown bowl of Central Otago was too dry for my great-grandfather. He had come from Ireland and he needed the friendly damp of the Coast to put down his roots and grow.

Boots remained his trade. In a subtle way his hands helped the feet of others alter the shape of the landscape about him, for without boots there could have been no diggings, no roads, no towns and no farms (not to mention breweries and racecourses), though it is unlikely the thought ever struck him quite like that. He was more preoccupied with matters of pride – he never sent more than one bill to a Coaster for his products, on the grounds that if they couldn't afford them they were welcome to them, and if they were too dishonest to pay the same sentiment applied anyway. His son Rob was the second white child to be born west of the Southern Alps.

Humans are a migrant species, and human history, so far as we can piece it together, is largely a tale of the sometimes sudden, sometimes systematic, movement of people across the face of the planet. The curious feature of these travels is the way that migrant people, while often retaining a dream-notion of the area they have left, so soon adapt physically and psychically to their new landscapes. It is as though the land has a magical power to print itself upon us. It takes only a single generation to produce this "native" effect – on those who are willing to submit to its unconscious force.

Soon after her first sister was born, my mother went to stay with her grandmother on the West Coast. More than sixty years later she wrote me an account of what she described as an "almost mystically beautiful memory" of the journey across Arthur's Pass. The Otira tunnel was not completed until 1923, and in the days before the First World War stagecoaches were still being

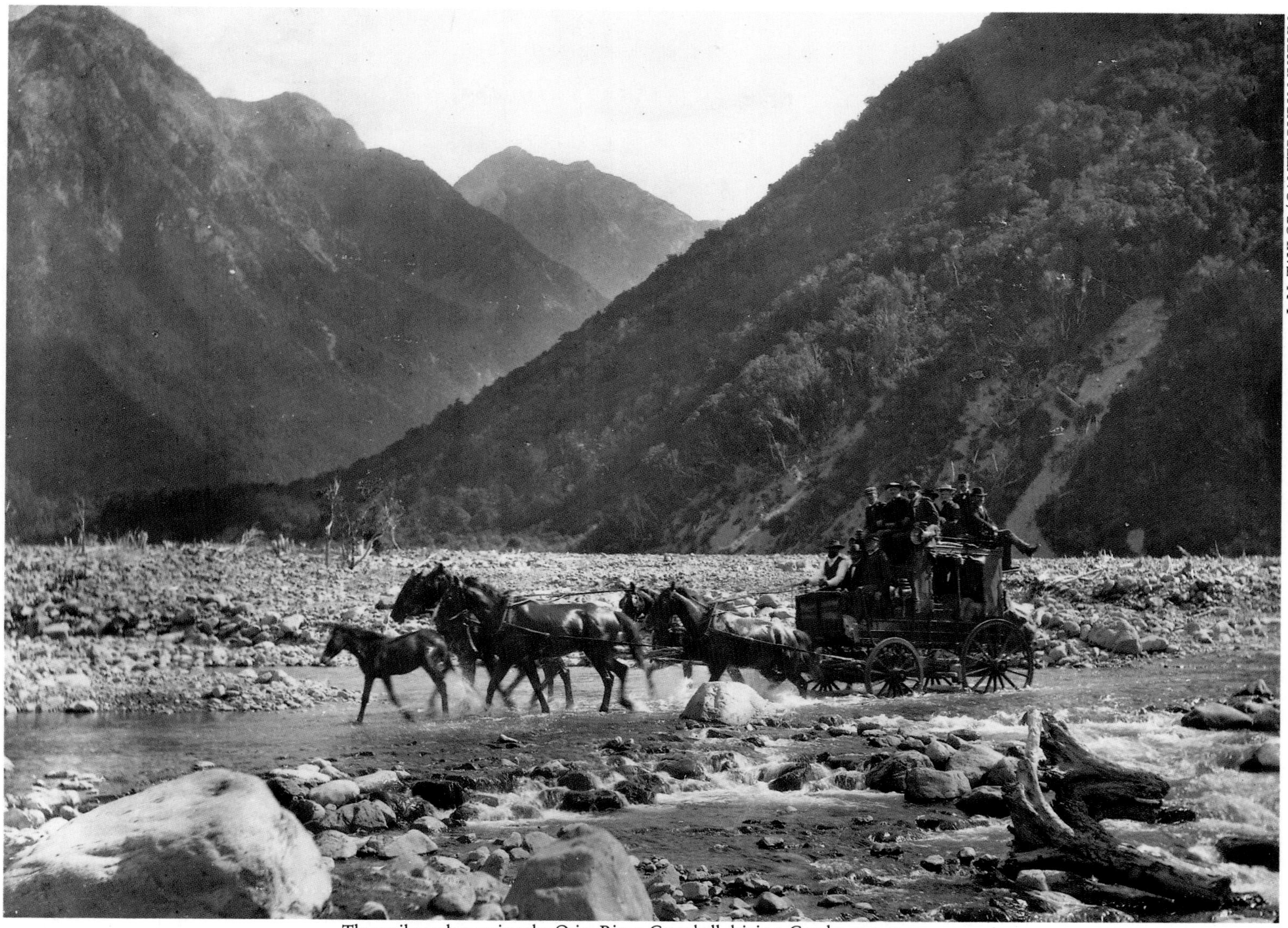

J. N. TAYLOR/CANTERBURY MUSEUM

The mail coach crossing the Otira River, Campbell driving. Coaches ran over Arthur's Pass until 1923. Sometimes snow falls closed the route for months on end.

used to make the connection between the two railheads on each side of the Southern Alps. She writes:

"In a coach we are on our journey homewards across the Alps in piercing weather. I am squeezed in between Mum, with the baby on her knee, and Ellen [an aunt], my hands in a warm fur muff. My head turns and for a moment as we flash past I am caught in the magic of a vision – a little tiny dark tree, branches covered with snow, standing beside the road alone against a background of chasm and mountain. So intense is the thrill of that perfect vision that I think it will be the last memory of life . . . Odd little girl, not three years old. For a moment I'd known ecstasy – an indelible impression of beauty."

WHEN WE ARE OPEN to such ecstasies, and their lasting visions, we are no longer migrants – we are bonded to a place as surely as if the experience of it is in the marrow of our bones. The alienation of which the European is sometimes self-accused has always seemed to me to be a grotesque, and even mischievous, literary invention. The only alienation New Zealanders – of all colours – suffer is that produced by the inexorable separations, confusions and tensions of our century. No race, no society, no culture on Earth has entirely outwitted them. The past preoccupations of a few older writers with "belonging" to a new land where landscapes have been deserted by the old gods and the new have made no impact, are brilliant metaphors for neurotic isolation, a hazard of post-eighteenth-century art everywhere.

The concept of "man alone" in a "far-pitched perilous hostile place" – to run together two unsophisticated yet highly literate, young, New Zealand, urban-dwelling males' descriptions of a largely sexual unhappiness – became for a while a powerful and fashionable romantic literary posture. It inspired some bowel-winding imitations, it had the neatness of suggesting a problem with a built-in no-answer clause (New Zealand was simply too far away from the rest of the world) and its comforting despair was only a variation on other popular artistic snobberies of the times.

My maternal grandfather would have laughed at such a notion. His connection to the land and to its entire human heritage, including its relatively short, exclusively Maori occupation, was biological and geological. He was as much part of his landscape as a tree, a hill or a river. He never thought of himself "apart" from anything. When, in his sixties, he had to fell a giant rata, he *was* the axe – just as he *was* the tree, and felt for it as it arced towards the ground, and spoke of it forever after with the respect you would pay to a friend who had died. It never occurred to him that he was "man alone".

Two generations later, living here and abroad, the notion never came to me that I was in any way different to him.

LANDSCAPE IS NOT JUST a picture-postcard collection of stunning views, it is also a collection of ideas about the form of the world and our feelings about ourselves inside that form. There are reference points within us without which landscape is simply shape without meaning. Landscape begins in the interior of the person who looks upon it, just as it accounts crucially for the way that person relates to a notion of his or her own existence. The place people feel close to and are nurtured by gives them a large part of their self-definition; in turn they pass this landscape-ness on to others they raise, look after, work with and love.

My mother describes how she once travelled with her father south on the Main Trunk railway. An elderly and distinguished-looking Maori man, accompanied by a young Maori woman, boarded the train and sat in the seat facing them at the end of the carriage. Years of outdoor living had burnt my grandfather to a shiny mahogany and age had turned his face round and wrinkled. He never went outside, even to the shops, without his pipe, a bowler hat and a walking stick (though he would sometimes pop out in a pink woollen singlet, properly buttoned up to the top), and he carried himself with great dignity. He was often taken for a Maori.

Because the two men were accompanied by attractive young women of different races there was a slight embarrassment between them and their conversation began in a desultory way, without the normal exchanges of where they were from. As the train headed south their conversation grew more animated. They spoke entirely in Maori. When it came time for the Maori gentleman to leave the train he asked my grandfather the delayed question of what tribe he belonged to.

"Ngati Porou" was the proud prompt reply.

My mother knew the language imperfectly, but well enough to understand what had just been said and to recognise that her father had told a lie.

"Goodness!" she objected when they were alone. "Should you have claimed to be Ngati Porou like that?"

But Maori had been my grandfather's first language. He had been born posthumously when his army officer father had tried, for a drunken bet, to ford on horseback the Hawke's Bay Wairoa River in full spate. His mother had let him run wild and finally abandoned him to the irregular care of an older brother. For several years he had been brought up in Maori care and custom.

He answered my mother: "Well, what the hell else could I do? I couldn't humiliate a decent chap like that by letting on I was no Maori when he hadn't picked it for himself.

"Anyway, and another thing, a God-damned hard time of it I'd have had when I was young if it hadn't been for the Ngati Porou. They fed and looked after me like one of themselves in times when my own people couldn't have cared a bugger or less if I had perished or went to hell. I *feel* Ngati Porou."

The self-definitions this man achieved so early in Hawke's Bay and Poverty Bay brought some curious later flourishes to his notion of what was achievable in some extraordinary landscapes. Some years prior to this conversation my grandfather had become one of a battalion of farmers defeated in a now famous bloodless twentieth-century land war. This time the enemy had not been Maori or European, it was the shape and character of the land itself – and the land had scored a spectacular victory.

In 1912 he had run into a certain Mr Rawlinson in Te Kuiti who had built up a deliriously optimistic picture of the opportunities for breaking in new farms in deepest Taranaki. He enthusiastically described the grandeur of the landscape. Spectacular hills, fertile valleys, virgin bush – all of it aching for the axe and the match. The only things you needed were nerve and capital.

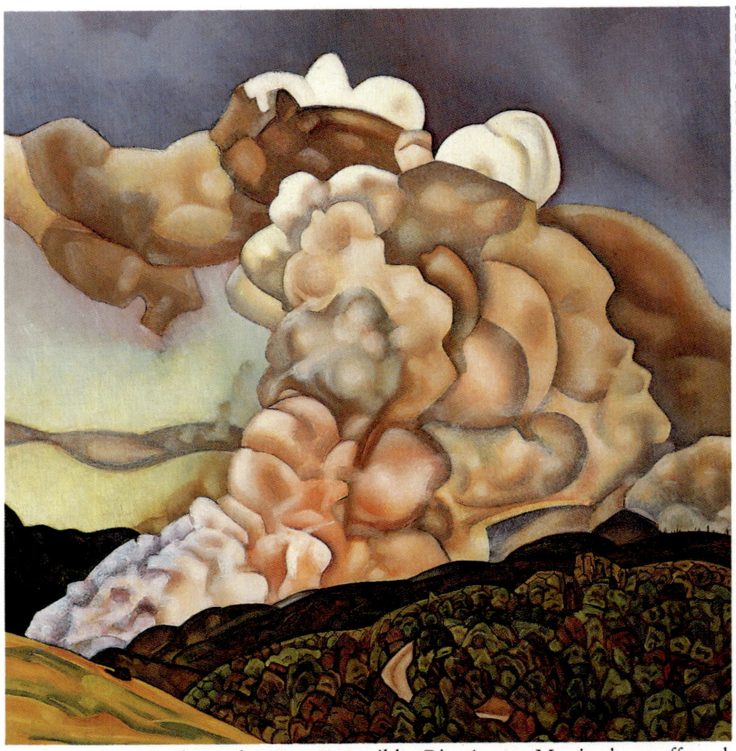

AUCKLAND CITY ART GALLERY

Scrub Burning, North Hawke's Bay, 1965, oil by Rita Angus. Massive burn-offs and milling reduced New Zealand's native bush from 14 million hectares in 1840, to 5.9 million in 1980. After burning "drives" came the back-breaking work of digging and blasting out the stumps.

My grandfather had a good friend called O'Dea, a well-known Taranaki solicitor who, like himself, fancied his chances as a cute man for business. The pair of them became Rawlinson's (truly) sleeping partners on a 500-hectare hill farm at Whangamomona. Two years later my grandfather, with O'Dea and the Loan and Mercantile mortgage company heavily involved, took up an option on a neighbouring farm as well. Visions of the splendid hills of Whangamomona persecuted him day and night. Dream landscapes ate into his every thought. It did not trouble him that his experience of farming and animals till that time consisted entirely of a bit of tuition from the unreliable Rawlinson plus his early days in Hawke's Bay and Poverty Bay as a goad-boy on a bullock team, jockey, horsebreaker and musterer – poor preparation for what came to be called "the heartbreak hills" and the Taranaki "tiger country".

THE PAST THOUSAND YEARS of human habitation have altered the New Zealand landscape for all time. The huge burnoffs in the South Island, probably part deliberate and part accidental, in the moa-hunting period of extensive Maori occupation, destroyed the bush cover and opened the plains and inland basins for tussock grass. Contemporary cities and towns, roads, railways, pine forests, dams, introduced animals and plants, and above all the destruction of the native bush, particularly in the North Island, and its replacement by farms, have worked such changes on the appearance and character of the land that it could never be restored to what it was. Even Whangamomona, as its hills have largely reverted to second growth and bush, has been marked forever. Change is permanent.

Curiously, it is now only by human agency that we can preserve in our wilderness and national parks a glimpse of pre-human New Zealand. In the absence of

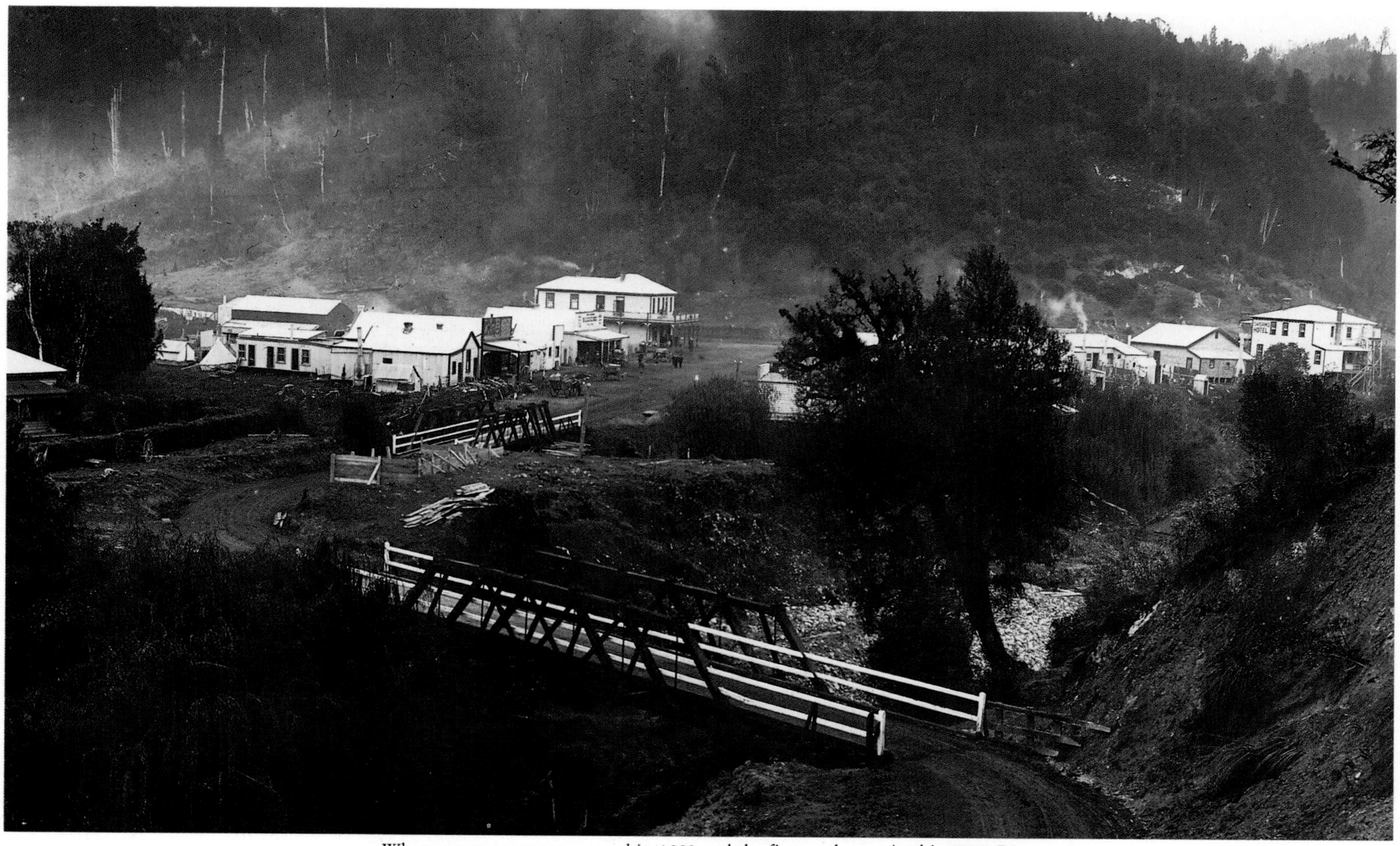

McALLISTER COLLECTION/ALEXANDER TURNBULL LIBRARY

Whangamomona was surveyed in 1883 and the first settlers arrived in 1895. By 1911 there were stores, post office, stables, a school, cheese factory, hotel, billiard room, hall, rugby club, bakehouse, racing club and bank. By the 1960s, most of these had disappeared.

our own species, the other introduced animals – rabbits, goats, deer, possums, cattle, sheep, pigs, and dozens of others – unchecked would probably take only a few centuries to gnaw and trample the whole land as bare as a Greek island.

At Whangamomona my grandfather's enthusiasm increased as farms failed in the valley which ran through to Aotuhia and from there to nowhere. As families simply walked off the triumphant hills, so his empire grew – though it was only ever his in name, for the Loan and Mercantile supplied the title and kept the deed. And when they saw at last that he too could not win in such a landscape they withdrew their support and off he walked like the others.

Behind him he left his response to the rivers, trees and hills in the days of his glory – standing amongst the stumps, fallen logs, wash outs and the weeds and scrub were his huge poems, painted on boards, now peeling in the sun before an audience of hawks, wild cattle and rabbits. Part of a passing landscape, part of the shape and colour of his own interior.

TO TRAVEL THE MISNAMED "Highway" 43 today, from Ohura to Stratford – large sections of which are still rough metalled surfaces, with the occasional slip and blind hairpin bend – is to journey into the dreamland of our recent history. It is as haunting as the old gold fields of the West Coast or Central Otago. Whangamomona is now a pub and a garage, a road works depot, a small school, a few houses and halls, derelict shops and a recently closed post office – a memorial to eternal optimism. A huge steep blob of a hill rises at the end of the village. It punctuates the broad main street as surely as a full stop.

And Highway 43, as an added bonus, has one of the North Island's scenic secrets: the stretch of road known as the Tangarakau Gorge through which my grandfather travelled by horse, mule, dray and coach before the railway was linked, and which he helped keep open by pick and shovel during the Depression. Gigantic rock bluffs are stacked unsteadily in layers which seem about to topple over. Ferns and bush crowd the road and the chasm of the gorge. Dull gummy water slushes over rocks and lies heavy in deep rusty pools. The air can be so still and oppressive it is as though it is stifled under the weight of the sky.

From Tangarakau it is a relatively short distance to Lake Taupo and the Tongariro National Park. Here mankind's efforts to transform landscapes to his needs and purposes are put into perspective.

The three neighbouring volcanoes, Ruapehu, Ngauruhoe and Tongariro, have all erupted in the past 100 years. A faultline of fire, with geysers and boiling mud, runs all the way to Wairakei, north of Lake Taupo, to Rotorua and on to White Island, the active volcano 50 km off the coast from Whakatane. The landscape is the creation of this long narrow furnace; sheets of lava flow are its basis, earthquakes and eruptions have twisted and pleated its surface, pumice showers have buried it. When Lake Taupo erupted during the second century AD, somewhere between seventy to ninety cubic kilometres of volcanic material were hurled across the land. It marked New Zealand's first recorded impact on the world: from these unknown islands volcanic dust circled the planet and changes in the skies were noted in Rome and China.

Mount Ruapehu has always had a private magic for me and many times in many lands over the years I have closed my eyes and summoned a more perfect vision of it than if I had carried an album of photographs with me. As an Auckland boy, I was sixteen before I first saw snow. My education took place before the days of school parties to remote areas. We had to make our own way about the country, and on the few occasions I passed Ruapehu it was hidden in cloud. Then came a blinding day of ecstasy similar to the one my mother had known so long ago at Arthur's Pass. I was hitchhiking to Wellington when suddenly the whole body of the mountain came into view. I blinked and gawked and rubbed my eyes. It was so perfect. I remember laughing with joy. It was unlike snow in books or on films. I was unprepared for its spotless ultimate whiteness – for such flawless colour pulsing from within, as though from an unstained heartbeat. I felt its radiance reaching for me, entering and filling me. Only the imagery of the mystics can convey a sense of that absolute identity with perfection – that moment of communion – when you look upon an ideal form and become it, as it becomes you forever.

I spent a good number of weekends on Ruapehu over the years following. On one trip I went for a quick though memorable swim in the crater lake while it was briefly non-sulphurous enough to risk a dip. A cliff of blue ice at one end of the crater kept cracking and roaring as if the mountain was going to split apart, and from it small icebergs peeled off and plunged with a huge hollow wallop into the lake. A unique waterline view of a landscape which makes my hair bristle to remember.

Nowadays it is in the waters below the mountains that I feel more at home, in the Tauranga-Taupo and Tongariro Rivers and on the southern end of Lake Taupo itself. The added pleasure of these landscapes is the possibility of a fat trout.

THERE IS NO EXPLAINING the attraction of fishing in the half light of a cold morning, standing up to the waist in a fast river, casting a few feathers over the waters. For those who are addicted, it is the most inwardly satisfying of solo human activities.

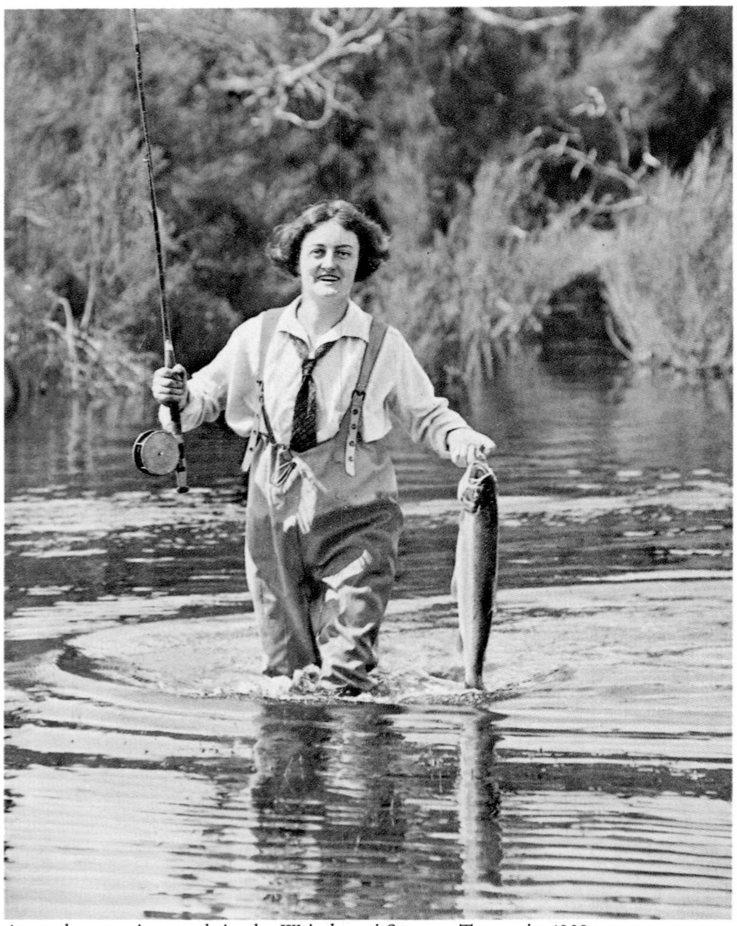
AUCKLAND WEEKLY NEWS

An early morning catch in the Waitahanui Stream, Taupo, in 1929.

The early mist rises over Taupo as silver light filters through a slit in the eastern sky and the distant bluffs of Waihi jut from the dark. It is as though the daylight we lost yesterday is being reinvented for the glory of life on Earth. The river is innocence and we who lean into its embrace feel we are made complete again . . . then, the strike of a trout. The rod bends into a hoop. The fight is on. The surface boils. There is no language of mysticism for this event. We are killers.

Yet not entirely without conscience. There are rules and those who break them are utterly unworthy of the river. Recently I took six trout from the Tongariro – a day's work. Yet every one of them went back. They were a bit on the small side, and I went home empty-handed. It is not enough just to be able to do this, you have to be prepared to look inside yourself and feel good about it.

And even on days when there are no fish, the rewards pile up like a bounty. Always there is the sight of a bend in the river, of a curl of water on a rock, the line of a tree against the clouds, the shadowed fold of a hill, a reflection of a leaf, to dazzle the memory with intimations of perfection.

And once, fishing the mouth of a small creek at night, I became aware of a presence behind me – inhuman, mysterious, yet not frightening. I turned slowly to where the huge black hills masked out the stars. The darkness of the land seemed to have slunk closer and to loom over my shoulders. And there I saw the unbroken frosted-grey arc of a night rainbow. Its pearl and oyster span was entire and flawless. It gave off a gauzy shimmering radiance. At first it seemed to hold the vaguest hint of the colour spectrum, yet the more I stared the stronger grew its single glow of mica. It began to sparkle. It was like the descriptions of the incandescence in the nimbus of a saint. Later, I had no conversation for the fishing. All I could remember was the lustre of a rainbow. A landscape with visions.

Fishing the Hopkins River, in its broad wind-tormented bed of stone, beneath an angular view of a tent-shaped Mt Cook, with the mirror of Lake Ohau curtained in the foothills of the Alps farther below, while monster trout attacked my dry fly as if enraged, remains a memory of superb sport in an inspiring landscape – yet a small Taupo creek with its mysterious rainbow shall always have that extra sense of revelation. It brought an intimation of the concealed landscapes inhabited by the spirit of the land. I know I have witnessed a marvel I shall probably never see with such radiant energy again, not even if I fish the same spot for a hundred years to come.

THE INTENSITY OF such experiences is rare. Silver rainbows, small trees under snow from a coach window, snowfields, mountains, rivers, are exotic and dramatic invasions into the depths of our beings. They possess us in rare encapsulated moments. Yet most of the pleasures of landscape are everyday and domestic and we can easily take them for granted. It sometimes takes a special effort of concentration to remind ourselves that what we are looking at or moving through is an unrepeatable event, a unique conjunction of form and colour.

Each day the most familiar view from our windows grows or decays. It never remains in every detail quite the same. Landscape is as impermanent as ourselves. A steep symmetrical hill begins to rise a few hundred metres from my verandah. It is known to me and to the once migrant people who brought my genes here as Mt Victoria, though it was known to previous migrants as Takarunga. These people had supplanted an even earlier group of inhabitants, who had also replaced others before them. Its summit looks down on the sites of many terrible battles. It is reputed to have had several names, and Takarunga is only the second-to-last of these.

Mt Victoria is one of Auckland's fifty or so extinct volcanoes, nearly all of which have been active over the past 30–40,000 years, and one of which – the island of Rangitoto – was active only a little over two centuries ago.

As my neighbouring volcano began to cool and weather many thousands of years ago, the next radical agent of change would have been botanical. The small plants, scrub and stunted trees which can be seen today on Rangitoto, took root, created soil and prospered. Eventually, a new tree-proud landscape emerged. Some time after the first people arrived – an event traced back to the coming of the Tainui canoe – they turned their attention to its defence advantages – its comparative security from attack and its marvellous command over the harbour. In a period when tribes all over the country began to create earthworks unequalled in the world using only wooden and stone implements, the cone of the hill was flattened and terraced.

When Europeans came they noticed the same advantages, installed guns and used the heights as a signal station to control the shipping below. They also discovered its value as a source of scoria. Takararo, its lower girdle, was quarried away. Two smaller sister volcanic cones have been entirely levelled and some of their substance undoubtedly helps knit the concrete wall of my garden – the perimeter of an old bear pit built as an eccentric early attraction for visitors to Auckland's North Shore.

There is now a road to the summit of Mt Victoria, the old defence terraces of its pa are grassed. Its violent origins and extraordinary contribution to life on the harbour can now only be guessed at. Yet its reshaping and recolouring continue. My view of it now and my memory of it as a boy when I went to the pictures and the woodwork school at its base are of two different hills. Slowly and slightly, yet surely, its shadows alter, and the trees and houses that frame it have given it subtle new perspectives.

In a central Auckland suburb some years ago, I visited a friend who spoke about his splendid new view. But there was no harbour, hill or bush anywhere to be seen. He had merely reorganised his furniture so that when he looked out from a side window he could see across his neighbours' tin roofs. Some were green, others red; they folded into strange angles and suggested curious planes and depths; alterations of light and shade jumbled and reformed the whole pattern. An abstract, geometrical, twentieth-century landscape charged with interest and movement, in a city backstreet.

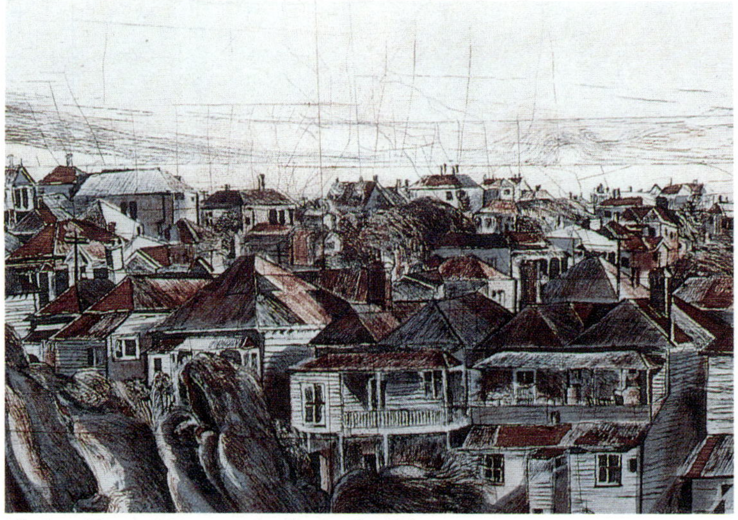

The Last House, 1974, engraving by Stanley Palmer.

Looking over a map of the whole country, I can tally the large number of places I have been and the spectacular sights I have stood in front of. But being somewhere is not necessarily seeing it – by which I mean that you can be aware of the impressiveness of a landscape without being able to make intimate contact with it. The view is there, but some inner part of you is blind to it. Its true quality evades you. Something which should move you leaves you, in fact, quite cold.

My own approach to landscape is largely to do with this special sense of intimacy – landscape becomes a personal matter of the way I feel inside it, and my interest in other people's landscapes is not to share the list of glorious mountains or rivers they have gazed on, but to comprehend the private point of reference from which they look. A Colin McCahon landscape is not a view of hills but a revelation of how hills "feel". A living world and a living response. A landscape photograph is only an optical catalogue until it makes us aware of the eye behind the eye in the viewfinder – that unmechanical gift of vision which locates the essence of a place.

LANDSCAPE IS ALSO a more active word than most definitions allow. It imposes itself on us, it can dominate our lives, it changes us. Its force is irresistible. Walk off Haymarket, in central London, into New Zealand House, and you are struck immediately by the New Zealandness of the faces. The difference from the people in the street outside is remarkable. The walk, talk, dress and manners have something to do with it, but the main distinction lies in the faces. It is as though the character of the landscape has begun to shape the bones, fill the flesh and rub off onto the skin.

It is something that happened within half-a-century of the European mass migrations of the nineteenth century. The photographs of First World War New Zealand soldiers show it clearly. Something had happened to the eyes, noses and jaws. A physical modification was taking place.

Diet and the sudden isolated genetic mix partly explain it. After all, the same thing had happened earlier to the Polynesians: the Maori are as different from the Samoans as they are from Tongans, and the paths of Polynesian migrations, alongside other evidence, can be traced accurately by these dissimilarities. However, the manner in which a migrant people begins to acquire an appearance that sets them physically apart from their root stock owes itself also to a host of other tiny pressures and chemistries. It is as if we absorb the place we live in. Over the years it seems to make a mineral change in us and shape us. Even within decades of arrival a population begins to evolve marginally but perceptibly towards a distinct type.

As we take our axes, bulldozers, machines, explosives, plants, animals, fertilisers and poisons to work on our landscape and shape it to our purposes, so too does landscape reply. It grips us and works us into its new mould. We become its native people. □

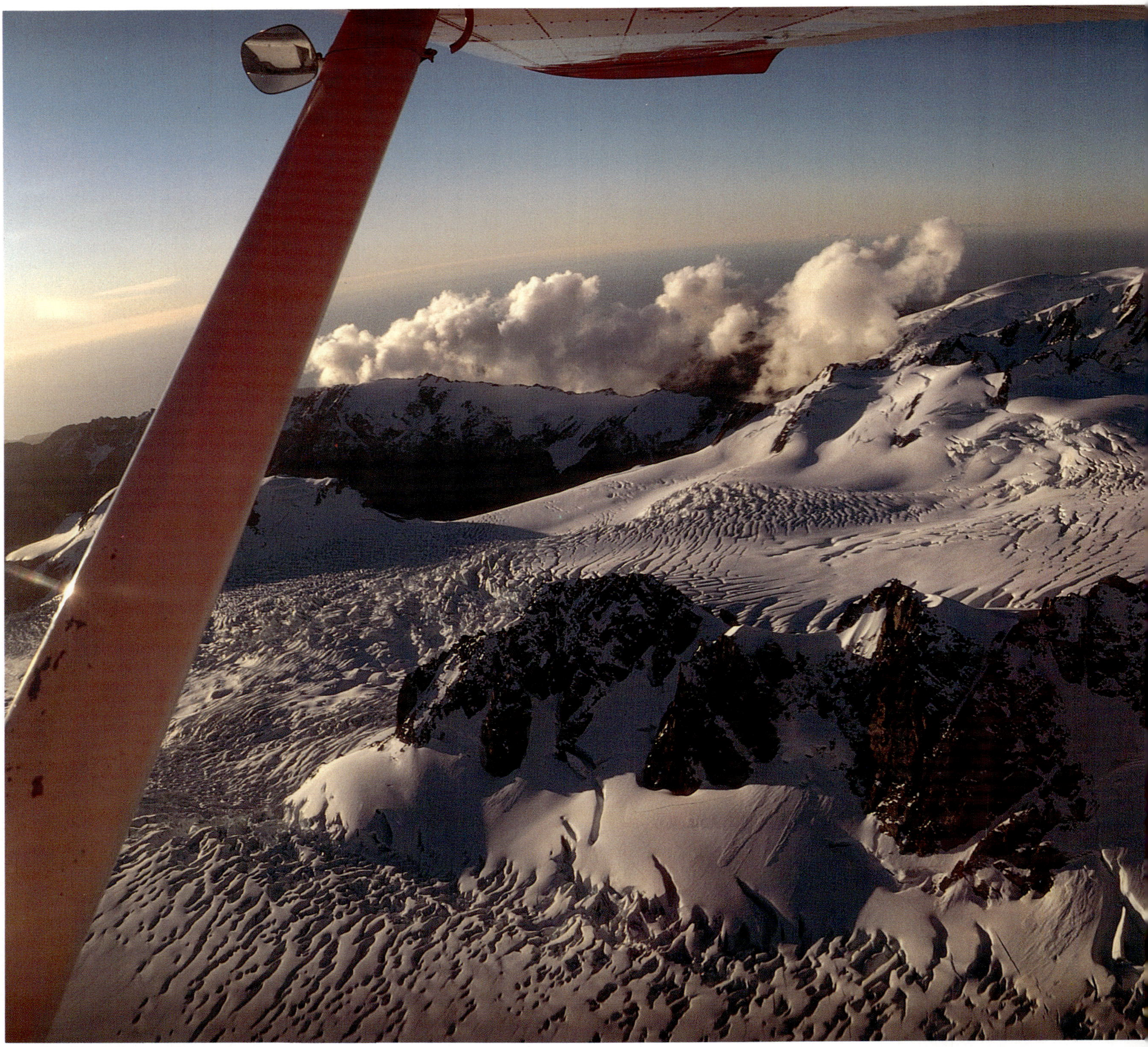

Ski planes over Mt Cook and glaciers GEOFF MASON

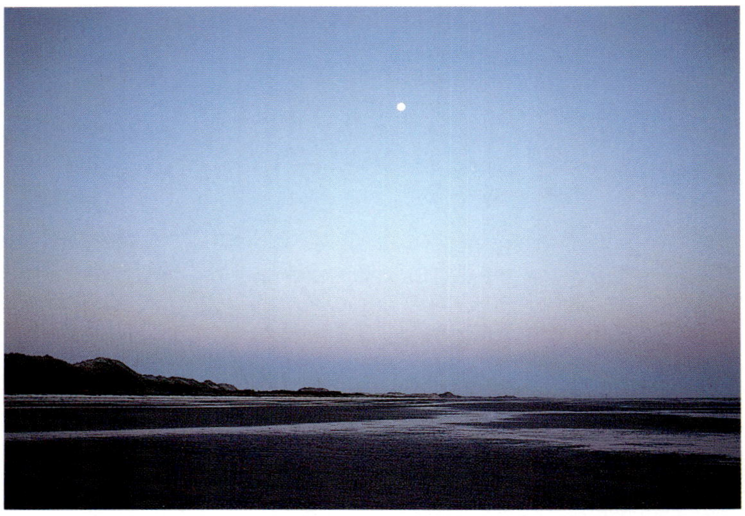

Farewell Spit at dusk BRUCE CONNEW

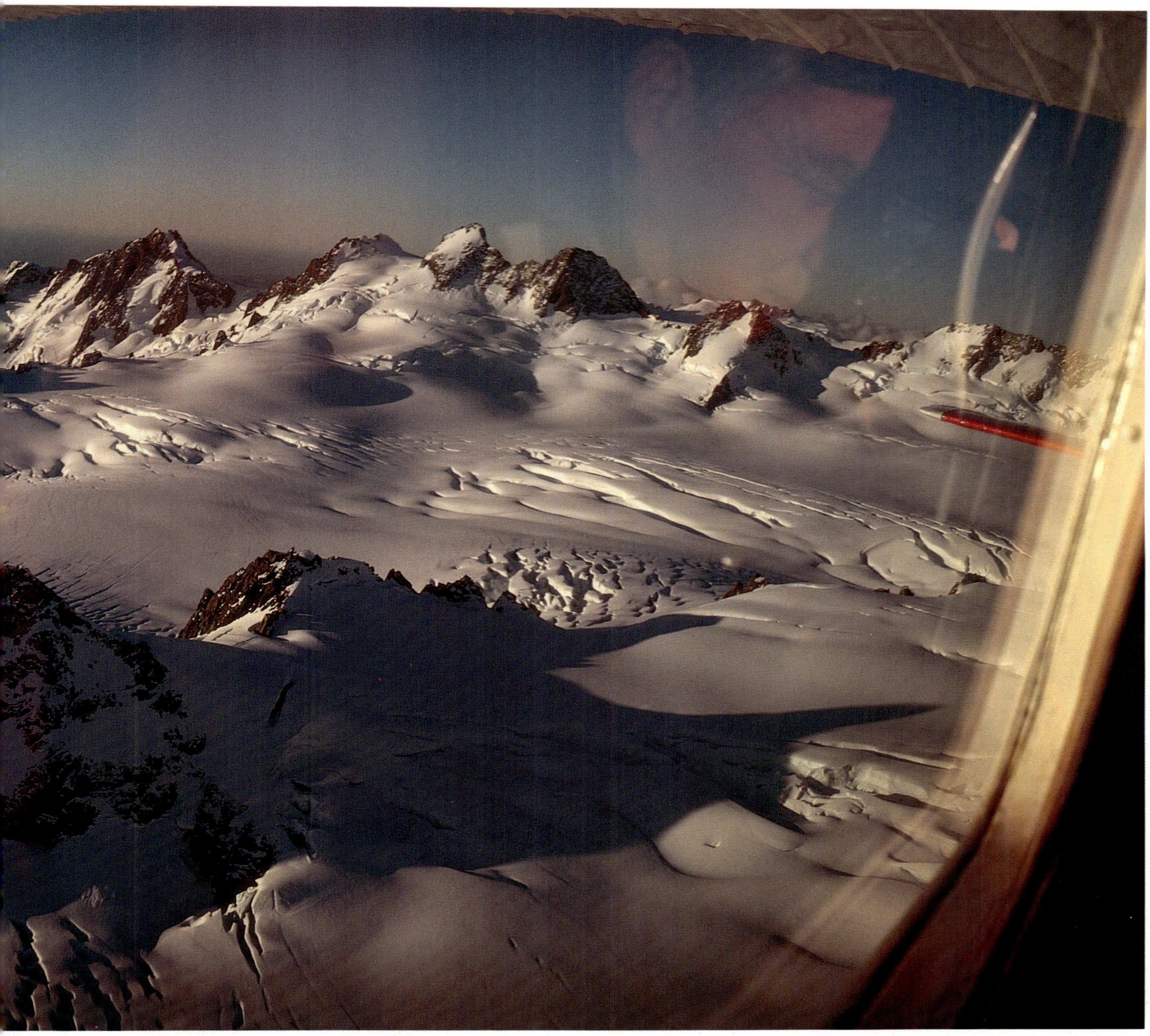

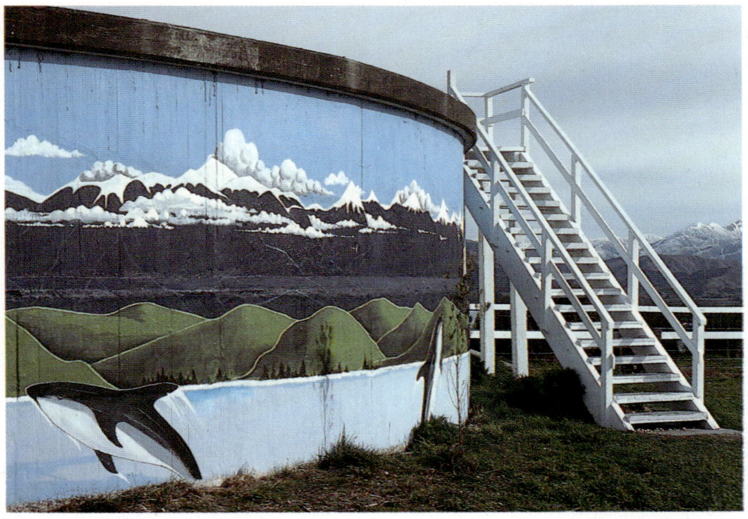

Water reservoir, Kaikoura ROBIN MORRISON

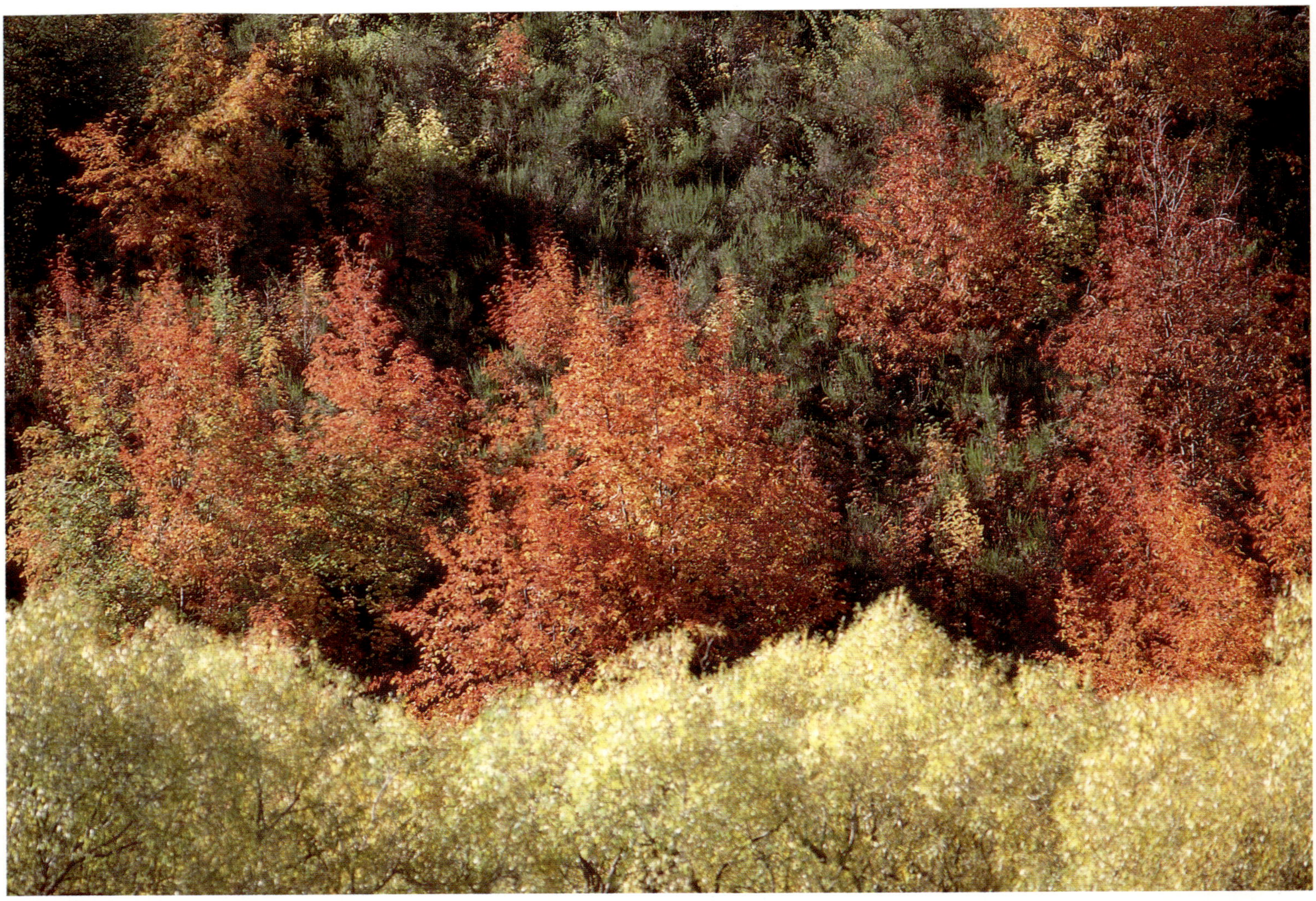

Hills of colour, Arrowtown GEOFF MASON

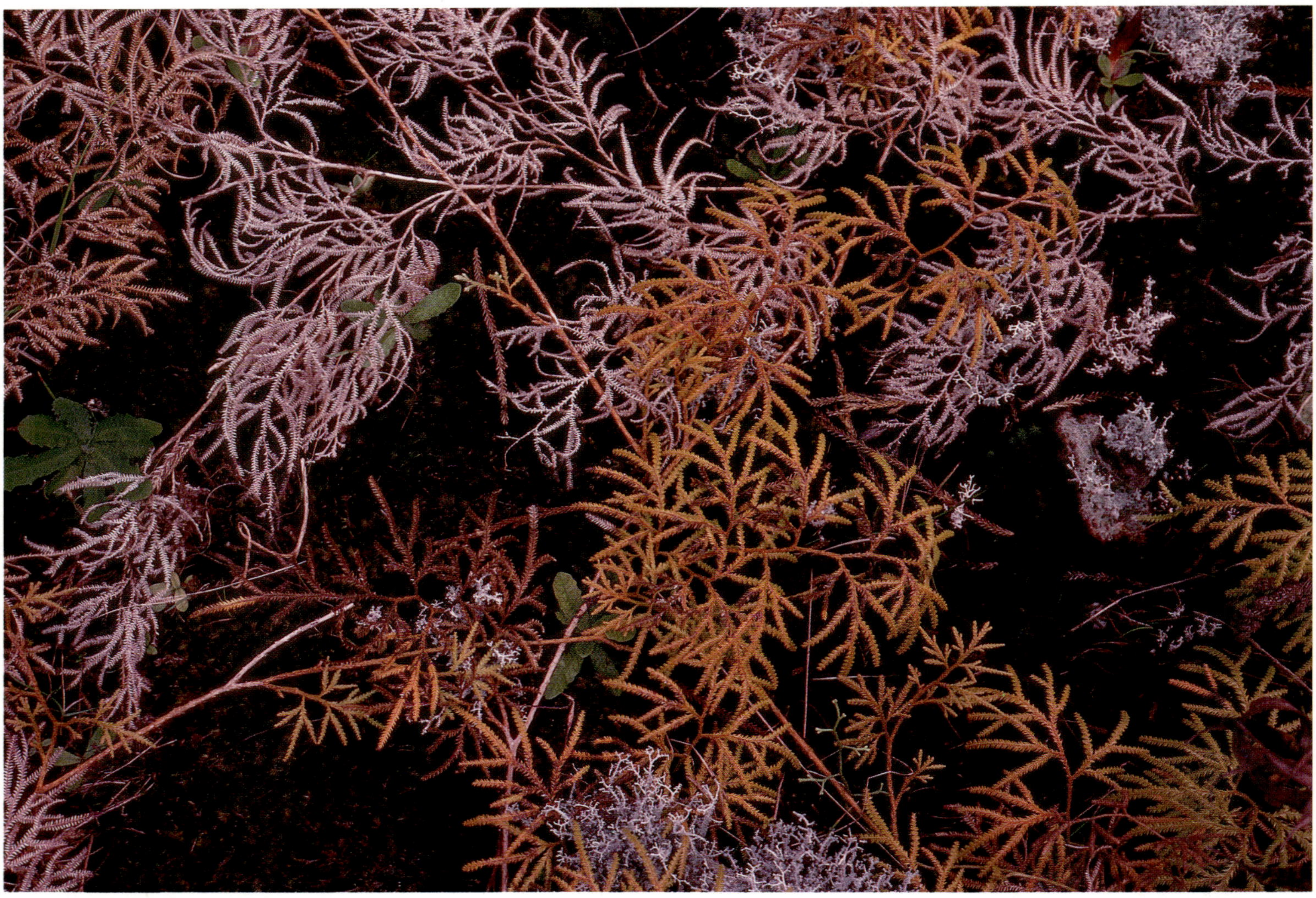

Lycopodium, Westland BRIAN ENTING

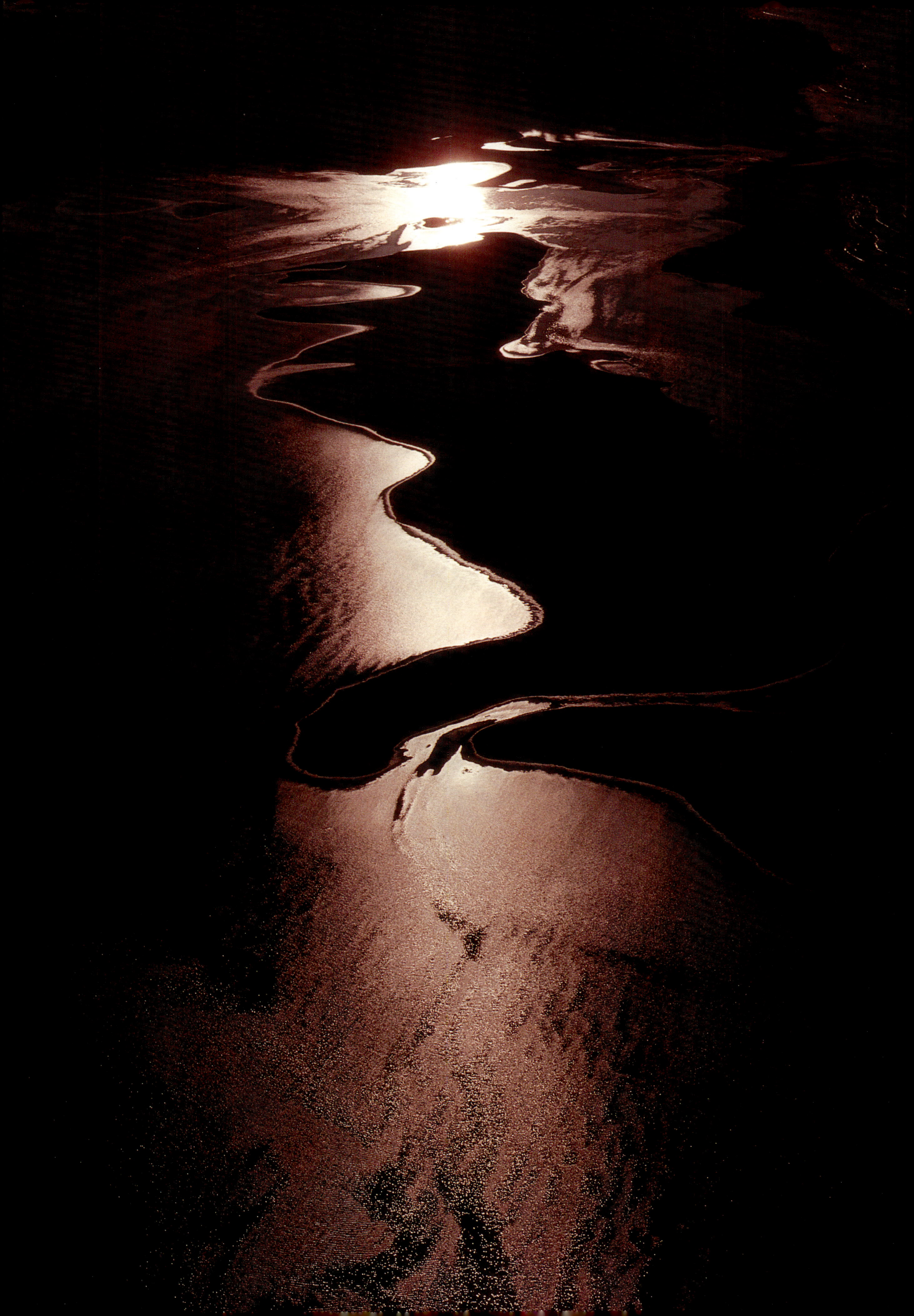

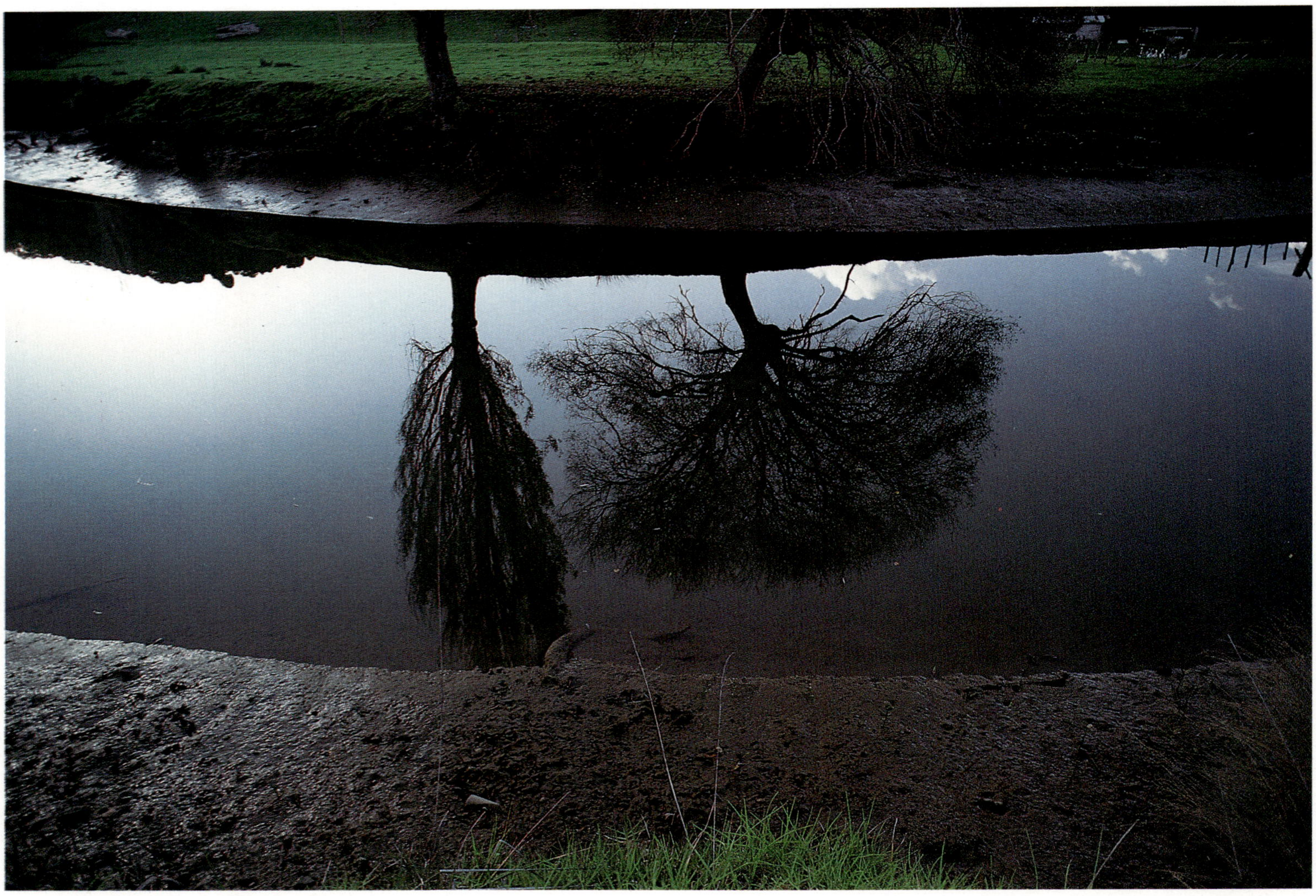

Waterway reflections, North Auckland TIM STEELE

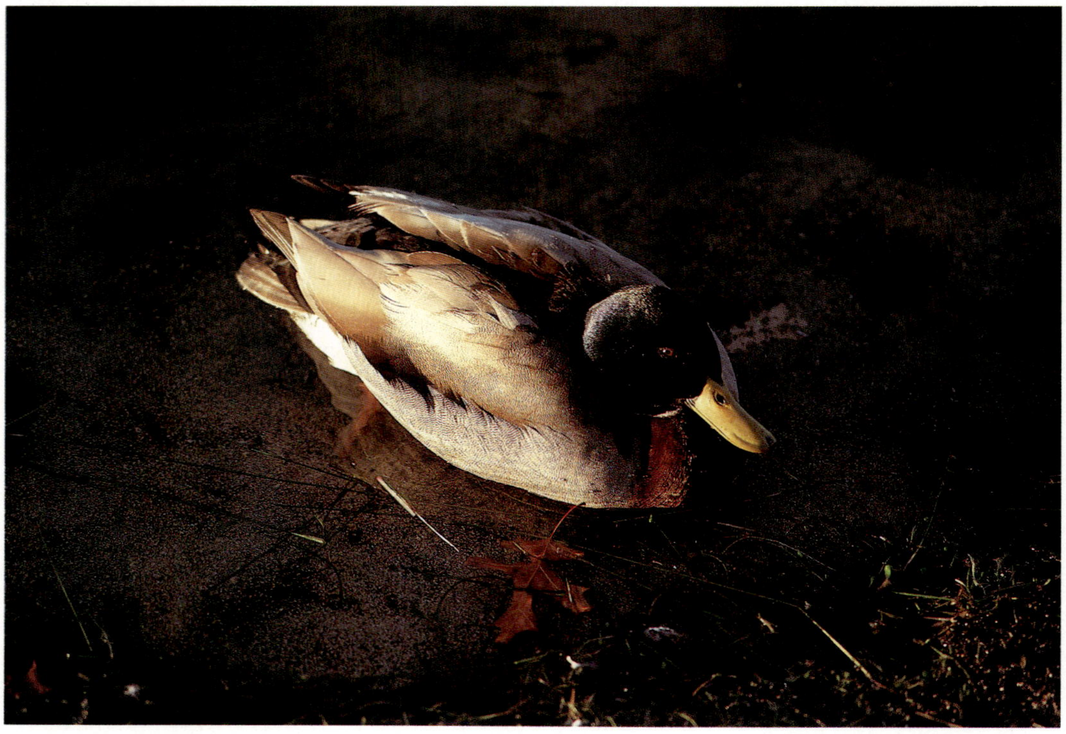

Duck, Lake Rotorua CRAIG POTTON

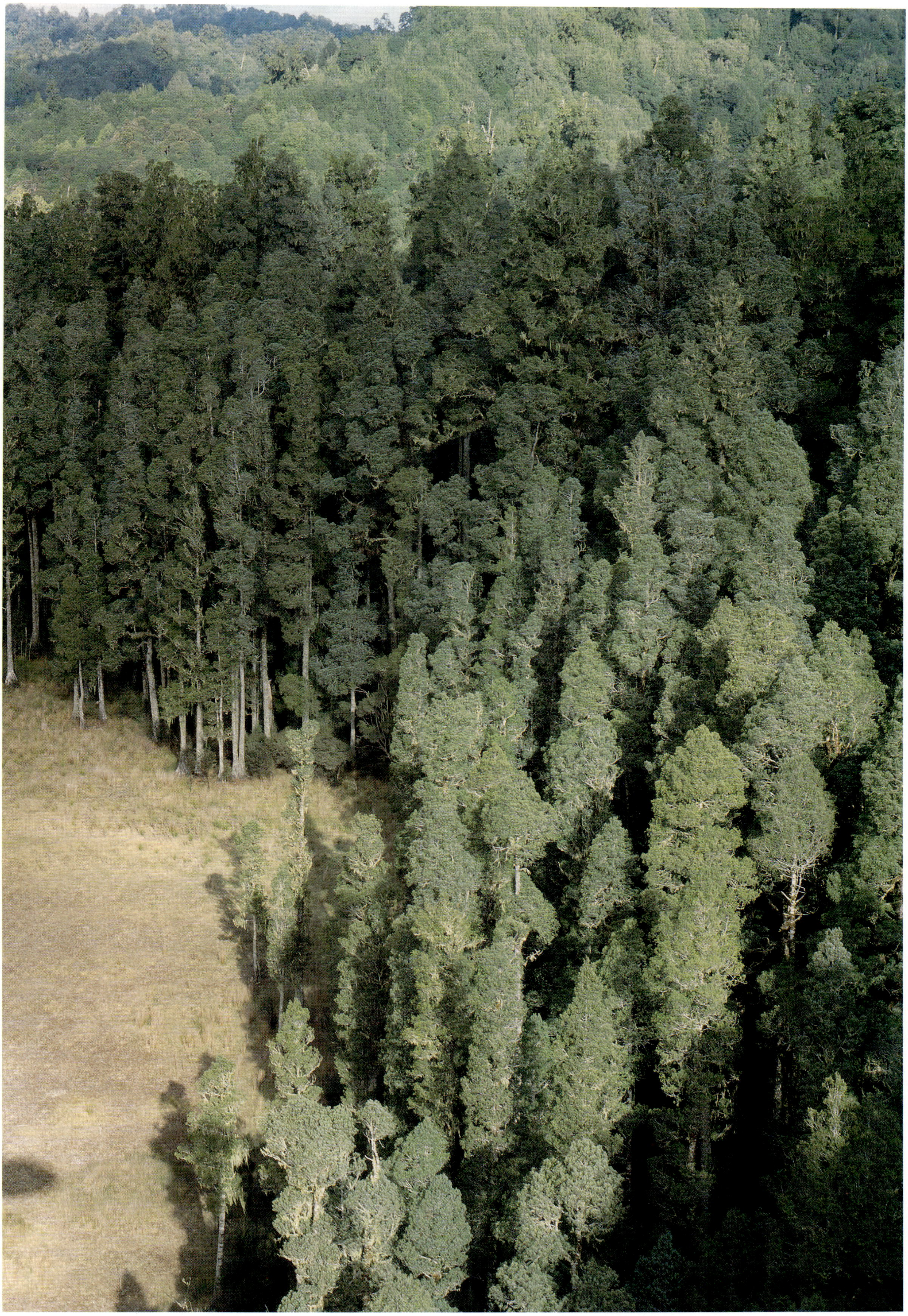

Whirinaki Forest, Urewera National Park

CRAIG POTTON

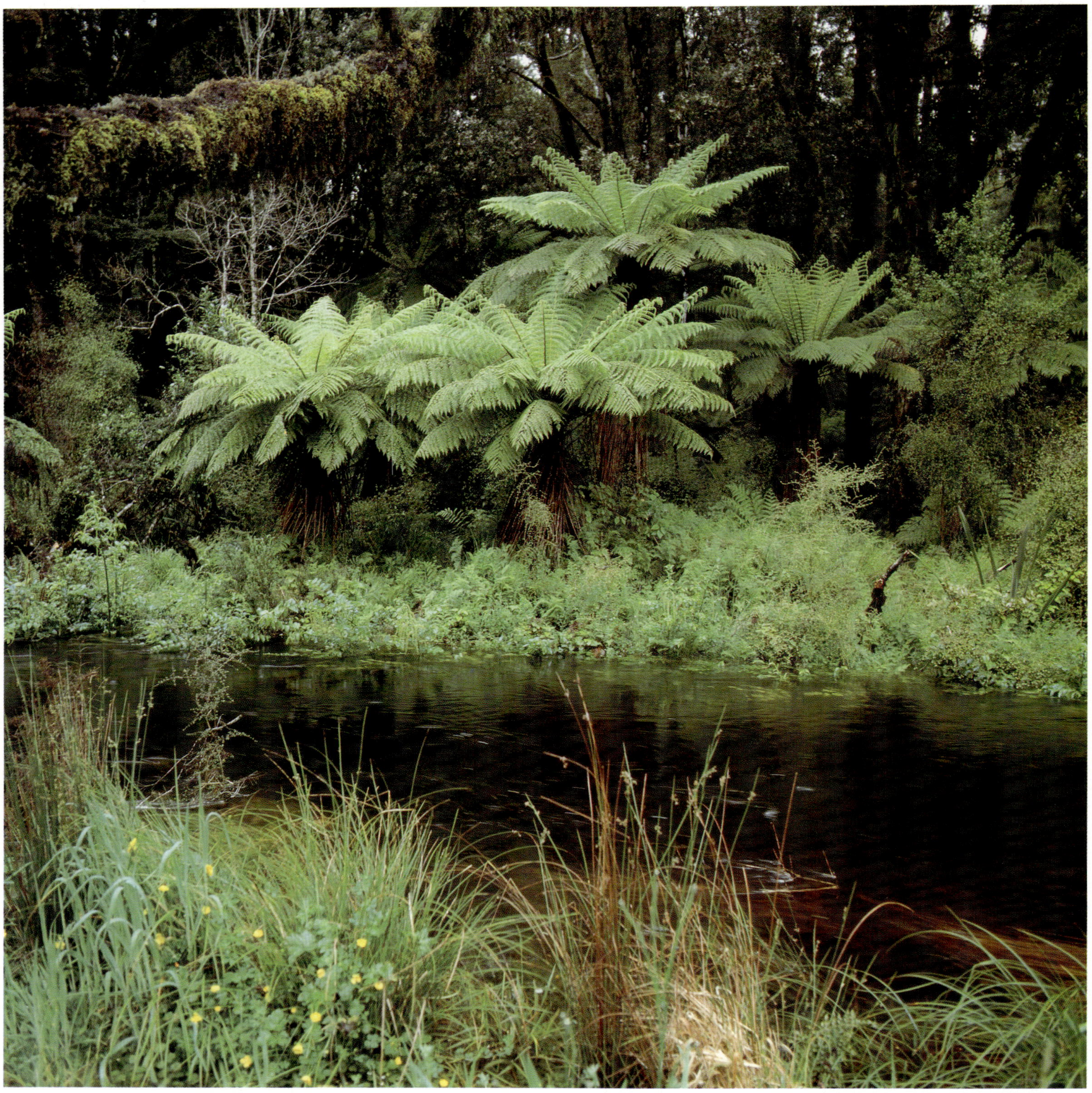

South Westland BRIAN ENTING

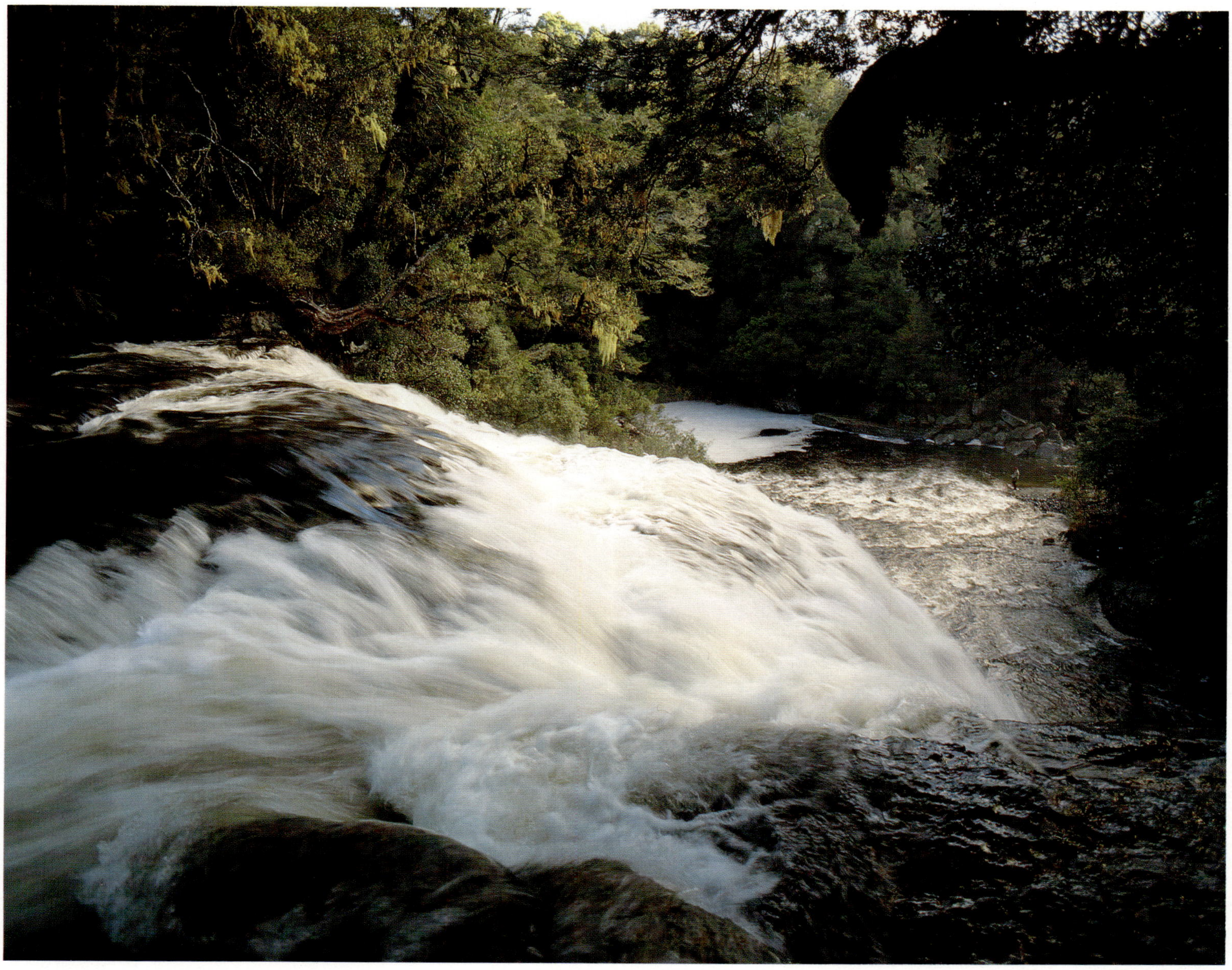

Tane O'Hinerau Falls, Aniwaniwa, Urewera National Park CRAIG POTTON

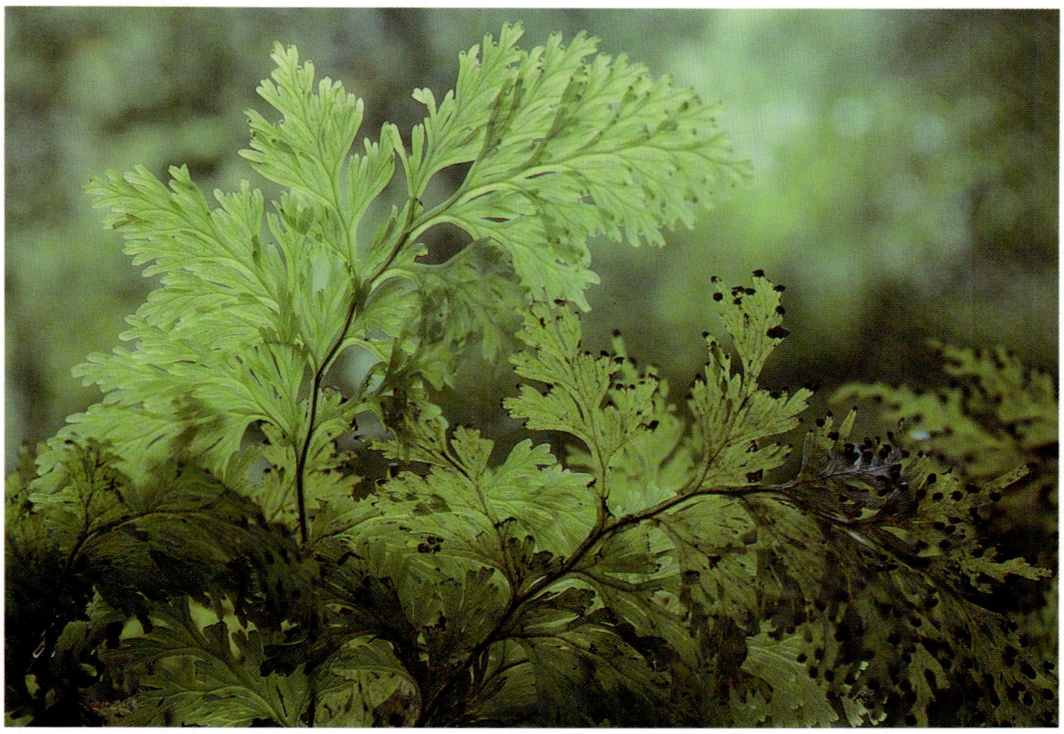

Filmy Fern, Ulva Island, Paterson Inlet, Stewart Island ROBIN MORRISON

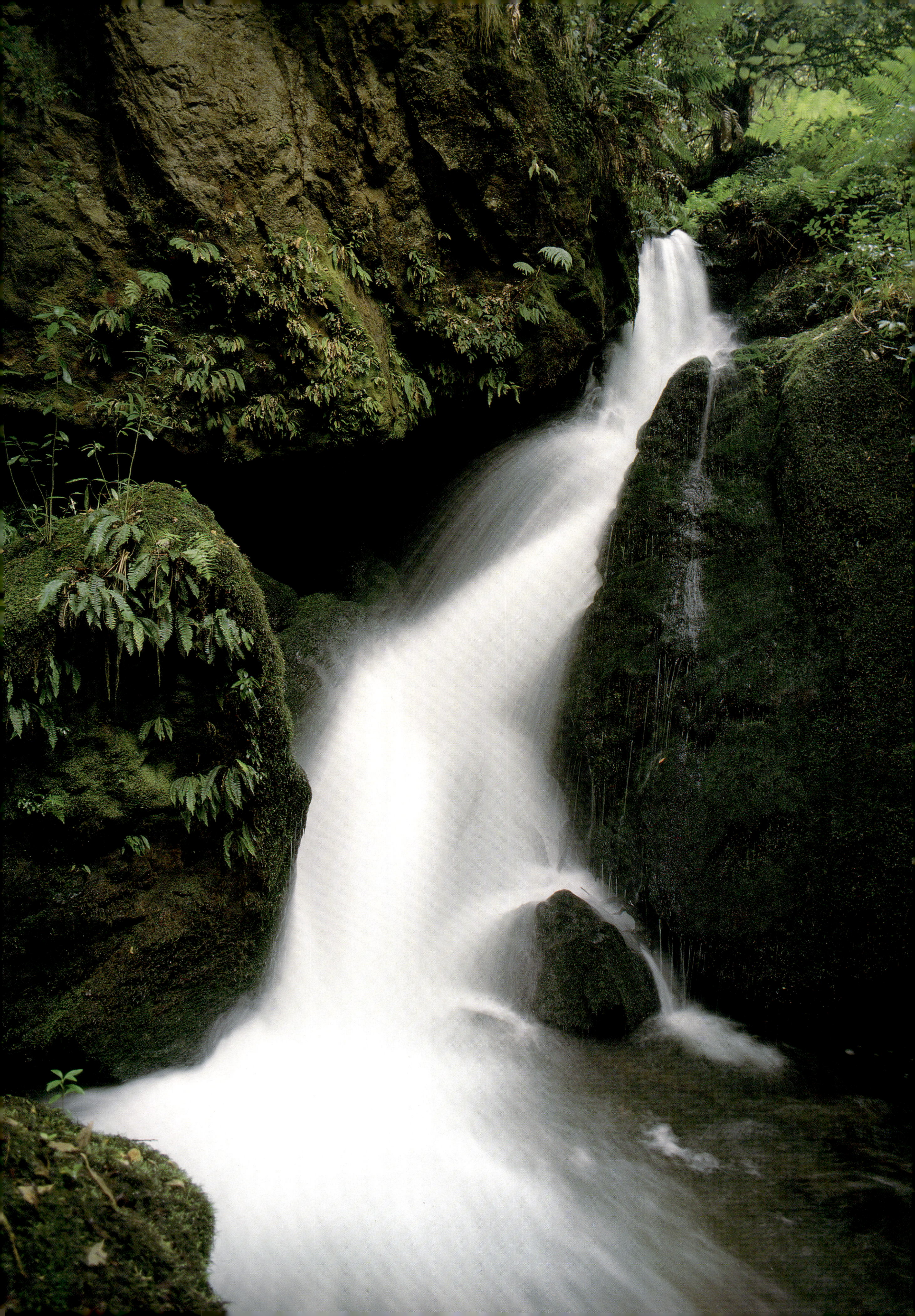

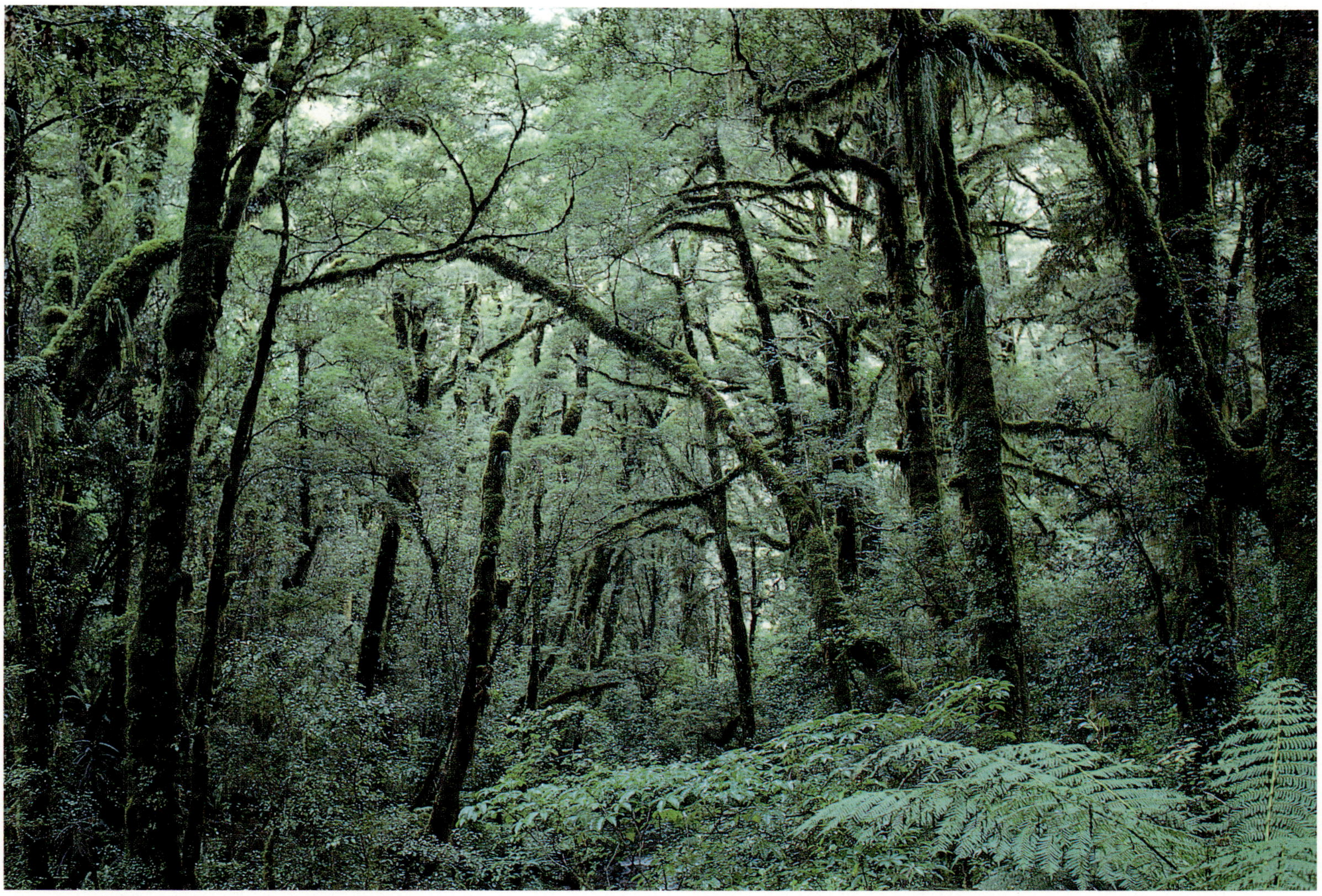

Podocarp forest, Fiordland BRIAN ENTING

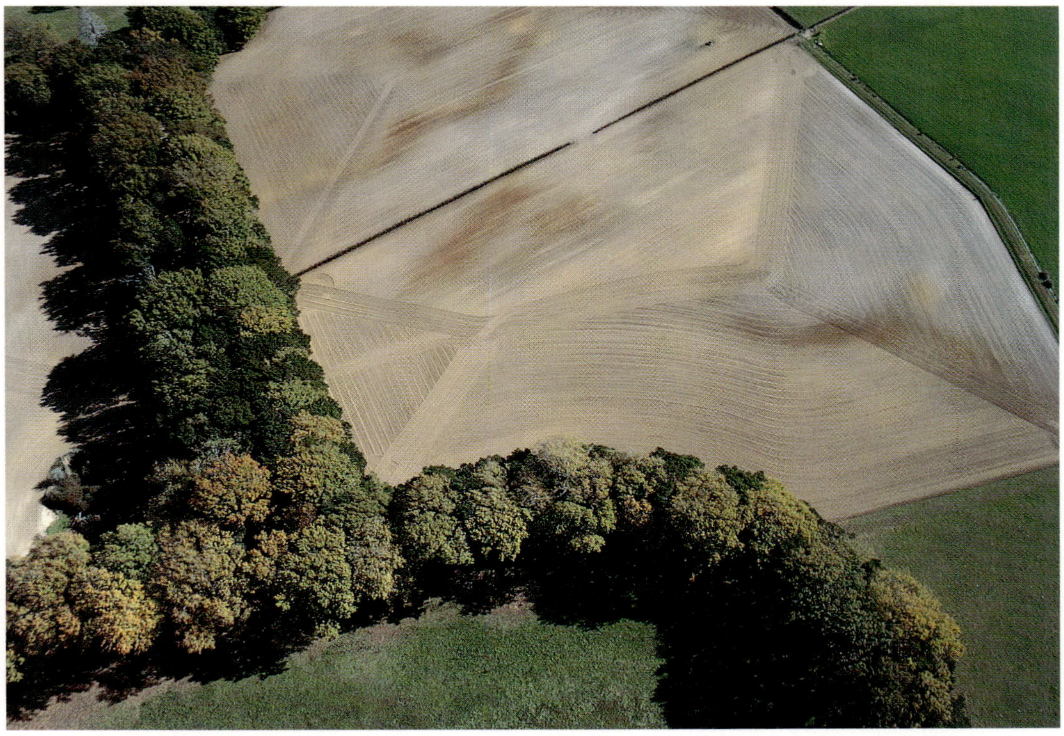

Aerial farm patterns in autumn, Cambridge ERIC TAYLOR

Te Wairoa Falls, Volcanic Plateau CRAIG POTTON

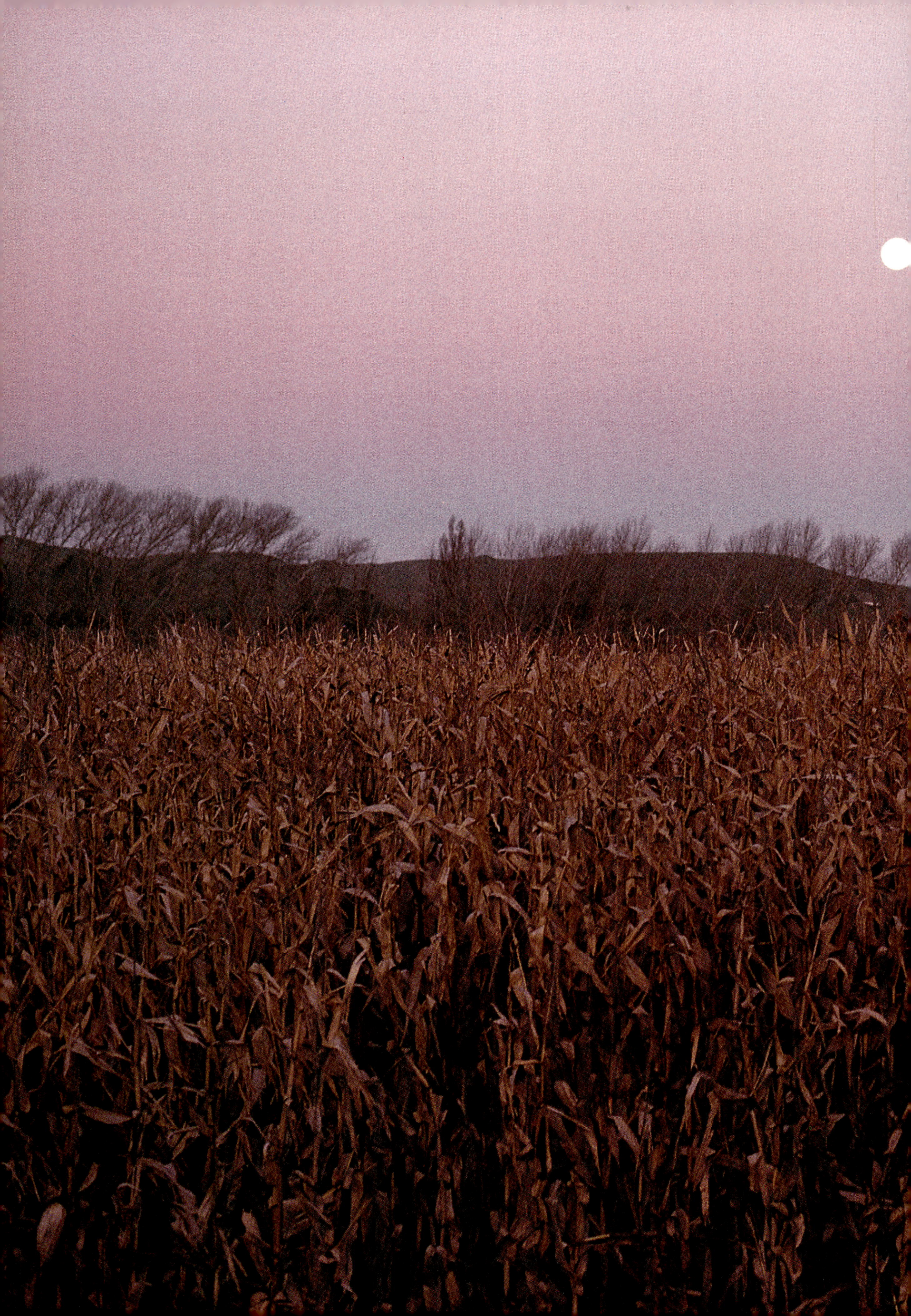

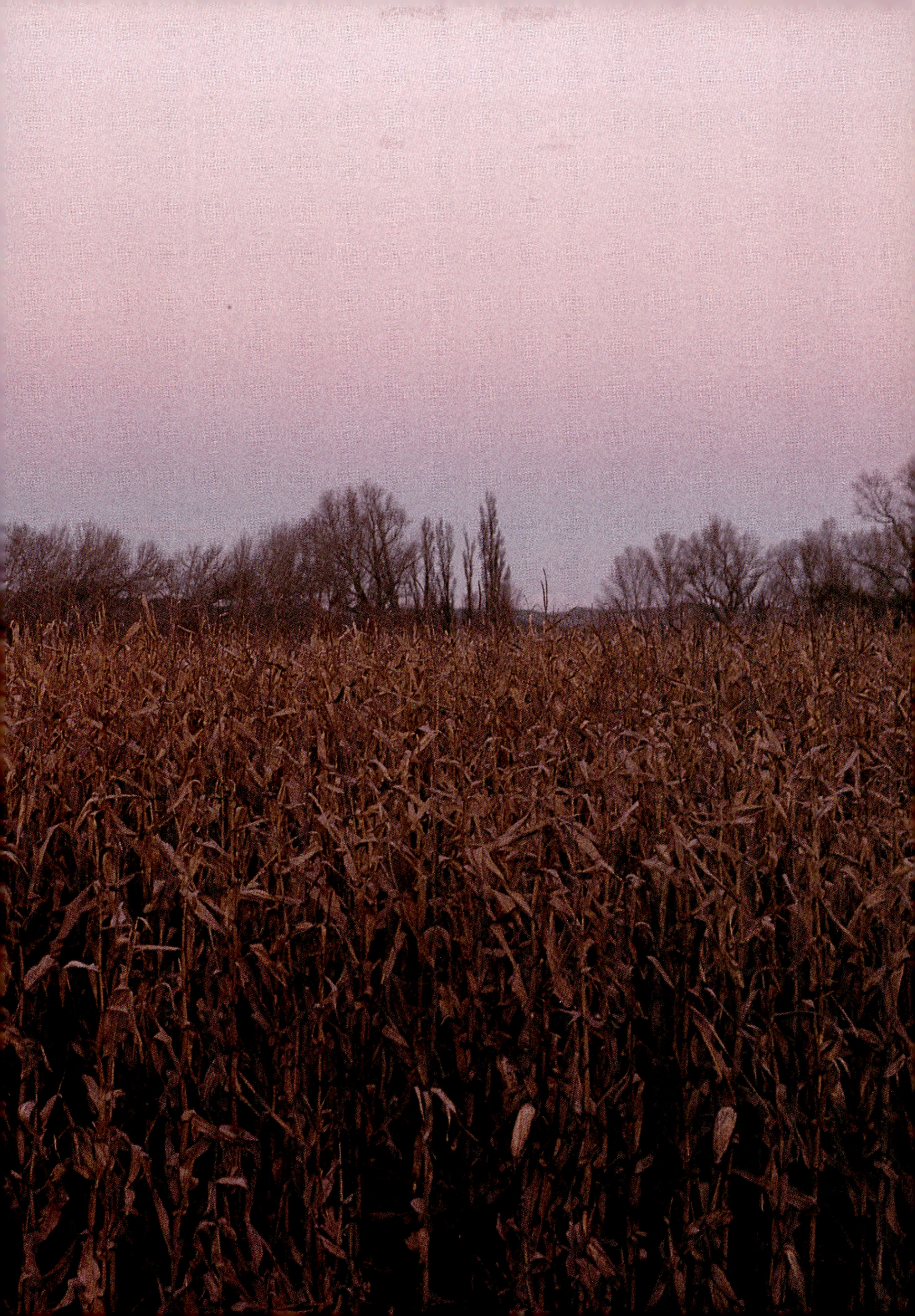

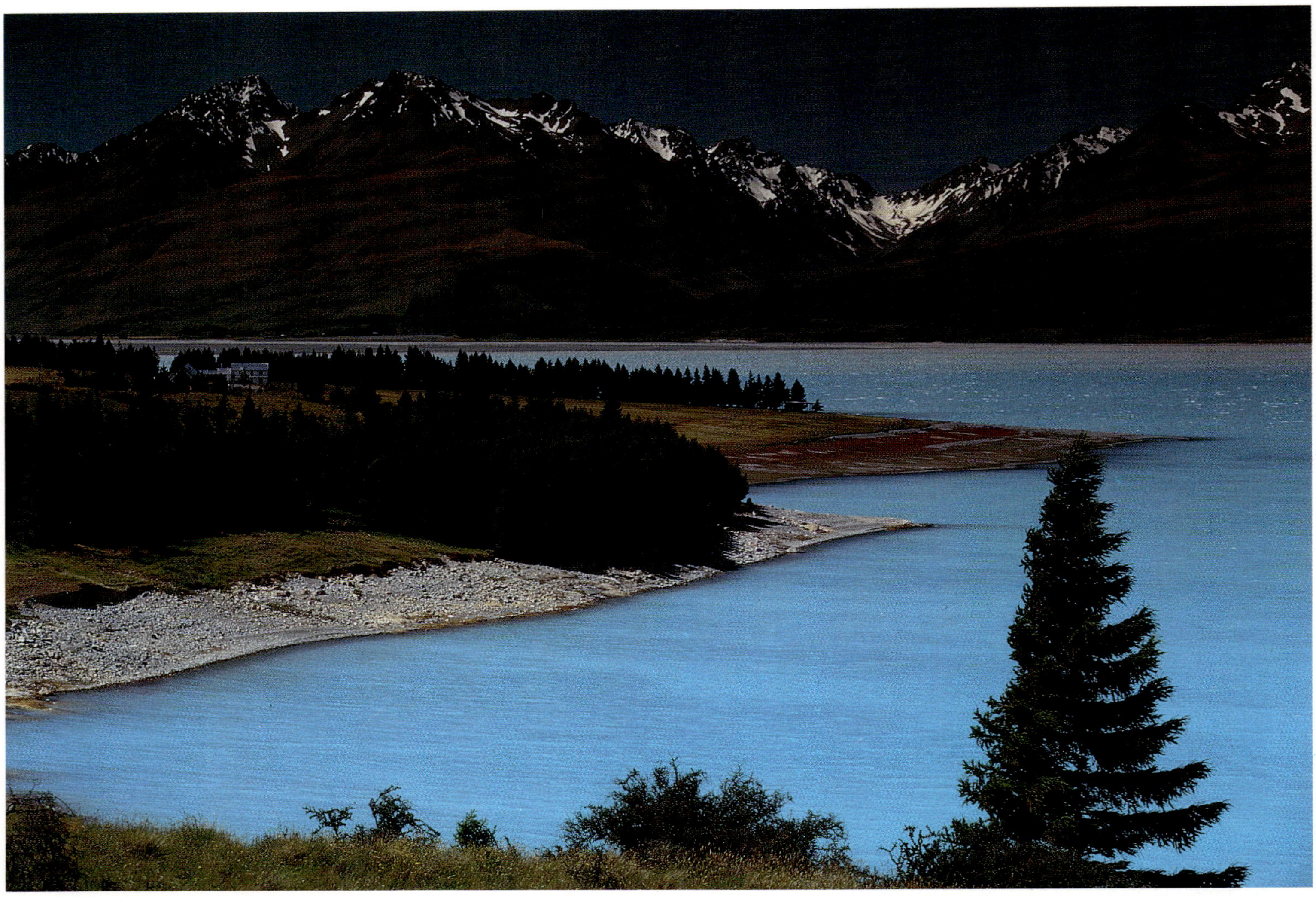

Fenntosh Station on Lake Pukaki, Mackenzie Country. The turquoise-blue colour of the water is caused by "rock flour" from the melting ice of the Tasman Glacier GEOFF MASON

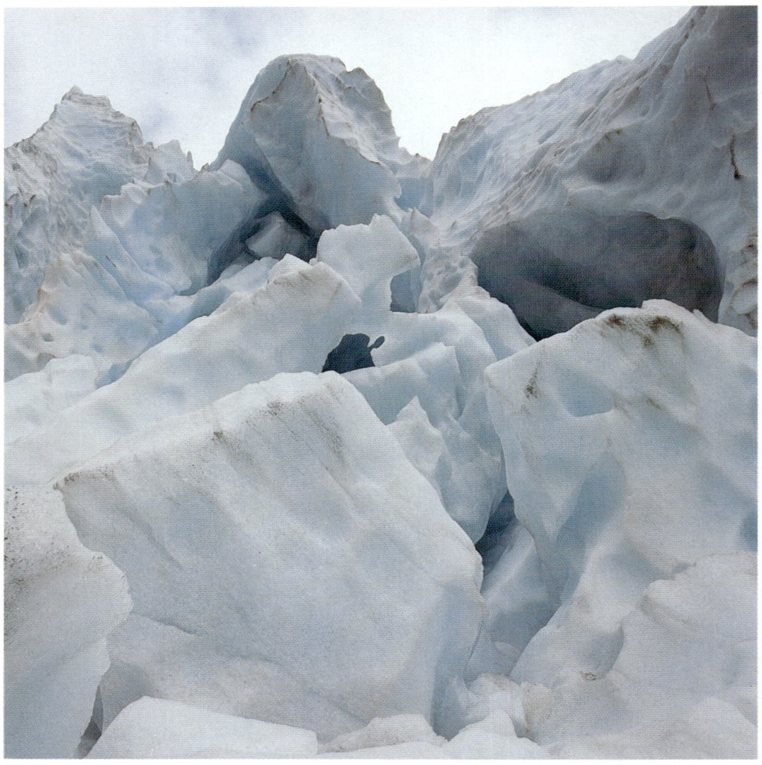

Franz Joseph Glacier BRIAN ENTING

Maize field, west of Wairoa CRAIG POTTON

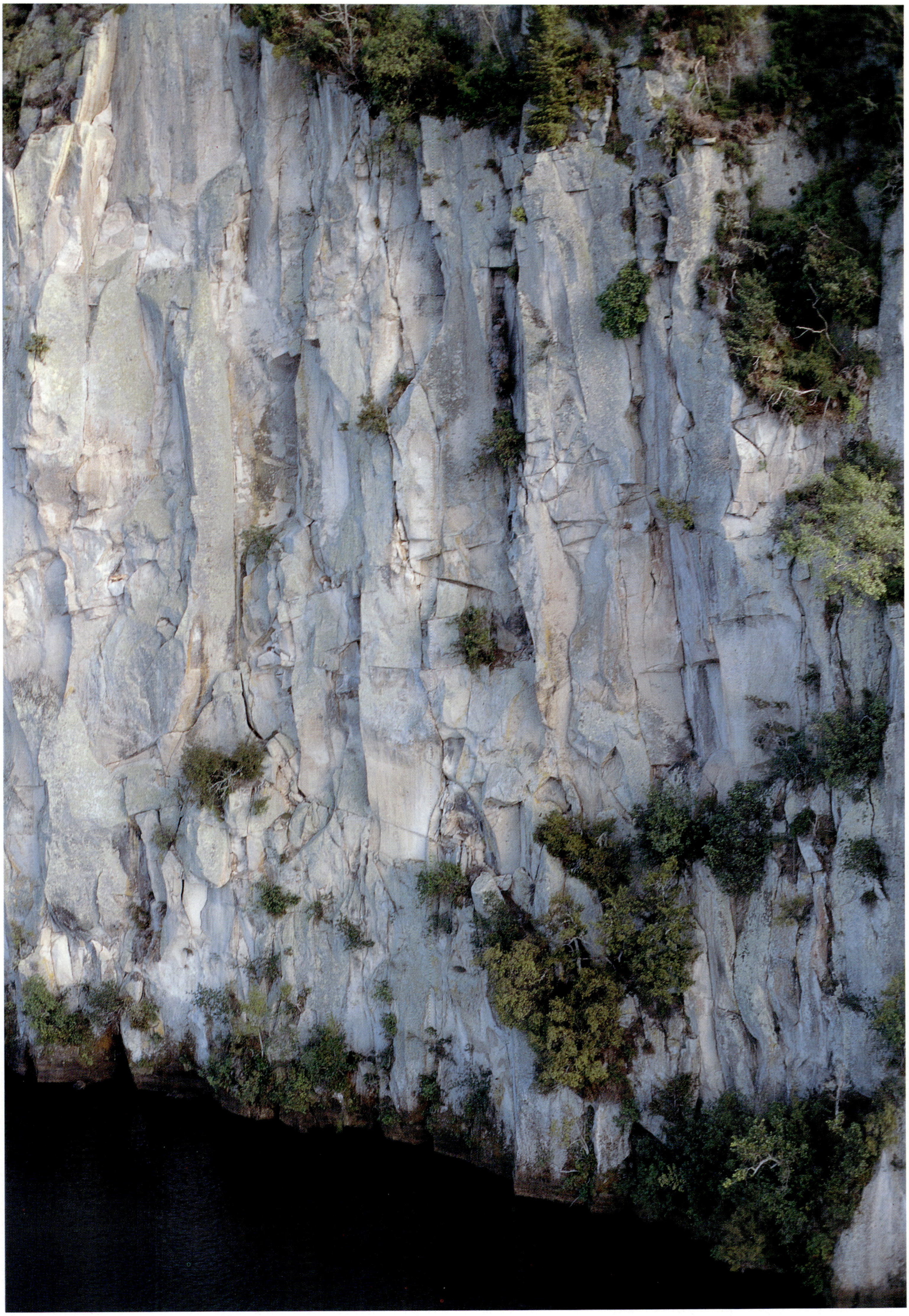

White cliffs on the western arm of Lake Taupo

CRAIG POTTON

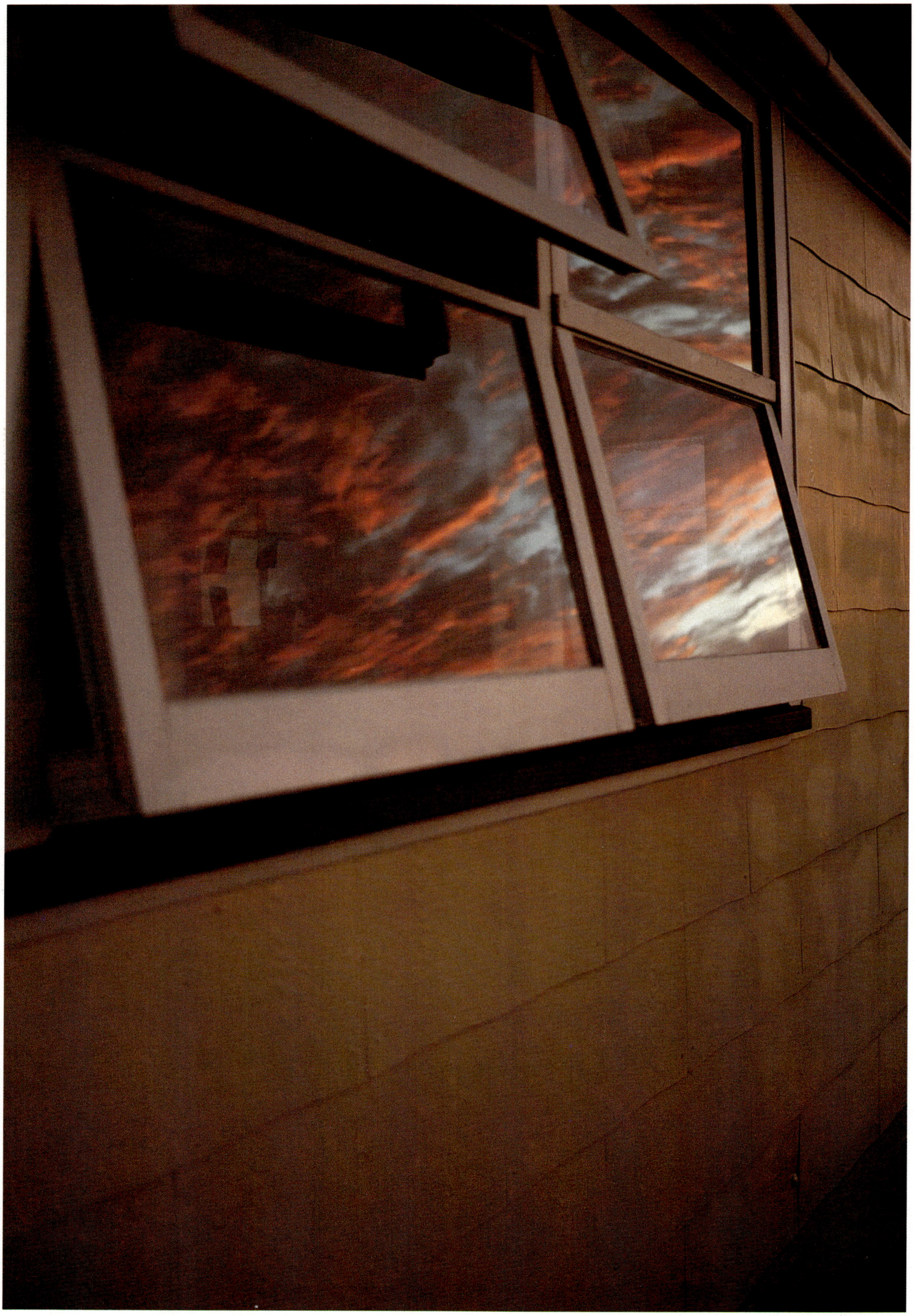

Sunrise at Te Hapua, Far North

STEPHEN ROBINSON

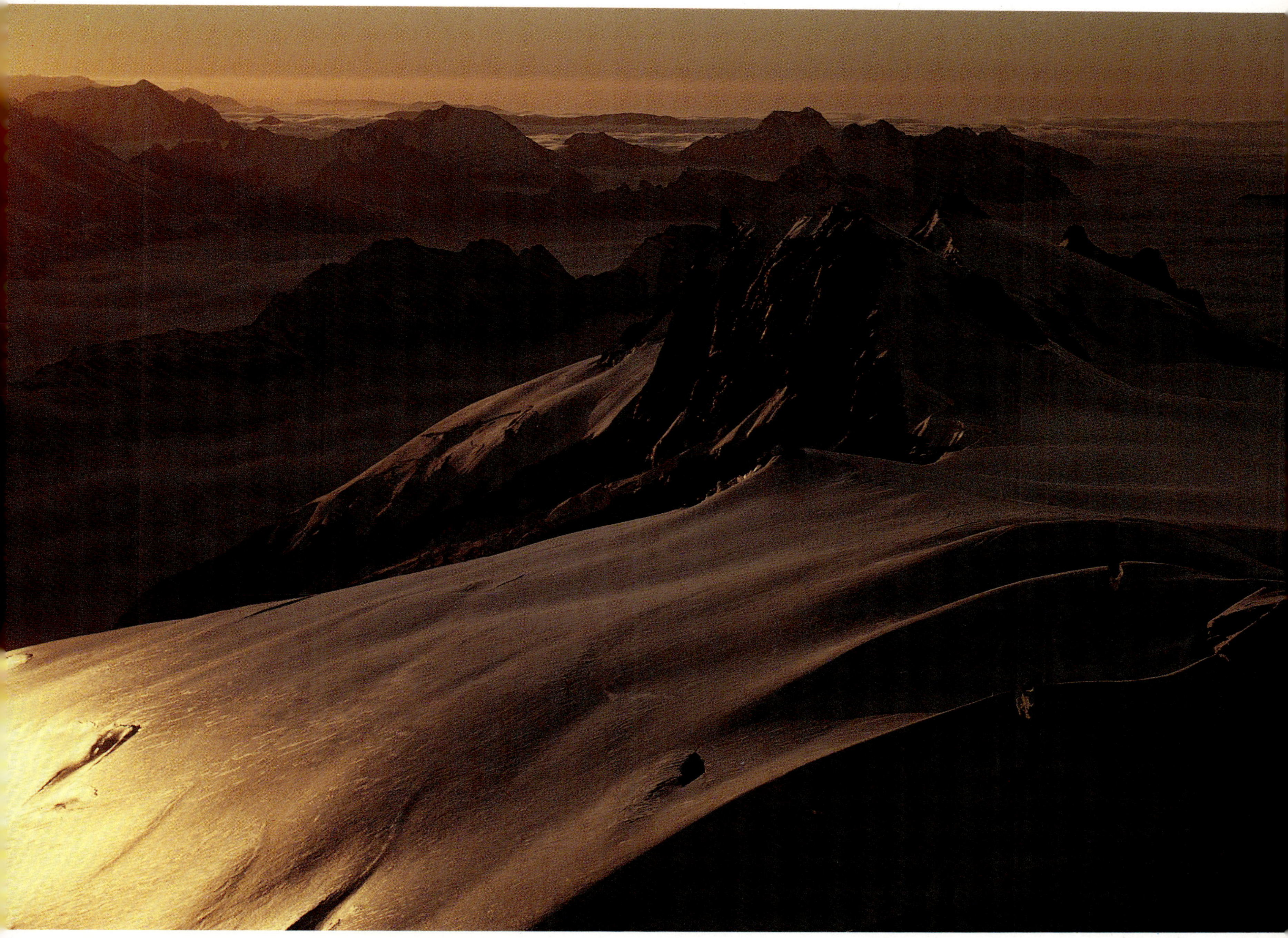

Sun on ice and snow near the Horace Walker Glacier GEOFF MASON

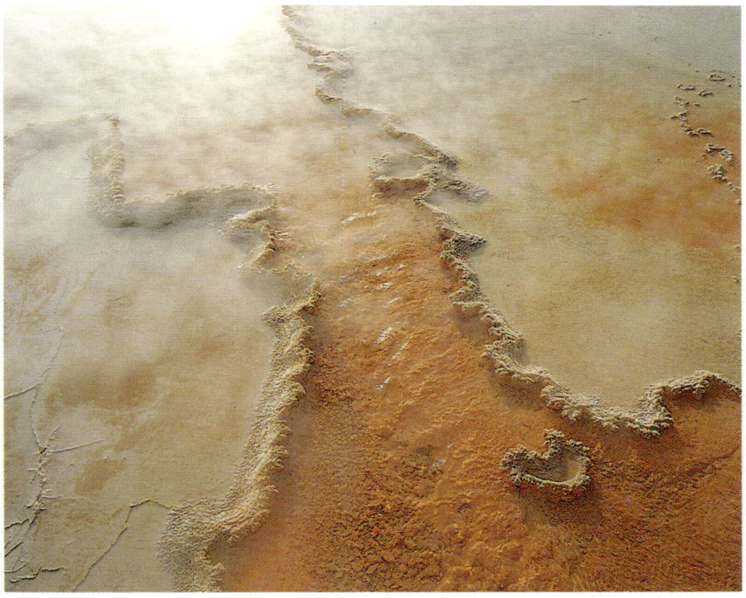

Waiotapu thermal area, Volcanic Plateau CRAIG POTTON

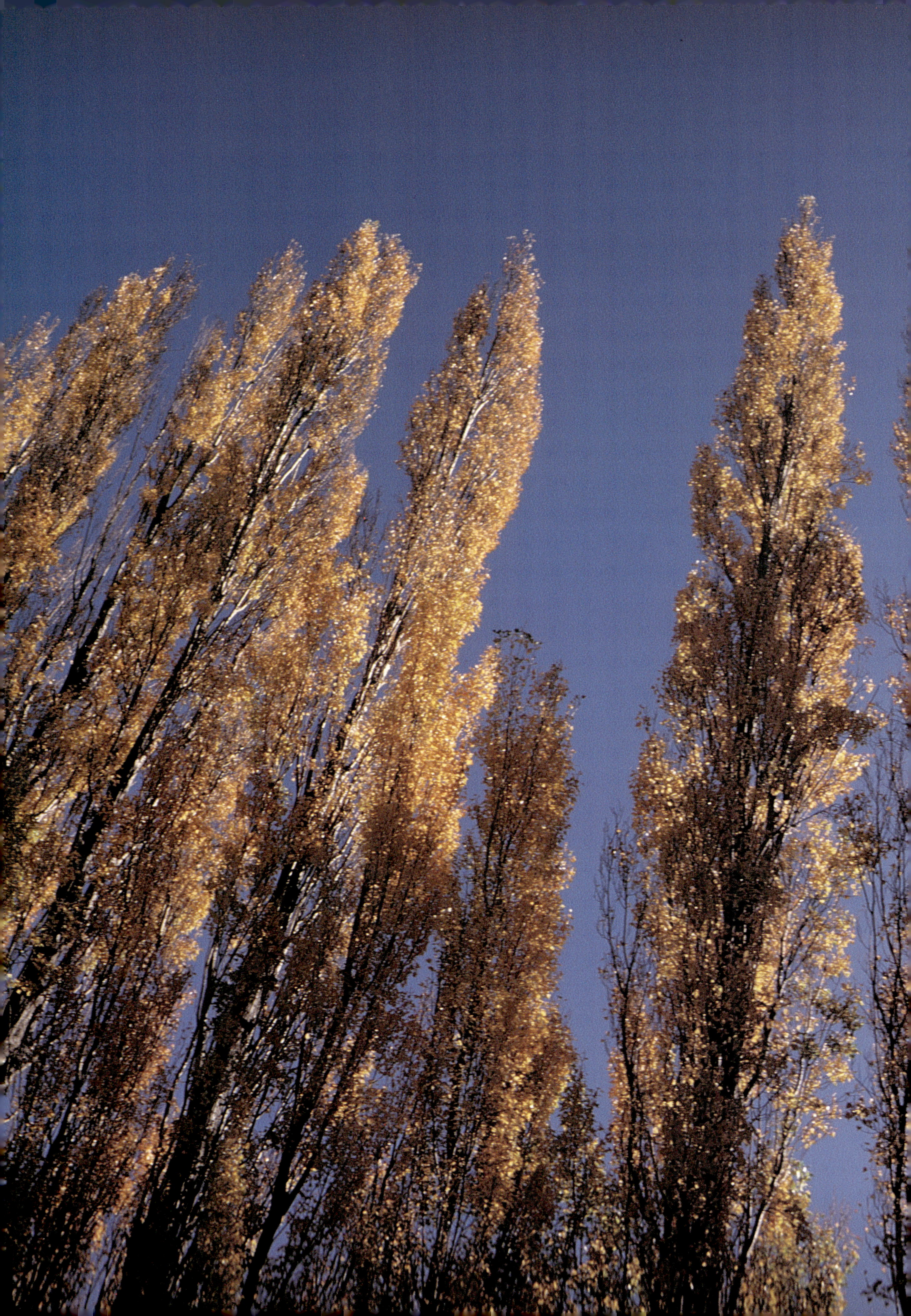

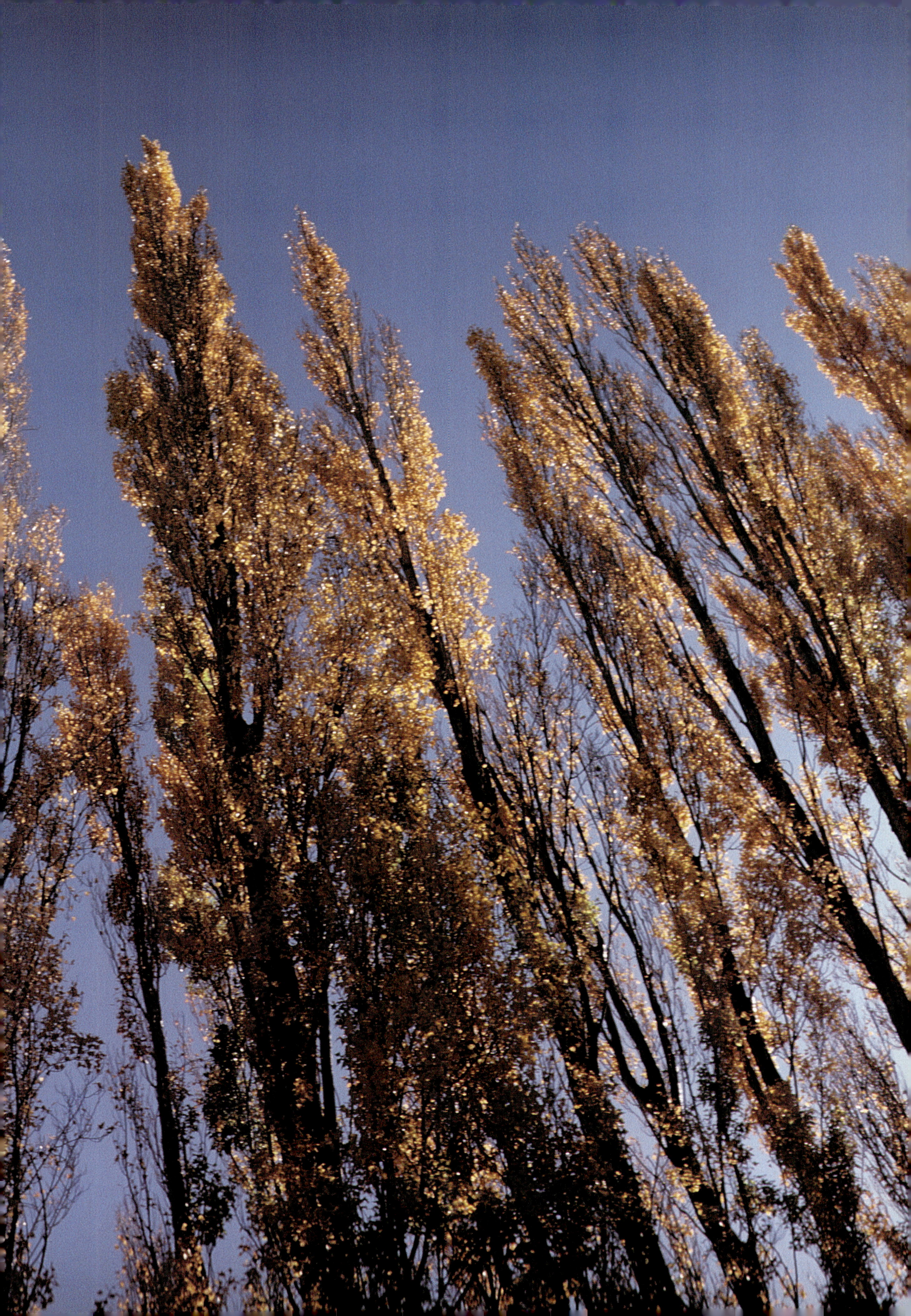

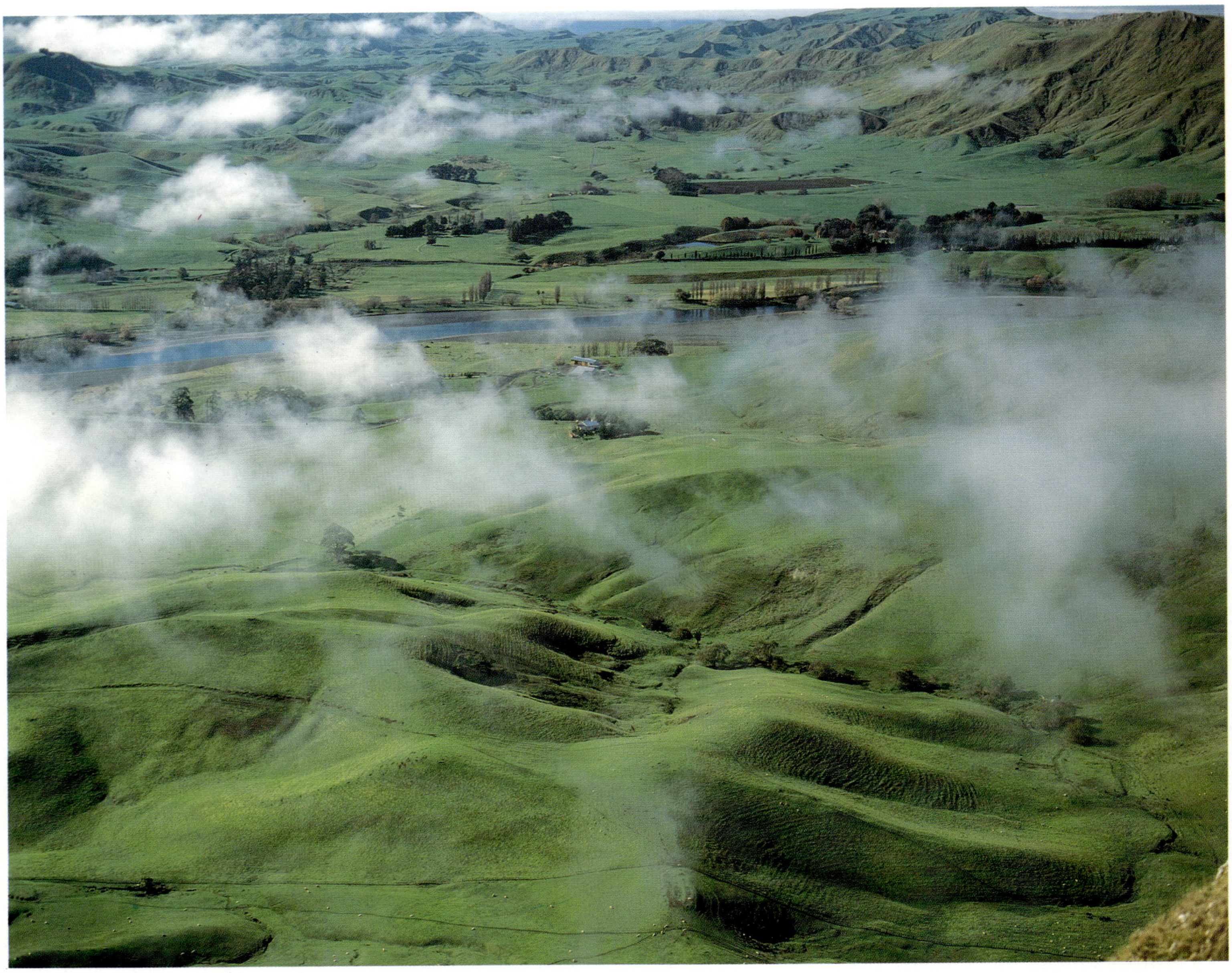

Te Mata Peak, Hawke's Bay CRAIG POTTON

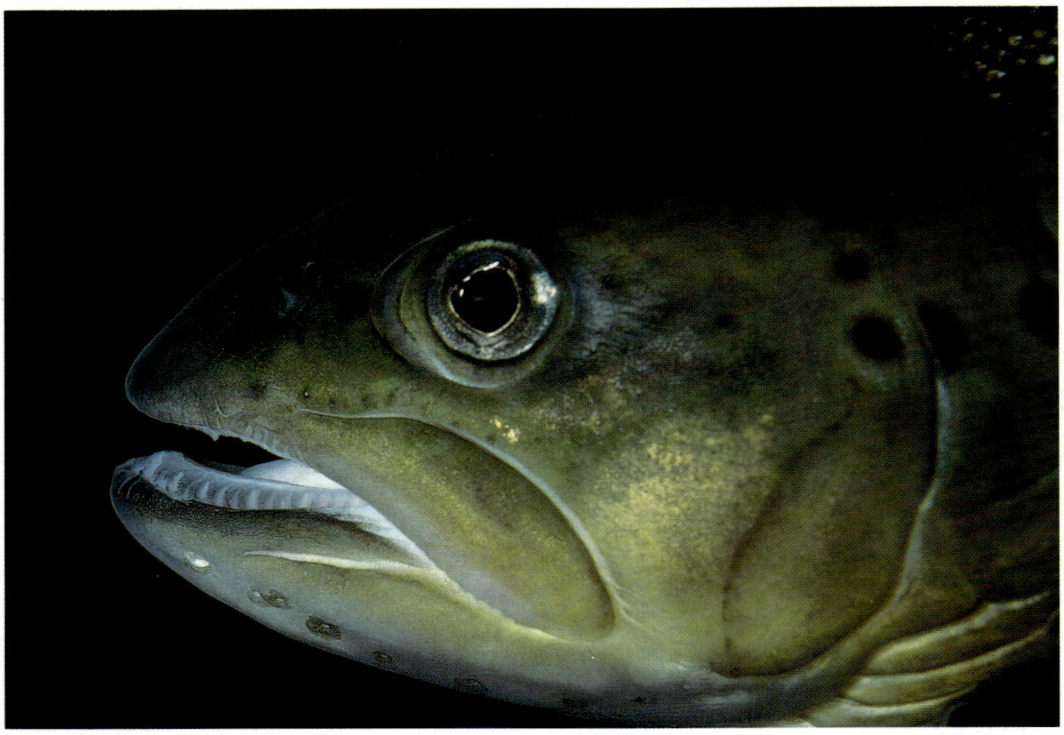

Trout, Te Anau BRIAN ENTING

Poplars near Cromwell, Otago GEOFF MASON

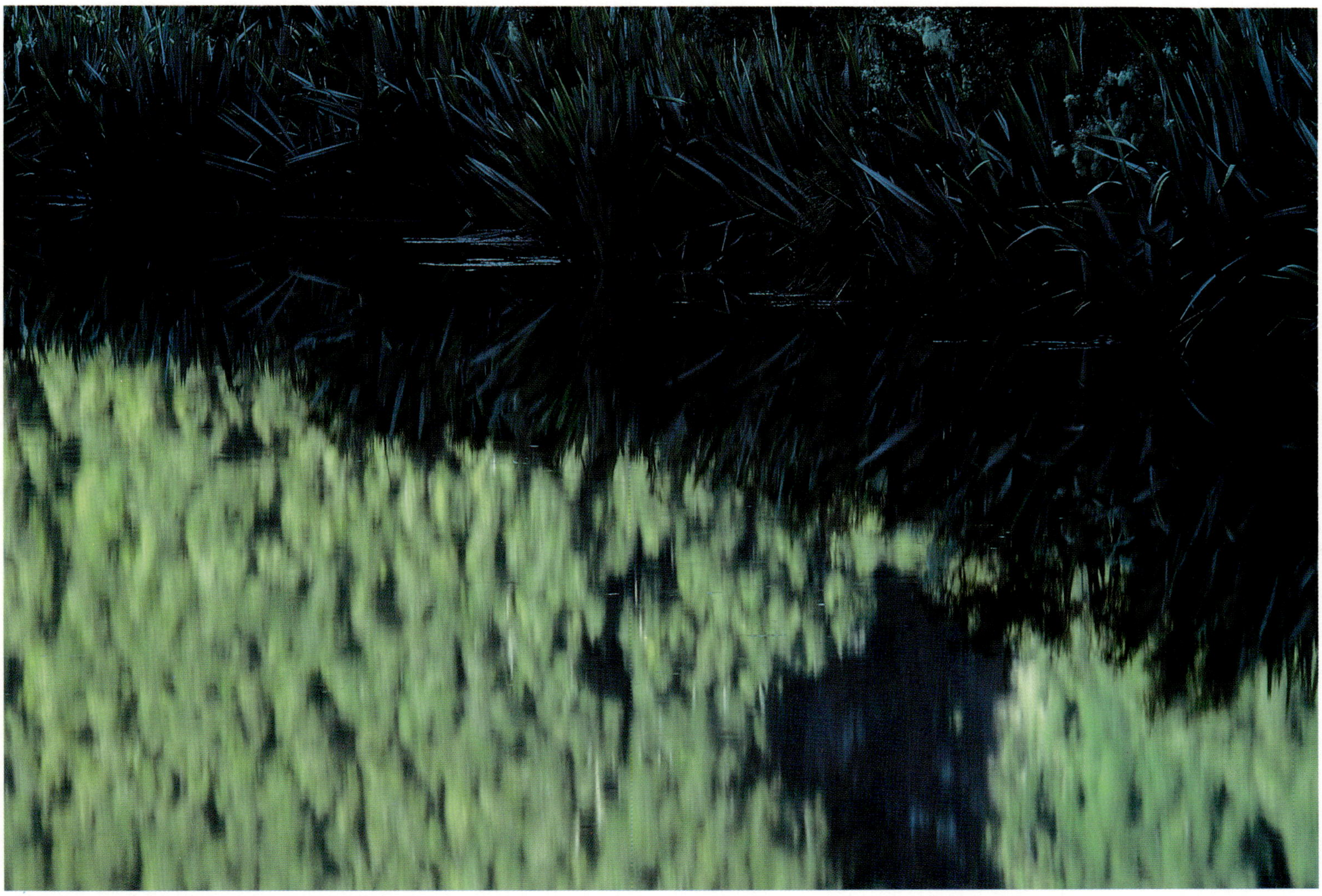

Mirror Lakes, Eglinton Valley, Fiordland GEOFF MASON

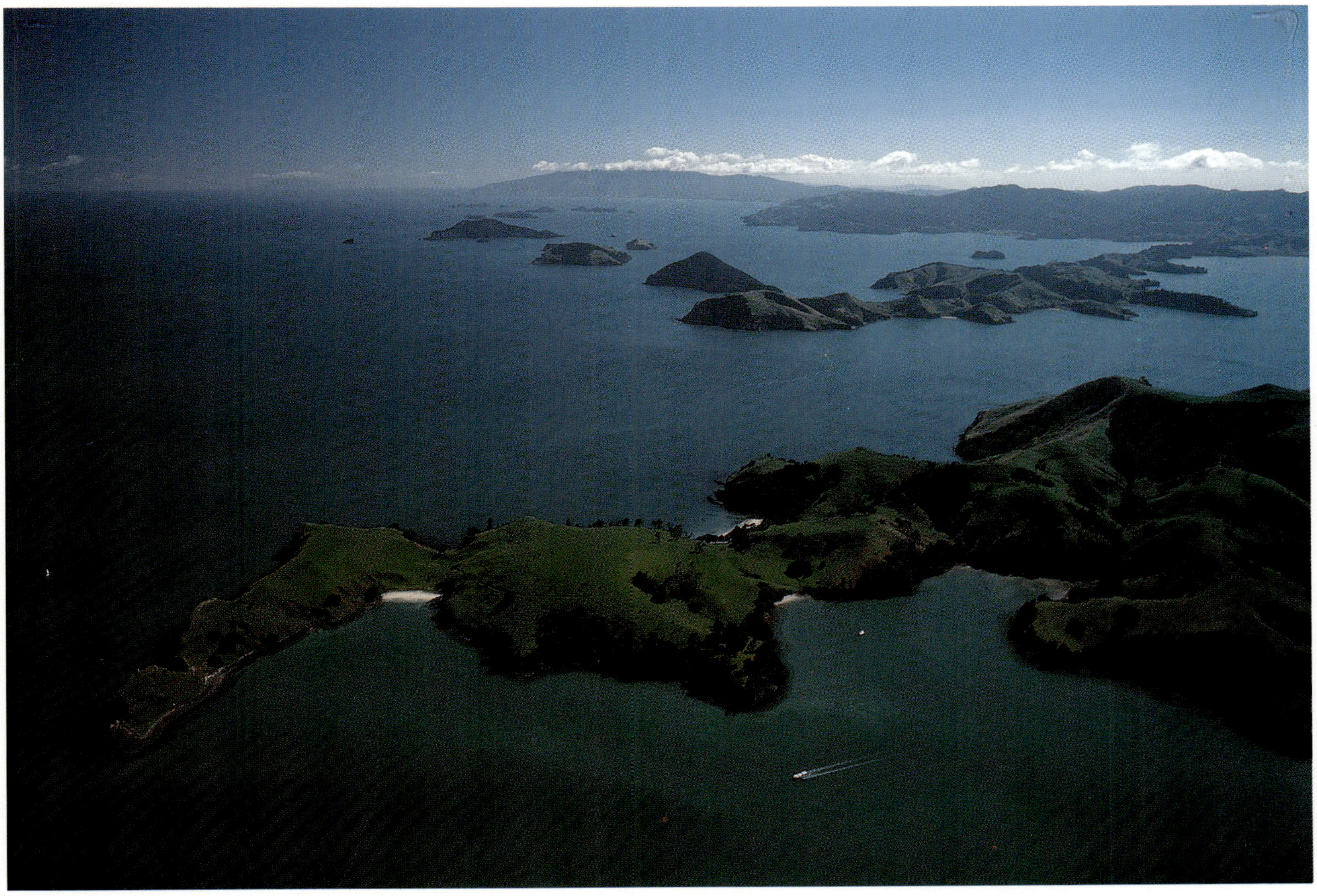

Aerial view of Manaia Harbour, Coromandel ERIC TAYLOR

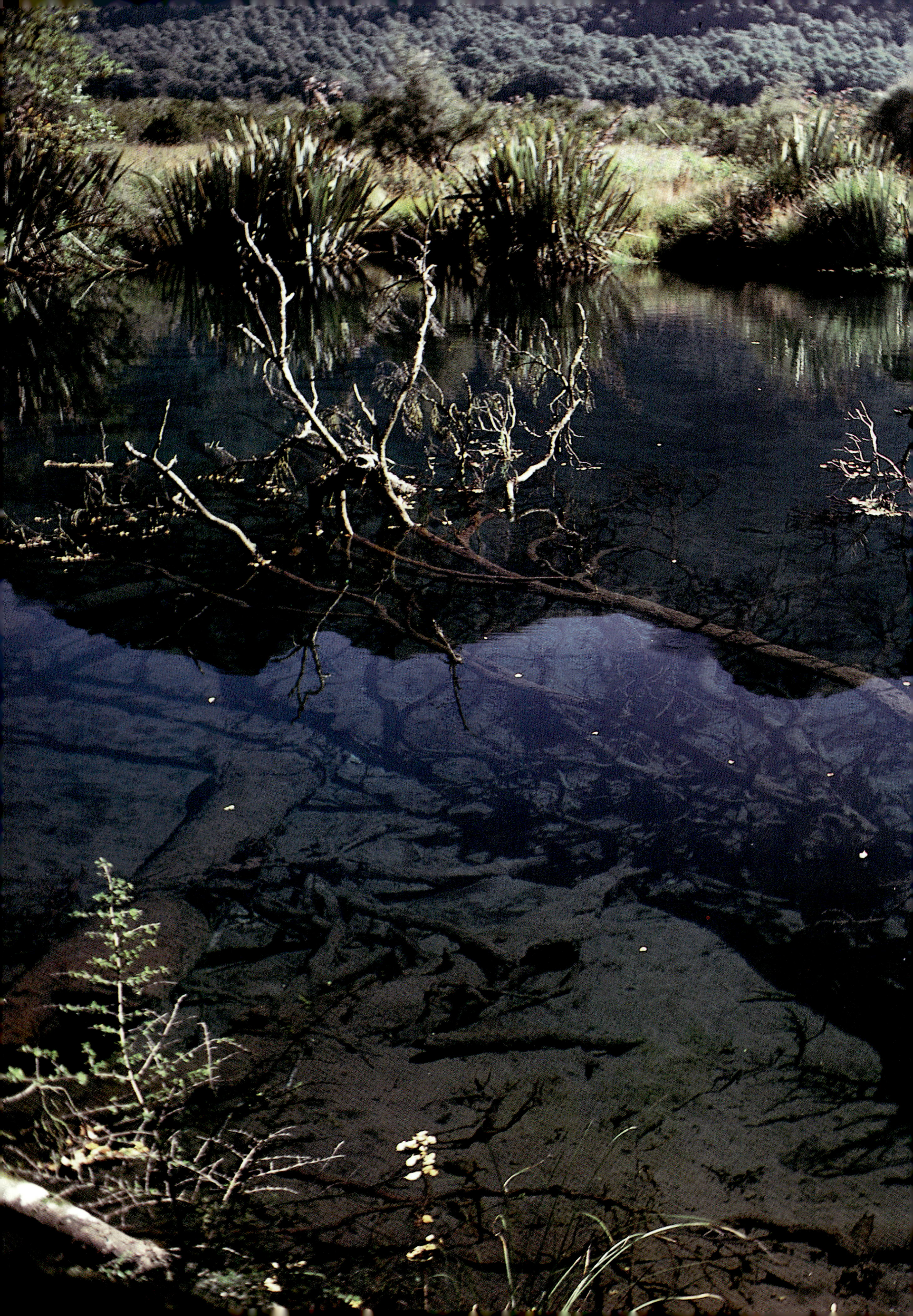

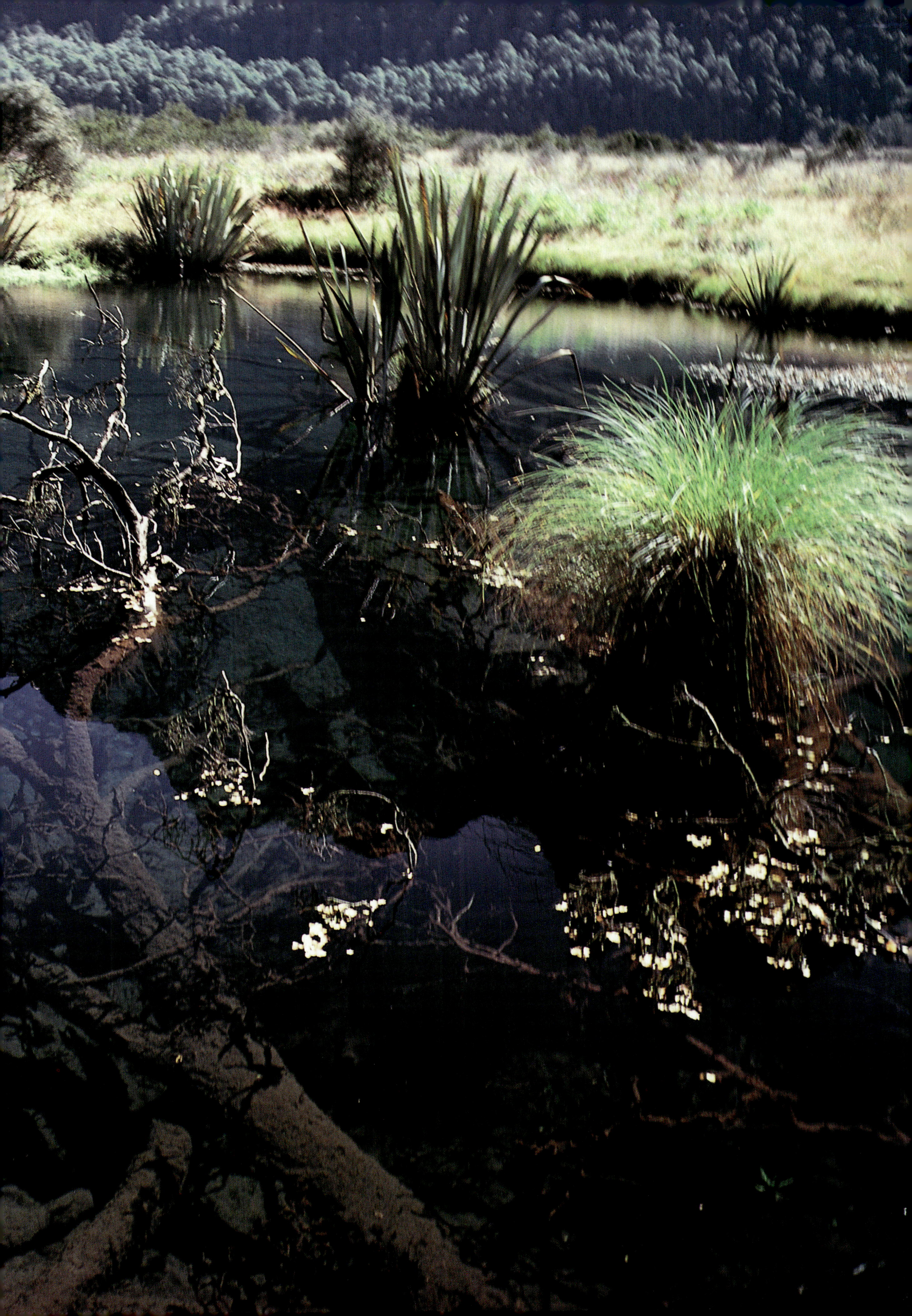

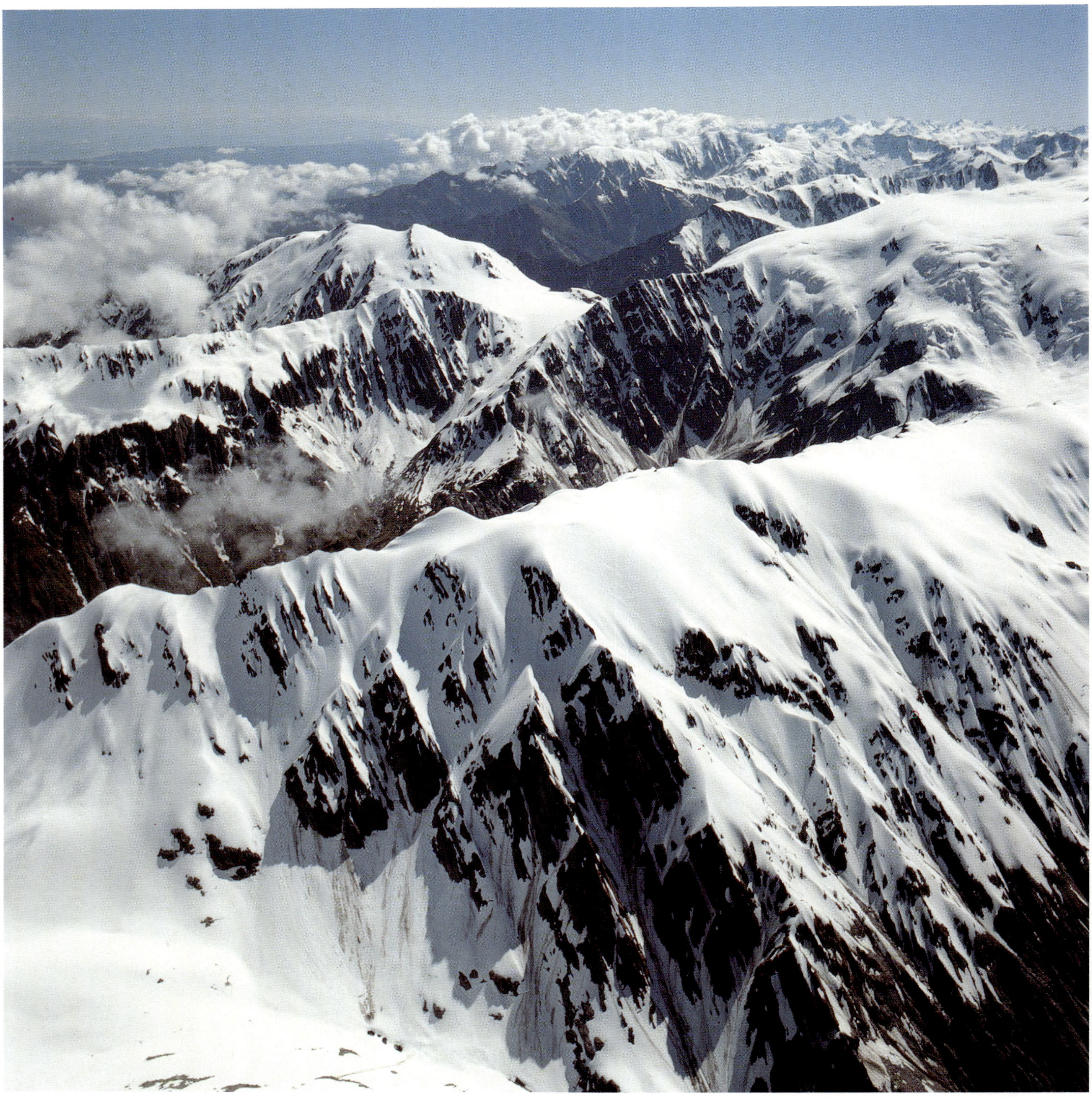

West of the main divide, Southern Alps BRIAN ENTING

Mirror Lakes, Eglinton Valley, Fiordland BRIAN ENTING

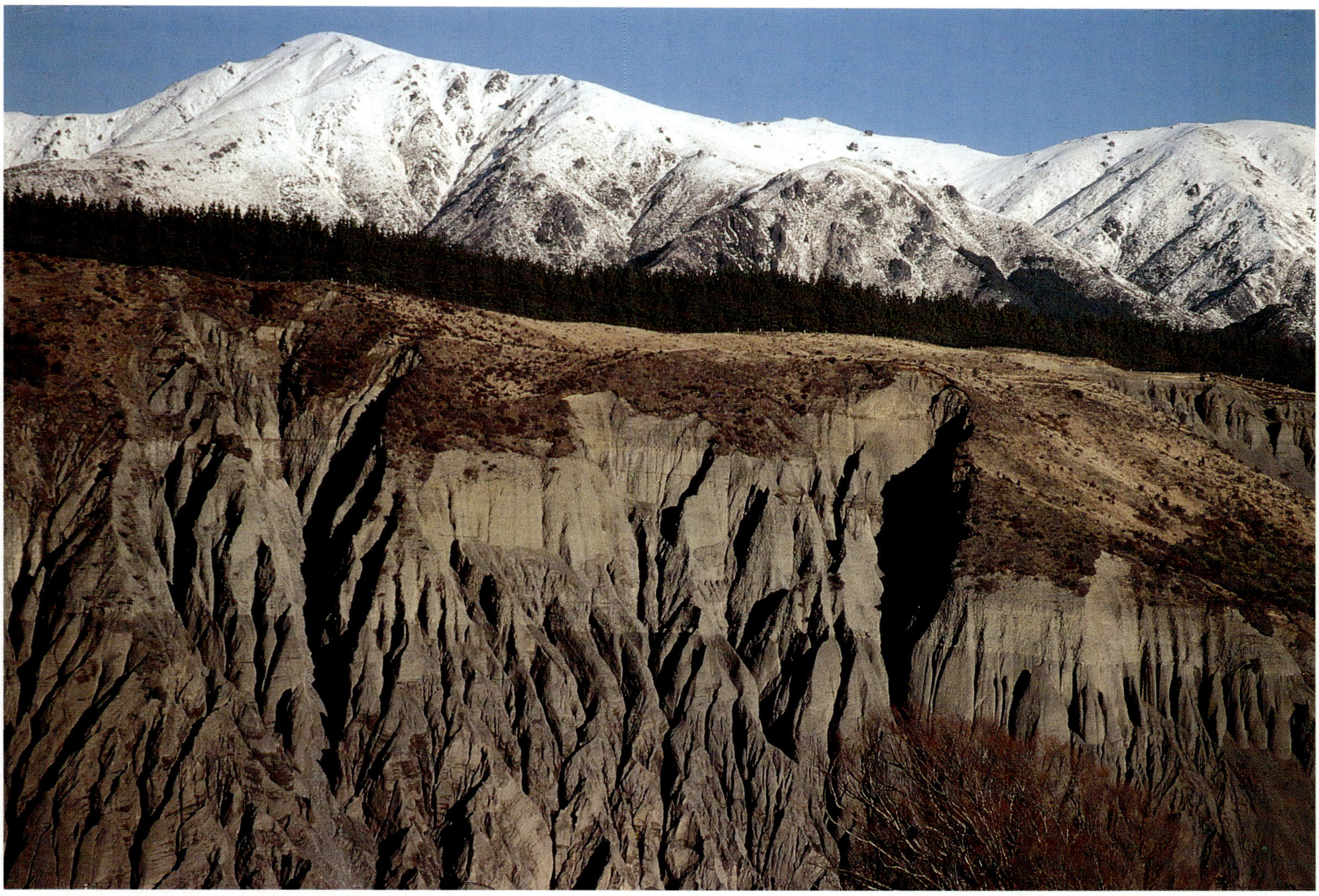

On the road to Lewis Pass, Canterbury ROBIN MORRISON

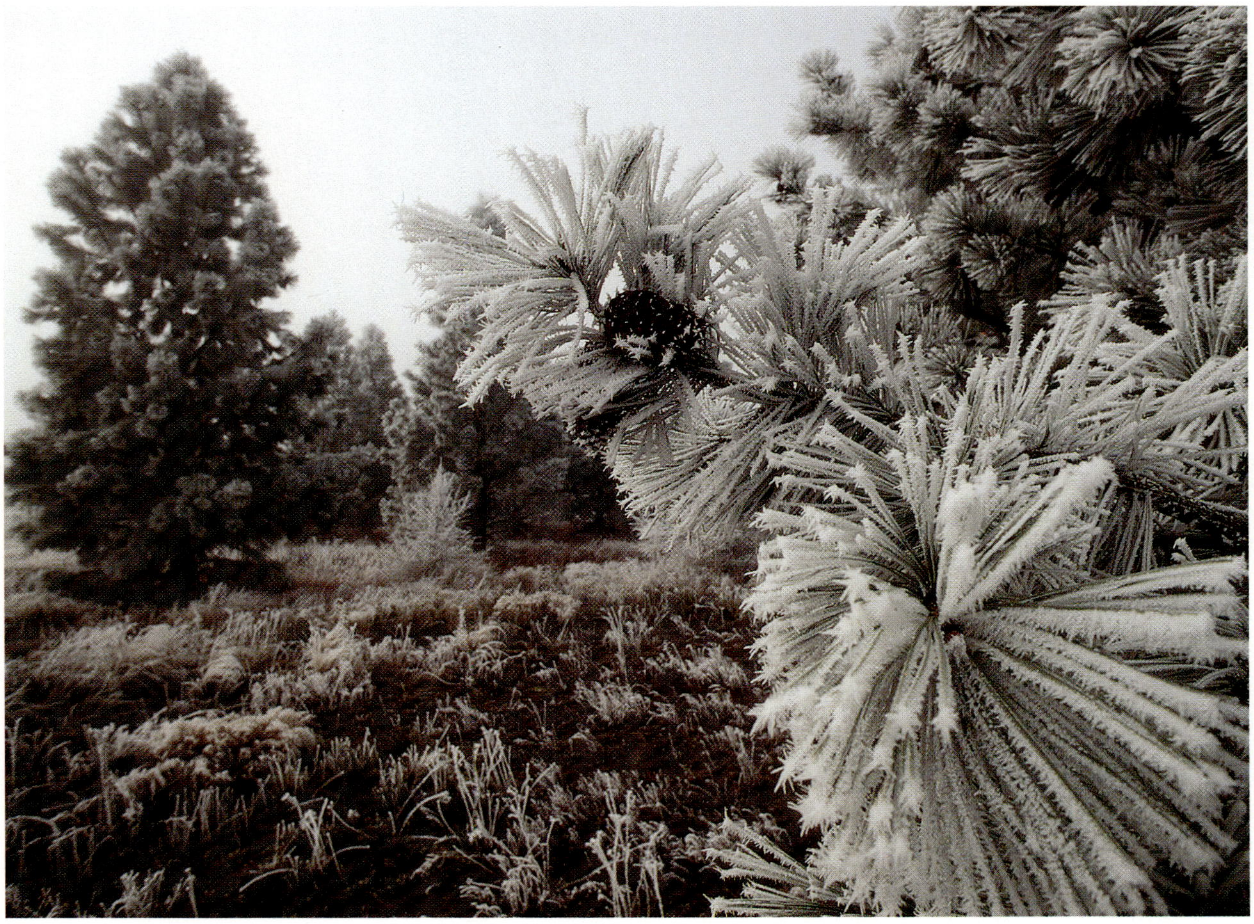

Hoar frost near Twizel, Mackenzie Country GEOFF MASON

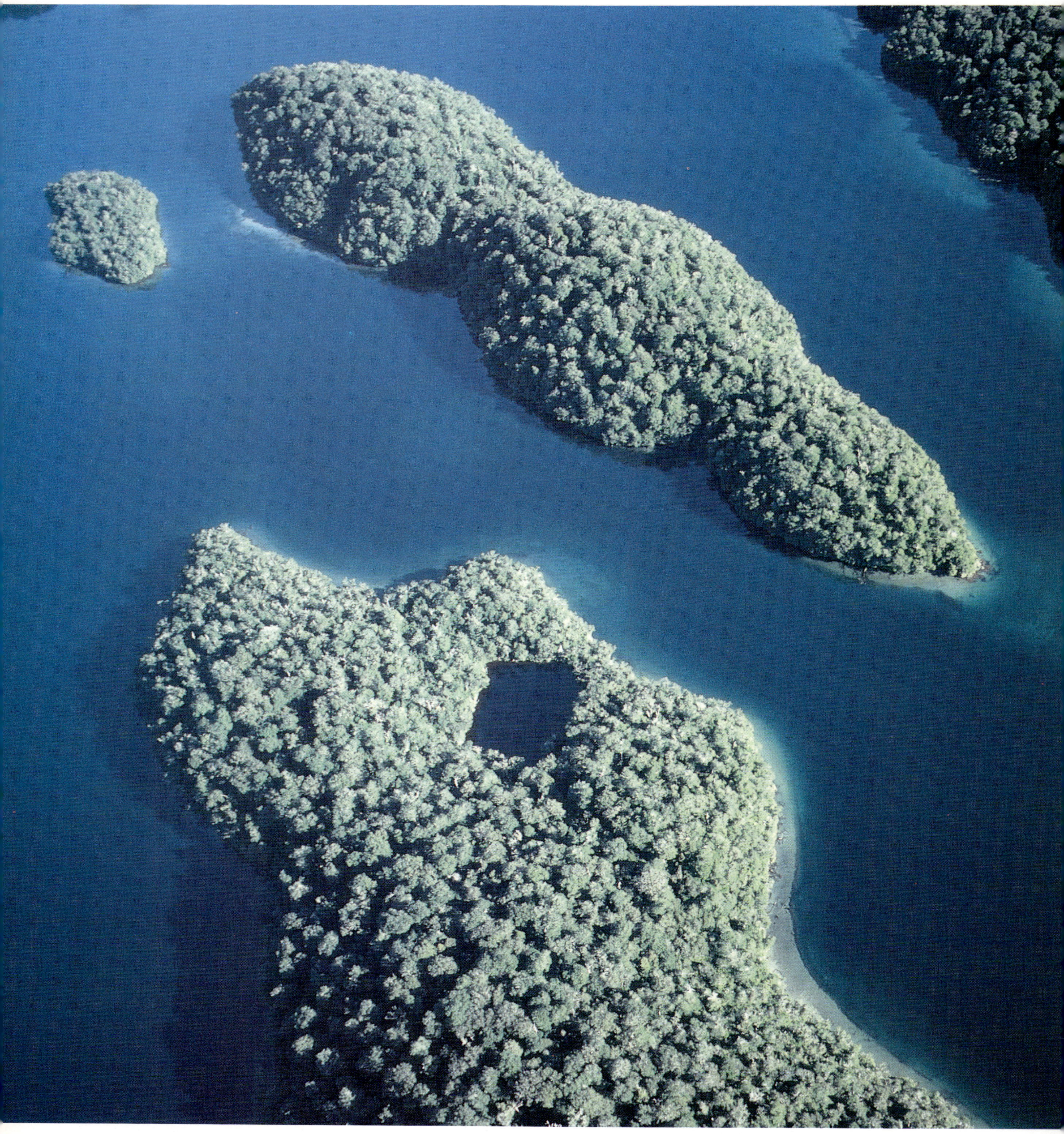

Lake Waikareiti, Urewera National Park

CRAIG POTTON

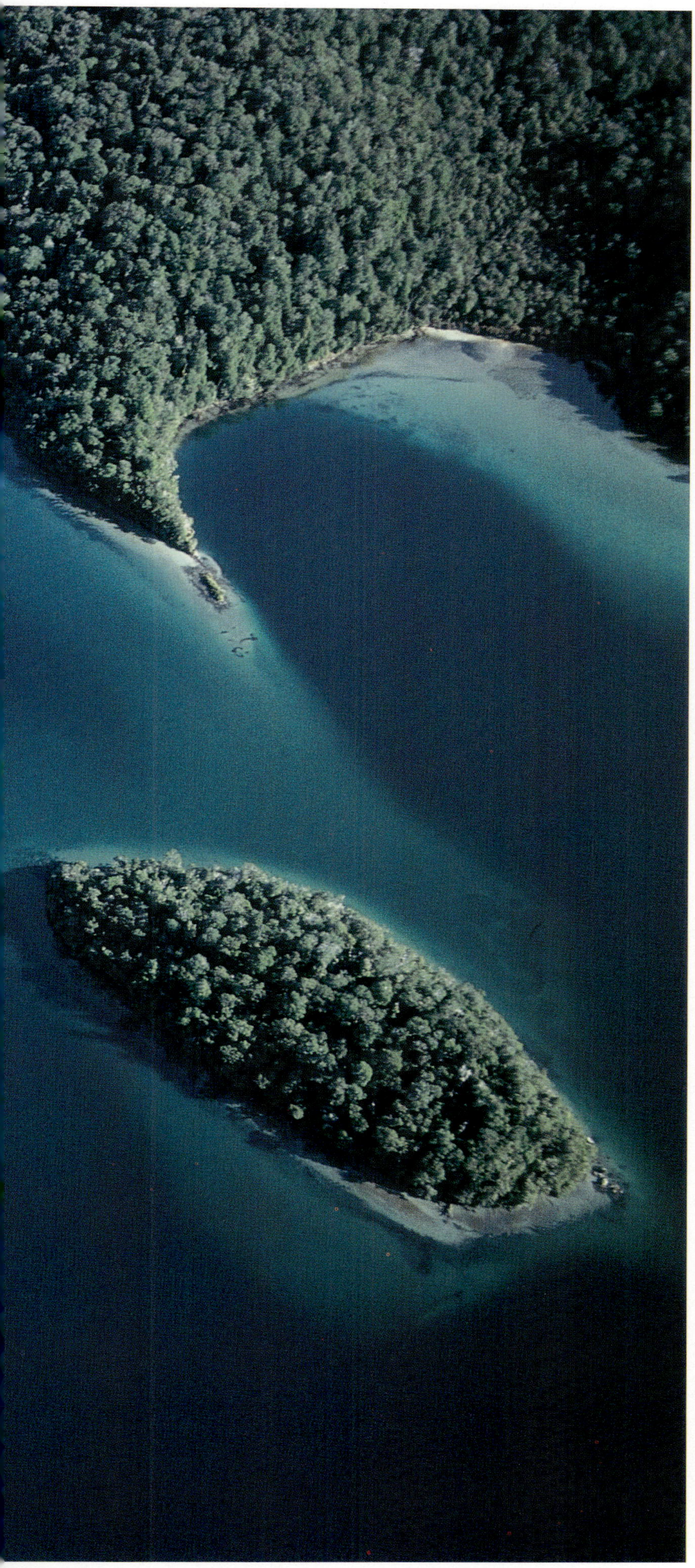

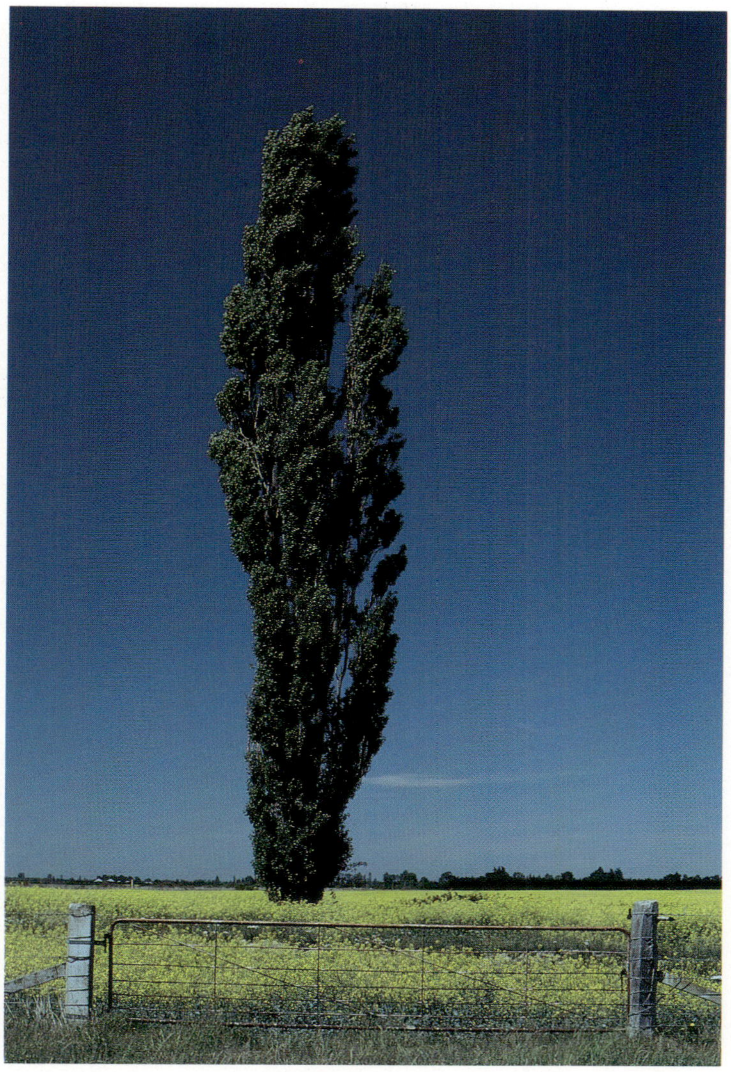

Poplars and rape fields near Fairlie, South Canterbury

GEOFF MASON

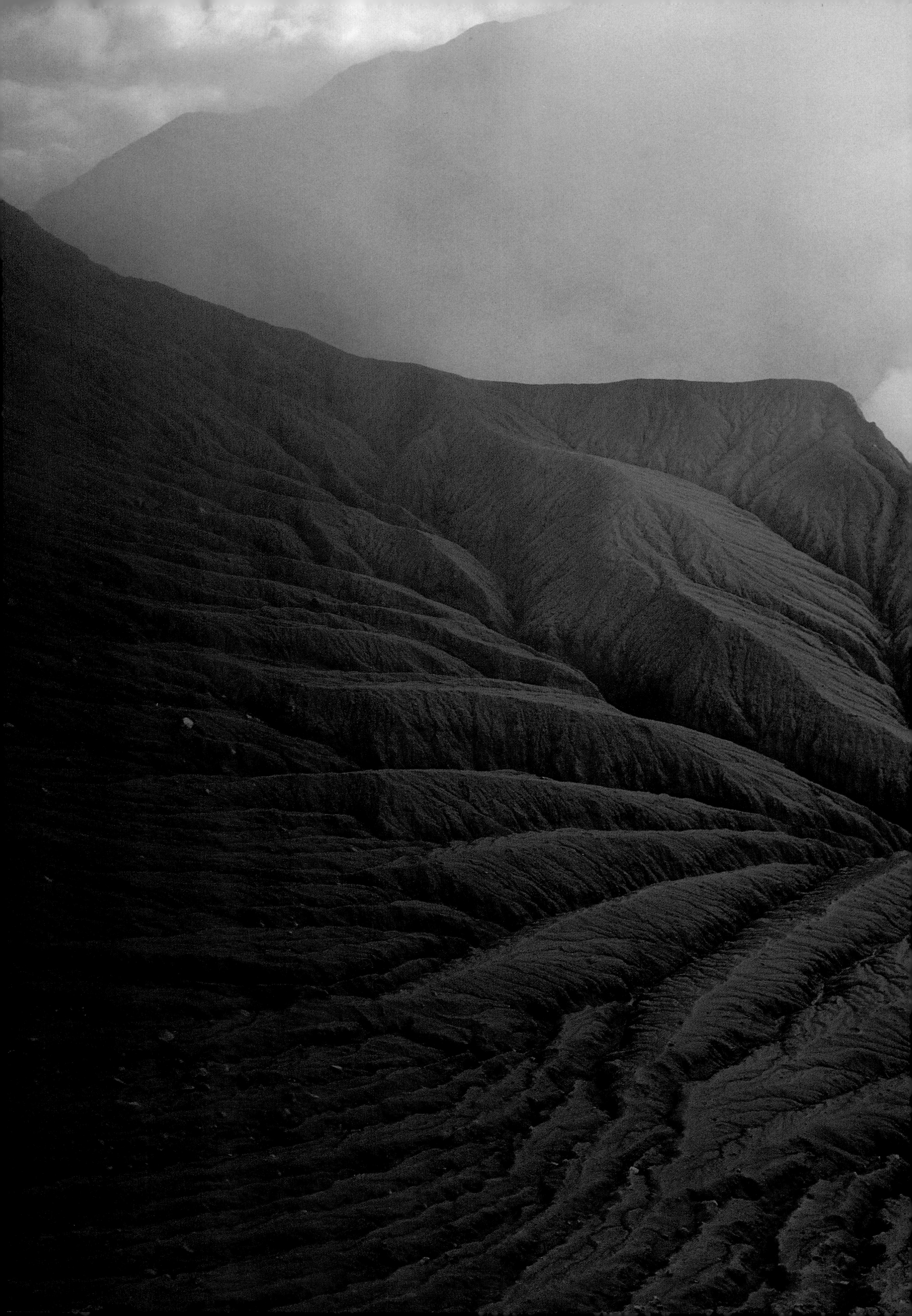

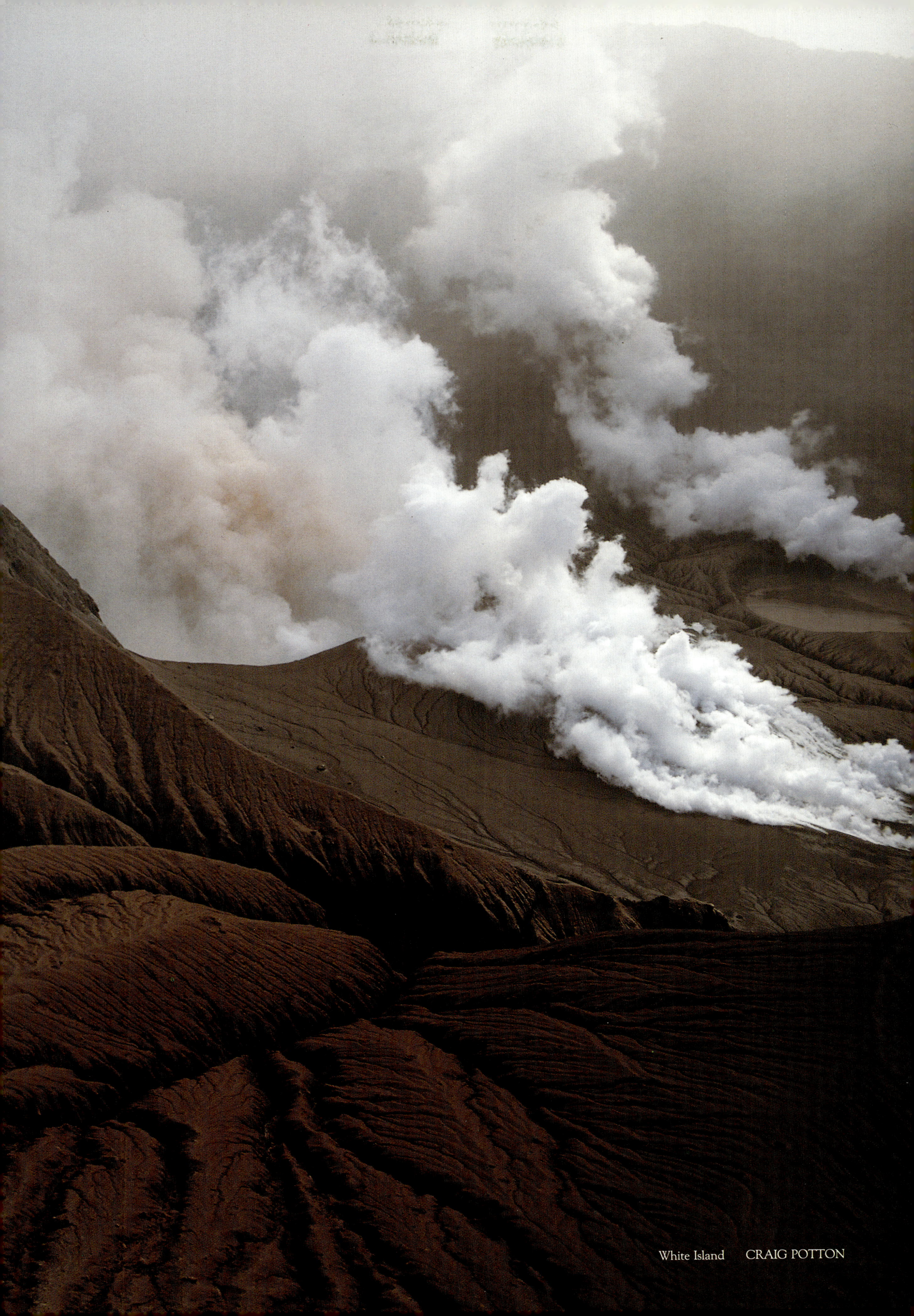

White Island CRAIG POTTON

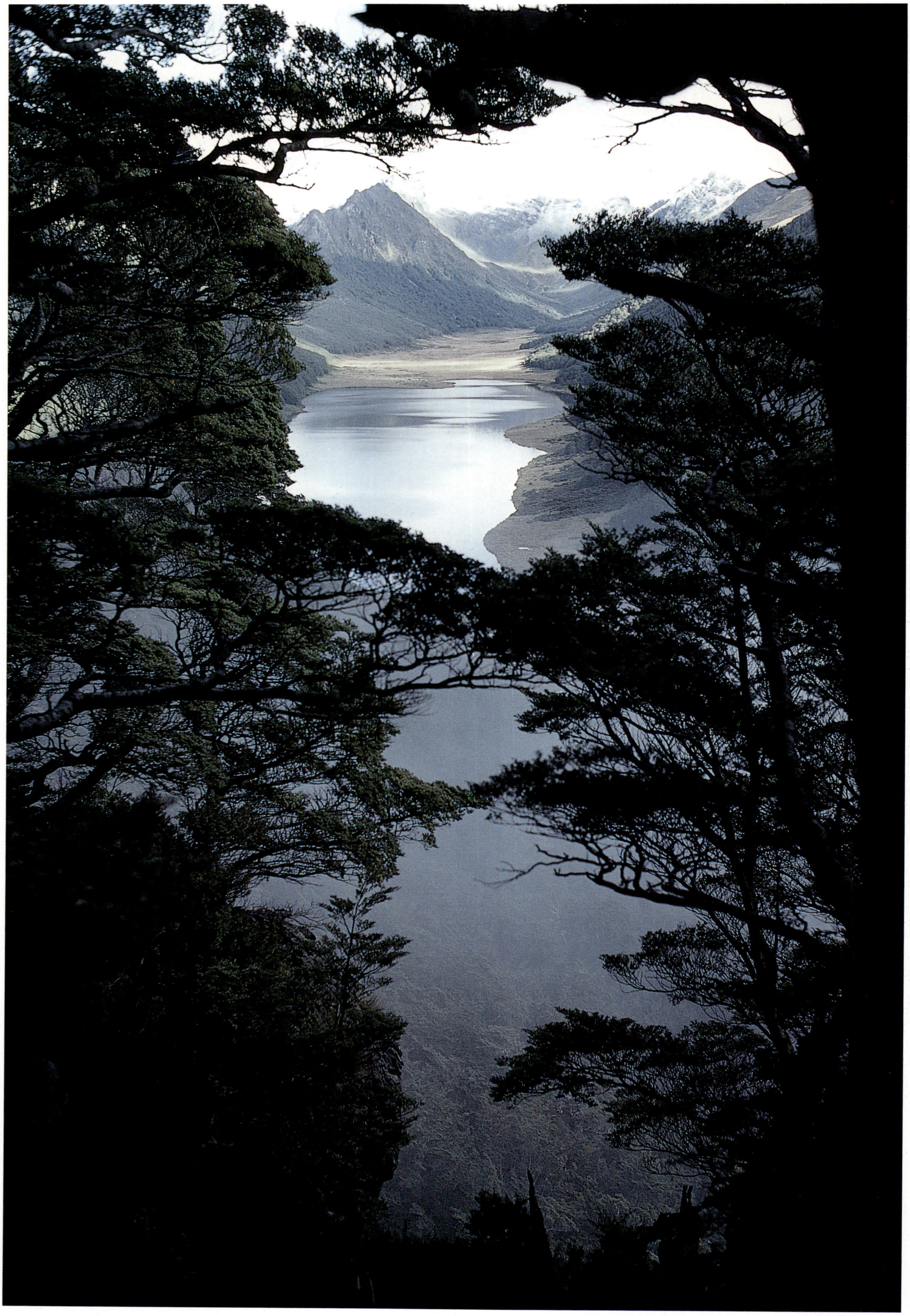

Takahe Valley, Fiordland

BRIAN ENTING

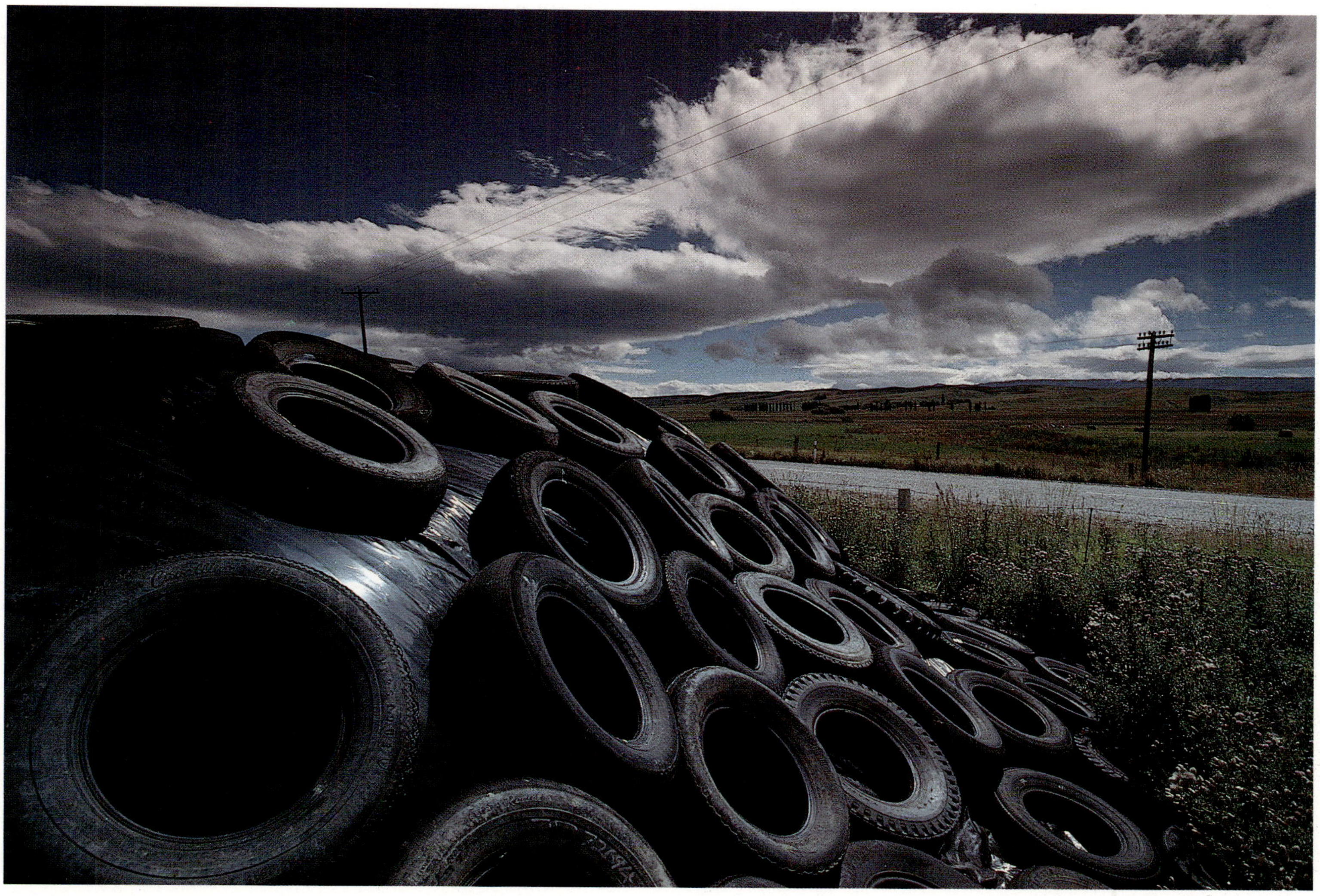

Ida Valley, Otago GEOFF MASON

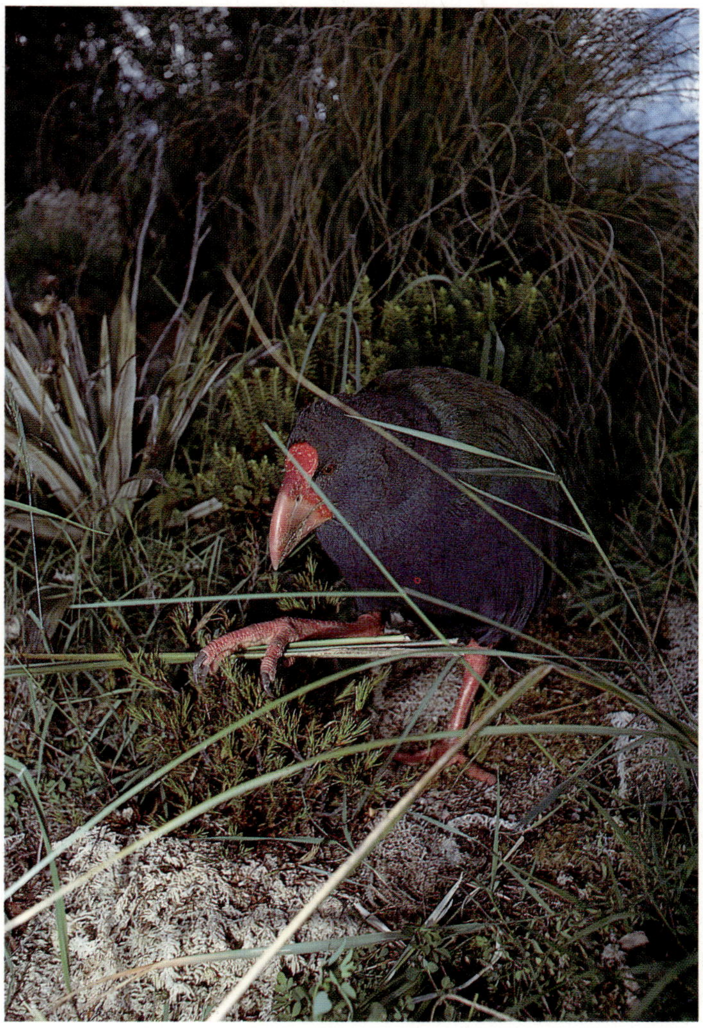

Takahe, Fiordland BRIAN ENTING

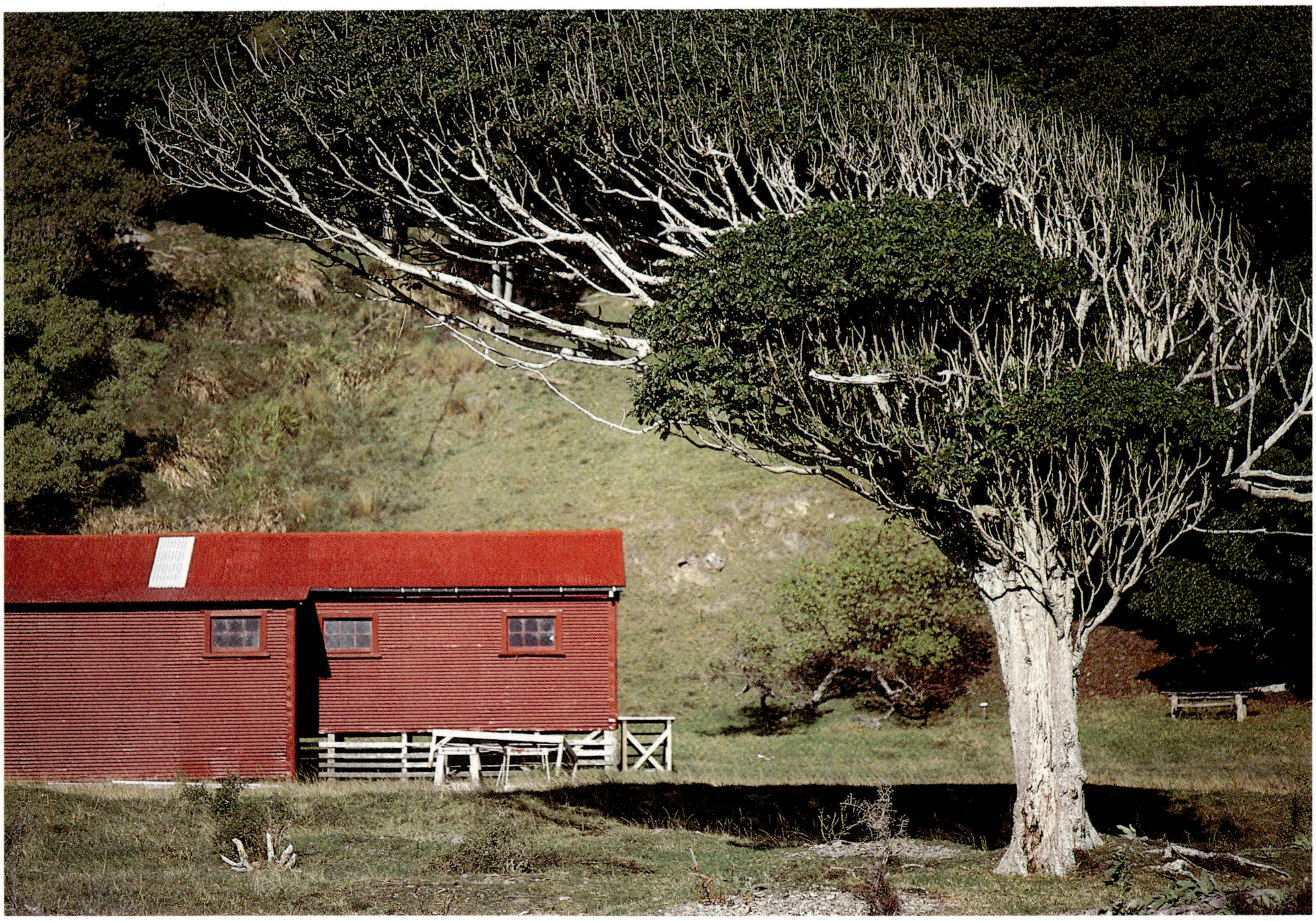

Titoki tree at Waihau Bay, East Cape — CRAIG POTTON

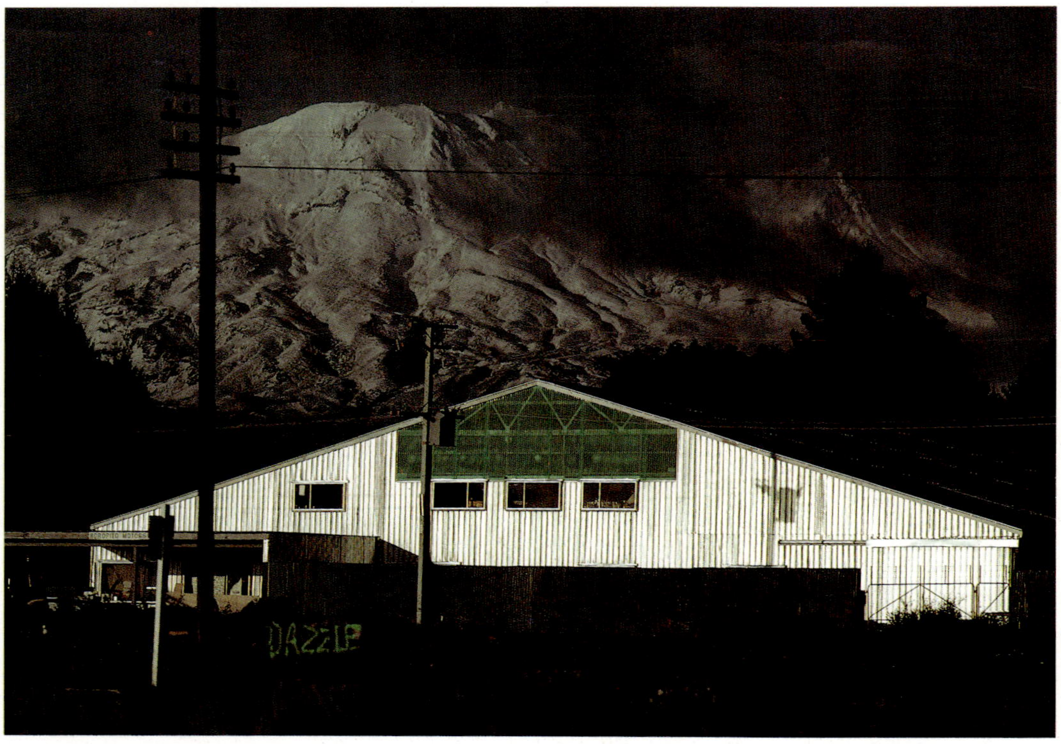

"Smash Palace", near Ohakune — CRAIG POTTON

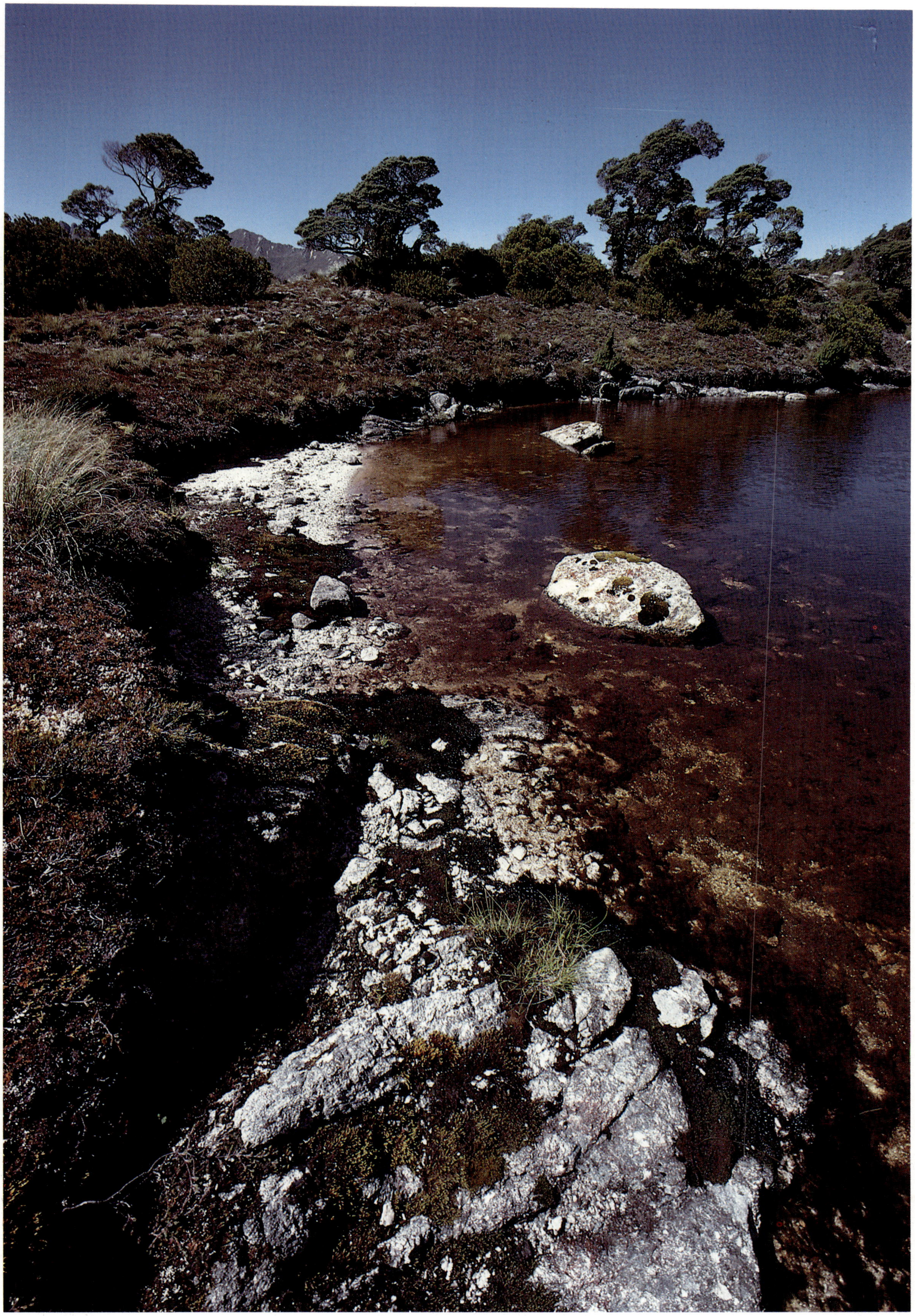

Sub-alpine tarn, Fiordland

BRIAN ENTING

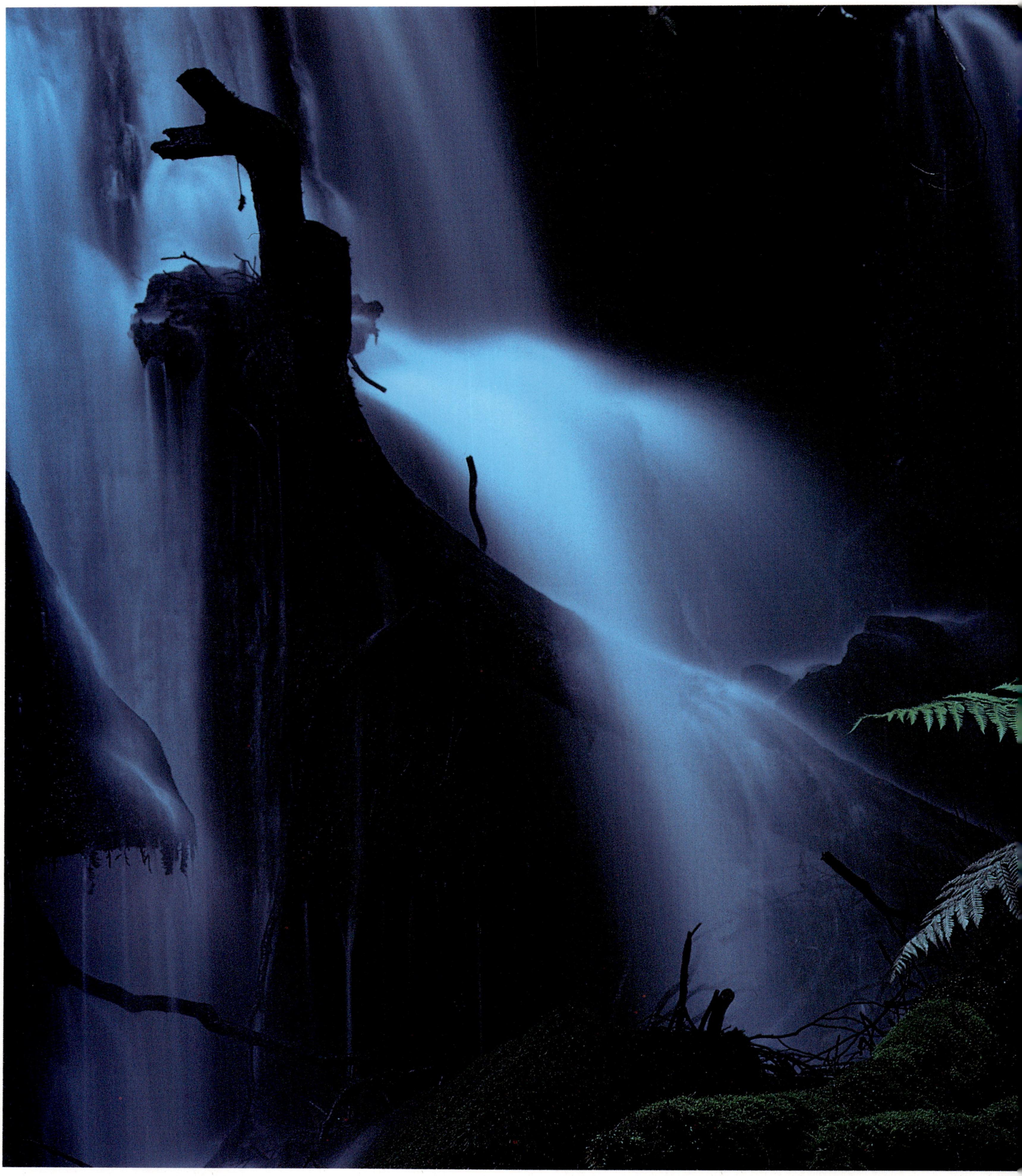

Purakaunui Falls, Catlins, Otago GEOFF MASON

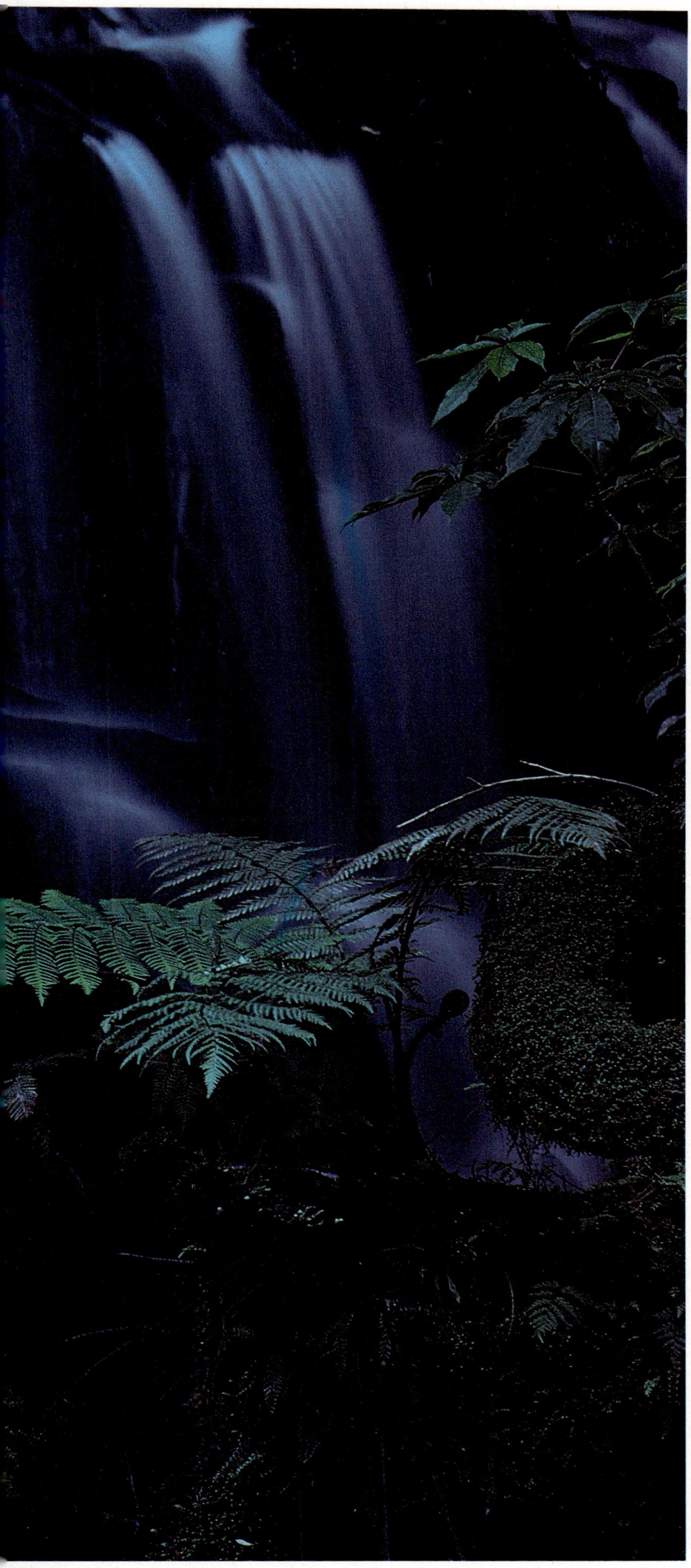

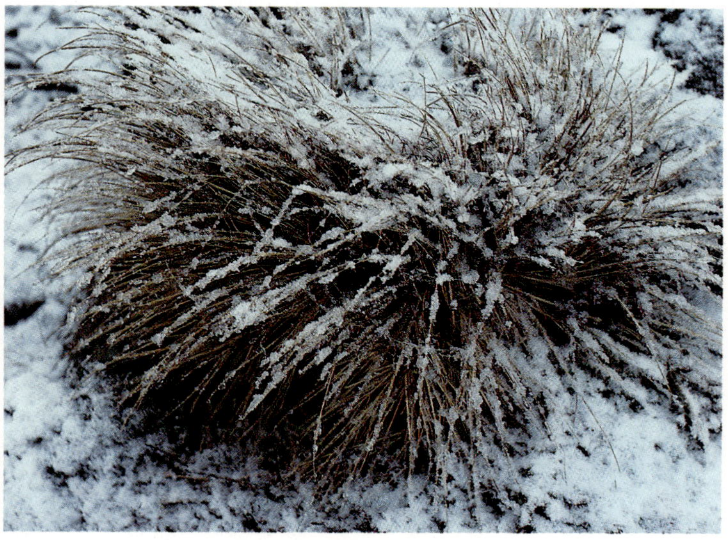

Whakapapa Ski Field, Mt Ruapehu STEPHEN ROBINSON

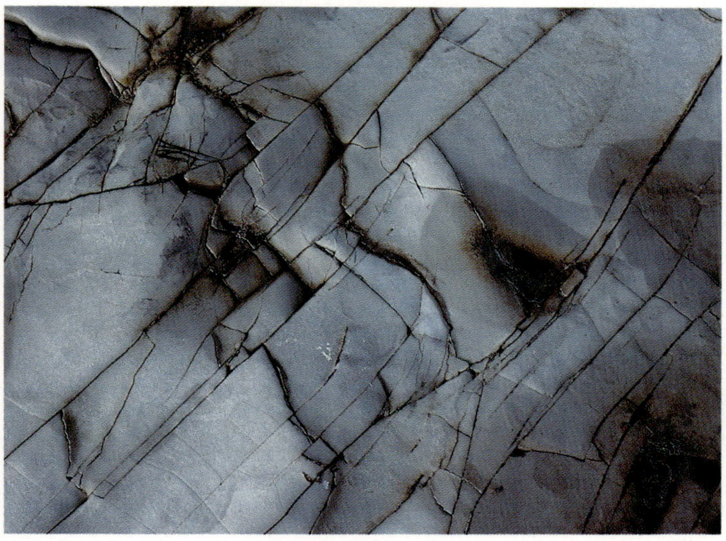

Mahia, Hawke's Bay CRAIG POTTON

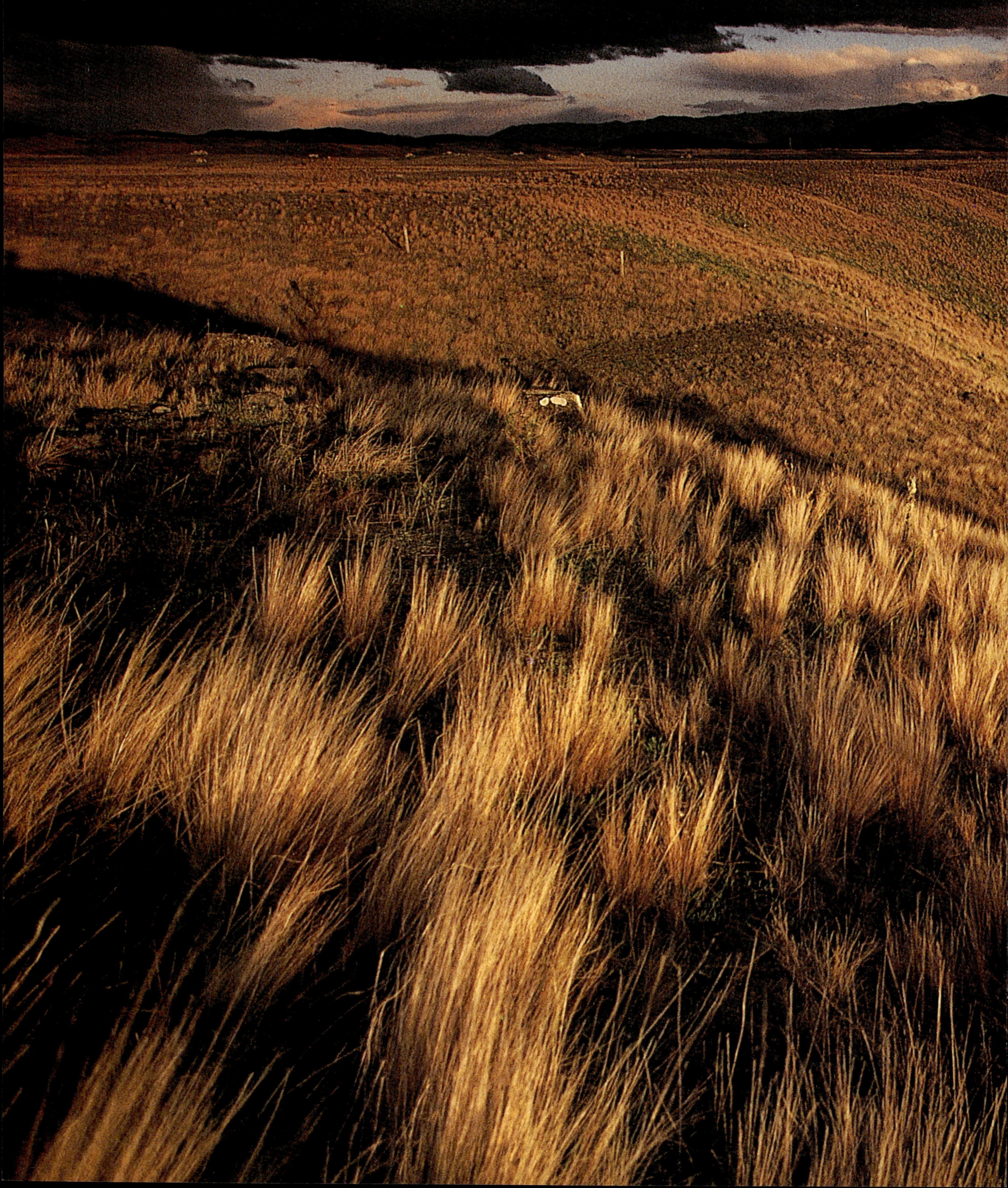

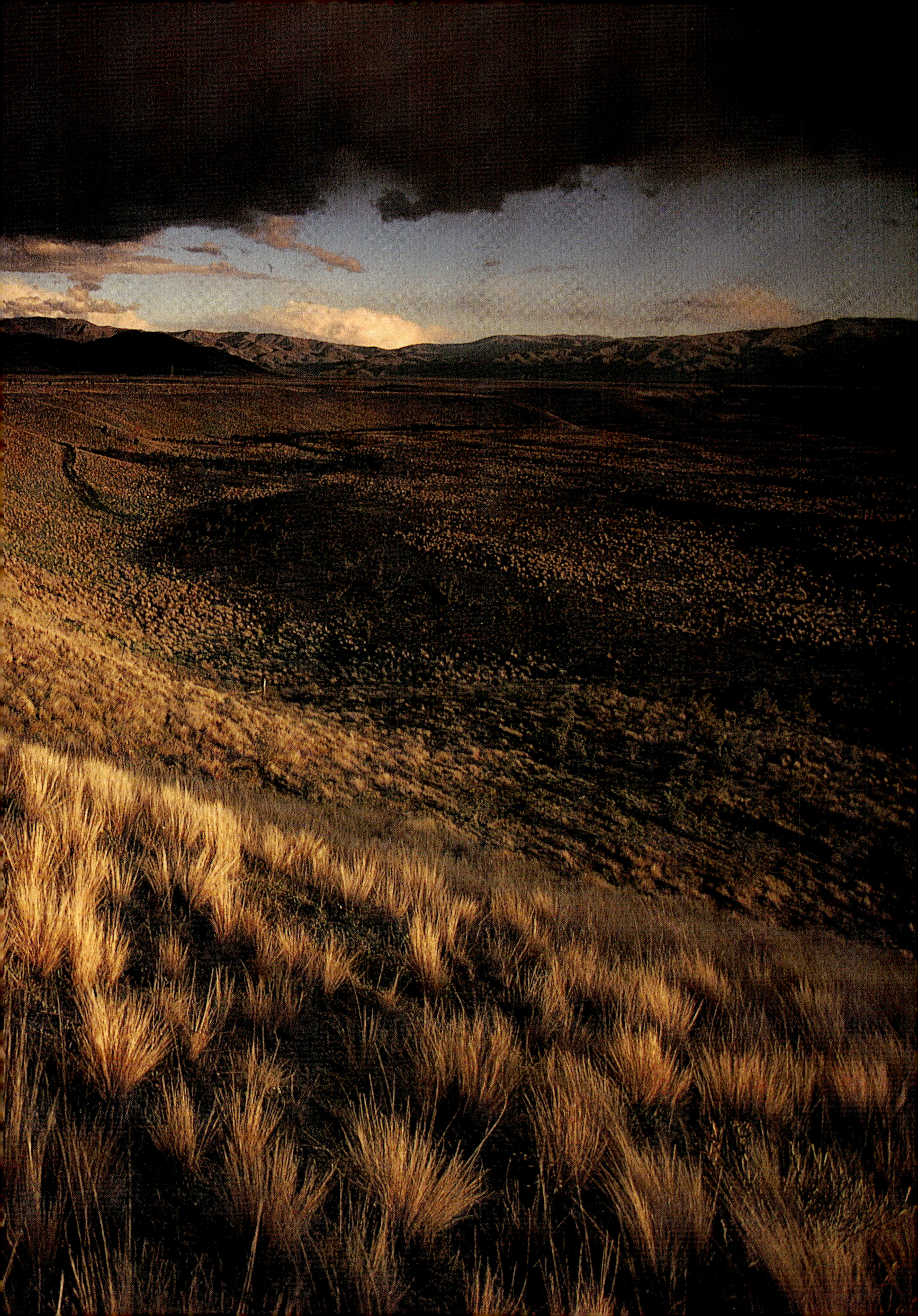

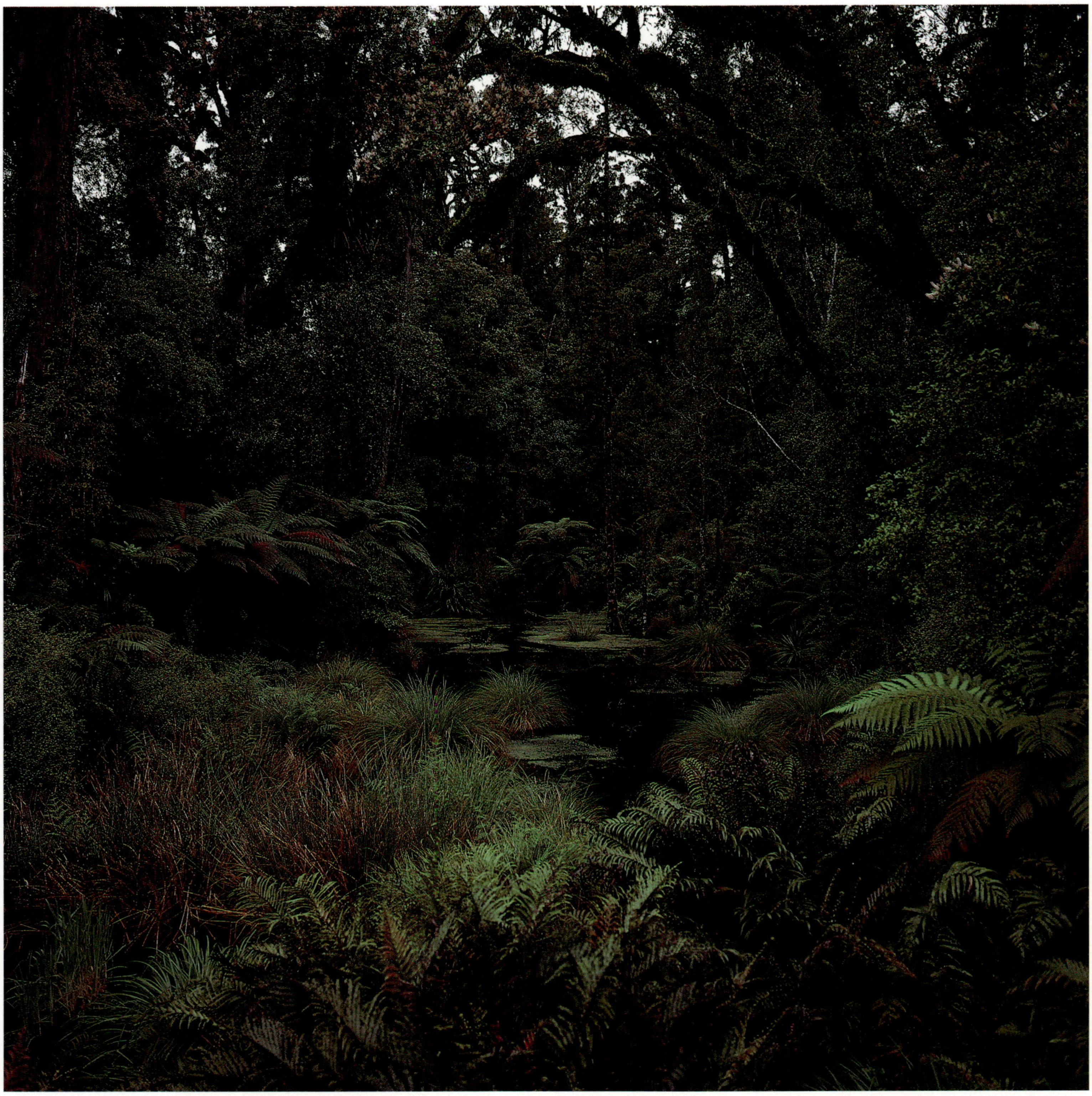

Near Ship's Creek, South Westland BRIAN ENTING

Tussock in the Mackenzie Country GEOFF MASON

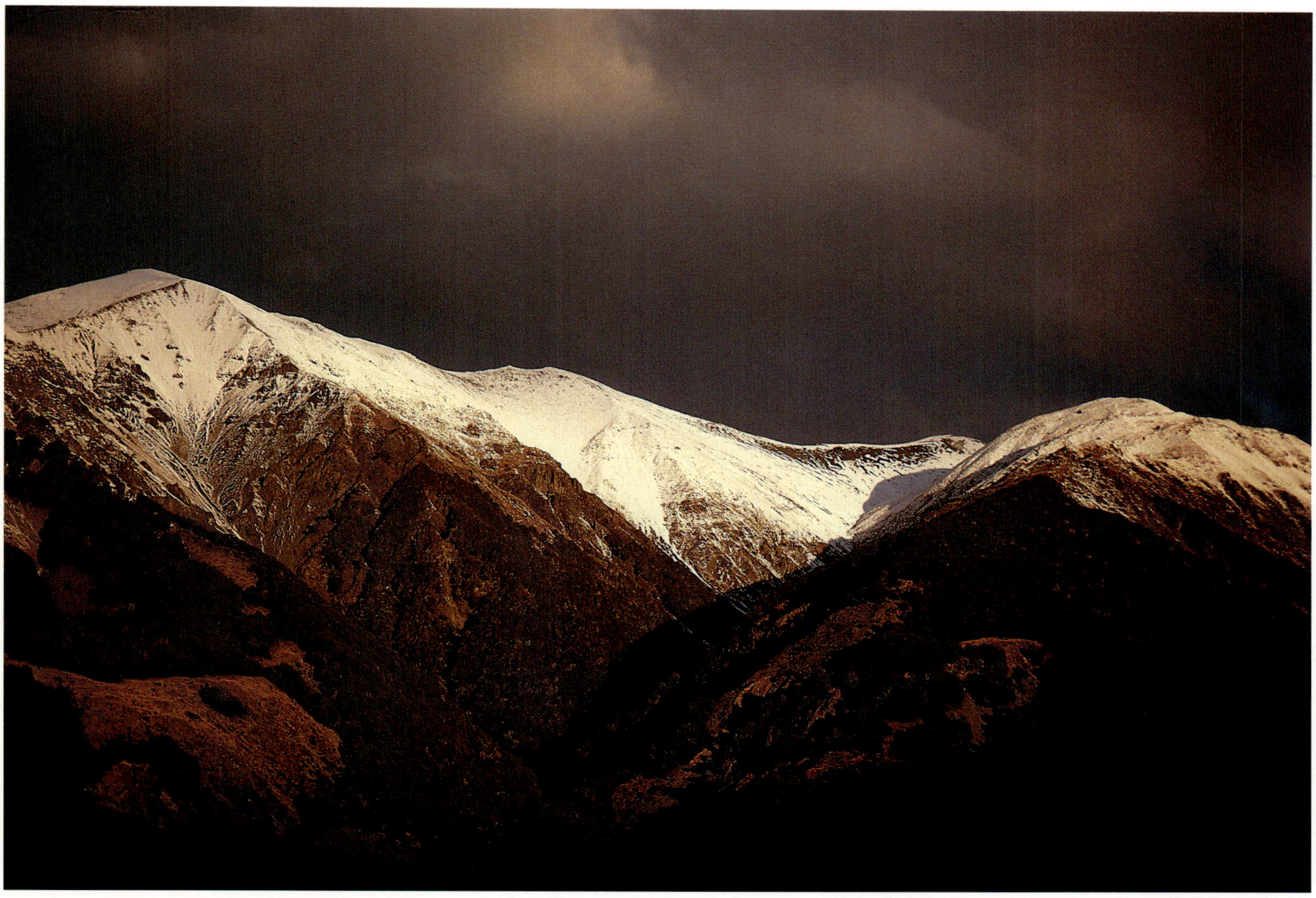

Craigieburn Forest Park, Arthur's Pass ROBIN MORRISON

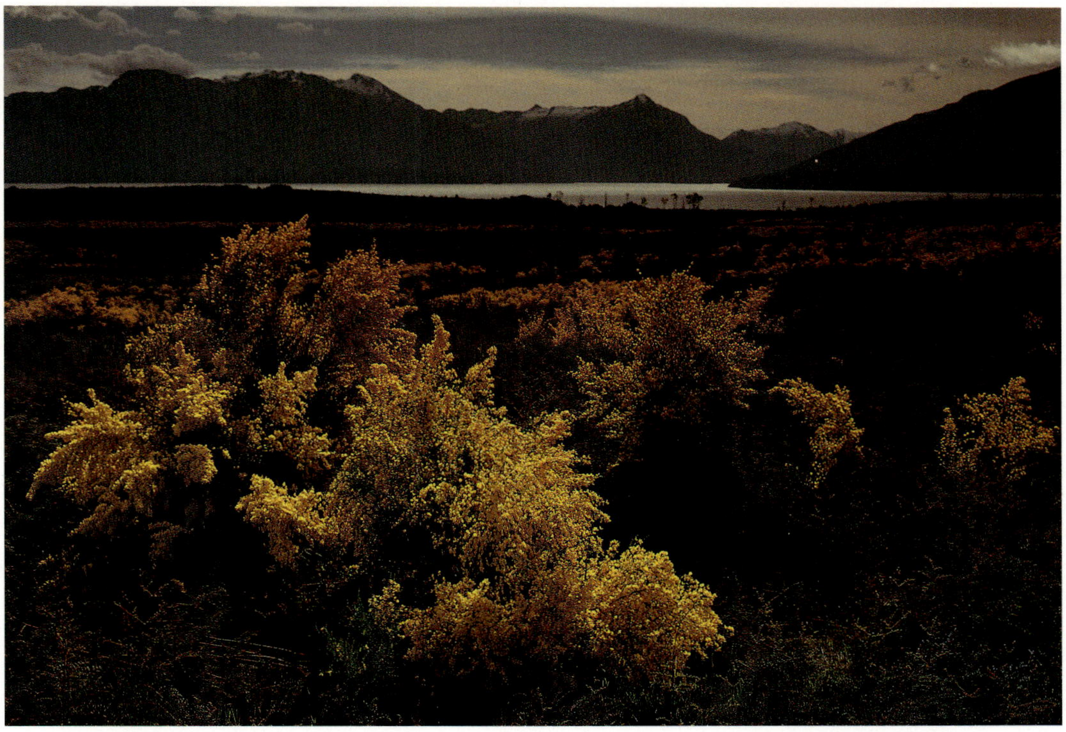

Broom at Lake Te Anau GEOFF MASON

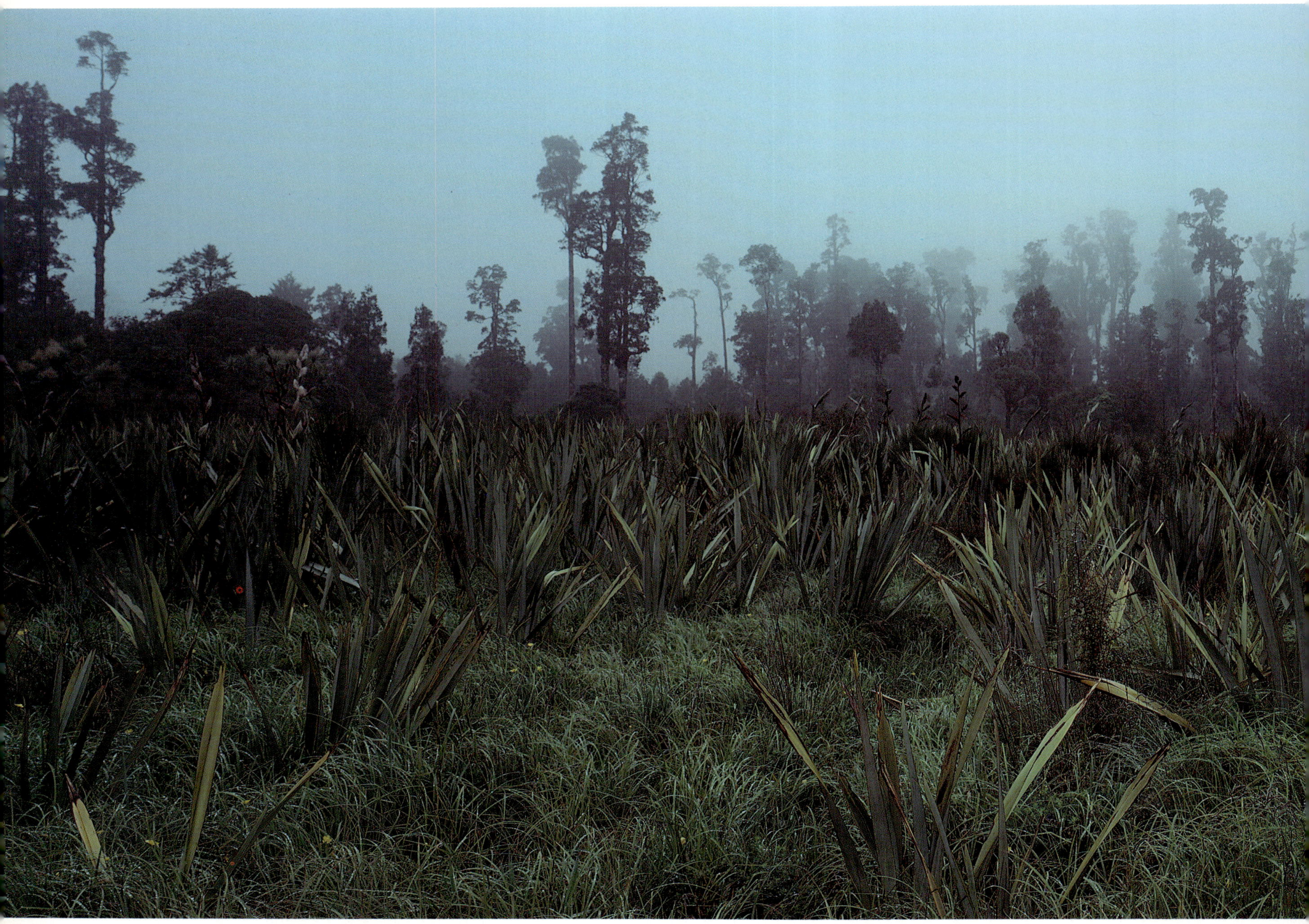

Kahikatea swamp, South Westland BRIAN ENTING

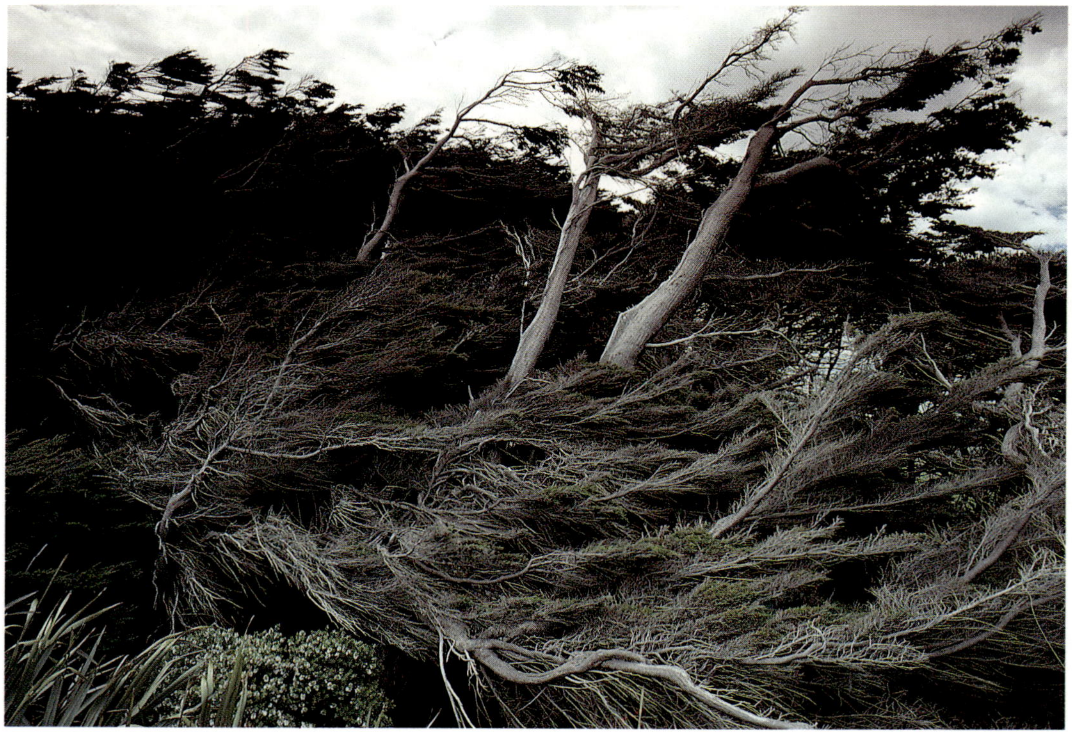

Macrocarpa windbreak near Orepuki, Te Waewae Bay, bent flat by gales from the Foveaux Strait GEOFF MASON

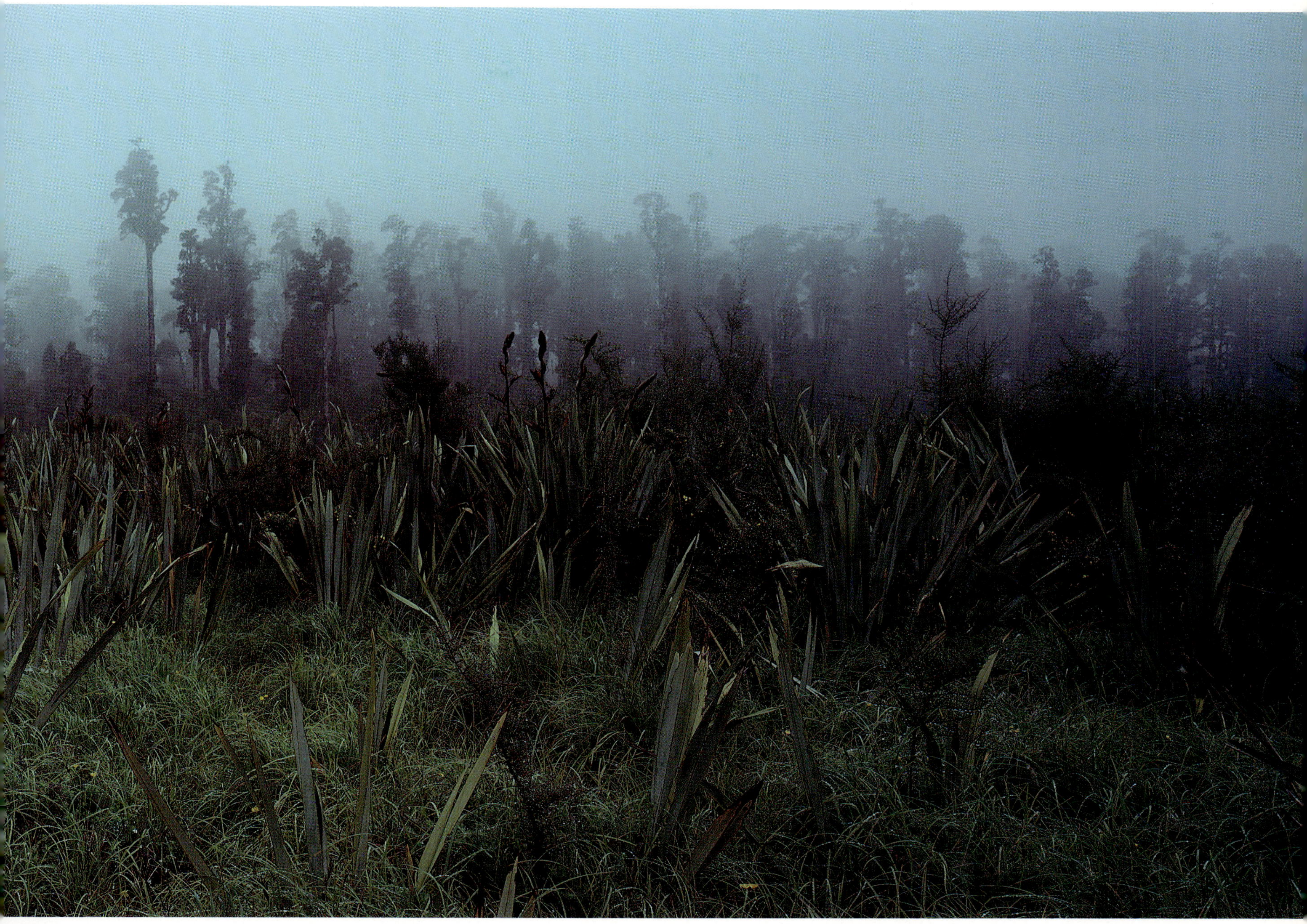

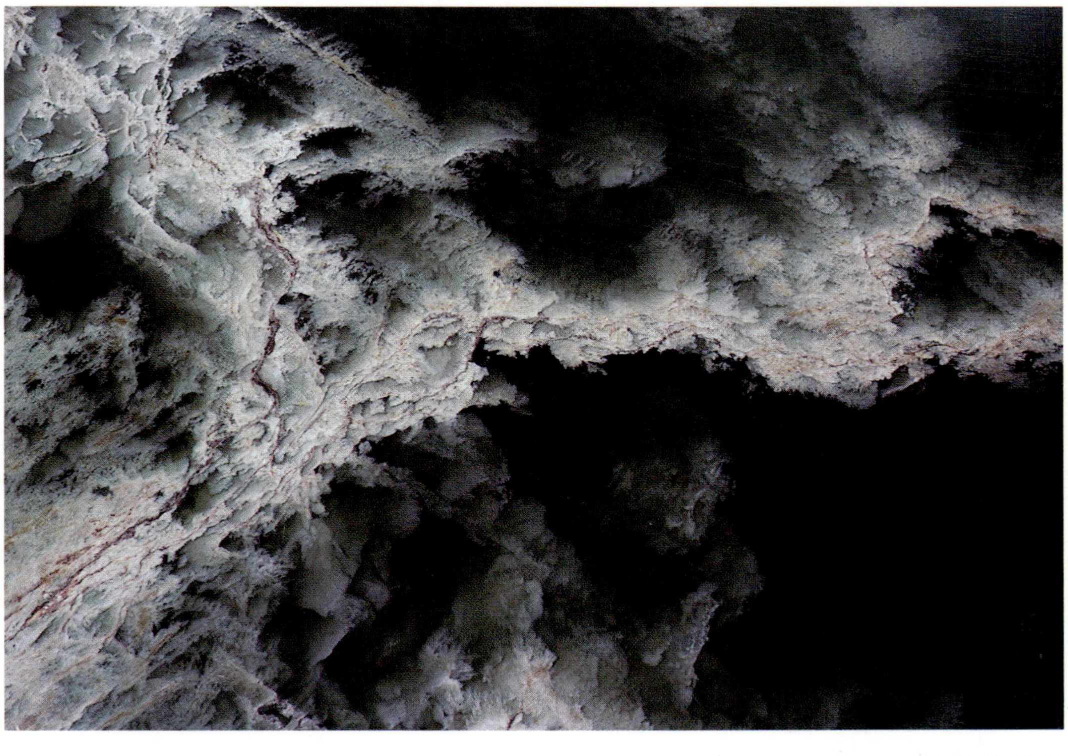

Greenstone, West Coast BRIAN ENTING

Mitre Peak, Milford Sound BRIAN ENTING

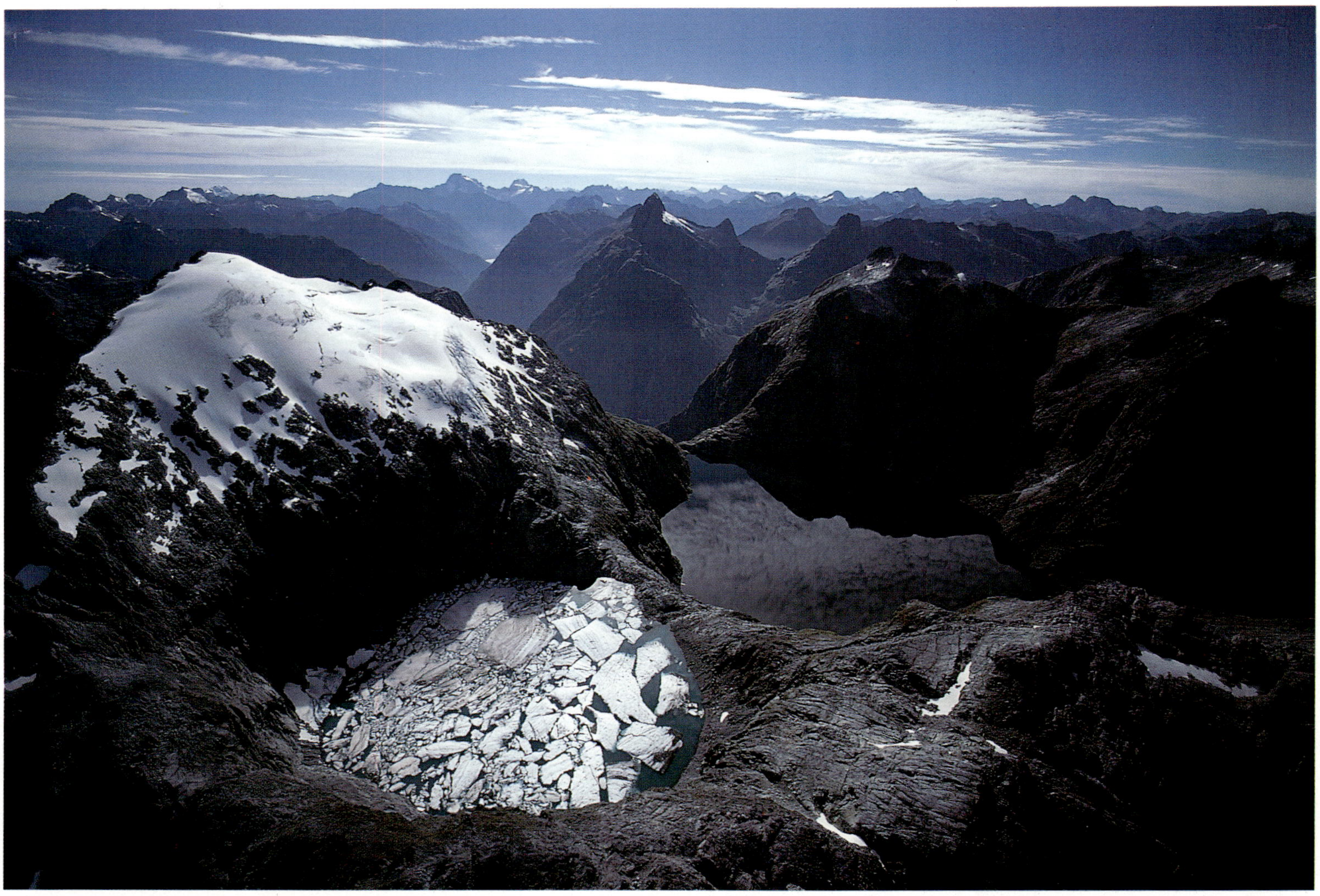

Source of the Sutherland Falls, Fiordland BRIAN ENTING

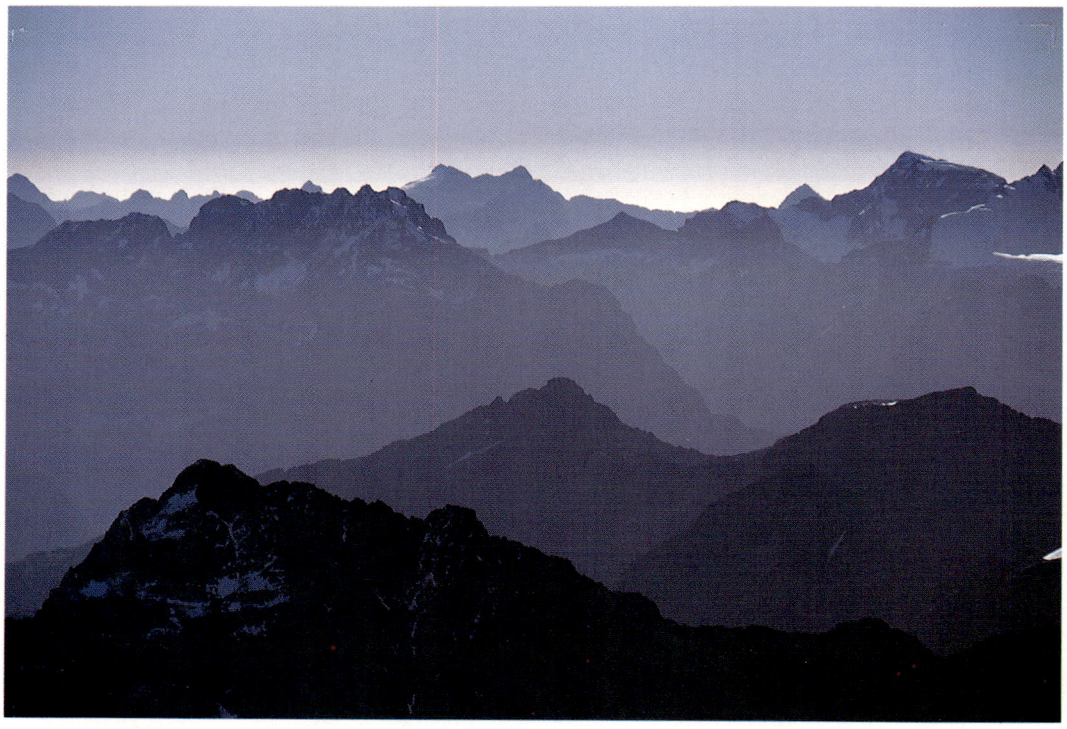

Fiordland BRIAN ENTING

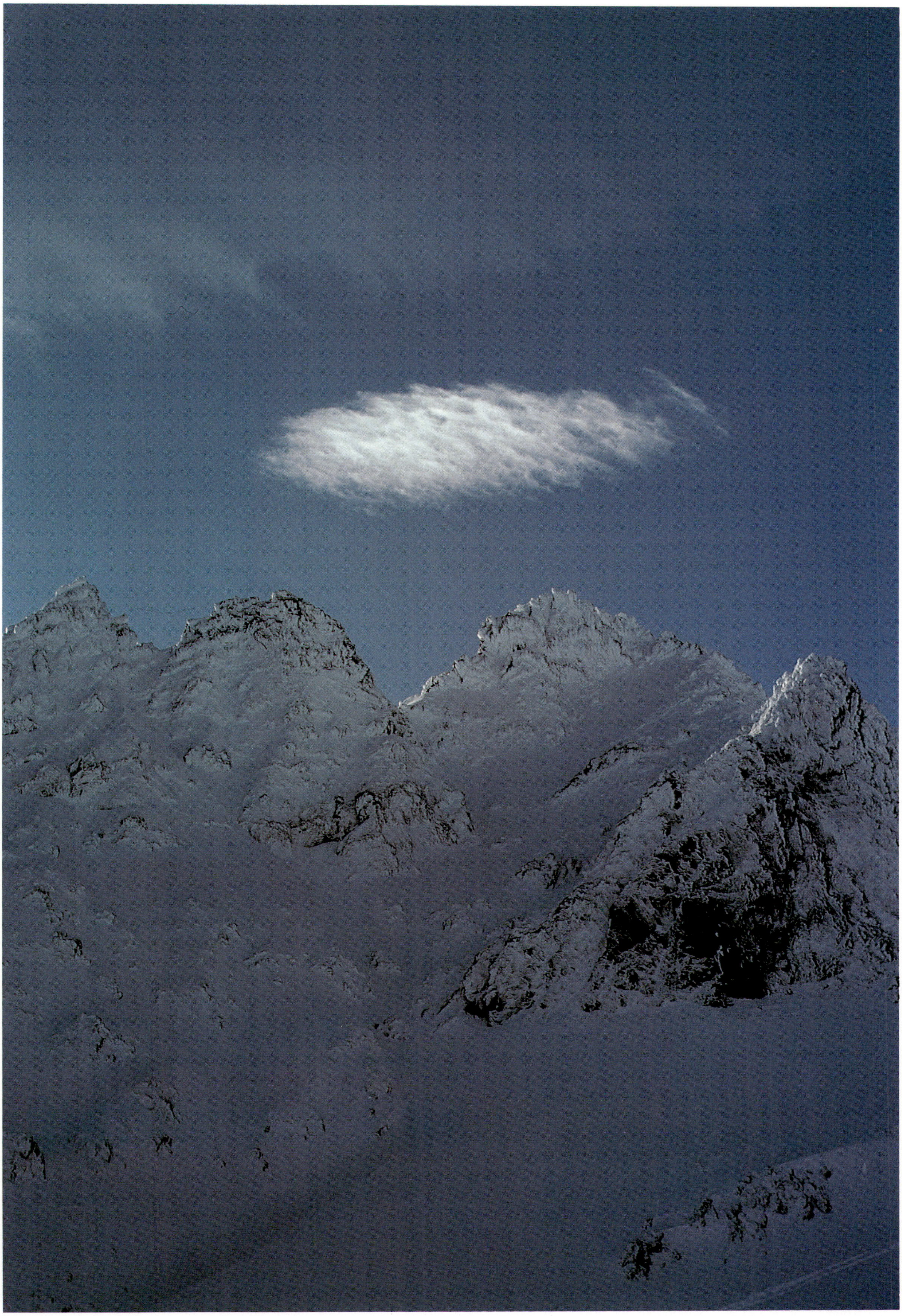

The Pinnacles, Whakapapa Ski Fields, Mt Ruapehu STEPHEN ROBINSON

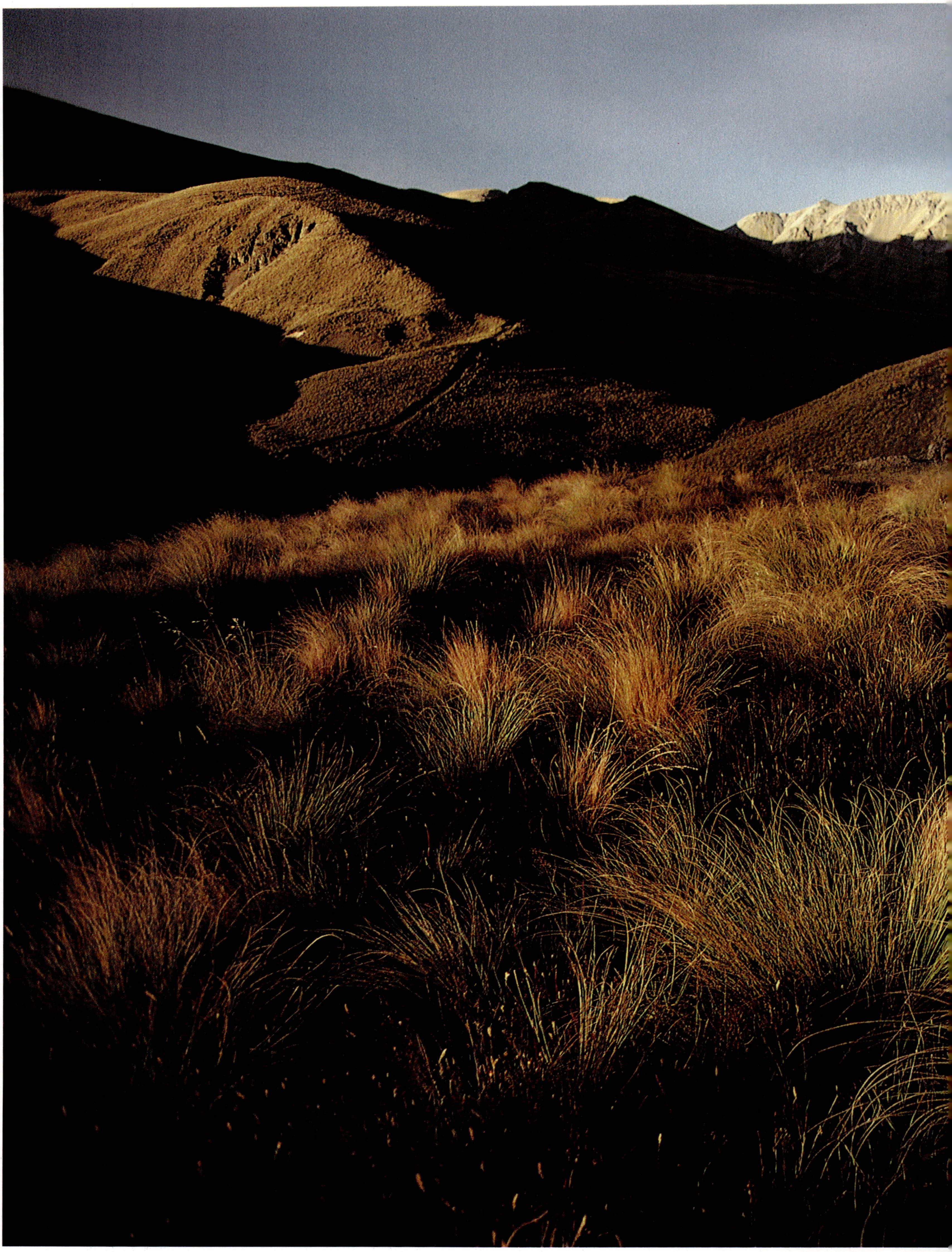

Golden sun on the tussocks at Dansey's Pass, west of Oamaru GEOFF MASON

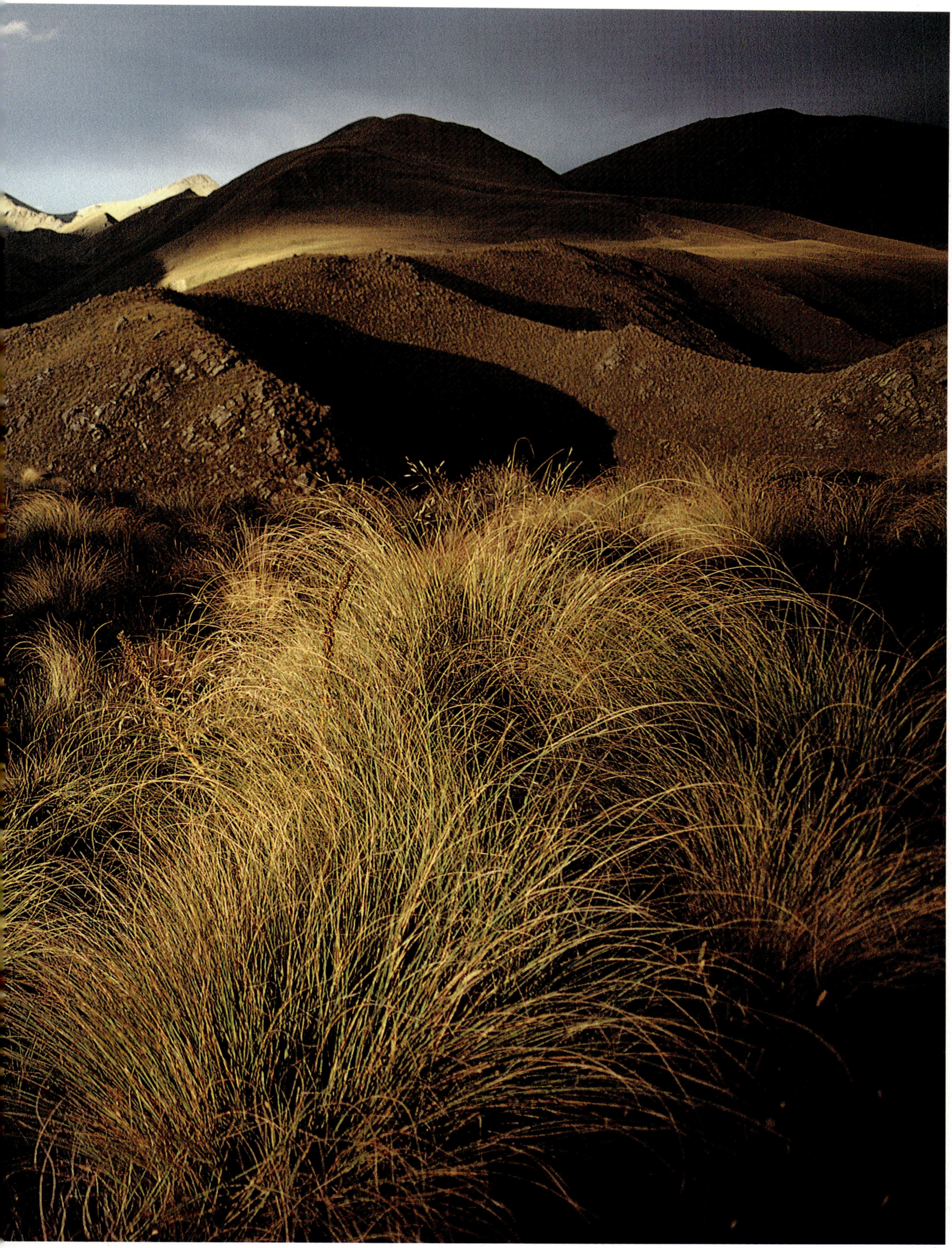

URBAN NEW ZEALAND

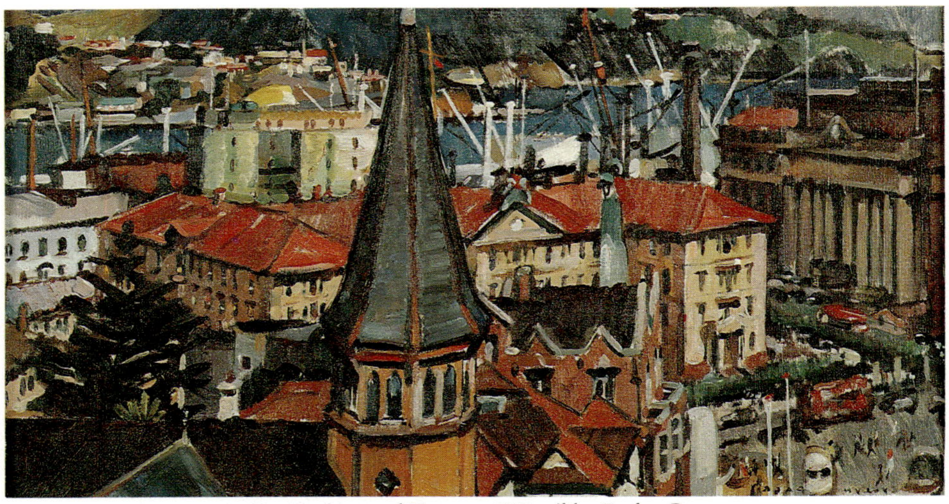

NATIONAL ART GALLERY

City Harbour and Tower, ca 1953, oil by Evelyn Page.

Colin James

START IN DUNEDIN. Compact, coherent, comfortable on its harbour, surrounded by light green hills of as seemly a shape as you find anywhere. There is an ageing at work here, a settling on foundations.

There have been great cities of Dunedin's size: Athens, Florence, even Edinburgh for which its founders homesickly named it. Dunedin was to be such a place: a university, industry, banks and a fine port. For a time it was the leading town in the new colony, stager of three international exhibitions in the late nineteenth and early twentieth centuries.

Its pretensions are smaller now, overgrown with provincialism. The bustle of ideas and invention and confidence that makes a city great has gone elsewhere with the gold that passed through from the hinterland 120 years ago. Gold glistens, but does not spark. To spark is a human energy.

After the gold had gone the hinterland was not rich enough to feed a big city. Set far to the south in a southern country, Dunedin was at the distant-most end of the trade routes. Its industry was overtaken by industry nearer the people. Head offices moved north. Factories closed. Despondency took root. Now Dunedin is fifth biggest.

But something was left and now people go to find it. There are many tales of people who have gone to Dunedin for a year or two and stayed to live. What draws them in? Is it retirement before their time? Or a quality that no other city in New Zealand can give?

By the standards of the rest of New Zealand, Dunedin has more than its share of theatre groups and museums. It has fine stone buildings – the university, the railway station, the law courts, Otago Boys High School – and they still stand uncrowded by the cacophony of glass and concrete which presses in on old buildings in other cities. Behind them, ranking up the hills, are stone and brick residences built to endure, of a grace and permanence not found in hastier cities to the north.

The people in Dunedin move more unhurriedly than in the north. Recessions and booms come and go; Dunedinites do not rant and rave as the cycles swing; they do not glow with the success of Scott Technology, which exports high-tech production lines round the world, or the emergence of their own home-grown multinational, Wilson Neill. They, like their houses, endure.

That lasting gives space for reflection. Robbie Burns, Scottish thinker and wit, who sits stonily in memoriam in the Octagon in the centre of town, lives on in spirit in a fellowship for writers down at the university. James K. Baxter was wrought here and wrote here, one of the foremost of the colony's raconteur-poets: he held the Burns in 1966–67. Frances Hodgkins, foremost among painters for half a century, grew up here and another university fellowship, for painters, is named for her. Colin McCahon spent the thirties here, drew on the hills as subject and inspiration as he started out on the country's most distinguished artistry. The university is the biggest business in town.

Dunedin knows its place. There are no kiwifruit bonanzas and slumps here, no shoals of flashy corporate raiders in big cars on tick. Nor is there much racial worry because Dunedin is overwhelmingly white. It preserves better than most the secure, generous, empty and green New Zealand of the 1950s.

It will accordingly settle better than the northern cities. In 100 or 200 years it will feel to have weight, much as a European city like Lübeck or York. It will stand as itself, as it now does, a city.

But York and Lübeck, though they were once places of decision, are not now. So with Dunedin: the decisions in New Zealand are made elsewhere.

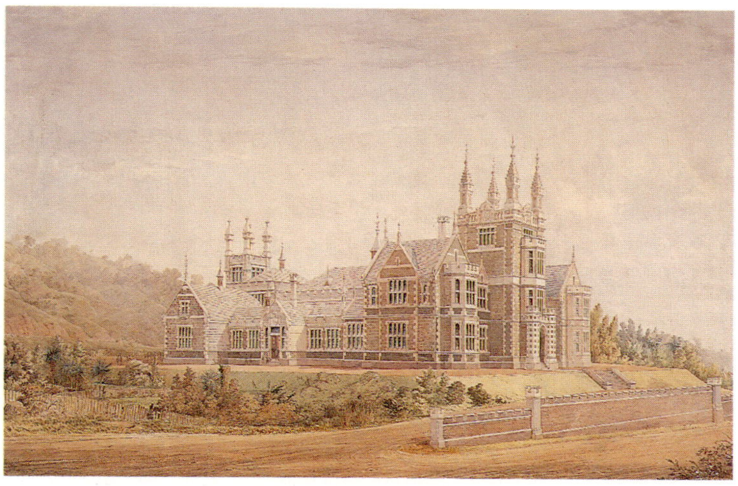

HOCKEN LIBRARY

Perspective drawing of Otago Boys High School, designed by R. A. Lawson, 1883, painted in watercolour by George O'Brien.

DECISIONS ARE MADE IN CITIES. In New Zealand for periods of its European history farmers could override the interests of those in the cities because they supplied the exports and because their outdoorness, their landed freedom expressed the colonisers' eagerness to escape nineteenth-century industrialism and social rigidity and oppression. But the country's pursuit of full employment in the 1950s forced farmers to subsidise protected industry and they lost their primacy. By the 1980s the ordinary city dweller determined the style of government.

New Zealanders live in towns and owe their allegiance to the towns, not to the surrounding country-dwellers. And the towns are increasingly self-dependent.

Hamilton is a case in point. It grew as a provincial farm-service centre. Its fortune went up and down with milkfat price. Farmers made the economic decisions of the town.

Now Hamilton is increasingly an industrial town. Industries developed to supply farmers have since become worldwide exporters – such as the Gallagher group, arguably the world's leading maker of electric fences. Auckland companies to the north are putting new or second plants up in Hamilton to capitalise on the more stable workforce.

Planners and civic dignitaries talk of the need for an adjustment of mentality. No longer can farmers expect to hitch their horse to a post right outside the shop they want to visit, is the usual way it is put. So Hamilton now has a big civic complex and an impressive new museum and art gallery.

But the compelling impression of Hamilton is the garish avenue of car sales, light industries and motels on the main route north. Hamilton is an overgrown town, not a city. It has the vigour to make a city but it does not have the heavy foundations that base a city. It keeps its university on the outskirts, pristine and quarantined. Don't look for a good bookshop in town.

Its elite treats it to some extent as a suburb of Auckland. An hour-and-a-quarter by car puts a Hamiltonian in a Queen Street shop or a restaurant or at a show or a friend's place for dinner. You can be back by midnight.

In its urban adolescence Hamilton is therefore a satellite. In its town-ness, it retains much of the old proximity to country. If New Zealand was still a place where the countryside was the determiner of decisions, Hamilton would be a lens through which to watch the meeting between town and country.

The main street of Hamilton has all the look of a saleyard in this early morning scene, taken on sale day in 1906.

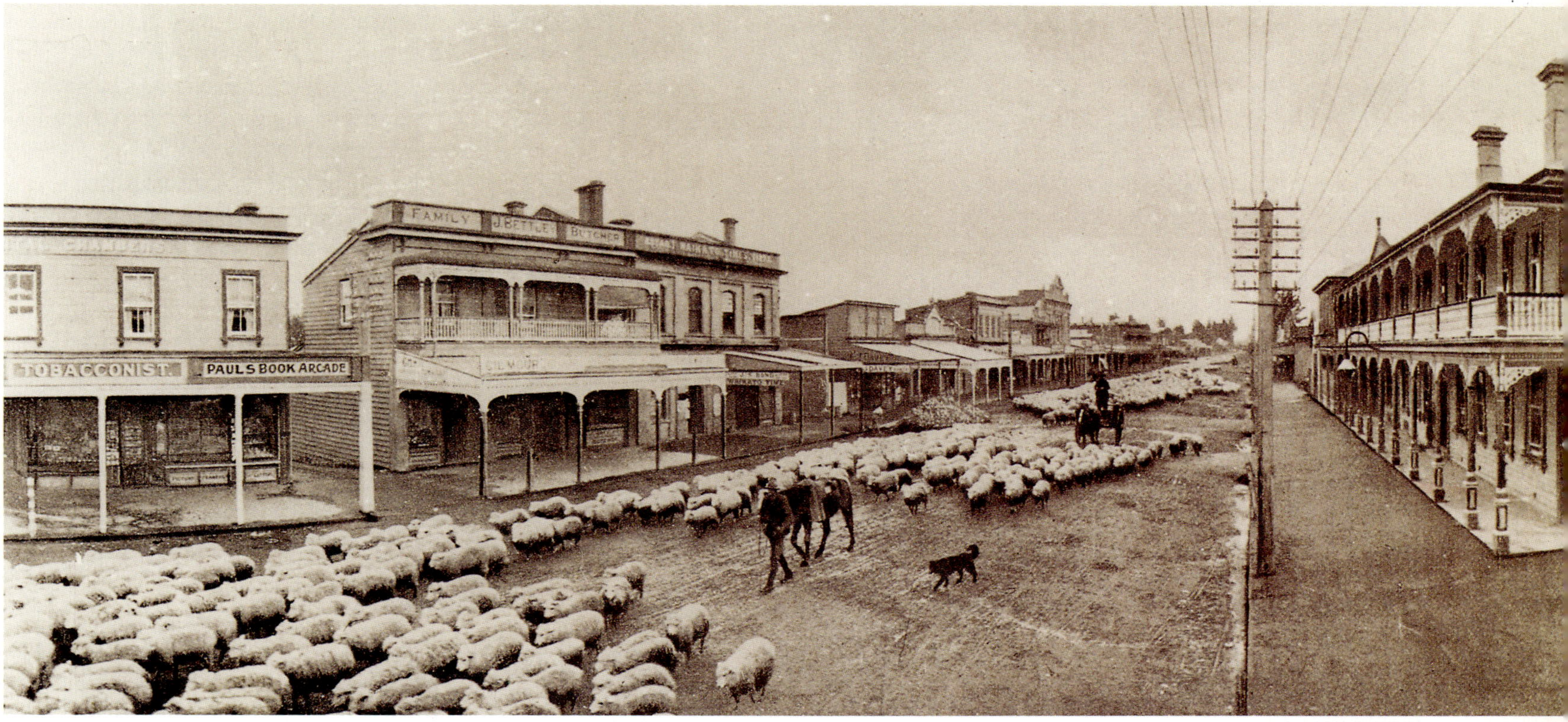

WAIKATO ART MUSEUM

But Hamilton is not such a focus. Its striving is away from the meeting place towards self-dependence. Its focus is increasingly a lens on Auckland.

So don't look to Hamilton for the decisions that will shape the country. For that you look to Wellington and Auckland.

WELLINGTON IS THE CAPITAL. So bureaucrats and lobbies and business head offices gathered here to advise and cajole the politicians. As the welfare state and the protected and regulated economy grew, so did the bureaucracy and the lobbies. Civil servants spilled in each day on the country's only significant commuting railway system to fill up an ever-increasing number of office blocks.

So voracious was the Government's hunger for bureaucracy that property firms have said, fatly, for years, the demand for new buildings will go on and on. And it did: for twenty years the centre of the city was a giant building site.

Cranes punched jagged holes through the skyline wherever you looked, pavements were pitted obstacle courses. Wellington was disorder – undisciplined, unimaginative and incoherent, with few oases of relief to blasted souls stranded here. So an ordinary town hall and the ordinary, but at least clean-lined, Bank of New Zealand head office stand out as slivers of taste.

The emergent Wellington is the creation of fast developers and architects racing deadlines posed by earthquake regulations for replacement or strengthening of risky buildings or to make as fast a dollar as they could while the property boom lasted. That creation scarcely paused, scarcely could pause, to ask what the total result should be, whether the buildings might be more than heavy boxes, tarted up a little in later times with glass facades or imitation Grecian excrescences.

PERHAPS THE HEAVY CONCRETE structures symbolise the deadening hand of the bureaucrats. Perhaps a slick glass facade reflects the zip, gloss and transitoriness of the neat-suited young traffickers in finance, the city's most expansive industry of the 1980s. Perhaps the excrescences express plausible property developers' desire for the respectability of taste. Perhaps the round hump, known as the Beehive, that houses the Cabinet (and is at least distinctive, if functionally infuriating) symbolises the circularity of all human affairs – and especially politics.

And perhaps the houses on the surrounding hills symbolise the transitoriness of a capital's population. Few people one meets in Wellington are Wellingtonians. Most have transferred from other places climbing ladders or pyramids in a career. Wellington dwellers are on the move. Compared with Dunedin's, Wellington's houses are wooden insubstantialities, few with grace. They fight the contours of the hillsides resentfully rather than fit them respectfully.

Renovation is relieving some of this ugliness. There are even a few "painted ladies", gaily redecorated houses in the style of San Francisco, as Wellington dwellers learn to live with other ages, the structures of other decades or even another century. In the houses the process of integrating past and present has begun.

But it will take some decades yet for the layering of history to give a true soil. And in the central city most of the structures of past decades have been eliminated.

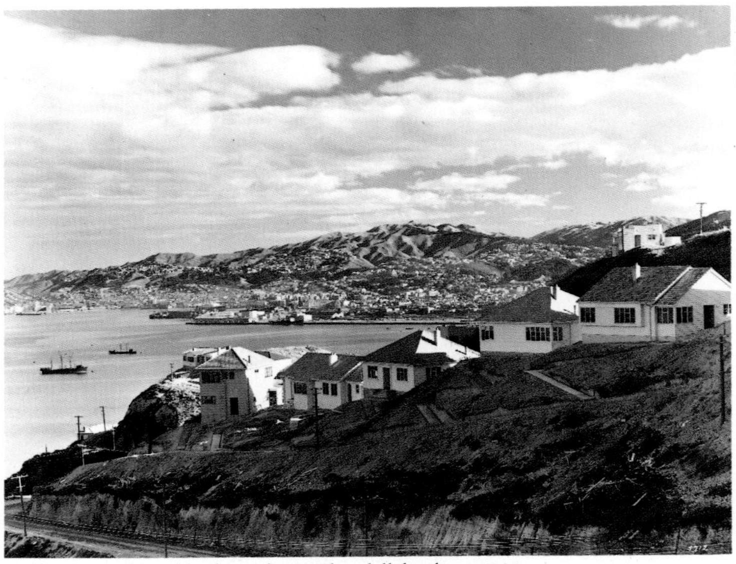

ALEXANDER TURNBULL LIBRARY

Wellington city and harbour from Khandallah, about 1936.
NATIONAL PUBLICITY STUDIOS COLLECTION

The result, as a glance from a room in the James Cook Hotel on the Terrace above the centre of the city tells the visitor, is a capital that looks just like that in any third world country – lots of new glass and concrete, reflecting the sun but with no history in the interstices. And, as one does in any third world capital, one wonders what substance there is to go with the newness. What sorts of decisions can be made in homogeneous but higgledy-piggledy newness?

The answer is in the living rooms and in the coffee houses and the bars and offices: there is the substance of conversation. Wellington dwellers jostle you with gossip: they talk more than those of any other place of theories and current events and economic matters. Wellington mixes diplomats, journalists, politicians, academics, financiers, economists and bureaucrats. It busies with the latest political breathlessness, policy initiative and twitch in the economy. It wants to know. It was to Wellington that Fletcher Challenge, the country's largest company, came to announce its 1988 profit, even though its head office had been shifted to Auckland, the new chief executive's home town, only a year before. In Auckland, the company reasoned, there would not have been the numbers or depth of journalists and analysts to listen.

And Wellington remains the financial centre. The big banks all have their head offices here. And the internationalised economy in which New Zealand is now enmeshed enhances the importance of the financiers.

That same internationalisation, however, requires a more competitive economy, which in turn requires leaner government. The inexorable rising tide of civil servants will ebb. The building of the world's most renewed capital will stop. Ugly holes will lie between ugly buildings. Wellington, then, will need to accommodate to a chill recessionary breeze. That will be a test of its substance.

Perhaps there is another symbolism in the rebuilding of the city centre. Sail into Wellington's harbour on a fine, still day and it is one of the most splendid in the world. From that generous and softening distance the city centre boxes give Wellington the look of a real city. Perhaps Wellington is best seen from a distance.

Which is appropriate for a capital, the place of feared and favoured decisions. For Wellington in a sense is New Zealand. If Wellington turns in on itself, New Zealand will, for Wellington is pervasive.

And in reverse, if New Zealand stagnates, Wellington

will, too. If New Zealand grasps the opportunity now before it and emerges into a post-colonial national adulthood, Wellington will, too. If Wellington lacks the coherence of a Washington it is because New Zealand is still not fully independent in spirit from its colonial heritage.

To achieve that coherence, Wellington will have to overcome its topography. Wellington is not one entity, but three: the municipality of Wellington city, the Hutt Valley at the other end of its harbour and a cluster of satellite cities and towns along the main route north up the west coast.

Wellington sprawls.

So does all New Zealand. New Zealand towns luxuriate in space and in the car that allows them to expand and yet remain close. New Zealanders are the second-highest travellers in cars after the Americans.

You can tell the age of a town by its sprawl. If it grew early, then slowed, the sprawl is less. Wanganui is a good example. Like Dunedin, it had an early advantage, its waterway, the Wanganui River at the mouth of which it stands. At the turn of the century it was the fifth biggest urban centre (which, like Dunedin, has left it with a better civic and cultural infrastructure than cities twice its size). Now it is fifteenth. Its hinterland, like Dunedin's, was too narrow to build it big as a service base. And, also like Dunedin, Wanganui, having peaked early, is contained relatively close to its city centre.

AT THE OTHER END of the scale is Tauranga. Down by the waterfront one- and two-storey shops and offices of fifty and sixty years ago dominate, tarted up a bit, but with the "est 1935" still rudely visible in the concrete or roughcast above the verandahs.

But once you get up the bank inland two or three streets back you see the growth that has come from the kiwifruit boom of the surrounding countryside in the 1970s and 1980s: new hotels and motels, offices, car saleyards, lots of bright signs and bright lights. Then to the south and west are wide acreages of houses for the new Taurangans – youngish, a bit flashy and a bit loud; or retired to the sun with a packet from a good income or a big capital gain.

At the north of the town the new Tauranga is symbolised in a slender cross-harbour bridge most towns Tauranga's size (population: 42,000) would only dream about. The bridge links the town with its twin, Mt Maunganui (population: 12,000). "The Mount" has its own substantial shopping centre, its own bronzed-bodied beach-resort life in the summer, its own long sprawl to the south. Yet it is also part of Tauranga. For a time they shared a mayor.

Between the extremes the pattern is repeated all over the country. There is not much to distinguish one town from another, apart from topography and specialities, such as tourism in mountainous Queenstown, the monumental white stone buildings of Oamaru built from the quarries nearby, the one-industry timber or coal towns, Kawerau, Tokoroa and Huntly – and perhaps, for Blenheim, a special wine status in the decades to come as the grape-growing excellence of the plains around is exploited. Regional variations in such a small country where modern communications homogenise thinking are small and subtle – the solidity of Invercargill in the far south or the high proportion of Maori in Kaitaia in the far north.

BARKER COLLECTION/CANTERBURY MUSEUM

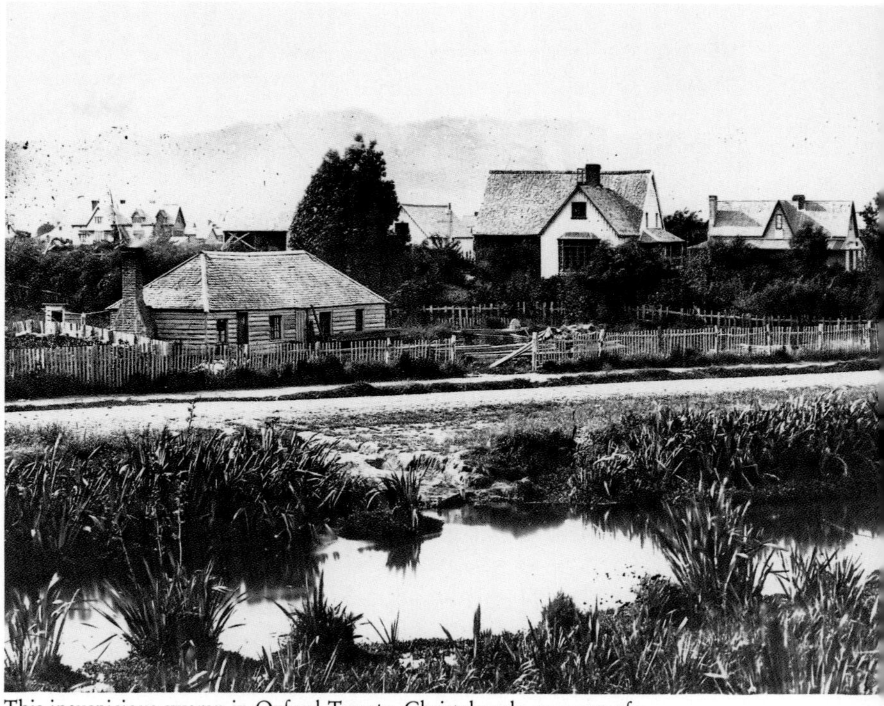

This inauspicious swamp in Oxford Terrace, Christchurch, was part of a panorama of central Christchurch created by the pioneering photographer Dr A. C. Barker in 1863.

The variations are mainly a function of size. Christchurch (population: 300,000), the largest urban centre in the sparsely populated South Island, has a few high-rise office blocks to compete with its cathedral and claims, with indifference to independence, a mythical Englishness on the strength of a replica of an English public school, a park of English trees and an eccentric public figure, the Wizard. But in reality Christchurch manages only elements of the stuffiness and snobbishness of an English society long decayed; it smells of hayseed – a supplier of goods and light engineering products to its once-rich cropping and pastoral farming hinterland.

At the level of Putaruru (population: 4000) or Ashburton (population: 14,000) the farm suppliers occupy an important status. If there is a big factory – pulp and paper at Mataura (population: 2100) in Southland or two dairy products factories in Te Awamutu (population: 8000) – it commands attention.

ONCE THE SMALLER of the towns defined New Zealand, so the folklore told us. There farmers, who made the exports, sold produce to middlemen and bought the necessities. So those towns are grander than you would build them now: concrete, brick or stone two-storey buildings housing spacious stores, self-important banks, a cinema or two, a post office built to last, often a hospital.

But the car has carried the activity away. The larger provincial towns are sucking in shoppers as travel becomes faster and cheaper in relation to incomes. So, for example, Hamilton grows fat at the expense of surrounding Morrinsville, Matamata, Cambridge, Ngaruawahia and Te Awamutu; New Plymouth at the expense of Stratford. Centralisation of government and administration on bigger towns has marched alongside. Rural depopulation – of little settlements – is being superseded by provincial drift – from smallish towns.

There are pretensions to special status. Te Puke near Tauranga proclaims itself the kiwifruit capital of the world. Turangi, on the country's largest lake, Taupo, claims to be the trout-fishing capital of the world. Taihape, a small railway and agricultural service town in the centre of the North Island, has declared itself the gumboot capital and has an annual festival to celebrate. Gisborne is the first city in the world to see the light (the sunrise), being the easternmost. Naseby, a tiny hamlet of 133 (shortly to be forcibly decommissioned by bureaucrats who don't like untidy excrescences), may have been the world's smallest independent borough.

One provincial city does have a claim to world status: Napier is the "art deco capital of the world". Devastated in an earthquake in 1931, Napier was rebuilt all of a style, a sort of cleanly provincial art deco. Most of it still stands, for Napier has not grown very fast and so has not knocked it down to make space for new buildings, and now new buildings are built in neo-art deco to maintain the lines. Specialists came from the other side of the world to view this microcosm of a period of taste.

But mostly sameness and predictability predominate, characterised by sprawl. Sprawl also characterises the biggest city, Auckland. But there the sprawl has a different effect.

IN THE PROVINCIAL TOWNS AND CITIES, sprawl still leaves those at the edges in touch with the centre, ten to twenty minutes away by car at the most. In Auckland powerful centrifugal forces are at work.

Drive round the vast reach of Auckland (as long north to south and wide east to west as London, with one-eighth the population) and you pass through a series of towns and villages. Auckland is not one metropolitan area but many. Huge shopping centres suck in surrounding populations and suck them away from central Auckland, severed from its surrounds by motorways.

So within Auckland, which sucked in people from all over the country as it grew fat on its sub-tropical warmth and industrial protection in the decades after the Second World War, a reverse magnet from that in the provinces is at work. In Auckland the suck is outwards to the suburbs. It is easier shopping there for all but the chic-est stuff. And one can be among one's own kind. Auckland is being segmented into villages, each homogenised in itself, but each of a different stamp from the other.

So Pakuranga, newly affluent and yearning for real money, is flashier and less substantial than Remuera, where the money sits heavily behind leafed fences and two-decker mansions. Titirangi, among the wooded hills of the west, encourages idiosyncrats and eccentrics and takes a more generous view of life than the tight-garbed yuppies of inner-city Parnell in their BMWs, or the trendy liberals of Ponsonby, now largely cleared of the immigrant brown life that poured into what was then a slum in the 1950s and 1960s. Flat, working-class Onehunga, in small wooden boxes, has not the respectability of Mount Albert to its north. Topography has sliced Auckland, too, the Manukau Harbour in the south cutting in from the west and the Waitemata Harbour in the north cutting in from the east like deep knives. Beyond these harbours the population consciously feels different from the isthmus dwellers. They even have separate representative rugby teams to prove it.

Other great sprawling cities of the world have managed to contain diversity within oneness. In Auckland, however, there is more than diversity. There is also a huge, gaping split.

One Auckland looks out over a magnificent harbour. In the Hauraki Gulf outside that harbour there is safe water for forty to fifty kilometres, scattered with beautiful islands. On a weekend, particularly a summer weekend, the water is flecked with yachts of all sizes. That Auckland is called the City of Sails.

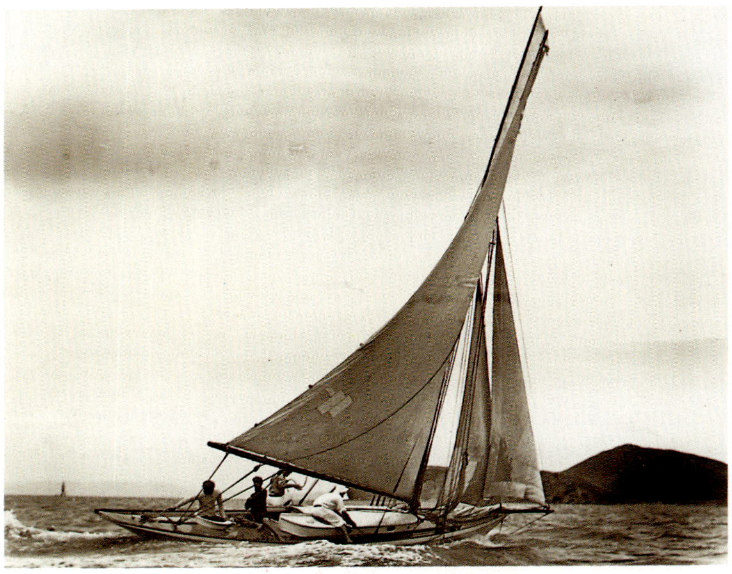
WINKELMANN/AUCKLAND INSTITUTE AND MUSEUM

The yacht *Rarere* in the Auckland regatta, 1902. The photographer, Henry Winkelmann, lovingly recorded almost every regatta from 1893 to 1928. The first regatta was held in 1840, and in the years following, races have been held for Maori canoes, whaleboats, large sailing ships and scows, as well as yachts.

YACHTING IS IN THE BLOOD of those Aucklanders. So Auckland has become one of the great yacht design centres of the world. Leisure and sport have been married with technological innovation and a fine sense of line. Yachts made here, sailed by yachtsmen brought up here, dominate international competitions.

It is a signal of excellence. In a country which for much of its life has valued mediocrity everywhere but in sport, yachting has extended excellence beyond sport into design, technological development and into business behind that design and development. At the end of the world, small and provincial, New Zealand has badly needed more than sport to make it feel good about itself, make itself feel a world leader.

We have been with the best in dairy industry product and machinery development. We invented the jet boat. We conquered Mount Everest. A New Zealander split the atom. But we have not celebrated those things: calling Auckland the City of Sails celebrates the yacht business with triumph.

It is also an active celebration. Christchurch celebrates rest as the Garden City. Wellington is recipient-prisoner of its weather as Windy City. Auckland does not rest or reflect or gossip on big events. It acts.

That Auckland is affluent. It is a bit brash, almost in an unseemly Australian manner as it apes the second hand California lifestyle of Sydney. In Queen Street the women dress snappier and look leaner, freer than anywhere else in the country. There is a pace here – not the pace of New York or Rome or Hong Kong or Tokyo, but enough to shuck the provincialism of elsewhere.

The best-off of those Aucklanders live in tree-lined suburbs along the Waitemata Harbour and the bush-lined beaches facing the Hauraki Gulf. For them Auckland is an agreeable place of comfortable cars, expensive and in some cases good restaurants, good money, a benign climate, fast fads and fine sailing. The less-well-off live in tighter suburbs on the rolling country of the isthmus between the two harbours and out to the west reaching towards the ranges – or on the fringes to the north-west.

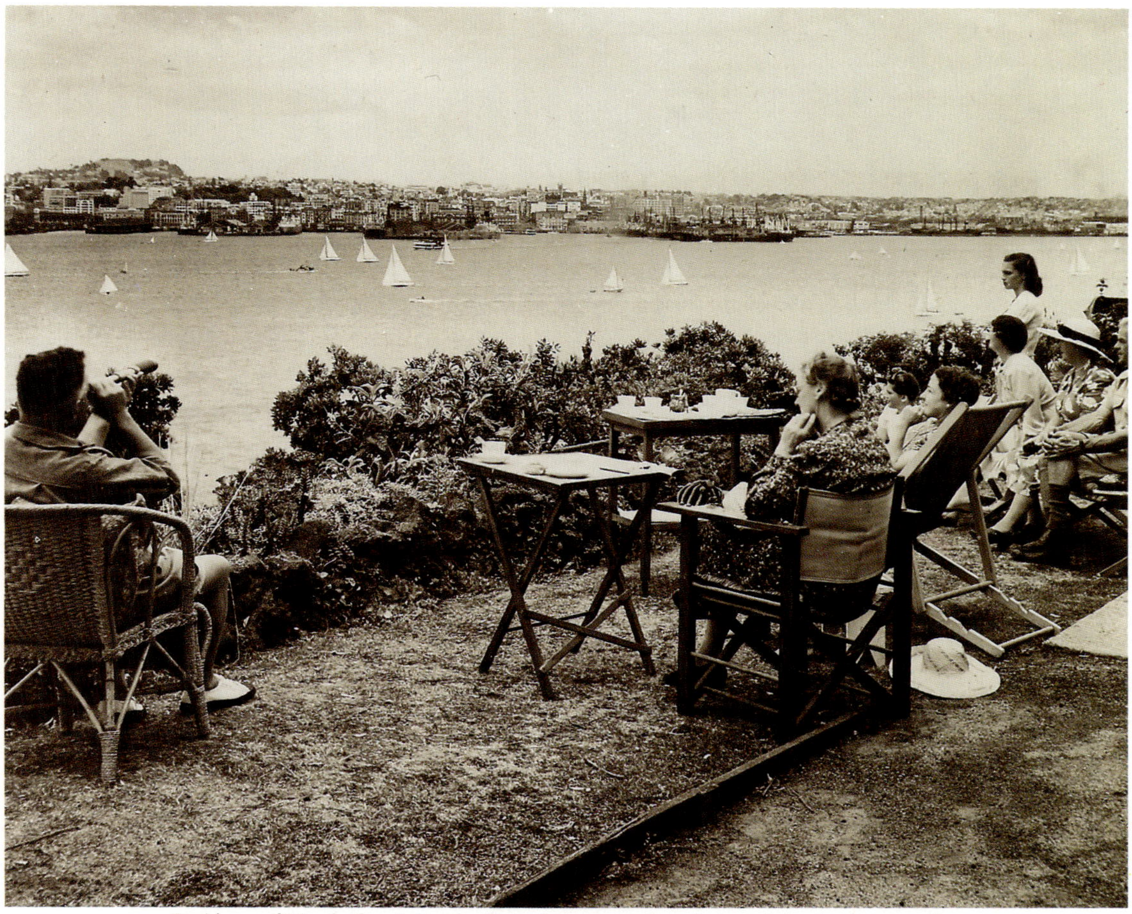

Residents of North Shore's Stanley Point have a grandstand view of the Anniversary Day regatta, ca 1953.

Their cars are second-hand and they eat out at "family" restaurants. But there is also a sense among these varied people that they belong to the same lot. They are where it's at – and the "it" is money.

They make up the biggest city in European New Zealand – living closer to the edge of their credit than the rest of the country. Their decisions, left to themselves to make, would be for a one-culture society dedicated to safe jobs making more wealth. Barbecue, boat and a bash on the beach.

They are white.

There is another Auckland. Some children in that Auckland have little to do with the sea, though they live a half-hour bus-ride from it. They do not live in the City of Sails. They live in the Polynesian capital of the world.

Stand in Otara in a side street near its junction with East Tamaki Road at 8 a.m. Behind and around you are vigorous brown faces and bodies, many neat in the blue and maroon uniforms of Hillary College, chattering in groups. On the side streets the cars are battered and old, full of kids, driven by people with brown, often tired, faces. On the four lanes of East Tamaki Road white, set, single faces are at the wheels of new sedans cutting through. They whizz through Otara to and from white Pakuranga and Howick and the white central city – the City of Sails in its safe transit zone through the Polynesian capital.

Walk a little way along East Tamaki Road from the side street and the spick new Lion Brewery comes into sight. Small dilapidated two-storey houses stand opposite. The brewery is an opiate for those in the dilapidated houses and they are machinery fodder for it – and all the manufacturing industry in the industrial areas of south Auckland.

Down a street to the south of East Tamaki Road a white tower looms distant. Centre of the Manukau City administration complex, where the local bureaucrats plan with white liberal authority, it is as remote as a medieval cathedral spire from village peasants.

A little way in the other direction and, among a clump of churches, you will come across the Presbyterian Church shared by Pacific Island groups. Well-built, new and spacious, it is the product of island immigrants' respect for christianity, the priests of which provide the social glue and discipline in a strange, cool land. Many islanders, particularly Samoans, are achievement oriented, having no place to stand here.

But as a group they share with the Maori around them underclass status. Too many houses to each side of East Tamaki Road need painting, too many need some trees and shrubs to lighten them. Otarans do not have great material riches. The manufacturing which sucked them in from their country marae in the 1950s and 1960s is throwing them on to unemployment heaps as it contracts. Their children are too often to be found out of work and in prison.

WHAT DECISIONS WILL BE MADE in that Auckland, the Polynesian capital of the world? Decisions to overcome their handicaps, some imposed, some self-imposed, and to match the City of Sails in affluence? Or decisions to turn away to another society, sometimes violent towards the City of Sails?

And if the decisions for New Zealand are to be made in the cities and if Auckland, being the biggest city, is likely to make some of the biggest decisions, what decisions will it make? If it makes the decision not of strengthening diversity but of division, what positive counter can there be in Wellington, with its third world towers, and in the smaller centres, now deprived of their once-weighty economic influence?

Those questions will be answered during the lifetime of this book. They are as big questions, as vital for the society around them, as any posed to any cities in the world.

OLD CITIES, DEEP CITIES are used to decisions. They have made myriad decisions, each adding another layer to the deep subsoil that makes up each city, makes it different, gives it a special character. New Zealand's cities are young, unsettled, uncertain, fragile: the luxuriating sprawl of the provincial towns, the provincial smallness of Dunedin, the glassy transitoriness of Wellington, the division of Auckland.

Youth gives sudden depression, sidetracks, dangerous risks. Youth often comes unstuck, goes the wrong way, damages what is around it. That is part of growing up. But youth also gives energy, excitement, hope, the space in the mind and heart to grow, develop, grasp opportunities, reach for the unknown.

Within those cities there are the seeds for destruction and decay and the seeds for richness and enterprise. The Maori renaissance, the recovery of mana, culture and confidence in a new leadership, suggests the decisions in the Polynesian capital of the world and its offshoots in the other cities and towns could be strongly positive. But they will not be easy decisions for the youthful City of Sails and its sibling cities and towns.

Young cities are unhampered by past straitjackets. They can choose what mould they will have for their ageing. That is the state of New Zealand cities and towns. Before them they, particularly Auckland, have the possibility of being a force not just in New Zealand but in the region around New Zealand.

There is a positive symbolic sign.

Hitherto in New Zealand towns and cities the waterfront has been the back end of town, a grim or derelict place. When Wellington built its new town hall, it was squashed into a small patch of land beside the existing one, when just across a four-lane street was a patch of potentially enchanting waterfront no longer used for shipping; the harbour board and the city council could not agree. Auckland has built its new Aotea Centre not on the waterfront, where Sydney built its renowned Opera House, but in a dip halfway along Queen Street.

Why this inland complex, this turning away from the sea and the wide horizons? Perhaps it was a rejection of the pre-colonial past, an unwillingness to be reminded of the conditions the immigrant colonists had left. If so, it was paralleled in narrow provincial sameness and an obsessive search for security in social and economic policy.

Oamaru has been redeveloping its waterfront area. Wellington has planned a project to develop the waterfront for recreation. Auckland has managed at last a restaurant on the harbour and has restored an old customs building near the ferry wharf.

Perhaps we are now ready to look outwards. If so, the decisions the cities will make will have a positive ring to them. And if so, they will be fine cities. □

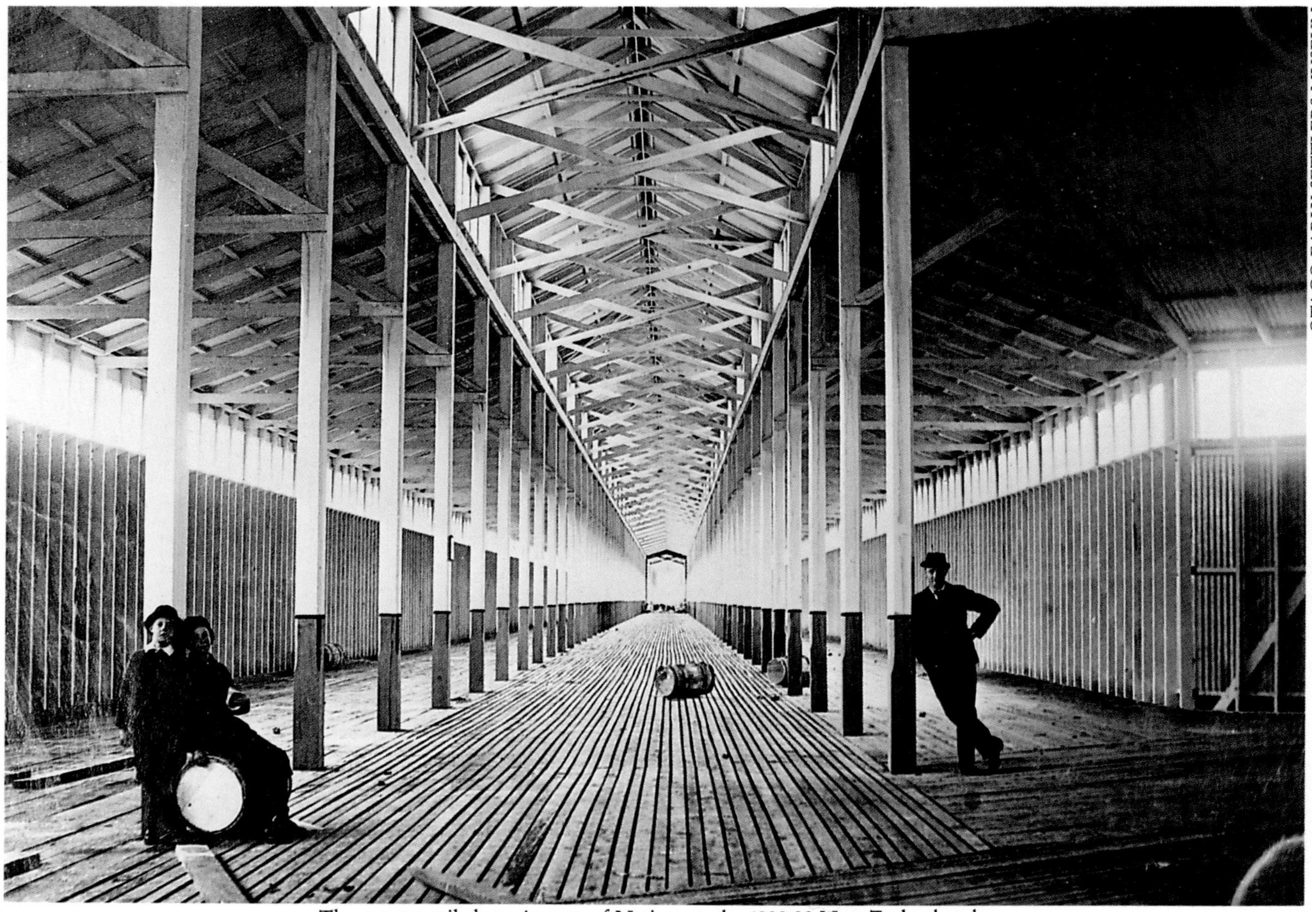

OTAGO EARLY SETTLERS MUSEUM

The quarter-mile-long Avenue of Nations at the 1889-90 New Zealand and South Seas Exhibition, the second of Dunedin's great exhibitions. The exhibition buildings covered ten acres, three million feet of timber and 330 tons of galvanised iron were used to construct them.

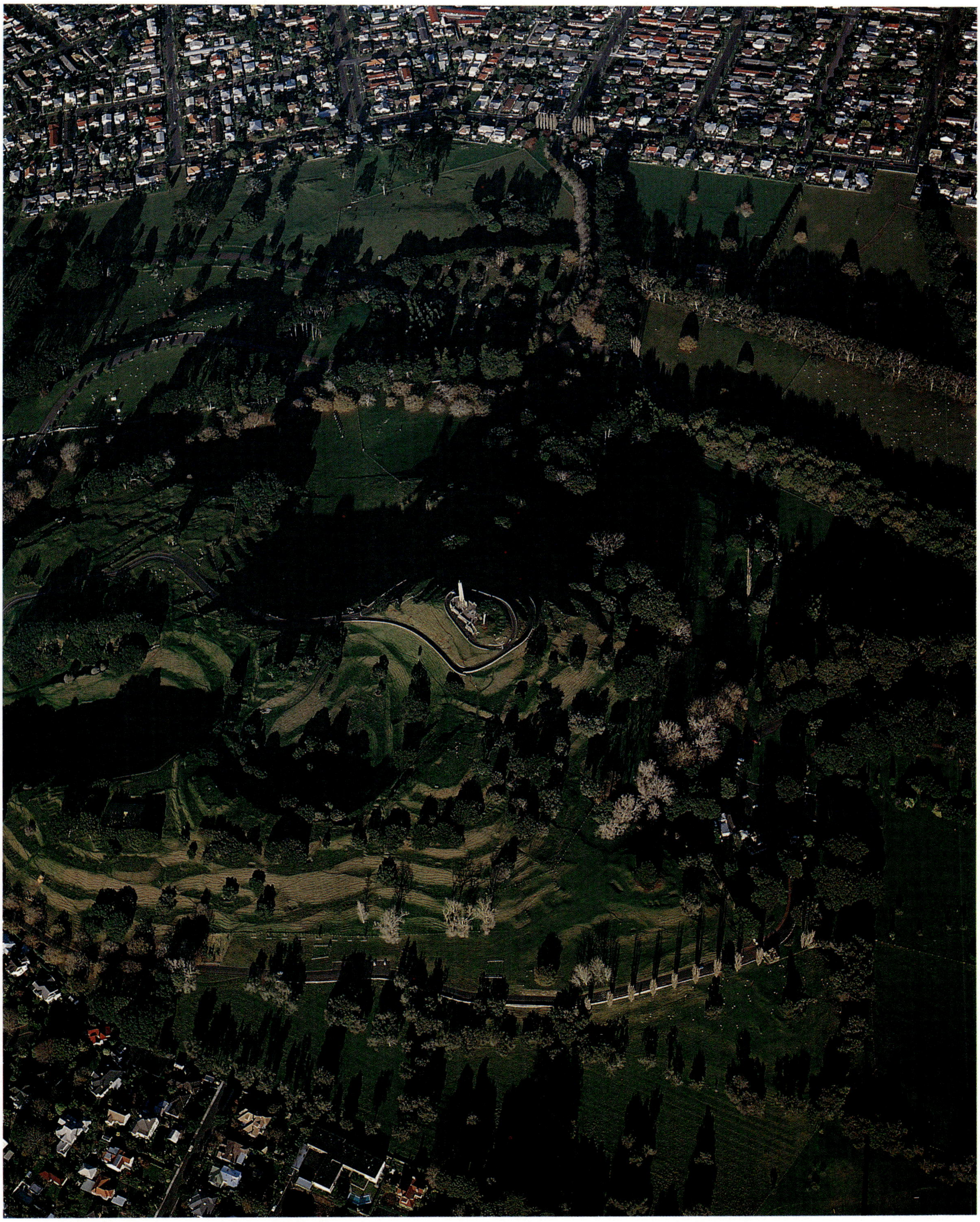

Aerial view of One Tree Hill and Auckland suburbs ERIC TAYLOR

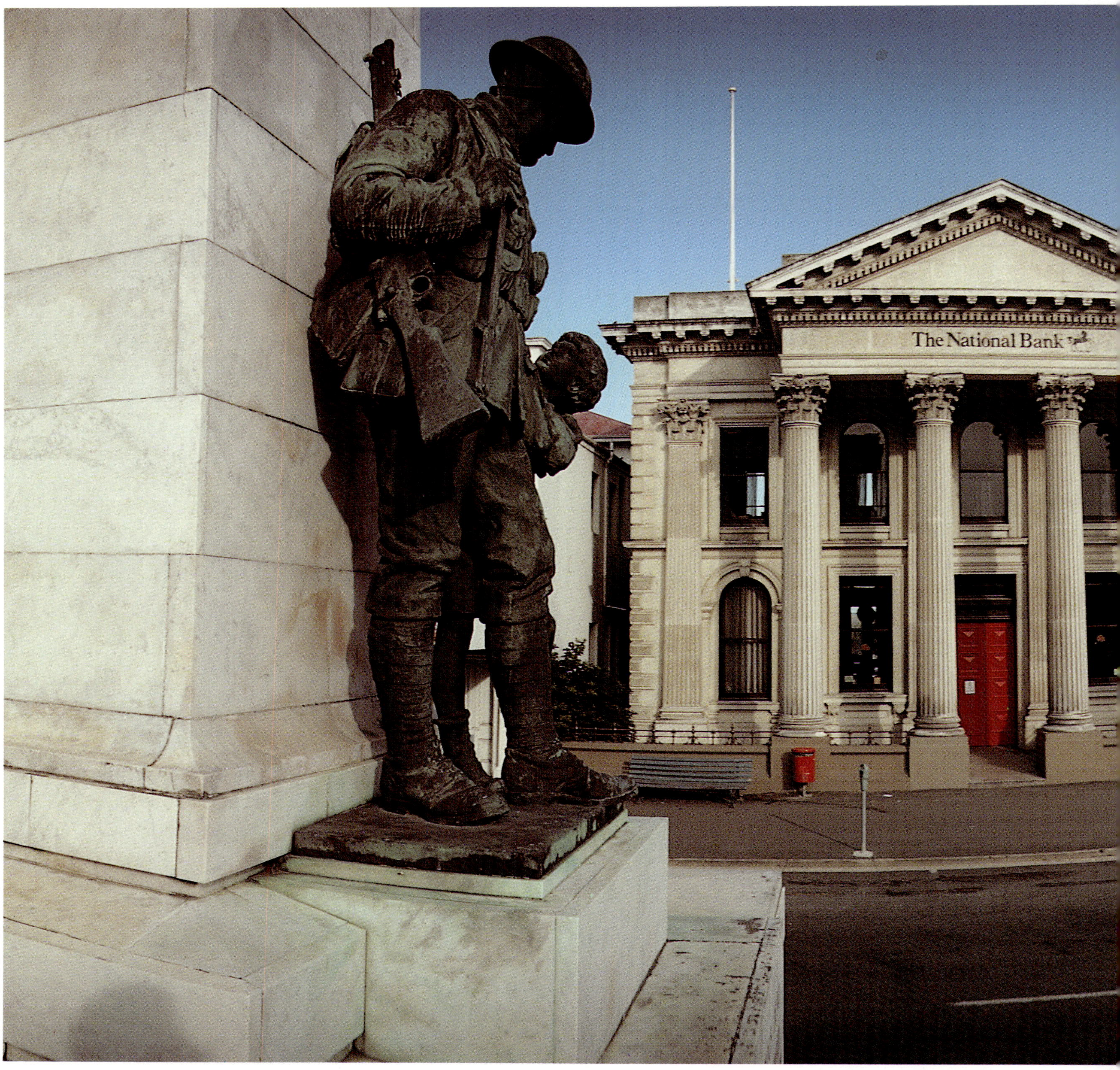

War memorial and old banks, Oamaru

GEOFF MASON

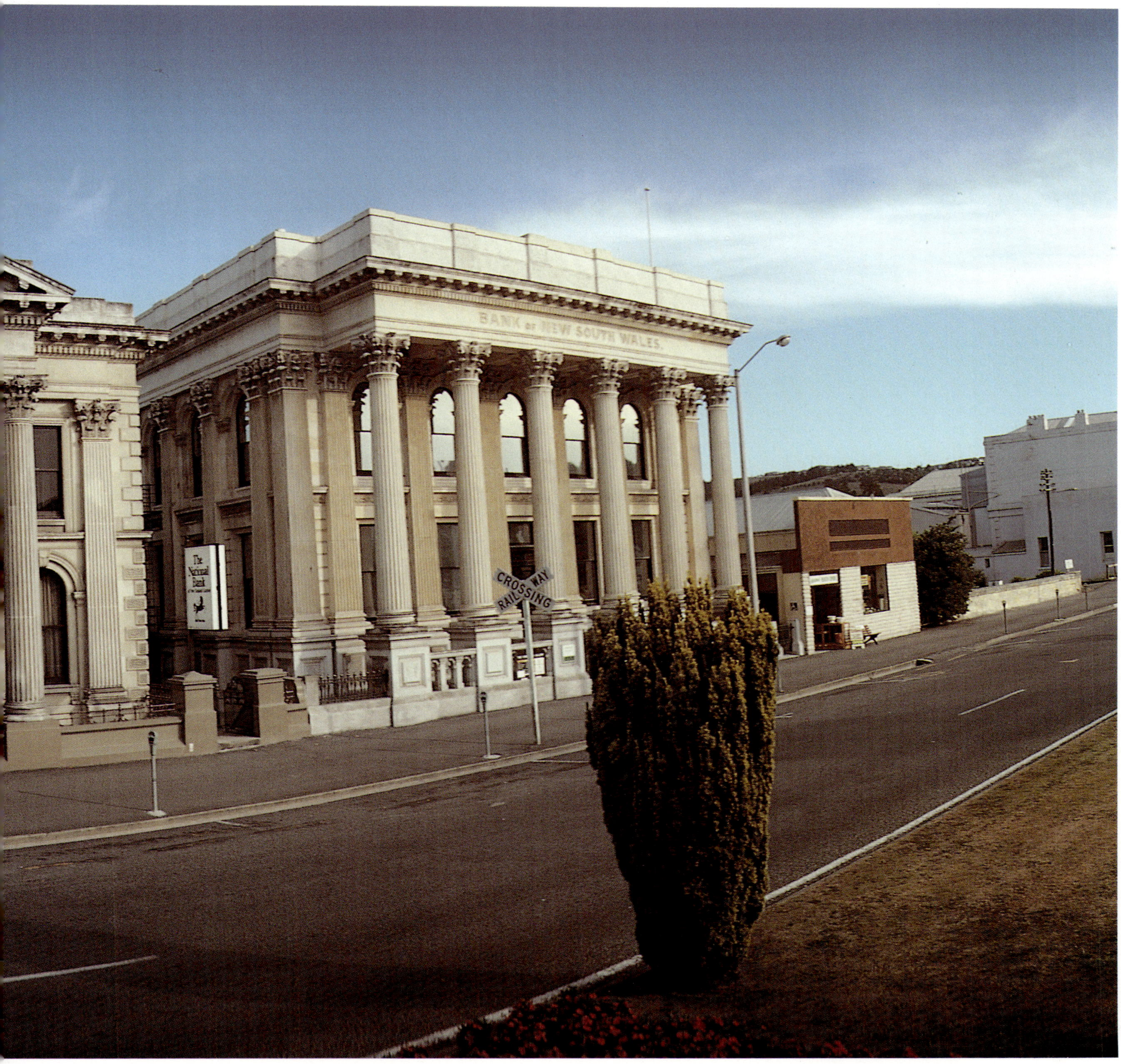
BANK OF NEW SOUTH WALES.
The National Bank
RAILWAY CROSSING

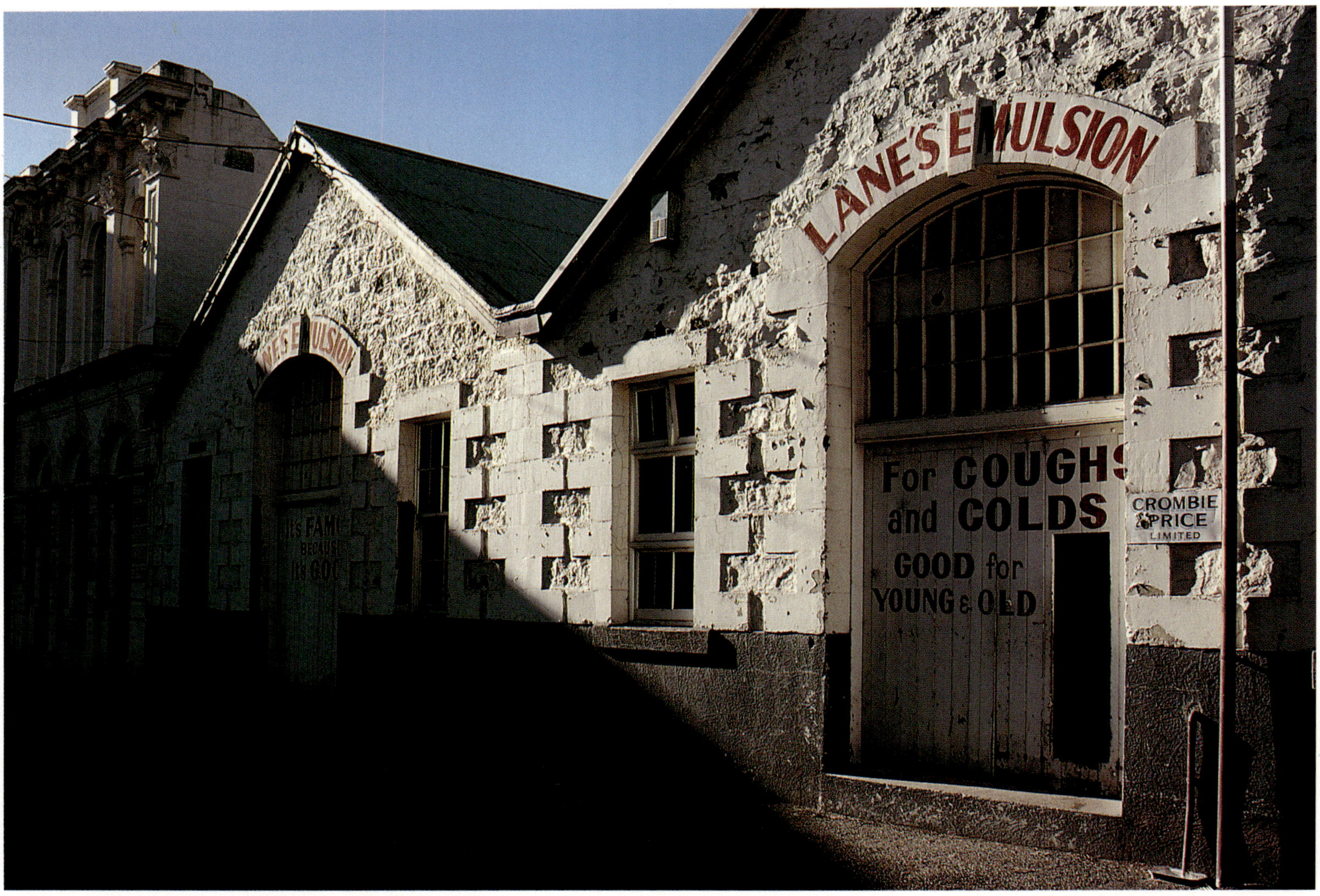

The original Lanes Emulsion warehouse, Oamaru — ROBIN MORRISON

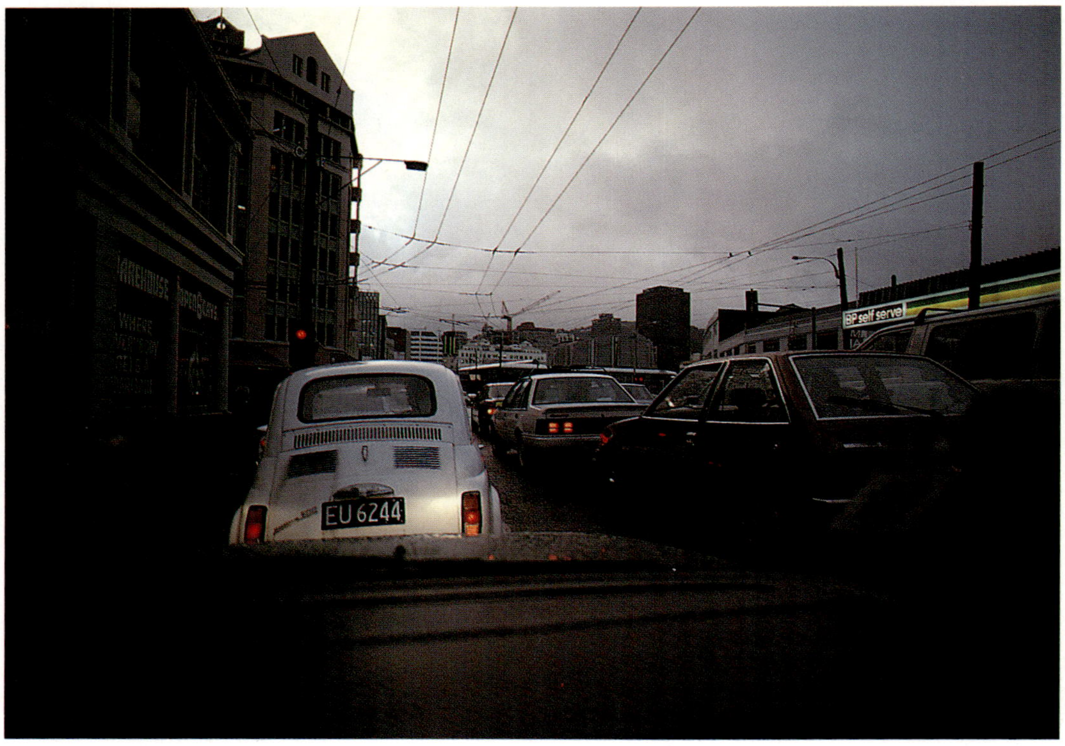

Twilight traffic jam, Taranaki and Wakefield streets, Wellington — TIM STEELE

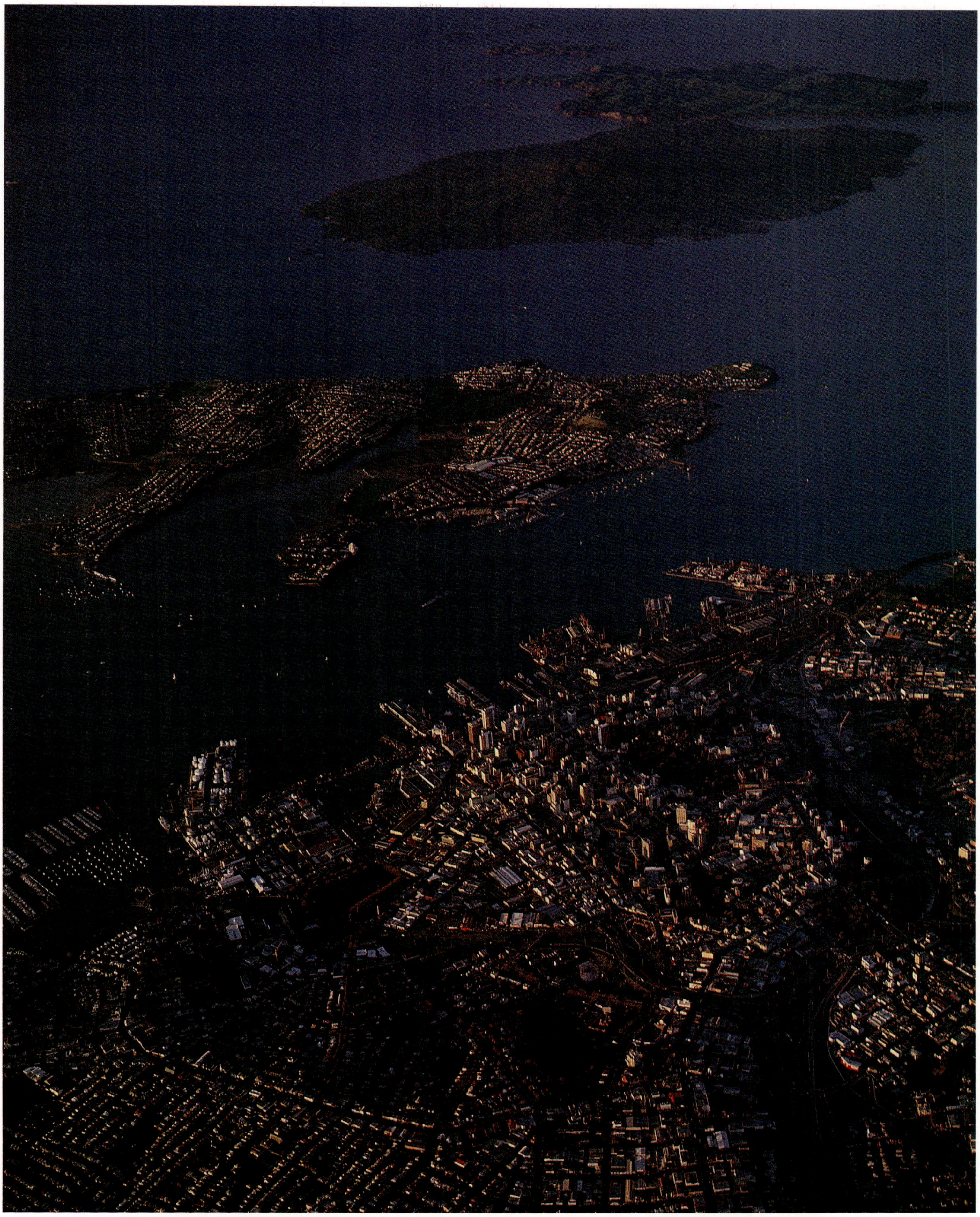

Downtown Auckland from 10,000 feet ERIC TAYLOR

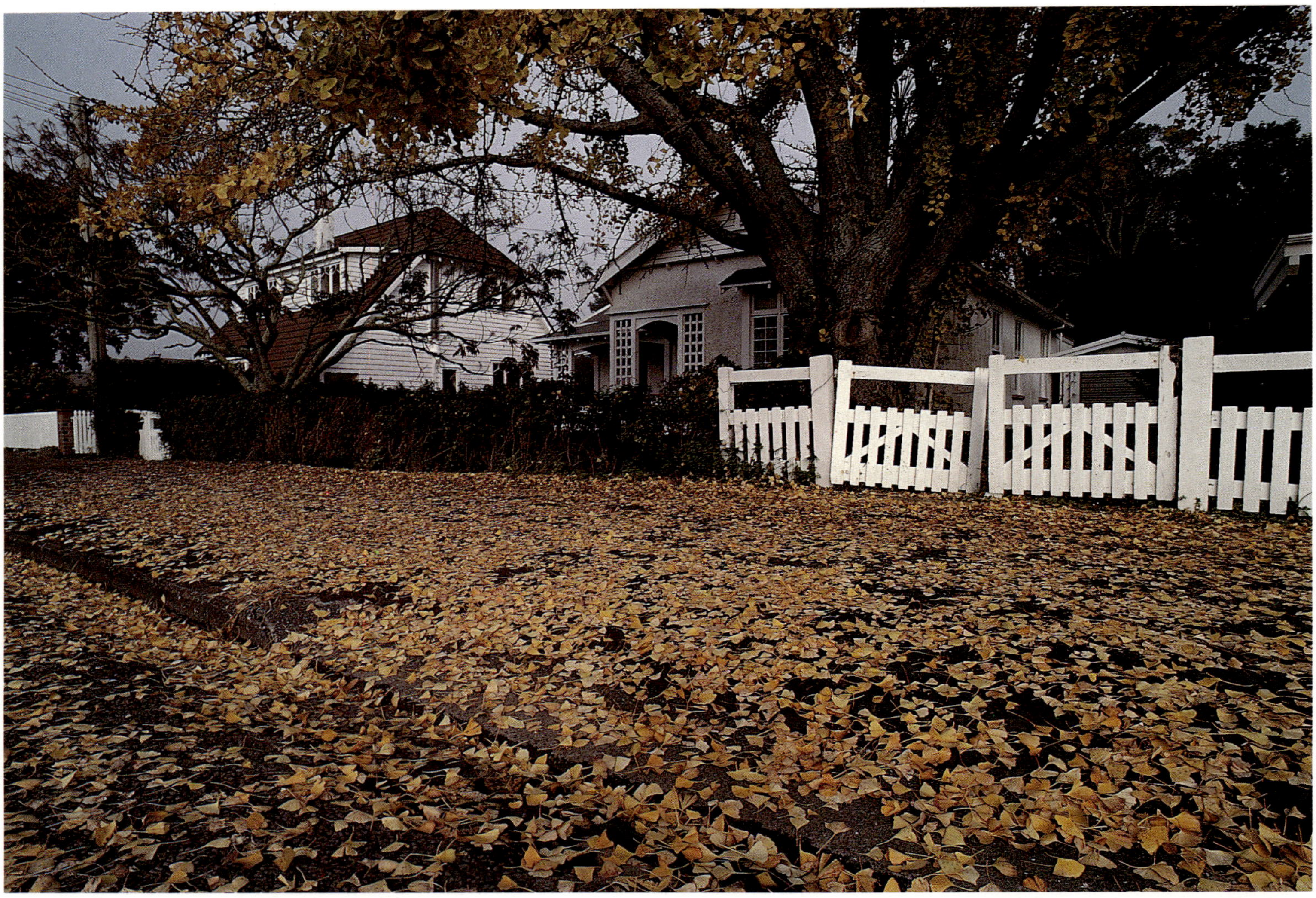

Autumn leaves, Narrow Neck, Auckland TIM STEELE

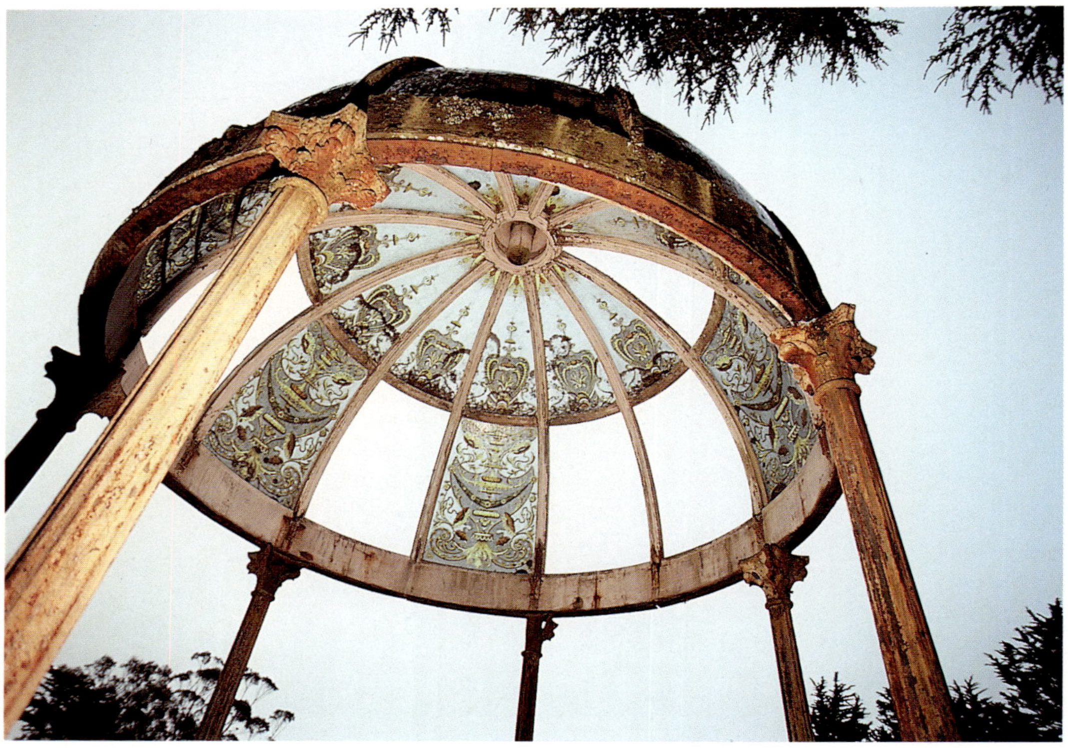

Larnach's Castle, Otago Peninsula GEOFF MASON

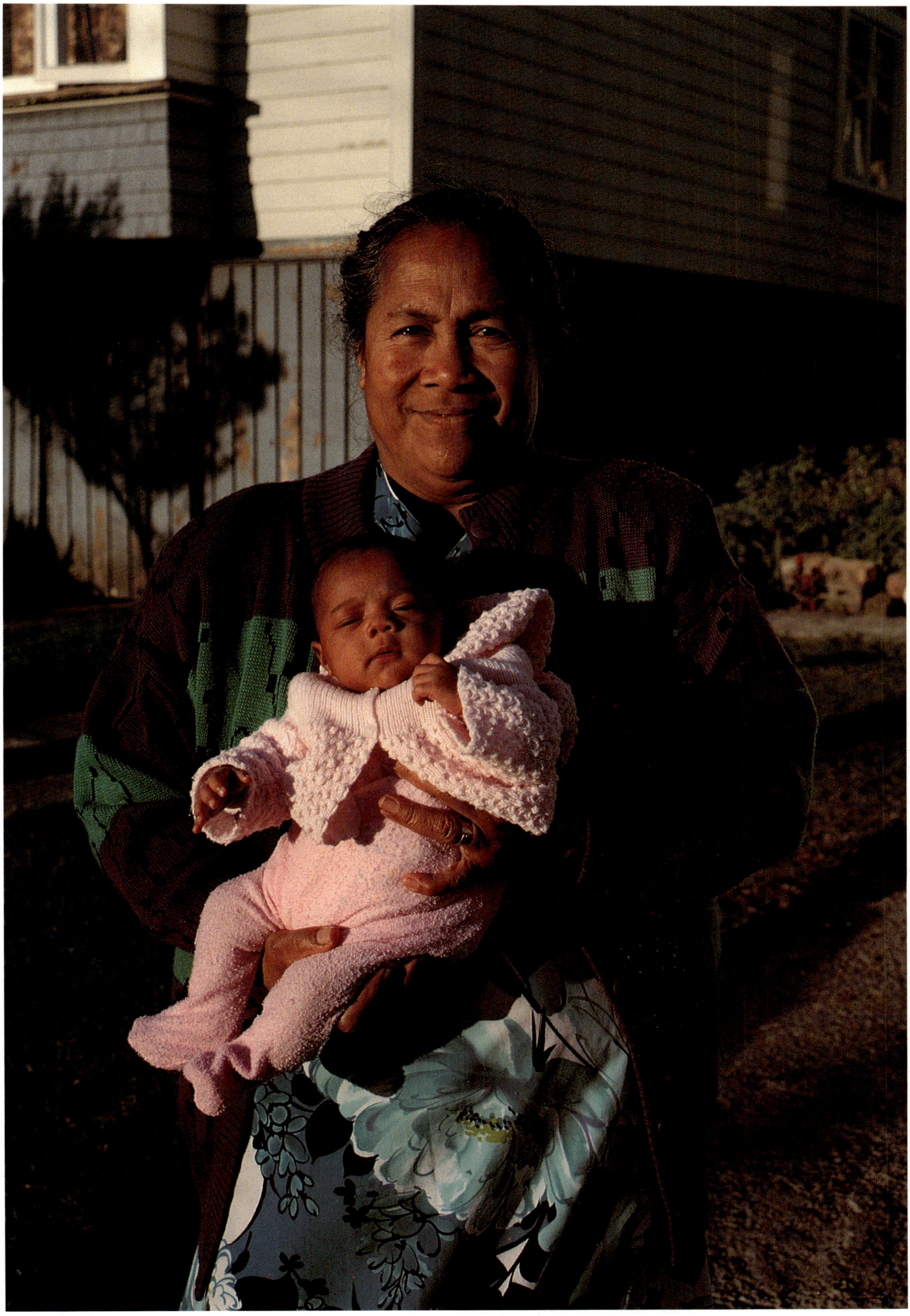

Samoan woman with her granddaughter, Grey Lynn, Auckland

ERIC TAYLOR

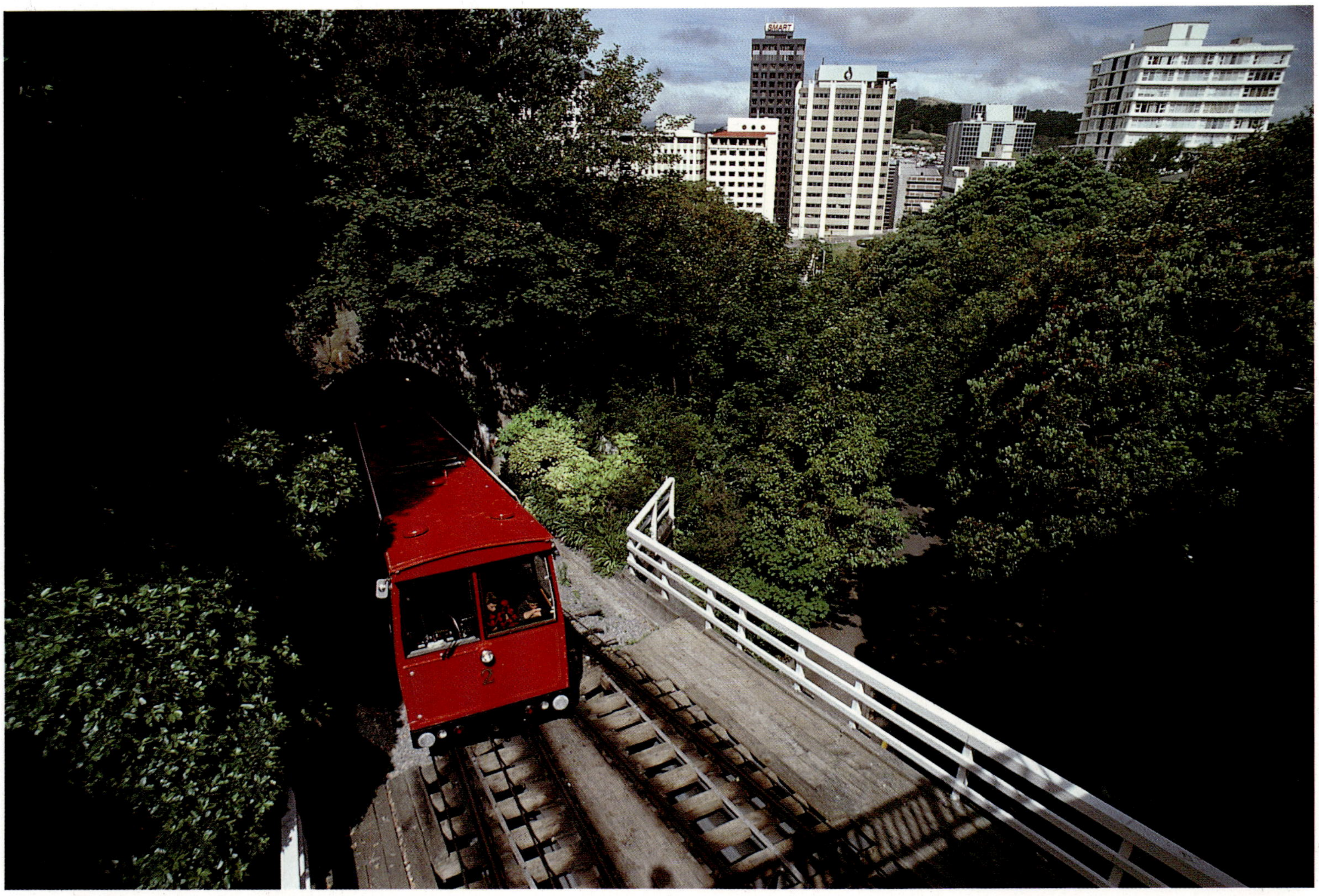

Cable car, Wellington — TIM STEELE

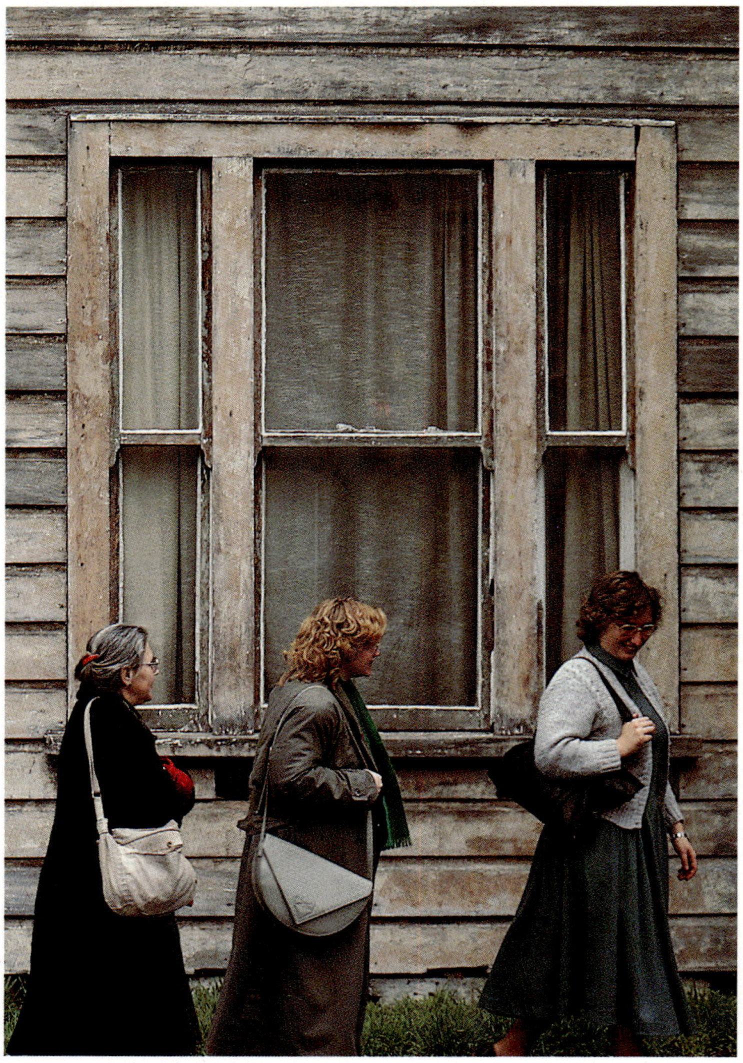

Tinakori Road, Wellington — TIM STEELE

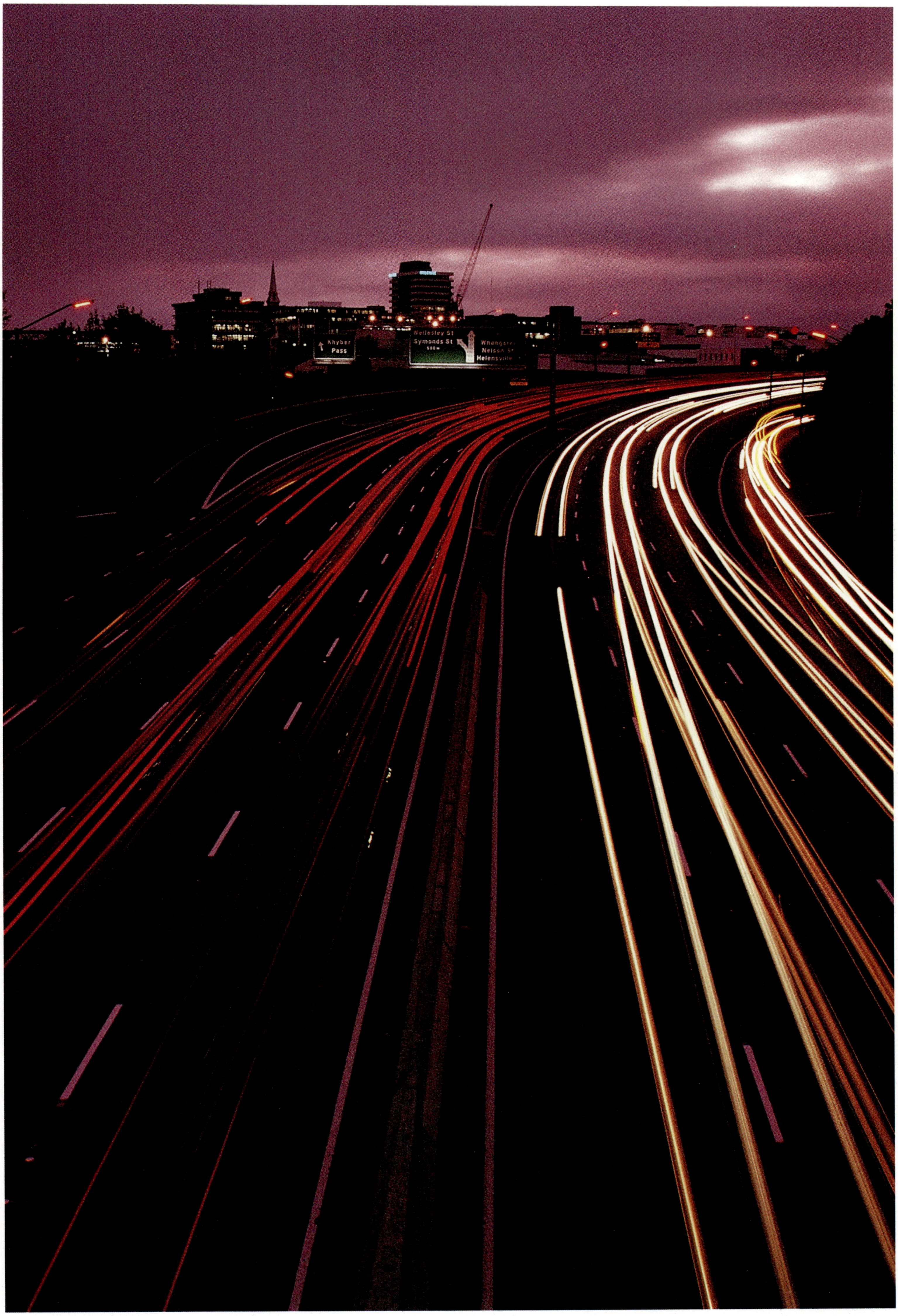

The Khyber Pass section of Auckland's southern motorway at sunset ERIC TAYLOR

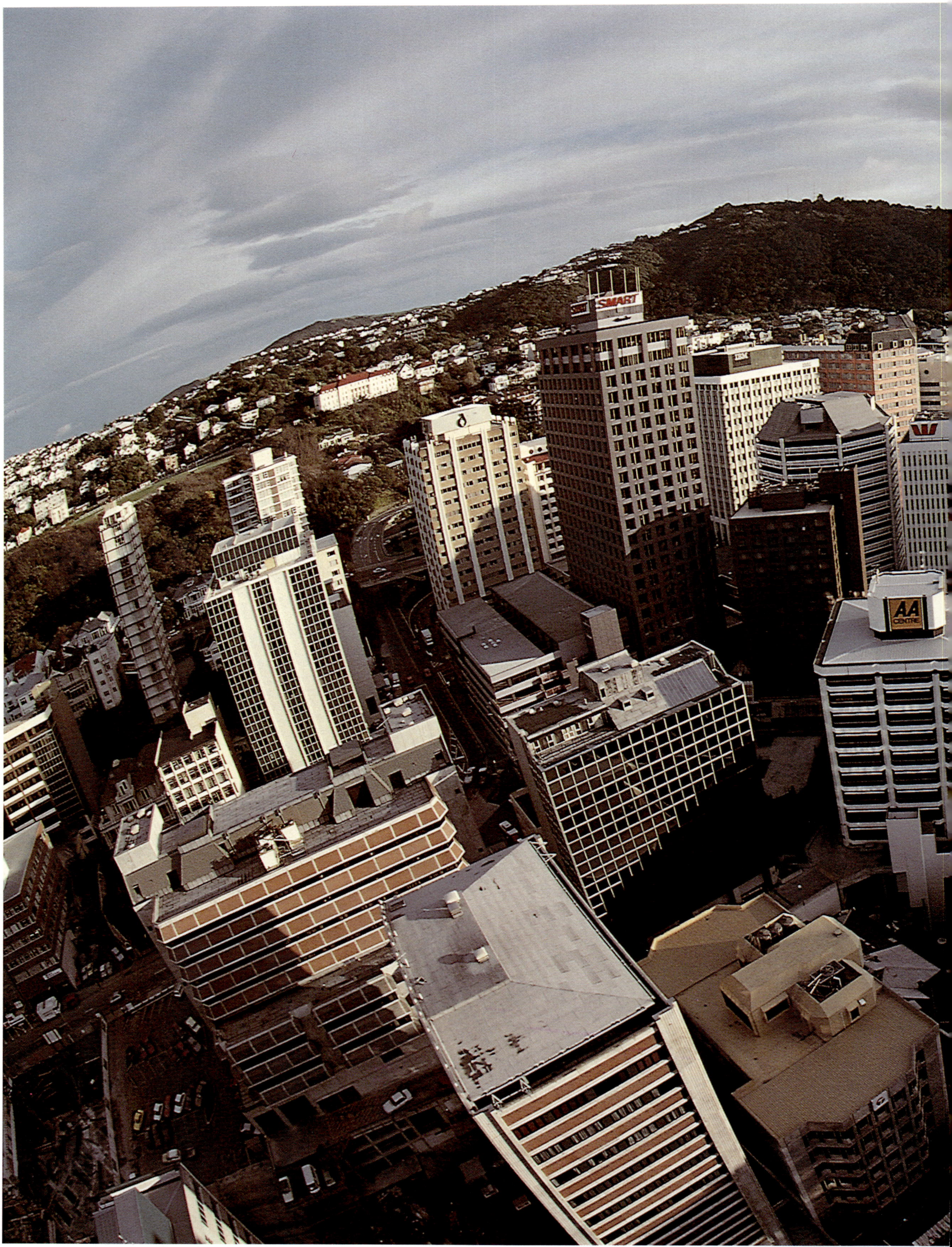

An early morning view of Wellington, seen from the roof of the Bank of New Zealand TIM STEELE

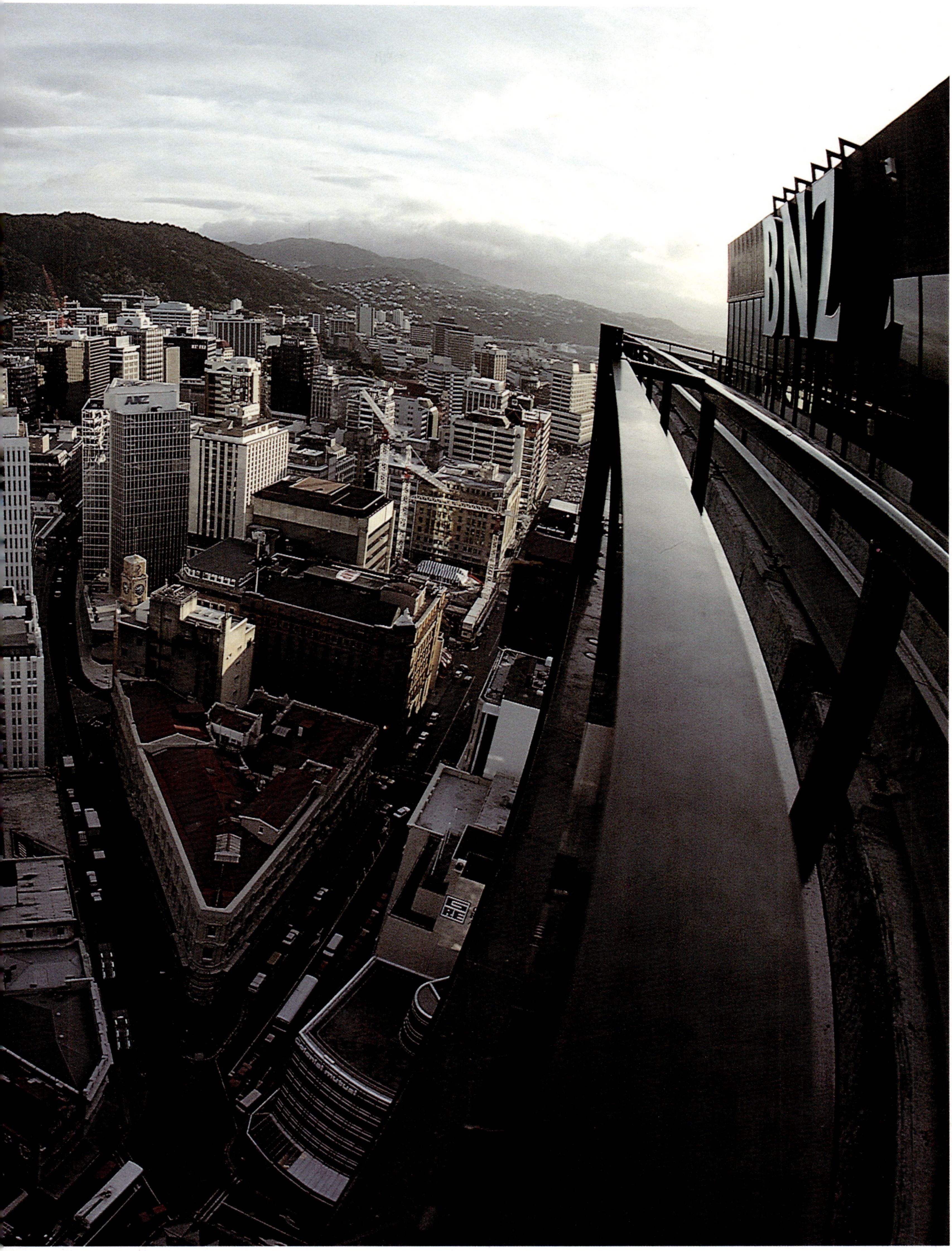
BNZ
ANZ

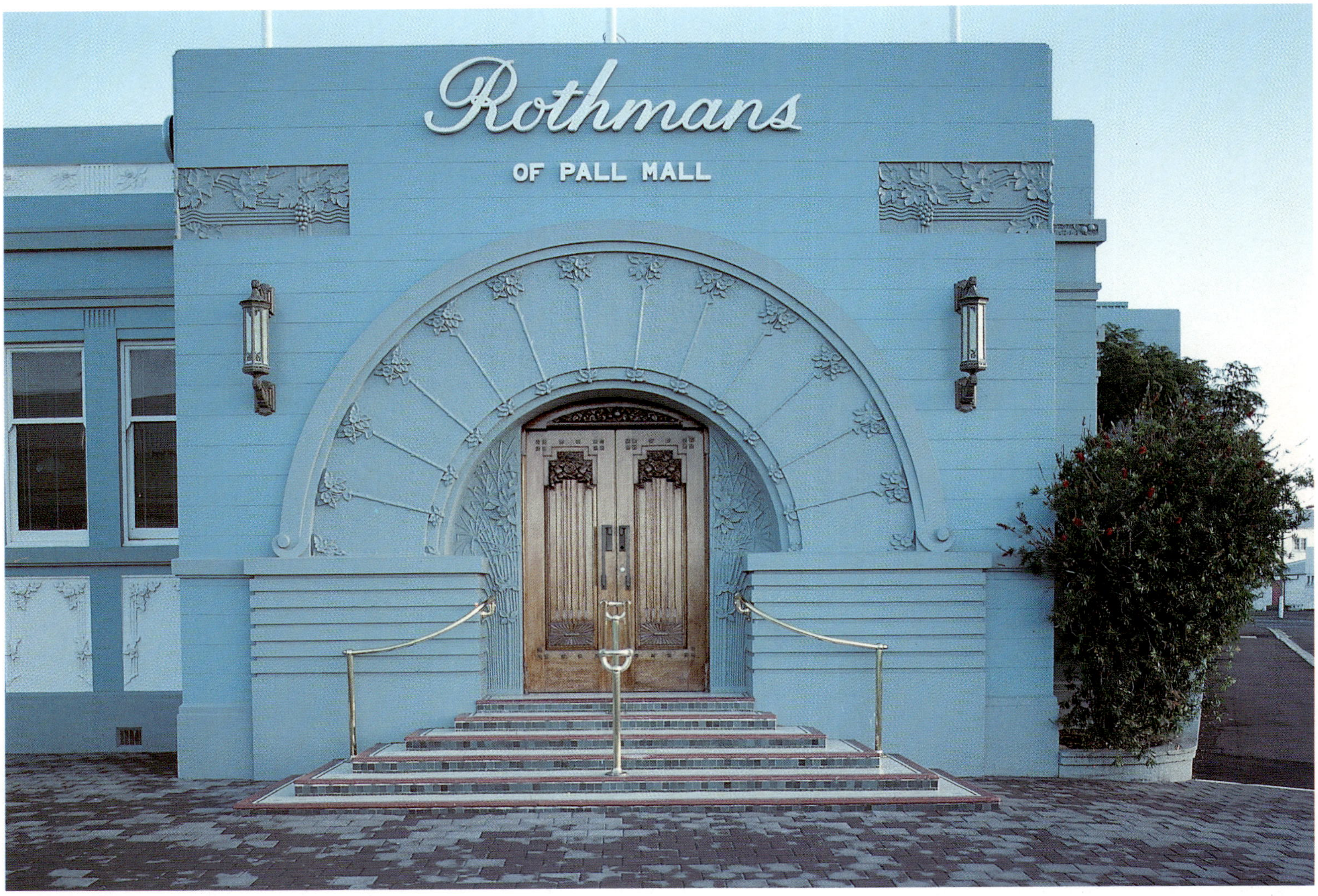

National Tobacco Company Building, now Rothmans, Napier — CRAIG POTTON

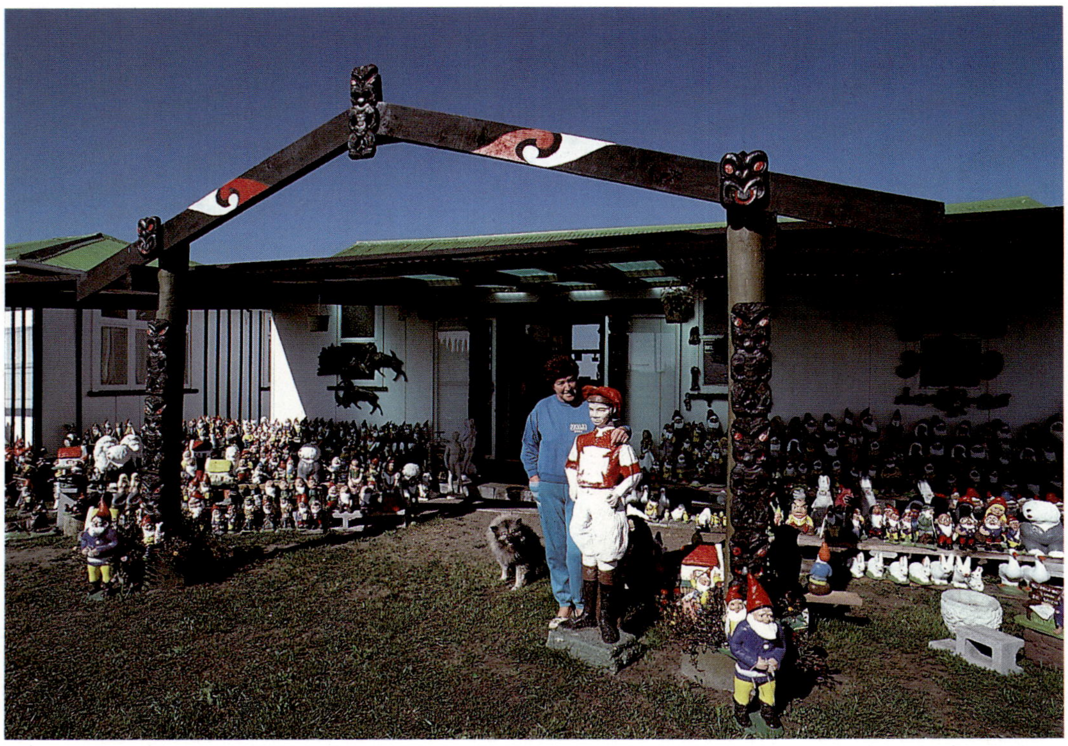

Ruth Harris, Pikihuia Arts, Rangioutu, Palmerston North — TIM STEELE

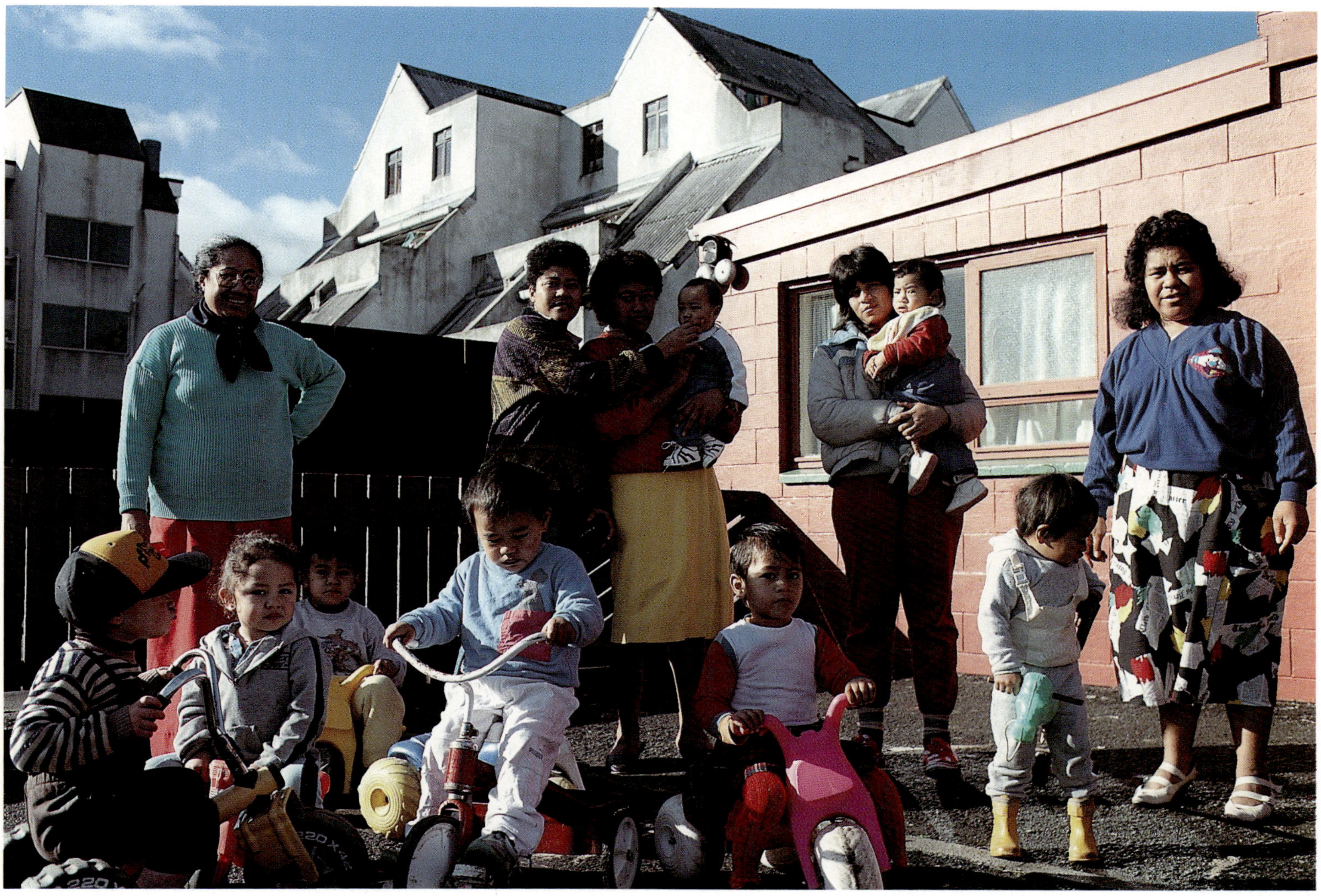

Mothers, helpers and children at the Pacifica Creche, Newtown, Wellington TIM STEELE

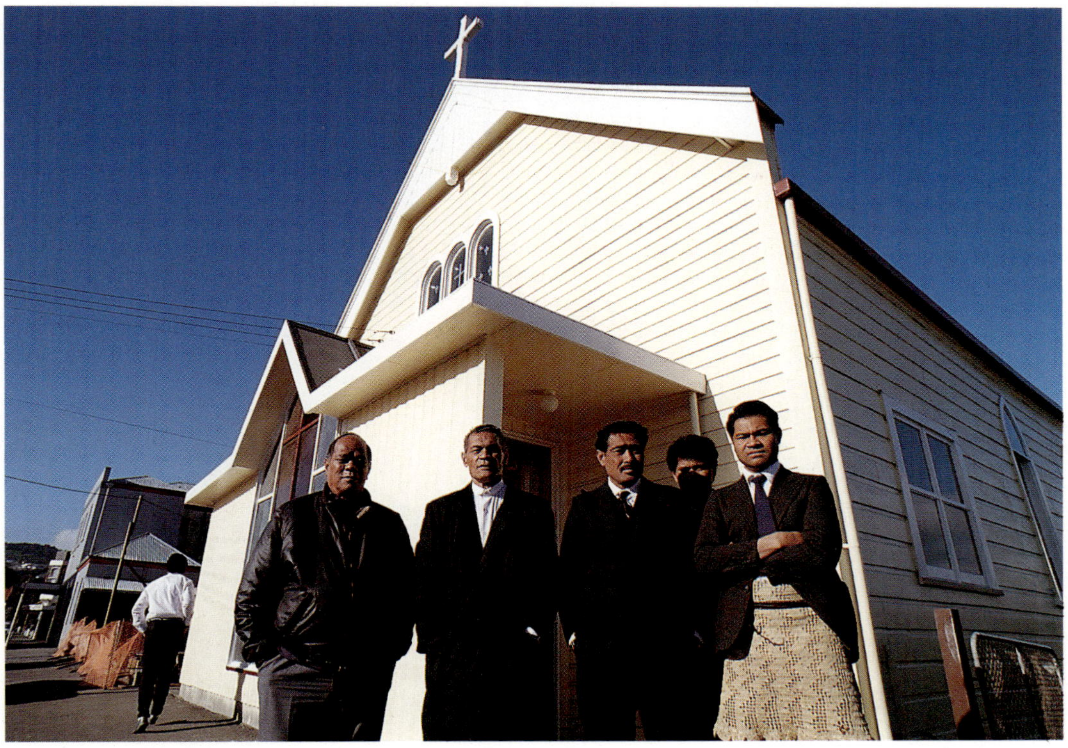

Worshippers outside the Wesley Chapel, Petone, Wellington TIM STEELE

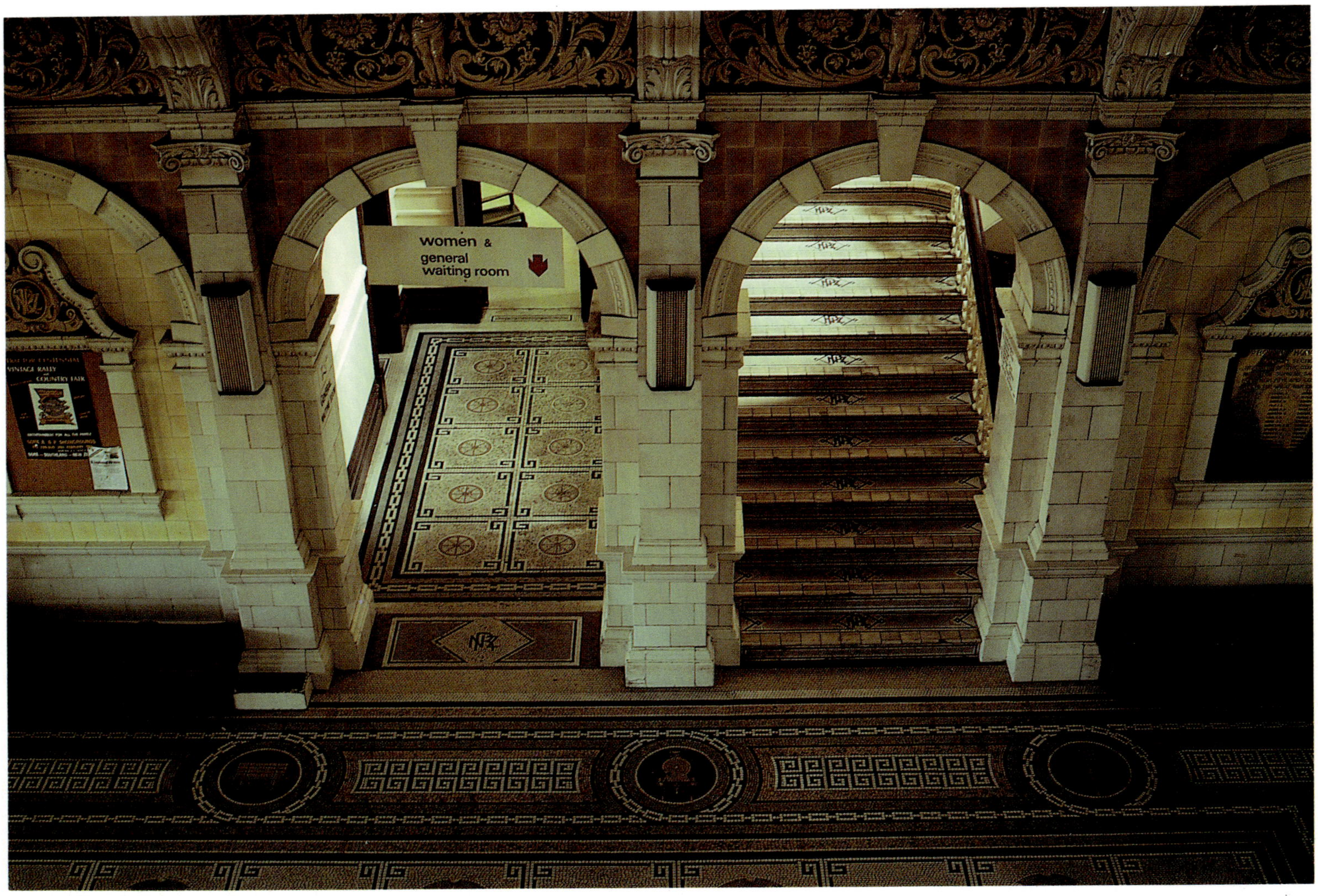

Dunedin Railway Station, designed by George A. Troup and completed in 1907 GEOFF MASON

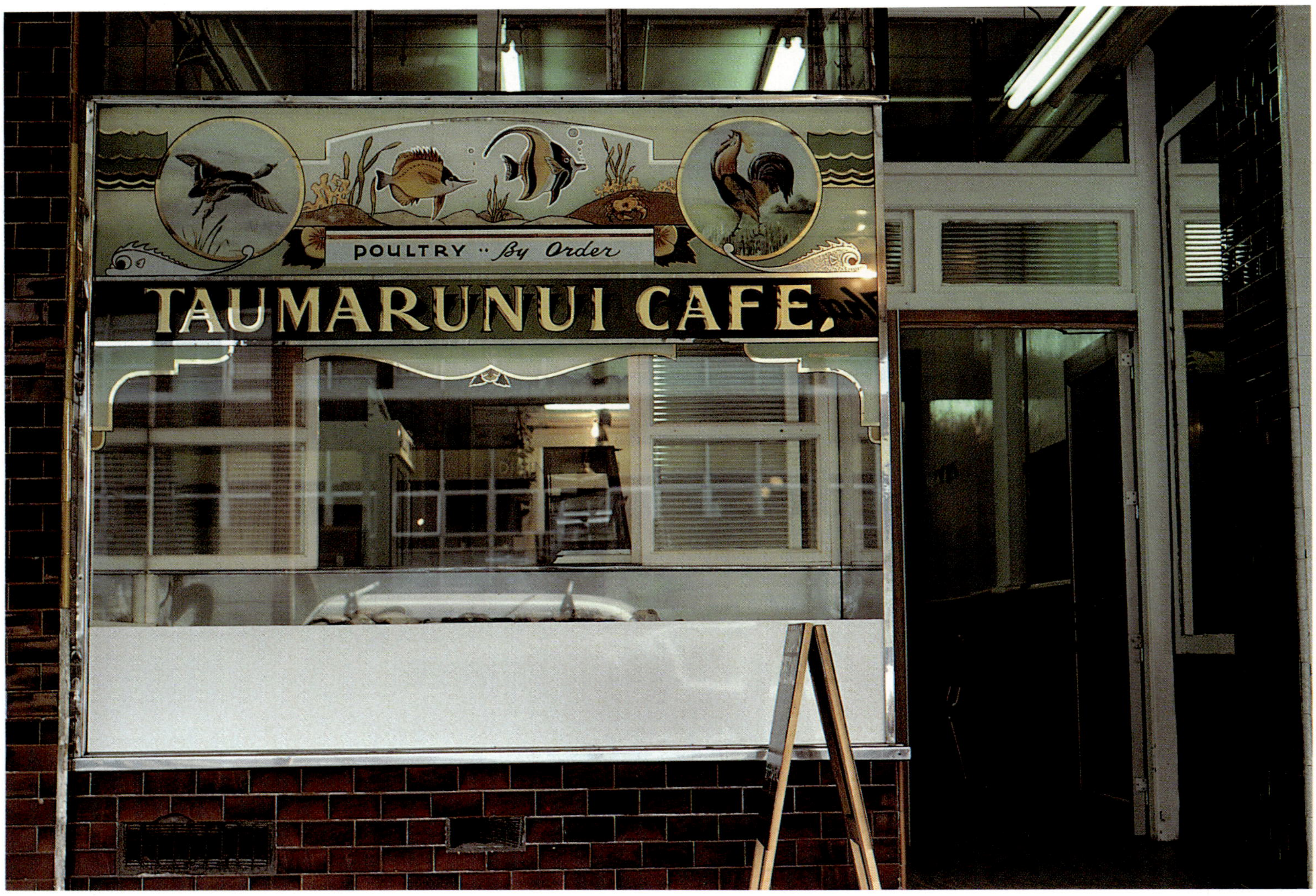

Taumaranui Cafe CRAIG POTTON

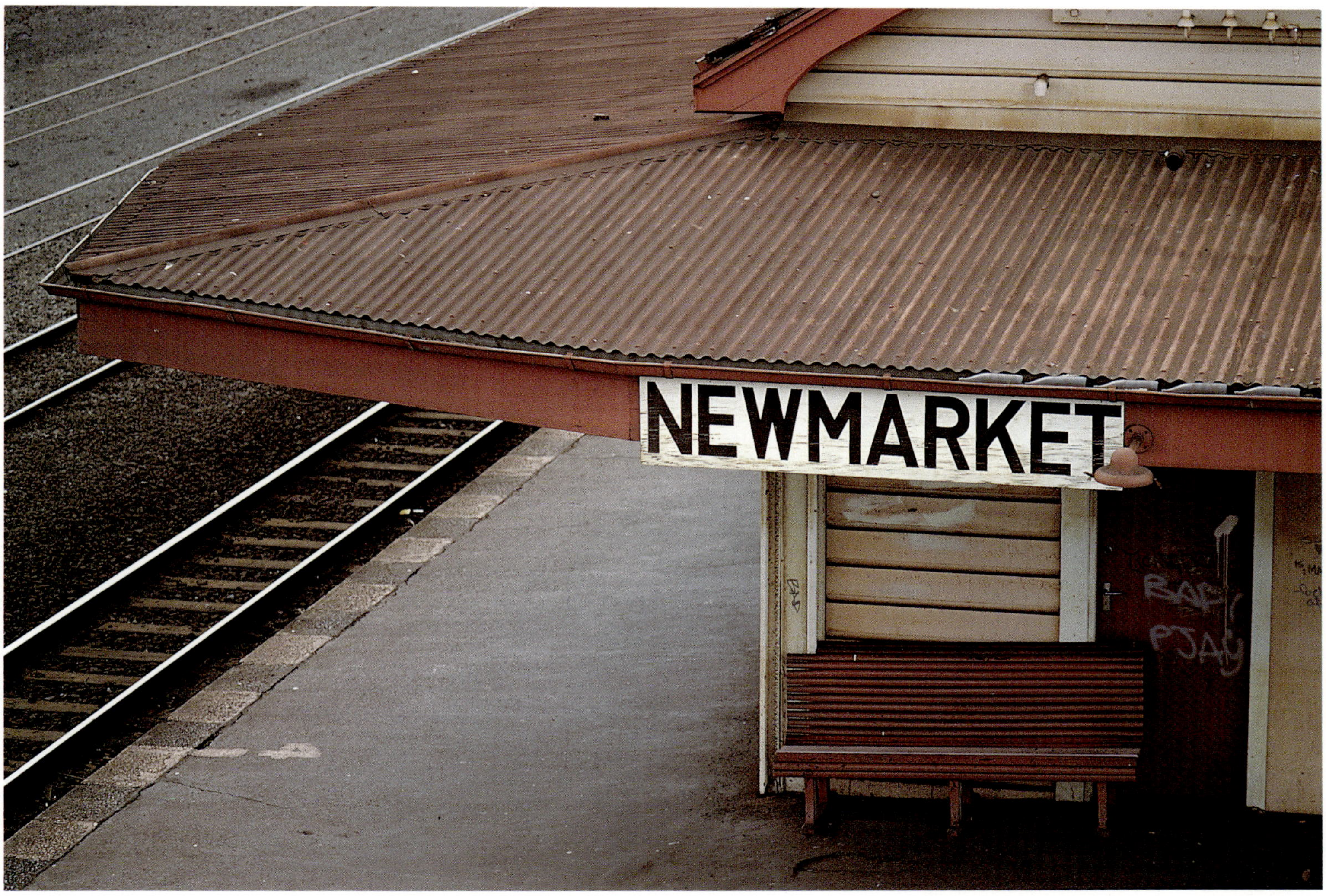

Newmarket Railway Station, Auckland — TIM STEELE

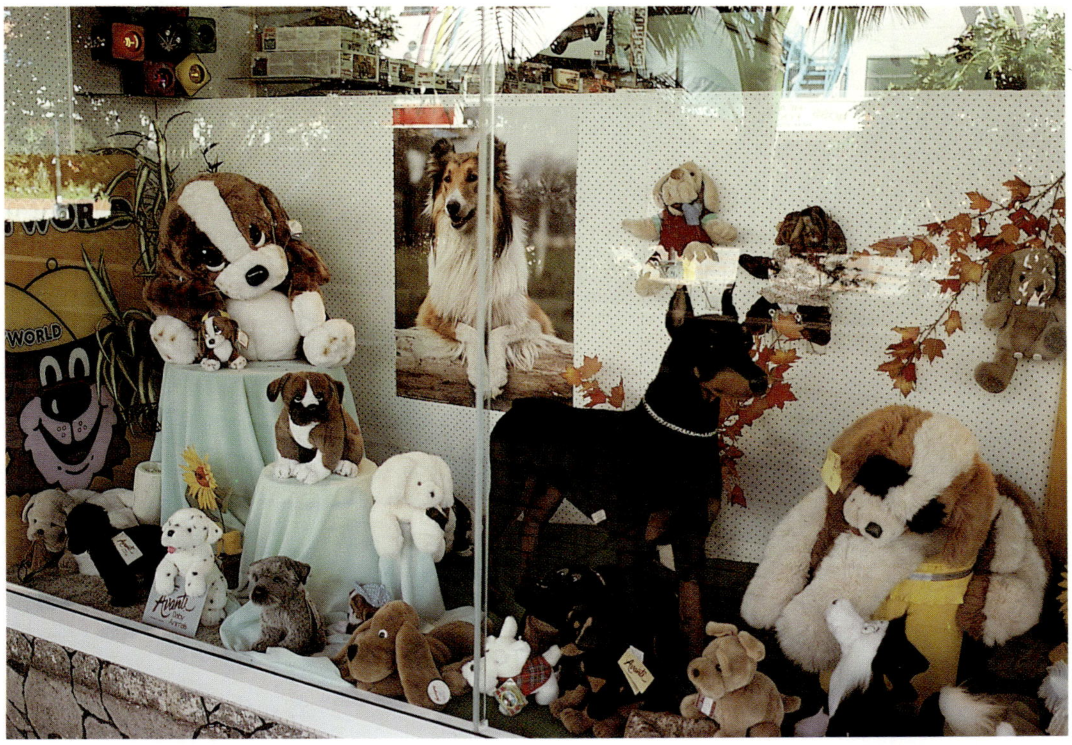

Shop window, New Plymouth — CRAIG POTTON

A NATIONAL PASSION

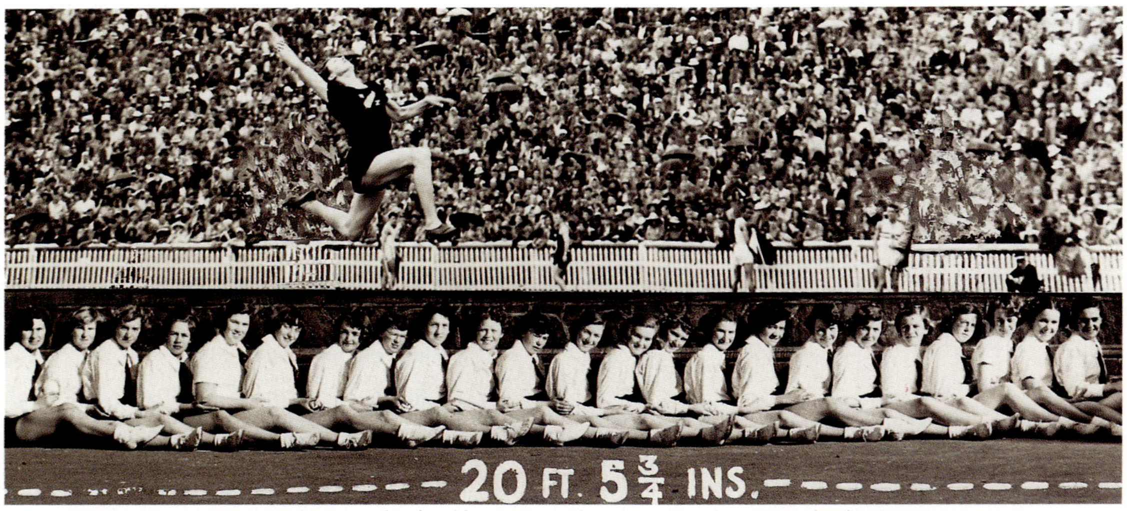

N.Z. HERALD

Twenty-three pupils of Seddon Memorial Technical College show the distance spanned by Yvette Williams when she won the Olympic long jump title and the Olympic record at Helsinki in 1952. She was one centimetre short of the world record.

Ron Palenski

IT WAS MID-AFTERNOON in Melbourne and late afternoon in New Zealand on 2 November 1983. It was the top hats and ultra fashion of Flemington racecourse, the public bar of a Lyttelton hotel, the poolside of a Remuera cup party, and the sweeps in thousands of offices. When the chestnut gelding with the appropriately patriotic name of Kiwi raced home for the most classic of last to first sporting finishes, the roar from watchers of the Melbourne Cup, wherever they were, was the same.

It was only a horse-race win, but there are few occasions when a nation is more at one than at the time of sporting success. There are other times when a nation thinks and concentrates as one. Sometimes the moments are of great significance to the country: Michael Joseph Savage proclaiming on 3 September 1939 that where Britain goes, we go, had the apprehensive ear of the nation; so did Robert Muldoon in 1984 when he, out of the blue and other colours, called an early election. The same attention was apparent when acting-Prime Minister, Keith Holyoake, announced on state radio in 1953 that "the New Zealander, Hillary, has reached the top of Mt Everest"; and when Richard Seddon on 17 December 1905, read on the steps of Parliament the text of a telegram he'd received from Cardiff: "Wales beat New Zealand by three points to nothing, one try. It was a very hard, fine game. No score was made in the second half."

Olympic events, big rugby matches, other major international sporting events in which New Zealanders compete successfully or just compete, provide the vehicle for a nation to focus its concentration, if only fleetingly.

IT WAS NOT ALWAYS SO AND INDEED, one of the earliest sporting achievements of some magnitude went unrecognised and almost unnoticed. It's but a footnote in history that in 1831 a Maori youth, one Whakarua-tapu, became the first person to swim Cook Strait. He'd been one of many captured in a raid on Kaiapoi by Te Rauparaha and was being taken back to Kapiti Island. As the canoes carrying the prisoners neared Kapiti, Whakarua-tapu dived overboard and started to swim for the North Island shore. Fearing recapture by Te Rauparaha's party, however, he changed course and headed for the South Island, apparently making a landfall in Queen Charlotte Sound.

When the first European, Barrie Devenport, swam Cook Strait in 1963, it was sport. For unfeted Whakarua-tapu, it was survival. Unlike Devenport, Whakarua-tapu had no television crews, newspaper photographers or reporters waiting to record the end of his historic swim. Sporting achievements in New Zealand only began to be documented with the arrival of the Europeans from the 1840s, and even then only sparingly. It was not until the 1880s that newspapers began to devote columns to leisure. But the absence of documentation didn't mean the absence of sport.

Elsdon Best, one of the finest early chroniclers of life in New Zealand, wrote of Maori sports like wrestling, boxing, running and swimming. Maori games would have been as competitive as anything we know today, even more so, according to one story Best was told. He related how young women took part in wrestling and that, usually, it was a case of two women versus one man. But one female wrestler, Kurawha, was enough for any man to handle. "She might be termed a good all-round man, for she shouldered a musket in the Mohaka raid, and she and Whaitiri (another Amazon) were two of the leading spirits in the vigorous rearguard action when Te Kooti retreated from Rotorua, pursued by Te Arawa under Tawa the Tireless," Best wrote.

He also recorded boxing matches in which sparring and parrying were dispensed with and it was straight-out trading of punch for punch; and of running races, usually endurance ones. He told of one in which the participants ran to a point about 40 km distant, scratched a mark on a tree to prove their arrival, then ran back to the start.

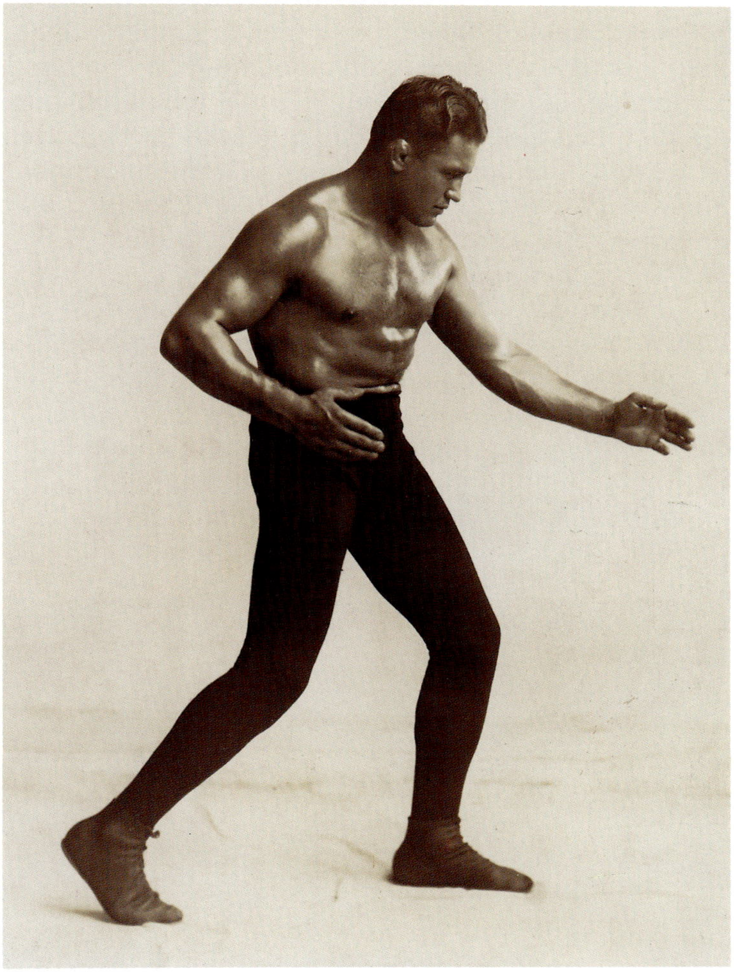

SCHMIDT STUDIOS/RON PALENSKI COLLECTION

Boxing was one Maori sport which had a European parallel. Tom Heeney's illustrious career spanned thirteen years from 1920 to 1933, much of it overseas. When he challenged the heavyweight championship of the world, he stepped into the ring wearing a Maori korowai cloak.

It was with the beginning of the British influx in the 1840s that sport began to take a codified form. Wherever the British went in their desire to see as much of their maps painted pink as possible, sport or games were an essential part of their baggage. The diaspora of the British coincided with the time in Britain when sport gradually came to be available to the masses rather than being a pleasant pursuit for an elitist few. The industrial revolution and then later the cutting back of working hours gave more leisure time to "ordinary" people and it was they who provided the impetus for the rapid acceleration in the development of sport in the mid-nineteenth century.

THE PIONEERS IN NEW ZEALAND left at home the class distinctions that had been so much a part of sport in Britain. It was sports that were beyond the reach of the majority of people in Britain, like yachting and horseracing, which were first staged on anything like a regular basis in New Zealand. They were organised by those with the interests and money to do so, but participation was not exclusive: Te Rauparaha entered his own horses in the early race meetings at Petone and Maori were encouraged to take part in early yachting regattas, as were the skippers of schooners and sloops that normally plied what ports then existed.

Cricket too was an early entrant in the New Zealand sporting stakes and for the first twenty years of European New Zealand, it was the main sporting activity. Charles Darwin, during his epic voyage in the *Beagle*, saw Europeans playing cricket on a beach in the Bay of Islands in 1835.

Cricket also provided one of the earliest examples of international competition in New Zealand when a go-ahead Dunedin promoter, Shadrach Jones, acquired the services of an English professional team touring Australia in 1863–64. In a festive atmosphere that saw Dunedin decorated as if for a royal visit, George Parr's All-England Eleven beat Otago and Canterbury, each of which fielded twenty-two players, but drew with a combined Otago-Canterbury side. One of the English players was Teddy Grace, amateur "crack" of the team and an older brother of cricket's nonpareil, W. G. Grace; a prominent member of the Otago team was a cousin of the Graces and W. G.'s godfather, William Gilbert Rees, founder of Queenstown.

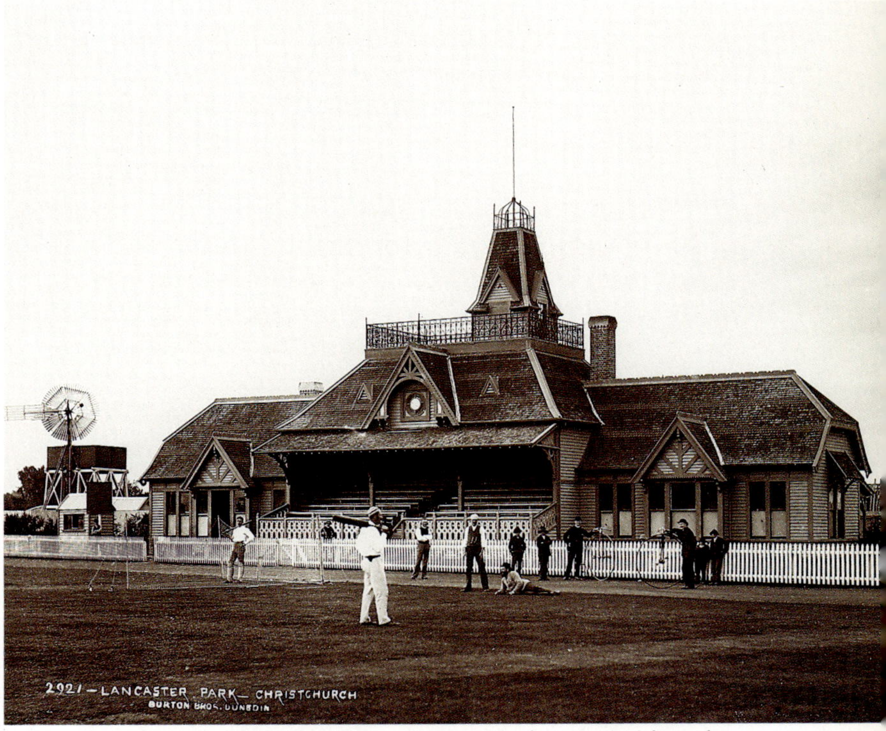

BURTON BROS/NATIONAL MUSEUM

Cricket is the oldest organised sport in New Zealand. The first provincial match took place between Auckland and Wellington in 1860. These turn-of-the-century players were photographed at Christchurch's Lancaster Park.

Rees was more than a pioneering pastoralist and an influence in cricket. His daughter, Isabel, was twice national women's singles tennis champion in the early 1890s but died at the age of twenty-eight from pneumonia. Her time at the top in New Zealand women's tennis came shortly before the thirteen-year singles reign of Kathleen Nunneley, the finest woman tennis player the country has seen. She was without peer through the 1890s and into the twentieth century and with Anthony Wilding showing his accomplishments in the male game (the pair combined twice for the national mixed doubles, winning both times), New Zealand tennis had a rare golden period.

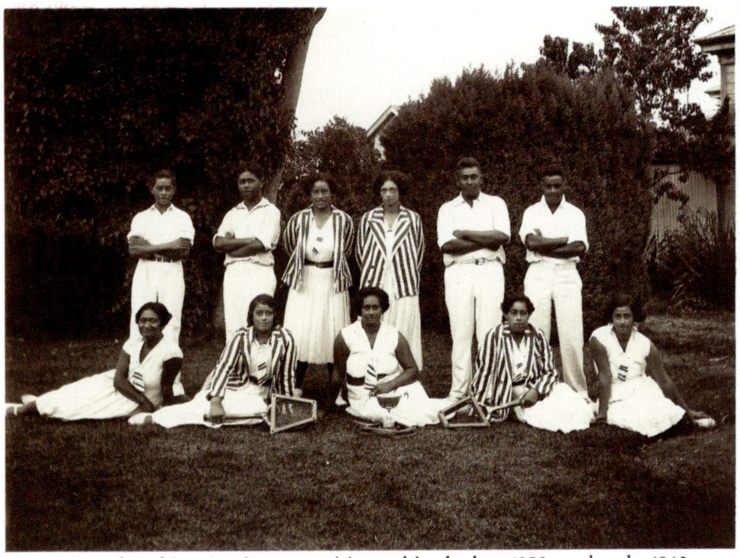

ALEXANDER TURNBULL LIBRARY

Tennis was played in Maori communities and in the late 1950s and early 1960s, the diminutive Ruia Morrison dominated New Zealand women's tennis. In 1957 she reached the quarter finals at Wimbledon. This unidentified winning Maori team comes from Hawke's Bay.

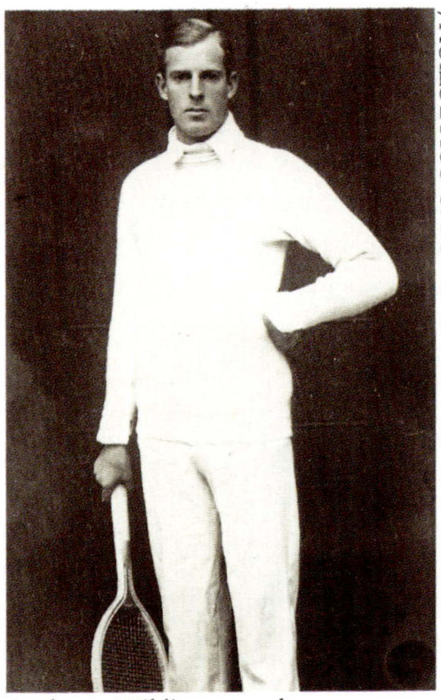

F. WILDING COLLECTION/ ALEXANDER TURNBULL LIBRARY

Anthony Wilding won the Wimbledon men's singles from 1910 to 1913. He was killed at Ypres in 1915.

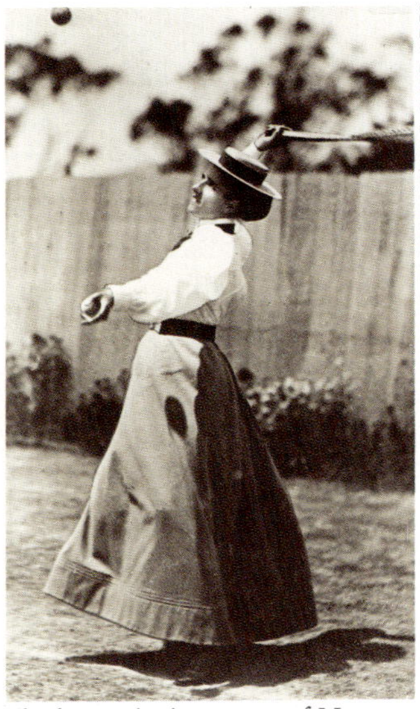

ALEXANDER TURNBULL LIBRARY

The long-reigning queen of New Zealand women's tennis was Kathleen Nunneley of Canterbury.

Wilding was of an unusual New Zealand breed, a genuine amateur of independent means in an age when New Zealand sport was proud of its egalitarianism. His father Frederick, a wealthy Christchurch lawyer, dispatched the younger Wilding to Cambridge to study law. Wilding did, but seemed to show more interest in courts than in torts. He resurrected the ailing Cambridge Tennis Club then spent most of his years travelling the then-exclusive European tennis circuit like a bon vivant. Wilding was not simply a gifted amateur. In between winning European tournaments and the Wimbledon singles title on four occasions, he was New Zealand's main contributor to combined Davis Cup success with Australia, and won a bronze medal at the 1912 Stockholm Olympic Games.

THE LATE NINETEENTH CENTURY was the era of the individual sportsman, with the emphasis on team games still to come. New Zealand had an early world champion. A young walker from Dunedin, Joe Scott, at the age of twelve in 1875 won what was grandly called a New Zealand two-mile championship. He later went to Britain where, through the 1880s, he held every distance walking record then in existence.

Scott was the first of several New Zealand athletes who, on times and performances (because they had few opportunities to compete competitively) could justifiably be ranked among the world's best. Billy McPherson and Jack Hempton were both sprinters of the now-comical upright-back stance who, from standing starts, recorded times over 100 yards that were then equal to the best in the world. So too were hurdlers Herbert Batger and Godfrey Shaw, although the latter returned to his native England at his peak and was Britain's best hurdler through the 1890s. Hempton, Batger and one of the remarkable men of early New Zealand sport, Leonard Cuff, were members of a New Zealand track and field team that toured Britain in 1892, an expedition funded by a public appeal and aimed almost wholly at trying to find out just how good they were.

Cuff was a long jumper and manager of the team, but he'd also played cricket for Canterbury and for New Zealand and made the first steps to get New Zealand involved in the Olympic movement. It was while he was in England as long jumper-manager that Cuff, then twenty-six, met the young French aristocrat, Baron Pierre de Coubertin, who was trying to revive the ancient Olympic Games. Coubertin told Cuff of his plans to stage a congress in Paris at which he would propose to representatives from other countries that the Olympics be re-established. Cuff could not go to the 1894 congress but he wrote to Coubertin: "I am sorry that this association [the New Zealand Amateur Athletic Association] cannot be represented ... but you have our hearty sympathy and best wishes for a successful congress."

Afterwards, when the first modern games were planned for Athens in 1896, Cuff accepted Coubertin's invitation to become the first International Olympic Committee member for New Zealand. Despite Cuff's enthusiasm, New Zealand was not to send athletes to an Olympics until 1908 (and then to be lumped in as Australasia), and it was not until 1920 that a New Zealand team competed at an Olympics in its own right.

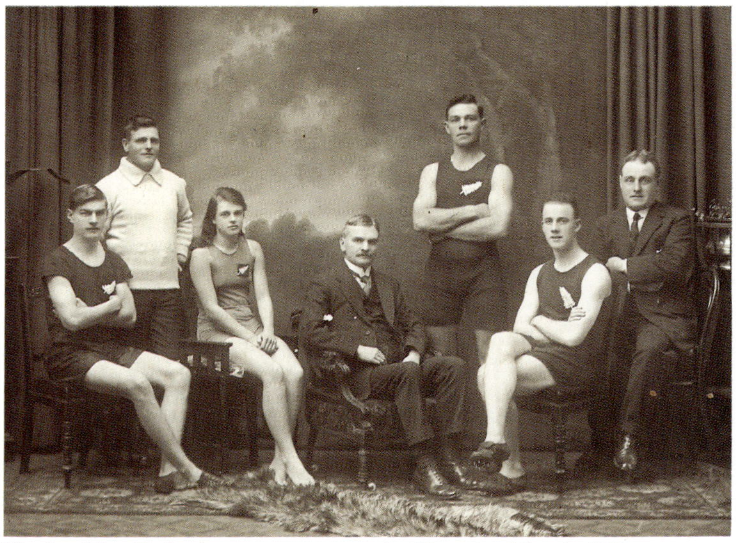

ZAC STUDIOS

The first New Zealand team to contest at the Olympics did so in 1920 at Antwerp. Darcy Hadfield (right back) was third in the single skulls; George Davidson (left front) was fifth in the final of the 200 metres sprint; H. E. Wilson (right front) was fourth in the final of the 110 metres hurdles, and 15-year-old Violet Walrond was fifth in the 100 metres freestyle swimming final.

Other individual athletes were making their mark during the same period. "Torpedo Billy" Murphy beat American Ike Weir in San Francisco in 1890 for the world featherweight boxing championship but lost the title later the same year in Sydney.

Bob Fitzsimmons, a blacksmith from Timaru, at various stages won the world middle-, light-heavyweight and heavyweight championships in a twenty-year career that ended in 1902. His most celebrated fight was that for the heavyweight title against James J. Corbett,

persisted with its invitation for the South Africans to tour and the National Government was steadfast in its declared policy of not interfering with the decisions of autonomous sports bodies. The tour carried on its sorry, sad way through New Zealand, the South Africans left and New Zealanders were left to count the cost. The result of the series was all but an irrelevance.

The four-yearly festivals of sport, the Olympic and Commonwealth Games, have not escaped the consequences of the politics either. The rugby issue kept about thirty nations away from the 1976 Olympics, east-west politics affected the Olympics of 1980 and 1984, and the question of trade sanctions against South Africa deprived the 1986 Commonwealth Games of some of the finest athletes.

NO SUCH WORLDLY, if peripheral, matters affected the performances of three of New Zealand's outstanding athletes, two men and a woman: Jack Lovelock in Berlin in 1936, Yvette Williams in Helsinki in 1952 and Peter Snell in Rome in 1960 and Tokyo in 1964.

To Lovelock, a supreme champion when he required himself to be, sport was a personal contest in which his opponents were as much the human psychology and physiology as they were the other people on the running track. He seemed to care not at all for the adulation that follows Olympic champions. After a series of successes in the 1930s, culminating in a decidedly emphatic win in the 1500 metres in Berlin, he said he would just quietly slip away. In a world that demanded fame, he chose anonymity.

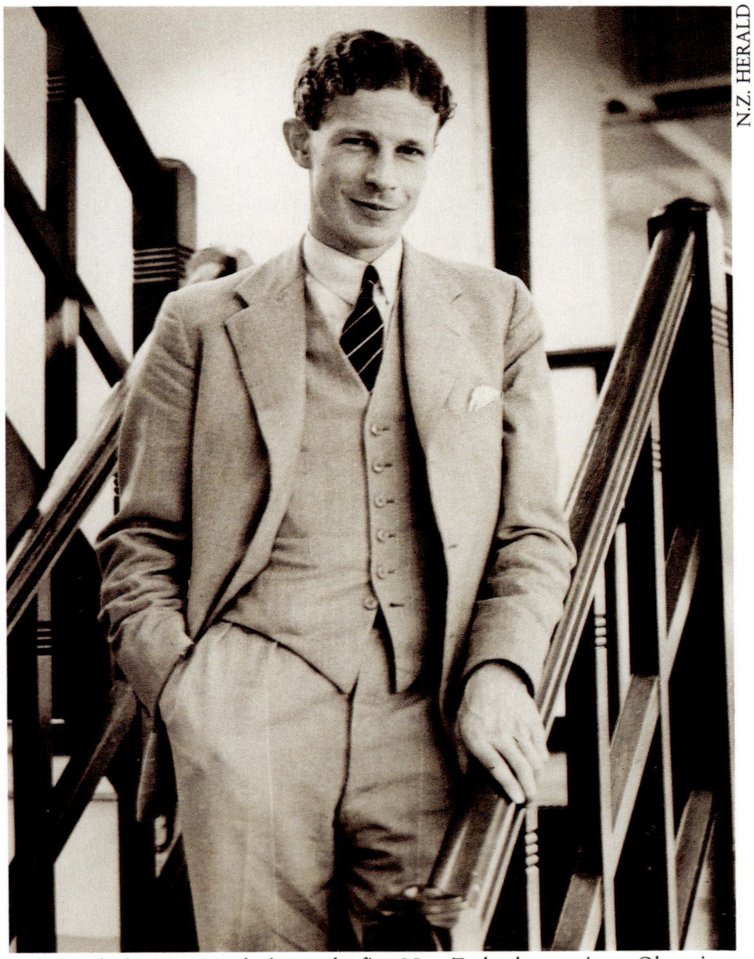

N.Z. HERALD

Jack Lovelock, 1936. Lovelock was the first New Zealander to win an Olympic gold medal on the track. He broke three world records: the three-quarter mile in 1932, the mile in 1933, and the 1500 metres in 1936.

There may have been much of that too in his successor as New Zealand's world champion miler, Peter Snell. He won the 800 metres at the Rome Olympics as an unknown, as much in his own country as in the world at large. He broke world records on grass tracks in New Zealand, he won the half mile-mile double at the 1962 Perth Empire Games. And in Tokyo in the 1964 Olympics, he overcame indifferent form and self doubts to win both the 800 and 1500 metres, both in entirely dominant fashion.

Snell did not remain long on the world's running tracks after Tokyo and neither did he remain long in New Zealand. The status of Olympic champion can be a burden in elements of society that are sport-besotted and perhaps Snell knew, as Lovelock did, that it is necessary to escape the adulation in order to get on with the business of living.

Yvette Williams was one of that rare breed of athlete. She was the club performer with ability well above the average who scaled the modern Olympian heights, won gold medals at Empire Games, and then returned to a normal, everyday sort of life in New Zealand.

New Zealanders had an almost blind faith in her when the New Zealand team left Wellington by flying boat on the first leg to Helsinki, not caring that the 1952 games were to mark the debut of the Soviet Union in the world's premier sporting event. Who knew what sporting Amazons lurked behind the iron curtain?

The faith was totally justified. With New Zealanders at home crouched around radios in the small hours of the morning and with sub-editors at Dunedin's *Otago Daily Times* poised for a special late edition, Williams on her fourth attempt hitch-kicked out to 6.24 metres for an Olympic record and the only Olympic gold medal won by a New Zealand woman.

Williams in 1954 broke the world long jump record and in Vancouver later the same year repeated her Olympic triumph and added the shot put and discus titles as well, confirming her as one of the Commonwealth's outstanding athletes.

It is only women of the calibre of Williams and, in later years, of Marise Chamberlain (also a world record breaker), Val Young (who repeated Williams' shot-discus double twice at later games) and the 1980s crop of world-class runners like Anne Audain, Lorraine Moller and Alison Roe, who gain widespread accolades. Women's sports in New Zealand tend to be participatory rather than spectator occasions. They tend not to get the large followings that the major male sports do. Thousands of netballers know, for example, how accomplished the New Zealand netball team is. But even when it's playing

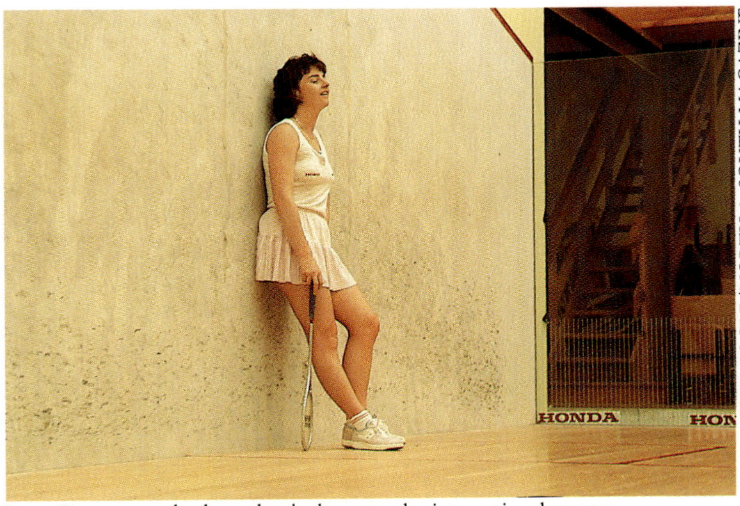

PHIL FOGLE/NORTH & SOUTH MAGAZINE

Susan Devoy, squash player, has had spectacular international success.

international matches at home, that team does not get support beyond a hard core of netball followers.

The 1980s provided another New Zealand woman absolutely dominant in her sport, Susan Devoy. While squash is one of the ultimate participation sports, Devoy's almost unbeaten progress through major tournaments, including world titles, earned her superstar status.

A CHARACTERISTIC OF SPORT in the 1970s and 1980s has been the vastly increased amounts of money involved, in sponsorships, in prize monies and in television fees. The development was tacitly encouraged when the International Olympic Committee revised its long-held amateur rules that had been instilled by the British early this century. Consequently sport became a big, commercial business, both for its practitioners and for its organisers.

An athlete like John Walker, another in the rare category of New Zealand world champion, wouldn't have stayed in the sport long after his world records and gold medal but for track and field's changing face. The advent of trust funds and commercial opportunities allowed him to continue doing what he did best, just as it's allowed people like Audain and Moller to run the American road circuit, once they'd deliberately broken the rules (in 1980) to point out the absurdities of under-the-table payments.

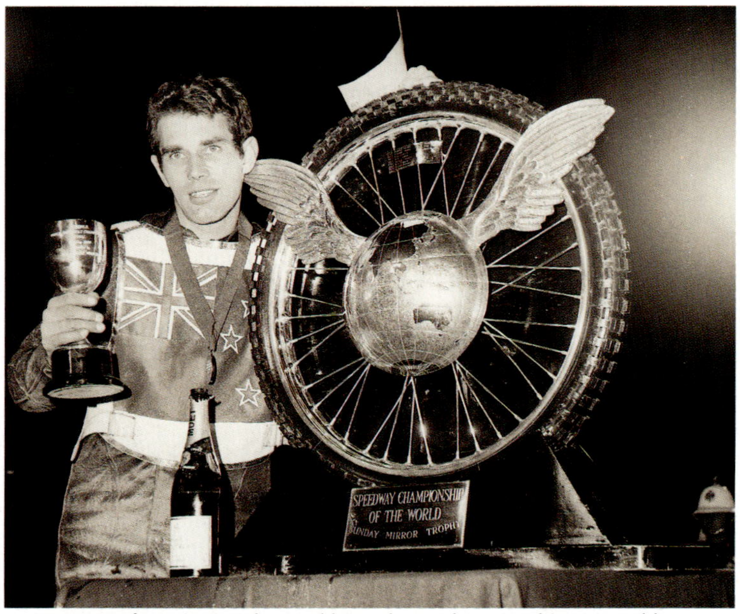

ASSOCIATED PRESS

Ivan Mauger after winning the World Speedway Championship at Wembley Stadium, London, September, 1969.

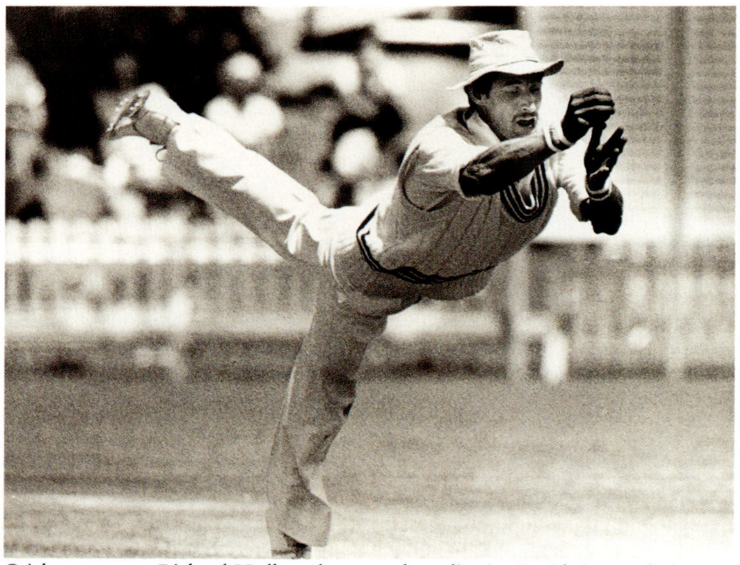

JOHN SELKIRK/DOMINION

Cricket supremo Richard Hadlee takes a catch to dismiss David Gower during the England v New Zealand test match at the Basin Reserve in January 1984.

Money made a vast difference in cricket too and for that the game has to thank mainly Kerry Packer, abused vehemently by establishment cricket when he set up his breakaway World Series Cricket troupe in 1977. When peace was declared two years later and the circus rejoined its parent, one of the prices the establishment paid was to accept many of Packer's innovations. Increased payments for players, a higher commercial profile for the game, more one-day matches, more television coverage – all of which led to a revolution in cricket and it was most marked in New Zealand.

The one-day series in Australia in 1980–81 that culminated in the Trevor Chappell underarm delivery to Brian McKechnie, Machiavellian act that it was, also contained some uninhibited cricket the like of which New Zealanders had never before seen live on their television screens. The coloured clothing, the bright lights, the all-action, was a far cry from the slow, gentle, polite game of the surburban ground and a whole new following was converted to the sport that was among the first to be played in New Zealand.

New Zealand had had cricket heroes before, men like Stewie Dempster, Martin Donnelly, Walter Hadlee, Bert Sutcliffe and John Reid, but they were history book figures to the new generation who could revel in the antics and successes of a Lance Cairns, a Glenn Turner, a Geoff Howarth, a Richard Hadlee or a Martin Crowe.

Money in sport also involved New Zealand in an entirely new venture. Yachting had always been strong in New Zealand since the earliest anniversary day regattas in Auckland and Wellington. Through the 1970s and 1980s, some of the world's leading designers were New Zealanders and the country had a high reputation for yachting expertise. When Australia prised the America's Cup from the hands of the New York Yacht Club in 1983, it led to yet another stage of sporting development in New Zealand.

For the Australian cup defence off Western Australia over the summer of 1986–87, yachting turned not to an orthodox administrator of the sport but to a merchant banker, Michael Fay. He had money and access to more, and he organised New Zealand's challenge. When that was deterred and the cup went back to the United States, Fay's involvement became even greater as he scoured the cup rules for a loophole for an immediate further challenge, which he found. Sport was being decided not by the sailors but by the bankers, the lawyers, the accountants and the judges.

But in those circumstances it's no longer sport. No yachtsman worth his salt would want his name on a cup that was won in a courtroom rather than on the water. Sport may need the bankers and the lawyers, but it needs too the same essential elements it's always had. However much money is involved, whatever political issues are attached to it, sport remains a basically simple contest, one that attracts competitors for the satisfaction and the joy of competing, either against themselves or against others. ☐

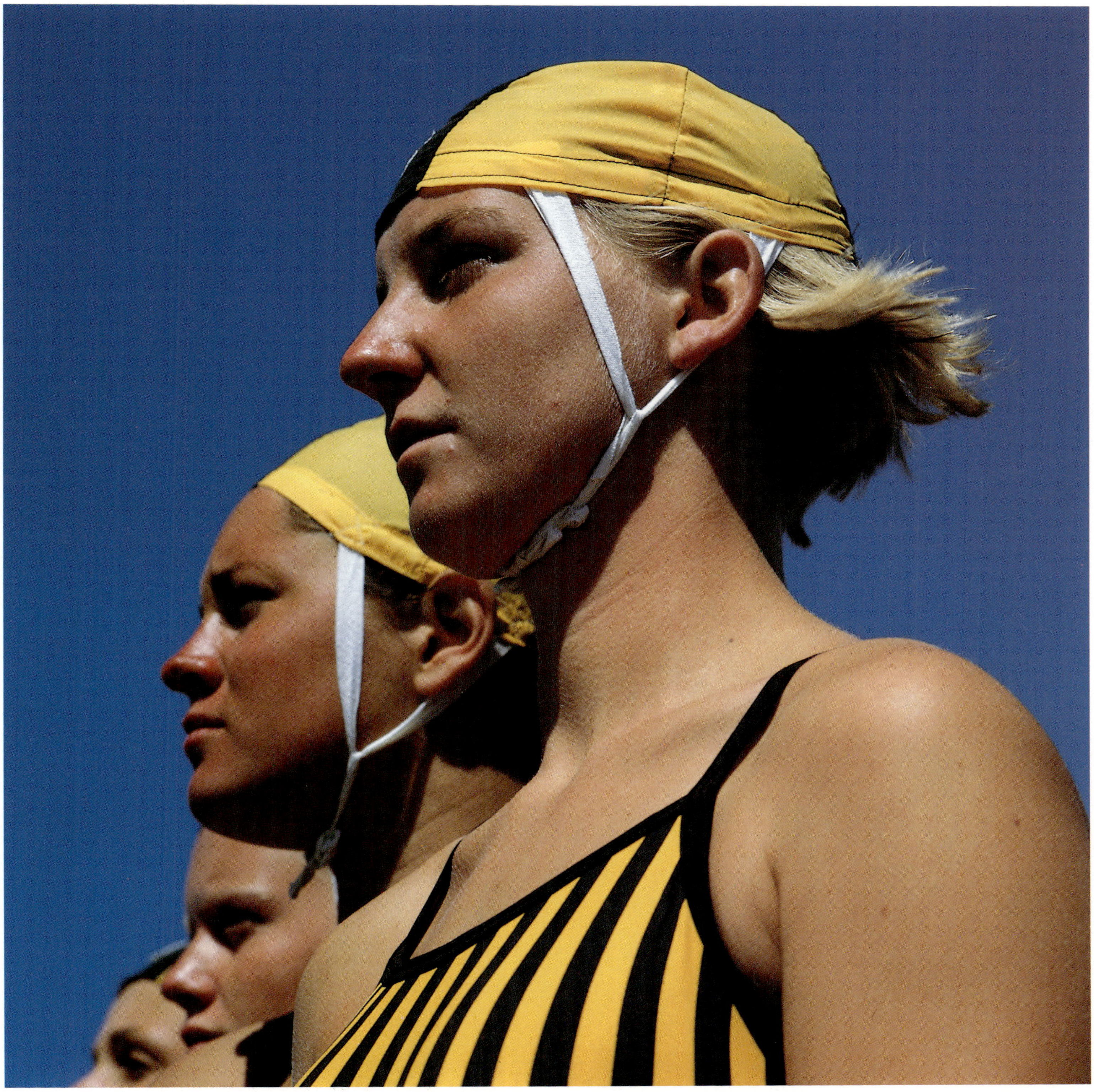

Women surf life savers at the national Surf Life Saving Championships, 1985 JANE USSHER

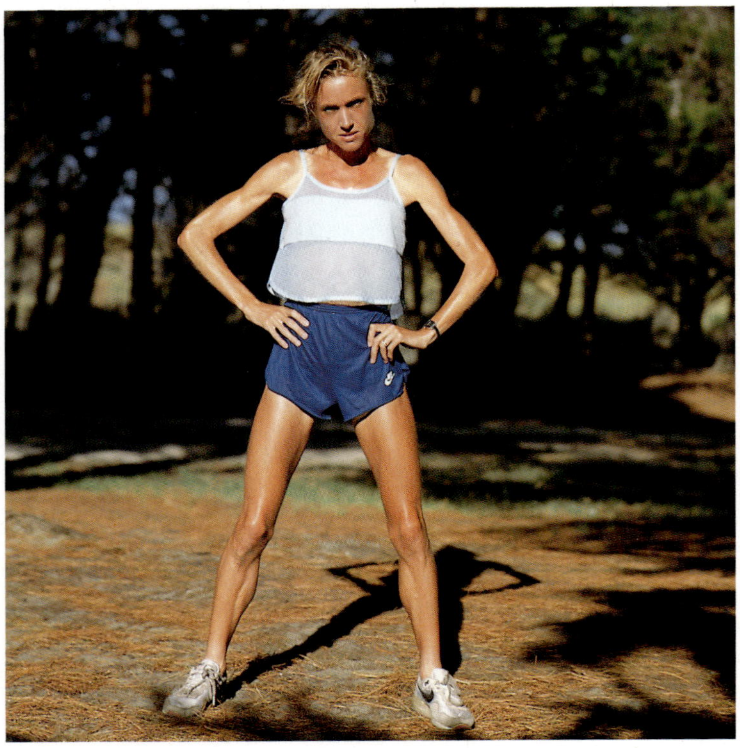

One of a new breed of outstanding runners, Anne Hannam — JANE USSHER

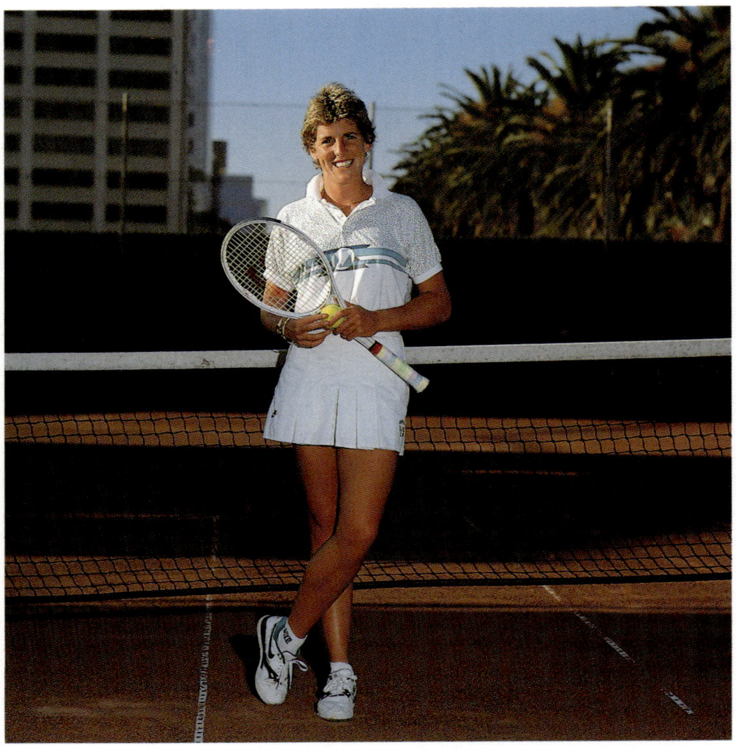

New Zealand's most prominent woman tennis player, Belinda Cordwell — JANE USSHER

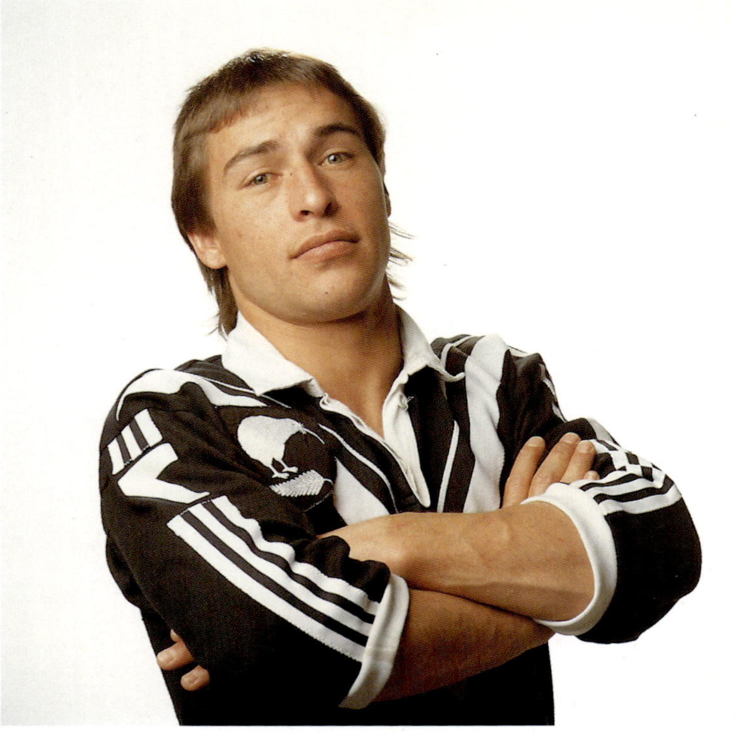

A standardbearer for rugby league in the 1980s, Clayton Friend — JANE USSHER

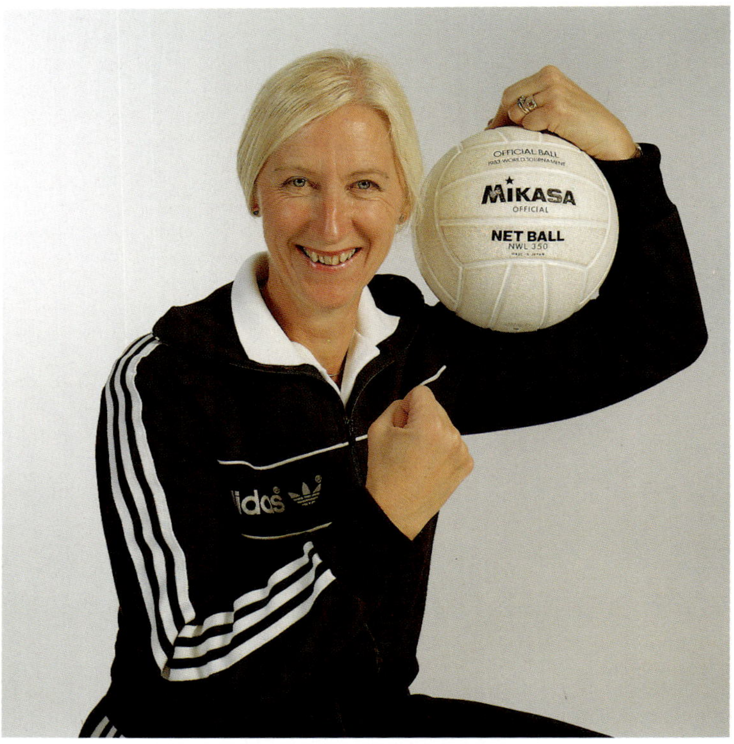

Lois Muir, who dominated netball for more than 20 years, first as a player and then as the country's most successful coach — JANE USSHER

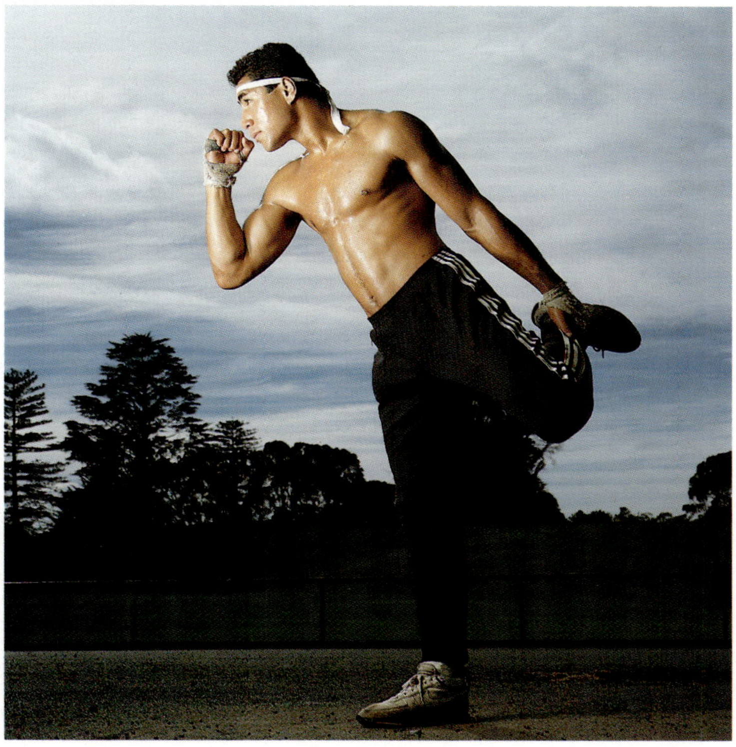

New Zealand's best known and most successful boxer of recent years, Jimmy Peau JANE USSHER

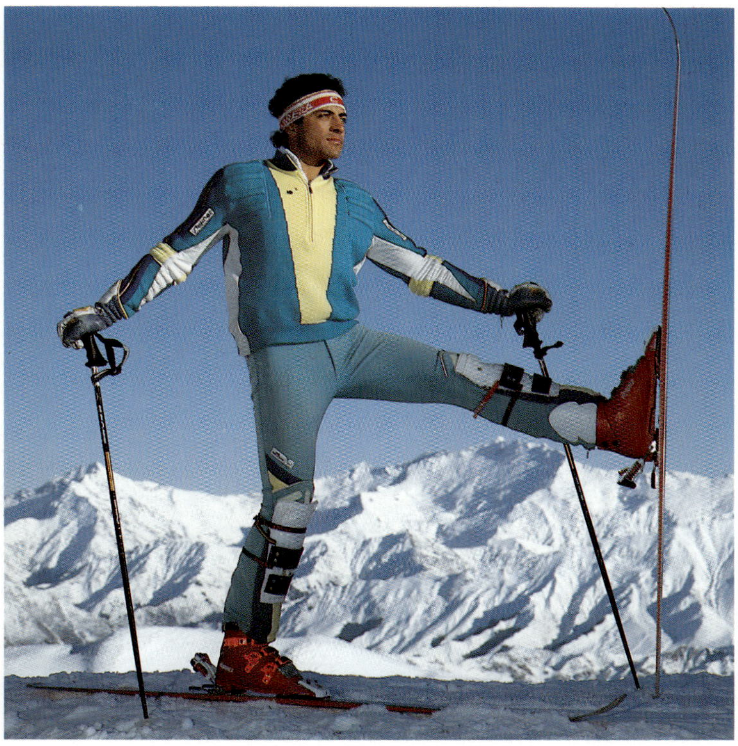

One of the few New Zealand skiers to rank with the best, Simon Wi Rutene JANE USSHER

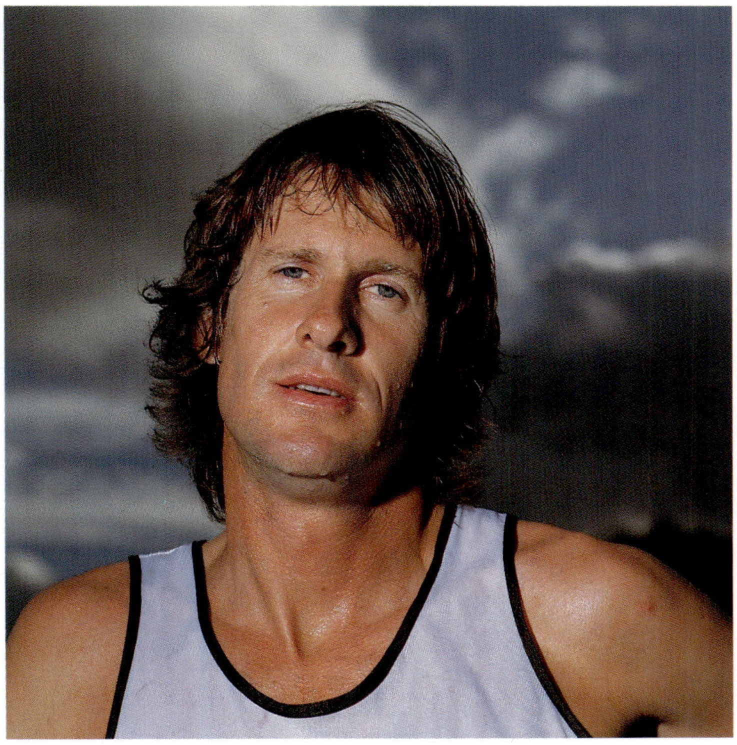

Track and field's most durable champion, John Walker JANE USSHER

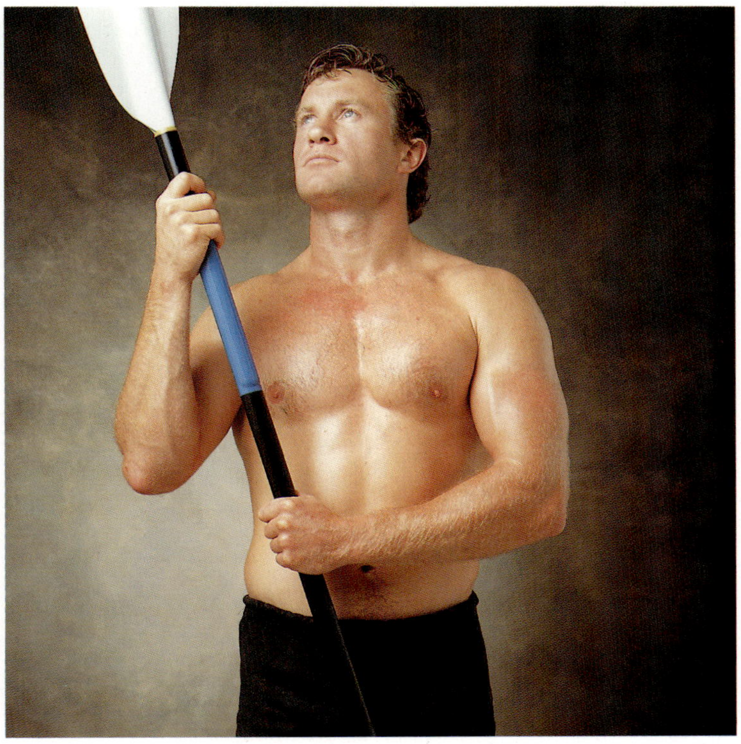

Canoeist Ian Ferguson, the winner of more Olympic gold medals than any other New Zealander JANE USSHER

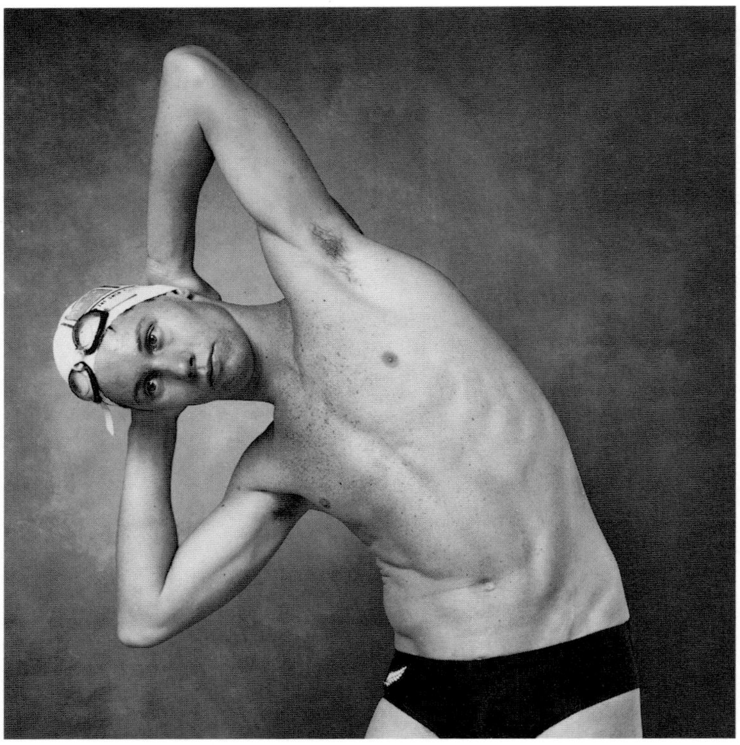

Olympic medalist swimmer Anthony Mosse JANE USSHER

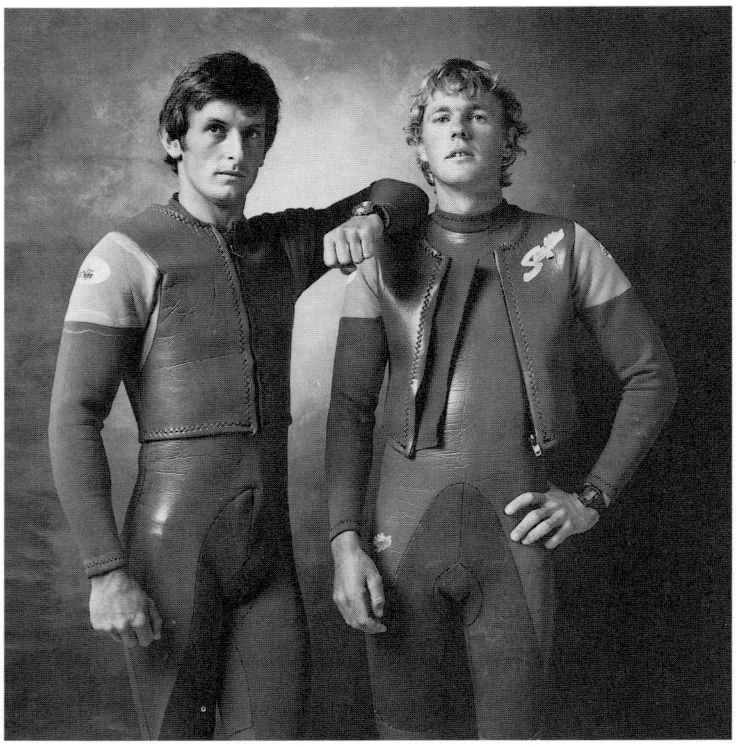

New Zealand's 470 class sailors at the Los Angeles Olympics, Peter Evans and Sean Reeves JANE USSHER

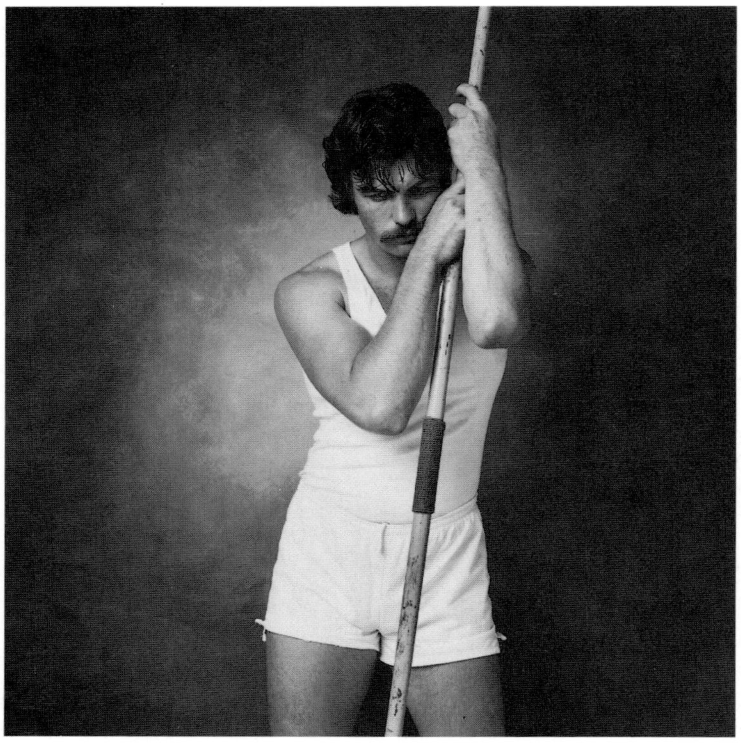

Commonwealth Games gold medalist javelin thrower Mike O'Rourke JANE USSHER

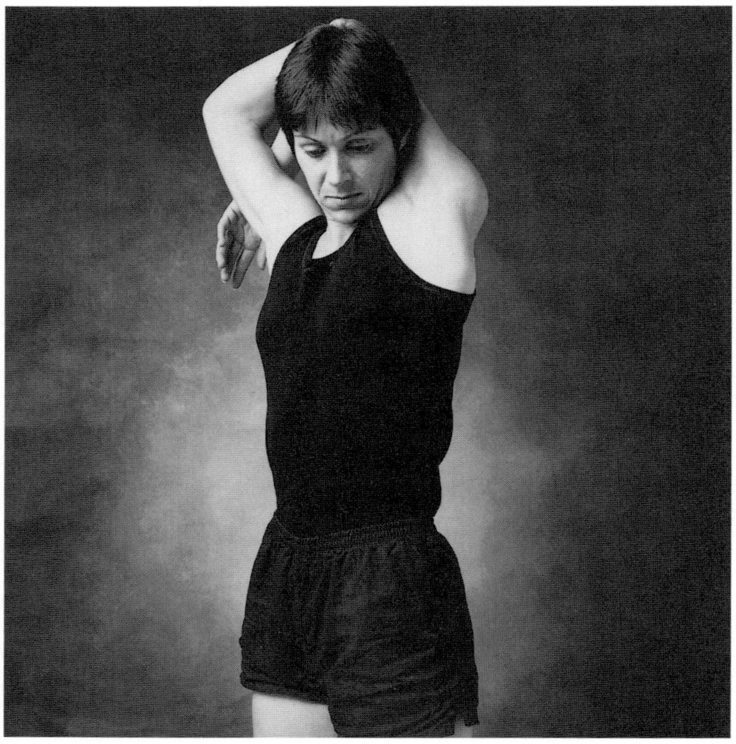

New Zealand's leading woman sculler in the 80s and Commonwealth Games gold medalist Stephanie Foster JANE USSHER

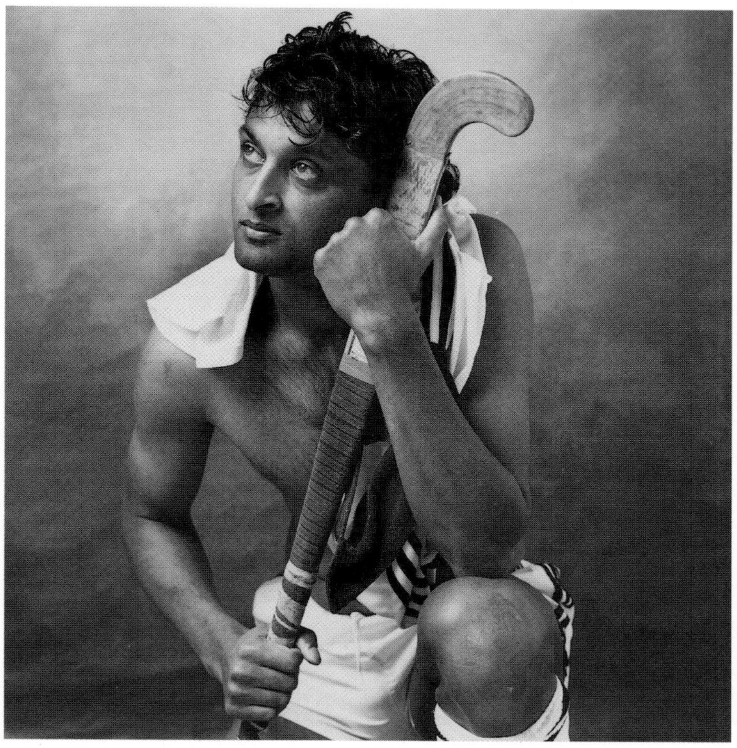

New Zealand hockey player Ramesh Patel JANE USSHER

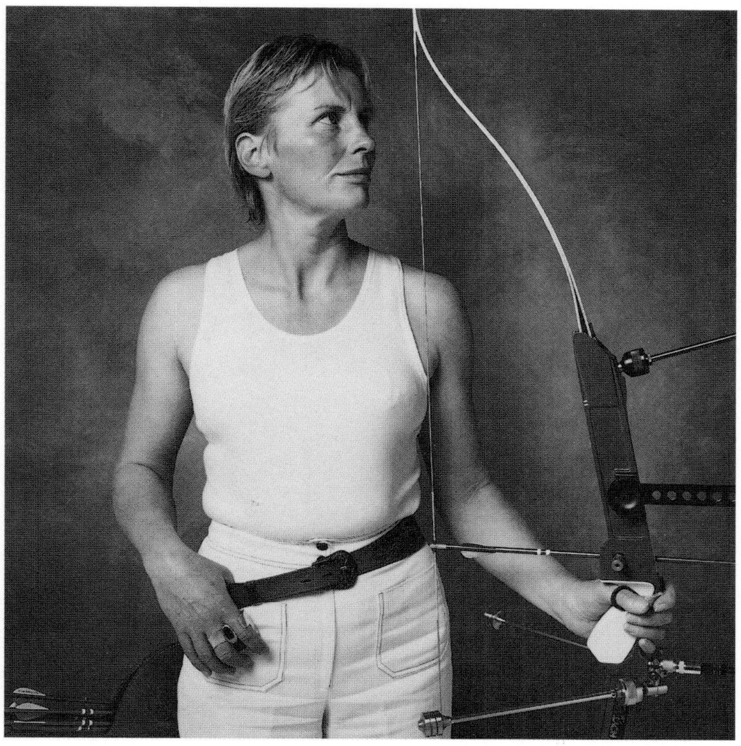

Olympic and Commonwealth Games archer Ann Shurrock JANE USSHER

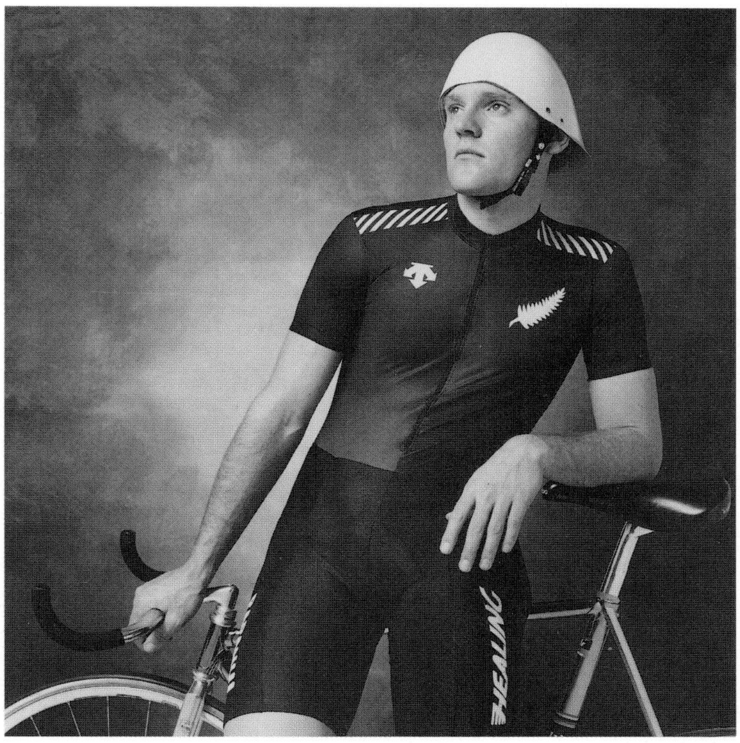

Craig Adair, the gold medalist in the cycling kilometre time trial at the Brisbane Commonwealth Games, 1982 JANE USSHER

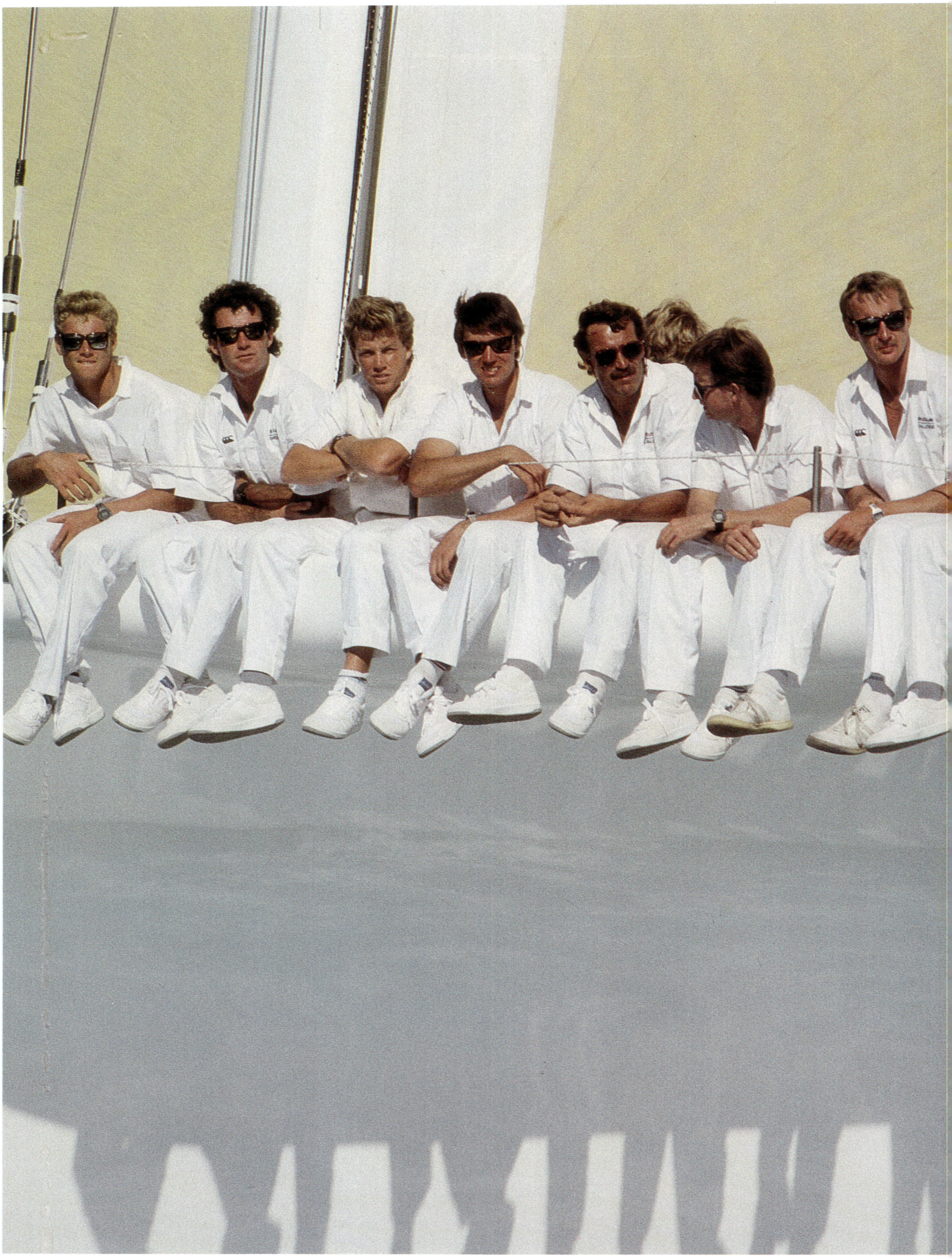

New Zealand, the challenger for the America's Cup, at Auckland STEPHEN ROBINSON

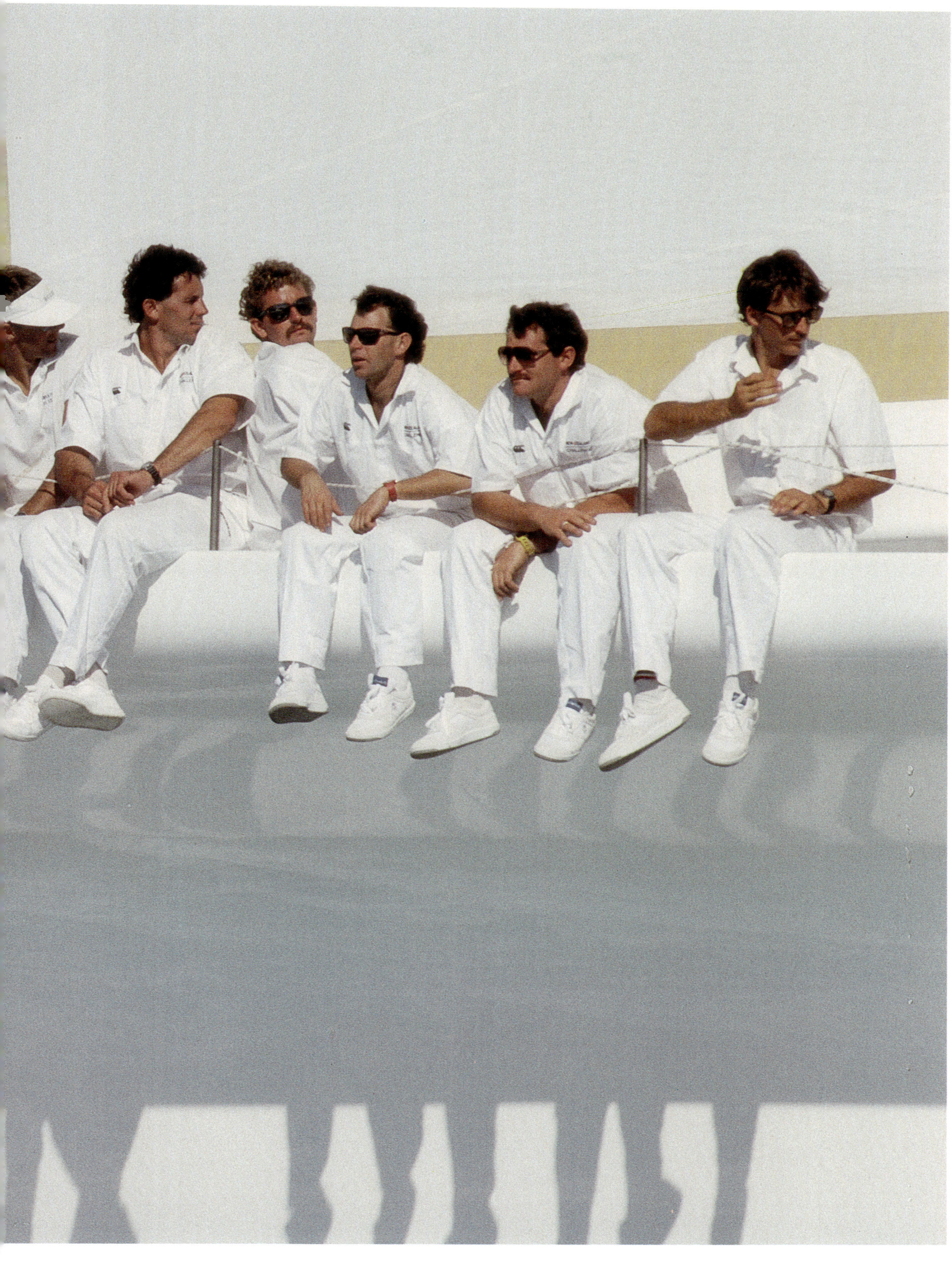

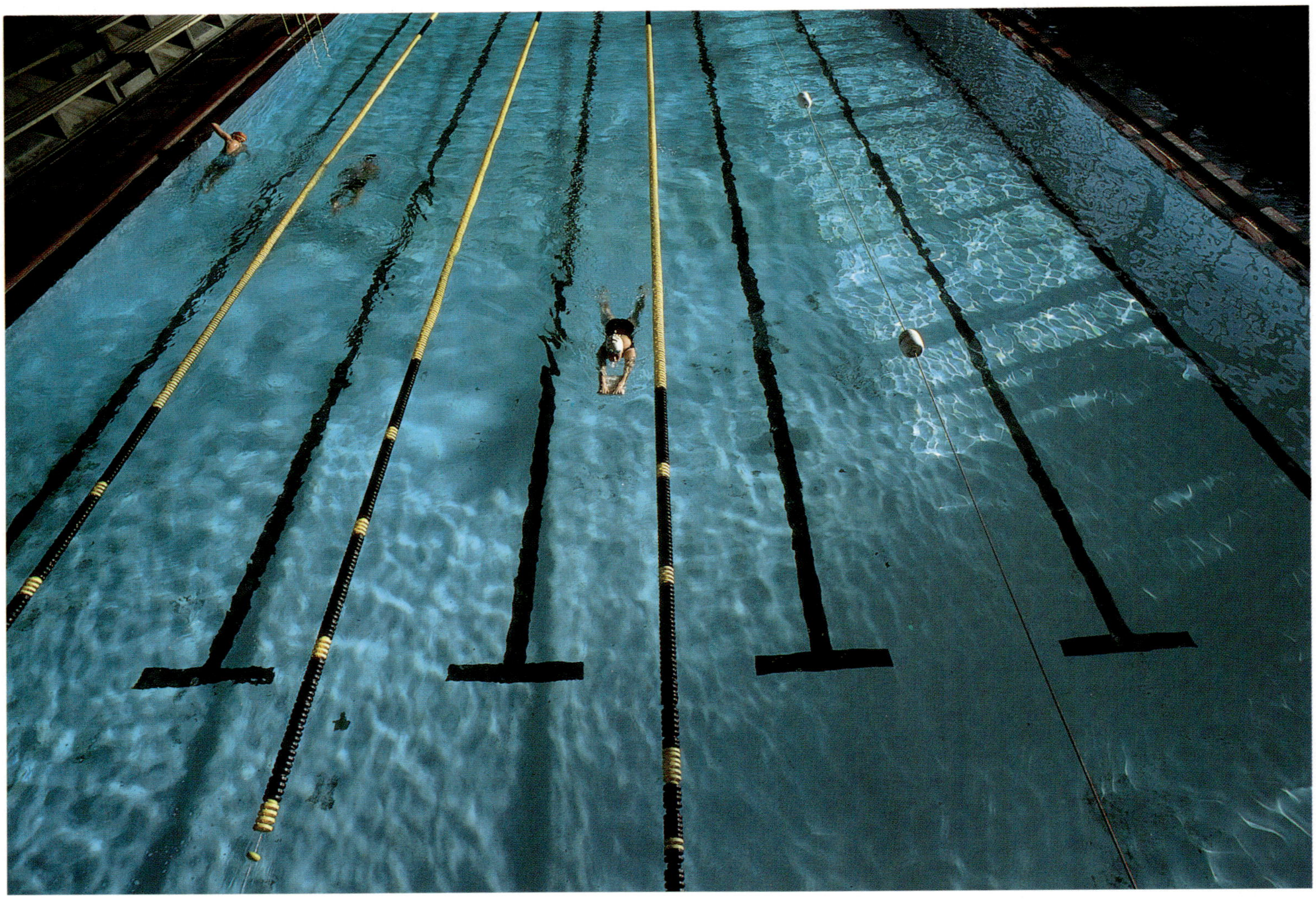

Freyberg Pool, Oriental Bay, Wellington — TIM STEELE

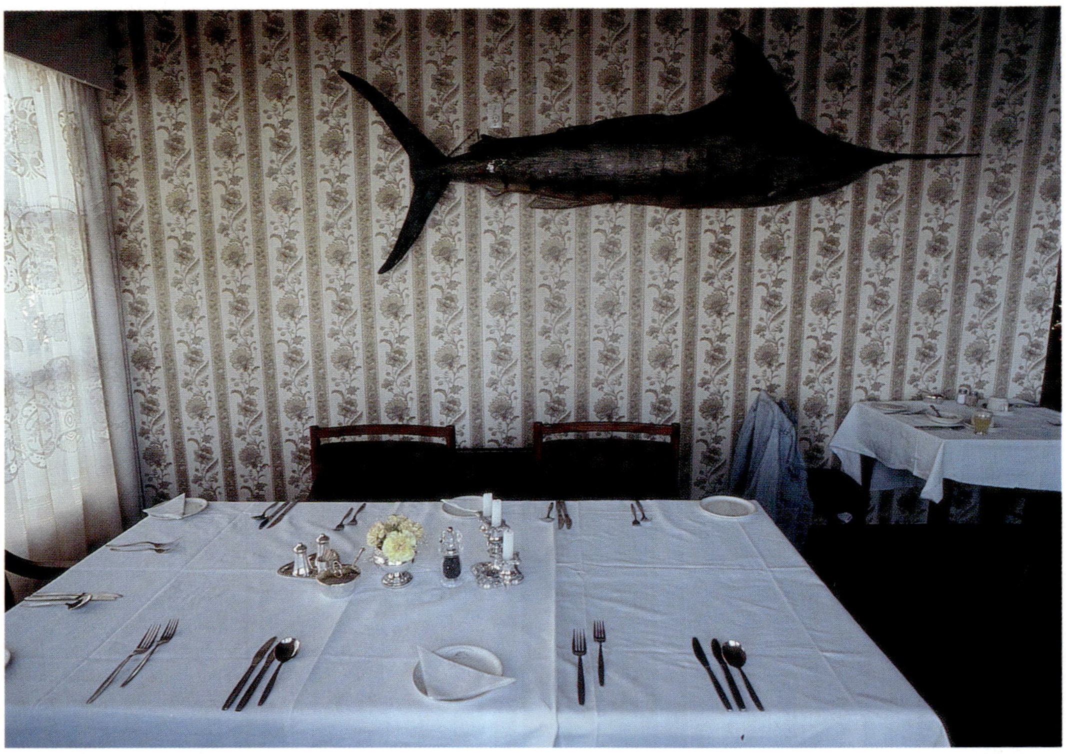

Marlin, Russell — STEPHEN ROBINSON

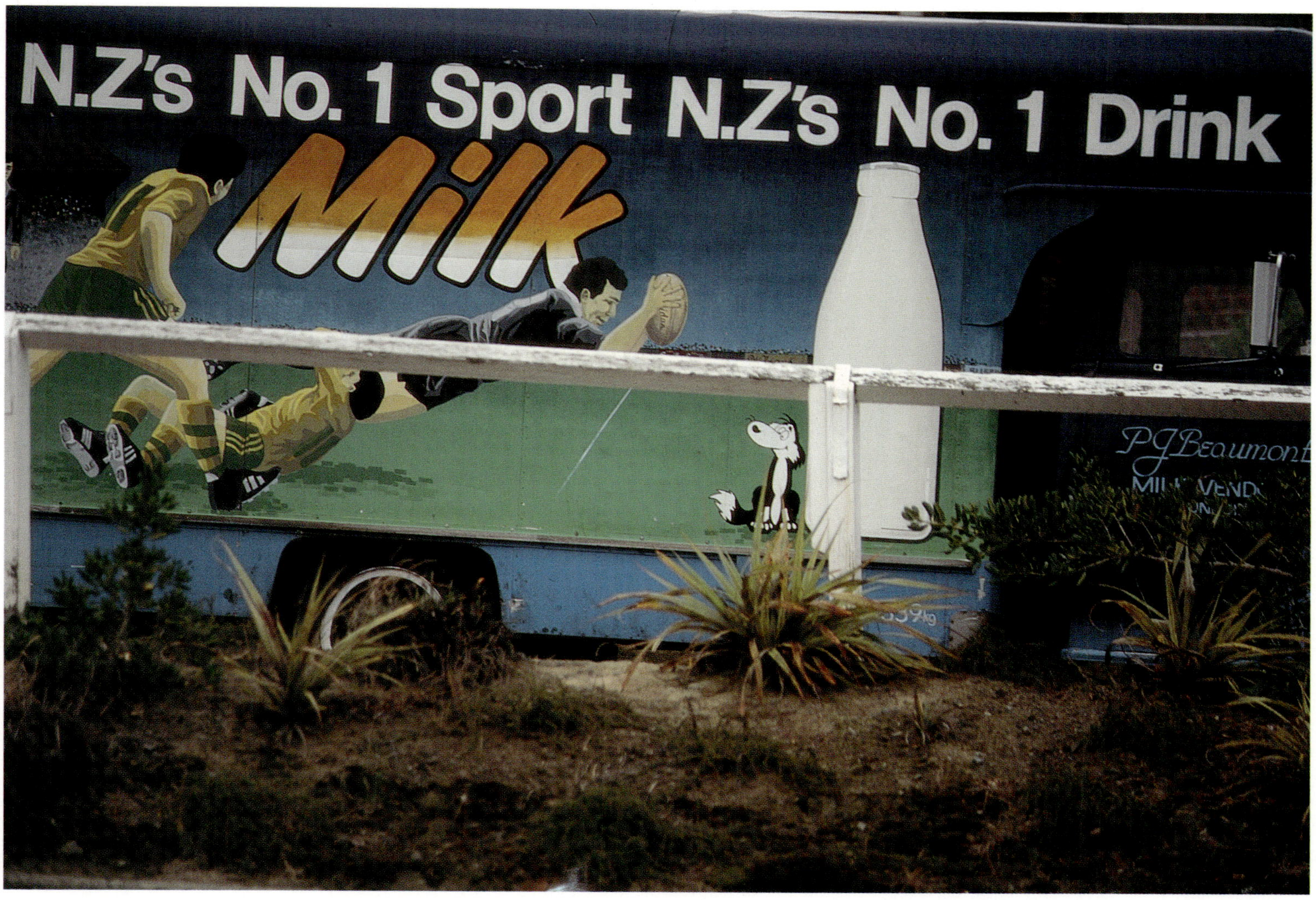

Milk vendor's truck, Dunedin GEOFF MASON

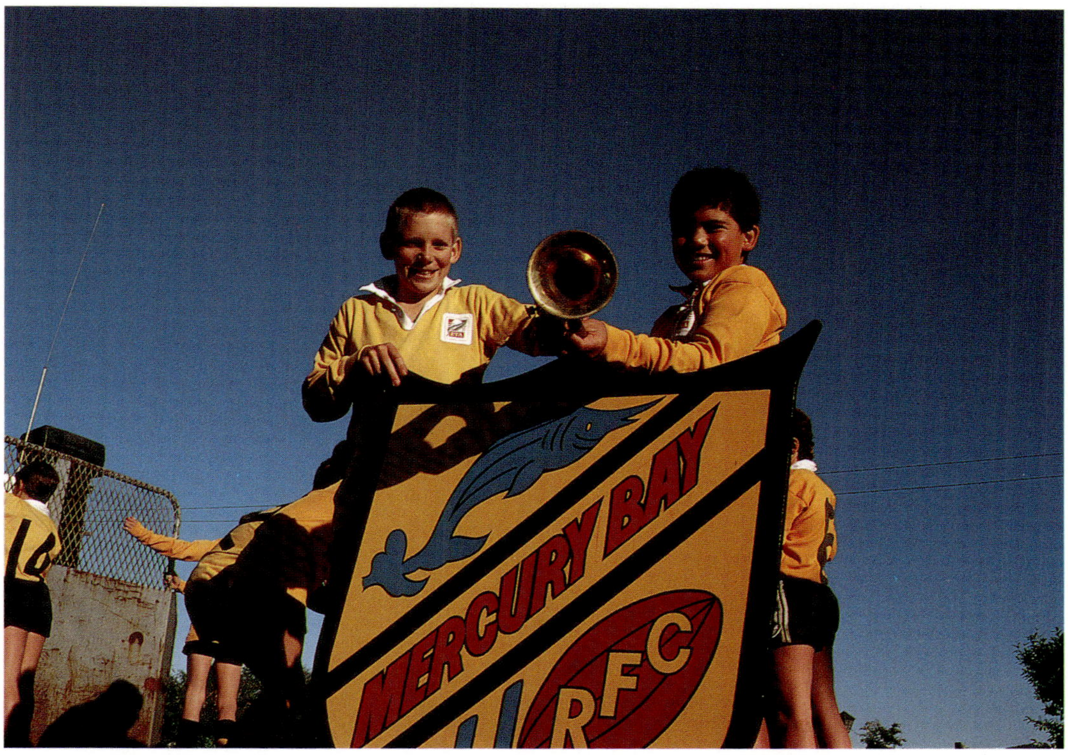

Schoolboy rugby players at the Mercury Bay club's centenary celebration ERIC TAYLOR

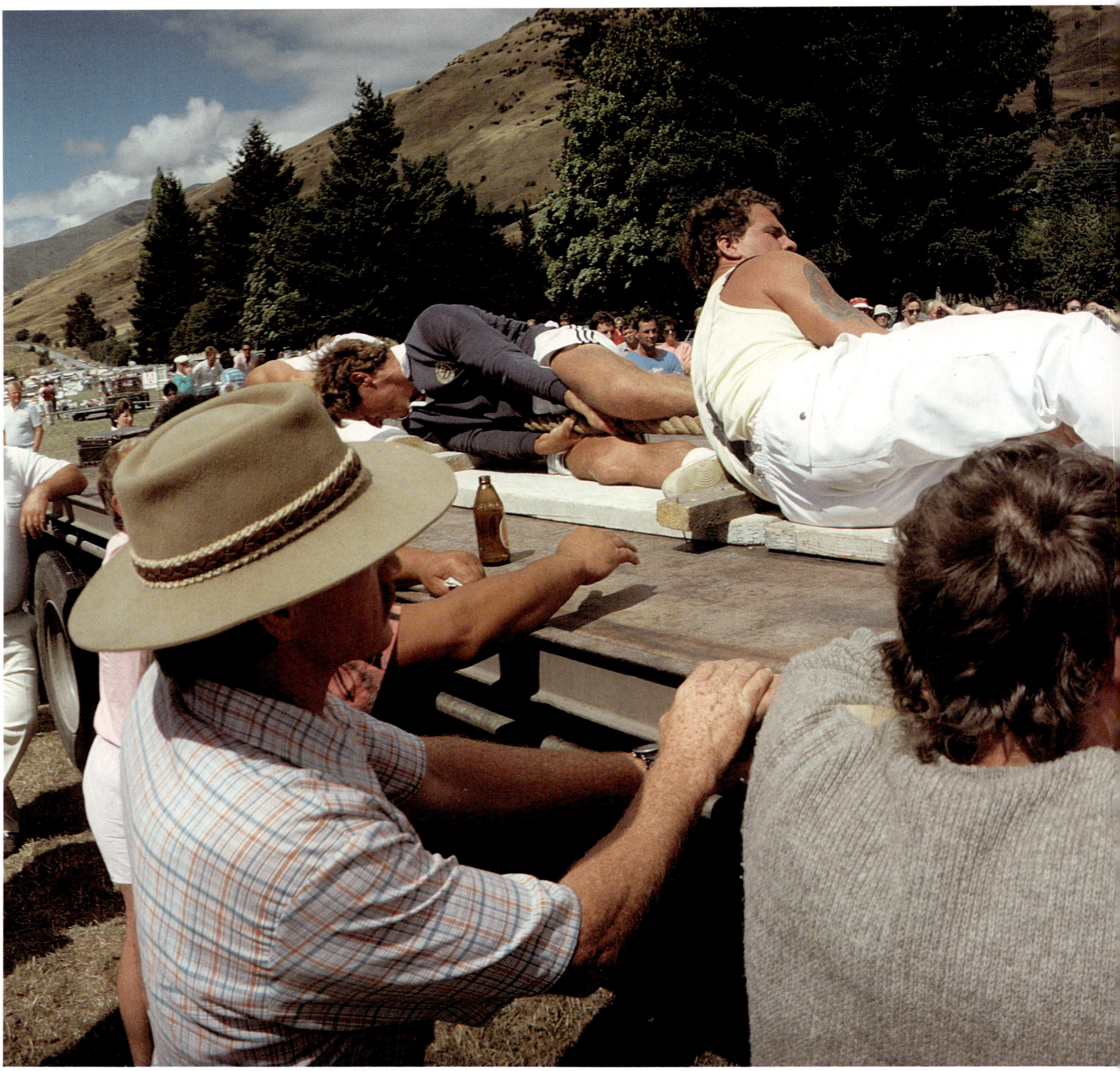

Tug of war, Lake County A & P Show, Lake Hayes GEOFF MASON

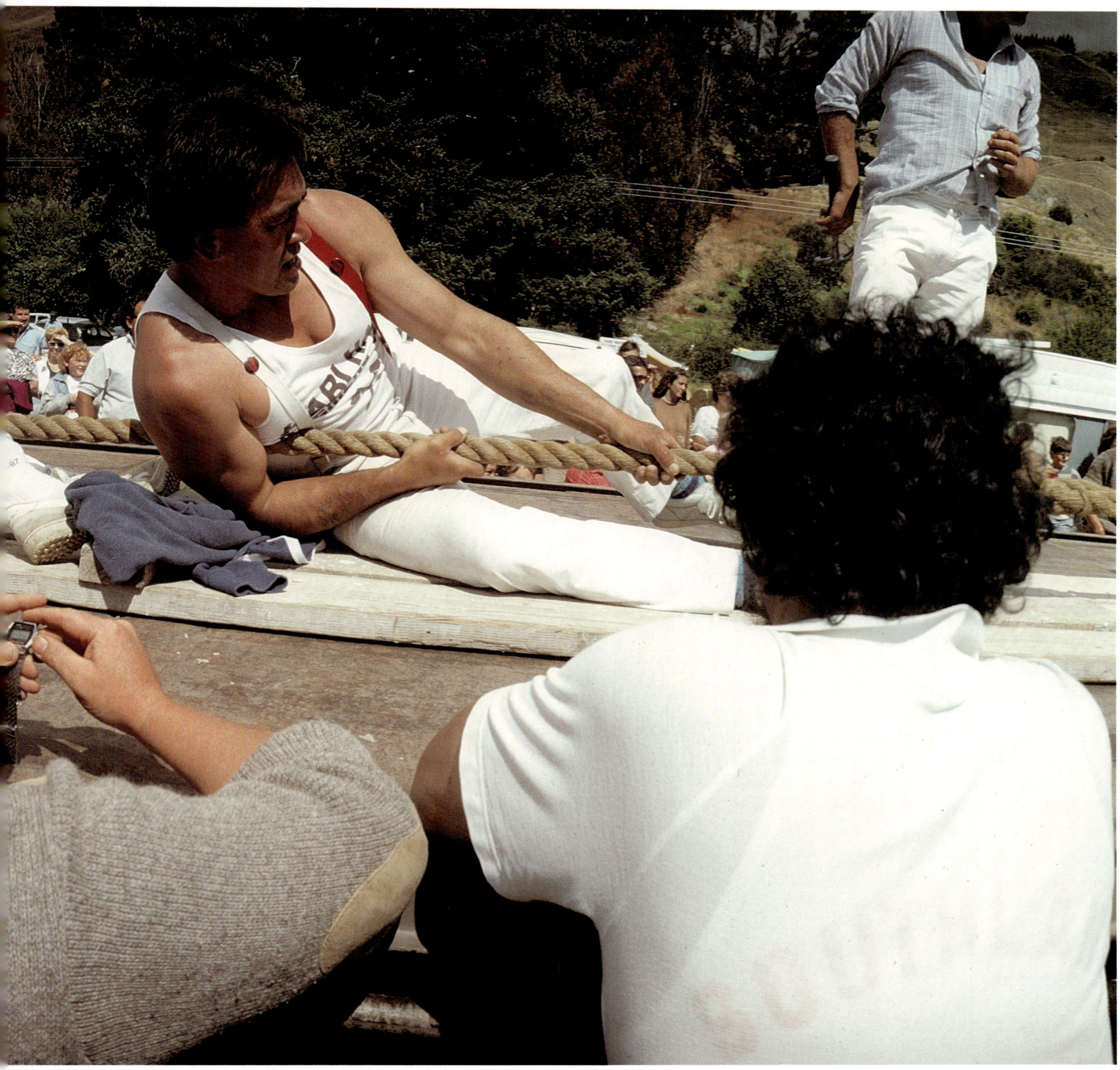

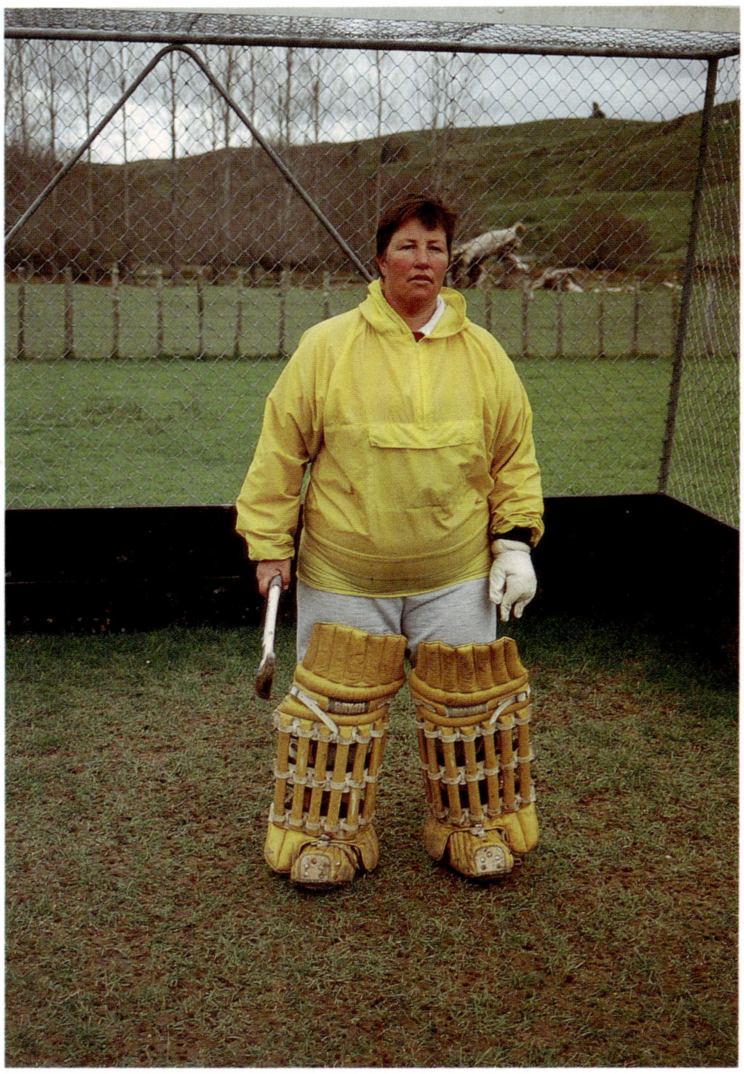

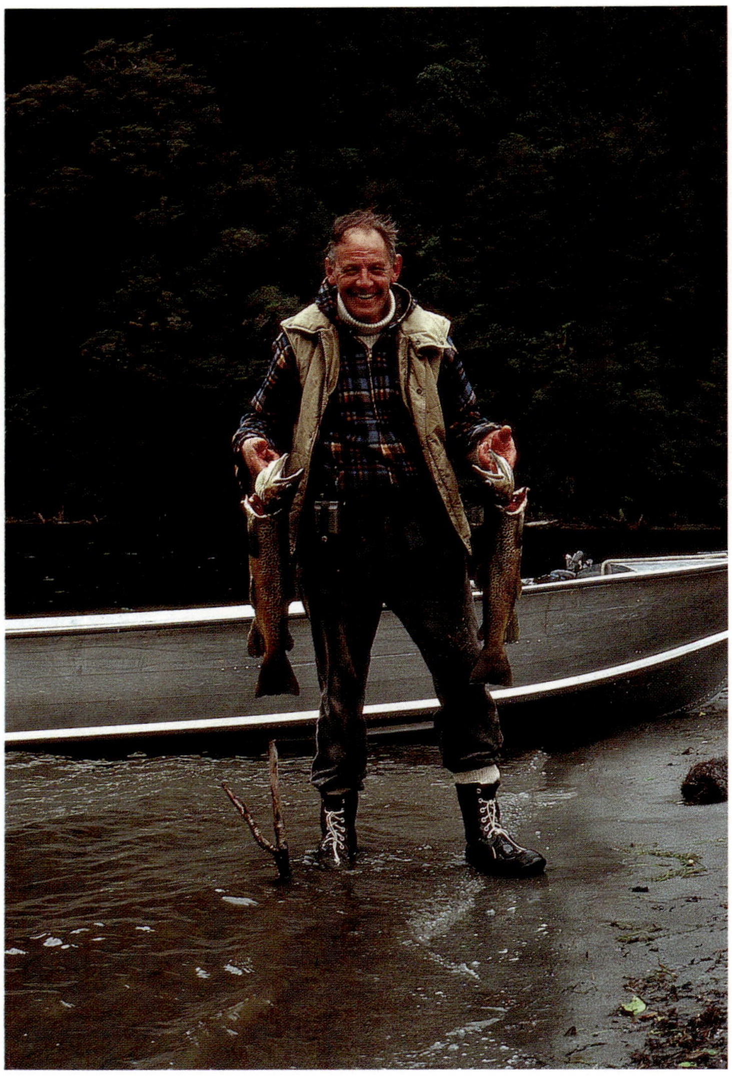

Goalkeeper, women's hockey, Marton — ERIC TAYLOR

Arthur River, Milford Track — BRIAN ENTING

Setting off down the Shotover River, Queenstown, from the Skippers Road — GEOFF MASON

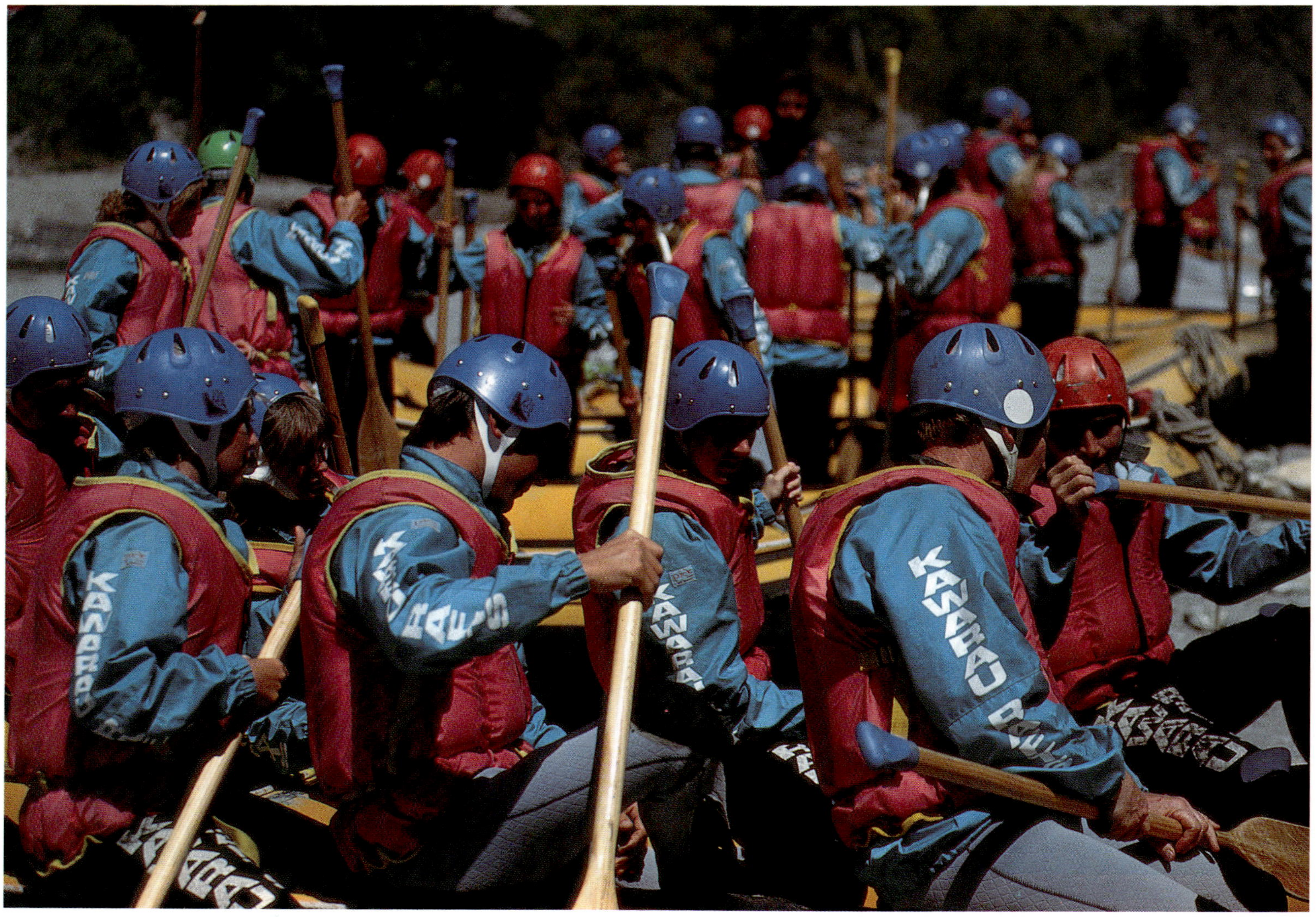

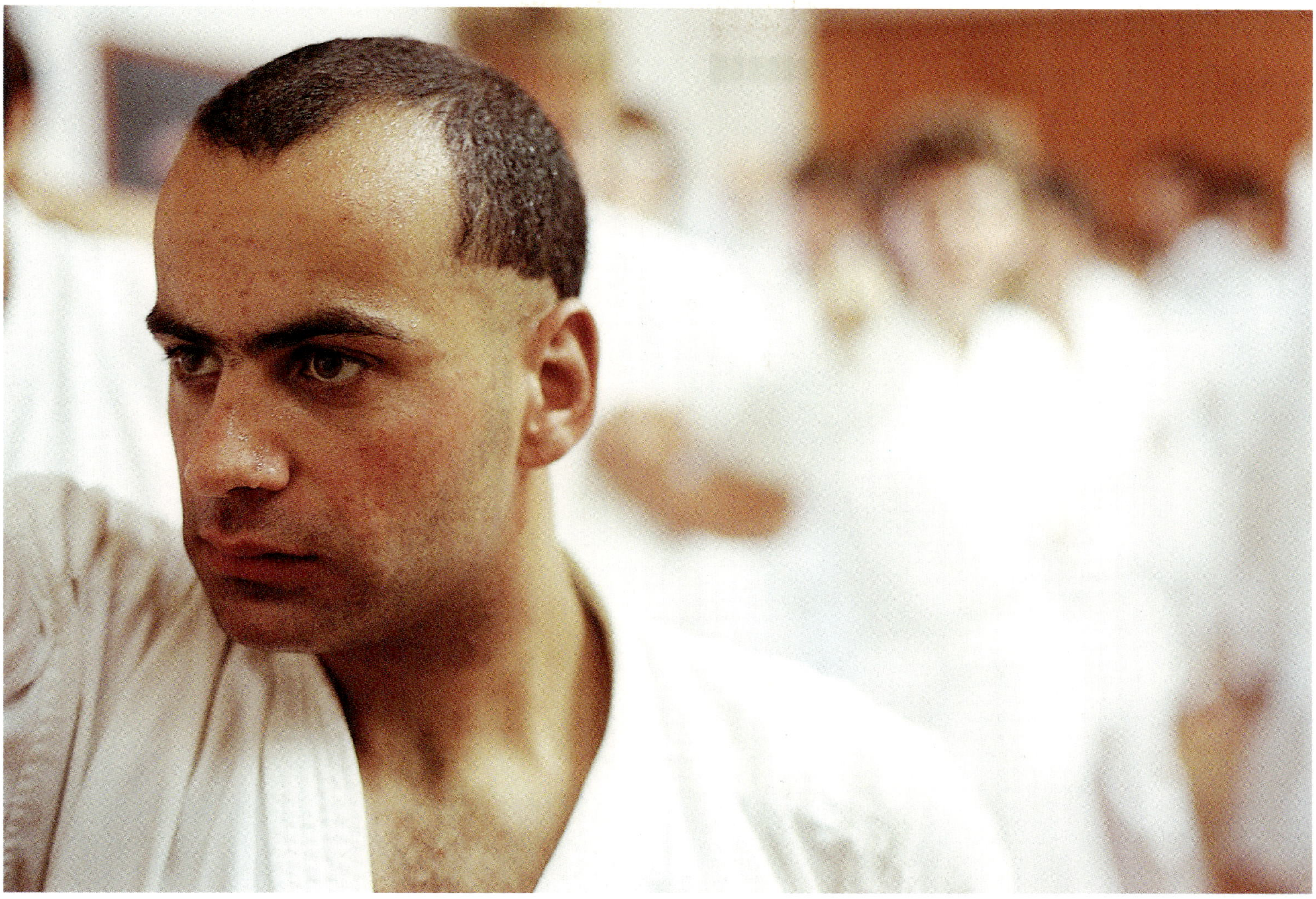

Seido karate training, Nelson BRUCE CONNEW

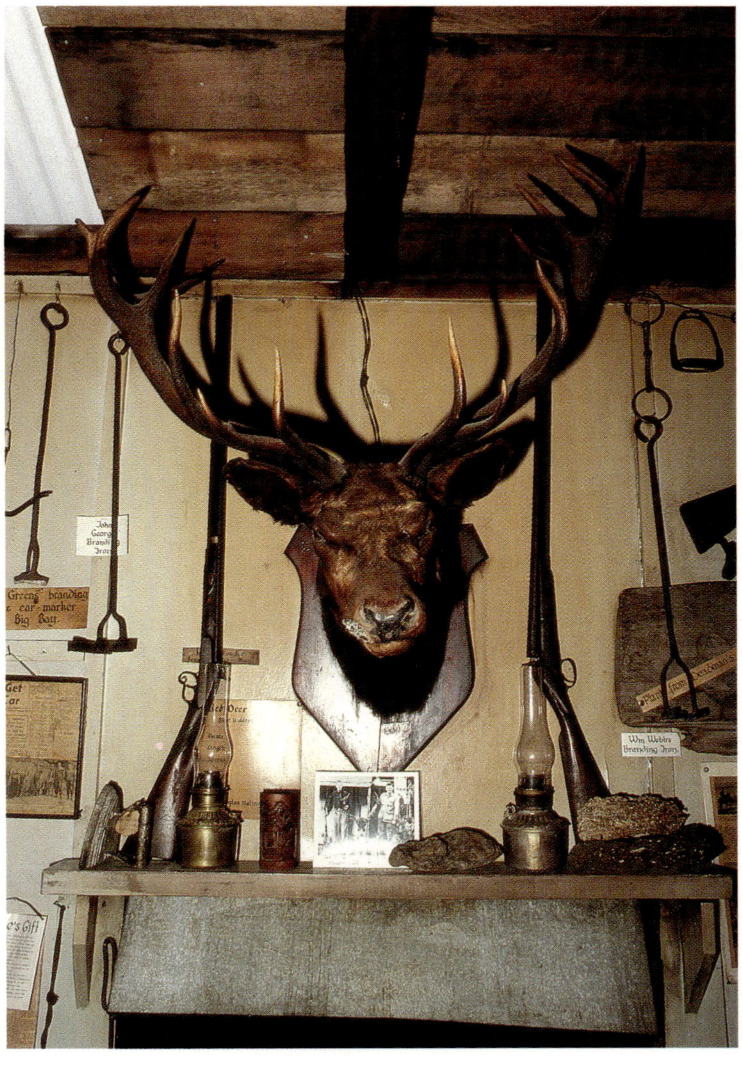

Murray Gunn's museum,
Hollyford Valley, Fiordland BRIAN ENTING

All Black haka before the second test against Wales at Eden Park, Auckland, 1988. The New Zealanders had a victory ERIC TAYLOR

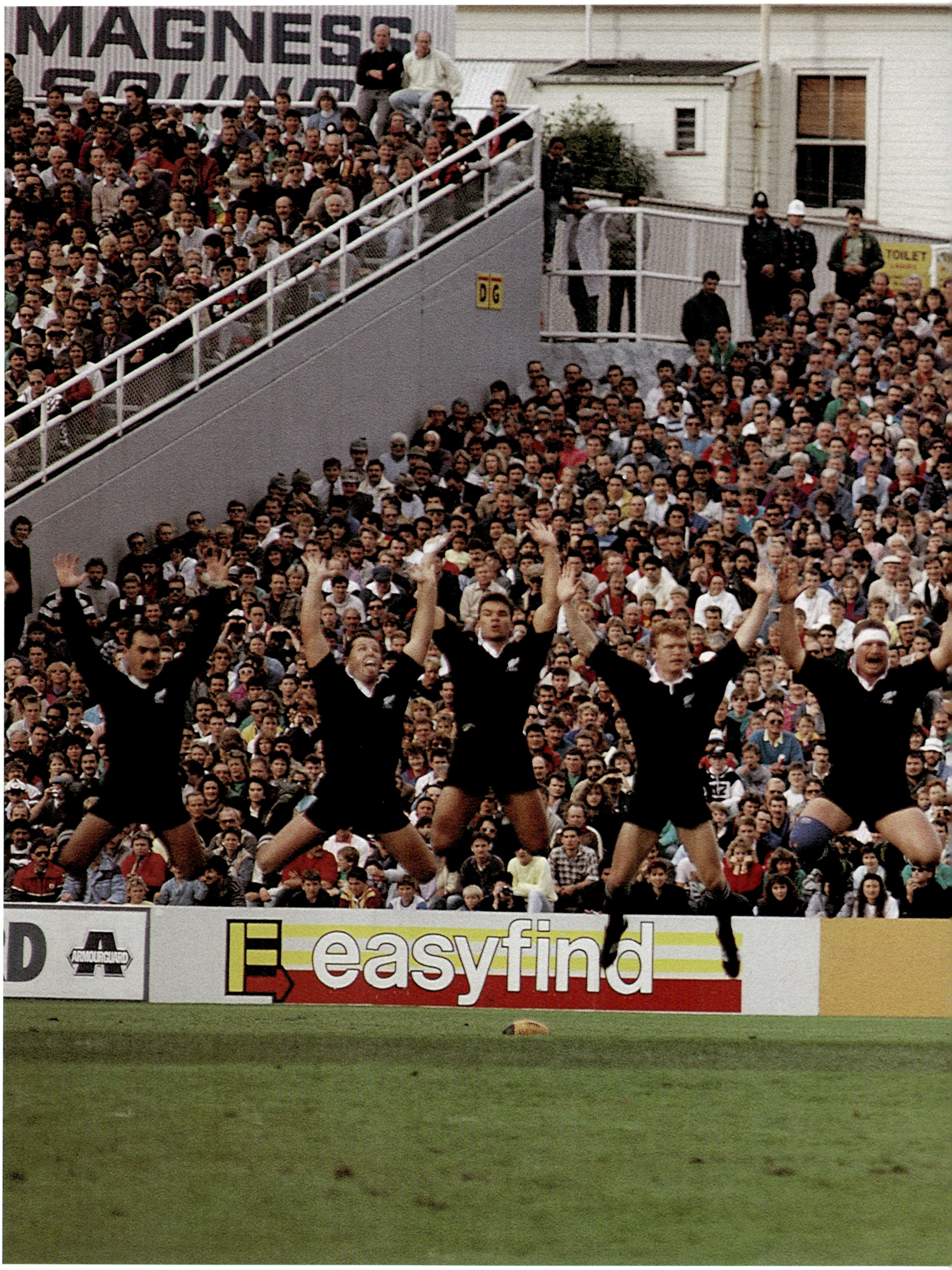

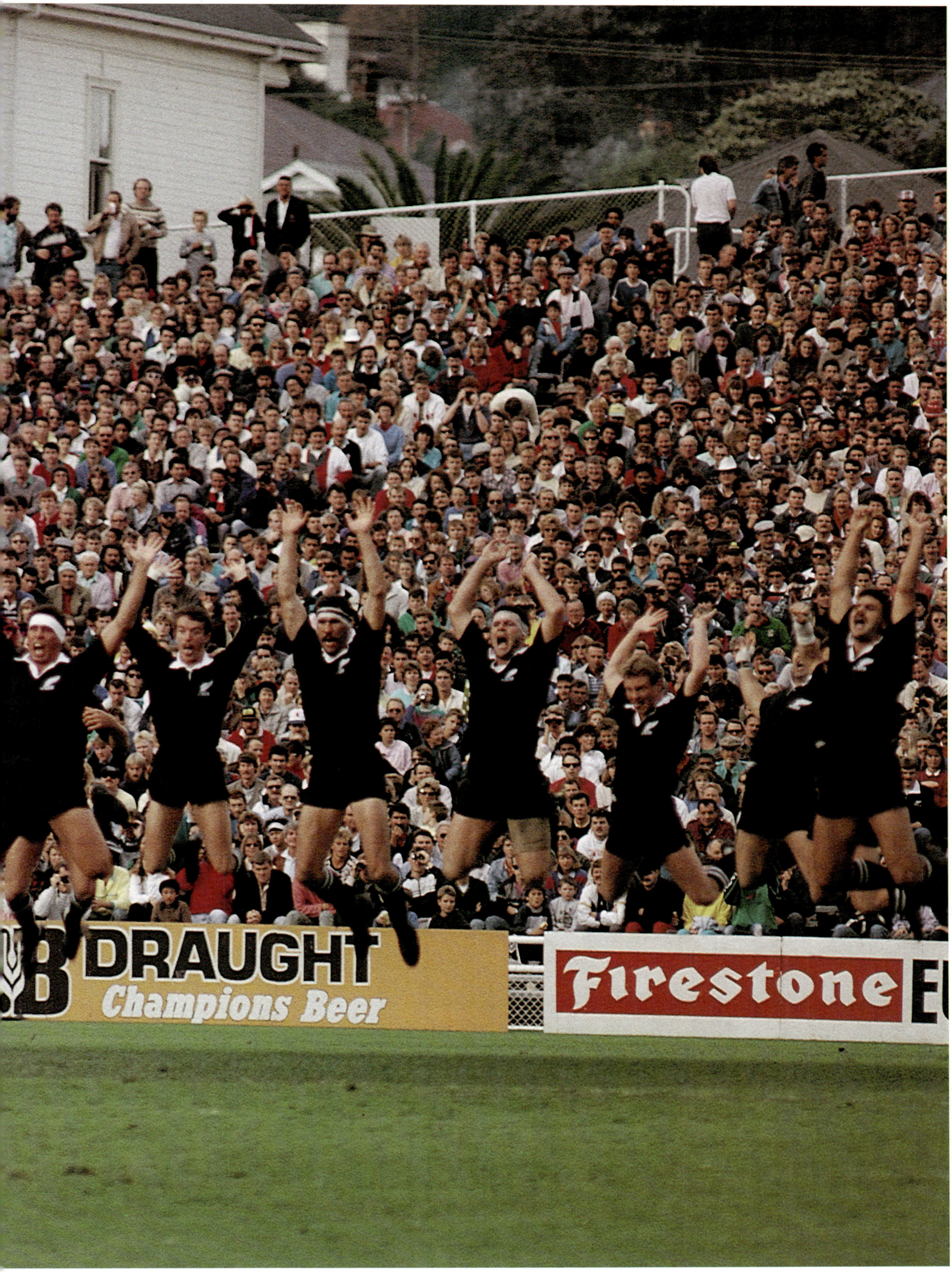
DRAUGHT
Champions Beer
Firestone

A STRONG AND VITAL PEOPLE

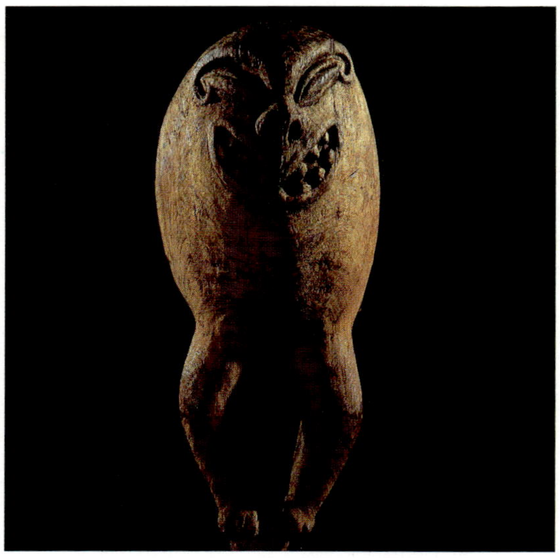

AUCKLAND MUSEUM

Wooden bone box, from Northland.

Buddy Mikaere

THE FIRST SCHOOL I went to was in rural South Waikato where most of the kids were Pakeha. Their parents were mainly cockies or tradesmen. But some of them worked as bushmen in the forests or in the local timber mills like most of the Maori fathers. My parents insisted that I go to school every day and learn to be a Pakeha. They didn't tell me any Maori history. We lived distant from our relatives and my grandfather was dead, so there was no one else to tell me either. Perhaps I wouldn't have listened.

The first things I learned about Maori history were from Pakeha teachers. They told me about Maui and how he hurt the sun and made it limp across the sky to make the days longer. I drew pictures of the trees in the great forest of Tane. We faithfully copied into our history books *1350AD The Coming of the Great Fleet* and traced a map to show where the seven canoes landed. It was all nice stuff. But that school, though it never knew it, also gave me my first lesson in what Maori history *really* meant.

One year we re-enacted the Battle of Gate Pa. I had to take my shirt off and be one of the Maori warriors manning a "pa" on the edge of the footy field. It was built from sawn up pine logs borrowed from the school woodpile. Our teacher let me use my Hopalong Cassidy cap pistol. The Pakeha kids got to dress up in bright red and white uniforms their mums had sewn for them, with tall hats made out of cardboard and coloured sticky paper. We were given blue-black crayons to draw moko on our faces. The headmaster told us that as the battle progressed, we Maori all had to be "killed", and that it was very important that we should die "well".

The engagement started with an artillery bombardment. The Pakeha kids all rushed off to stand importantly around their cannons, bits of drain pipe with sawn rounds of pine for wheels. On the count of three they shouted out in unison – Boom! Some boys made whizzing noises, while others threw handfuls of flour in the air to make the smoke of battle. In our pa, we waved a flag made from an old sheet. Like the real flag at Gate Pa it had on it a moon, a cross and a star, but ours were drawn in red lipstick.

Meanwhile the brave Pakeha soldiers who had been marching around the dead-ball line came striding up to our pa carrying their wooden muskets with cardboard bayonets tacked on. Every now and then they stopped to point them at us and shouted "Bang! I gotcha!" We dozen Maori boys charged out of our pa yelling and slashing about with our cardboard tomahawks and dying in heaps, just as the headmaster told us to. I managed to kill Johnny Woolnough and David Stannard before I expired. Those of us who had seen the last Audie Murphy picture got shot in the shoulder but fought on bravely, clutching the wound.

Well, the battle was soon over, The victorious Pakeha marched off, except for those who had decided to die for the Queen. The teachers and parents clapped and cheered, and the Maori warriors all came back to life and got in the queue for a drink of orange cordial and a tennis biscuit. It was a green day and the sun was shining. I found out much later that the battle we had recreated was the very one in which some of my own ancestors had fought the British and died. Gate Pa had been a famous victory for the Maori side.

THIRTY YEARS ON, I can look at the history of my people with a discrimination beyond that of a school kid, happily collaborating in Pakeha myth making. Maori have made myths to counter the Pakeha ones, and it's sometimes hard to find solid ground. We have to stand between two worlds. This is about the Maori one.

Three thousand years ago our ancestors burst into the Pacific Ocean in a wave of settlement which hissed onto the shores of most of the islands of the Great Sea of Kiwa. We sing, we sing of Maui, who fished up the land, and of Kupe who made it lie still; of captains who, a thousand years ago, followed Kupe's directions and set off on the southern sea where there were dragons, maelstroms and whirling death pools. We sing of explorers who named the land, tohunga who tamed it, and chiefs who claimed it.

Life in Aotearoa was harsh and short. The climate was cold. There were different fish, different birds and different trees. We burnt off the southern forest, destroyed the moa and the eagle, and learned how to look after one plant, the kumara. For much labour the return was one annual crop of thumb-sized tubers. We were born into squalor, our companions fleas, lice and hunger. We slept, ate and squatted on the ground, and our imagination was dominated by fear.

Kinship gave us humanity and human rights, but outside the kinship circle we acknowledged no one. Our hapu prospered as long as we had the power to defend our possessions by strength of arms. We were a neolithic culture, stone age man, and we died at the age of thirty with our teeth ground down. What we had – our jade ornaments, our fighting weapons, our bone and stone fish hooks, our carvings – were beautiful, but we hardly had anything.

THAT IS WHAT WESTERN scholarship tells us about ourselves, and from the scientific point of view maybe it's true. But it's not how we thought of ourselves then, or how we think of ourselves now.

Once the land was all alive. Mount Taranaki stood in the centre of the North Island where he fell in love with beautiful Pihanga. Tongariro loved her too and the rival volcanoes quarrelled and fought. After a great battle Taranaki was defeated. He lumbered off sadly to the sea, gouging out the bed of the Wanganui River as he graunched along. His journey took him up the coast, but, overtaken by the dawn, he was transfixed by the sun. Now he stands splendid and alone, on the edge of the western sky.

Mahi-Aotea came to the South Island, where he met Te Aitanga-a-Hine-mate roa and Te Ti-a-Tauwhetekui. They were tribes of enchanted trees who walked about, and danced in the shimmer of summer days.

The forest was full of fairies, who laughed in the mist at night. They came down from their mountains and toiled at tasks their chiefs commanded. Tokaroa, the black lava reef that juts out across the upper Waitemata harbour, is a half-finished fairy bridge. The Patupaiarehe were set to build it in one night, but daylight came too soon and they fled forever. Patupaiarehe took human lovers and when people have reddish hair, we say they are descended from a fairy marriage.

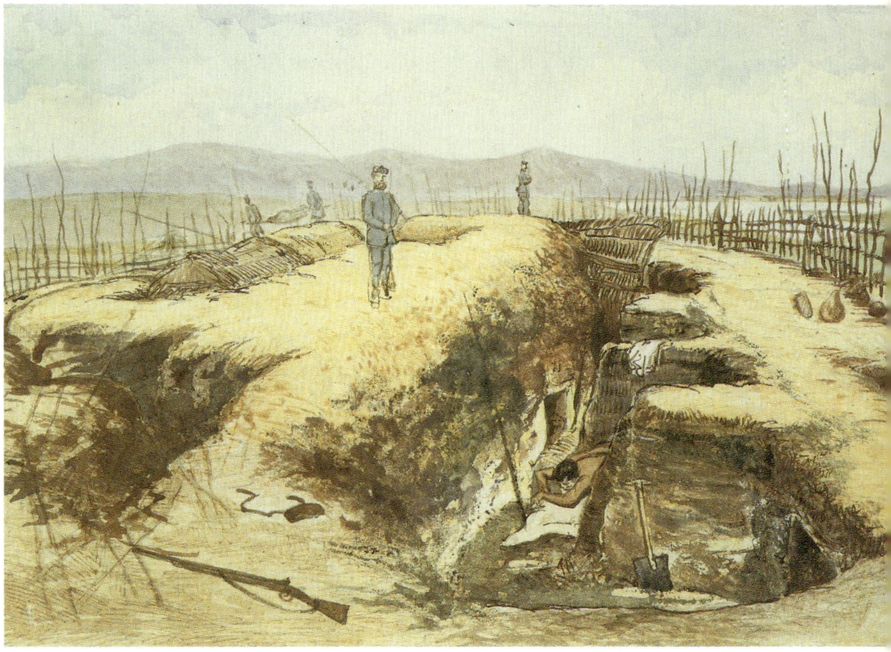

NATIONAL MUSEUM

Breach of the Gate Pa, April 30th 1864, by Horatio Gordon Robley. Although at the time the British called their defeat "perhaps unparalleled in the British military annals", Pakeha history redefined the battle at Gate Pa as a British victory.

There were giants in the earth in those days. The Maero were huge wild men whose bodies were covered with long matted hair and they lived high up in the southern mountains. Sometimes they came down to the coast to fish, and on still nights you could see their lights twinkling as they walked along the waters' edge spearing flounders with their long fingernails. It was better to close the door and stay at home when the Maero were about, for they ate men and fish alike.

Kura-ngaituku, Clawed Kura, was a winged ogre who lived in a cliff cave deep in the bush. One day she caught Hatupatu and made him look after her pet lizards and birds. But when she went away hunting, he killed as many of the lizards as he could and let all her pet birds go free. In a rage she flew after Hatupatu. She nearly caught him near Atiamuri, but he hid inside a hollow rock and she passed him by. He ran on towards Rotorua and at the top of the Waipa valley, Kura snatched at him again. He jumped behind a rock as her great talons scrabbled for him. You can still see the marks. At Whakarewarewa, Hatupatu leapt high across Whangapipiro's steaming mud. Kura misjudged the jump and was boiled.

Our history is not only in the land, it *is* the land. Takitimu canoe was beached at Murihiku in the far south and left there as a mountain range to mark its captain's journey. The giant waves which had carried Takitimu ashore are now the folds in the foothills.

Somewhere near Takapo in the heart of the South Island there are two standing rocks. They are the chiefs Te Rua-taniwha and Mauka-atua, who set out one bitter night and froze to stone. When the people found them, they were so grieved that they abandoned their lake home for the sea coast that very night. That is how Taka-po was named. It means "Preparing to leave in the night". Someone wrote it down as Lake Tekapo, and now people say the name of that lake means "darts in the night", and tell you a story to prove it. They also tell you that Te Rua-taniwha, the taniwha's lair near Takapo, means "two taniwhas". It's depressing.

When Tainui canoe visited Tauranga it grounded on a sand bar. That meant danger, and the crew worked desperately to refloat her. Hoturoa the captain seized one of the old women in the canoe and threw her under the bow for a roller. Tainui was free, and Wahinerua's spent body floated out to sea and turned to stone. She's the Kuia rock at the harbour entrance. My relations throw her an offering every time they rev up the outboard and go fishing. Her aroha to her mokopuna is calm seas and a safe return.

Our parents last century thought of our history as three things – the deeds of the ancestors who brought us here, the genealogies and stories which bind us to them and the land, and the record of war. Above all else, war. We were a warrior society.

Engari, kia mate-a-ururoa te tangata!
But let a man die like a shark!

That is, fighting to the last.

LISTEN TO THE STORY of a shark. Te Waharoa was named by his mother to remember that his father was crucified in the gateway of an enemy pa. While still a baby, he became a slave of Te Arawa. They were out raiding when a warrior called Pango found him crying in the burning pa and put him in his kit to save him. It was an act of kindness. But that baby grew up, returned to his own country, and later descended on Te Arawa at Rotorua. His army left behind them a valley of stinking bones and rotting green flesh. That was Pango's reward.

Te Waharoa fought with his neighbours on all sides. He also had enemies come at him from afar. When a Ngapuhi army arrived before his pa, he retreated behind its defences and ignored the challenge. The lack of action made Ngapuhi careless, and then Te Waharoa raided their camp. The prisoners he took he crucified after the manner of his own father's death, leaving them screaming on his palisades. Watching their kinsmen die, Ngapuhi decided to have nothing further to do with this madman. But Te Waharoa wasn't finished with them. He sent the Ngapuhi leader, Tareha, a message.

I hear you fight with the long-handled tomahawk. I fight with the same; meet me.

Te Waharoa's message was cool and even, I think he might have smiled. But Tareha, a huge man who liked to eat young children, declined to make Te Waharoa's day and Ngapuhi vanished.

Hongi Hika of Ngapuhi was another shark. In 1820 on his way home from England, he travelled back from Sydney with Hinake of Ngati Maru. Hongi's friendship, like his English manners, lasted only until he stepped ashore and learned that Ngati Maru had killed his son-in-law. He went to war and killed Hinake by slashing off his head. Then he drank the hot blood which spurted from the neck of the corpse and, holding up the head, scooped out the left eye with a pocket knife and swallowed it. Revenge wasn't just a matter of keeping a score sheet; it was satisfaction.

These stories come from the time our Pakeha manuhiri were starting to arrive, and I mean it to show how close are the days of our savagery. Dear friends, we were warriors in the time of your great-great-grandmothers, and we lived by our own rules.

Hongi's nephew Hone Heke was another kind of shark. He had a soldier's confidence which mocked men and gods, Pakeha and Maori. When the old warrior Te Kahakaha was killed in battle, Heke was the only one brave enough to save his body from enemy hands. "If you go you will die," said the tohunga, because Heke had looted a dead enemy and lost his spiritual protection. Heke, the protector of missionaries, ground his teeth and rolled his eyes to heaven:

What care I for either men or spirits? I fear not. Let the fellow in heaven look to it. Have I not prayed to him for years? It is for him to look to me this day.

Heke got shot through the thigh for his impiety, and had to be rescued himself. Gazing upon him, an elder observed:

. . . there is nothing in this world so deaf to reason as a warrior when he is enraged. He only listens to his own courage, and, being led away by it dies.

Fighting was men's work. But women shared the exultation of victory and the malice of revenge. A war party which attacked a steep pa on Tuhua (Mayor Island) by night were driven back by an avalanche of rocks hurled down on them by the defenders. In the morning the women of the pa raced out to lick the damp enemy blood from the stones.

When a Tuhoe woman mourned the death of her sons, her "flock of high born ones", she spat out a menu for the revenge to come:

The teeth of the widow of Mate-haere shall be sharpened . . .
Te Huri-kino shall swallow
The brains of Paia.
All the gleaming eyes of Mura-hioi,
By Hine-ringa shall be eaten raw!

Yes, our history is soaked in blood.

The whole race . . . is madly fond of war, high-spirited and quick to battle, but otherwise straight-forward and not of evil character . . . at any time or place and on whatever pretext you stir them up, you have them ready to face danger, even if they have nothing on their side but their own strength and courage . . .

That's what the Greek historian Strabo said about the Celtic tribes of Europe, but he might as well have been talking about us. Like us, the Celts were quick to take offence and prone to exaggerate their own importance while looking with contempt on others. They were boastful and vain when the luck was with them, and cowardly when it was not. So were we. They bore pain stoically and faced death with courage. So did we.

But war wasn't all gore and glory. It was often ridiculous. Ngaiterangi planned a surprise attack on Papaka, a pa perched on a cliff above Whakatane, and Tamapahore was sent at dusk to spy out its defences. While he was creeping around in the shadows he came across a woman at the latrine. He stretched up and gave her a prod in the backside with his taiaha. He just couldn't resist it! But she squawked so loudly that Ngaiterangi's surprise was ruined.

THE PEOPLE I BELONG TO are sometimes called Hamuti-wera, Hot shit. This recalls a time we had arranged to fight at sunrise. Just before dawn, while the men were preparing for the morning's work, our chief scouted the enemy camp and found that we were well outnumbered. What could a prudent tribe do but turn for home? And quick! When the enemy came over the hill there wasn't one of us in sight. All that faced them were the steaming piles of our morning's toilet. That's how we got that name.

We admired winners, and we especially admired tricky winners. Maui set the pattern when he tricked his mother into revealing the secret entrance to the Underworld, and when he fooled his grandmother into giving him all her fire. But cheek was also his undoing. He tried to climb back into the womb of Hine-nui-te-po and become immortal. The Goddess of Death squeezed him dead between her thighs, and now we must all die. The moral of the story is: don't push your luck.

We admired trickery in love. Rau and Uenga, who lived on the northern bank of the Patea river in Taranaki, were rivals for the affections of Tane-roroa, whose home was on the southern bank. The two men decided to visit her but lacked a canoe to cross the river. Rau couldn't swim. Uenga thought this was his chance to cut his mate out of the contest, and plunged into the river. Aue! the murky water was only up to his knees! He crawled across, flapping his arms mightily. Uenga won the lady while Rau lamented on the farther shore.

Kahungunu stole Rongomai-wahine away from her husband with a most famous ingenuity. Kahu had heard that Rongomai was beautiful and set out to see her for himself. Unfortunately she had just taken a husband, but Kahu decided to press ahead anyway. He started by showing the local people how good he was at providing food. In one day he gathered so much fern root that when the bundles were rolled down the hill they blocked the doorways of the houses. Working alone, he gathered enough paua to feed all the people. They began to say what a catch Kahungunu would make.

That night, when the paua were eaten, Kahu deliberately took only the roes. Now paua roes give you the wind, and during the night Kahu had a terrible attack. He crept over to where Rongomai and her husband were sleeping, lifted their mat, farted under it, and crept away. They woke up gasping, each blaming the other. Eventually they went back to sleep. Up creeps Kahu, lifts the mat again – another haunga blast! Rongomai woke up furious, would listen to nothing, and kicked her husband out of the house. Poor Tama! And Kahu moved smoothly into the space beside the lady.

The descendants of Kahungunu and Rongomai-wahine live mainly on the eastern coast of the lower North Island and this story is told wherever Ngati Kahungunu gather. All Maori think of Kahungunu as a great chief, but tribes have their own tales of how they bested his children. Ngati Whare took on a Kahungunu war party and were getting the worst of it. Suddenly their chief Taketake stood up, naked, and paraded on his ramparts with his ure erect. Well! Kahungunu were so confounded by the size of his taonga that they stopped fighting. And while they gazed, some of the Ngati Whare soldiers crept around and attacked from behind, and Kahungunu were defeated.

We appreciated nature's magnificence as well as its jokes. But our relationship with nature was one in which we were often overmatched. The harshness of our existence meant we didn't have the energy to put ourselves safely beyond want; surviving the days was sufficient labour. But we stripped nature where we could, in order to show we were people of consequence.

We used feasts to woo our relations' support for a war, or to thank them for past help. It took months to assemble the giant piles of food we displayed on scaffolding which might be ten storeys high. The feast held by Wiremu Tamihana Tarapipipi Te Waharoa to mark the peacemaking between Ngati Haua and Te Arawa boasted one thousand pigs, fifty thousand eels and a stack of potatoes and kumara two hundred yards long, five feet high and five feet thick. The climax of the peacemaking was the presentation of forty umbrellas to the leading Te Arawa chiefs who opened them and walked, with great dignity, two by two to the church.

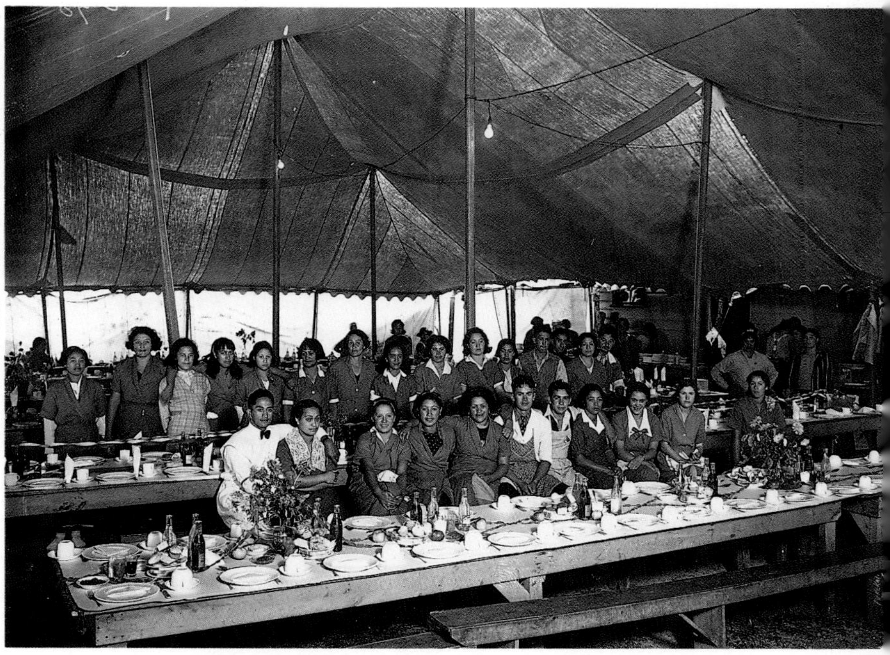

HALL RAINE COLLECTION/NATIONAL MUSEUM

Feasts on a grand scale have been a feature of Maori social life in both historic and recent times. This hui took place at Otaki in the 1940s.

Kororirori used to be a favourite at feasts. It was flour and sugar stirred up with hot water, made by the ton and served in fishing canoes. At a wedding in Taranaki, a small boy eager to get his share overbalanced and fell in. The bride's father snatched him out by the foot and, to save waste, carefully licked him clean.

Nature wasn't "she" to us, it was a family full of conflict. The children of the Earth and Sky were the natural forces of our world, and they set things up the way they were supposed to be. Tu-matauenga demanded the first victim in battle as his tribute. Bad Whiro drew the lost souls of men to the Underworld and Ruamoko the earthquake shook the land in anger. Overhead Tawhirimatea hurled the wind and storm against his gentle brothers Tane of the forest and Rongo of the gardens. They teach our kids a version of this in school and countless cute books as "Maori religion", because the personification of nature is an idea that Pakeha approve. But it's too remote, too abstract, and it misses the connection between the gods and us, which was the karakia which invoked their powers.

KARAKIA BROUGHT THE PAST to life again, so that the powers of the gods could work for us. For instance, when a Wanganui warrior needed strength to turn back a surprise enemy attack he re-kindled the ancient anger of Tu-matauenga:

Tu's face is angry!
Tu's face rages!
O Tu, cleave the heavens.
Give me my strength to be bent up,
To be wrapped around.
A fierce prayer, a raging prayer.
An army devouring prayer!
A prayer to engage the land.

Tapu, or supernatural restriction, made the rules for our relationships with each other and with nature. Near Te Kouma, not far from Coromandel, there is a stretch of coast which my family regard as being very tapu. Nothing is ever taken from there, so as kids we pretended that the summer peaches we could see growing on the hillside were not real. When my grandfather was alive he said that Sonny Williams went fishing one day and on his way home he cut some flax to string his fish with. He forgot about the tapu. As Sonny walked along the riverbank, he saw a queer foaming whiteness in the water and he told his parents about it when he got home. "Take your flax string and throw it back in the river!" they said, and when he had done it, at once the colour disappeared and the river cleared. It was Whai-a-roa the white stingray, the guardian of Te Kouma. Our kaitiaki was protecting Sonny from the tapu.

Our own immediate past ancestors were our household gods. We carved them and placed them outside our whare, but they would protect us only if we did things according to the tikanga we inherited from them. That is one reason tangihanga are so important to us. These days most of us just feel we haven't done right by our tupapaku if we don't farewell them with Maori honours, but there's an older reason for our unease. If the souls of the dead were not properly despatched on their lonely journey to their kindred, belonging nowhere, they became full of malice, and tried to destroy their relations who live in the world of light. The spirits of the stillborn were always dangerous, because they died before they had a chance to learn to behave like human beings.

Tena koutou i o tatou tini mate,
Takato, takato, takato i re rangimarie.

Night was a time of danger from the spirit world, so we were scared of the dark. Journeys were dangerous, because any ordinary piece of landscape might be a wahi tapu, a sacred place which, if trespassed upon, meant misfortune or death. Ignorance of the law was no excuse. Our territories were studded with the eerie tombs that housed the corpses of great chiefs, and we would pass them walking close together with our heads down. If a bellbird should happen to sing, it was a signal of danger. Walk faster, brothers!

What made our culture so secure was that we had an answer to every question; nothing was unknown. For example, our carvings were our ancestors, powerful gods. Why then could they not talk? Ah, but they could once, when all carvings lived under the sea. We discovered the art of carving by accident, when a father went looking for his son.

Rua Te Pupuke was the father of Te Manu-hau-turuki who was caught by Tangaroa and taken down to his home in a land under the sea. Tangaroa stuck him on top of his house as a tekoteko. After a long search Rua found his son, and while he sat inside Tangaroa's house thinking how to rescue him, he found that the carved posts inside the house could talk to each other. The outside poupou were dumb.

That night, while Tangaroa and his family slept, Rua set the house on fire. Tangaroa's children were burnt up, except for those, like the mullet and the flying fish, who fled before the flames. Rua snatched up his son and an armful of the poupou from outside the house and ran. As he looked back, the carvings inside the house stamped out a haka as they burned, and sang to him through the flames.

And sang to him through the flames. This story kind of haunts me. It's saying something we used to know, but I don't know what. We have only got the silent carvings, and they've been made to tell us something else.

Witness in the Native Land Court: The god of whom I speak is dead.
The Court: Gods do not die.
Witness: You are mistaken, gods do die unless there are tohungas to keep them alive.

Looking back, our gods had died when carvers started having to put names across our ancestors' chests, or add other props to jog our memories. I should say our old way of thinking about the world had died rather than the gods, because the forms remained; it was just that a new spirit came to dwell in them. How many times have you heard an older Maori person explain that carvings have three fingers to represent the Father, Son and Holy Ghost? Beliefs like that make life meaningful for many people; it's a true Maori culture, and the certainty of the believers is the descendant of the certainty we once had in our ancient ways. Their world still hangs together through faith.

It's the fragmentation of my world which draws me so strongly to my aunties, who are in their eighties. They know their lives have been hard, but they are matter-of-fact talking about it, and they don't grumble about the parents who married them off too young, the relations who sponged off them and the Pakeha connections who ended up with the land. But I don't share their uncomplaining acceptance of a raw deal. For me, their Maori Christian God – the one who is present in the three-fingered ancestors in the meeting house – their god, too, is dead. We seem to be evolving a new spirituality now – composed of respect for the past, love for people and protection of the environment. But there's an old current just beneath the surface. Many still fear to desecrate a tapu.

HOW DO I FEEL ABOUT THE PAST? Societies whose ways are too fixed are doomed to endless repetition, and there is no special value in that. Our ancient life was not, as some people like to think, carefree and harmonious, because we were such a confrontational people, and because we had to struggle with nature to survive. But neither was it, as others suspect, brutish or especially cruel. It is the human past everywhere, but we did not know it, because at the time we thought we were humankind, all of it, all the people in the whole world. In 1769 nothing from the outside had touched us. But from that year we were not alone.

The moment the Pakeha came, what we saw was a better way: iron tools, food, boats, horses, books. We wanted it. We went flying from the stone age through the industrial revolution, climbing in fifty years the mountain which had taken Pakeha society centuries to scale. We had a culture which approved change, loved freedom and desired wealth. We were prepared to act in order to achieve; our ancient story of the beginning of the world confirms that.

The close embrace of Earth and Sky deprived their children, who lived between them, of liberty, light and experience. Tu-matauenga, the god of war whose offspring is all humankind, discovered light when his father stirred, and then he could not live without it:

... It was light, my brothers. Light.
A most beautiful sight infiltered past
the armpit hairs of the father. Why, I could
even see to count all the fingers of my hands
held out to it, see the stain – the clutch of
good earth on them.

But then he moved.
And darkness came down even more oppressively
it seemed and I drew back tense, angry.
Brothers, let us kill him – push him off.

Hone Tuwhare wrote this a few years ago, but the life in the story comes all the way from Hawaiki.

Above all we were practical. At the same time that Charles Darwin was realising that the reason for adaptation in nature is that only the fit survive, we were finding it out in practice. We were not fit to compete in the world of the Pakeha, and we had to make some fast adjustments. But not everyone adjusted.

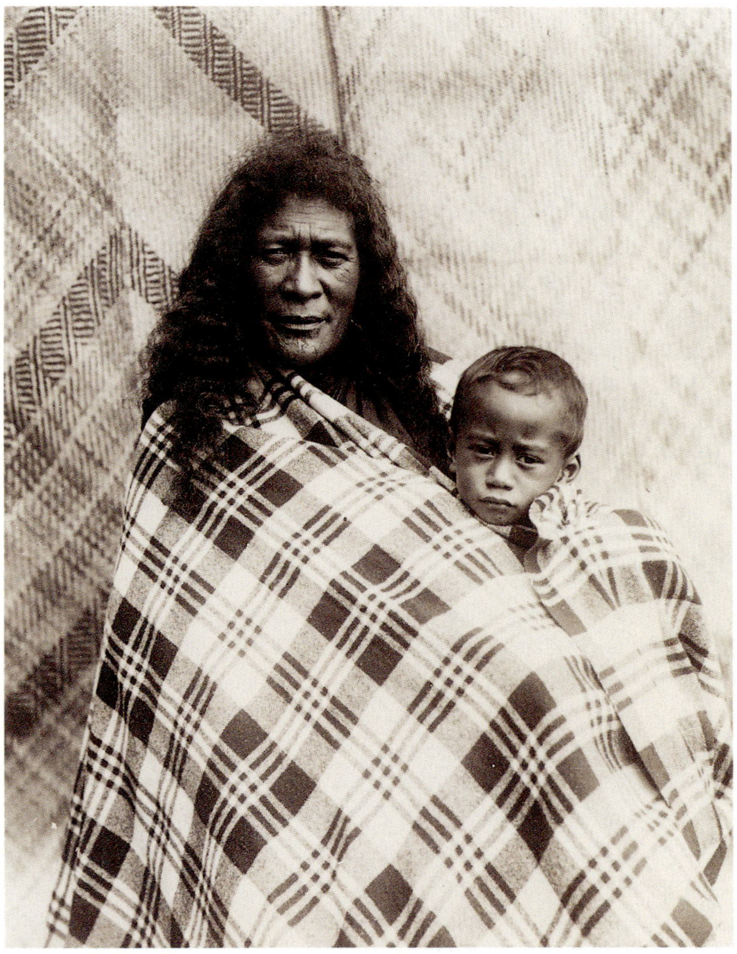

H. J. THORPE COLLECTION/CANTERBURY MUSEUM

The Maori were willing to acquire Pakeha commodities, technology and know how. This woman poses before a traditional floor mat while wrapped in a blanket – a popular item in the British trading repertoire.

I've already mentioned the Ngapuhi chief Tareha. He was nearly seven feet tall and weighed over twenty stones. Such a large man required hefty feeding. Once he pulled alongside a ship just as the cook was cleaning out the galley. Tareha grabbed the slops bucket and swallowed its contents entirely. Then he handed it back and enquired if they had any more. Tareha was keen to take advantage of Pakeha weapons and a new range of food, but it never occurred to him to change his ways or his values. Pakeha technology simply enlarged his warrior life, not to mention his frame.

Tareha was well aware that new ideas were abroad in the land. In 1840 he attended the Treaty deliberations at Waitangi, getting up to speak wearing his usual piece of dirty old matting. In one hand he carried a canoe paddle and from the other dangled a bunch of fern root tied with a piece of flax. If Ngapuhi signed the Treaty, he said, the Governor would be like the canoe paddle, standing tall above the chiefs:

We will not be ruled over. You high, and I, Tareha, the great chief of the Ngapuhi tribes, low? No, no, never, never ... Go back, go back, you shall not stay here ... !

The officials were so ignorant as to bribe this glutton with promises of free food. He shook his bundle of fern root under their noses and dismissed their simplicity.

As a chief, Tareha had less reason than others to feel there was any value in change, but the thing was, the rest of the world was passing him by. The twenty years that followed the Treaty were in many ways years of hope. We appeared to be in control of change. Our land was planted in wheat and other crops which supplied the young towns, and Maori-owned ships carried produce to the goldfields of Australia. We were secure enough to experiment. That was the time when a nation should have been born. Instead the twenty years culminated in a bitter, bloody war.

Ka po, ka po te ao.
The world grows dark.

We must now enter for a while the valley of the shadow, and talk about some harsh matters which explain some things about the present.

WHAT WENT WRONG? It was the surfacing of the unfinished business of Waitangi, where we were made fools of by a mock serious ceremony and a piece of paper. On 30 January 1840, Captain Hobson signed a proclamation declaring himself Lieutenant Governor of New Zealand and announced it to a meeting of Pakeha gathered on the beach at Kororareka. We were consulted six days later. So 6 February 1840 doesn't mean much to some of us; the Treaty must stand on its power among Maori living now.

Nominal legal equality only leads to actual equality if the parties are equal. Where one is unsophisticated in the forms of western government the only consequence of establishing the same rights and obligations for both will be to destroy the weaker under a show of justice.

That was the Reverend Montagu Hawtrey's version of Tareha's opposition to the annexation of Aotearoa. He said it all. For most of its subsequent history the Treaty of Waitangi has not protected us in courts of law. We had to become Pakeha if we wanted to be free of the Paheka and that is still largely true. So in recent times some of us wrote on walls: "The Treaty is a Fraud". Then the fourth Labour Government committed itself to the principles set out in that document, and practical as ever, we changed our call to "Ratify the Treaty", and it became our ancient treasure. The Waitangi Tribunal was empowered to investigate breaches of the spirit of the Treaty back to 1840, and as I write, there are claims before the Tribunal covering about seventy per cent of the country. We are fifteen per cent of its people. Will the government's commitment encompass the millions of dollars and the shift in the balance of power that sticking to principle might require? Would yours?

Principle as the basis of government was first introduced to Maori as stemming from Christianity. I wish I could meet a man who believed it: Wiremu

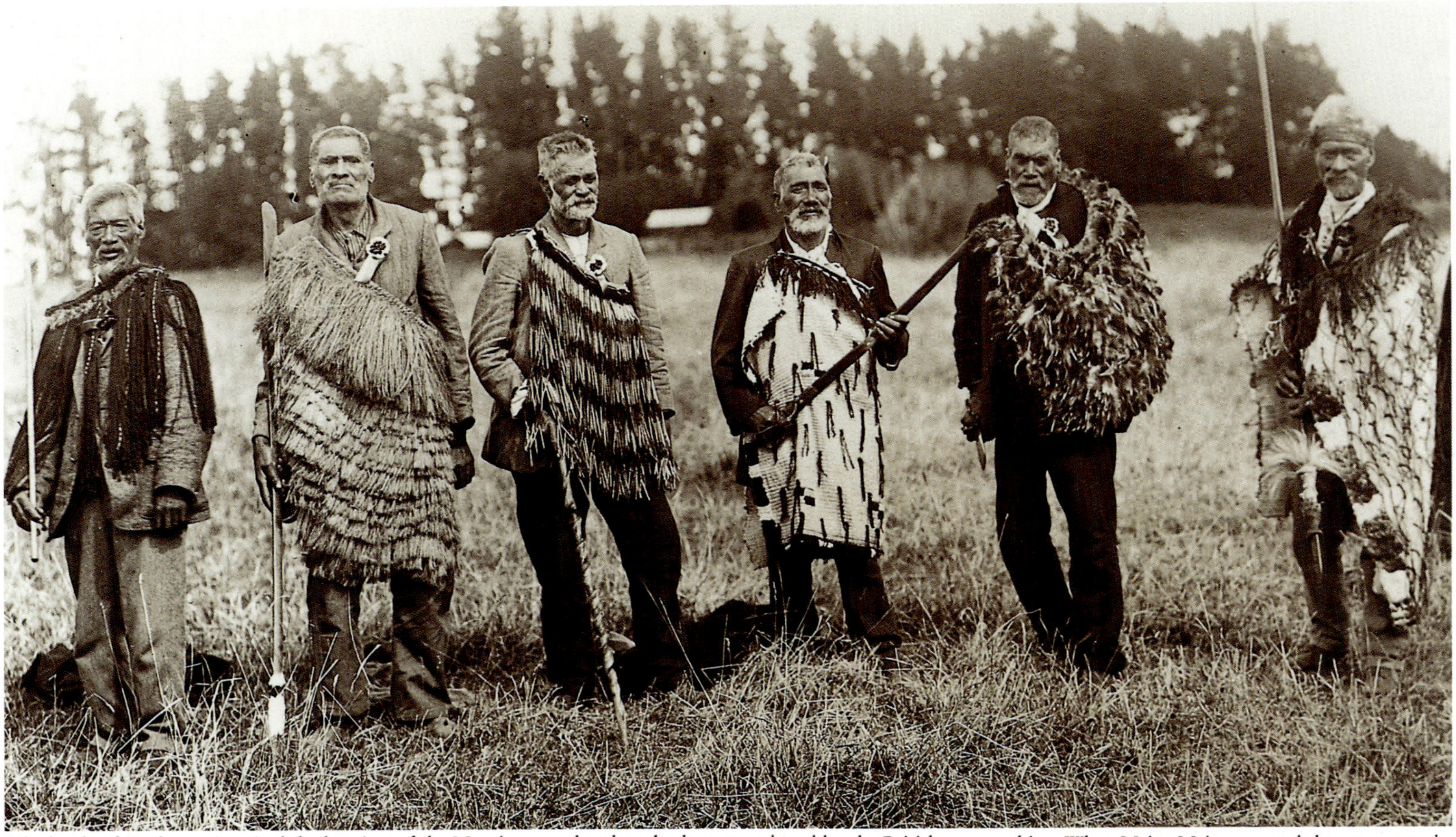

COWAN COLLECTION/ALEXANDER TURNBULL LIBRARY

The battle of Orakau epitomised the heroism of the Maori, even when hopelessly outnumbered by the British war machine. When Major Mair suggested the women and children be sent away, Ahumai spoke for the women and said: "Let us die with the men!" These Ngati Maniapoto survivors of Orakau were photographed fifty years later.

Tamihana Tarapipipi Te Waharoa of Ngati Haua, the son of Te Waharoa mentioned before. Tamihana became a Christian in the 1830s and made the word of God the guide and law of his life. He made peace with his father's enemies, and built a new pa where Christians could break with their past. He grew wheat to fund a boarding school for his people to grasp the future. The best building in his village was a church with glass windows and a code of laws based on the ten commandments nailed to the wall. Tamihana thought that having banished those things in Maori life which were contrary to the gospels, he could live in harmony with the Pakeha. But he did not contemplate dependence any more than had Tareha.

In 1860, after the Governor abolished the right of chiefs to veto the sale of tribal land, war began in Taranaki. Wiremu Tamihana tried to stop his people from going to fight, and fled to his Bible for guidance:

. . . I wish to understand the case, but do not see it. They [the Pakeha] have forsaken the right way, they have become deranged like the King of Babylon who was turned into the forest. But let us not take up arms in an unrighteous cause . . . I do not forget some of the Kings of Judah who engaged in unrighteous war, how they perished in their sin. Therefore I hesitate, and say let us see our way. I also remember the words of Paul, "Let every soul be subject unto the higher powers, for there is no power but of God; the powers that be are ordained by God".

In 1861, Tamihana arranged a truce between Taranaki and the government, but war burst through the shaky barrier and spread to the Waikato when British troops crossed Waikato's border on 12 July 1863. Tamihana was at Rangiaowhia when the troops set the houses on fire. Old people were shot as the flames forced them out, while others chose to be burnt in their houses, rather than fall to enemy weapons. Tamihana's imagination was tortured by this tragedy and for a few months he lent his authority to the war.

But his soul was in torment: "the powers that be are ordained by God". Tamihana could not live in disobedience to the word, and in November though he feared to be hung, he arranged for his mere to be handed to General Cameron. His act of surrender was rejected, to teach him the depths of his powerlessness; nevertheless Tamihana fought no more.

Required to make a formal surrender in 1865, Tamihana laid his taiaha before General Carey. The officer said:

You caused your people to go to war. You have now ended it by making peace.

That was a victor's lie. Tamihana had tried to prevent a war that most of the Pakeha wanted. Only it wasn't called war, it was called a rebellion, because the Treaty of Waitangi said we were one people. Don't talk to me about he iwi tahi tatou just now. Let me grieve for my brother Tamihana, who was destroyed by men who preached a religion they did not observe, made laws which they did not keep, and arranged matters so that they could not lose.

Tamihana leased out vast acres to a Pakeha, Josiah Firth, and, reviled by his people, died in 1866 in the ruins of his deserted village. Within another twelve months Firth had converted his leases to freehold. His improvements to his property included a handsome blockhouse, right next to the house.

WE WERE PUNISHED for defending our right to our land with confiscation, but worse was the requirement that all Maori land be held under grant from the crown. Families used to hold rights to food resources on tribal land, but after 1867, when the Native Land Court was set up, ownership became a question of shares in a block. Every generation increased the number of owners, the shares became smaller and more scattered. People say you can tell Maori land by its lack of development. Sometimes that's true, but this is a situation which has been created by law.

My great-grandfather had a block of land of over 350 acres. When he died he left it to his twelve children. Their children numbered more than fifty.

In my generation, we number in the hundreds, all of us holding onto our turangawaewae with a steely grip. Anyone wanting to farm that land or even to put up a house on it, has a huge battle to get title to a piece big enough, to raise the money for the survey and to win the arguments with relatives who will oppose any land claim or succession order. We're still a confrontational people and arguments over land make old jealousies hatch out like huhu grubs. Some are defeated by the huge frustrations: they can't farm, they can't develop, can't consolidate shares, can't raise money on it. You'd be surprised how many family heads steeped in tradition sell land. Tamihana sold his people's birthright in his hopelessness, and it's still going on.

Wiremu Tamihana Tarapipipi Te Waharoa is not now remembered as well as the prophets who promised Maori people the earth if they lived in the spirit. Yet he has his legacy. It was Tamihana who consecrated the first King of Waikato in 1858, and who shaped the principles of the King Movement:

Te aroha, te ture, te whakapono.
Love, law and faith.

Today the Kingitanga is the identity of the Waikato people. It is a repository of custom and values, and a concept which makes space for individuals. It provides a unity which chiefs can no longer command. My grandmother's hapu, Ngaitamarawaho of Ngati Ranginui, are included in the first circle of King Movement tribes because we fought on the King's side. Every year we host the Maori Queen at our marae at Judea for the Poukai, a hui which keeps the relationship warm. The Queen's approach is heralded by her uniformed silver band. This is a tradition from the 1850s, when we felt independent enough to make a bit of Pakeha culture our own. Some of us today are trying to get back to a "pure" Maori culture, which makes you wonder if they've forgotten that their tipuna of the last two centuries ever lived.

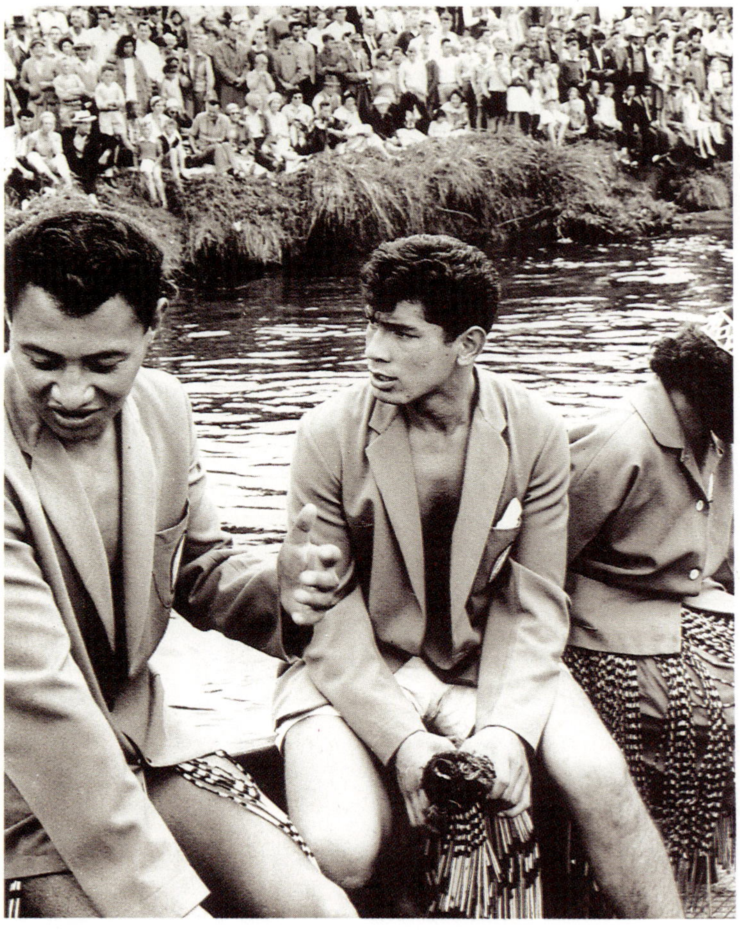

Contestants in the annual regatta at Ngaruawahia, early 1960s.

We used to go to Ngaruawahia, the home of the King Movement, for the summer regatta. When the power boats and canoes were racing on the river, all us kids would climb up on this big round steel thing to get a good look. I know what it is now. It's the turret from a British gunboat that cruised the river during the years of war. I'm not flattered by Pakeha attempts to rewrite the history of that war and make us the winners; we have our honour in defeat. The British were able to field an army of thousands, veterans of Crimea and India, backed up by artillery and naval forces. We struggled to put 600 soldiers in the field at any one time. Outnumbered, outgunned and out-organised, we were steamrolled by the war-machine of the greatest military power on earth.

But moral victories shape a people too. At the Gate Pa, Ngaiterangi and their allies fought under a code of laws devised by Henare Taratoa. The laws protected the captured, wounded or unarmed, and, most touchingly, the man overcome with fear:

Rule 3. The soldier who flees, being carried away by his fears, and goes to the house of the priest with his gun (even though carrying arms) will be saved; I will not go there.

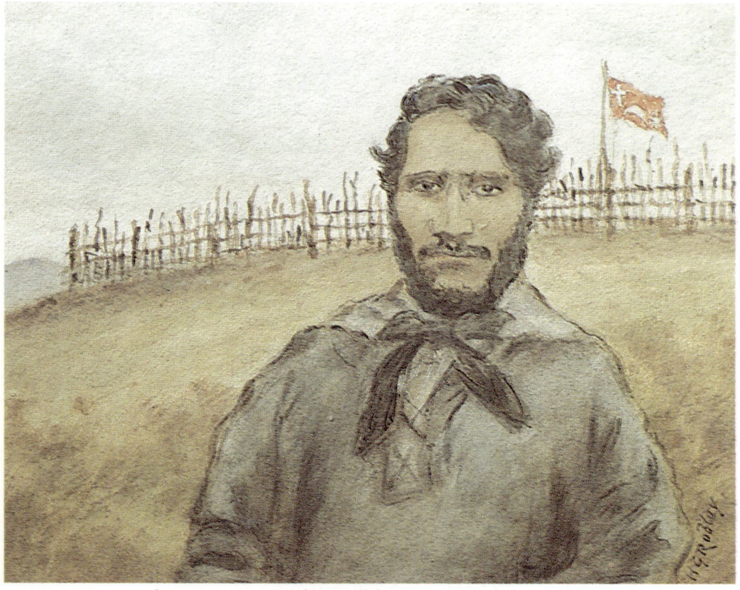

AUCKLAND INSTITUTE AND MUSEUM

Henare Taratoa, by Horatio Gordon Robley.

"Ngaiterangi kupu tahi" – Ngaiterangi of the one word, Ngaiterangi the Upright. In victory, Ngaiterangi were true to their proverb, and Gate Pa is best remembered now because during the night and at great risk the Maori soldiers tended the wounded Pakeha who lay about the battlefield. This is the story I wasn't told at school: *that my ancestors routed the British at Gate Pa and were merciful in victory.* But Ngaiterangi were crushed, Christians and heathens together, when we next faced the British at Te Ranga, and Henare Taratoa died with his rules pinned to his shirt.

WE DID NOT TURN AWAY from God in the 1860s, because by then our spiritual life depended on Christian belief. But the war meant that we needed to think more independently about religion, for while we had been welcomed into the Christian family with the news that God belonged to everyone, he turned out to be on the other side:

The Gospel is a scabbard for the sword. These men showed us this beautiful scabbard, all adorned with gold and jewels and we admired it, and hung it up in our whare, and then came a man in a red coat, and took it down to look at it, and, all of a sudden, drew a sword out of it and cut off our heads.

A feeling of betrayal shaped all the Bible-based movements that proclaimed Maori independence – the Hauhau faith, Tariao, the Ringatu church and the teachings of the Parihaka prophets, Te Whiti and Tohu. In the Old Testament we found the story of a tribal people like ourselves from which we could draw inspiration and identity. Conquered, dispossessed and declining, we yet had hope in the promises of God. Te Ua Haumene, the prophet of the Hauhau, said:

God has told me twice that his lowly, naked-standing people in the half-standing land shall be restored, even to that which was given unto Abraham, for this is Israel!

Israel and Canaan, the chosen people and the Promised Land. Te Whiti said it, Te Kooti Rikirangi said it, Rua Kenana said it. Formerly when a calamity befell a hapu, their name became tapu, and they would take another until the tapu was lifted. It's as if being Maori became tapu in the wars of the 1860s and we took refuge in a new identity which healed our wounds. The loss of land was transformed into a vision of paradise, and our bleak future was remade into the certainty of deliverance:

Te Whiti says that the great power and lordship of Israel has come to pass. The white skin is vanquished. The black skin will ascend, and the Maori will have wealth. The Pakeha will have nothing!

Waiting for deliverance was a balm which helped us survive defeat, but it was a trap in the end. By 1900 the followers of the King Movement in Waikato, Te Whiti and Tohu in Taranaki and Te Kooti on the East Coast, were among the poorest and most helpless Maori in the country. Choosing to turn our backs on the Pakeha world did not stop its power in Maori life, but just our ability to cope with it.

I CAN'T SEE THE SHAPE of the present clearly. All this century our lives have become more and more like those of the Pakeha. I think that this is the only thing I can say which will still be true at the next anniversary. It's hardly a fashionable view. But if you look at the work of the great leaders of Maori society this century – Te Puea, for example, who revived Waikato pride, or Ratana, who revitalised Maori Christianity, or at the great events to which we responded – the two world wars and the migration to the cities are the most significant – the end result is the same: *our lives have become more like those of the Pakeha.*

But most of us are still poor because we haven't got the education. Creating an education system that works

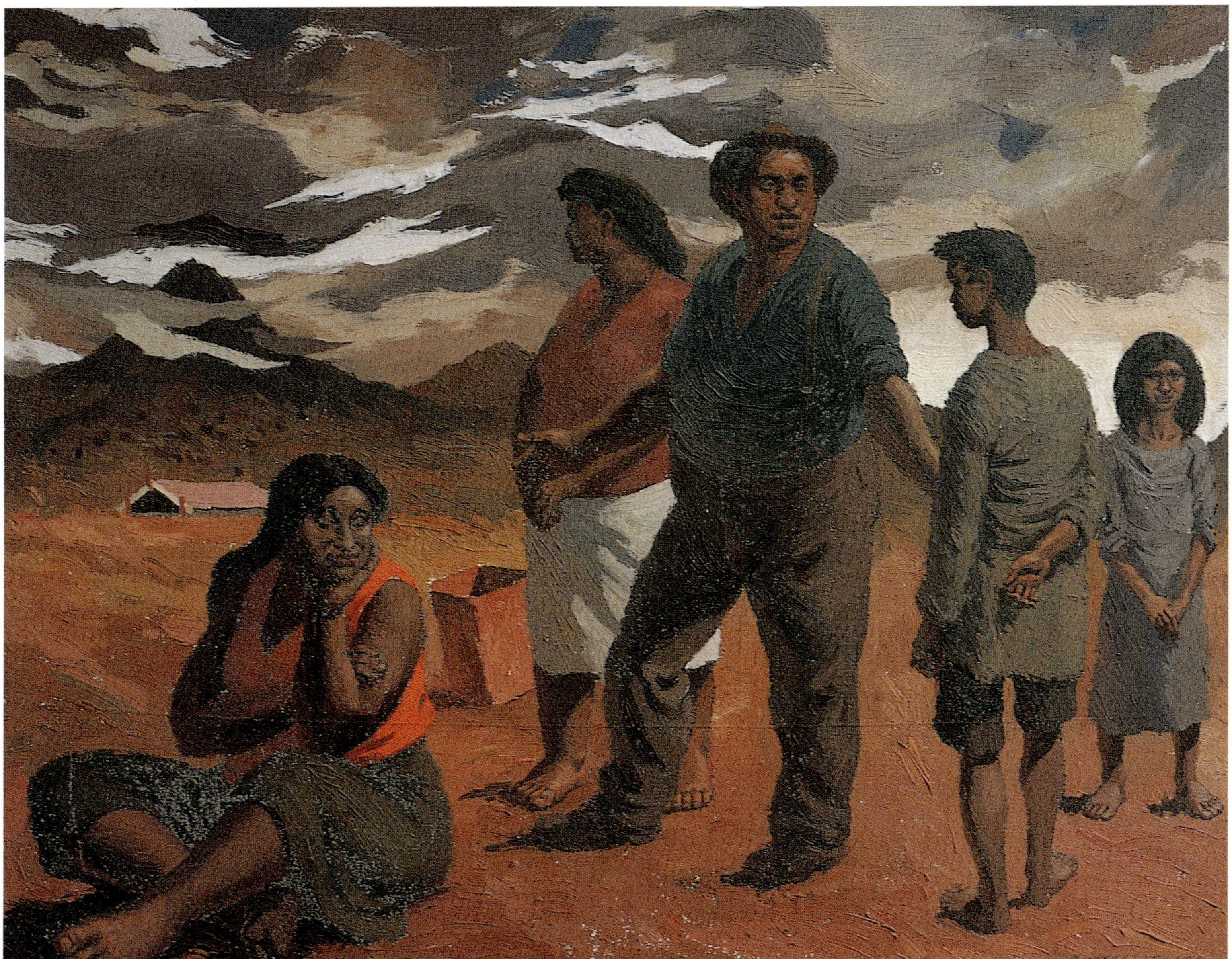

SHIRLEY SMITH COLLECTION

Manihera's Family, ca 1950-51, oil by Russell Clark.

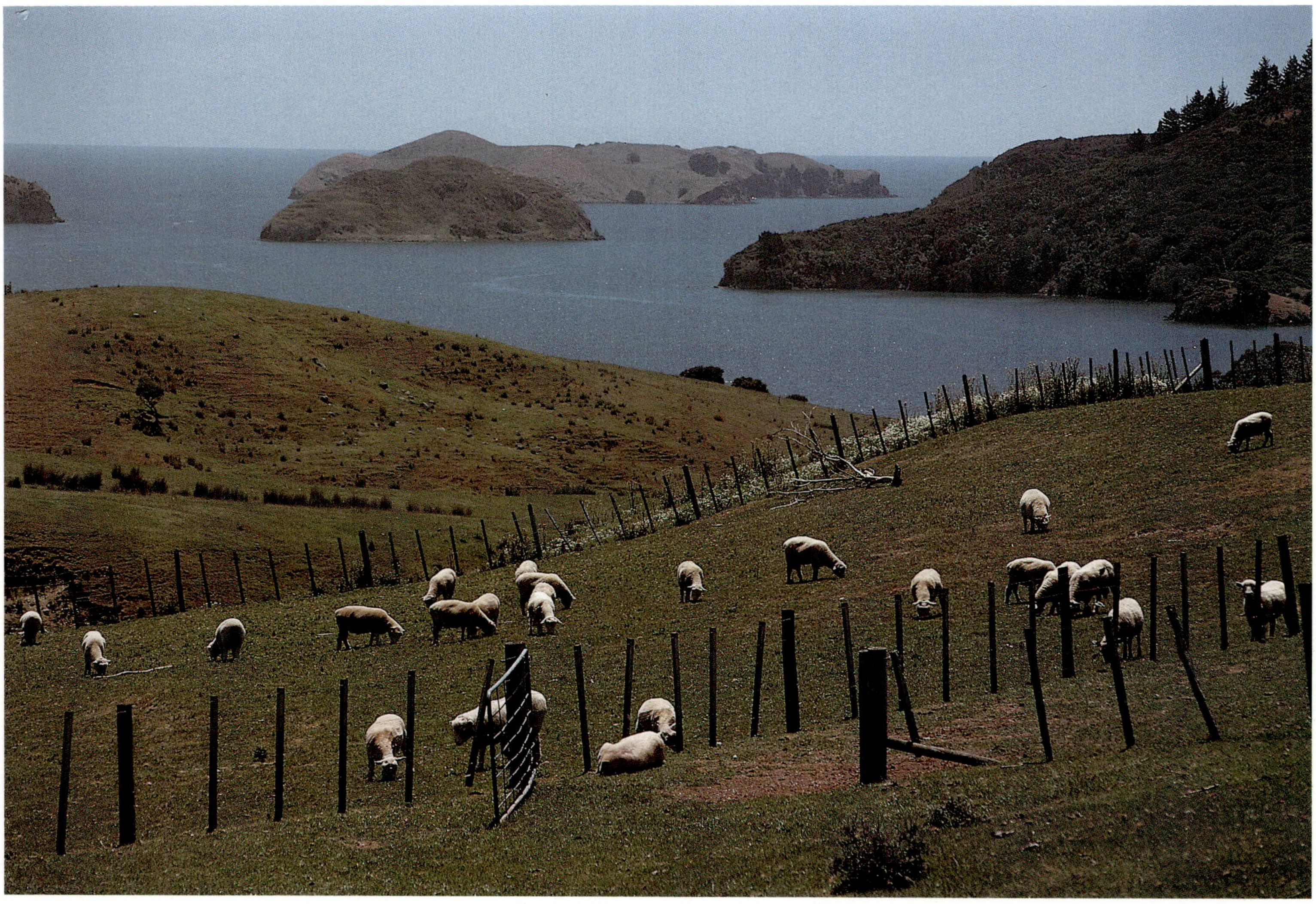

Manaia, Coromandel — ROBIN MORRISON

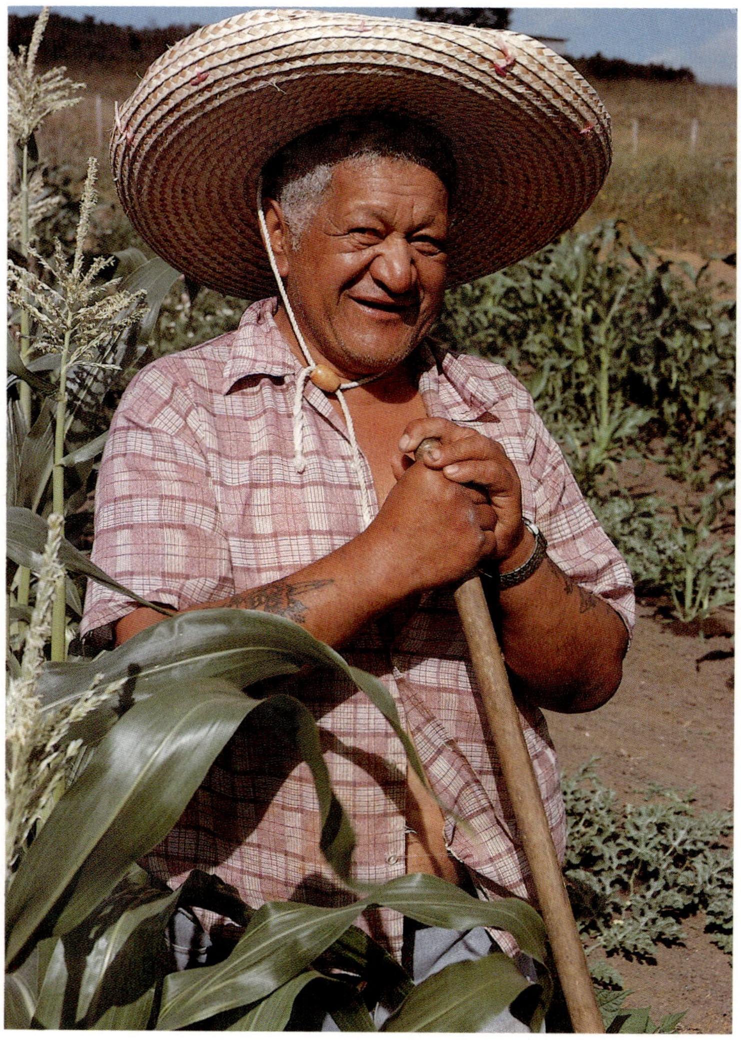

Kingi Mikaere,
father of Buddy Mikaere, at Manaia — ROBIN MORRISON

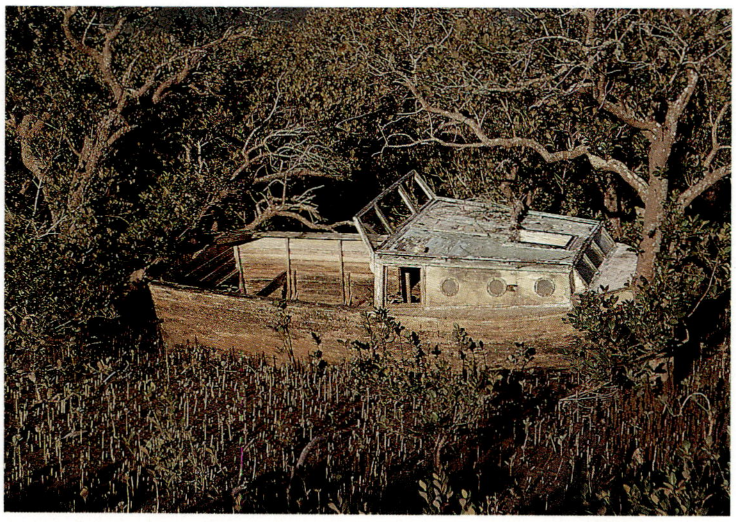

Manaia — ROBIN MORRISON

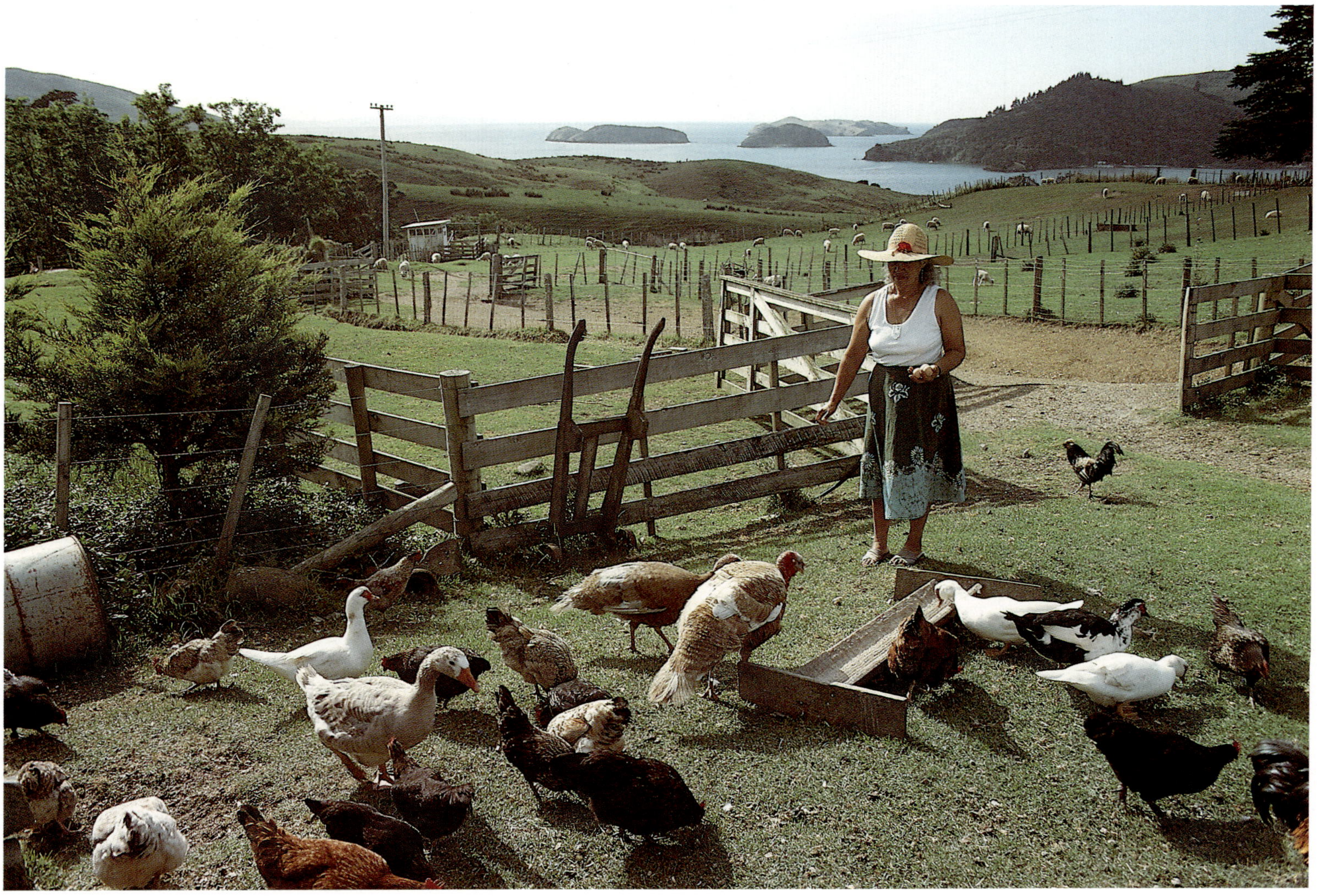

Buddy Mikaere's mother, Ada, feeding the hens at Manaia

ROBIN MORRISON

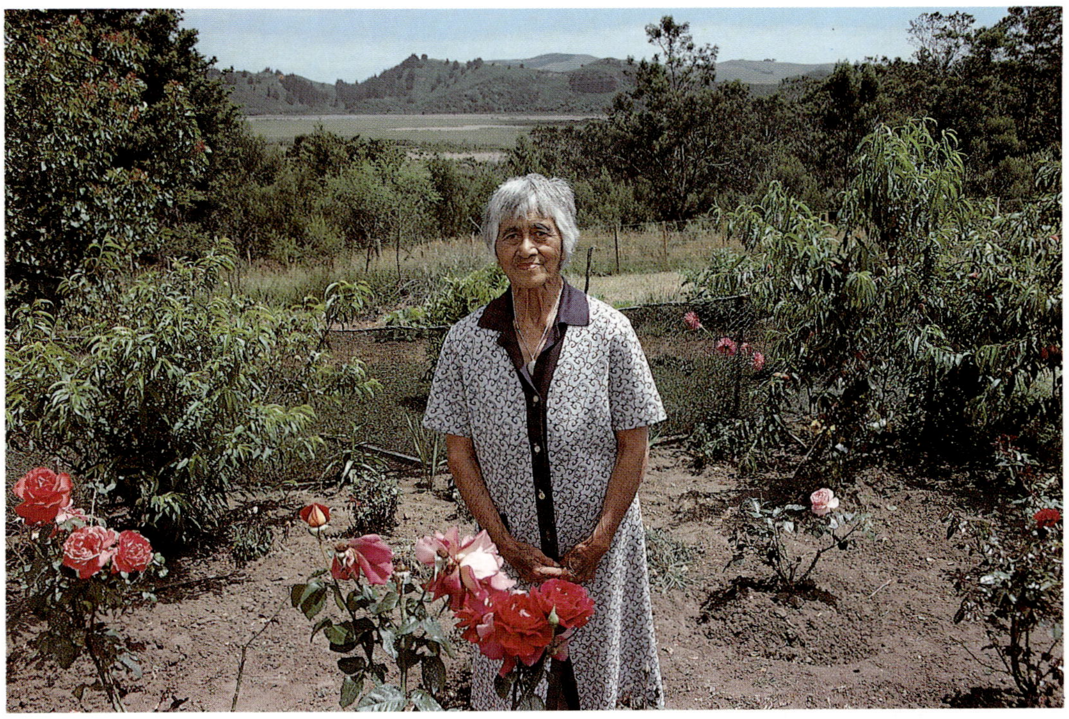

Te Oriwa (Olive) Forsman, Ngati Pukenga, Manaia, 1901-1989
". . . our old people die here with dignity." Haere ra e kui.

ROBIN MORRISON

the tip of the peninsula, the blue bulk of Moehau shoulders the horizon – the burial mountain of chiefs and heroes. To the south are the remnant forests of the Manaia sanctuary, where the last of the kokako sing to the last of the giant kauri.

In the bush below the fortress is the cave where our bones lie, and a landslide has uncovered a great midden of shells several feet thick on the slopes of the pa. Down by my father's bach is the little hollow where my great-grandfather, Taoki, had his whare, and that little terrace on the hillside, sited to catch groundwater, is where he grew kumara. The deep narrow foot-track winding through the manuka stands is the daily path he and others walked to fetch springwater. The humble little basalt adzes which I keep in a drawer were found by my mother under the Manaia blackberries.

When I pick up these adzes, they speak of the unbridgeable gulf between my ancestors and me. But if I hold them long enough, they start to spin a dream of the people who make me real.

Ko Aotearoa te whenua e mihi ana au.
Tihei mauri ora! □

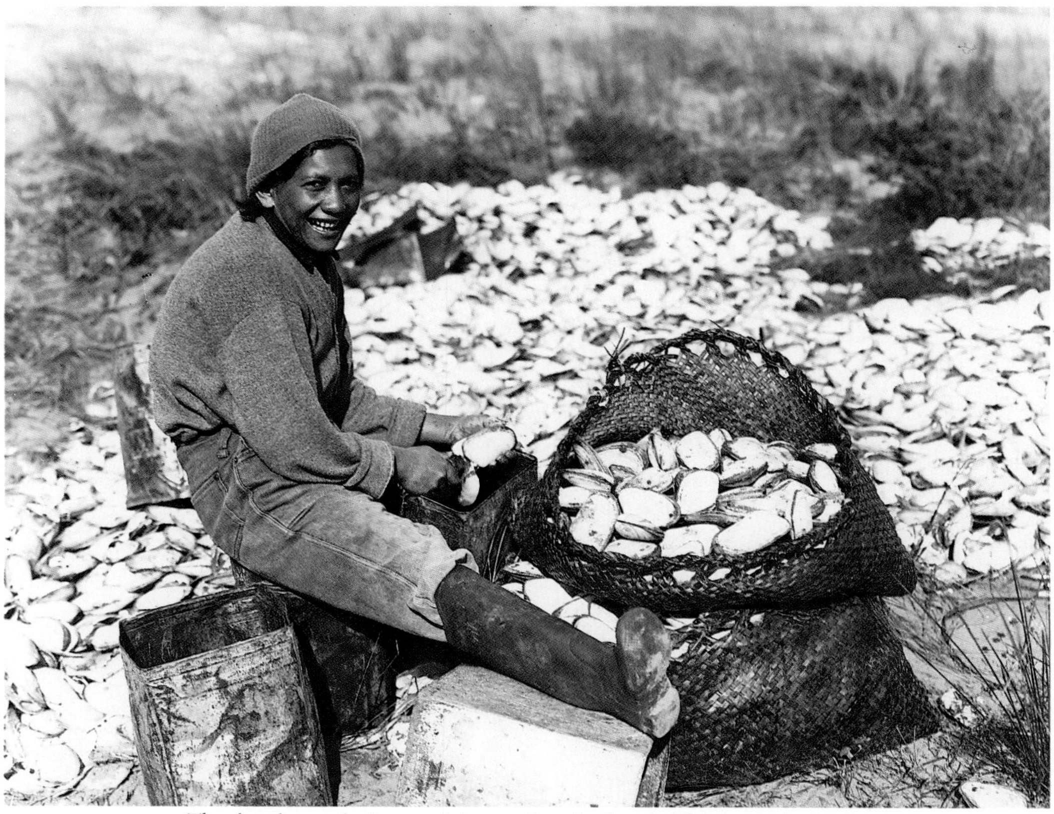

The abundance of toheroa, pipi, mussels and other shellfish is seen in the deep middens which punctuate the coast in many parts of New Zealand.

for Maori is maybe our biggest challenge, so that we can be both Maori and full members of society. And no, I don't think changing the language of education, its cultural content or the colour of the teacher is the key. We need to want to succeed again, as much as we used to in, say, 1850, when a higher percentage of Maori than Pakeha in the country could read and write.

Sir Apirana Ngata dominated Maori education policy for much of this century. Apirana was a glittering academic success, in an uncompromisingly Pakeha education system. This gave him great personal security, but it made him look at his relations like an educated Pakeha of the times, and from that point of view he concluded that most Maori children could never make it. He decided that they should be trained for a life of rural subsistence, housewives and farmers, and generations of school kids grew up without any goals outside their own community: boys and girls expected to live the same lives as their fathers and mothers, and for them the house of learning had no doors.

MY FATHER GOT TO STANDARD TWO aged twelve in 1940. By that time he felt big enough to stand up to his father so he left home and went to work for local farmers. Forty years on, he still points out to me ditches which he dug by hand and the straight fences he put up steep hillsides. My mother left with her Proficiency.

My parents married as teenagers. For a living they gathered Jew's Ear and sold it to the Chinese storekeeper in Coromandel. They picked blackberries into kerosene tins. They gathered kauri gum, packing it through the bush on their backs because the horse couldn't get up the creek bed. They shot pigs and pigeon for food. One of my first memories is being put into the branches of a tree while my mother shot a sow that had been bailed up by our fox terrier.

When I was a baby we lived in a tent in the scrub. My mother cooked on an open fire in a billy made from a milk powder tin. We sometimes walked the twenty miles to town, and on the way home we would sleep in a cave near the roadside. That was before my father got his Indian motorbike with no brakes. He'd stop at the top of our hill, cut a big manuka branch and tie it on and fly down the road in a cloud of dust. Cars would queue up at the bottom because they thought the dust meant the cream truck was coming.

My parents had a hard life in the 1950s, the decade we're told when New Zealand really was God's own. That's why they eventually moved to town, and joined the national economy: it was a better way. Neither of them yearns for the old days, and they tried hard to save their children from repeating them. I am their eldest. When I was born they made a pact to swear off alcohol forever, and they still don't drink.

I've reached an age to be thoughtful, and I think of the shape of the future. Assertiveness, independence, the ability to change, are the qualities which shaped our traditional culture and which saw us through cataclysmic change. They are human qualities which may or may not continue to wear a Maori cloak. Our culture will flourish as long as the Maori who live in towns – three-quarters of us – need it to. We have to need it enough to stand for it against the rush of life. The support we need from the government is to sort out the laws and policies which have made it hard to be both Maori and a full member of society. Then maybe we could shed the anxiety complex which makes some of us deeply conservative, and others, extreme.

Pakeha society has its own conservatism, but it's early days, and as a nation there's hope for us yet. We all cheer the All Blacks' haka. We want long-haired women wearing swinging grass skirts to tell the world who we are at trade shows. It's Maori culture Pakeha define themselves with when they try to express pride of country, because there's something in their hearts that belongs not to England, but to Aotearoa.

Kia ora koutou, e aku whanaunga!
Noho mai i konei, kia korero ai tatou ki a tatou ano.

Greetings, my relations!
Sit down here so we can talk together.

One thing we should talk about is how the loosening of ties with our tipuna, Great Britain, has made some Pakeha feel insecure all alone and 12,000 miles away. Western thinking has changed a lot since 1840, and cultural history, not conquest, is now considered the moral basis of sovereignty. Our history here is more than one thousand years old and so we Maori are the guardians of a treasure which Pakeha cannot have except by our gift – the gift of belonging. Friends, it is blessed to receive.

I COME FROM MANAIA, a small settlement at the head of Manaia Harbour on the western side of Coromandel Peninsula. The people I belong to, Ngati Pukenga, are members of Te Tini-o-Awa, who sailed to Aotearoa in the Mataatua canoe. Toroa, its captain, was the great-grandfather of Pukenga our ancestor. We have lived here at Manaia since the seventeenth century.

We gained the land as a reward for fighting in the ranks of Ngati Maru of Hauraki. We were a small tribe who battled hard to gain a foothold in a land desired by many. One of our strategies to achieve it was to fight as mercenaries in other people's wars. Many tribes claim victory over us, from Ngapuhi to Tuwharetoa. But there is also a list of their defeats.

On 29 January 1832, less than one hundred Ngati Pukenga men, women and children under their chief Nainai faced a great war-party of Ngati Haua, Ngati Maniapoto and Ngaiterangi soldiers at Maketu in the western Bay of Plenty. The situation Ngati Pukenga faced was hopeless and Nainai said to his people:

Let me die on my land.

And the whole hapu knew to run meant dishonour; it would be better to die. Battle was joined and by nightfall, Pukenga-ki-Maketu had ceased to exist. Nainai was beheaded on the thwarts of his own canoe.

The lands that the morehu of Ngati Pukenga hold at Manaia are precious because of the blood we spilt. My mother's father carried the name Maketu in memory of the fallen soldiers of Pukenga. But the blood does not make Manaia a graveyard. Manaia is a place to live in a world where for many Maori there seems to be no place. Maori are the majority here. For my kids it means a holiday, but our old people die here with dignity.

There are reminders everywhere. I can see on the skyline above the valley the Tomo, the rock fortress, still standing guard. When the day is clear, you can stand on the top defences and command a warrior's view. Towards

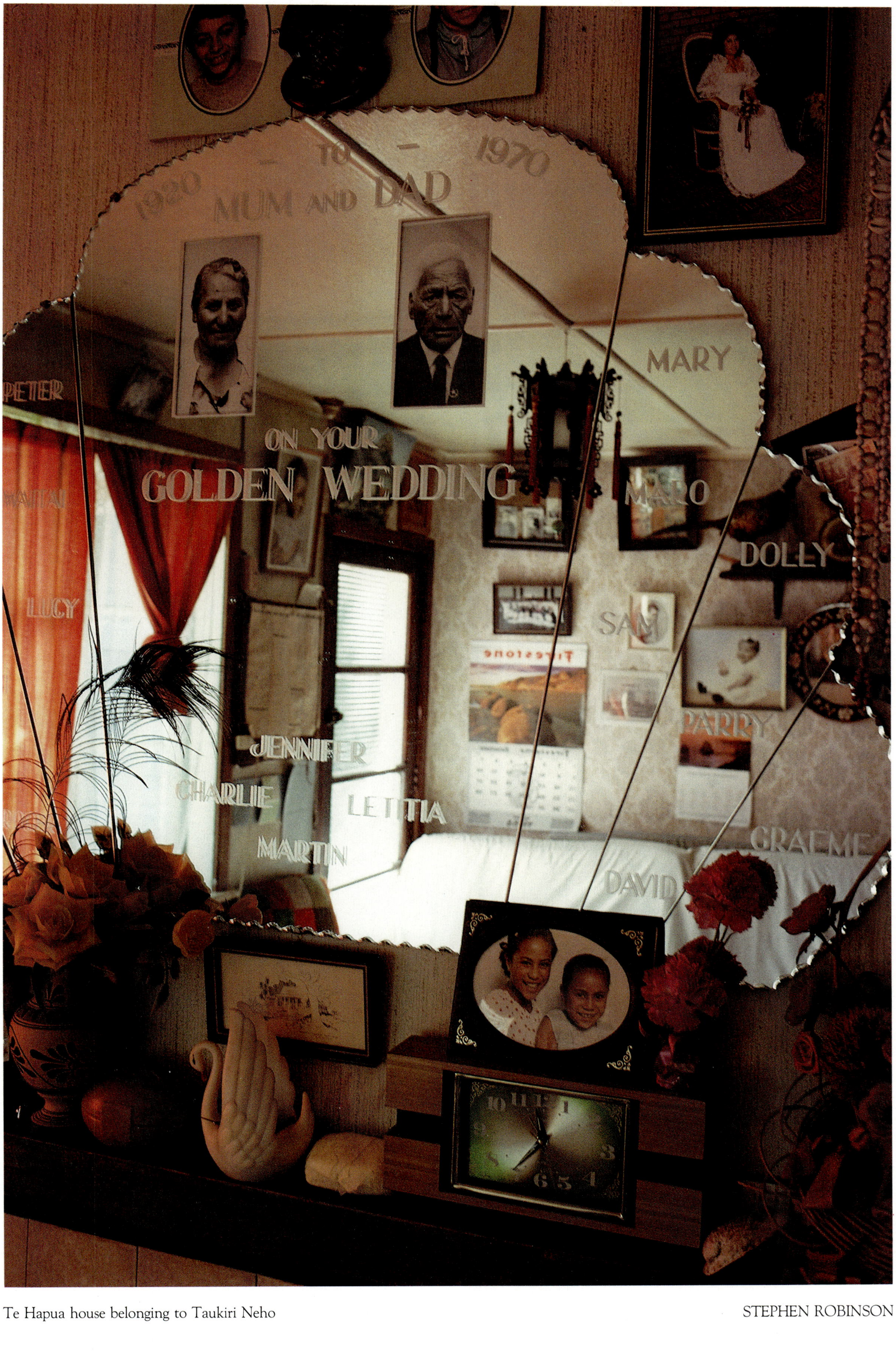

Te Hapua house belonging to Taukiri Neho

STEPHEN ROBINSON

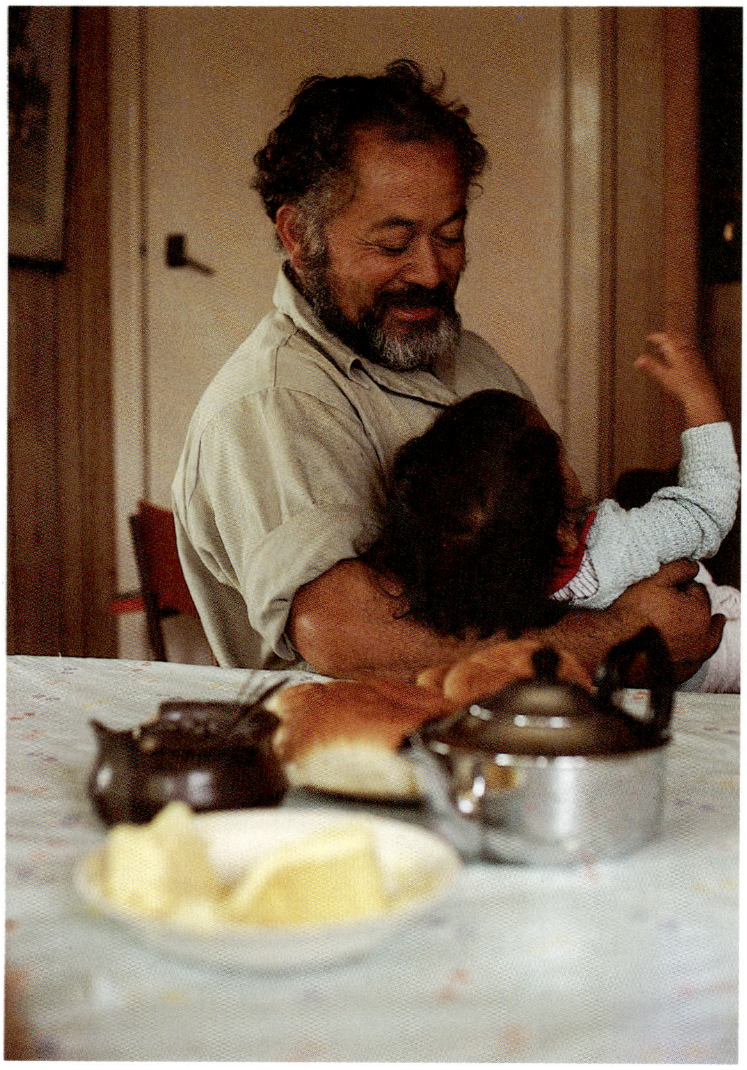

Walter Anderson with grandchild, Waitomo — STEPHEN ROBINSON

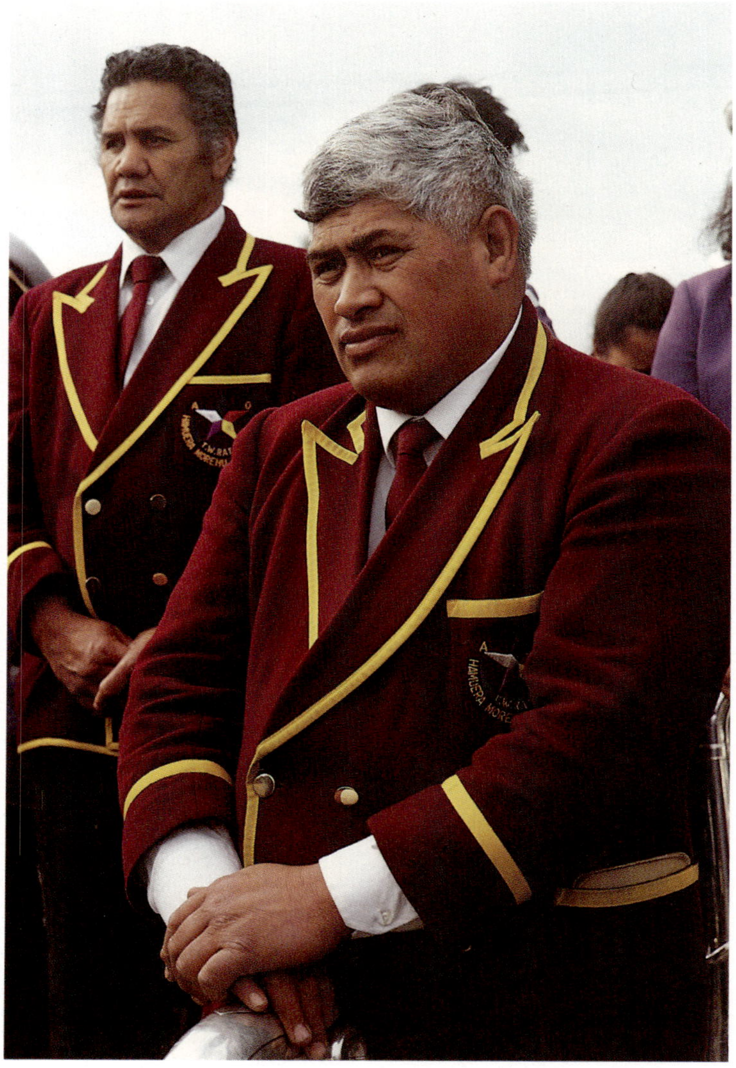

Ratana Band, Turangawaewae Marae, Ngaruawahia — ERIC TAYLOR

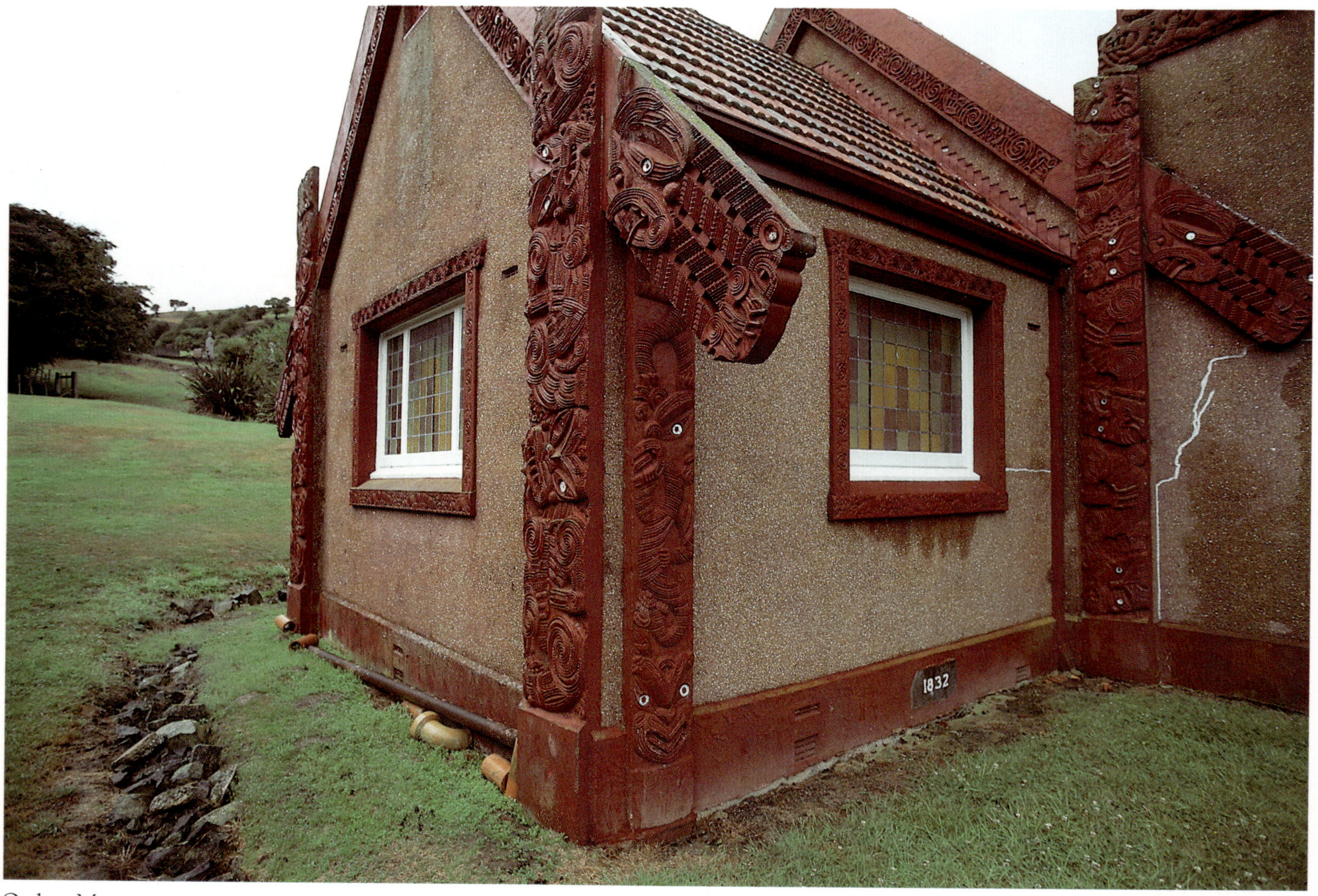

Otakau Marae — GEOFF MASON

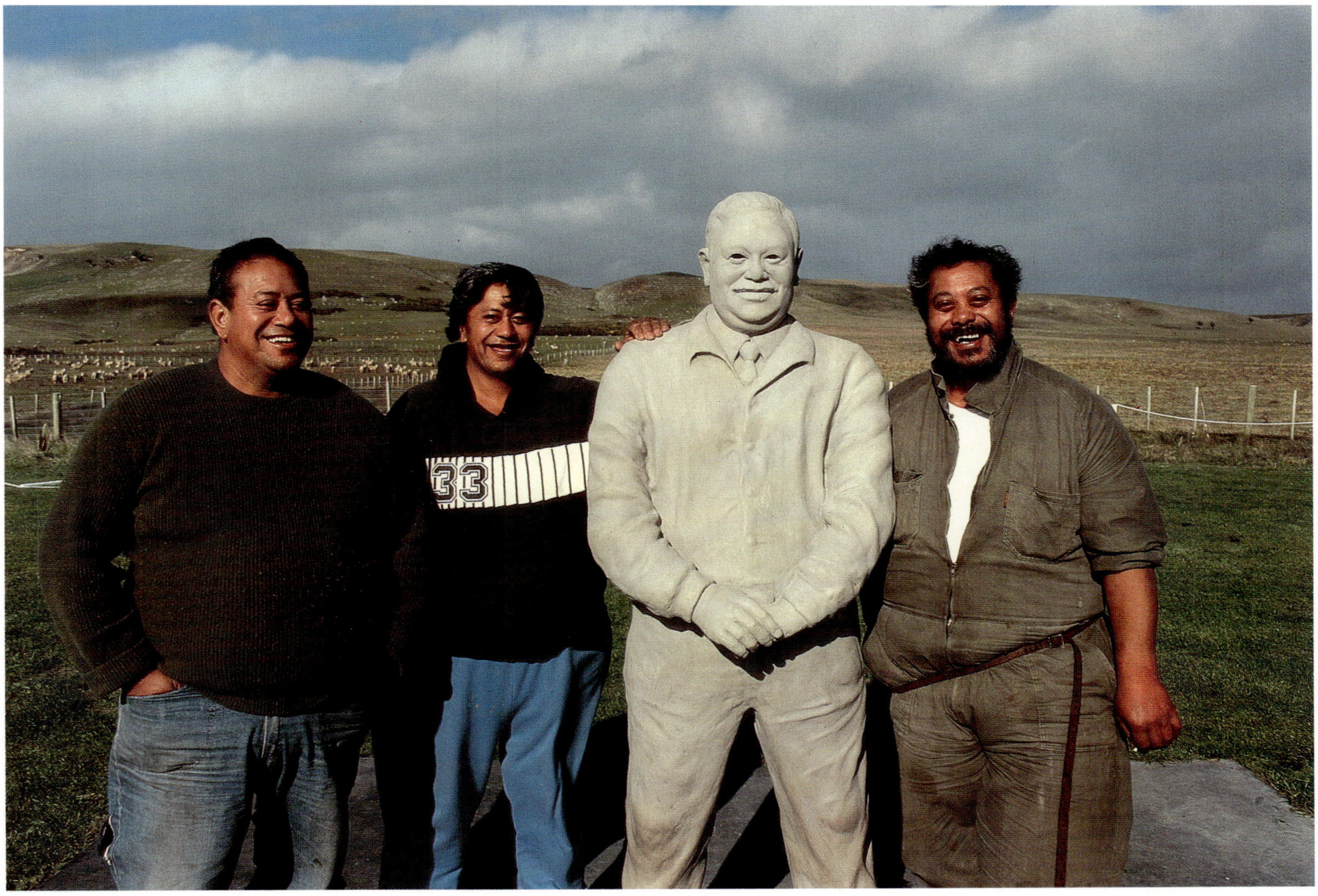

Tommy, Denis and Garry Solomon, with the statue of their grandfather Tommy Solomon, the last full-blooded Moriori, Chatham Islands

ROBIN MORRISON

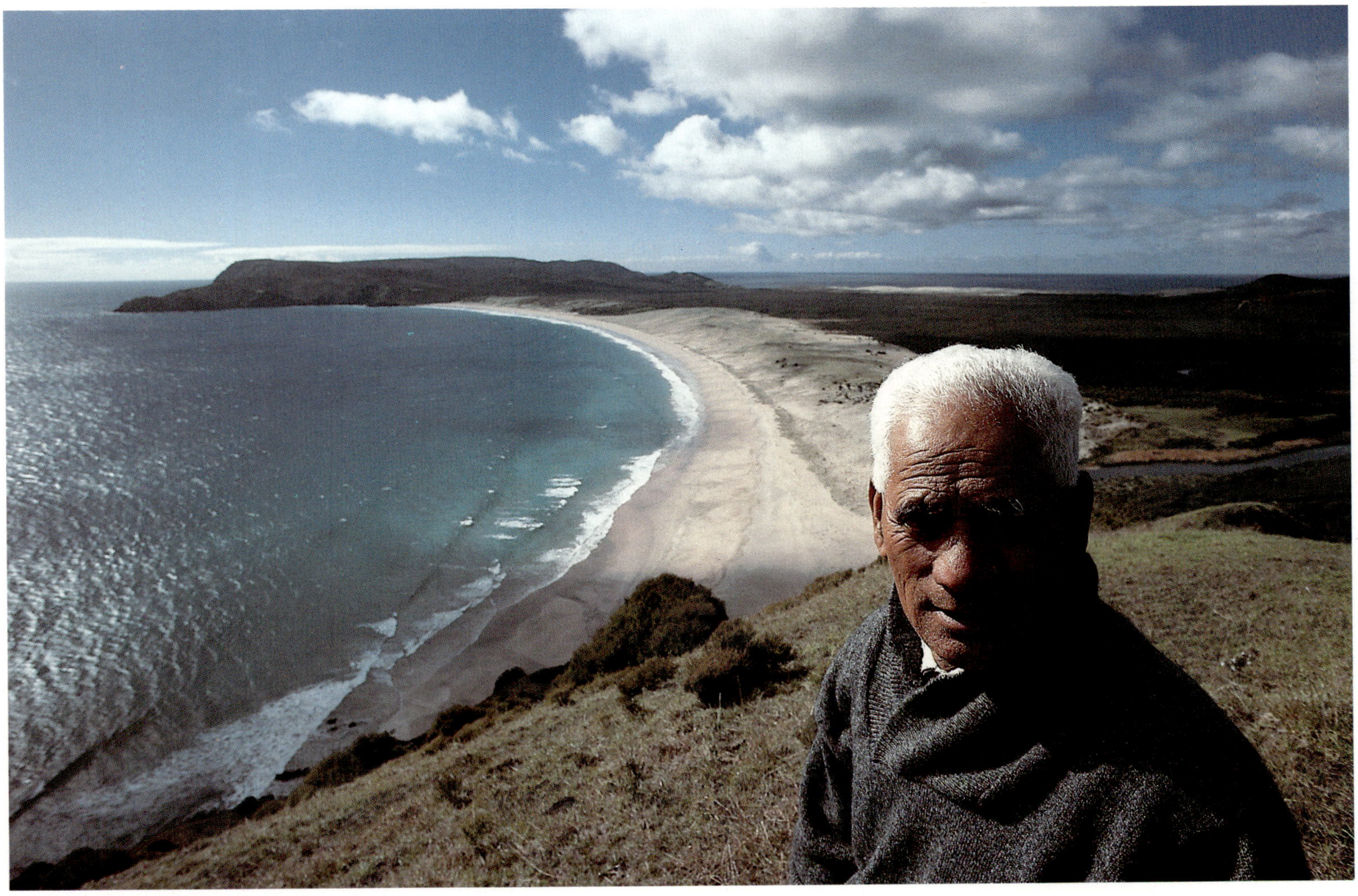

Whio Motu at Waitangi Pa site, Tom Bowling Bay, Far North

STEPHEN ROBINSON

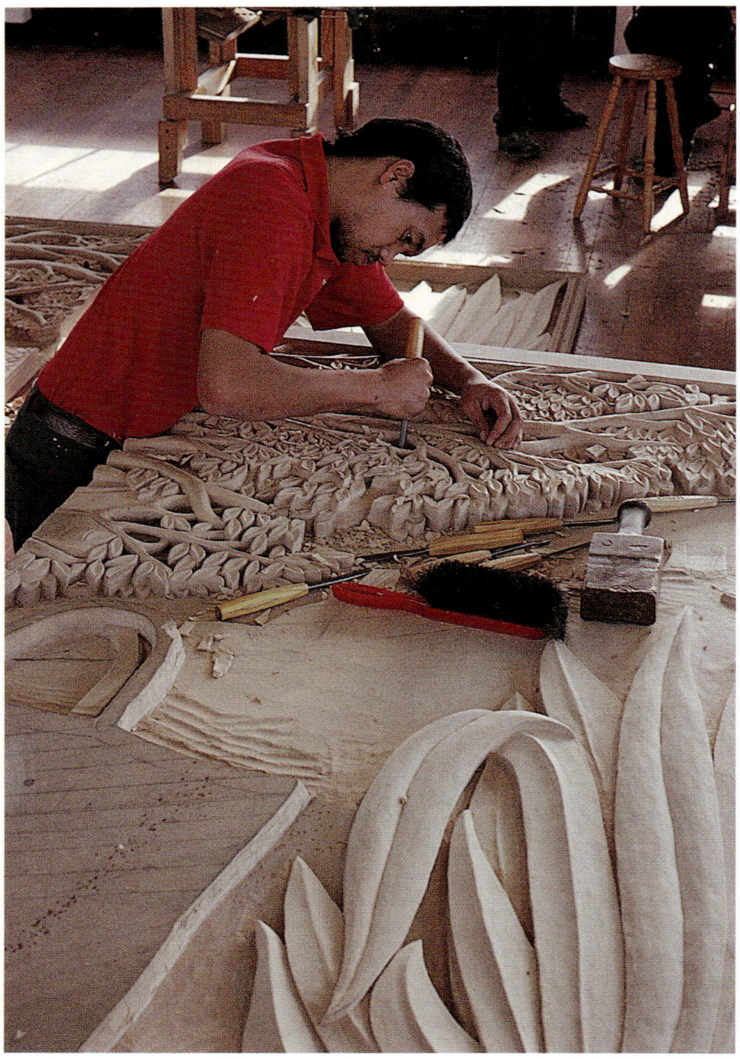

Maori Arts and Crafts Institute, Whakarewarewa — CRAIG POTTON

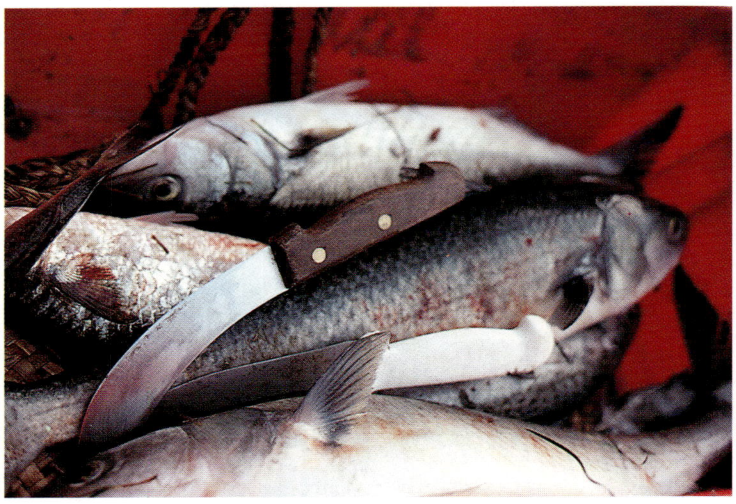

Fish for breakfast, Te Hapua — STEPHEN ROBINSON

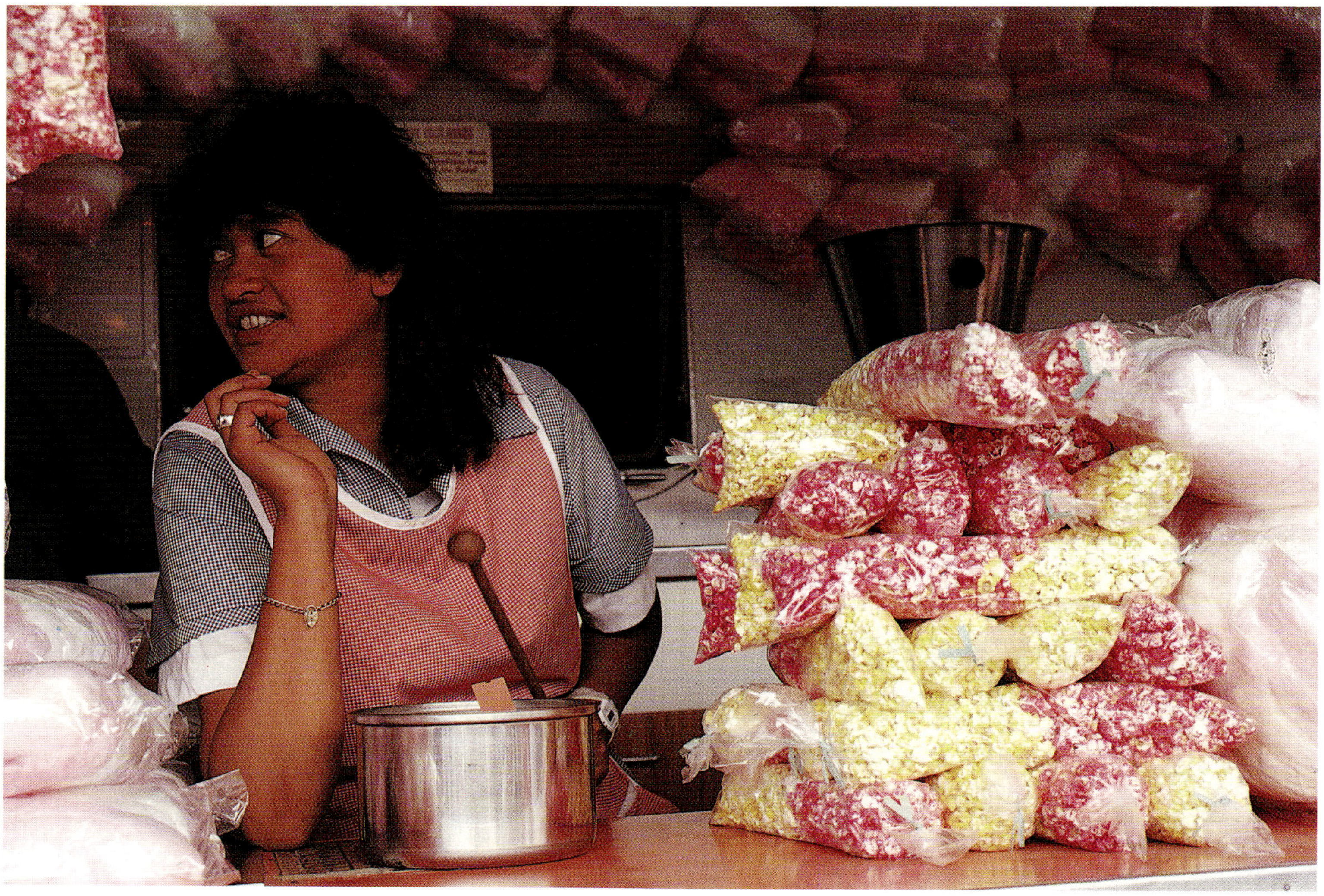

Candy floss stand, Easter Show, Auckland — ERIC TAYLOR

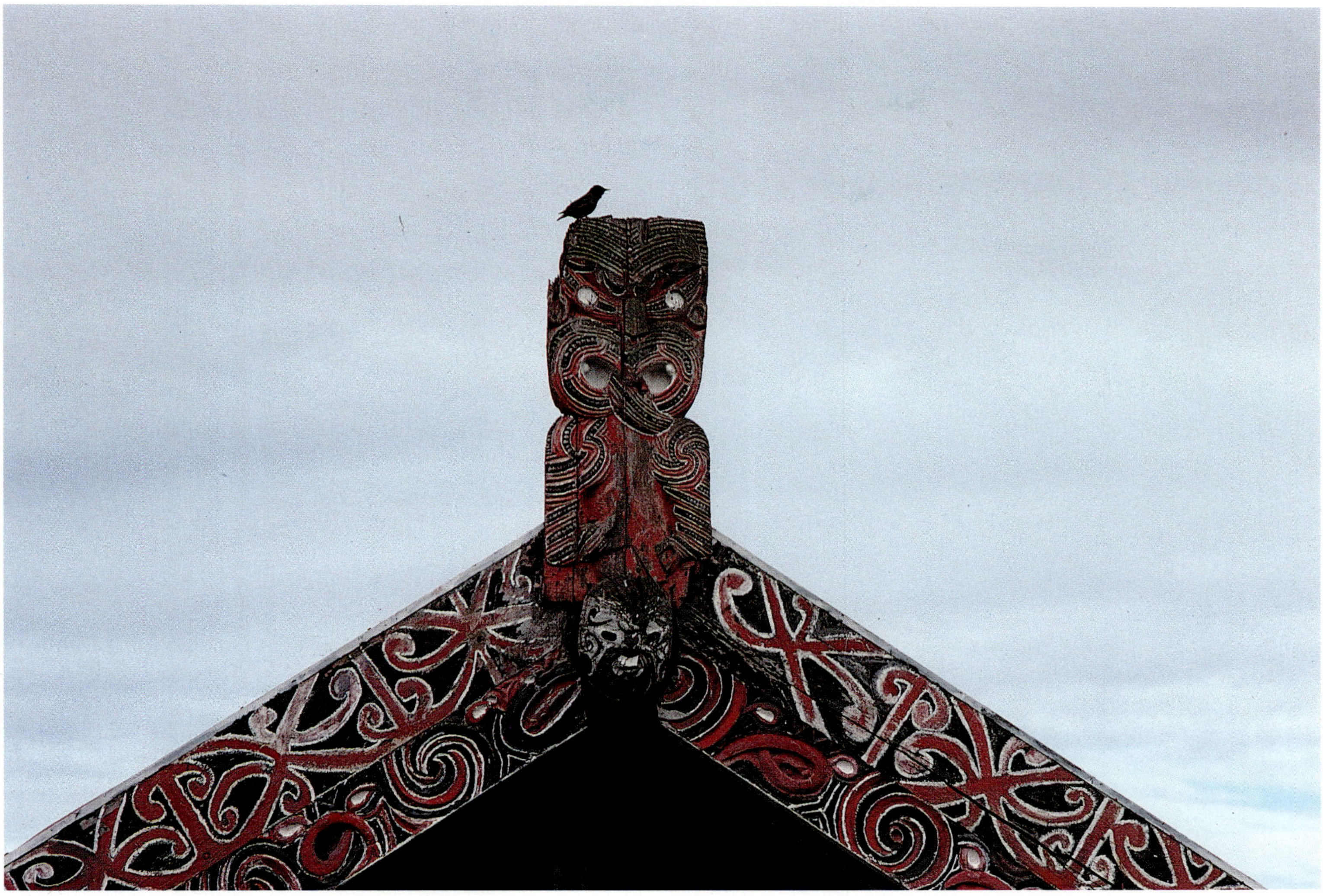

Ratana CRAIG POTTON

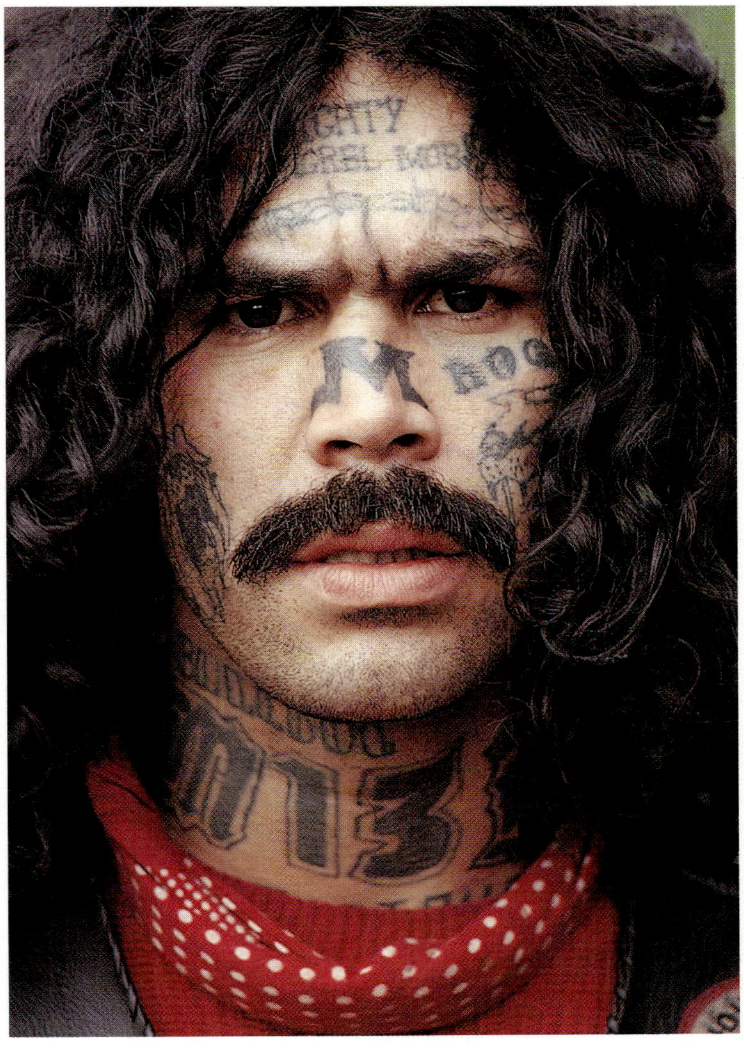

"Doc", Mongrel Mob, Ngaruawahia ERIC TAYLOR

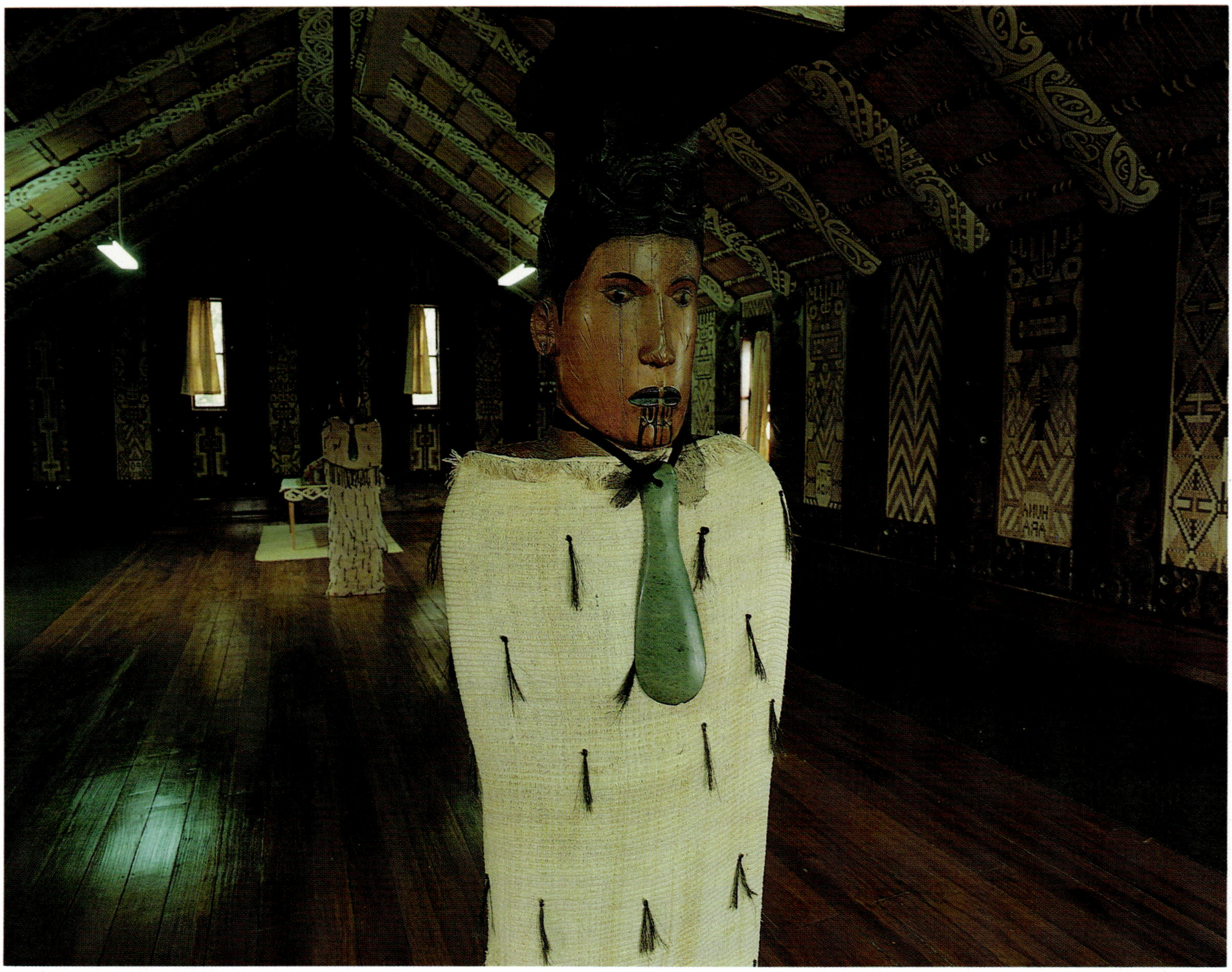

Ngati Porou's Poroutangi Meeting House, Ruatoria, East Cape — CRAIG POTTON

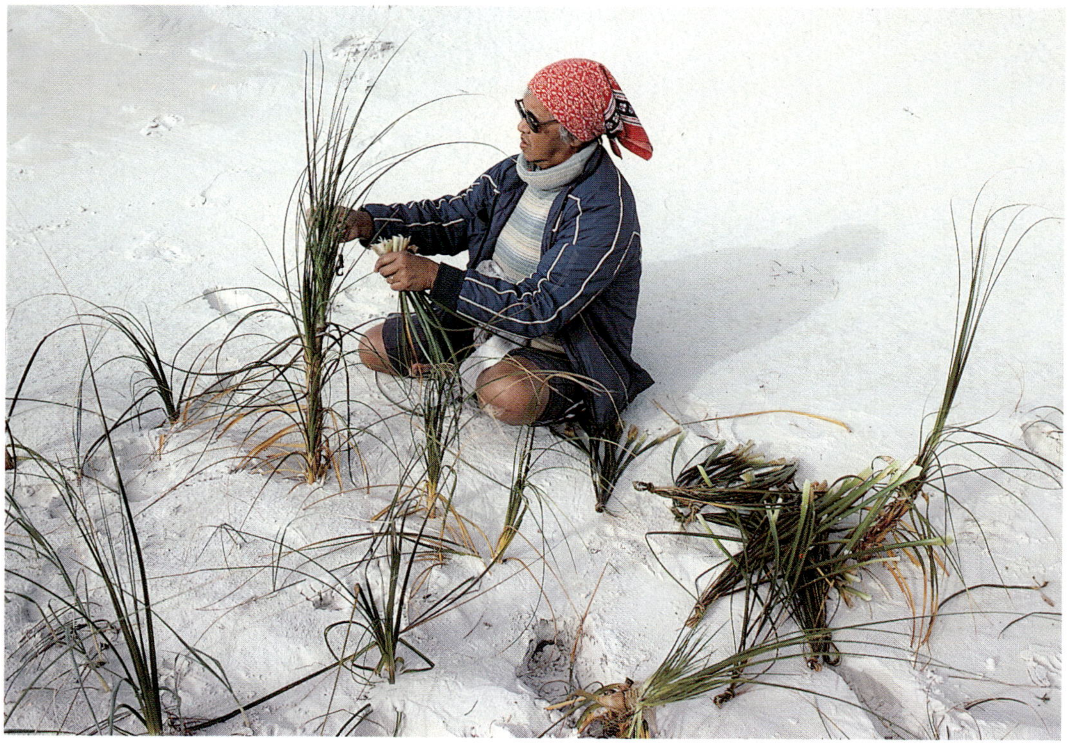

Rangi Motu with pingao, Te Hapua — STEPHEN ROBINSON

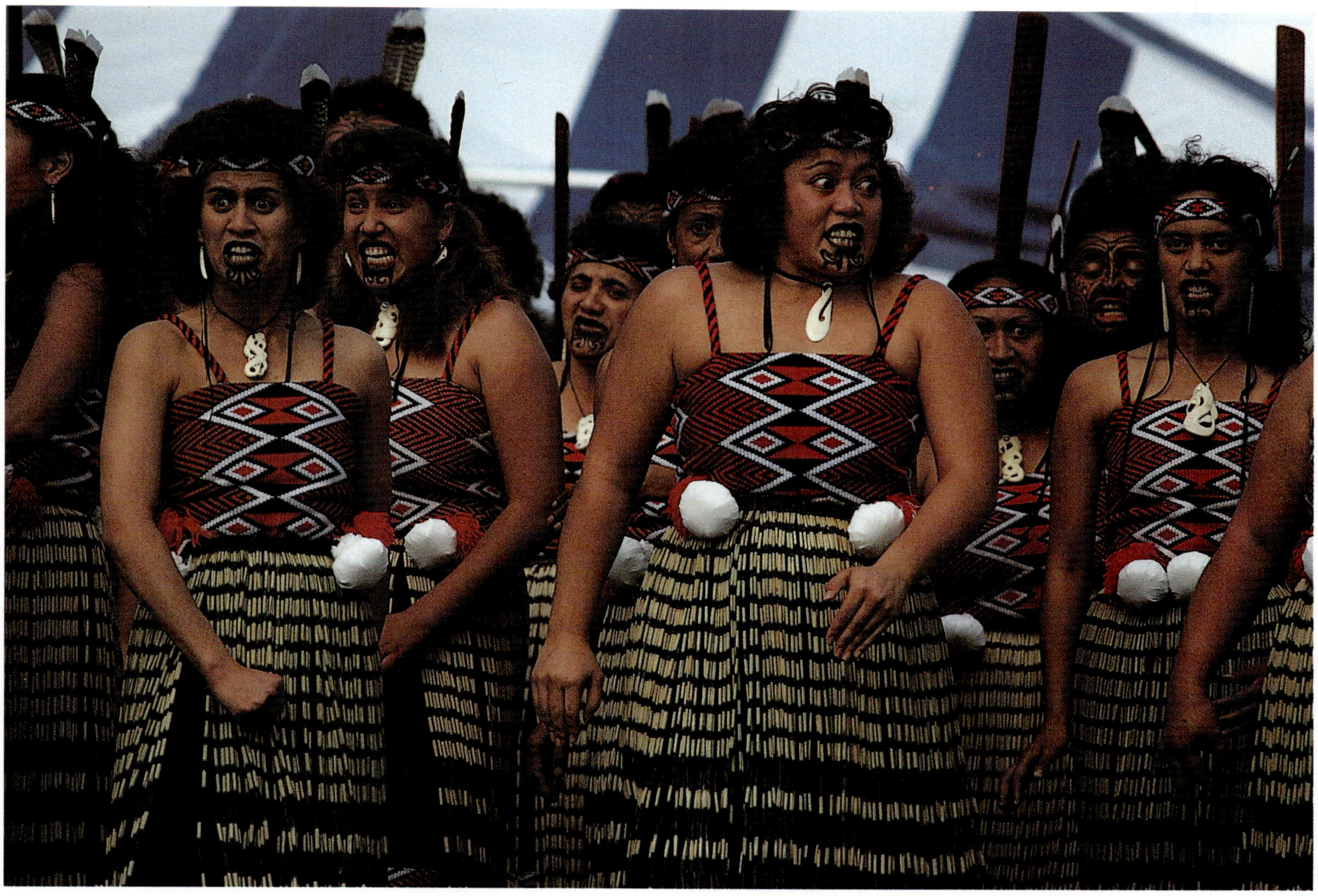

Concert at Turangawaewae Marae, Ngaruawahia ERIC TAYLOR

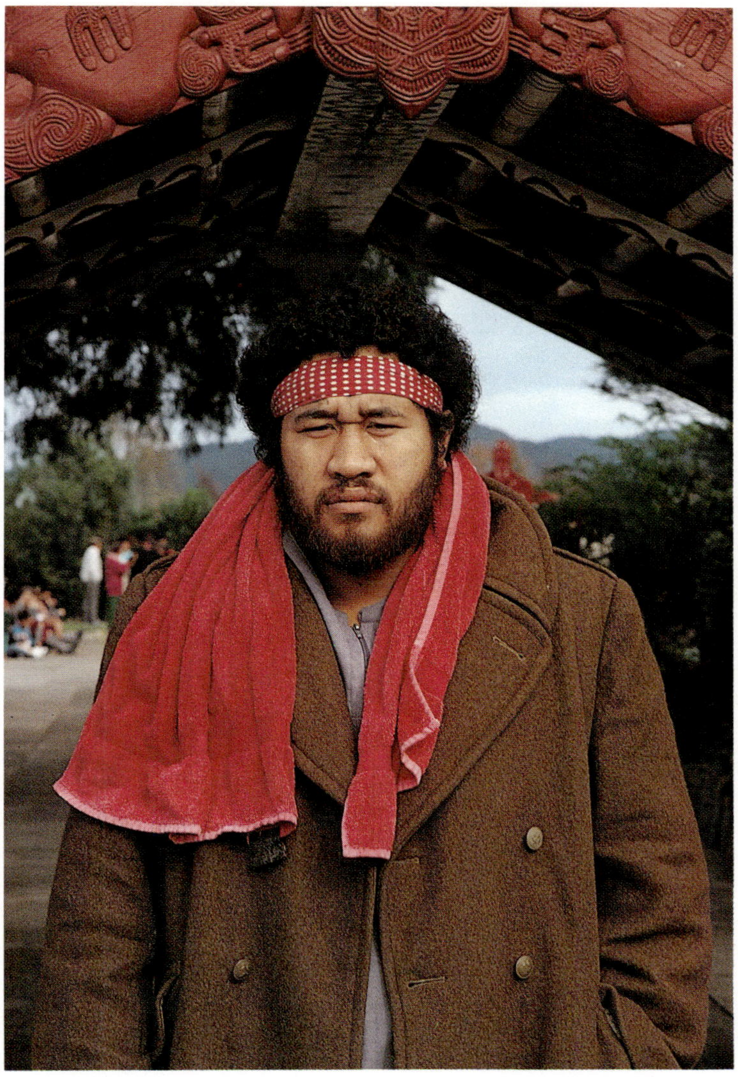

Ngaruawahia ERIC TAYLOR

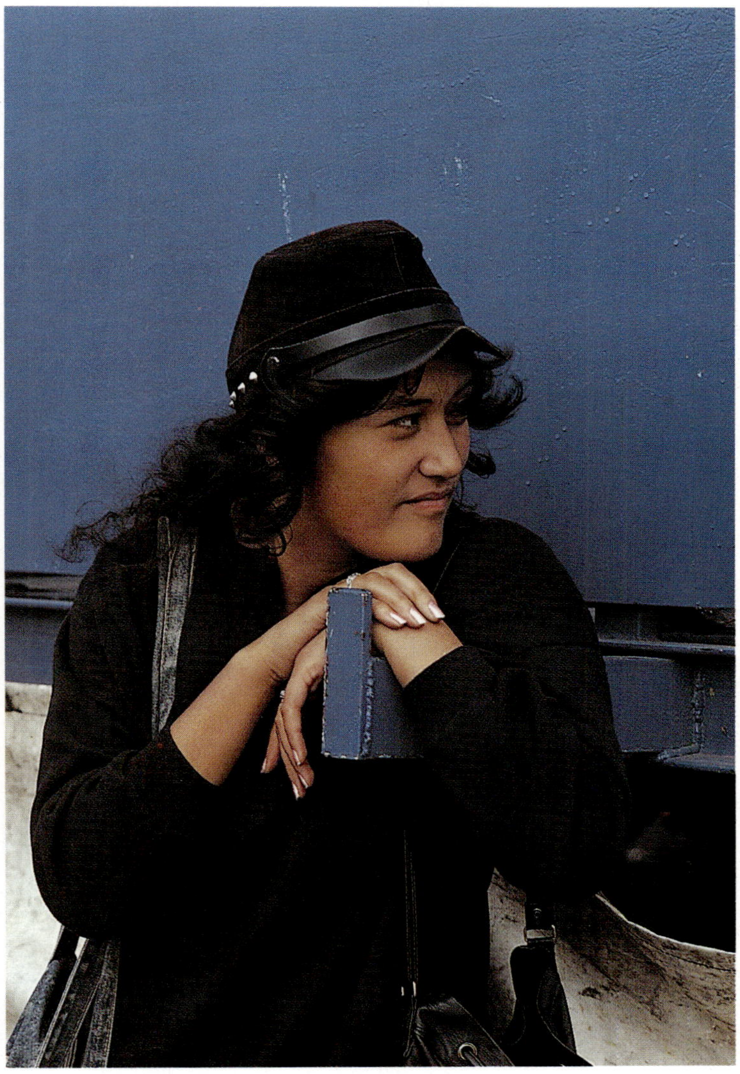

Spectator, Easter Show ERIC TAYLOR

THE PAKEHA INHERITANCE

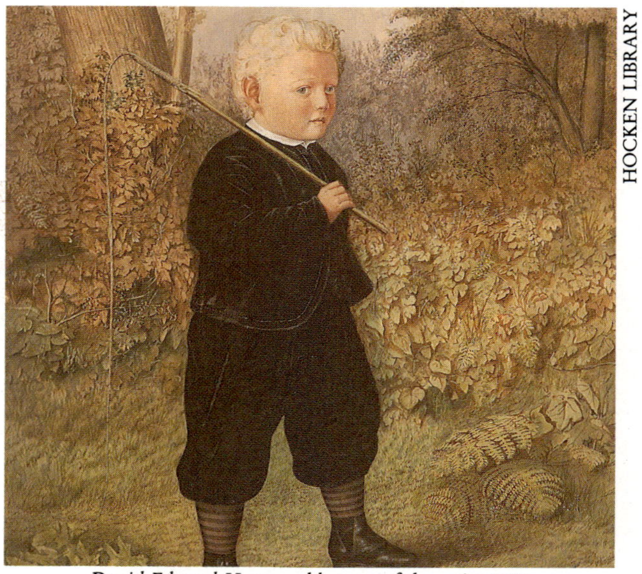

David Edward Hutton, eldest son of the artist, 1873,
watercolour by David Con Hutton.

Laurie Barber

A "PAKEHA" IS A "white" New Zealander. Although Maori language scholars dispute the word's origin, they agree it was in use in reference to the hatted, totally clothed and strangely mannered Europeans who came to Aotearoa in the late eighteenth and the early nineteenth centuries. Pakeha were fair skinned persons of European descent. They were oddities, ignorant of the lore and law of the tangata whenua. Through the nineteenth century and into the twentieth, the term Pakeha was accepted and adopted by settlers of Anglo-Saxon and European descent, who came to claim New Zealand as their homeland.

In the latter part of the twentieth century, most non-Maori and non-Pacific Island New Zealanders accept the designation Pakeha. A minority of Pakeha refuse the designation and insist they are "New Zealanders of European descent".

THE PAKEHA HAVE made New Zealand their home for 150 years. At the turn of the eighteenth century, sealers, whalers, traders and absconders had built their shacks on Kororareka's beach. Missionaries arrived soon after, mostly evangelical protestants of the Church of England. Wesleyans were quick to follow. From homeward ships and Sydney gossip, Britons learnt of the existence of a temperate, bush-clad, potentially farmable, South Sea Islands group, sparsely populated by a warrior race. Curiosity and entrepreneurial interest were awakened. In the 1840s planned colonisation by the Wakefield scheme settlers – in Wellington, Wanganui and Nelson – and by church-sponsored settlements at Canterbury and Otago, brought a constant flow of migrants to the new land.

The colonists immediately assumed that untitled, unfenced and unhedged land was "wasteland". They failed to understand that the forest, plains, bracken-clad hills, river plateaux, swamps, mountains and seashores, all had their particular place in a Maori economy. Each geographical division was a peculiar food source, and the mountain ridges provided timber for canoes and greenstone for ornaments and implements.

Land was the lure that drew Pakeha to New Zealand. Landless Anglo-Saxons sought to become what they could never be in Britain: land owners with their own homes, their own town acre, and perhaps even a farmer with the social status of a squire.

From the viewpoint of the Pakeha of the mid-nineteenth century, the Maori were treated well. Christianity, literacy and numeracy were offered and taken. Tribes of illiterate cannibals, victims of destructive superstition, dispensers of utu (revenge killing), doomed to short and primitive lives, were offered warless unity under the law and order of the British Crown. The newcomers assumed the more intensive the Pakeha settlement the greater would be the colonisers' prosperity and the quicker the assimilation of the Maori to Anglo-Saxon civilisation. Indeed, they believed that without this assimilation the Maori were a doomed race.

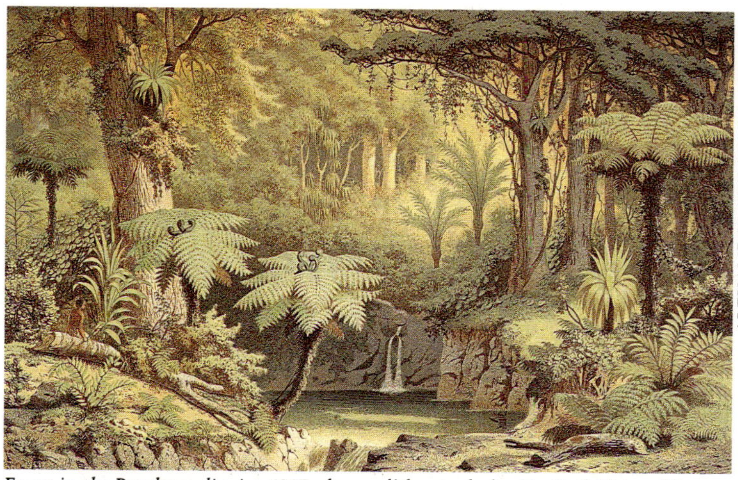

ALEXANDER TURNBULL LIBRARY

Forest in the Papakura district, 1867, chromolithograph, by Dr Carl Fisher. The settlers saw the native forest as vacant and unused, and thus lacking ownership, an idea that persisted until the resurgence of Maori land claims in the 1970s.

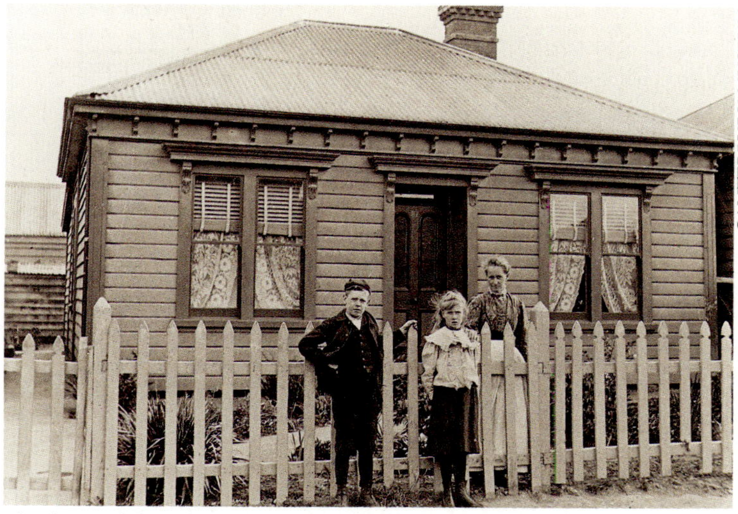

CANTERBURY MUSEUM

The dream of their own town section brought many Pakeha from the slums of industrial Britain. The Kiddey family were snapped outside their cottage in Byron Street, Sydenham, Christchurch.

From their perspective, Hone Heke's "Flagstaff Rebellion" (1844–46) was the troublemaking of a reverted savage rather than a contest over sovereignty. Te Rauparaha's attempts to confine the Wakefield settlements were regarded as murderous attacks on civilised outposts. The Taranaki, Waikato and Bay of Plenty resistance in the New Zealand Wars of the 1860s were seen as last ditch stands against the frontiers of a better life.

The Pakeha boat people were children of their age. They were pre-Social Darwinists, or Social Darwinists, convinced of the inferiority of those with darker skins. At their best they were humane and patronisingly concerned for the "Native Race". At their worst they sabred Maori adults and children and confiscated their land.

ON THE 150TH ANNIVERSARY of the signing of the Treaty of Waitangi the Pakeha contribution to New Zealand's development is undervalued and misinterpreted. A Pakeha "cultural cringe" distorts history and impairs the current dialogue with Maoritanga. While the prophets of Maori renaissance offer a grouping of culturally binding myths to emphasise the nature of Maoritanga, Pakeha New Zealanders make little of their culture. Much of the present Pakeha applause for things Maori and confessed guilt for Pakeha shortcomings is insincere. A romanticism that affirms that before the Pakeha came Aotearoa was a Garden of Eden, a conservationist's delight, and a diseaseless place of joy and family unity, flies in the face of history. Civil war, cannibalism, cancer, dietary disorder, rape, incest, revenge killings and "black magic" were a strong part of pre-European contact Maori lifestyles. It is true that the Pakeha overturned the old Maori order and transformed the landscape. There is no doubt that confiscations of Maori land were often unfair, and that some Crown purchases amounted to appropriation. For all that, however, the Pakeha brought to Aotearoa a transforming heritage that few New Zealanders, Maori as well as Pakeha, would renounce.

Pakeha technology, in 1990 offering computers, teletext, video recorders, microwaves and communication across the globe, is a continuation of the technological input of the pioneer Pakeha immigrants. The white skinned brought iron and steel tools, printing presses, wheeled transport, oxen and horses to draw ploughs, as well as firearms. From the beginning of the nineteenth century sealers, whalers and traders bartered for provisions, flax and timber, with nails, axes and spades. Before the second decade of the nineteenth century, Maori demand for muskets and gunpowder was insistent. The "Musket Wars" enveloped the North Island in unparalleled tribal military opportunism. Those with firearms seized their chance for utu and for territorial gain. Those without retreated and desperately lured

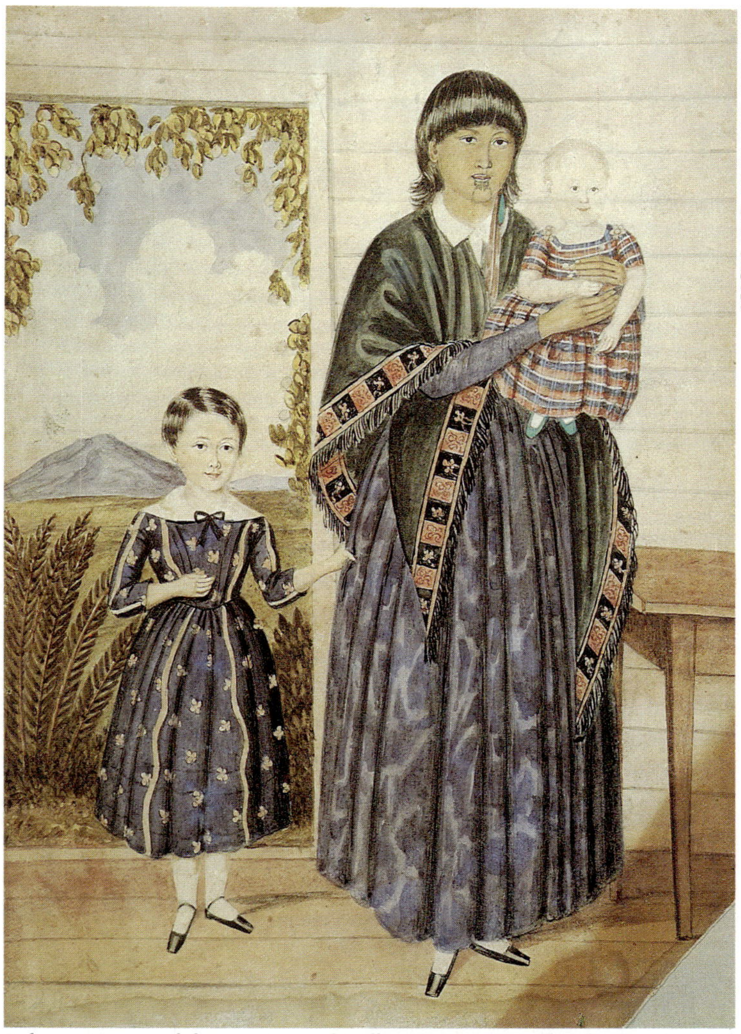

AUCKLAND CITY ART GALLERY

Rakapa Ngawai with her sons Eru and William, 1852, watercolour by Joseph Merrett. A cross-fertilisation of Maori and European styles marks the portrait of this Ngati Maniapoto woman and her children. The older boy is from her earlier marriage to a Mr Herslett; the boy in her arms is the child of John Edwards.

traders to them, to win equality of weaponry.

With missionary encouragement, the Maori, using horse- and oxen-drawn ploughs and iron tools, transformed a limited acreage into wheat and potato fields and into orchards. Imitation and adaptation of Pakeha entrepreneurial skills were speedy. Waikato Maori of the 1850s chartered schooners to transport wheat cargoes to Sydney and to the Californian coast.

New technology flooded into New Zealand with planned and unplanned immigration from 1840 to the 1870s. Pakeha capital investments, Pakeha preference for Pakeha farm products, and a growing displacement of the Maori away from Pakeha settlements, slowed Maori acquisition of the new magic. The wars of the 1860s brought a temporary close to interest in new farming technology. Wheatfields and kumara plots were neglected as the two races fought for sovereignty. New machinery arrived — threshing mills to flail grain, reaping machines and portable steam engines. Iron-screwed steamers linked Christchurch and Dunedin to Melbourne and Sydney. Sheep and cattle stations, often run by Australian "shagroons", enclosed the flat lands of the plains and the alpine hills beyond, and the repetitive clicking of blade shears accompanied the early dawns of summer. Flour mills, breweries, sawmills, brick and tile kilns, and woollen cloth factories appeared. Towns with brick and stone buildings, gas lit and streets cobbled, with newspapers, churches and cathedrals, banks and libraries, brought a replica of Britain to an antipodean setting. There were few Maori in the south and the transfiguration of that part of the country into a British cultural model was easily accomplished.

In the north, demoralisation followed defeat in war, as the Pakeha excluded the vanquished from their commercial world and from participation in a developing technology. The Maori were pushed to the outskirts of Pakeha frontier civilisation. And a Pakeha near-monopoly of machinery followed for close on 100 years.

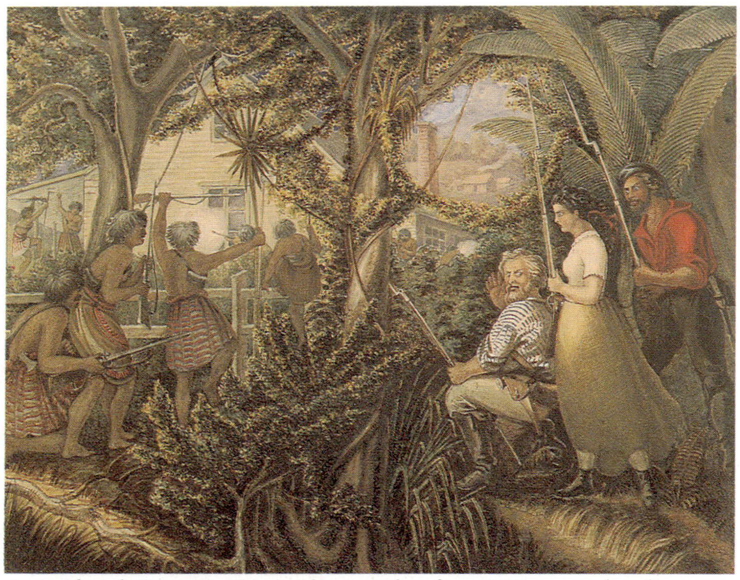

HOCKEN LIBRARY

An incident during a Hau Hau raid on a settler's farm, 1863, watercolour by Gustav Ferdinand von Tempsky. The future of the Maori hung in the balance as von Tempsky and his Forest Rangers engaged in guerilla warfare with the Maori. Ultimate defeat led to the isolation and demoralisation of many North Island tribes.

Monocultural though it was, the Pakeha achievement in this 100 years is impressive. By 1890 a rail network linked many of the settlements of each island. In 1890 £4,000,000's worth of wool was exported overseas and £1,000,000 of meat products. In the first years of the twentieth century the last of the North Island's frontier land was divided by the Pakeha – in the King Country, Urewera, Volcanic Plateau and hinterland Taranaki. W. F. Massey's Reform Government (1912–1925) followed the policies of the Liberal Party Government (1891–1912) by alienating hundreds of thousands of acres of the remaining Maori land. The advent of the dairy industry, made possible by refrigeration, exacerbated this last seizure. Dairy factories dotted flat land at about 15-kilometre intervals. New small settlements abounded. On the eve of the First World War (1914), motorcars, buses, rail transport and telephones integrated a rural lifestyle and closed the gap between town and country in New Zealand. But from this new prosperity the tangata whenua were largely excluded.

In the 1950s and early 1960s Pakeha technology brought an agricultural revolution to New Zealand that further enhanced farming efficiency. Research scientists promoted intensive grassland farming, aerial topdressing, artificial animal breeding, careful attention to trace elements and fertiliser programmes, the introduction of new animal breeds, closer monitoring of animal production efficiency and greater disease control. Diversification in the agricultural sector and development of manufacturing industries have followed a decline in British demand for New Zealand farm produce in the late 1970s and the 1980s. Technological invention and the importation of advanced technology have augmented new trade developments. One hundred and fifty years of applied technology have given New Zealanders the highest standard of living in the South Pacific.

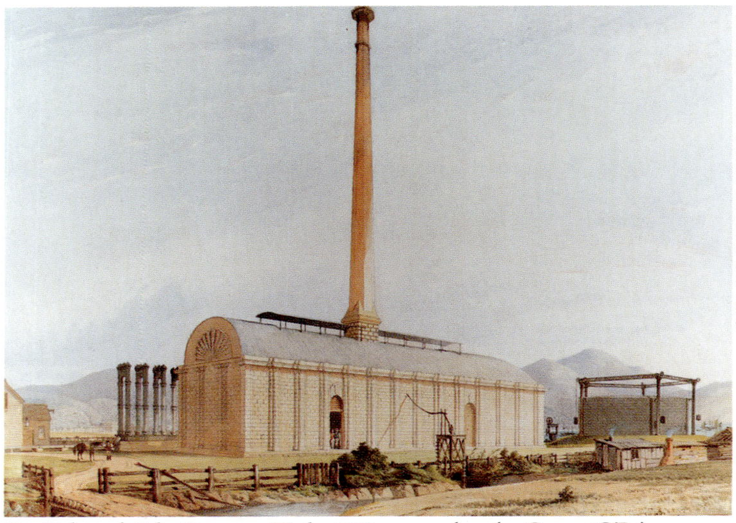

OTAGO EARLY SETTLERS MUSEUM

Gas Light and Coke Company Works, 1865, watercolour by George O'Brien. Pakeha technology permanently transformed the landscape and the way of life.

SOCIETIES SHOULD BE JUDGED more on the creativity and civilised behaviour of their inhabitants than on their technology. Western civilisation's invasion of Aotearoa's cultural life has touched and transfigured two races. The pioneer missionaries brought high "puritan" values to Aotearoa. In a prophetic role they confronted both wayward Pakeha and Maori with their rigorous code. Mostly artisans, lower middle class in origin, the first Pakeha had little appreciation of their own Western civilisation's music, art, literature, or performing arts. Pakeha society began with a Philistine base and has long manifested Philistine characteristics. Its slogans affirm its extrovert and unsophisticated emphasis: "Beer is best", "Rugby makes men", "It's the practical that counts", "Too much learning spoils a boy (girl?)", "Give me a good tune any day". Philistinism is still an apt description of the semi-cultured veneer of most Pakeha in 1990. A restaurant is still judged by many on the quantity rather than the quality of its food. *Crocodile Dundee* is counted immeasurably superior to a Fellini film. There is little respect for philosophers or poets (unless the poet is Sam Hunt, a "bar room balladeer").

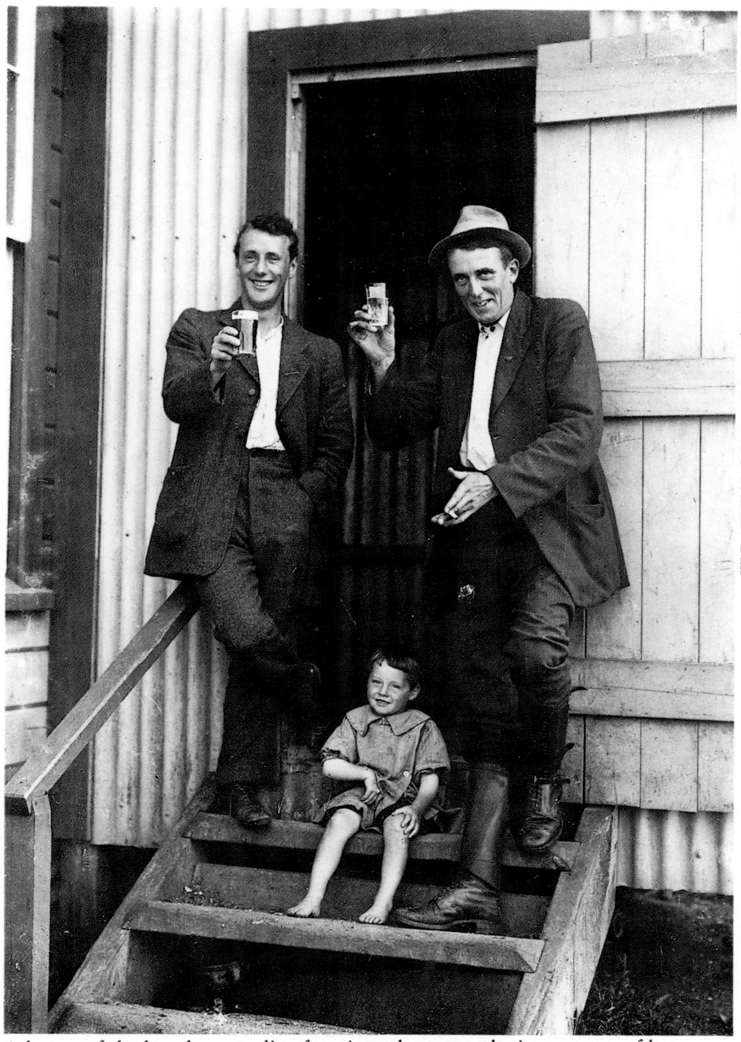

W.R. BURT COLLECTION/ALEXANDER TURNBULL LIBRARY

A legacy of the largely masculine frontier culture was the importance of beer drinking as a social focus. In 1911 Speight's Brewery in Dunedin alone produced 8,592,000 litres of beer. These cheery drinkers enjoy a pint in the Chatham Islands.

This Philistinism reflects the origins of the waves of Pakeha settlers. The public house, dance hall and church or chapel provided the early extent of their leisure time "cultural" activities. Aotearoa's opportunities allowed them to expand an extrovert lifestyle to beaches, sportsfields, bush and skifields. In a society where carpenters, plumbers, lawyers and medical general practitioners were, and are, of more worth than thinkers, planners and the practitioners of the arts, cultural values remain basic and undeveloped.

A "rural myth" that arose in the nineteenth century has reinforced this value system. Farmers were judged, and judged themselves, "the backbone of the nation", and the farming way of life was promoted as a no-frills, simple and in-tune-with-nature existence, superior to the artifices of urban culture. Stolidity took preference above political aptitude; prejudice and blind loyalty were praised, and any departure from a Calvinist social morality denounced. Most politicians, even the few refined ones, have accepted the reality of this Philistine base. In 1958 Arnold Nordmeyer, Minister of Finance in the second Labour Government, brought down a "Black Budget" that insisted that continued full employment could be bought with extra taxes on beer, tobacco and petrol. At the 1960 General Election the hedonistic Philistines took their revenge and dismissed his government.

A preference for mediocrity and distaste for elitism marks this aspect of Pakeha culture. In both Aotearoa and in Australia the cutting down of "tall poppies" is a national pastime. Anti-intellectualism is overt rather than covert within Pakeha society. Richard Hadlee is a folk hero – Ernest Rutherford is not. The cult of the common denominator is popular in 1990. Television, radio and newspapers reinforce its development. Some commercial radio stations promote their disc jockeys to guru status whereby they settle every problem; others assume that "talkbacks" can transmute collective ignorance into collective wisdom.

A culture that lacks both self-assurance and a strong and satisfactory link with its past is often a persecuting culture. Settlers from Dalmatia, Denmark and Norway were all made aware that Pakeha culture was monoculture. Social pressure was asserted to erode the conventions and verities of their imported lifestyle, and to assimilate the newcomers into a Pakeha ethos where English was the only language spoken, where Pakeha sport, Pakeha dances, Pakeha community good works, and Pakeha religious practices, were the only acceptable form of community involvement. In the First World War, anti-German xenophobia was endemic. Pakeha families with German surnames, despite several generations of settlement in New Zealand, were regarded as possible traitors. The miniscule Lutheran Church was spied upon and train passes to Lutheran children

A genteel boating expedition in a less than gentle environment, at Mirror Creek, Hokitika. The new immigrants took to the outdoors with gusto. Picnicking, tramping, camping, mountain climbing and swimming were accessible to every social class.

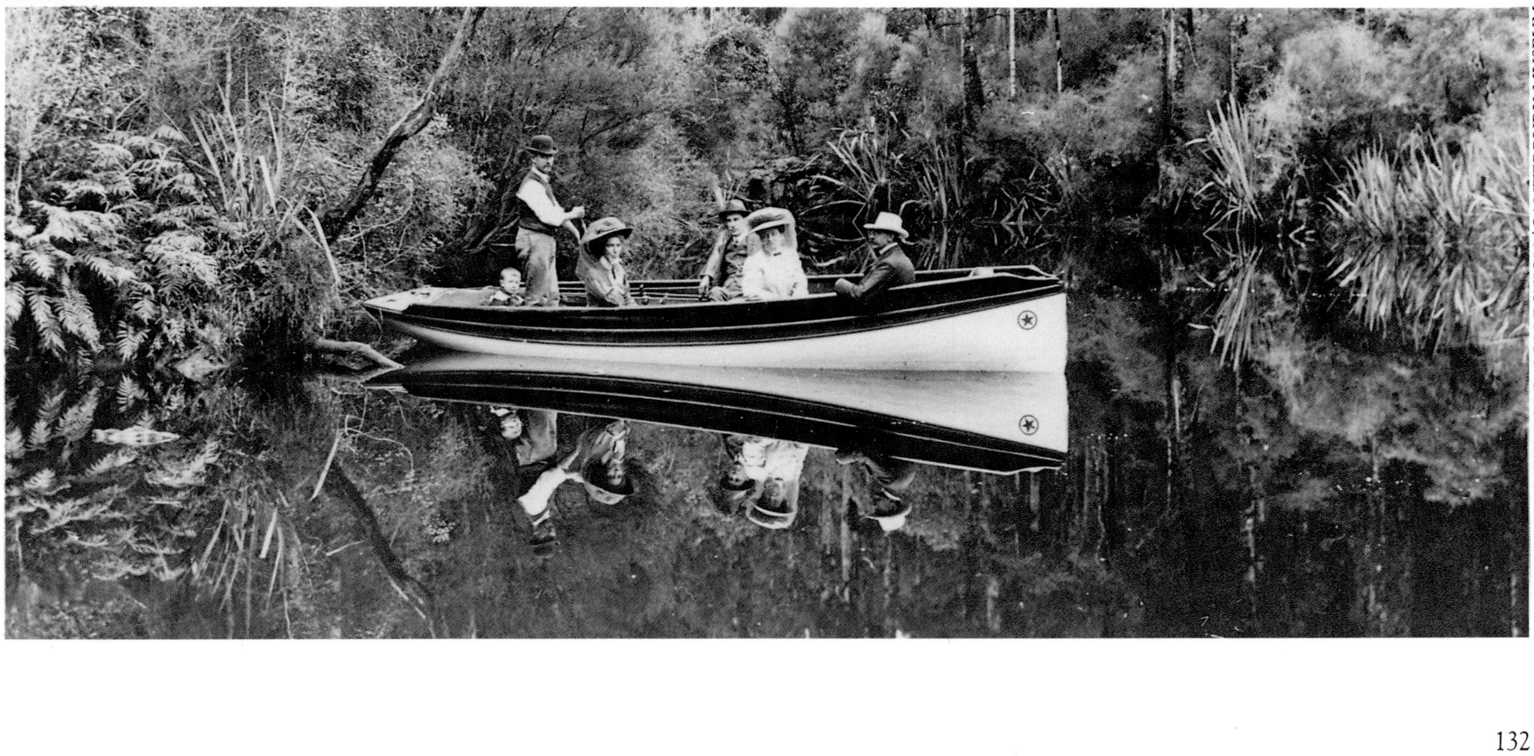

TELFORD COLLECTION/CANTERBURY MUSEUM

attending Lutheran schools were cancelled. Naturalised New Zealand citizens of German extraction had their citizenship revoked, their civil rights cancelled, and some were incarcerated for the duration of the war.

The wave of new immigrants that followed the Second World War were mainly British and Dutch. Their assimilation was easy and deliberately designed. Pakeha society had no room for separatist blocks or "foreigners" residing within New Zealand cities. But even these newcomers occasionally felt the acid tongue of xenophobia. A critical Briton became a "whinging Pom" and Dutch who offered advice on cultural development were told "to go home if you don't like it here".

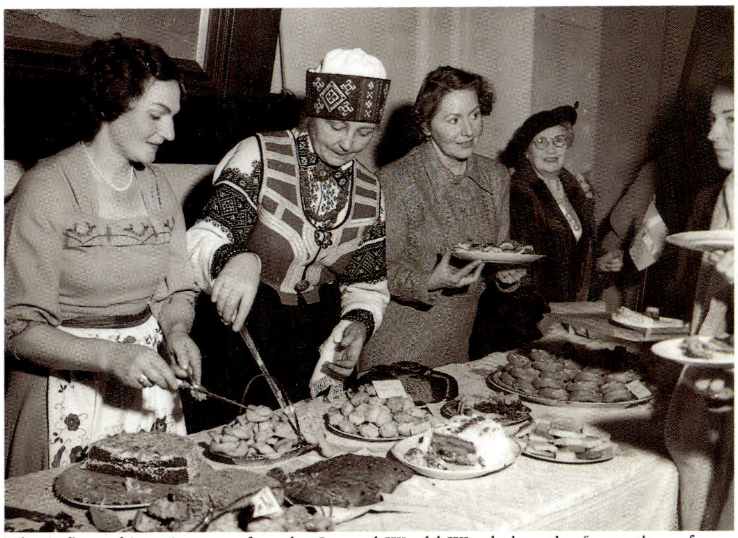

AUCKLAND STAR/AUCKLAND YWCA

The influx of immigrants after the Second World War led to the formation of ethnic clubs. These women at the Auckland YWCA's International Club represent Yugoslavia, Latvia and Egypt.

In the 1970s, with the downturn in the economy, Pacific Islanders, encouraged to work in New Zealand during times of labour shortage, were subject to harassment by Pakeha unemployed and by government agencies obeying the will of politicians eager to please Pakeha voters. "Dawn raids" by immigration officials to apprehend "overstayers" were a further manifestation of xenophobia.

AOTEAROA'S PAKEHA OF 1990 are not all blind to the shortcomings and aberrations of Pakeha culture. Cartoonists satirise them and Pakeha abroad denounce them. These deficits, real though they are, should not blind New Zealanders to the social merits of the Pakeha cultural contribution. The rule of law has replaced anarchy, social security provides a safety net for the needy (albeit with some tears), and a network of schools, colleges, polytechnics and universities spans the land. In 1990 it should be possible for New Zealanders to perceive the beauty and wisdom of Maori myth, proverbs and arts and crafts, without dismissing the riches within the well-filled Pakeha basket.

New Zealand's Pakeha should not disregard the essential "otherness" in their own culture. They should not be tricked into defining themselves exclusively in terms of their relationship to Maoritanga or to their antipodean placement. New Zealand's Pakeha need to rediscover their cultural roots and value them.

PAKEHA FAILURE to appreciate their own tradition and its historical input into New Zealand's growth has much to do with uncertainty over Pakeha attitudes to Britain. Ambivalence towards things British is a long-held symptom of Pakeha schizophrenia. For 150 years Pakeha New Zealanders had been mesmerised by a sense of duty to "the Old Country" that led to costly involvement in two world wars with the loss of thousands of New Zealand lives. Even in the 1960s, with Britain's entry into the European Economic Community imminent, few Pakeha were convinced that "the Motherland" would prefer Irish butter to New Zealand's, and European meat to Aotearoa's. For most it was inconceivable that Britain, supported with filial devotion in war and peace, would turn her back on the nation she had spawned. Tim Shadbolt voiced nationwide disbelief with his announcement that "Mother had run off with a Frenchman".

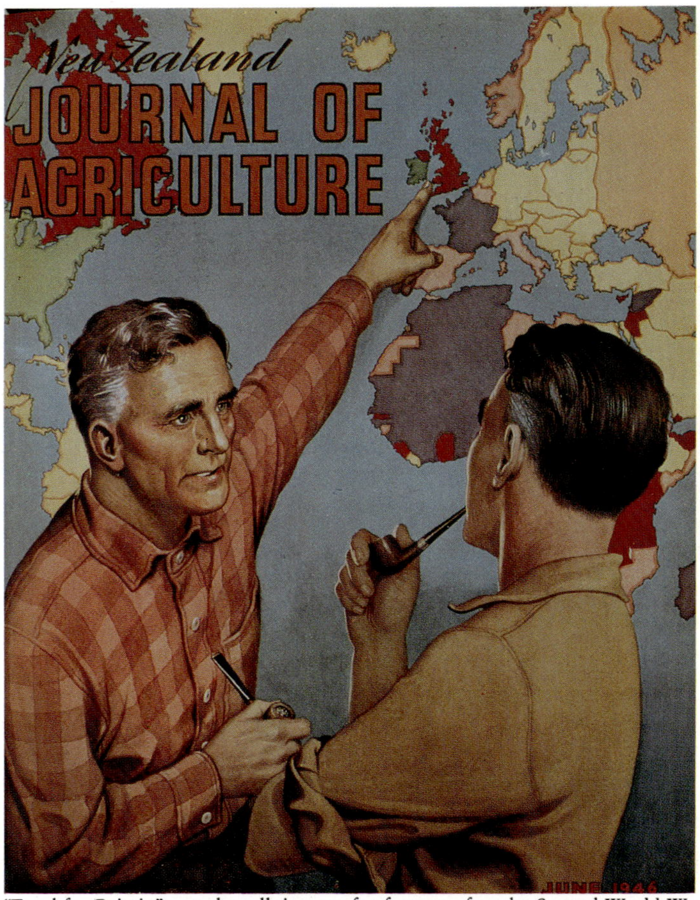

N.Z. RURAL PRESS/AUCKLAND INSTITUTE AND MUSEUM

"Food for Britain" was the rallying cry for farmers after the Second World War, as shown on this cover of the *New Zealand Journal of Agriculture* in June 1946. They believed they faced a bright future as agricultural producers for the old country.

For all that, Anglophilia was never total. Many United Kingdom migrants to New Zealand, whether from the Wakefield settlement boats, from assisted passage after the Second World War, or as private passengers, left Britain to escape from its social constriction. Poverty, a binding class system, lack of opportunity for upward mobility and the dread that their children's lot would be no better than their own, pushed them to the docks. To some, Britain was Dickens' urban rubbish dump, a cemetery of decay and ruin.

Away from Britain, in New Zealand, these migrants mostly rejoiced in Pakeha culture. Open spaces, uncrowded beaches with the sea sometimes warm enough to swim in, native bush close enough for weekend picnics, and boiling volcanic cauldrons – all these were theirs. Farm labourers became land owners, working-class children could proceed to secondary school and thereafter win better jobs than their parents.

Yet, these same ex-Britons, away from their "Motherland", idealised and mythologised Britain's virtues. British justice was judged unsurpassable – despite the treatment of Maori land protestors. The British Empire was supported as the bulwark of a *pax Britannica* that maintained world stability, despite the empire's maintenance of its authority by military intervention. The Crown and royal family were revered, almost deified. Distance from the Pakeha *Hawaiiki* brought distortion in evaluation. An almost blind loyalty to empire, then to commonwealth, grew, because the Anglo-Saxon Pakeha settlers lacked the mutual protection, economic self-sufficiency and social security, to make their own destinies.

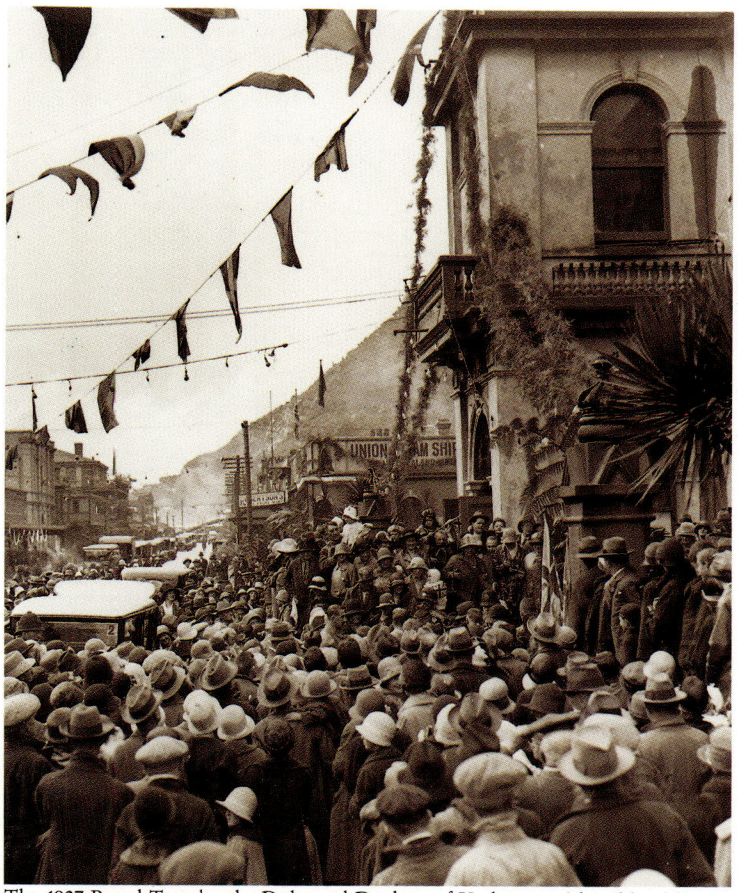
BOYER COLLECTION/N.Z. HERALD

The 1927 Royal Tour by the Duke and Duchess of York met with wild public enthusiasm. By the 1980s New Zealanders were much less devoted to royalty, nevertheless the visit of the Prince of Wales and Lady "Di" attracted rapt attention, perhaps provoked more by the princess's outfits than loyalty to the throne.

Britain's wars were the most powerful reinforcement of kith and kin unity. From 1899 to 1902 Pakeha fought in the Anglo-Boer War. New Zealanders fought farmer-soldiers who wished only to run their own affairs in their own way – an enemy who, apart from language and custom, very much resembled Pakeha New Zealanders. Volunteers fought the Boer because they were convinced that Afrikaaner independence threatened the British Empire. There was little reason and much emotion in the New Zealand commitment to this war.

In 1914 the breakdown of a European concert of treaties and guarantees, occasioned by an assassination, brought New Zealand into the First World War. It was taken for granted that if the king was at war, then so was his empire. War memorials throughout New Zealand pay tribute to the thousands who lost their lives in "the war to end all wars". Many were stupidly and callously committed to impossible tasks in a war of attrition where British generals and politicians treated human life with scant respect. Gallipoli is remembered each Anzac Day (25 April) as some sort of victory amidst tragedy. It was utter tragedy – Churchill's folly. Land forces, untrained in amphibious operations, were ordered to succeed where the Royal Navy had failed, against well-armed and better-placed defenders.

In 1939 the Polish crisis unleashed the Second World War. Michael Joseph Savage, the Labour Prime Minister, committed New Zealand to the war with the unforgettable words, "where Britain goes, we go, where she stands, we stand". His successor from 1940, Peter Fraser, was more reserved in his commitment of the Second New Zealand Division to Britain's care. Bernard Freyberg, the division's commander, was given a charter, with firm instructions that the New Zealand Government was the arbiter of the division's deployment. Even so, with Japanese bombing Australia's northern and northwestern towns, and with Japanese reconnaissance war planes over New Zealand, Britain's need to retain the division in the North African desert was accepted as of more strategic consequence than the division's return to Aotearoa. While Australian troops returned to fight the Japanese, United States marines deputed for New Zealand's natural defenders.

Britain was, from the mid-twentieth century, militarily incapable of defending New Zealand. The United States was the natural super-power ally in the South Pacific, and to maintain her protection a token New Zealand military presence in Vietnam was needed. ANZUS (1951), a consultative protective alliance between Australia, New Zealand and the United States, grew in importance during the Cold War, and as Chinese and South-East Asian nations appeared to fall to a mixture of communism and nationalism with great rapidity. Britain's flagging interest in New Zealand's farm produce, and military withdrawal east of Suez at last awakened Pakeha New Zealanders to their need to cut the historical apron strings.

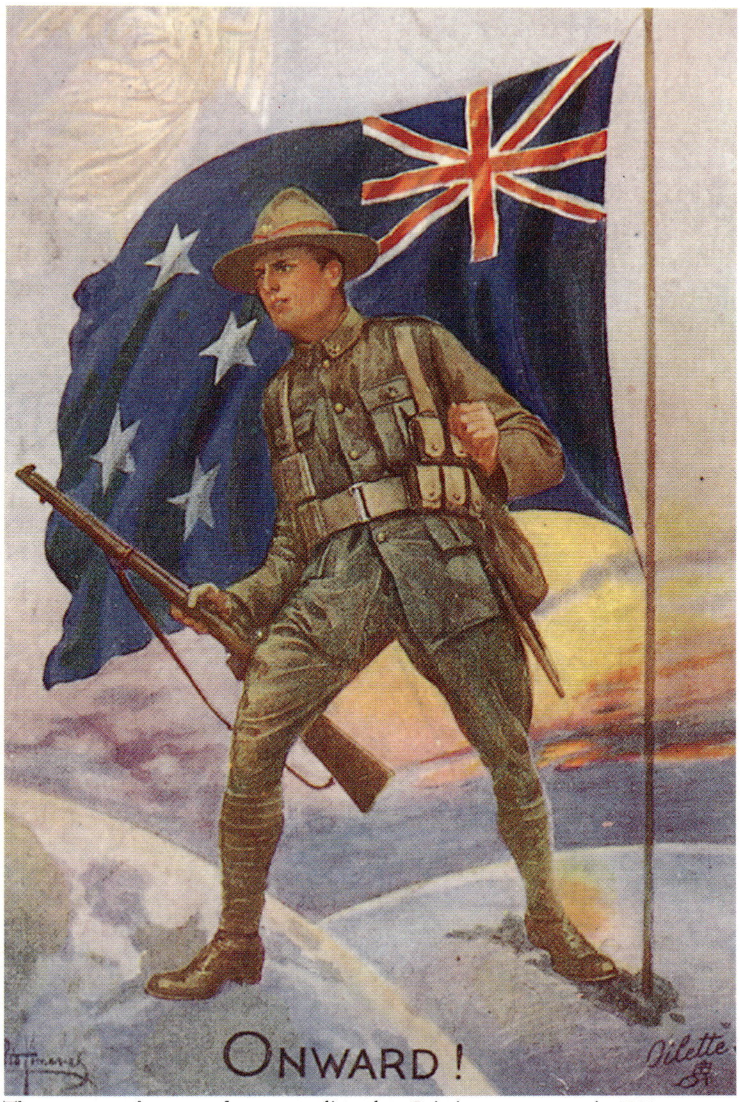

There was no shortage of men to enlist when Britain went to war in 1914. Ultimately nearly twenty percent of eligible men went and New Zealand suffered the highest casualty rate in proportion to population in the Empire.

PAKEHA NEW ZEALANDERS in the 1980s realistically expected little from Britain and Europe. While they clung to the trappings of a governor-general, appeals to the Privy Council in London in law cases, and to royal honours, political links with Britain began to erode. There is still little call for a republic in New Zealand, perhaps because an appointed governor-general's duties are exclusively ceremonial (and the incumbents are now New Zealanders). The monarchy's relevance has declined, paralleling Britain's distancing of herself from her Pakeha offspring. Only occasionally does a Pavlovian response to the imperial drum succeed. The despatch of a New Zealand warship to take station as a Royal Navy replacement during the Falkland Wars is the most recent and rare example.

For 150 years Aotearoa's Pakeha have been unable to come to terms with their British and European heritage. It has been a "love/hate" relationship. British constitutional, legal, educational and sporting values are links that have been valued. British patronage, class division and self-interest have been despised. The tensions of this volatile relationship have hindered the development of Pakeha cultural pride.

In 1990, unlike 1840, New Zealand's destiny is decided in Aotearoa, not in Whitehall. Maoridom asserts its right to legal, educational, welfare, linguistic and political equality. Pakeha reaction to this assertion is cautious, alarmed and lacking in understanding. This reaction reflects a Pakeha uncertainty of the values and roots of Pakeha culture. True biculturalism will be felt in Aotearoa only when the nation's Pakeha discover who they are and value the civilisation they have sprung from and adapted. The "white New Zealanders" need to discover their "Pakehatanga" before they can appreciate Maoritanga. Until this happens the Maori renaissance confronts a riven Pakeha society, where monocultural remnants and treacly sentimentality toward "our Maori" stand cheek by jowl. The cultural awareness that will make the Pakeha a worthy partner in the second century following the signing of the Treaty of Waitangi has yet to be realised. Until this cultural rediscovery takes place, a vigorous Maoritanga faces a Pakeha New Zealand guilty not only of repressing Maoridom in the past, but guilty of ignorance as to what its contribution to biculturalism ought to be in the future. In this situation, Jonathan Lamb's invented Maori proverb is applicable. In 1990, Aotearoa's Maori would do well to "beware of Pakeha baring guilt". □

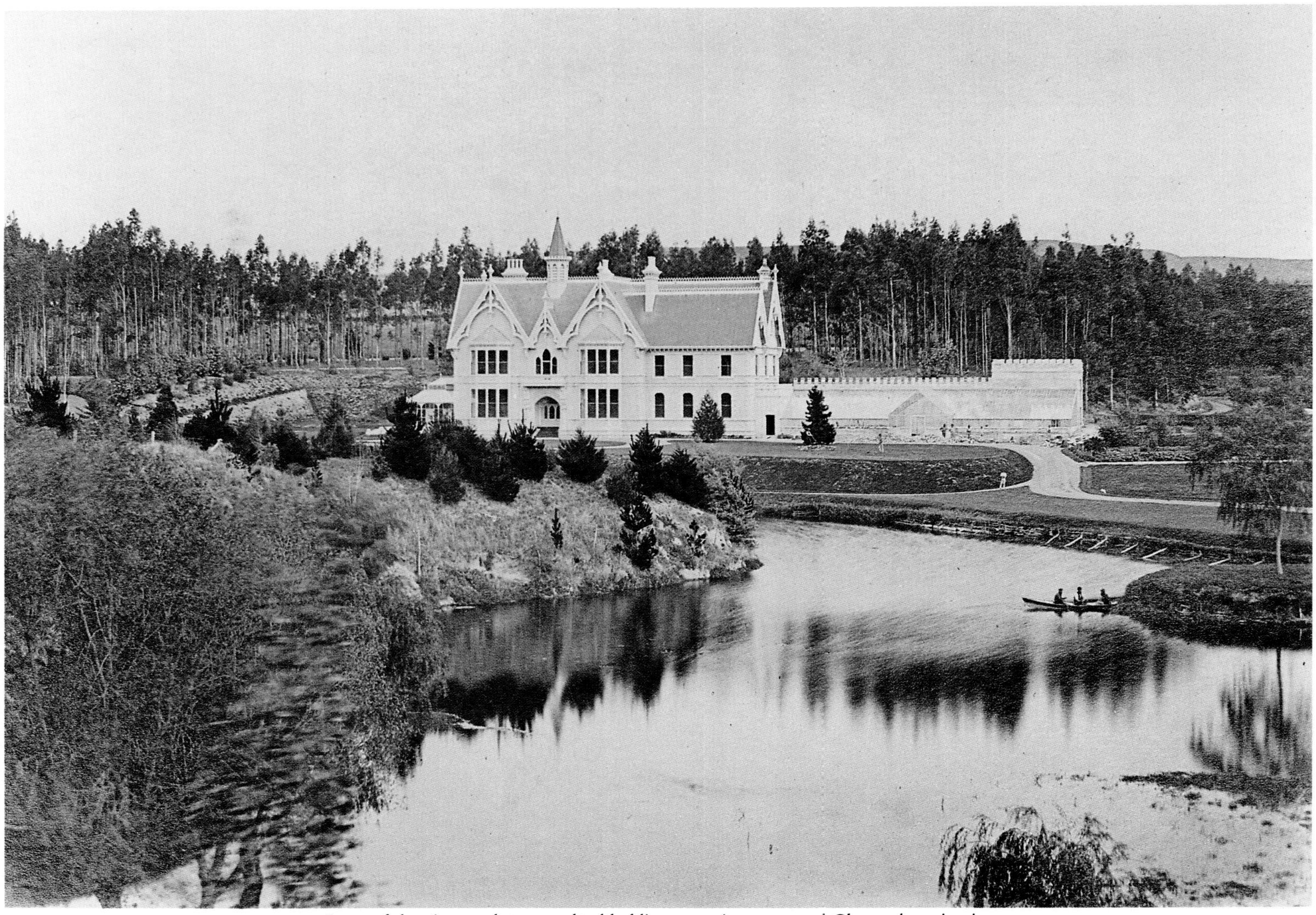
DUNEDIN PUBLIC LIBRARY

Some of the nineteenth-century land holdings were immense, and Glenmark station in Canterbury was one of the grandest. G. H. Moore bought 81,000 acres for 10/- an acre in 1854 and when he died "his was the largest fortune that had ever been made in New Zealand."

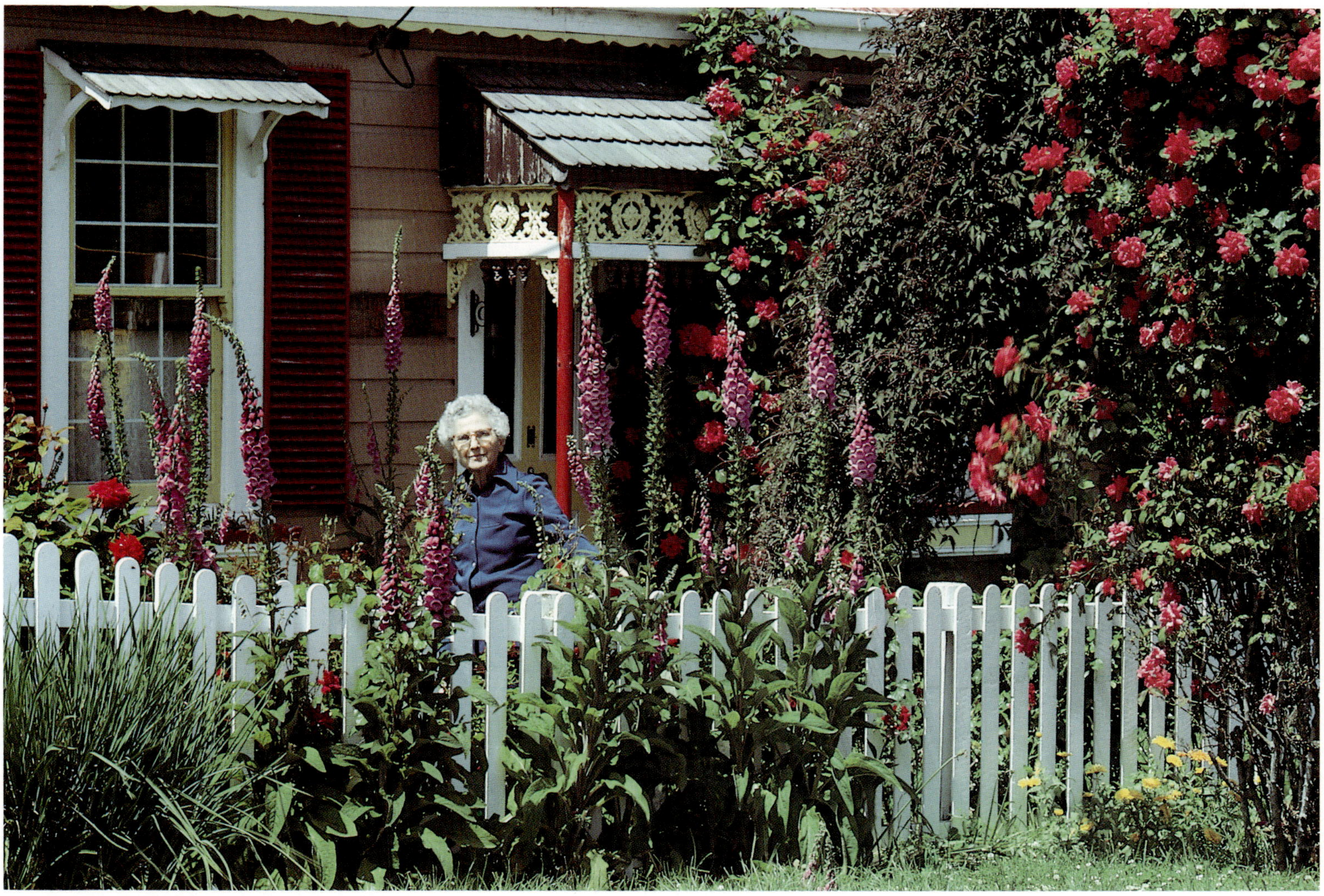

Colourful cottage at Kingston, Lake Wakatipu GEOFF MASON

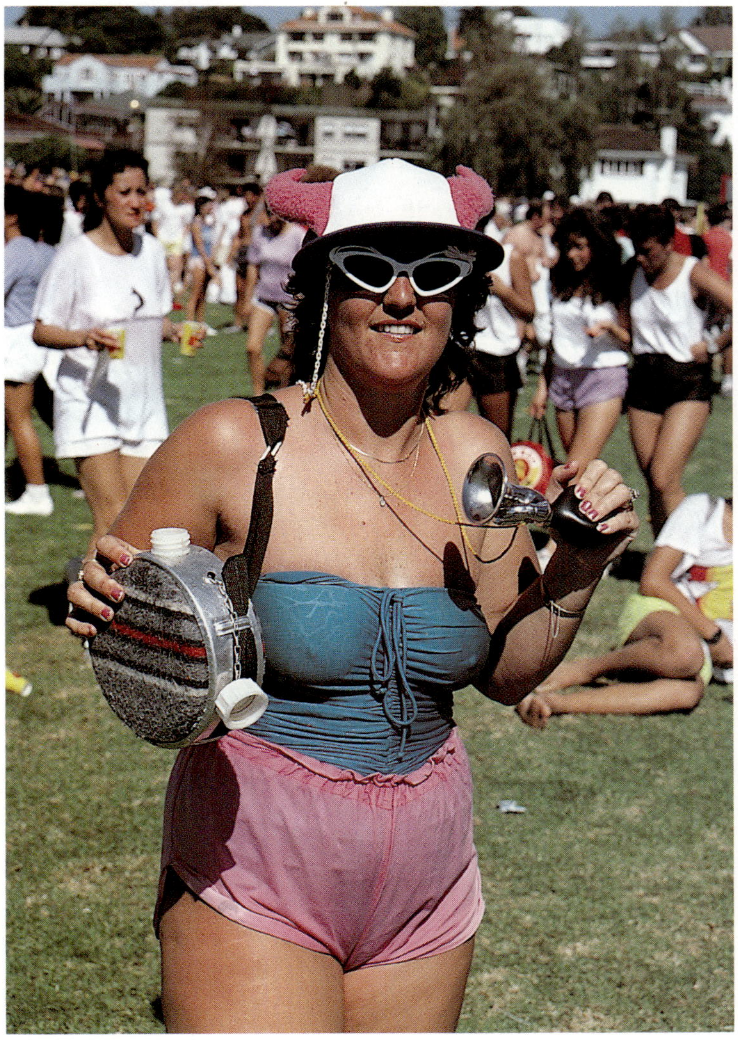

"Around the Bays", Auckland ERIC TAYLOR

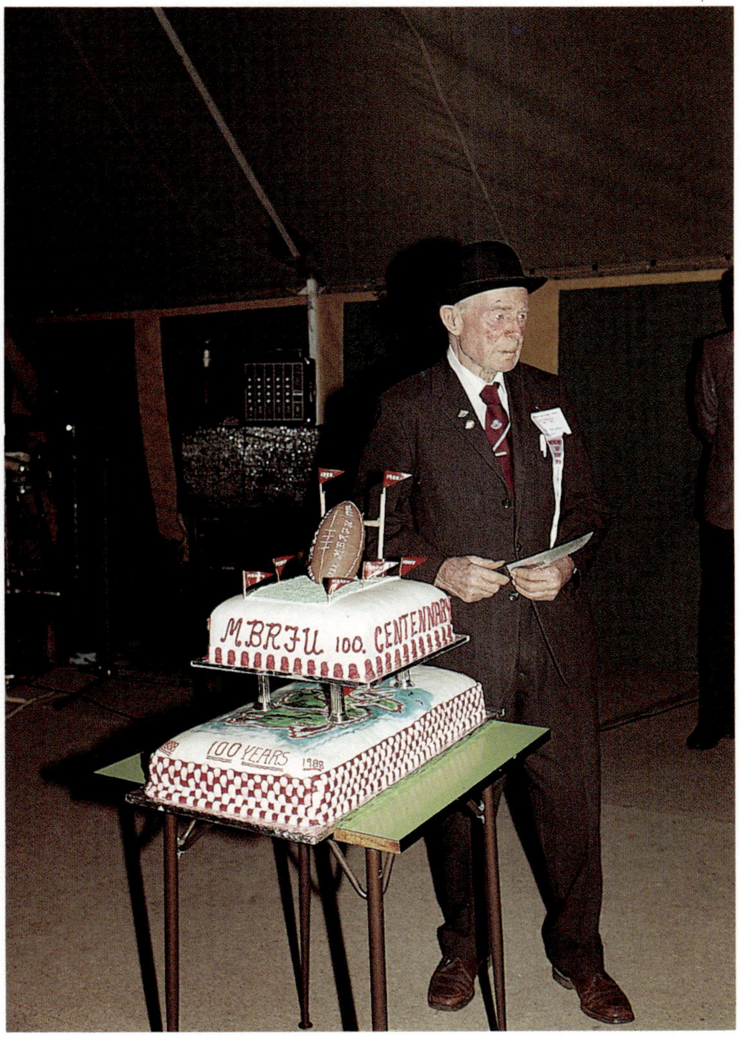

The oldest living member of the Mercury Bay Rugby Football Club at their centenary celebration. ERIC TAYLOR

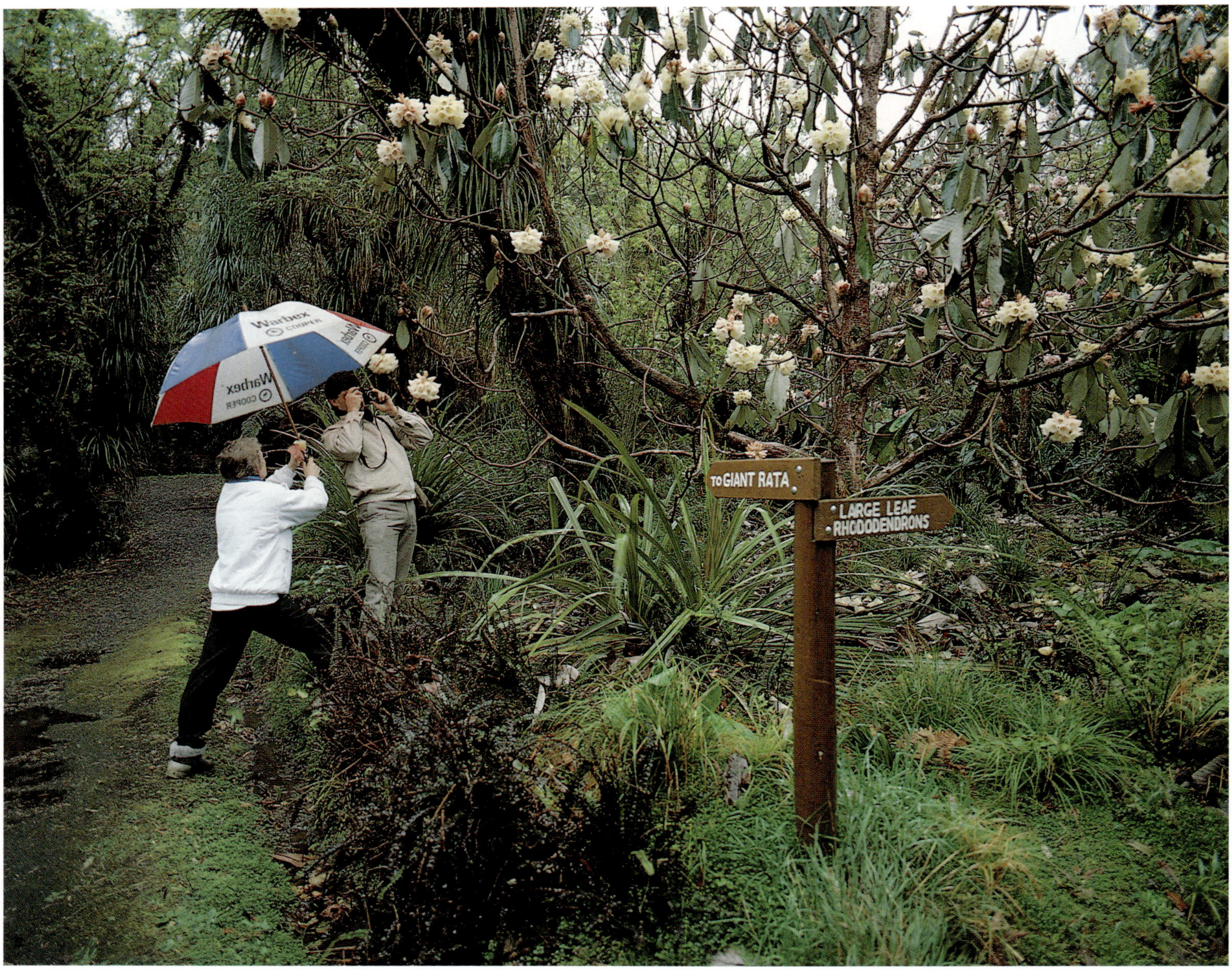

Puketi Rhododendron Trust, New Plymouth CRAIG POTTON

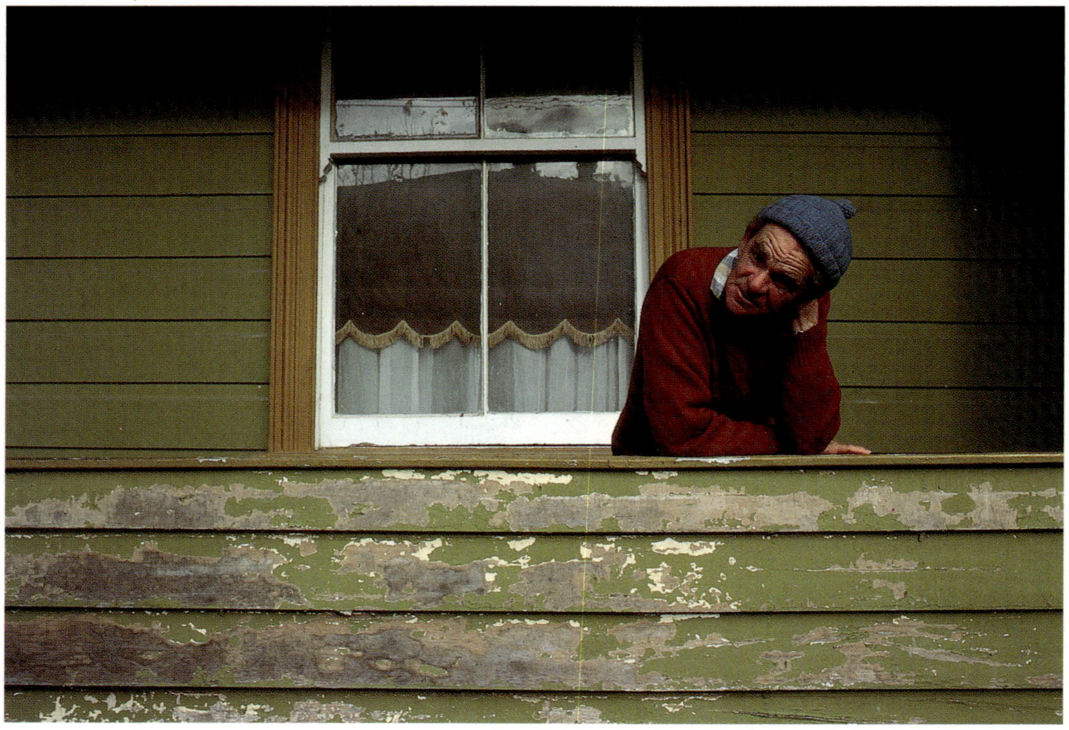

Arch Hill, Auckland STEPHEN ROBINSON

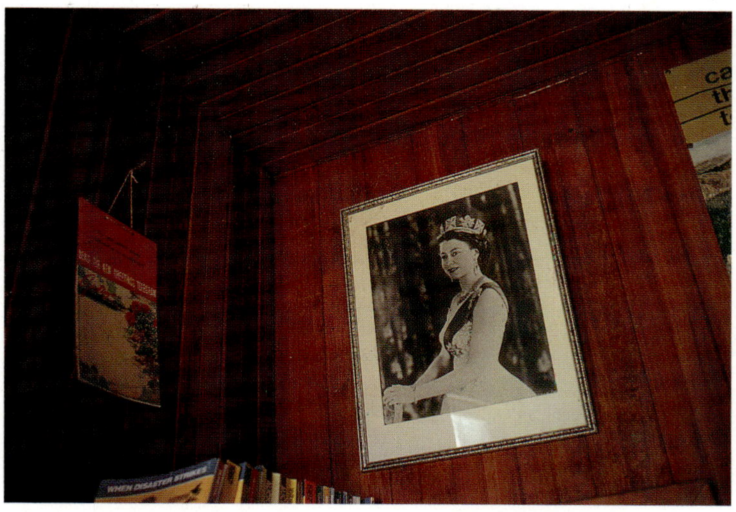

The Queen, Bainham Post Office, Golden Bay — BRUCE CONNEW

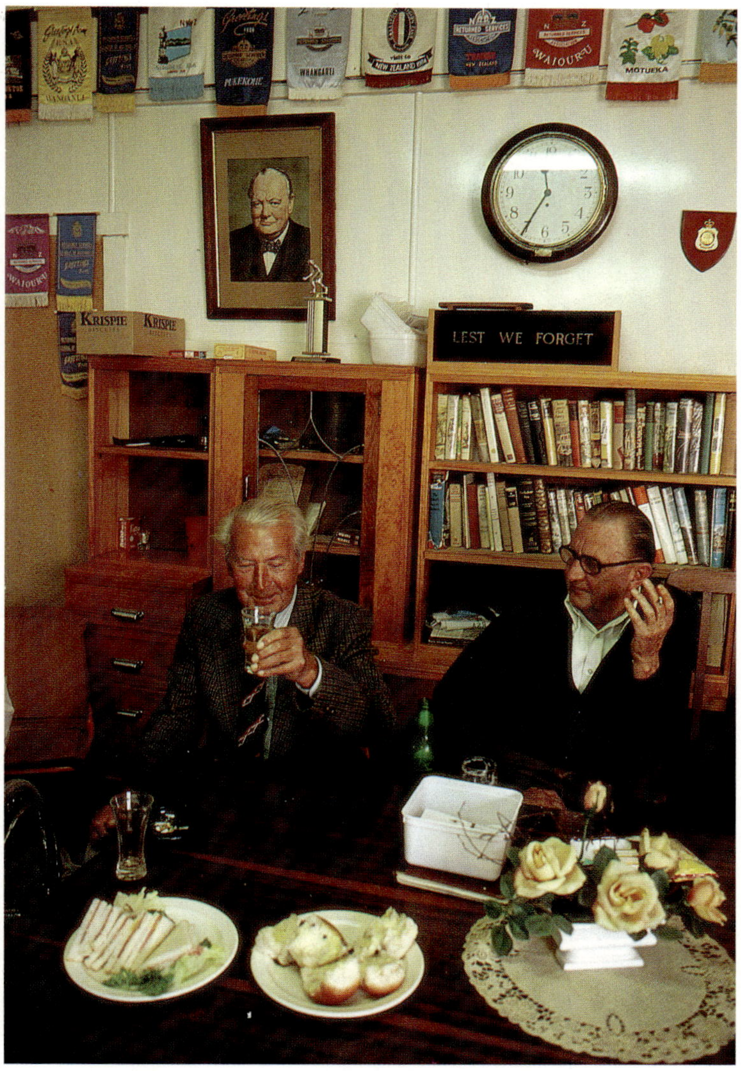

Anzac Day, Coromandel RSA gathering in the Town Hall — ERIC TAYLOR

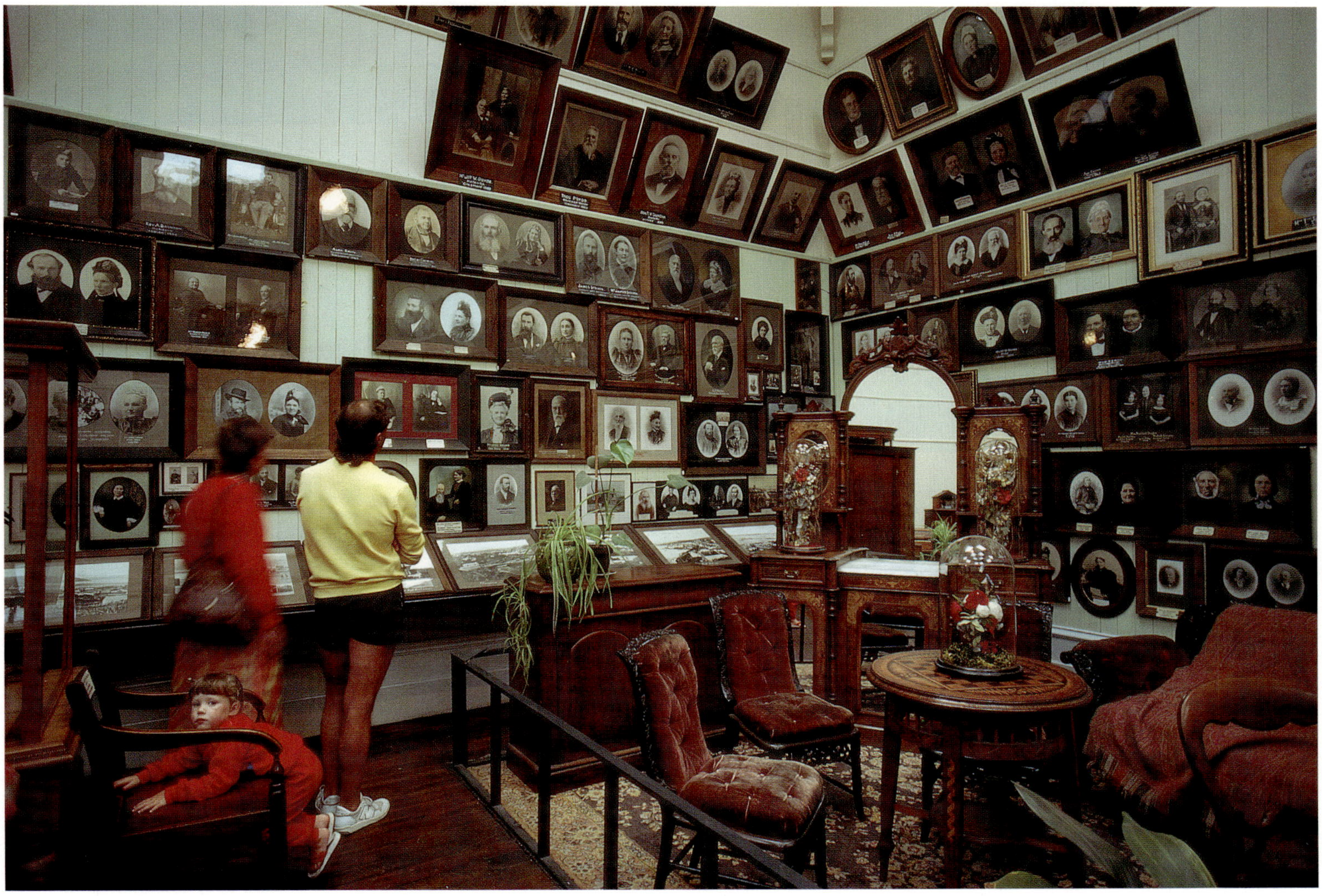

Otago Early Settlers Museum, Dunedin — GEOFF MASON

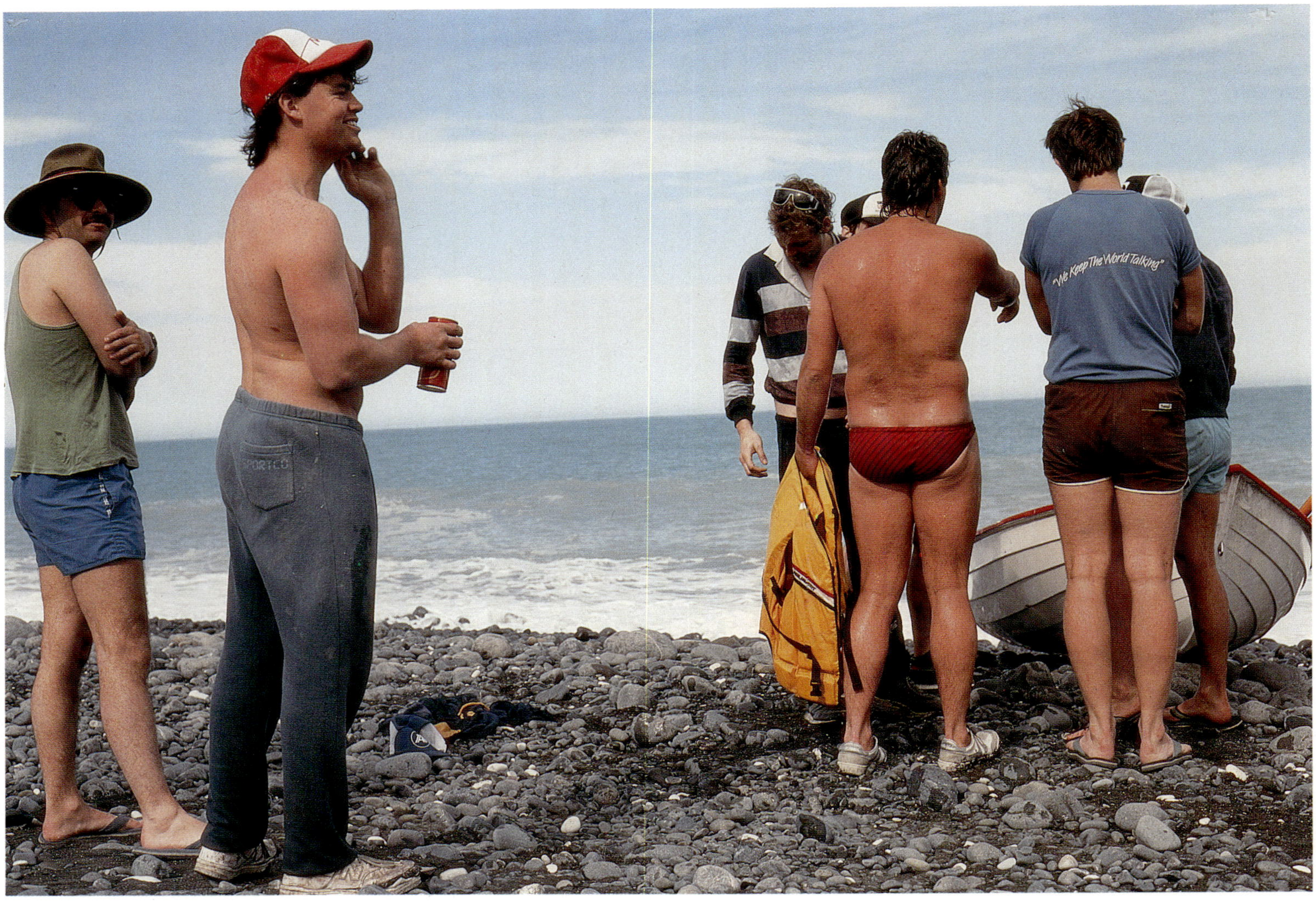

Holidaymakers from Christchurch at Kaikoura Coast BRUCE CONNEW

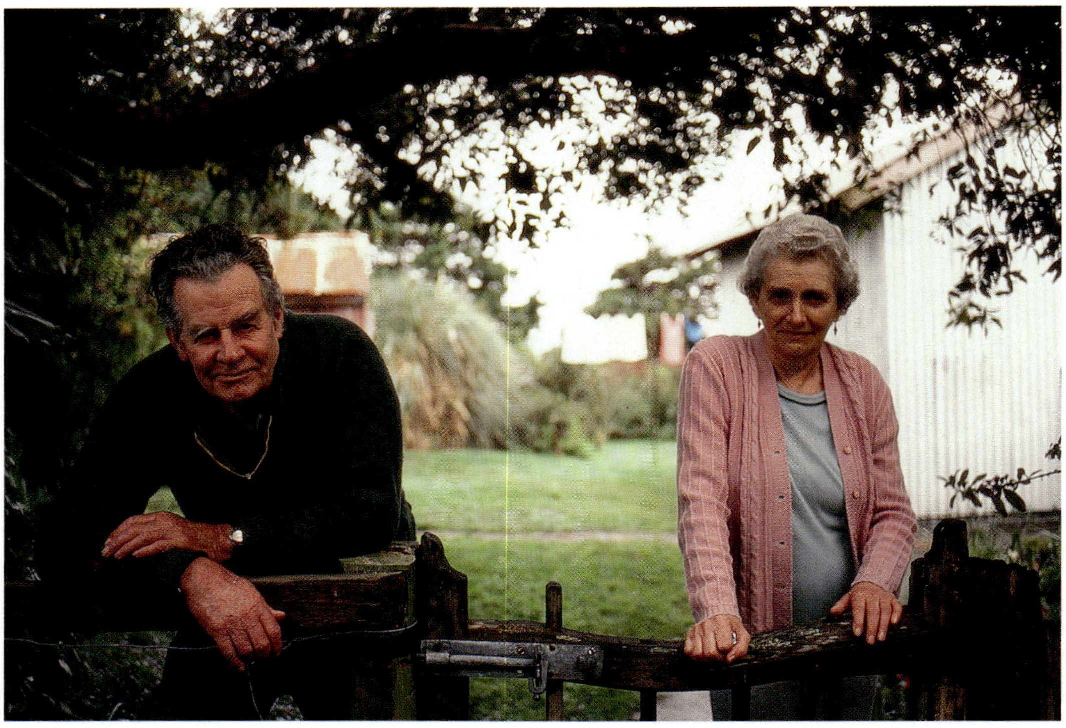

Oscar and Betty Climo, Pupona, Golden Bay BRUCE CONNEW

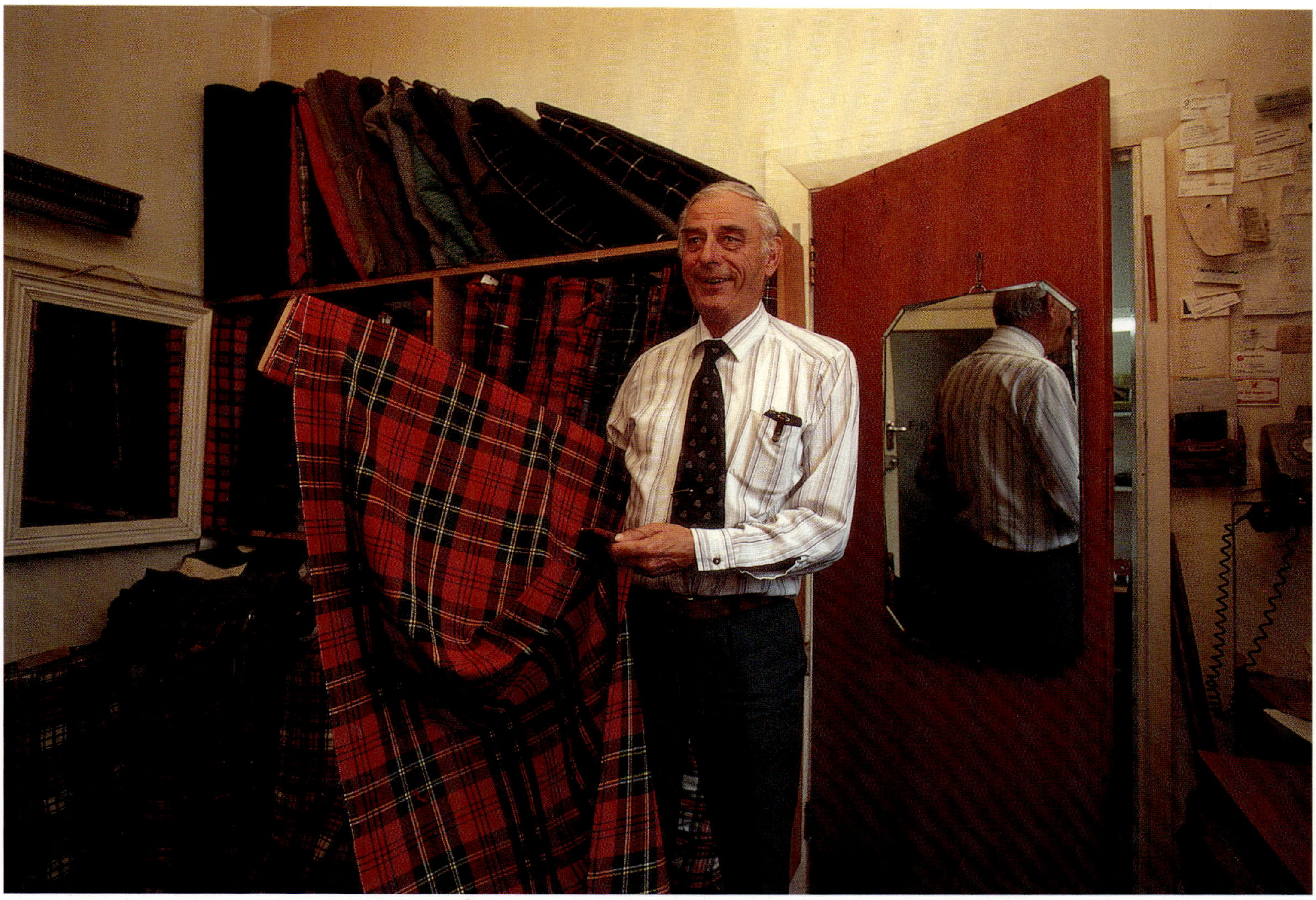

Storekeeper with a selection of tartans, Naseby, Otago GEOFF MASON

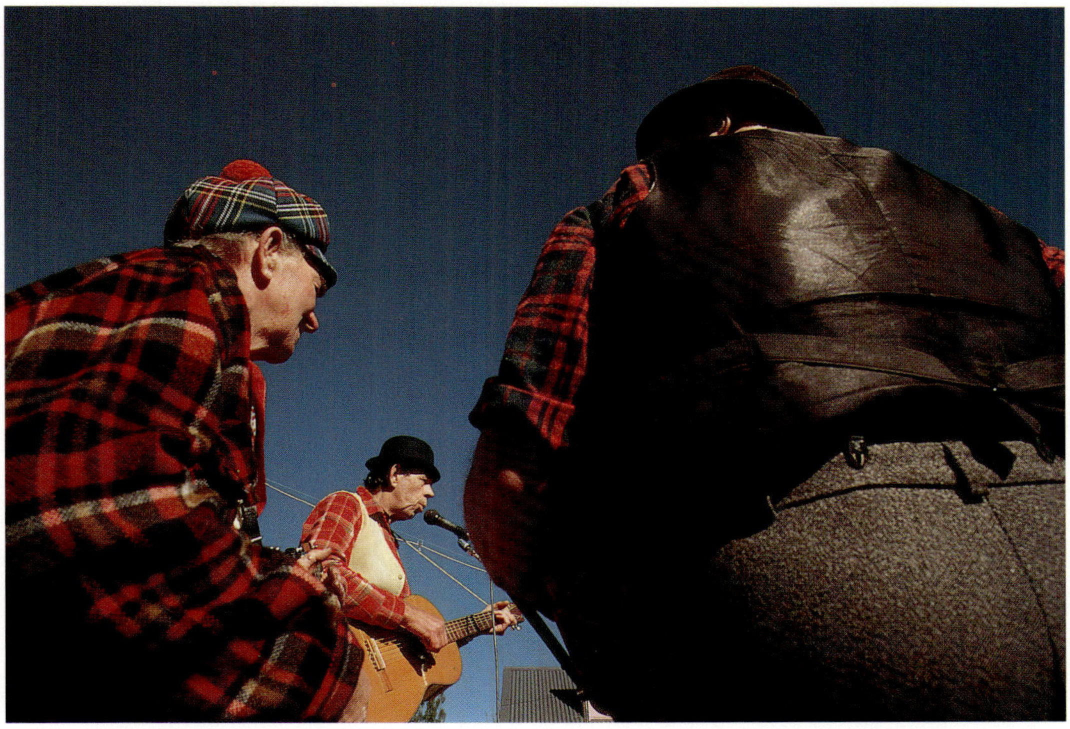

Old time band, Arrowtown Autumn Festival GEOFF MASON

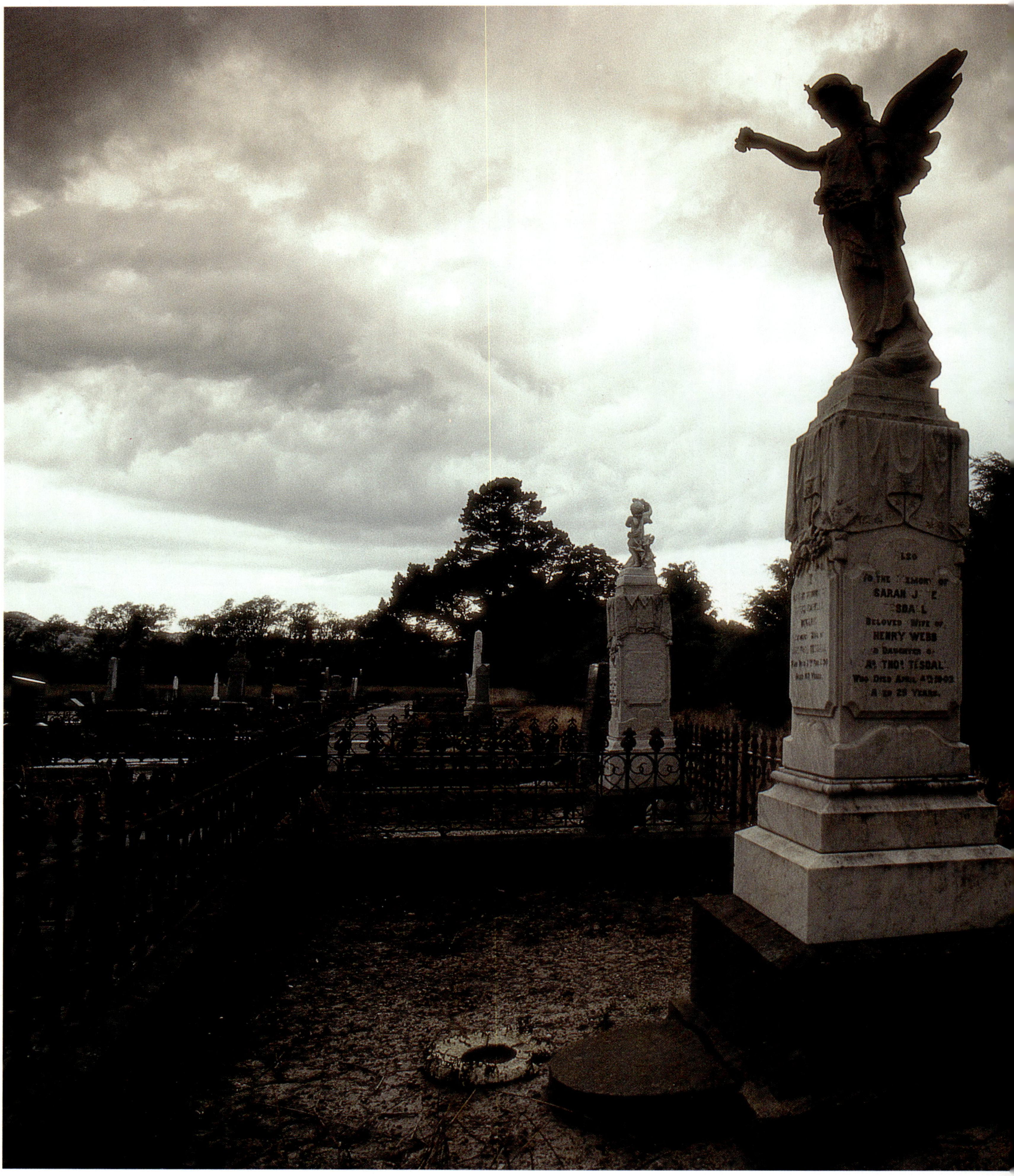

Early settlers graves, Middlemarch Cemetery, Central Otago

GEOFF MASON

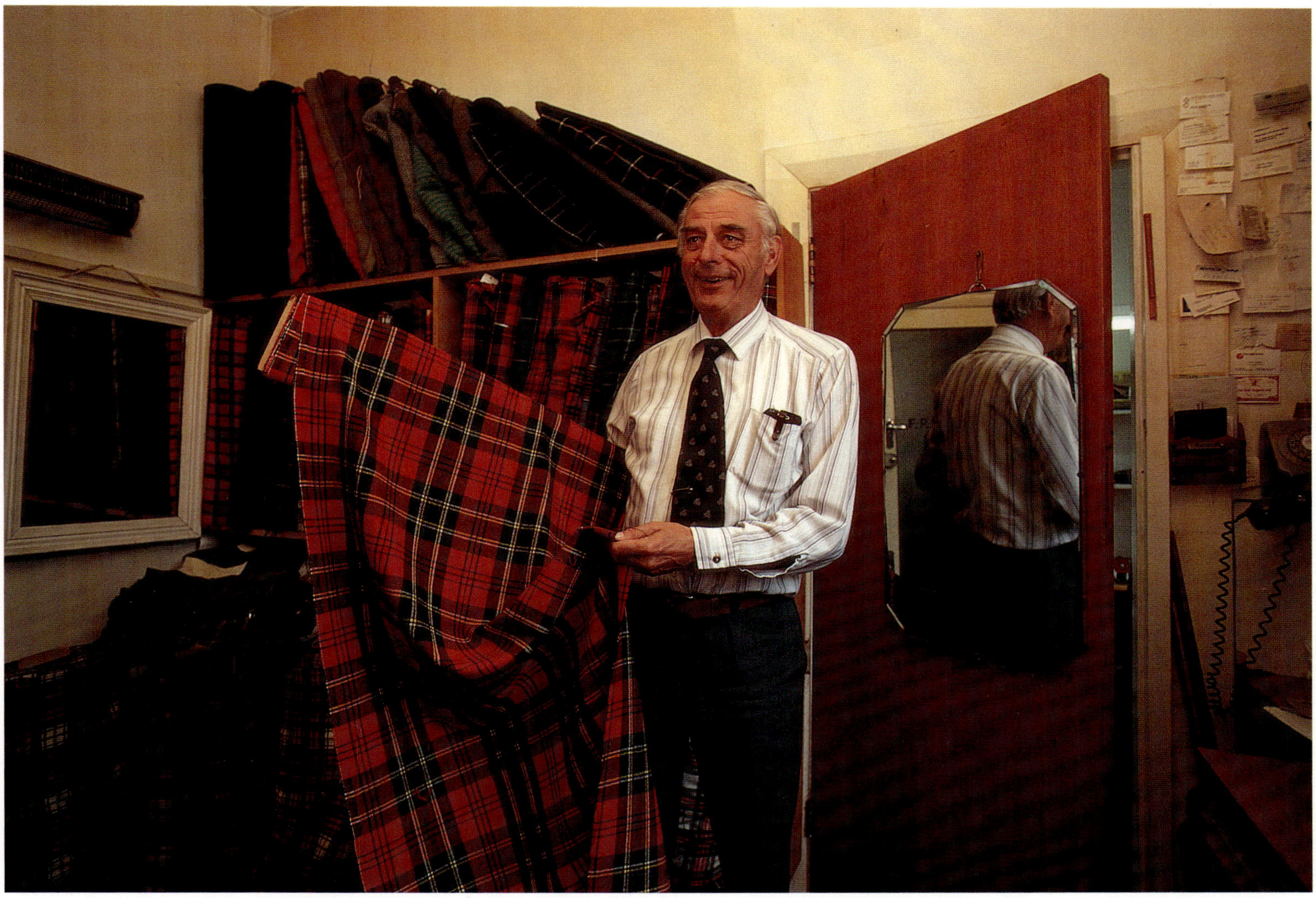

Storekeeper with a selection of tartans, Naseby, Otago GEOFF MASON

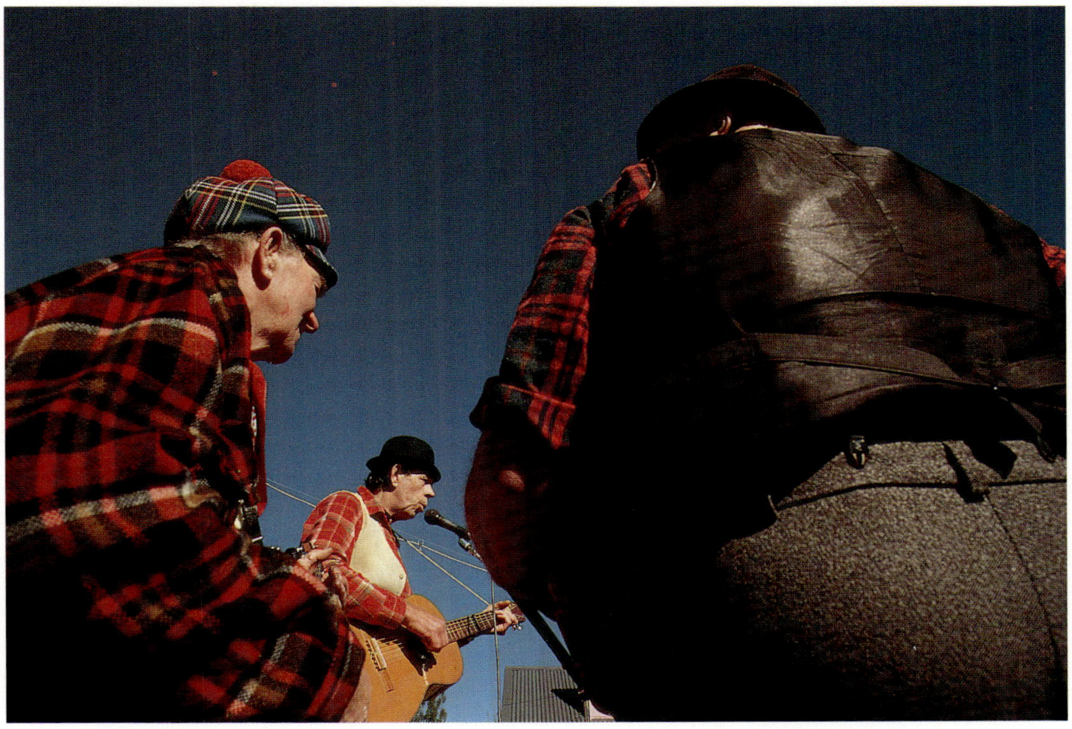

Old time band, Arrowtown Autumn Festival GEOFF MASON

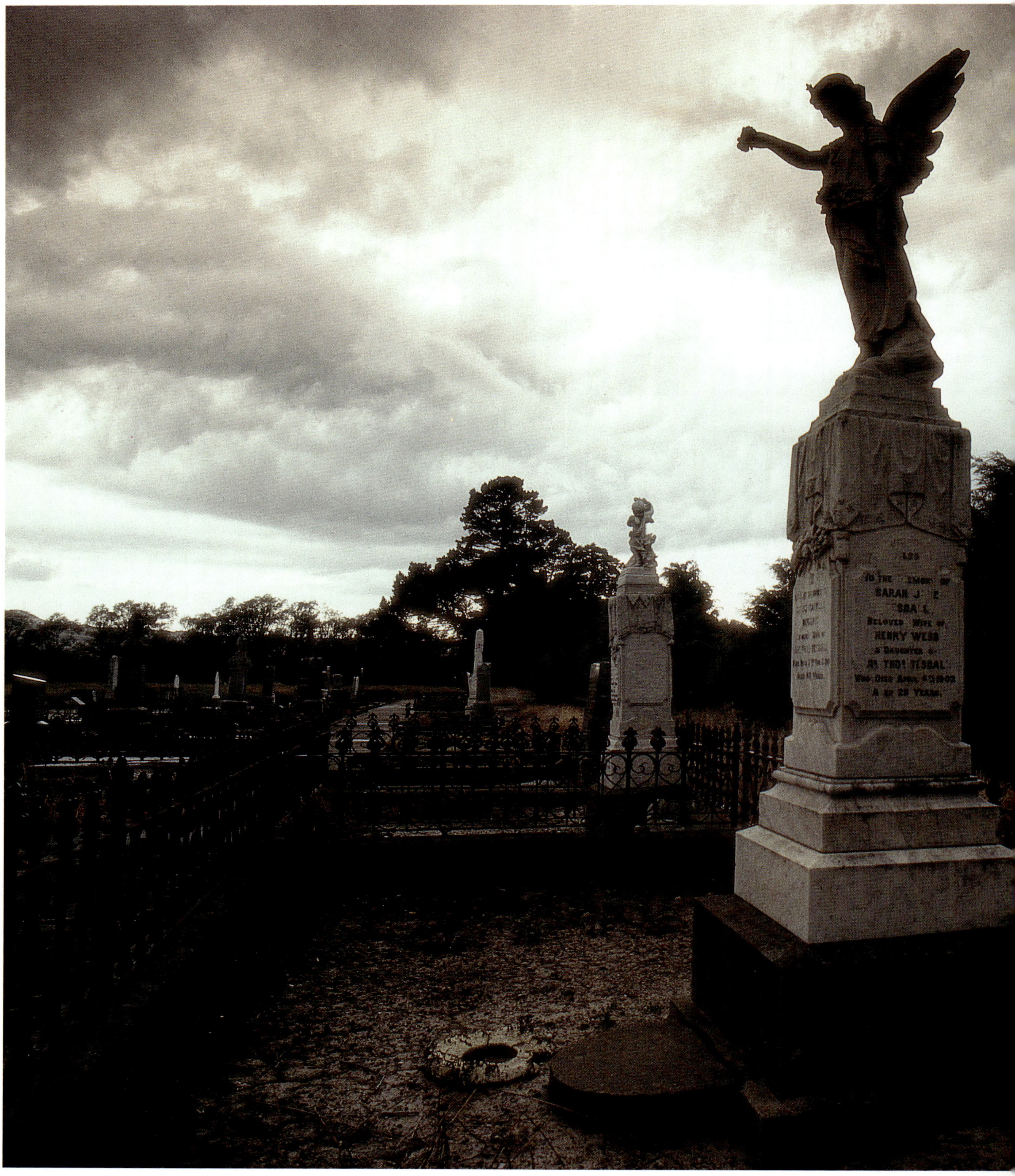

Early settlers graves, Middlemarch Cemetery, Central Otago

GEOFF MASON

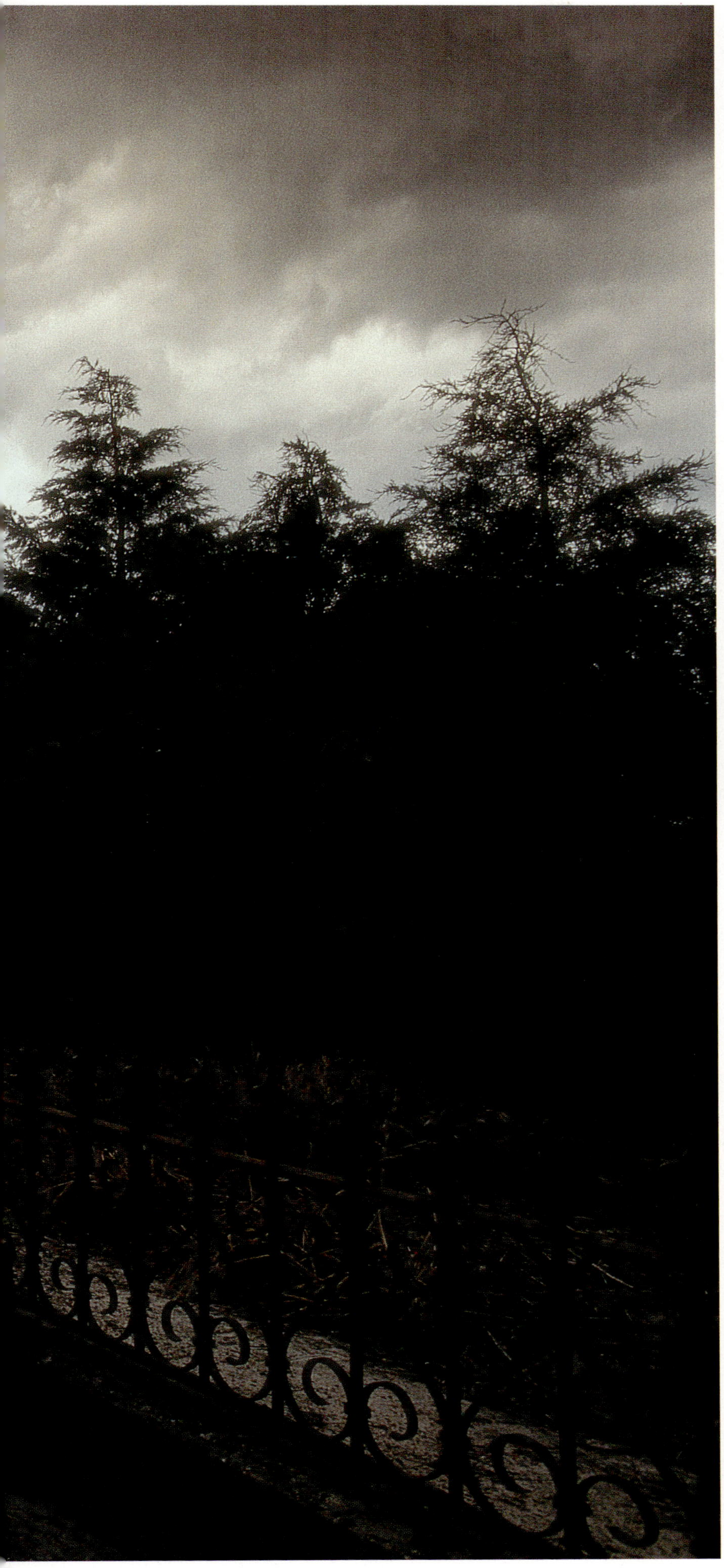

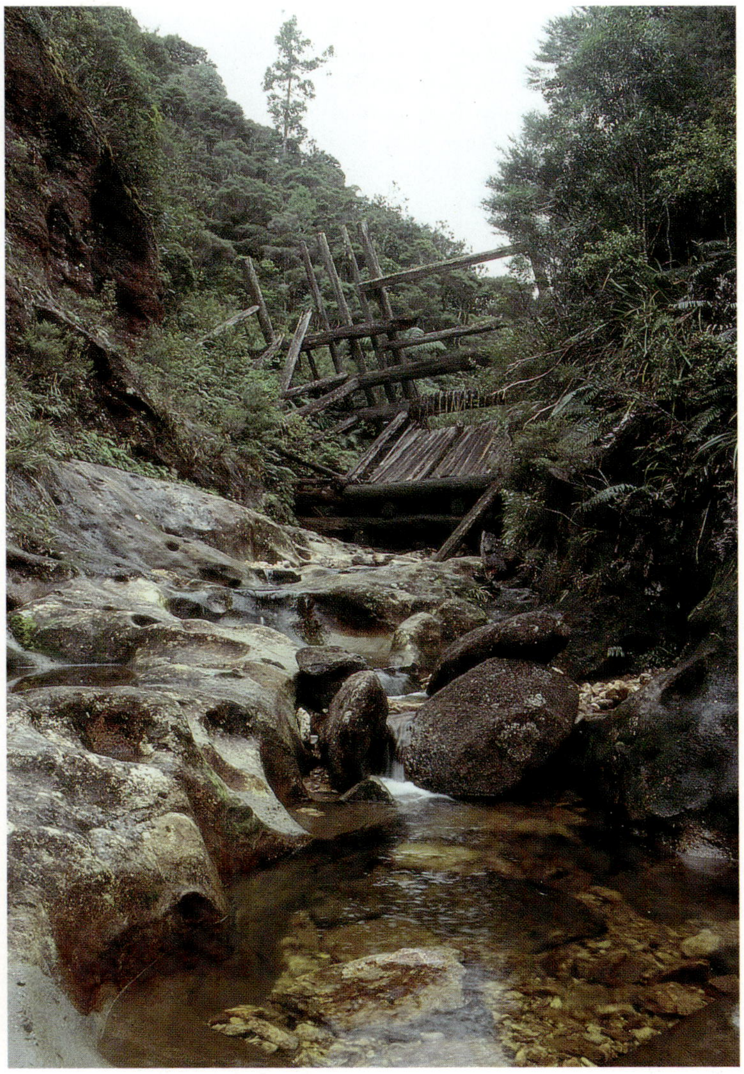

Kauri dam, Great Barrier Island ROBIN MORRISION

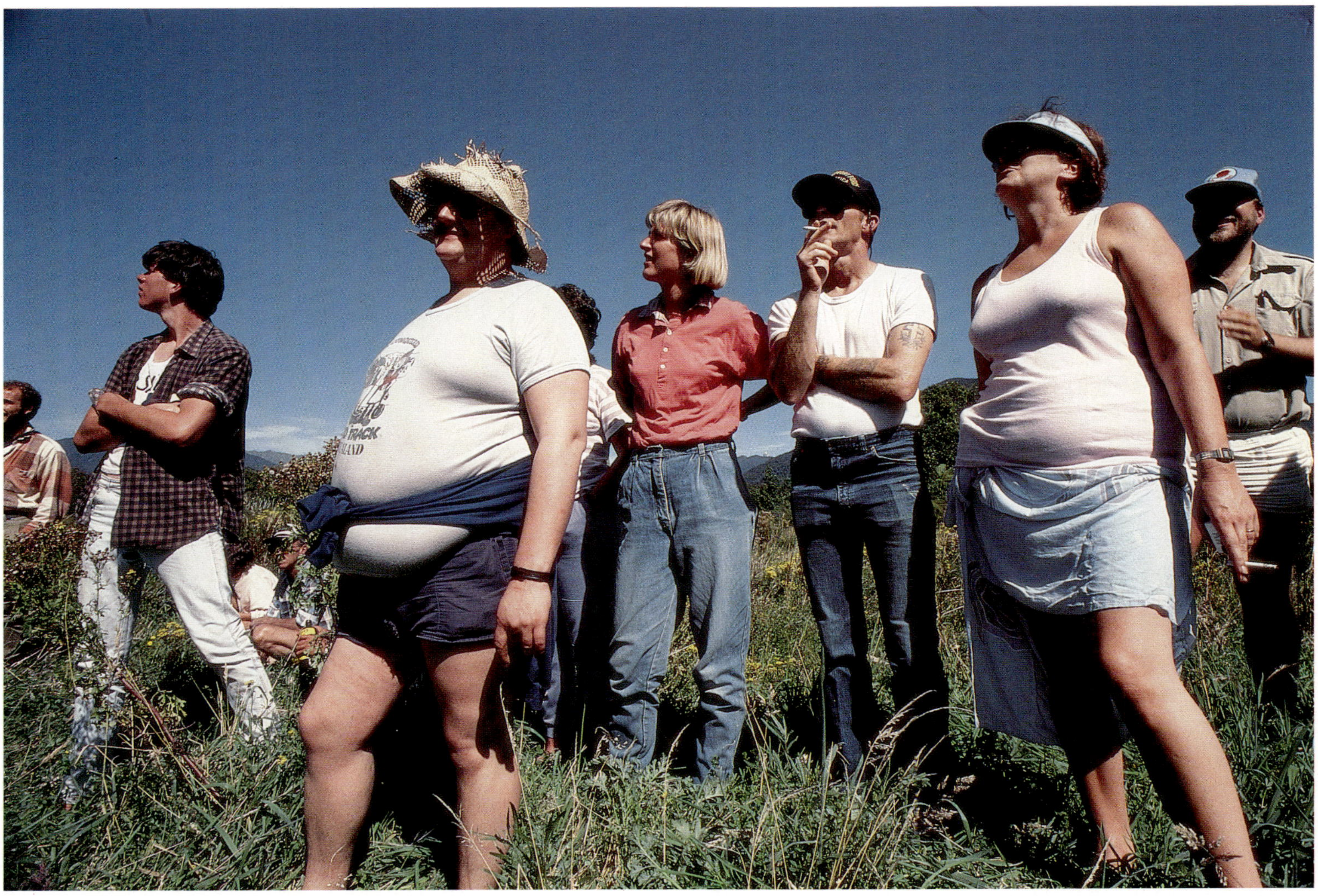

Spectators at clay pigeon shooting before the Martins Bay "golf match", Fiordland. There is no golf course at Martins Bay. All the equipment is improvised

BRIAN ENTING

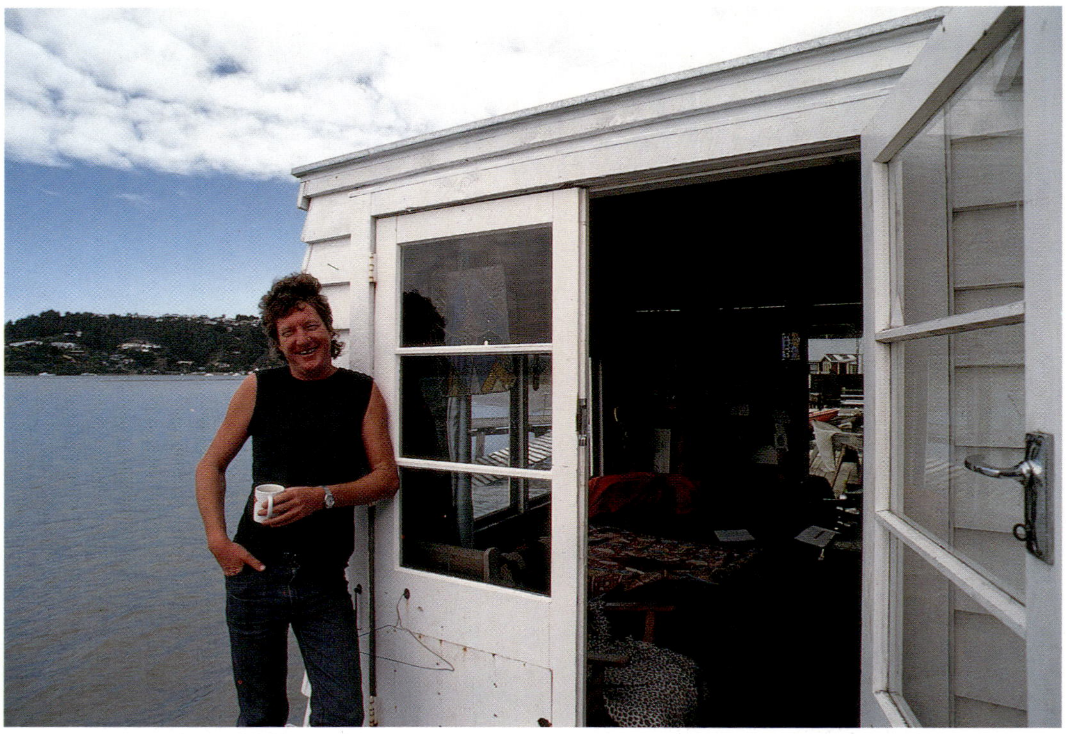

Sam Hunt at home, Paremata, Wellington

TIM STEELE

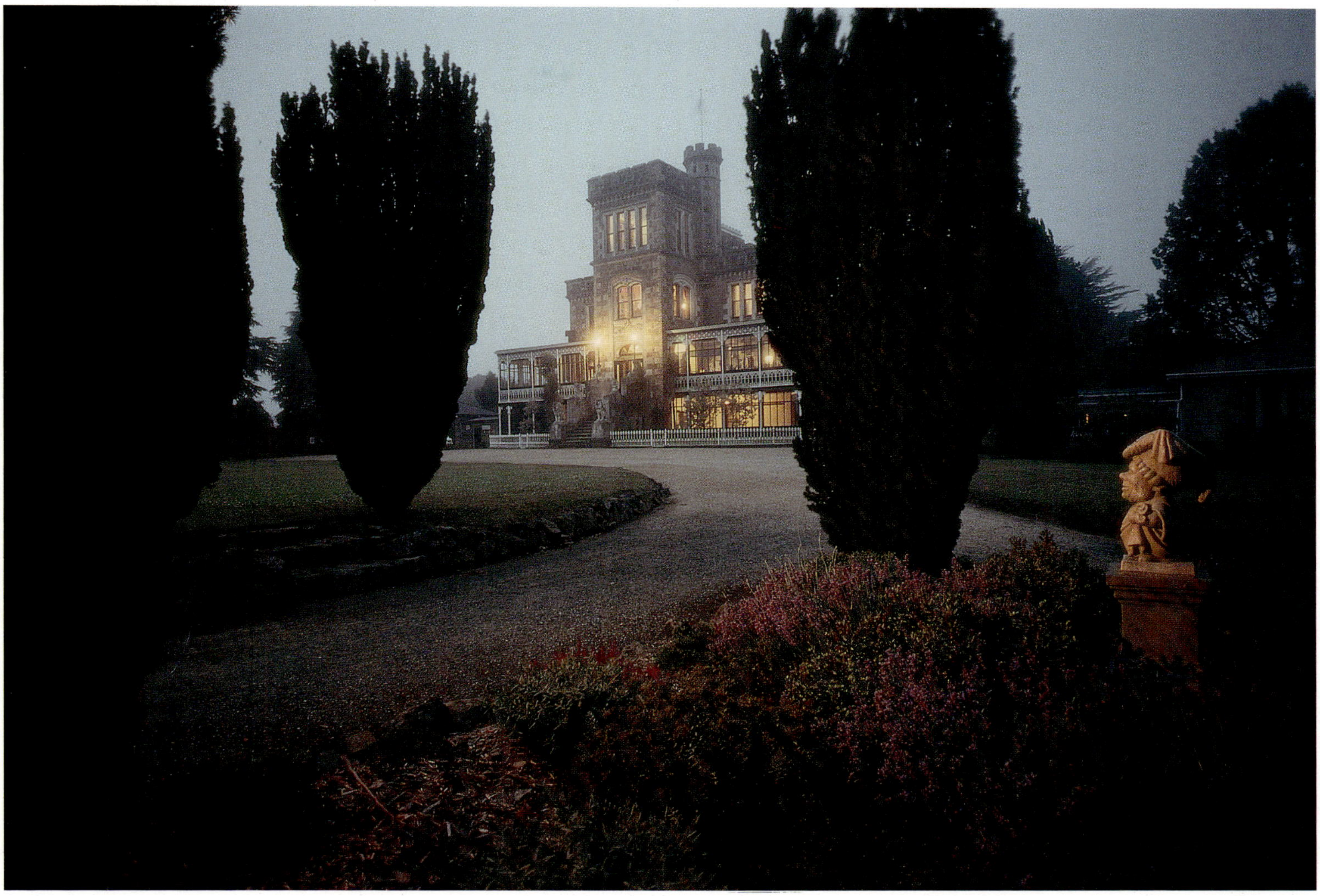

Larnach's Castle, Otago Peninsula, built in 1876 for the financier and politician William Larnach — GEOFF MASON

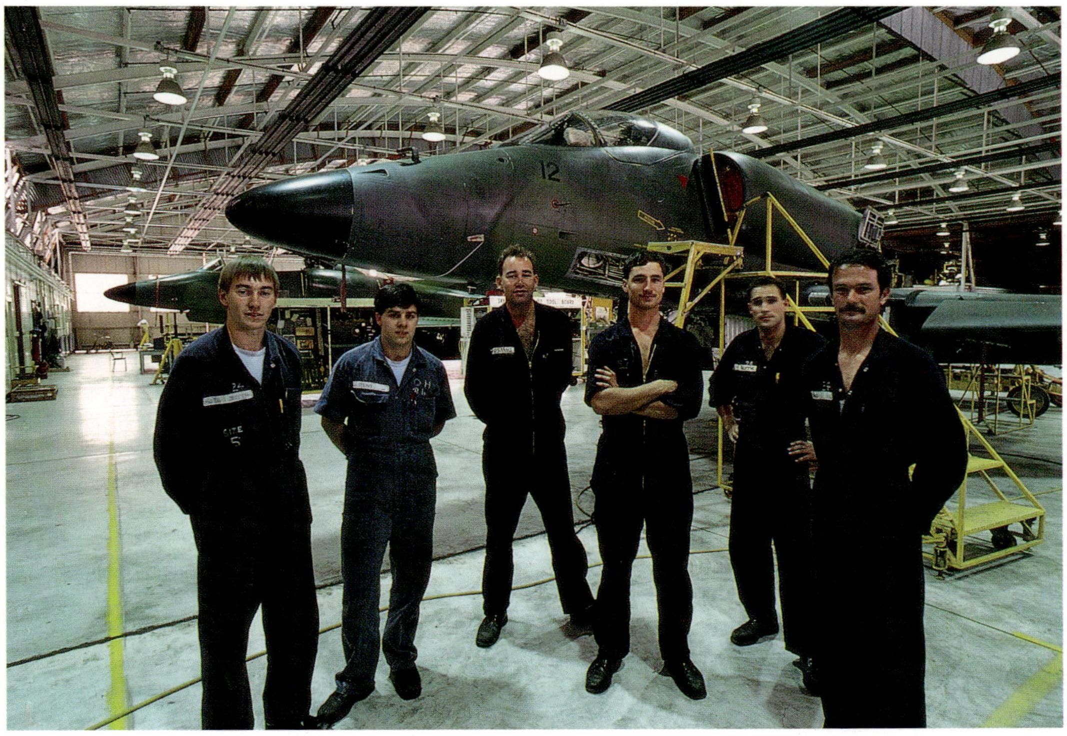

RNZAF technicians in front of Skyhawk NZ6212, Ohakea Airforce Base — TIM STEELE

TALES OF THE COAST

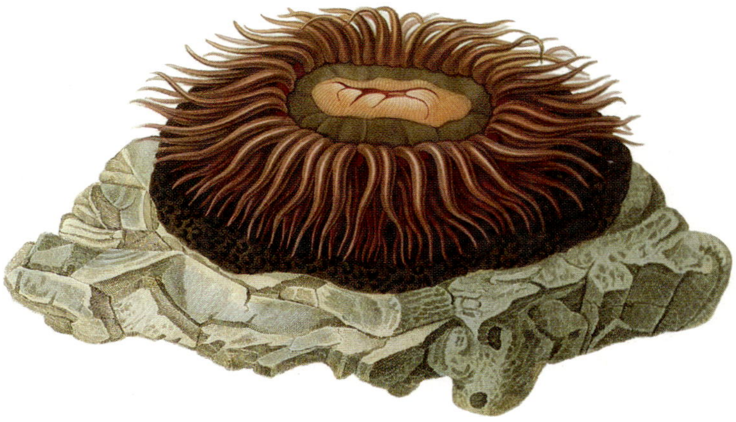

Voyage Autour Du Monde, L. I. Duperrey, 1826, Paris.

Keri Hulme

STEP OUT INTO the first light of day – tihei mauriora!

This morning, the Tasman is eery-quiet, and there is no wind. A line of shags, a living net, is working the little lagoon, and the flip and surface skittering of the flounder fry they're after comes clear and sharp to the ear.

Walk south, to the Sisters.

A benign overnight tide has spread dark sand over the shingle and rocks. "Black sand" we call it, and if this were 120 years ago, I'd be out with my shovel and table, digging instead of strolling. For black sand is quartz granules mixed with rutile and titanium, with ilmenite, garnet – and gold.

There doesn't appear to be much life around the Sisters as they squat, massive and shadowed, by the bluff. Some stout-shelled limpets on the landward side, and the limpets' nidamental coils in season, looking like onion slices with alternate rings removed: tiny black periwinkles, seed mussels, barnacles . . . the sand periodically scours them all away. Gulls fly over, the gulls fly back. Caspian terns yelp and swoop, and in winter, the solitary resident kotuku beats slowly past on its way to the lagoons. A desolate place.

And yet: I have found a living oarfish on this beach, and many whales have stranded here. Last century's horde of miners are long gone, but seals and penguins still haul out and shelter in the lee of the Sisters. The first people to walk these sands, over 700 years ago, may have sheltered there too.

Over the hill, on the other side of the island, two degrees of latitude south and about 200 kilometres away (as a kea might fly), is a different shore, another world. *This* beach is golden, a crescent of ochred sand ending in black rocky arms. The reefs, Te Karipi to the north and Tikoraki to the south, cradle the bay, but cannot ward off that occasional wind-driven sea which comes crashing past the high-tide mark and covers the kaik' cribs with spume. Ordinarily, the Pacific is as quiet as its name, and the little beach of Matuatiki sleeps in the sun.

But step along the tide-line at night: a thousand crabs and sandhoppers skip by your feet. On the reefs you may disturb octopi feasting on starfish, and, if you listen carefully, ear down by them as they move with a tiny heavy sucking sound, you can hear the green snails browsing. The dark is wound through with the cries of birds.

This place has been alive with people for a thousand years. We pick their handiwork off the beach, adzes and koauau and flake knives; we disturb their umukai when digging holes of our own, finding that old sand still blackly rich with sooted fat; their bones lie in the ancient urupa, just over the crib's back fence.

In one of the continuum I work in, and from, you go backwards into the future, the past is ever before you, and the present, the now, is only breath – hu! Tihei mauriora!

HOW TO CONVEY a land in words? More precisely: how to convey to you these sea-coasts in written words?

I could write,

The Okarito cliffs are recent 'piedmont' moraine, formed about 15,000 years ago, and weathered and sea-worn since. The Moeraki region has paleocene-eocene igneous rocks from the Waiareka volcanic formation, and conglomerates and concretions in confused strata and heaps.

(And geomorphologists could both see and wonder anew at the fascinating cycle of land formed and changed and reformed, and raise an eyebrow at the way I use their language.)

I could write,

Sea and air are rich with life. Ducks in the moult, and gulls' eggs; titi chicks, and kiwi, kakapo, and weka, and the many succulent smaller birds of the bush; whitebait in their myriads, and young kanakana; flounder and kahawai and silver-bellied eel, and shellfish from tuatua to the lowly titiko – all were taken and eaten in due season.

(And biologists could sadly ponder a view that sees life as food-flying, and food-swimming, and cooks recoil in horror at the thought of sullying their kitchen with mud-shitting snails.)

I could write,

We know about the swarms of gold miners, measuring their beach claims with plumb bob and rule lest an inch of valuable sand be forfeited: we know how they tried to keep the sandflies at bay, with a vile mixture of bacon fat and kerosene. But we know so little about the shadowy figures behind them – Kati Mamoe, Waitaha, Kati Wairaki, Ka Tini o Rapuwai, Te Kahui a Tipua . . . real peoples, and legendary goblins (or strangers): all they left of themselves were stone artefacts, and vast middens, and names.

(And historians could demand sources for the plumb bob and the bacon fat, and my elders rightly retort, "Kati Mamoe ma left behind more than names and rubbish – they left whakapapa and a considerable number of descendants, amongst whom you stand.")

All the preceding words contain truths. All illuminate shadows, cloud lights, at Moeraki, and Okarito. But English is a subtle language, and a treacherously variable one. New Zealand English is not fully understood by someone who doesn't know us. Maori English may be despised by someone who doesn't appreciate its pungency and rhythm. I'll choose words as best I can to give a certain shade of meaning to my sentences; you may freight those words differently, give them another sensory or emotional loading.

Well, given the above – and remembering that Okarito Free Republic is a state of mind, and that the ghosts of Moeraki are realities only to those who've met them – here are a couple of coasts, and an island or two, in a general salute to our land.

FROM THE DAWN of my life, is Moeraki. We went there on weekends and holidays, and in times of crisis. The name means, in southern dialect, "a place to sleep (or dream) by day", and the whole area has a curious, deeply restful, ambience – during the day.

Night-time is a different story.

The kaik' beach, where Matuatiki makes watery braids on the sand, was our playground, and when we were able to swim, and more or less trusted not to drown ourselves or each other, we ventured out on the reefs. You *could* play there, but we were interested in fishing, and fishing is not play. Cross over the little channel in Tikoraki that even in the lowest spring tide has a surge in it: go out past the blowhole where the scary tentacles of kelp writhe (we made slippers and pretend-poha and balls from the kelp on the beach, but somehow the same stuff became sinister round the blowhole): find yourself a seat or a perch just out of reach of the waves, and throw a hand line into the channel. Maori chiefs and kelp-cod aplenty and, if you were lucky, and had the right rig, and the fish were feeling like suicide, greenbone and moki.

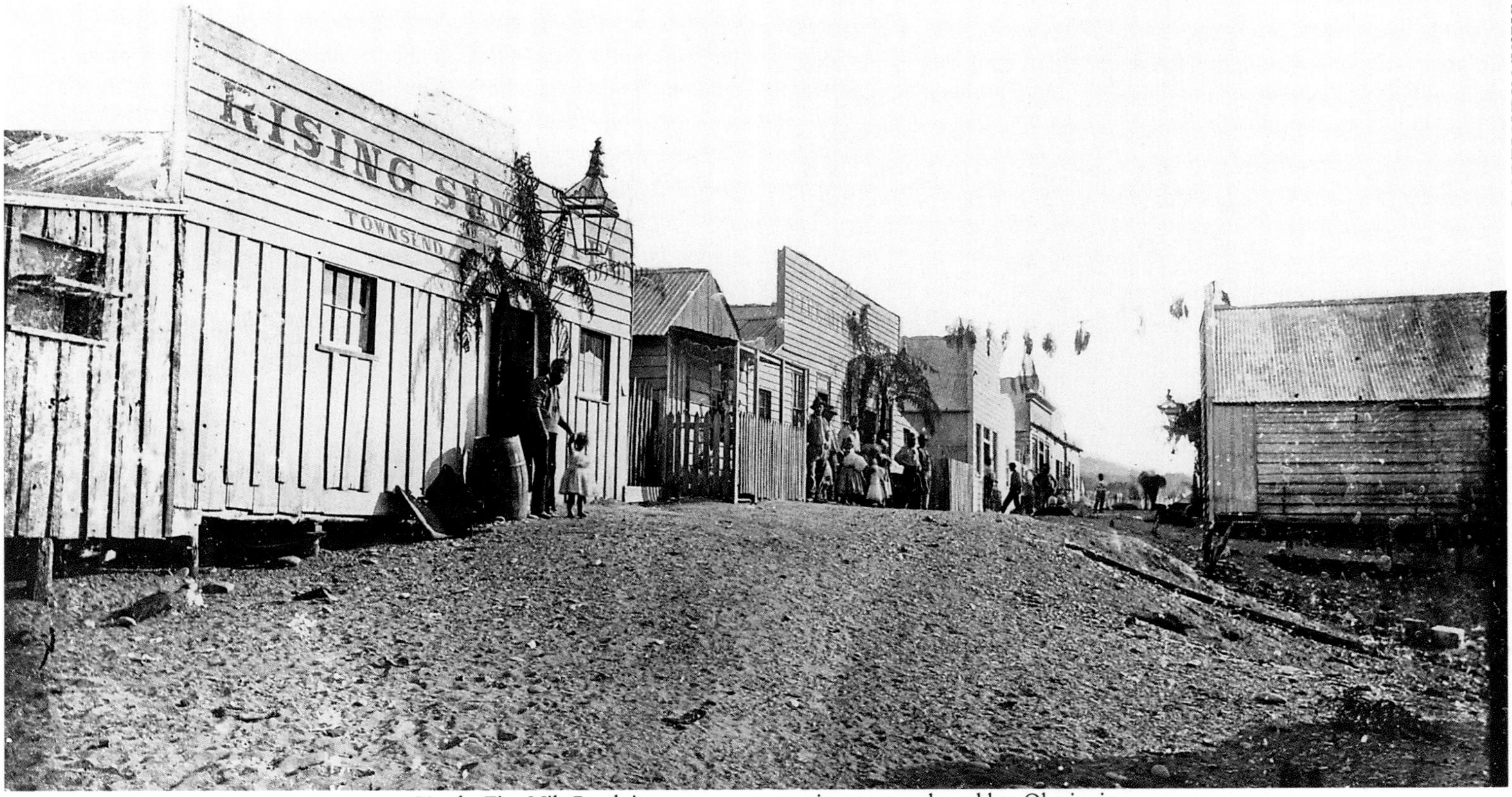

CANTERBURY MUSEUM

"At the Five Mile Beach it was common practice to carry the gold to Okarito in billies to sell because the ordinary chamois leather gold bags were too small to hold the splendid yields," said the *Cyclopedia of New Zealand*. This photograph of the Five Mile Beach township was taken in the 1870s, at the height of the gold rush.

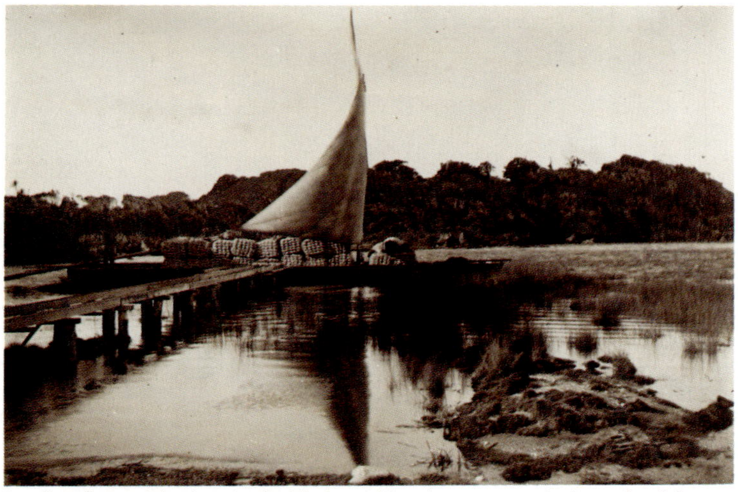

CANTERBURY MUSEUM

Loading flax at Okarito. As the black sand beaches were worked out, local flax provided alternative employment for some. At Kino Flax Mill at Whale's Beach twenty-five men were employed.
HAROLD HENDEY/LUCAS COLLECTION

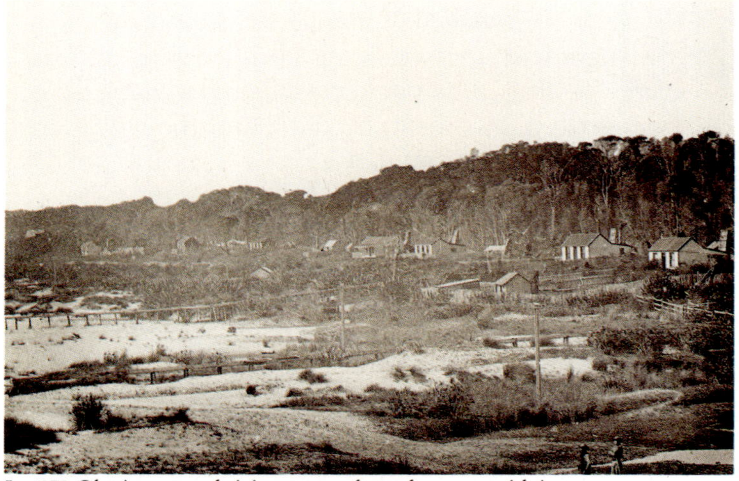

CANTERBURY MUSEUM

In 1870 Okarito was a thriving port and supply centre with its own newspaper, rivalling Hokitika and Greymouth. As the gold was exhausted the population dwindled, the land was cleared, and farming developed.

When you had enough, or all that were cooperative, you wandered back, relocating starfish and hassling crabs and (more peaceably) gazing for long minutes into the tidepools.

We graduated from fishing the reef to fishing out in the boat; the blue boat mainly, a clinker-built rowboat older than I was but beautifully seaworthy. And Moeraki became a whole new world, seen from the sea. The kaik' dwindled, seemed both vulnerable and a distant security. The hills, particularly Puketapu and Raumoa, became more than just names and dim background presences: they were friends, allies, who showed you where the fishing patches were. ("Put the lighthouse in the middle of Puketap' and those cribs left of Raumoa.")

It wasn't all fishing: we ate a lot, slept a lot, read a lot, and talked half the nights away. Sometimes you'd be chattering on and uncle Bill's dog would rouse and quite suddenly bark, staring hard at a corner with nothing in it. Or the cat would come in from molesting the mice, and settle down to cleaning herself in a relaxed sort of way, and then bristle and mewl deep in her throat. We'd joke, "The old fellas have come in for company again," but the jokes had undertones.

There was a beach too, where the sand whispered loudly as you walked on it, and you had an uneasy feeling someone was staring at your back all the time. You would be walking by yourself, and stop abruptly and turn round: nobody was there, and the sand-whisper continued too many seconds after your last footfall. The beach was (and is) starkly bare – no clutter of gaudy baches there – although in past centuries, it had been a major kaika.

If you walked that beach barefoot, the soles of your feet rapidly turned black. No mystery in that, however. The sooty fat exuded by countless cooked barracouta, and penguin chicks, and seals (and other creatures), was still thick in the sand.

I wondered, often, how had it been when the cooking pits were in use? And the village crowded and noisily alive? What did the people look like? Like my uncle Bill in a maro? Or my great-uncle Dave in a cloak? Katie Parati from up the hill without her blouse?

And I wondered what Moeraki was like when the southern right whales brought their calves in to play in the shallow waters of the port bay, and the humpbacks streamed past Tikoraki in steady procession. And, looking round the shaven hills, the only scrub imported boxthorn, how it must have been when the bush came right to the water's edge and the birds sang all day.

IT IS 1989, and the fishing is poor. There is plastic debris among the kelp, and more shags are dead or dying on the beaches than I've ever seen.

There are odd rays of hope: people have begun planting trees, and Cook's scurvy grass was recently rediscovered round by the lighthouse. There are a couple especially concerned with looking after the hoiho, the yellow-eyed penguin, a solitary determined species of bird which needs bush to breed in and freedom from interference by cattle or sheep or humans – or other hoiho in the near vicinity. And it is intriguing to learn that the remnant southern right whale population (a few individuals had habitually bred at Campbell Island instead of travelling to New Zealand, and so had escaped the general massacre of the late 1820s to 1845) – the southern rights are on the increase.

Maybe one of these days, instead of slack-spiritedly trudging through festivities which contain little of their original impulse and joy, and which have nothing to do with our climate or seasons, we will celebrate our own reality in our own way.

Waitangi, certainly, but also Tangiwai when we could remember and mourn for all those lost or broken in the disasters that come our way, and a day in June when the sun is lowest, the night is longest, to make bonfires for the dead and wildly, riotously acknowledge the fact of our own deaths, (a long way in the future of course – this is just to brighten up deepest winter you understand).

On The Whales Are Back! I'd fly kites and let off sky rockets and make music and dance: the First of Oysters would be for general feasting and merriment before winter sets in, and the spring Festival of the Clematis, Our Lady of October time, would be to welcome all new life and growth.

Meanwhile, Maukiekie stands staunch in the kaik' bay, white-topped in the sun.

I DIDN'T GET TO *the* West Coast until 1970. I knew little about it – my greatgrandfather Tieke Mira and his mother had come from there as refugees when Te Puoho raided, went the family story, and of course it was Te Tai Pouitini, home of the greenstone fish – and I didn't intend to stay.

It would be five years before I started building my home at Okarito (I still haven't finished it, but do you ever finish building a home?), and by that time, the place had seeped into my bones.

For one thing, I'd discovered whitebaiting, and had

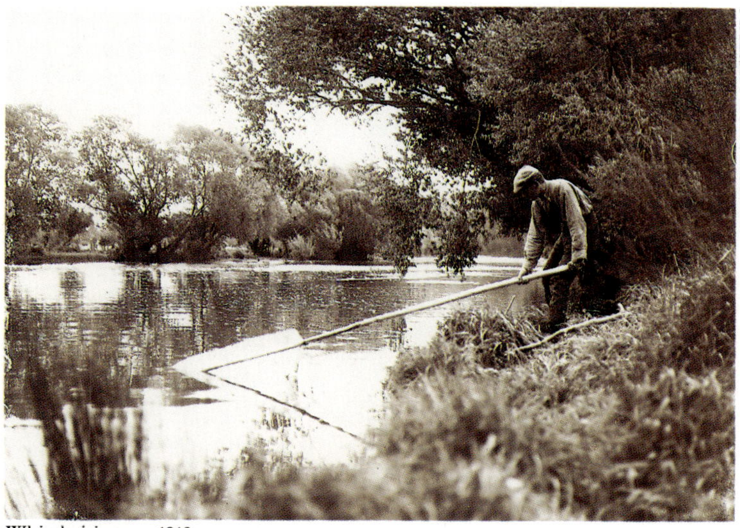

CANTERBURY MUSEUM

Whitebaiting, ca 1910.
CANTERBURY TIMES COLLECTION

caught and eaten enough of those utterly delicious little fish to literally be part'bait. For another, the pace of life on the Coast (which, at its best, is seasonally determined, slowed or quickened by the larger rhythms of the world), suited me down to the ground. For another, I'd fallen in love with Okarito. It was bleak and ascetical, shadow to Moeraki's light, but it was also untamed and floodprone and bushclad, and you could walk for miles on the beaches and never see another human being.

Okarito became a place of marvels for me, where a gull dropped a live fish at my feet (unintentionally, but it didn't dispute me picking it up), and a young female fur seal, flippers bound tight with that wretched plastic tape so frequently flung overboard by the careless and the uncaring, dragged herself past four other houses, through gorse, to warble for help outside my door. I still mourn her, because I was a coward afraid of her teeth, and wouldn't go close enough to hold her and cut through the binding. She lay there from dawn until the evening, and dragged herself away during the night. I found her skull a month later in the little lagoon, and have it still as a reminder of how not to behave.

I have watched the silken dancing of kanakana through the water (neatly avoiding the fyke net I had set for them in the main, although I did catch two and so can confirm what an elder told me years ago – young lamprey are even richer than their equivalent weight in sardines). I have seen a scoop-net with over 30 lb of bait in it, caught in one drag, and spent a season where we counted the catch on our fingers, and gave them names for fun.

I know now that some paradise shelducks are aware of the dates for duck-shooting – why else should that pair have settled onto the little lagoon (which is thirty yards away from the six houses and baches that line the road at the south end of the village, and thus not available to shooters) two days before the season began? And never left it in daylight until the day after the season ended? I know now that at least one white heron in the world knows what a camera is: Hieronomo, who overwinters in Okarito, will crane elegantly or fold his/her neck into that distinctive double-kink the instant a lens is aimed its way.

West Coasters tell marvellous tales, and most of them are more true than you would believe.

GETTING TO KNOW SOMETHING of a place over twenty years: it rains. Twenty-four inches in twenty-four hours. Three days of sunshine between May and October. But there can be droughts, when the bush dries out, and local authorities cart water for people in Hokitika, and the little crabs run round the cracked mudflats of the lagoon wondering in a dim way What happens before dying? Nothing human lasts here, very long. The stone artefacts, the midden heaps, the names . . . the bush and the rain and the highly mobile land take care of everything else. Great dredges that used to munch acres in the search for alluvial gold, flake away to heaps of rust. Neglected houses and sheds and farm buildings sag and collapse into piles of borer-riddled wood and rotten iron. In twenty years, there's a weedy heap: in fifty years, nothing.

Getting to know something more: you can't fight this land, and you can waste too much time and energy trying. Chop down the forests, and the slips and flooding increase and overwhelm you. Build beside a river that is known to rise ten feet overnight, or apt to change channel, and whether you're a town or a farm, you'll get drowned. If you live with the land, live lightly on it, you can thrive. Sometime in the future, maybe, a people will dwell here, a quiet, dry-humoured, amphibian people, who harvest considerately, with care not greed; who grow what is suited to the place, prawns and herbs rather than sheep and cattle; a people who will cherish what *is* here, rather than try to 'tame', 'build', 'develop' (and only succeed in spreading a miserable human ugliness).

Part of the present reality, however, is that people learn very little from the past: we introduced the rat and the dog, and killed off the moa, the flightless goose, and the giant swan. We introduced the stoat and the pig, and another twenty-odd species died out. The magpies have reached Harihari, and oppossums have at last managed to cross the Cook River, and someone wants to farm fitches, and someone else introduced a voracious fish to keep the ditches clear of sandfly larvae and mosquitos . . . there's a rumour those things are vectors, carry AIDS, and 'flu bugs, and economic deficits.

You acquire a strange sense of humour, on this coast.

IT'S NEW YEAR'S DAY, and the Okarito Free Republic flag is aloft and flying free. (The present flag, you understand, is not the definitive one – while it has three stars, and a brilliant yellow smiley-face, a bonfire and a spiral, and the OFR's motto FOREVER (a somewhat arrogant choice for people who live beside the sea on a notoriously unstable coast), we feel it lacks a certain – I don't know quite what. Space, maybe?)

Anyway, here we are, sitting in the sunshine watching the hangi flames grow. The stones heat to white-hot: the rata chunks turn to ash. The baskets (ex-millcrates) go down under sheets and sacks and flax, and the steaming pile is covered with earth. We'll lift in a couple of hours.

It isn't a long-planned celebration. Few of our affairs are. They tend to be spontaneous and sudden, though opportune, and this one got organised round the hogmanay fire last night – "How're you off for chicken, Judith? Feel like making a steamed pudding?" "What, a hangi?" "Why not? It's gonna be fine, and I've still got two kahawai in the freezer from that last catch." David offers corn and cabbage he's brought from Christchurch, and the Warden and Harbourmaster of OFR, W. P. Minehan Esq. says how about some mutton from the sheep he killed last week? And there's a bit of venison from Richard's deer-from-the-3-Mile, and I've plenty of kumara and spuds.

Visitors turn up for a drink and chat, and are invited to stay for the later food (we've never yet run out): the flag hangs limply on the pole, and the sandflies become bothersome. It's going to be a glorious sunset, you can tell by the way the clouds are starting to light up, and over the back of the lagoon, high above that bronze-and-dark-green bush-covered range of hills, a bright red rainbow is forming, like a tohu for the newborn year.

The summer flag of toitoi are at their best, silken and greenly blond.

Soon, the shining cuckoos will cease calling, ready for the far ocean flight.

In March, Bluff oysters: in April, hopu-titi, and the chicks available soon after.

By May, Hieronomo is the only kotuku left in Okarito, and I've wound up the waterbed heat by a couple of notches.

In June, we'll light a solstice fire, inside or outdoors, and keep a weather-eye out for frostfish.

In July, the shining cuckoo juveniles that have wintered over, start to call, tentative and thin. The toitoi plumes are bare and brown.

August: time to head for Moeraki, for the kareko and winter-fat cod.

The whitebait season begins on the Coast in September. The herons are already in nuptial plumage and are breeding in the Waitangi-roto stream. Spring growth among the birds, the grass, the sea: kamahi flowers are rampant, and the first new wheki-ponga fronds are unfurling.

The Lady of October is everywhere, and the best runs of 'bait begin.

November, and the kowhai's out; the kina roes are getting plump and sweet.

The rata begins blooming, and the manuka is riotously in flower. O Summer December, rich with new peas and strawberries. The kahawai are shoaling at Moeraki, and the salmon getting ready to run. And January is coming, stonefruit ripening, and it's time to think New Year, again.

EVERYONE HAS their own almanac, yearly pattern, book of days. Mine changes the more I learn from my beaches, the bush and and rivers around. And it changes as I grow older, changing views.

I could give you an immensely detailed pattern, narrowly based: life on one small reef jutting out from one small beach. Or smaller still: life *in* one tiny tide pool. I could give you that kind of record, which I've ignored almost entirely here, a chronicle of family, birthdays and hui and small people growing up and old people looking hard at illness and death (or vice versa). Whatever, it would be *a* New Zealand pattern, one of the many million (think how many you could weave from your own life and history and years!) generated here, that are melding, and, somehow, growing us. To quote some words written about the Cliff Whiting design on the cover of the Waitangi Tribunal reports, that tauira is

Original . . . invoking the signing of the Treaty of Waitangi and the consequent development of Maori-Pakeha history interwoven in Aotearoa, in a pattern not yet completely known, still unfolding.

Tauira is teacher, is pupil, and copy as well as The Pattern.

On the West Coast, te tai-tamatane, the boisterous young men's sea, is roaring again. The Sisters were awash in the surf last night, and there are flurries of foam bowling along the beach today. On the east coast, North Otago way, the woman-sea will be calm, saving its waves for the wild time later in the year. The shags wing out from Maukiekie unimperilled, and the white horses are stilled.

We are a sea-people, in a sea-land: islanders, not surrounded and cut-off by the sea, but linked to the rest of the world, by ocean. And by the air we breathe, and the ideas and lives that we share.

Step out into the light of midday, step out on a beach. I greet us all – kia ora tatou katoa. □

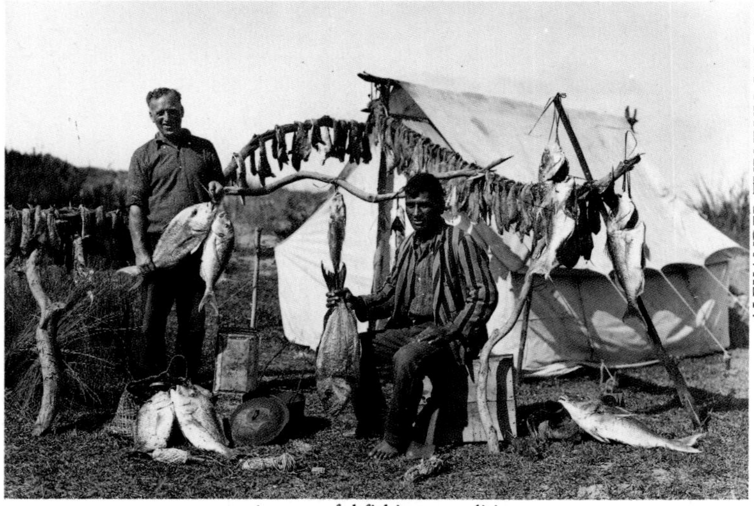

ALEXANDER TURNBULL LIBRARY

A successful fishing expedition.
NORTHWOOD COLLECTION

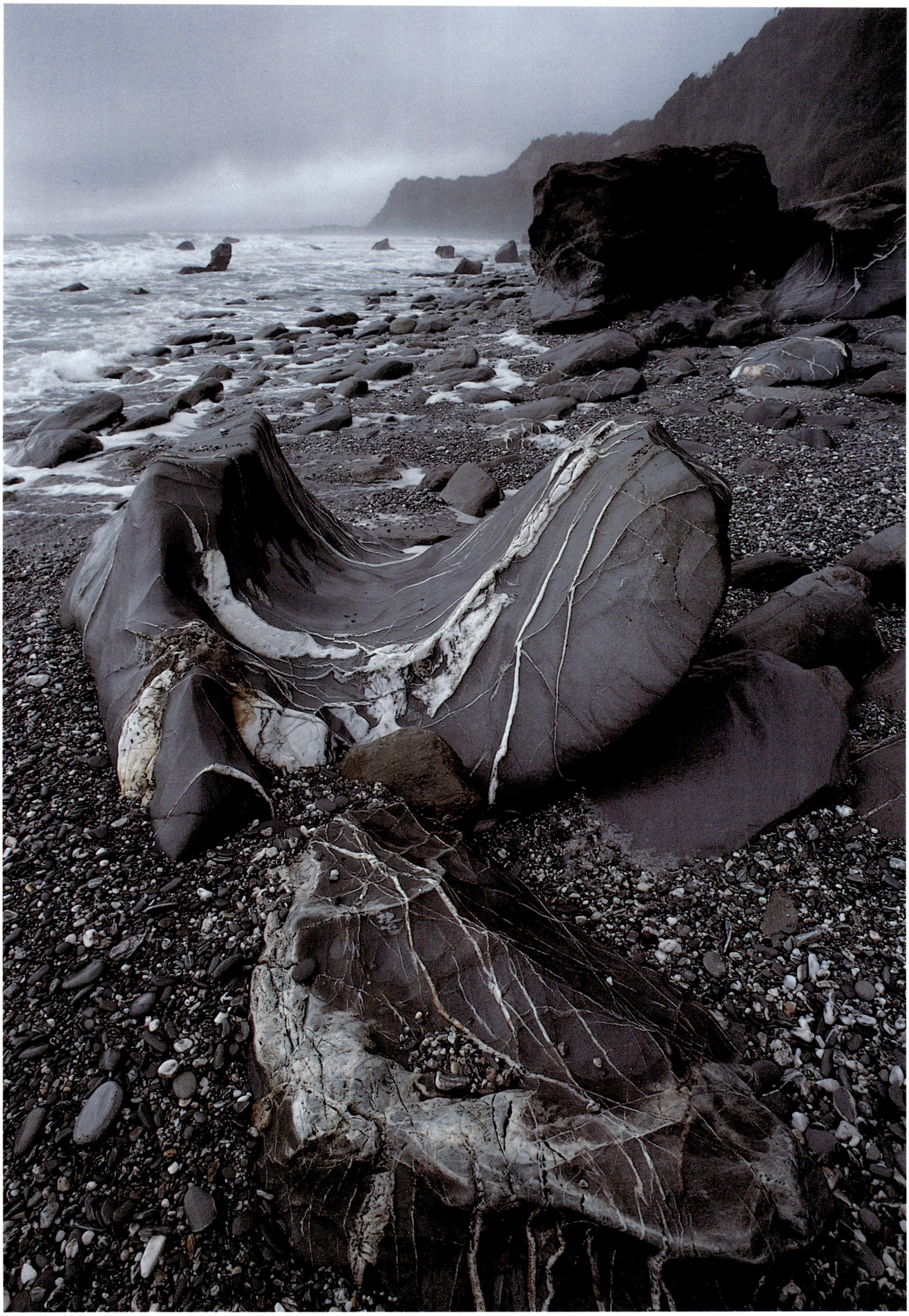

Okarito, West Coast

BRIAN ENTING

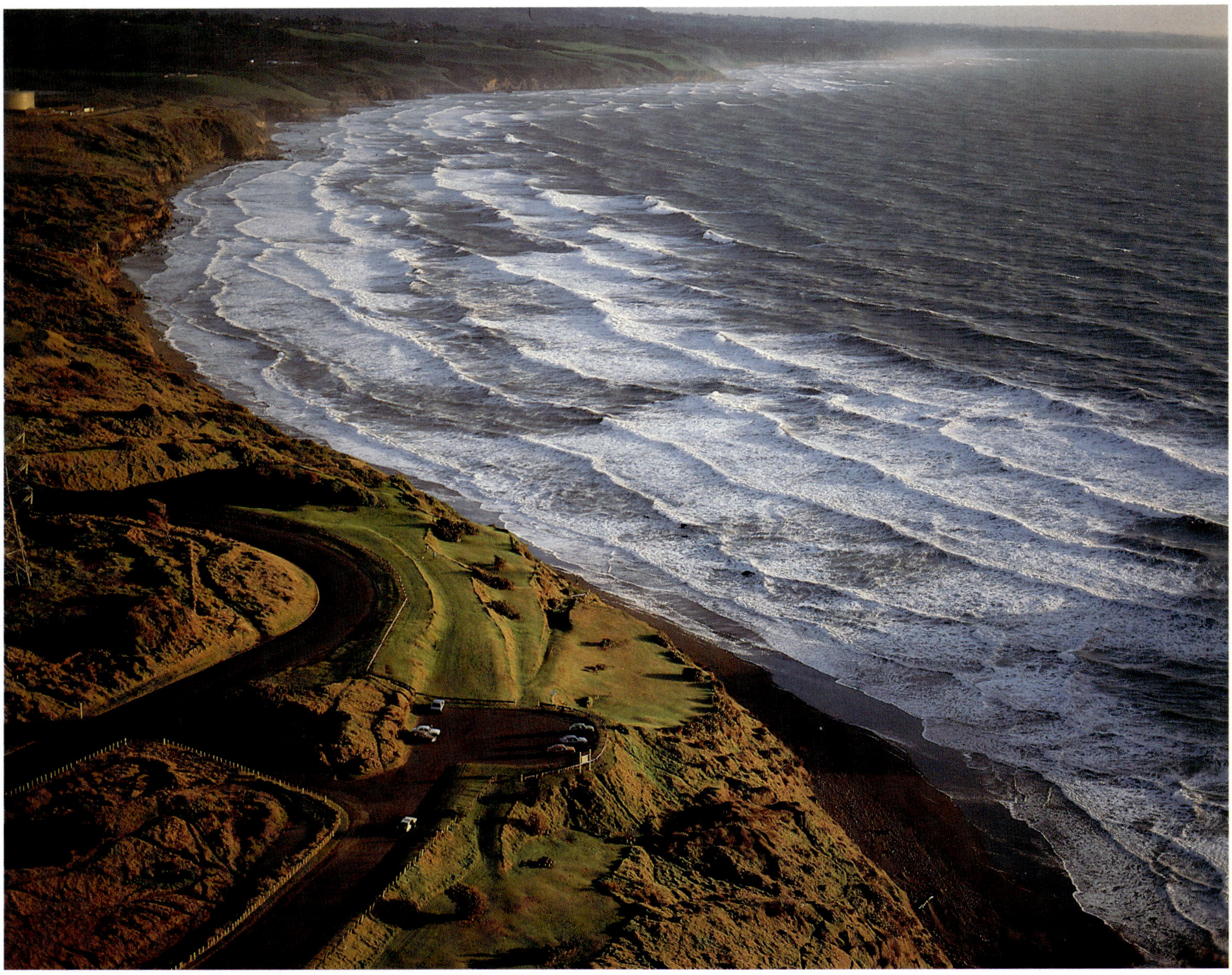

The coastline north of New Plymouth CRAIG POTTON

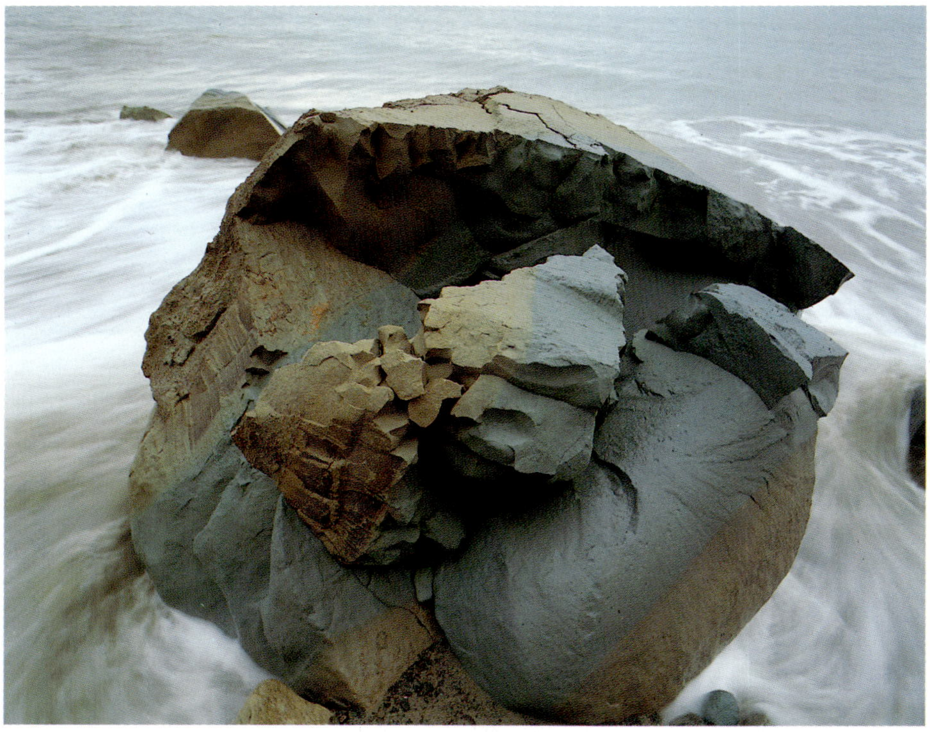

Cape Kidnappers, Hawke's Bay CRAIG POTTON

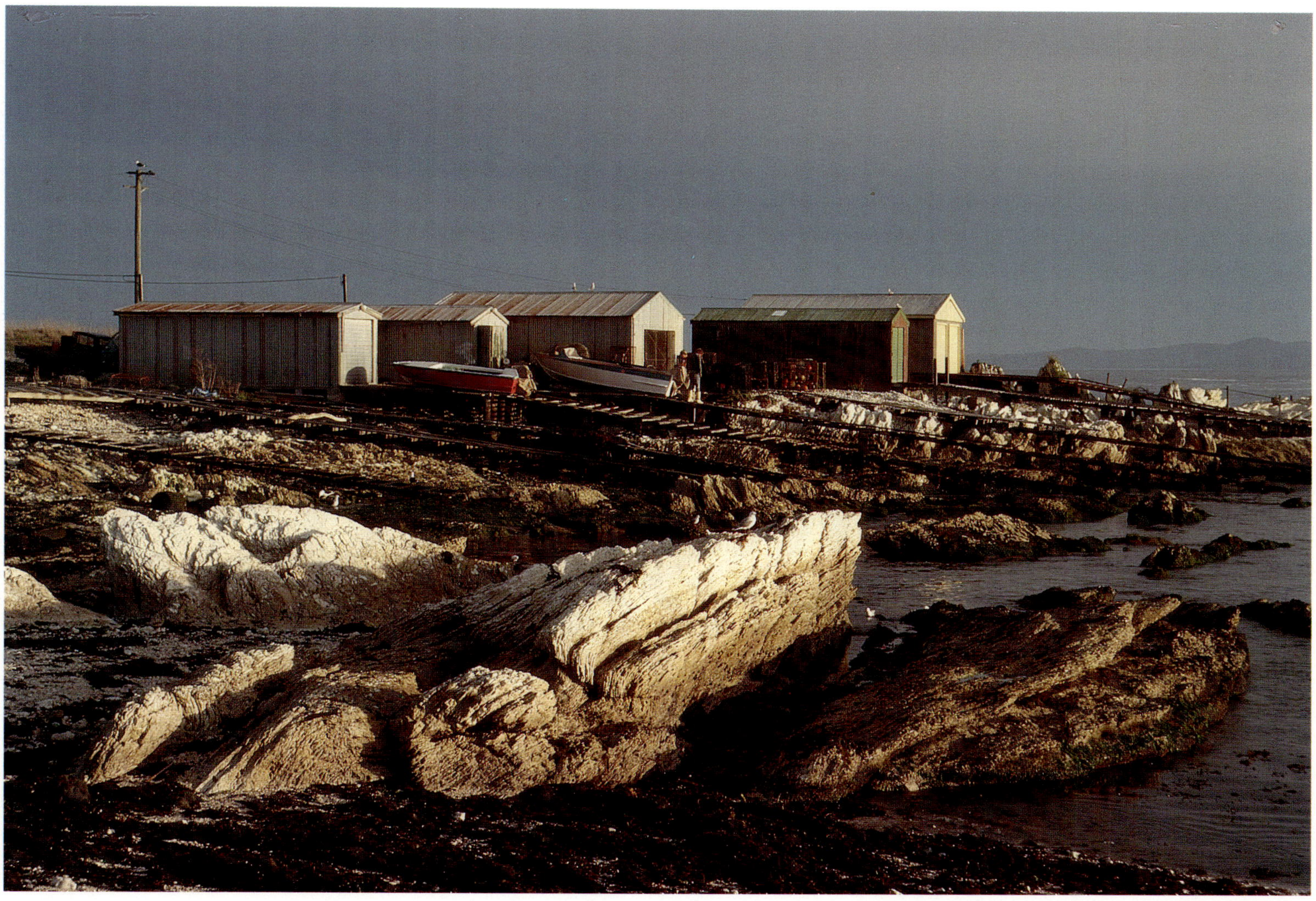

Kaikoura ROBIN MORRISON

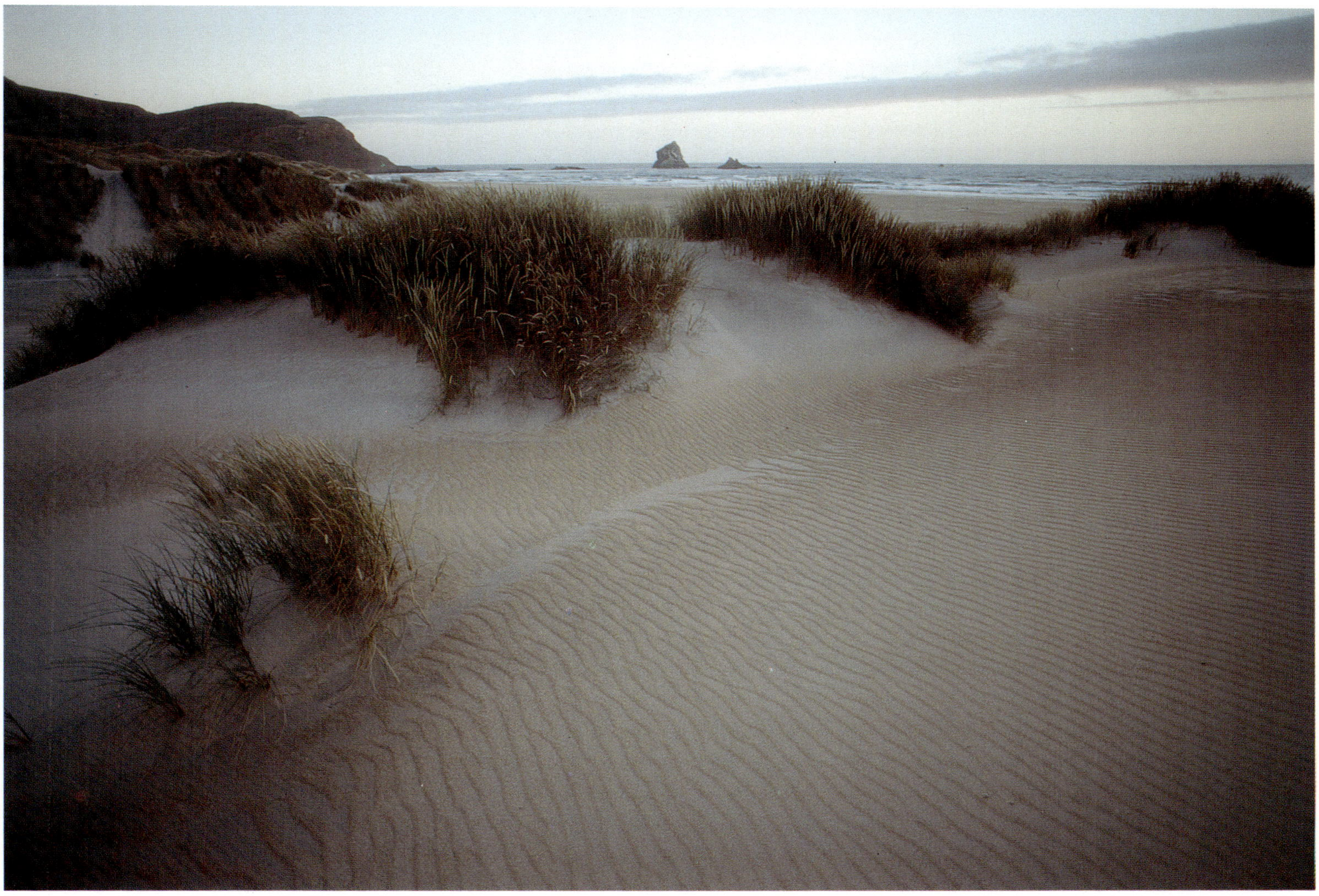

Sandfly Bay, Otago Peninsula GEOFF MASON

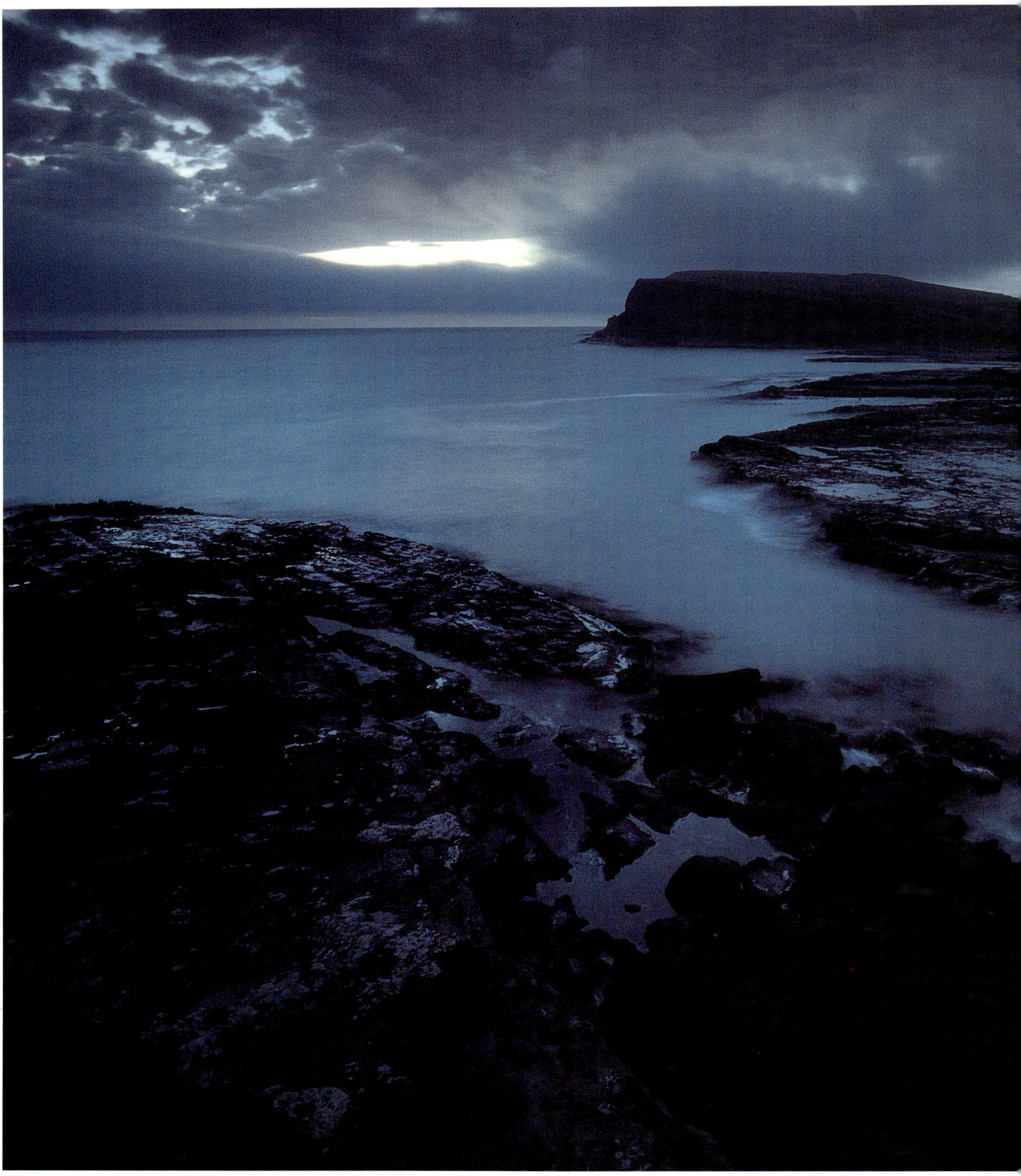

Curio Bay, Catlins, Otago

GEOFF MASON

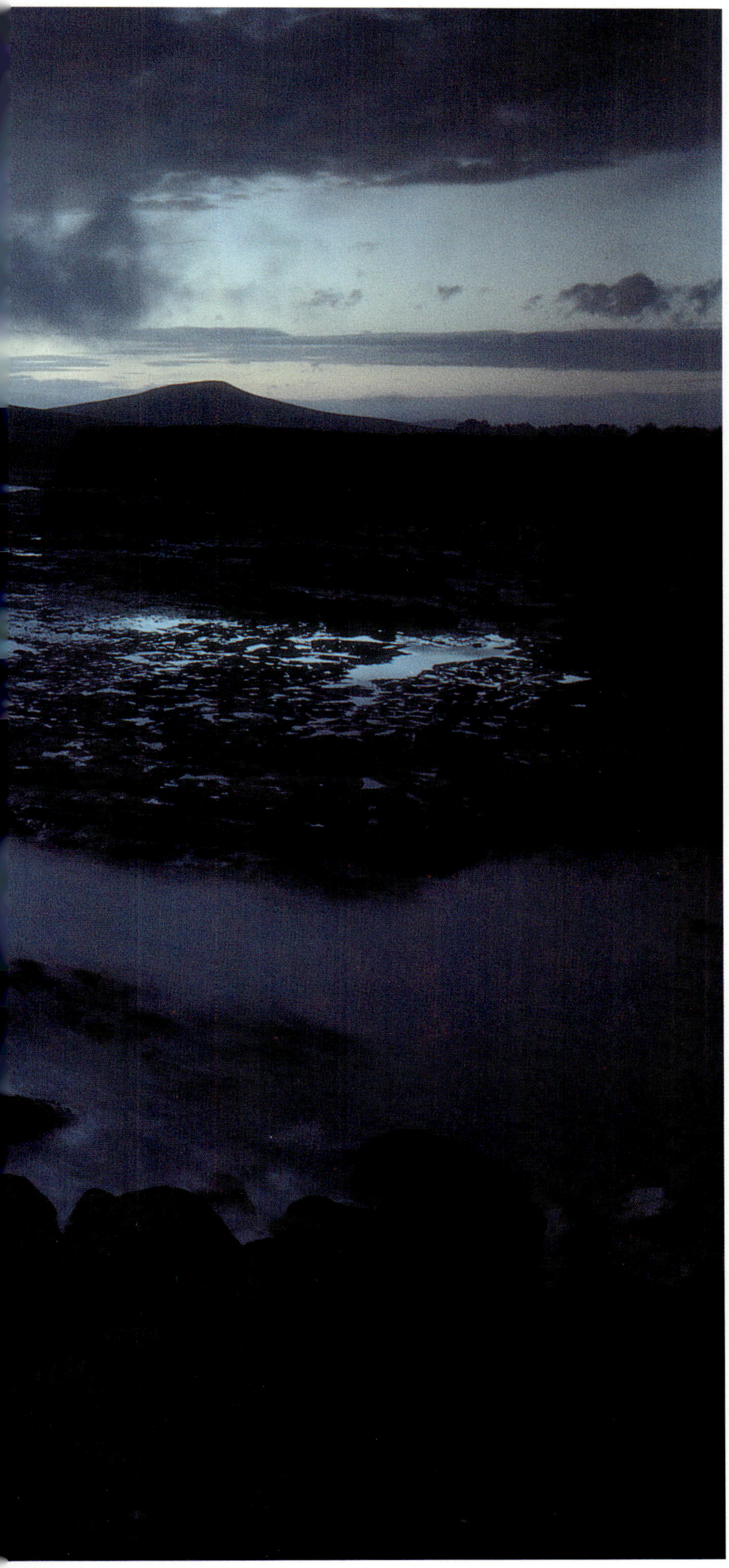

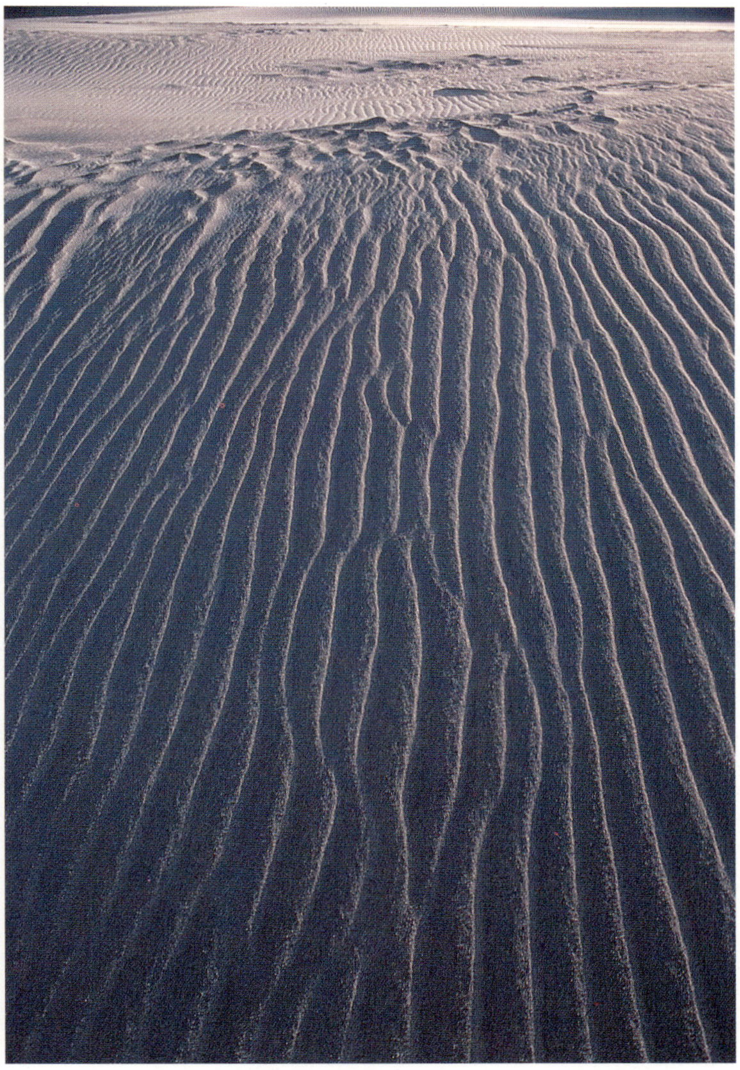

Martins Bay, Fiordland BRIAN ENTING

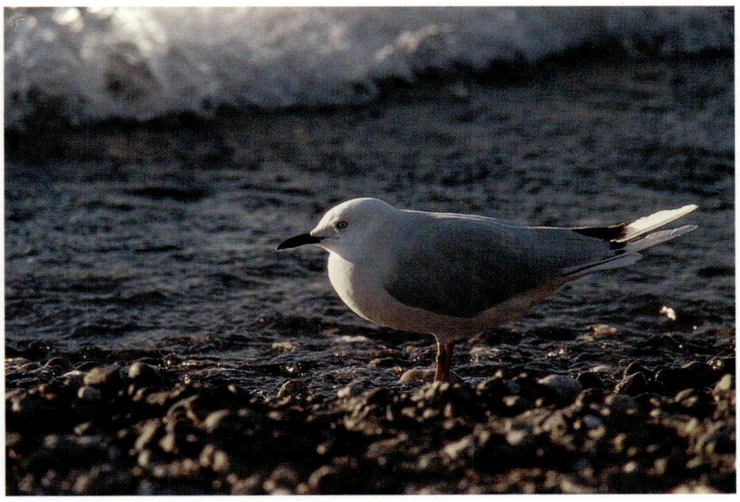

Black-billed gull, Te Anau BRIAN ENTING

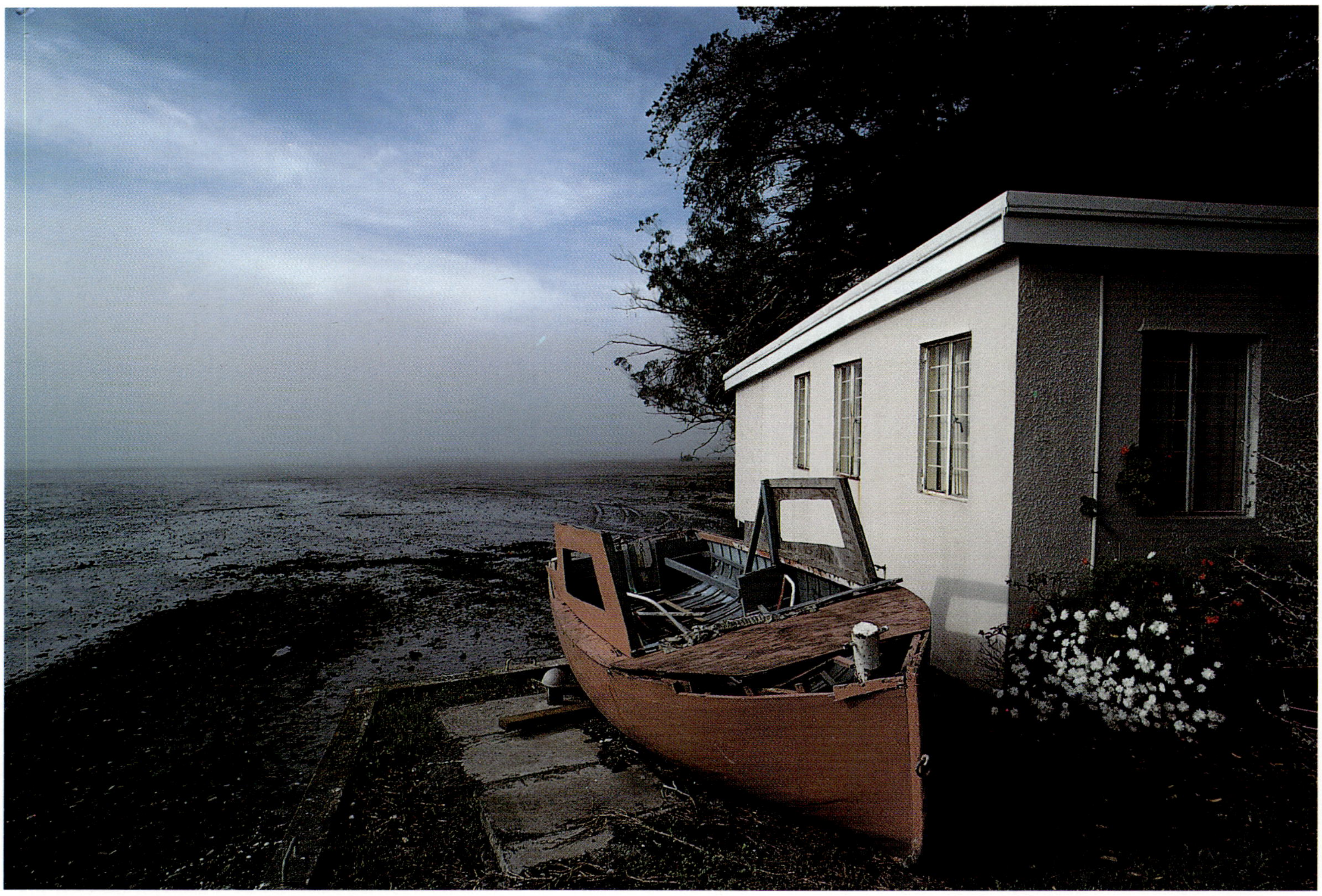

Laingholm Beach, Manukau Harbour, Auckland — TIM STEELE

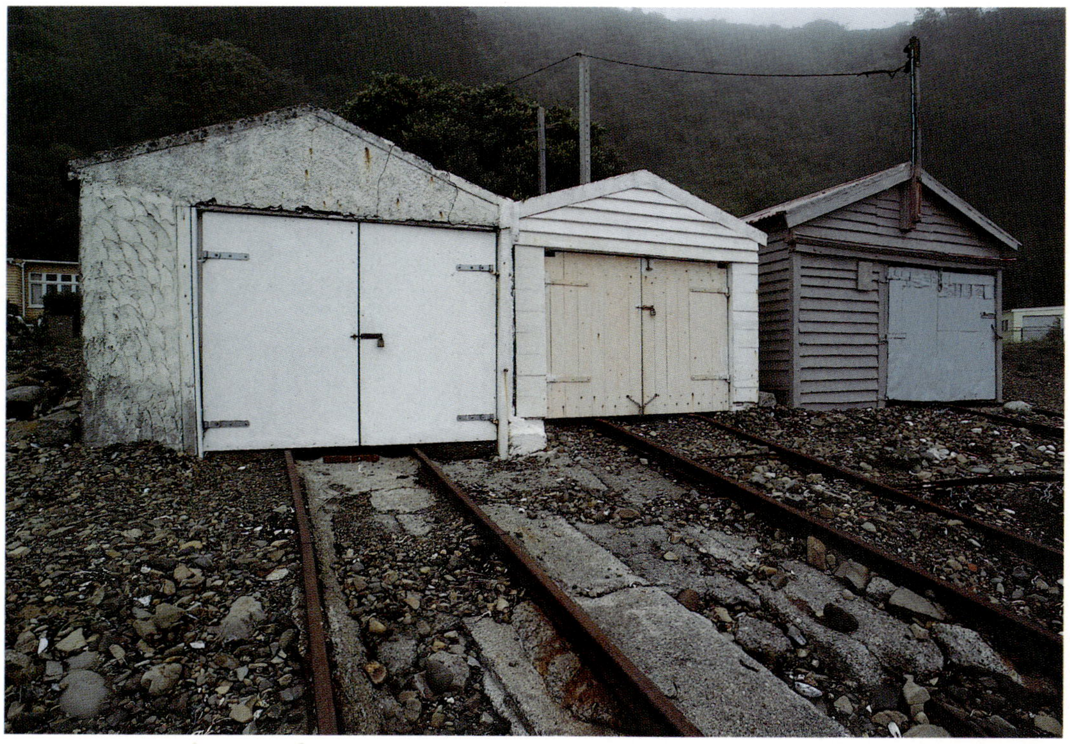

Boat sheds in the mist, coast south of Wellington — TIM STEELE

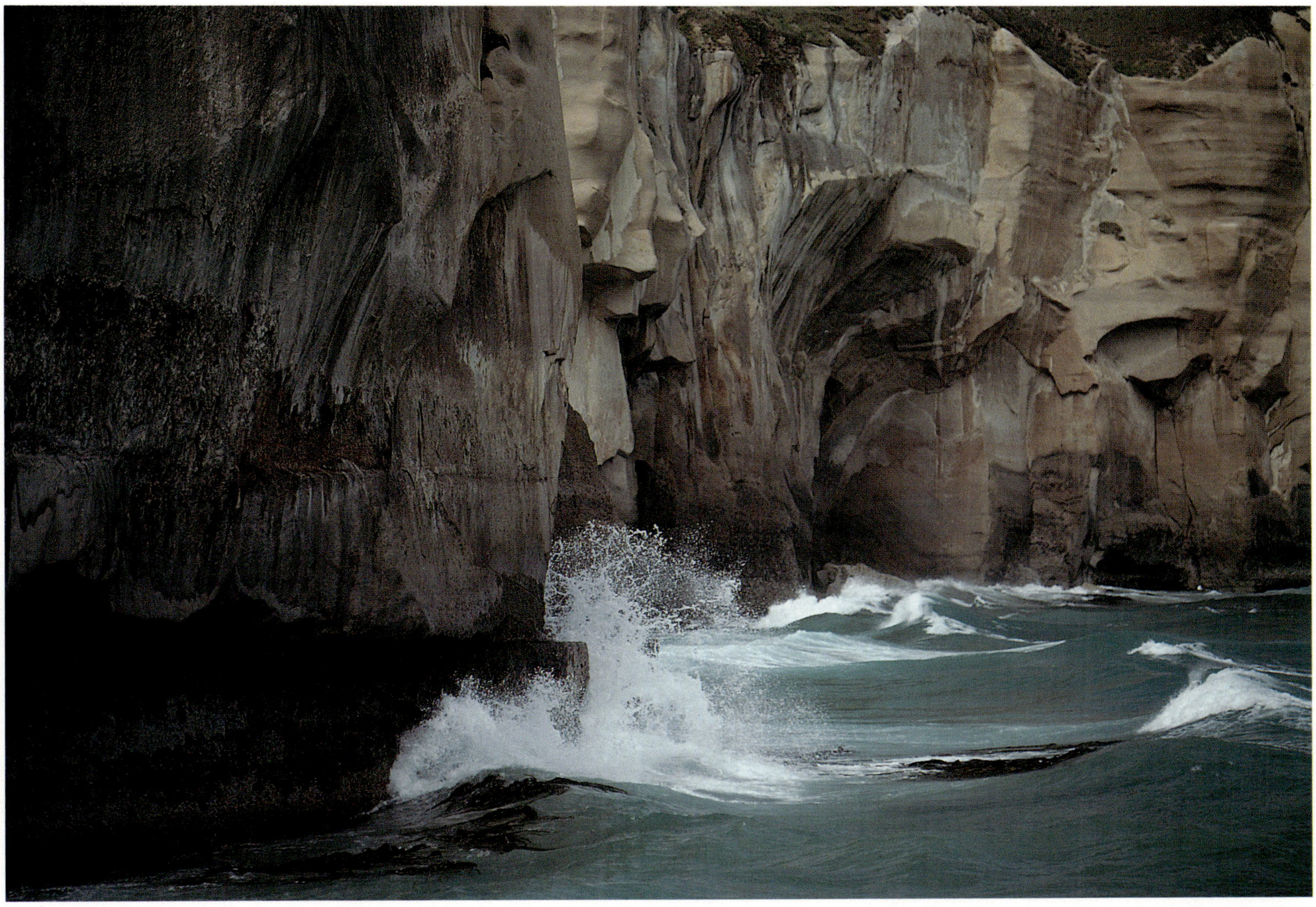

Tunnel Beach, Dunedin GEOFF MASON

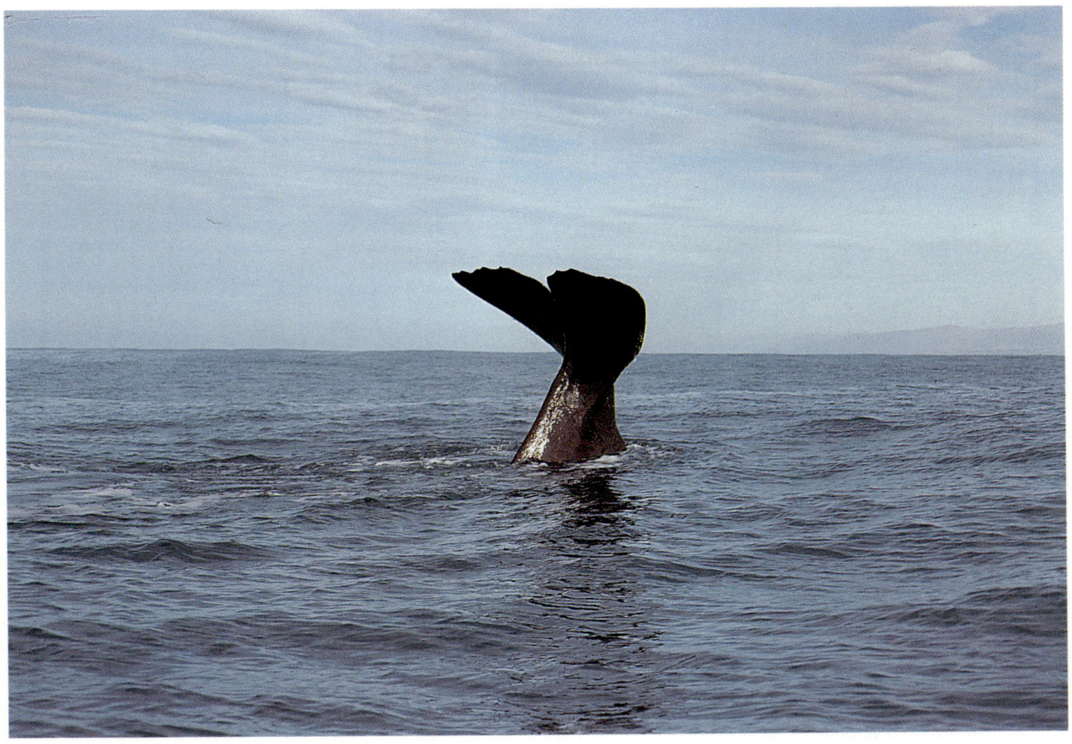

Sperm whale, Kaikoura ROBIN MORRISON

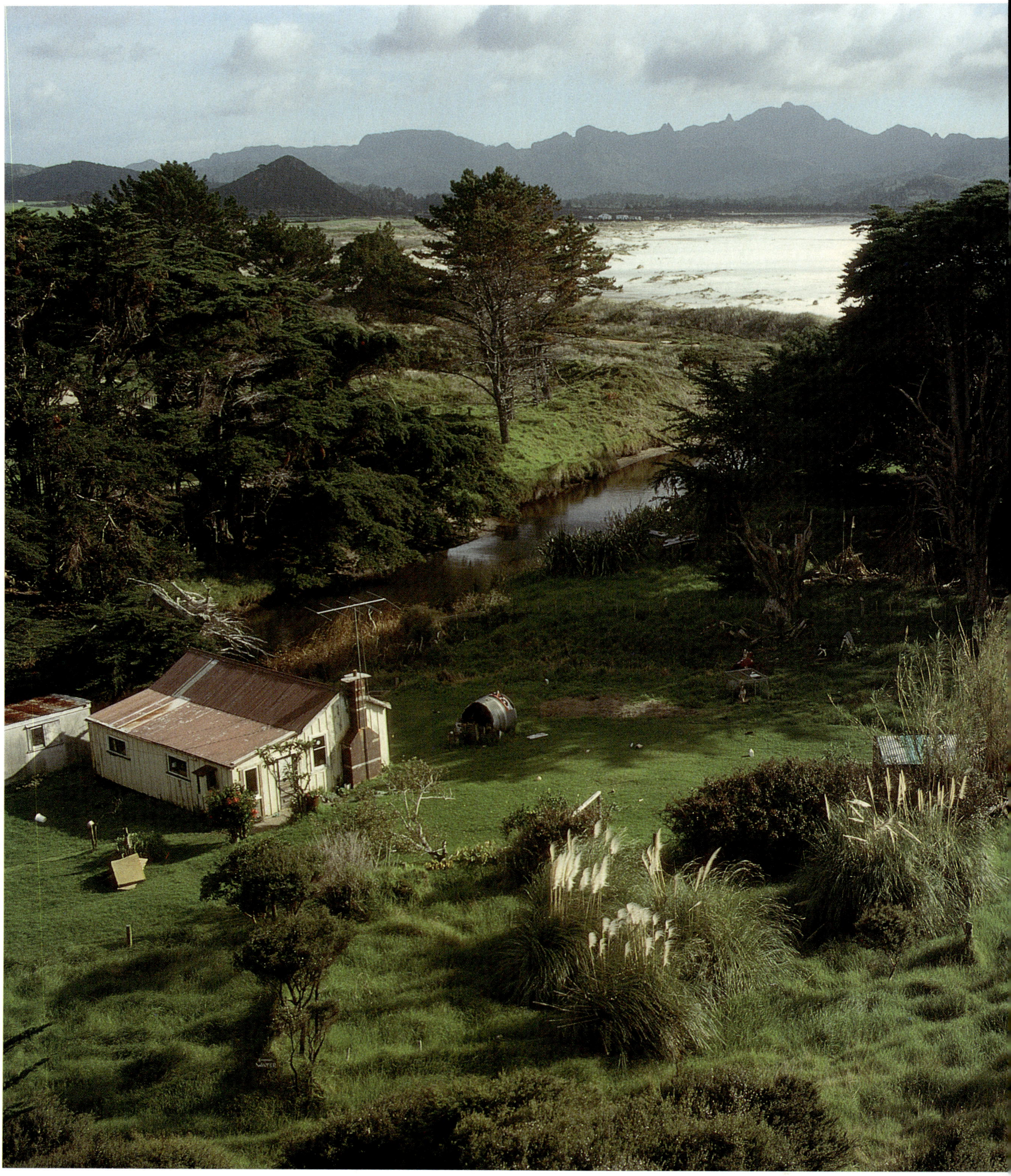

House on Kaitoke Beach, Great Barrier Island

ROBIN MORRISON

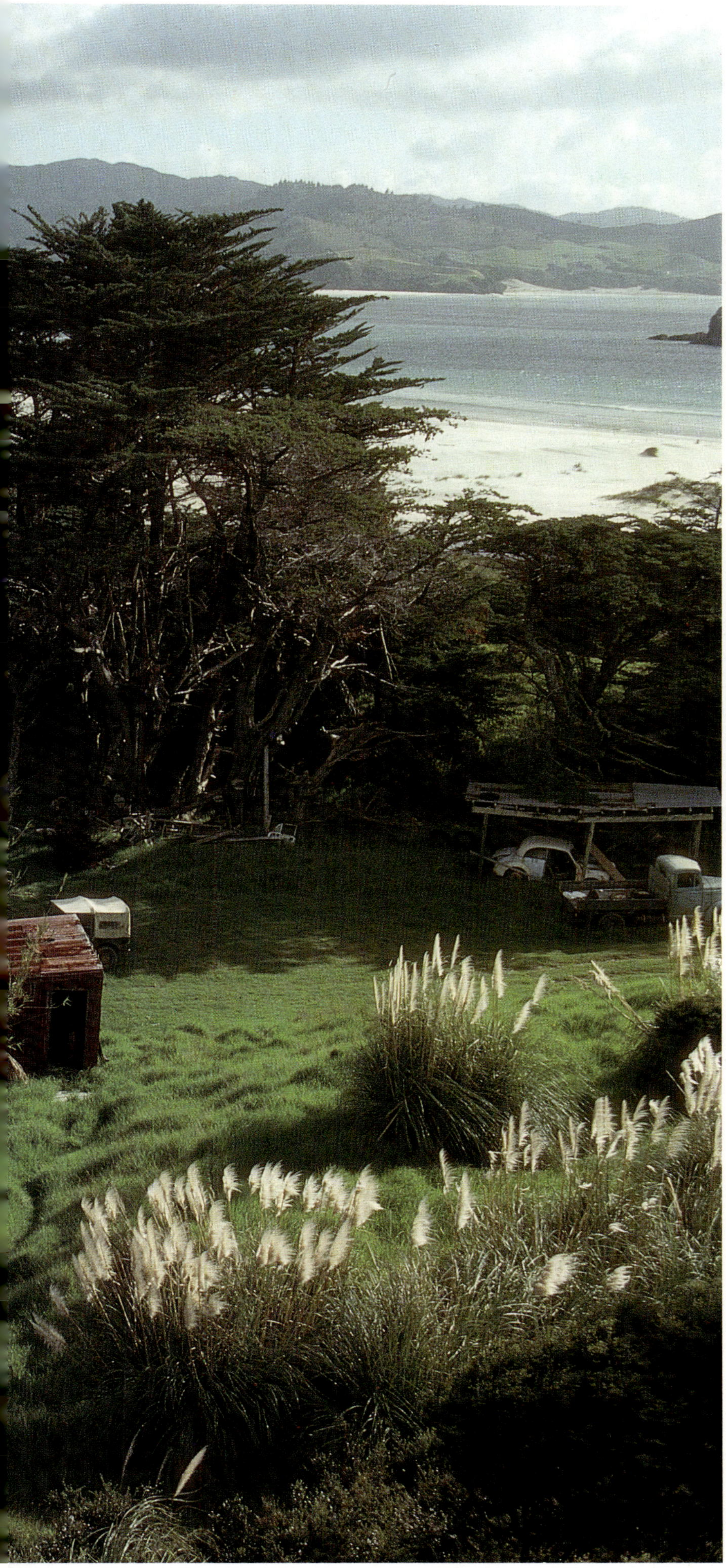

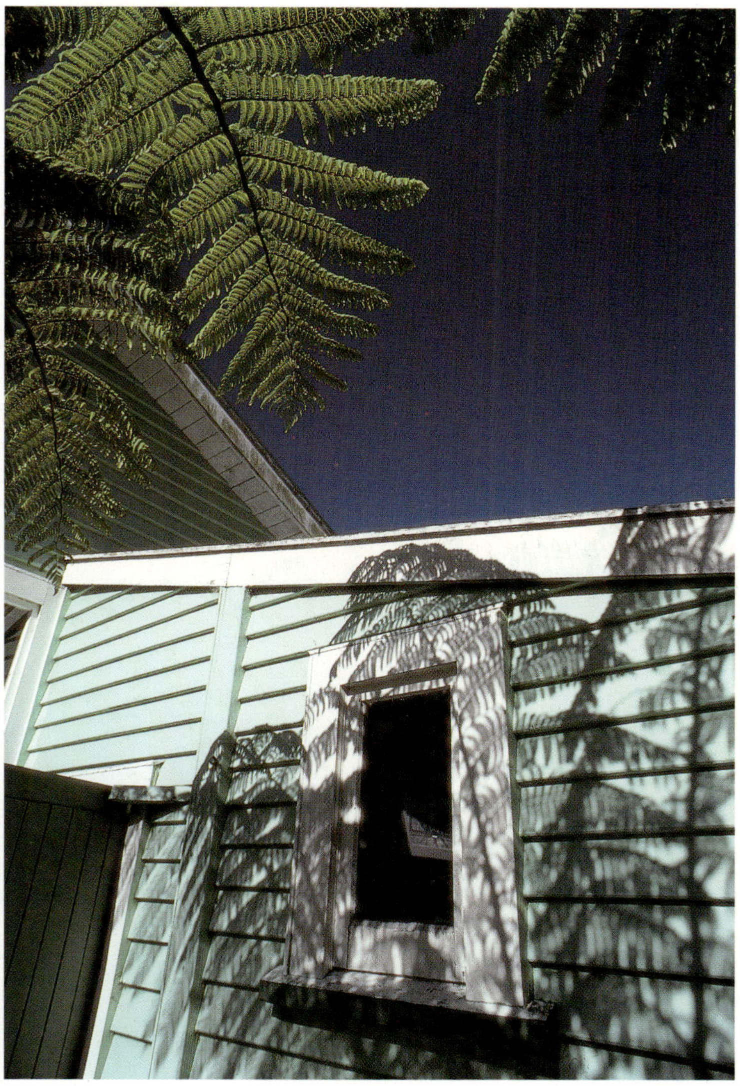

Fronds and weatherboard house, Wellington TIM STEELE

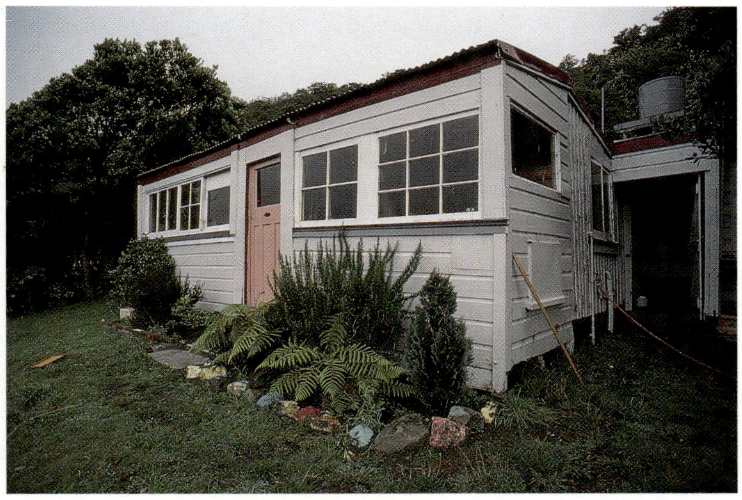

Early cottage, south coast of Wellington TIM STEELE

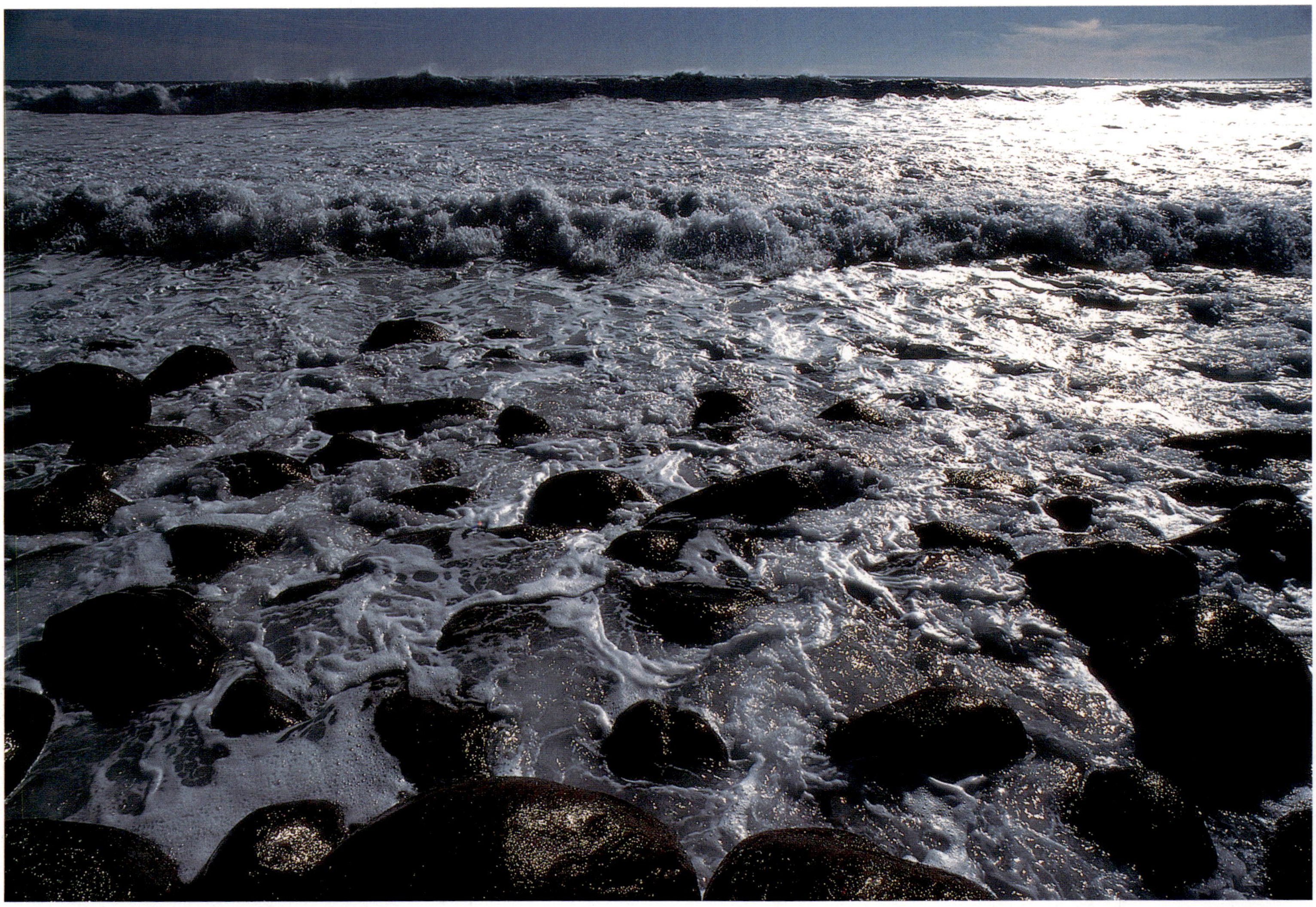

Fiordland coast BRIAN ENTING

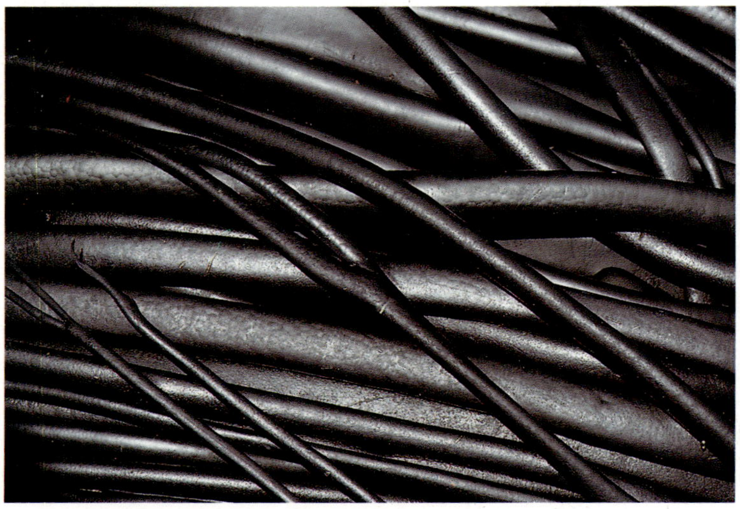

Kelp, Curio Bay, Catlins, Otago GEOFF MASON

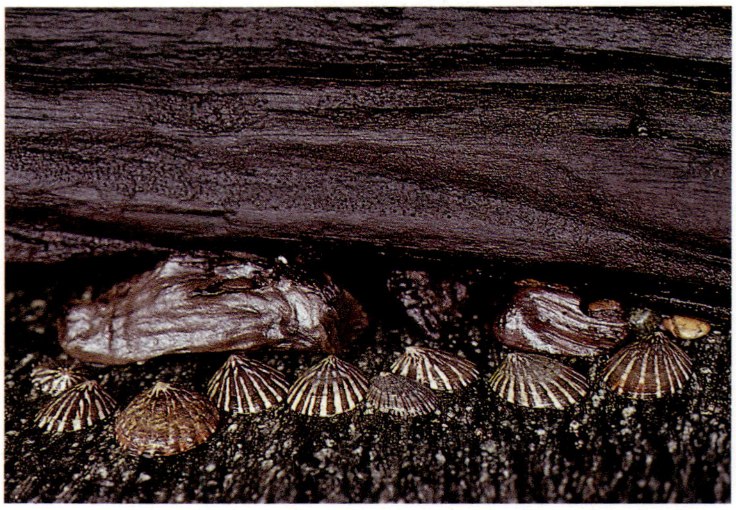

Limpets, West Coast BRIAN ENTING

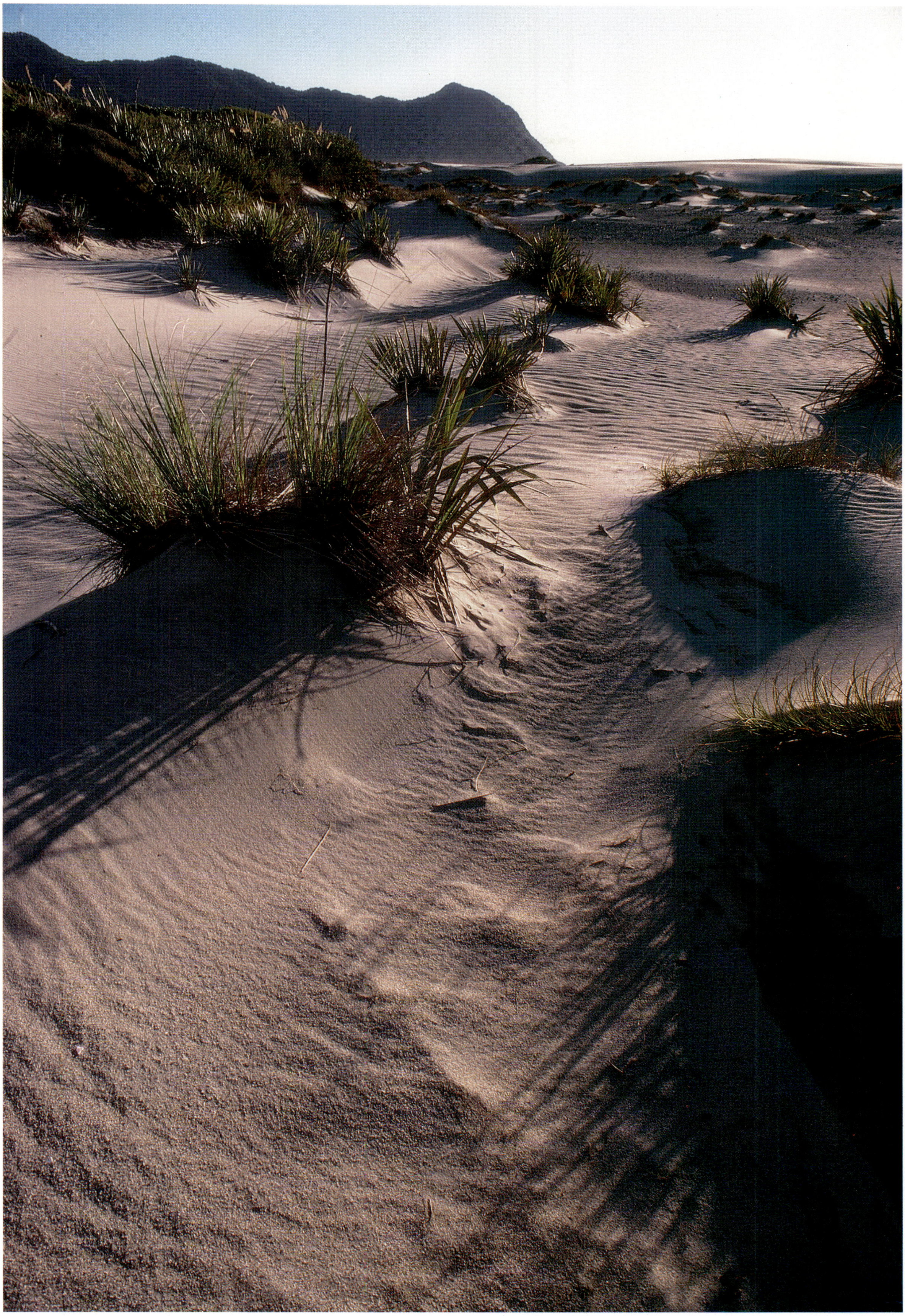

Martins Bay, Fiordland

BRIAN ENTING

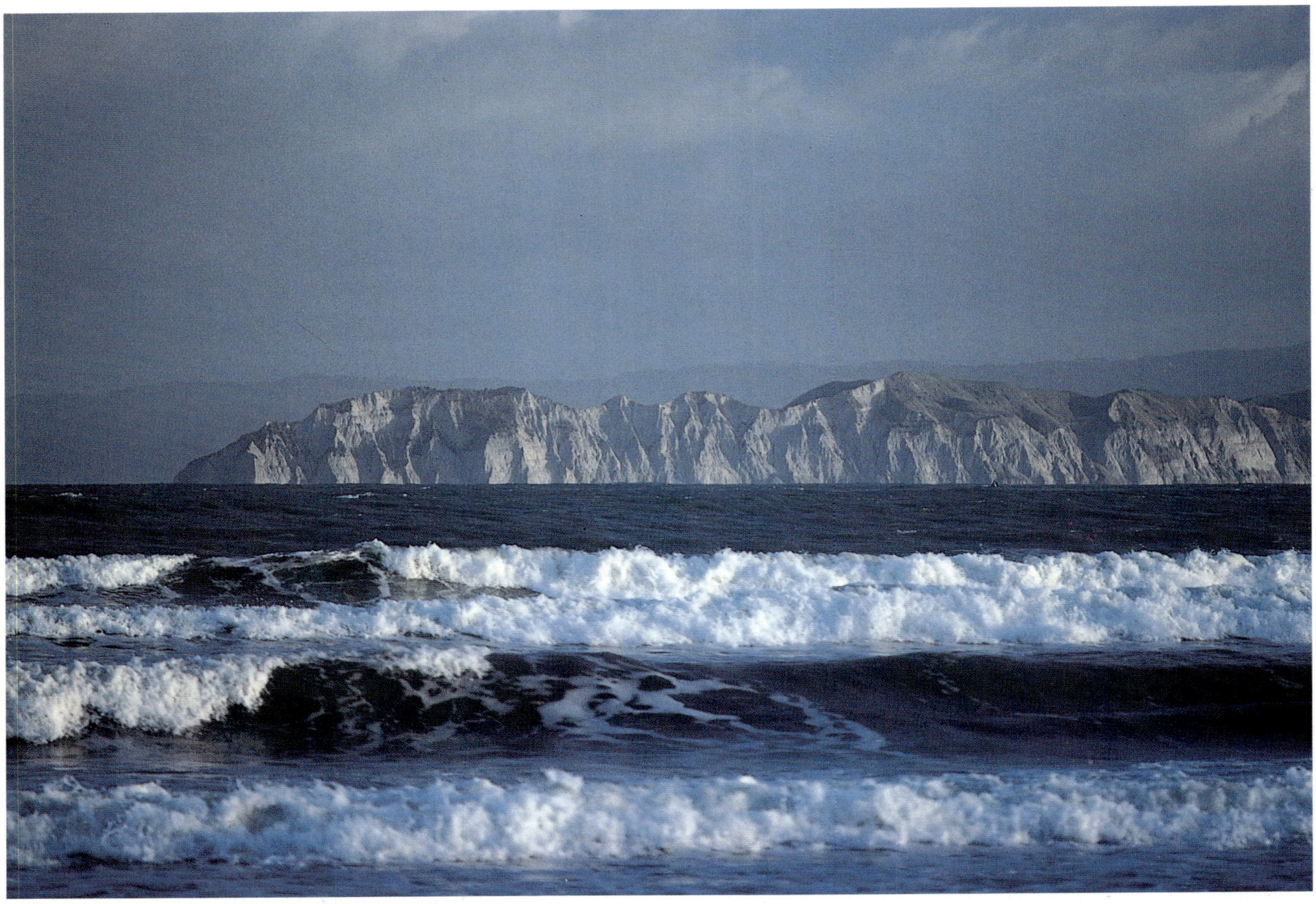

Gisborne CRAIG POTTON

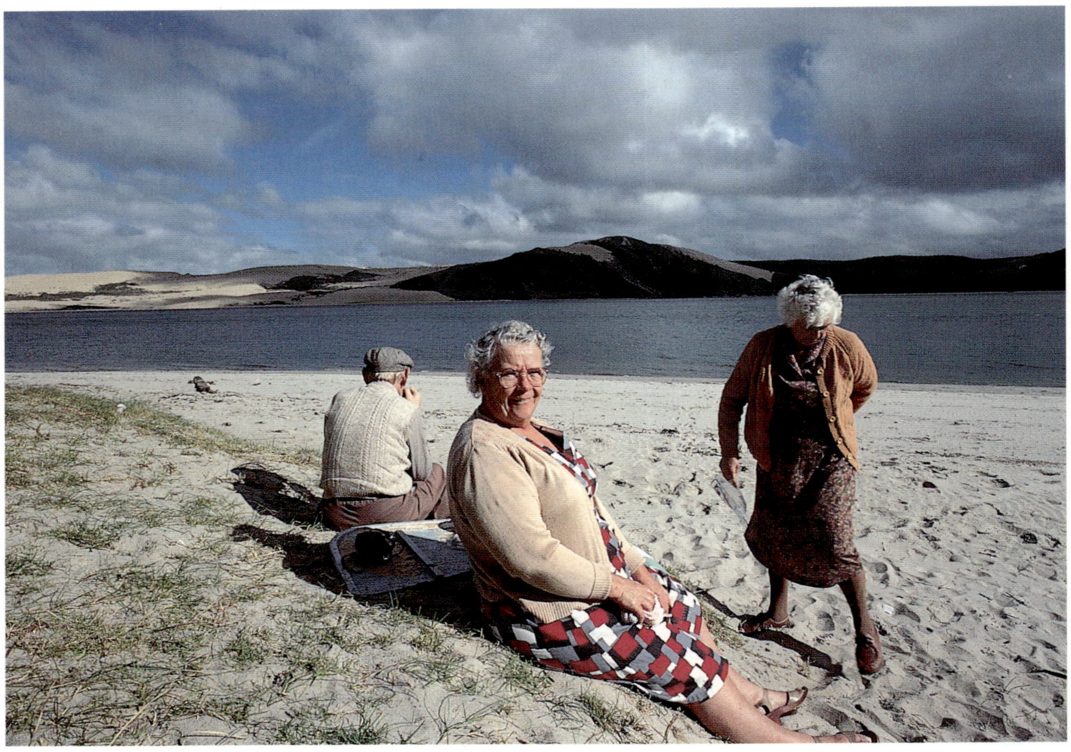

Opononi STEPHEN ROBINSON

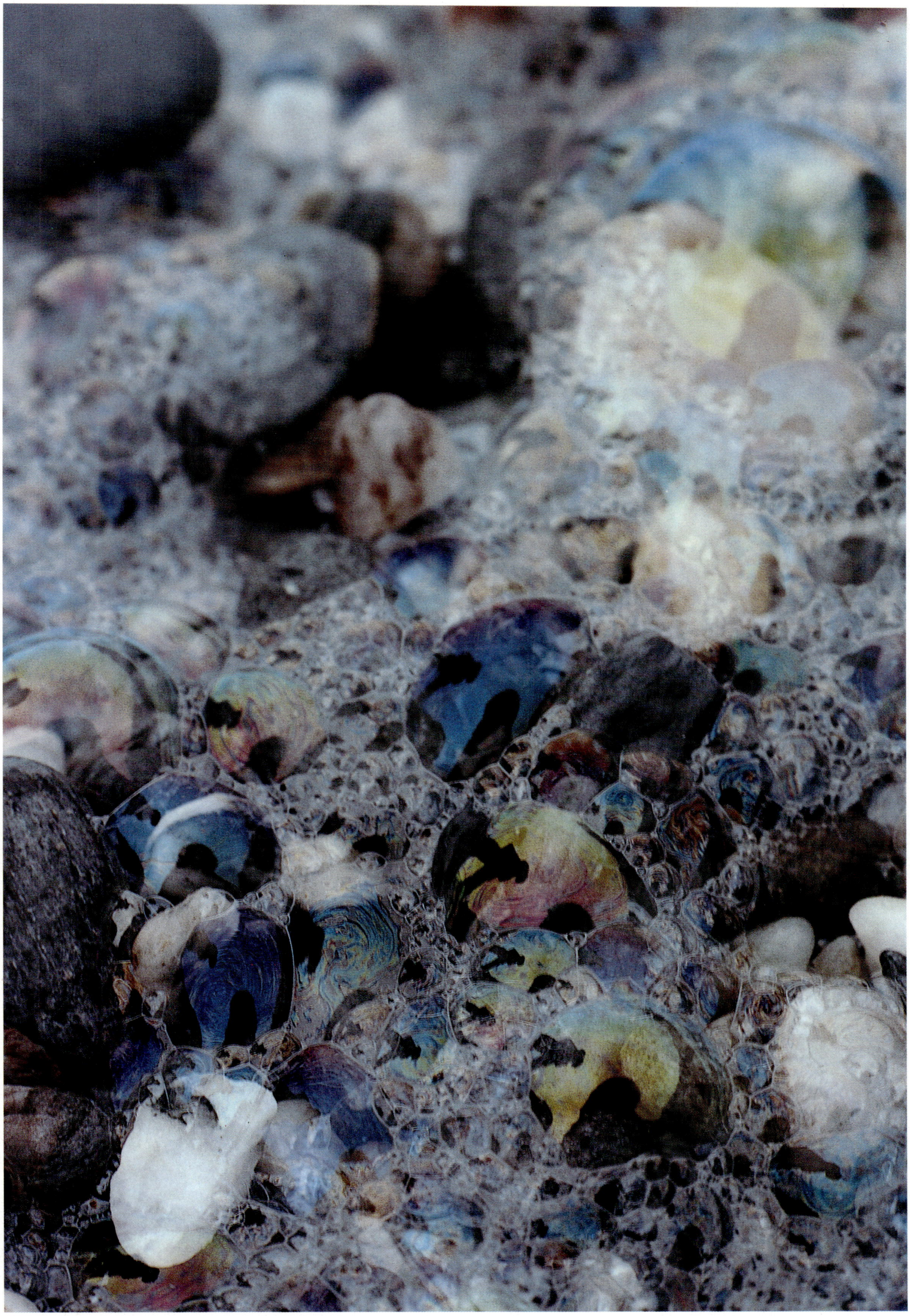

Naturally formed bubbles, Okarito Beach BRIAN ENTING

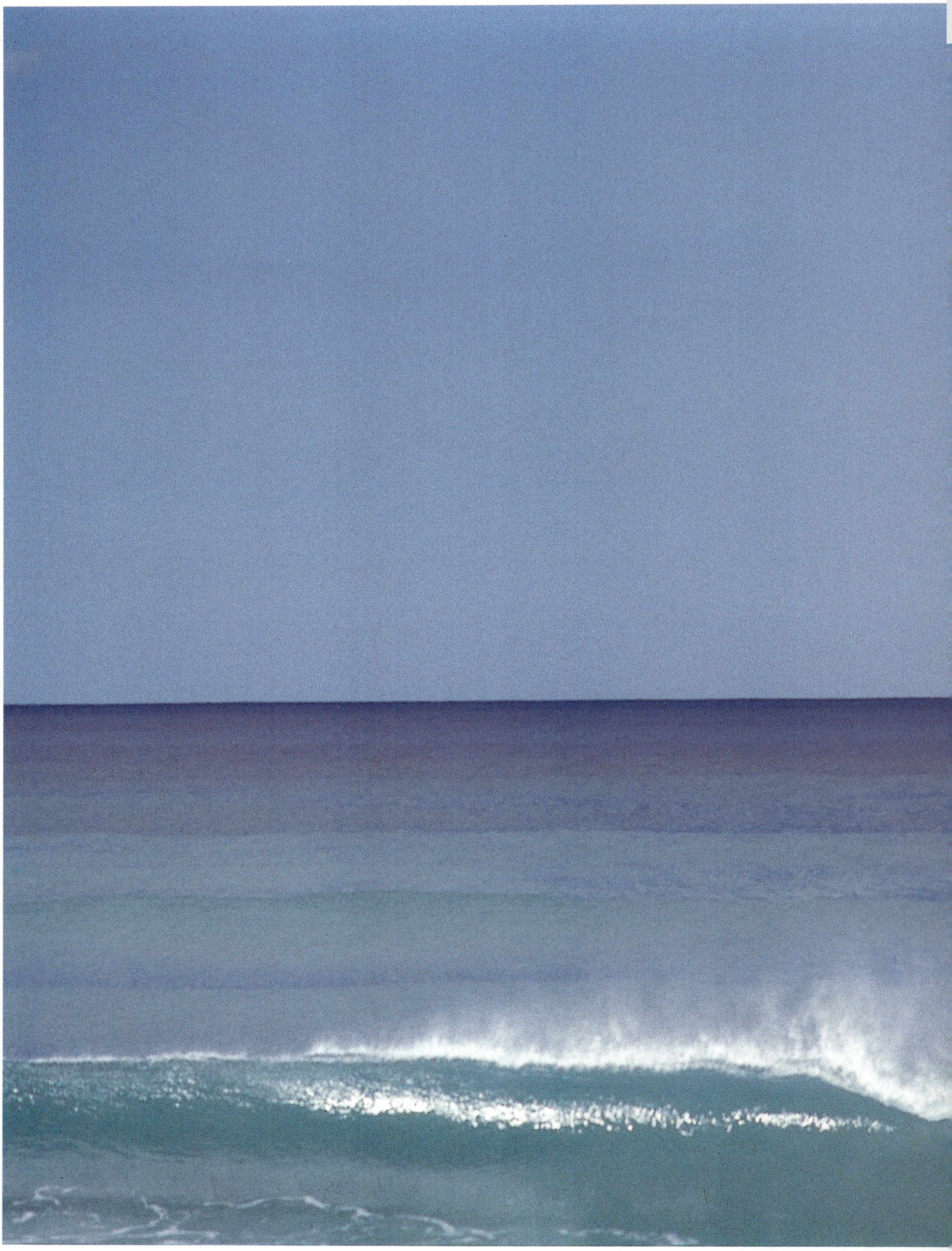

Opoutere, Coromandel Peninsula ERIC TAYLOR

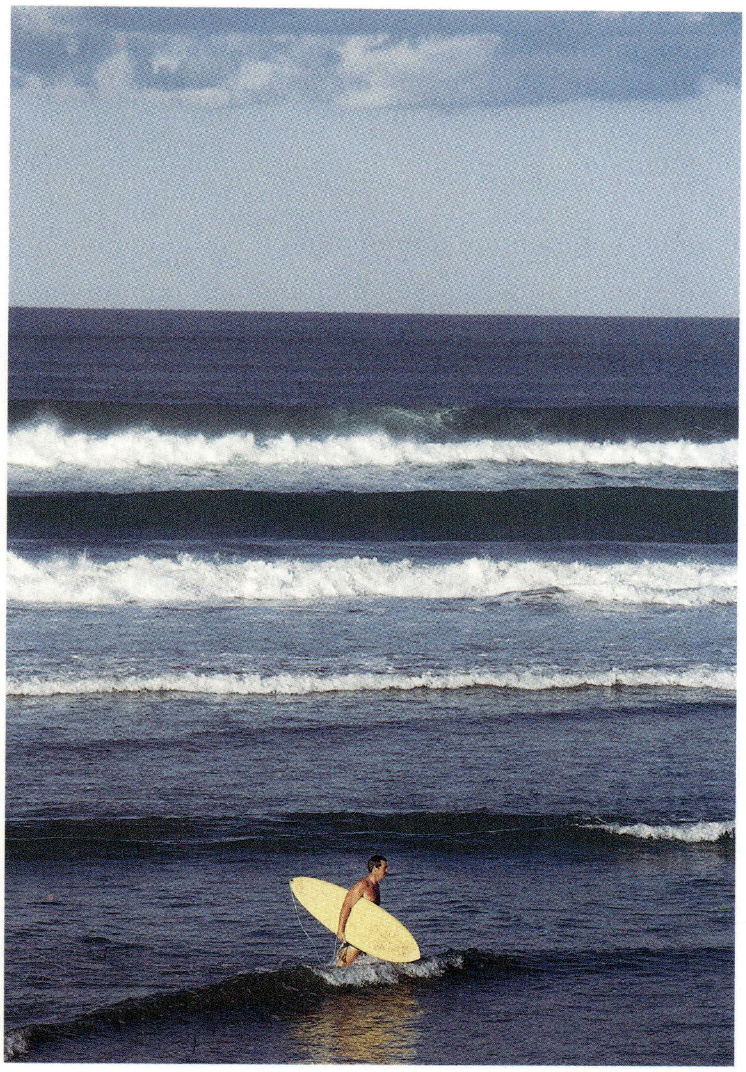

Surfer, Whangamata, Coromandel Peninsula ERIC TAYLOR

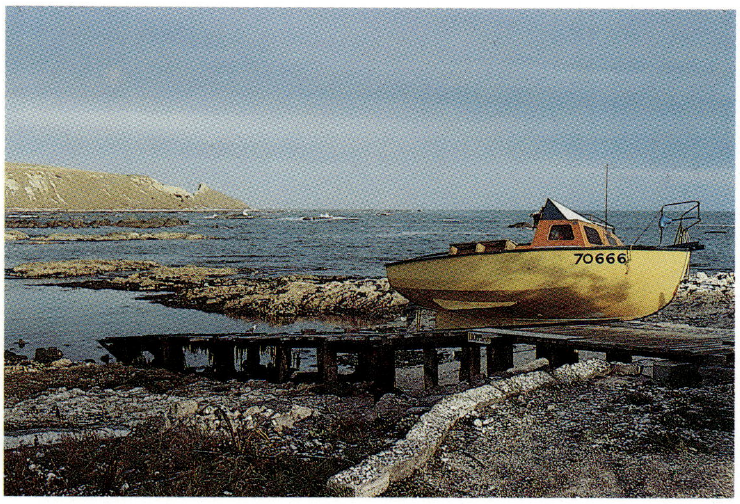

Kaikoura ROBIN MORRISON

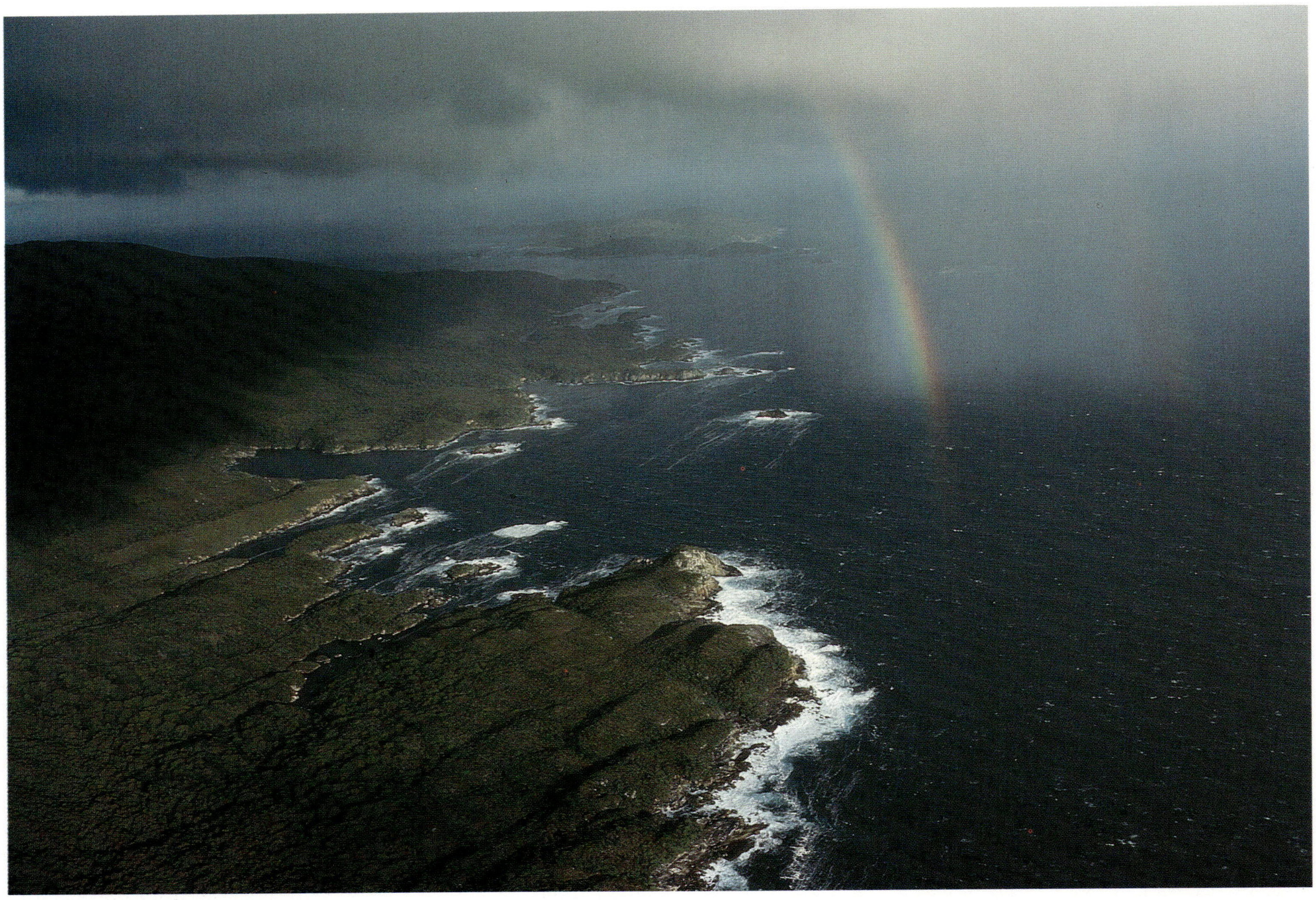

Southern Coast of Stewart Island ROBIN MORRISON

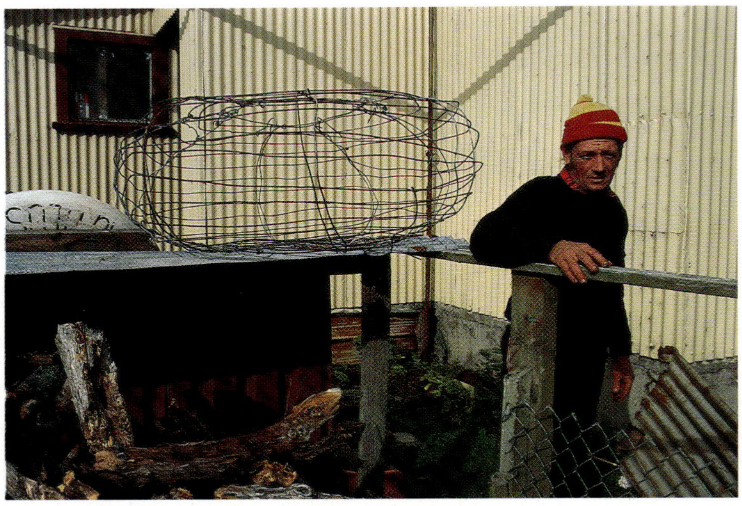

Graham Ayton, Port Hutt, Chatham Islands ROBIN MORRISON

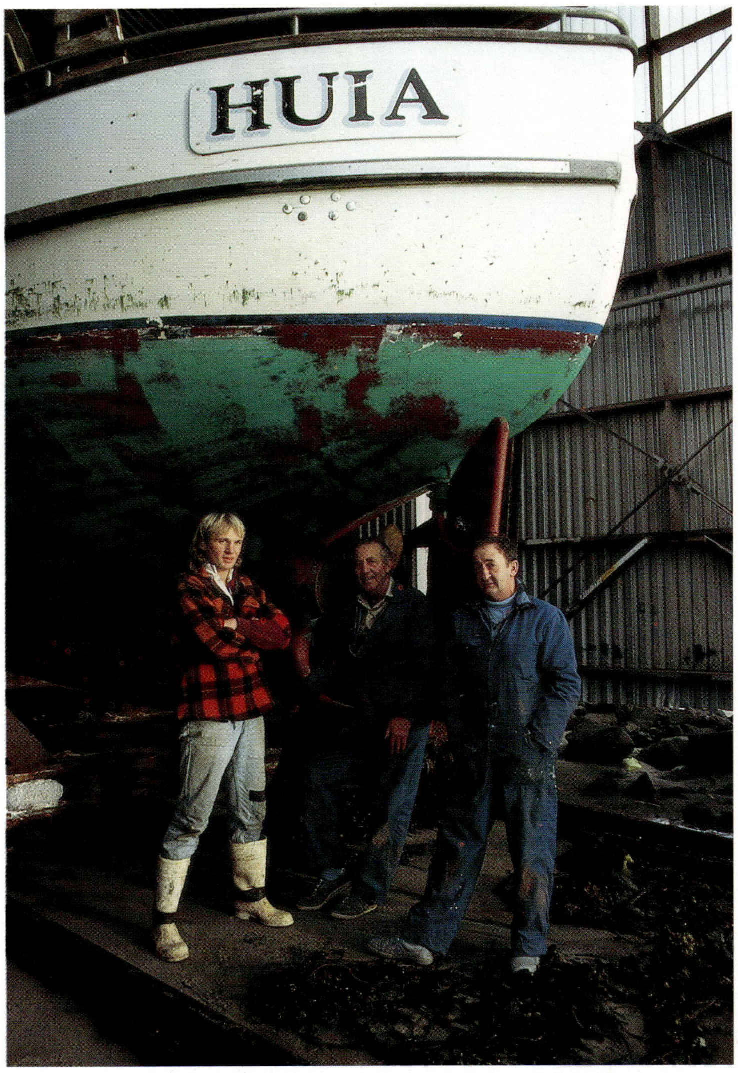

Boatyard, Halfmoon Bay, Stewart Island ROBIN MORRISON

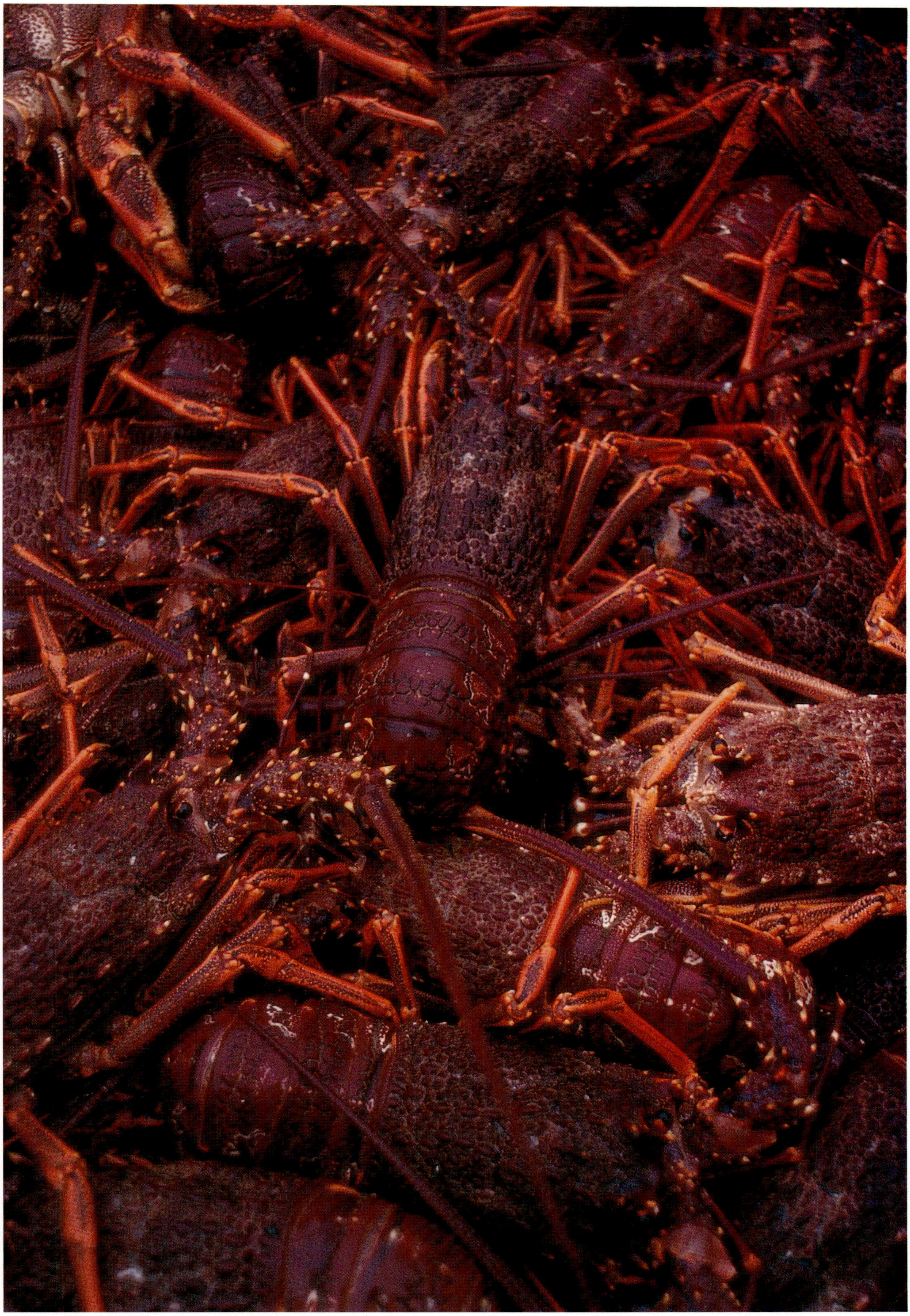

Crayfish, Jackson Bay, West Coast

BRIAN ENTING

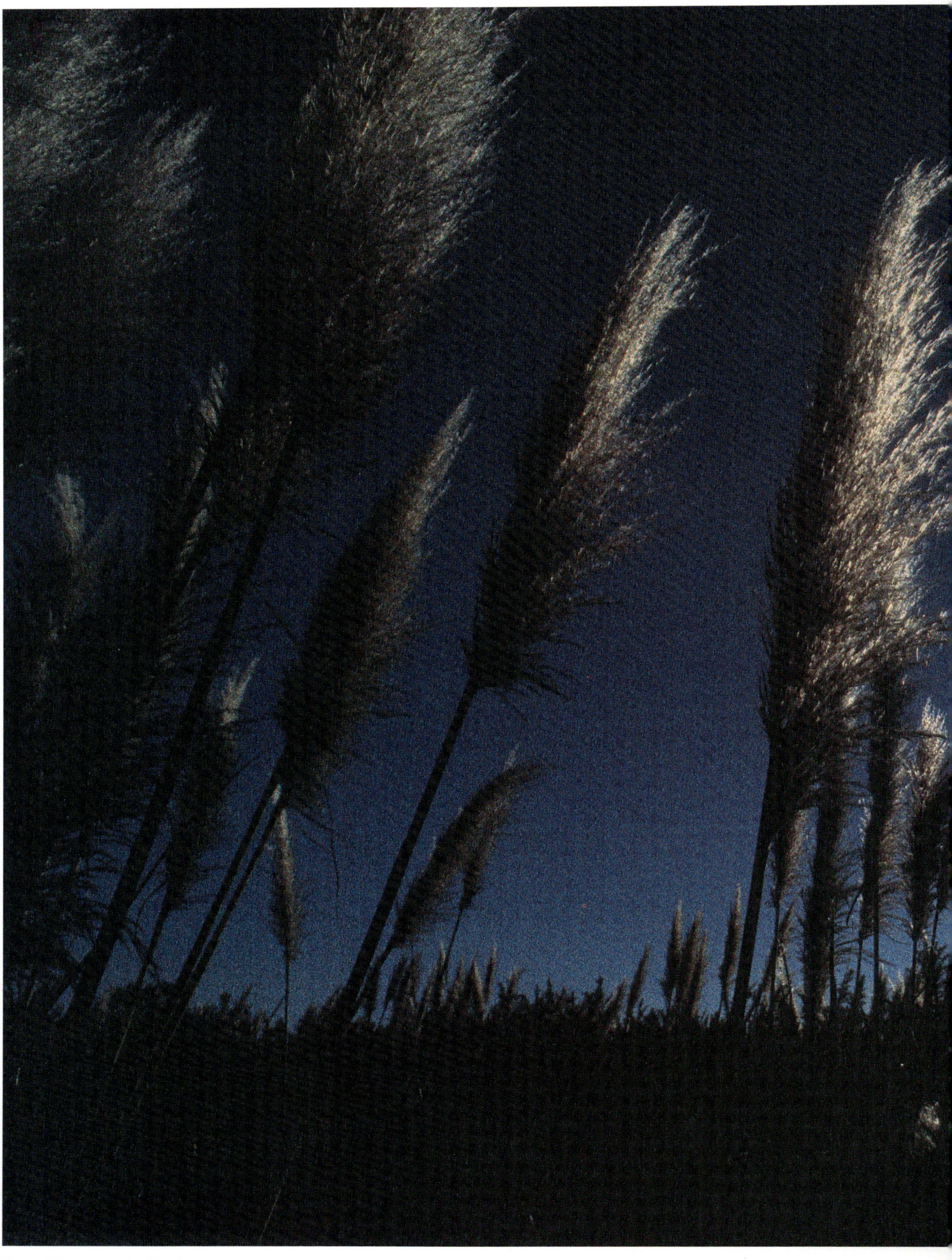

Toitoi, West Coast, Auckland TIM STEELE

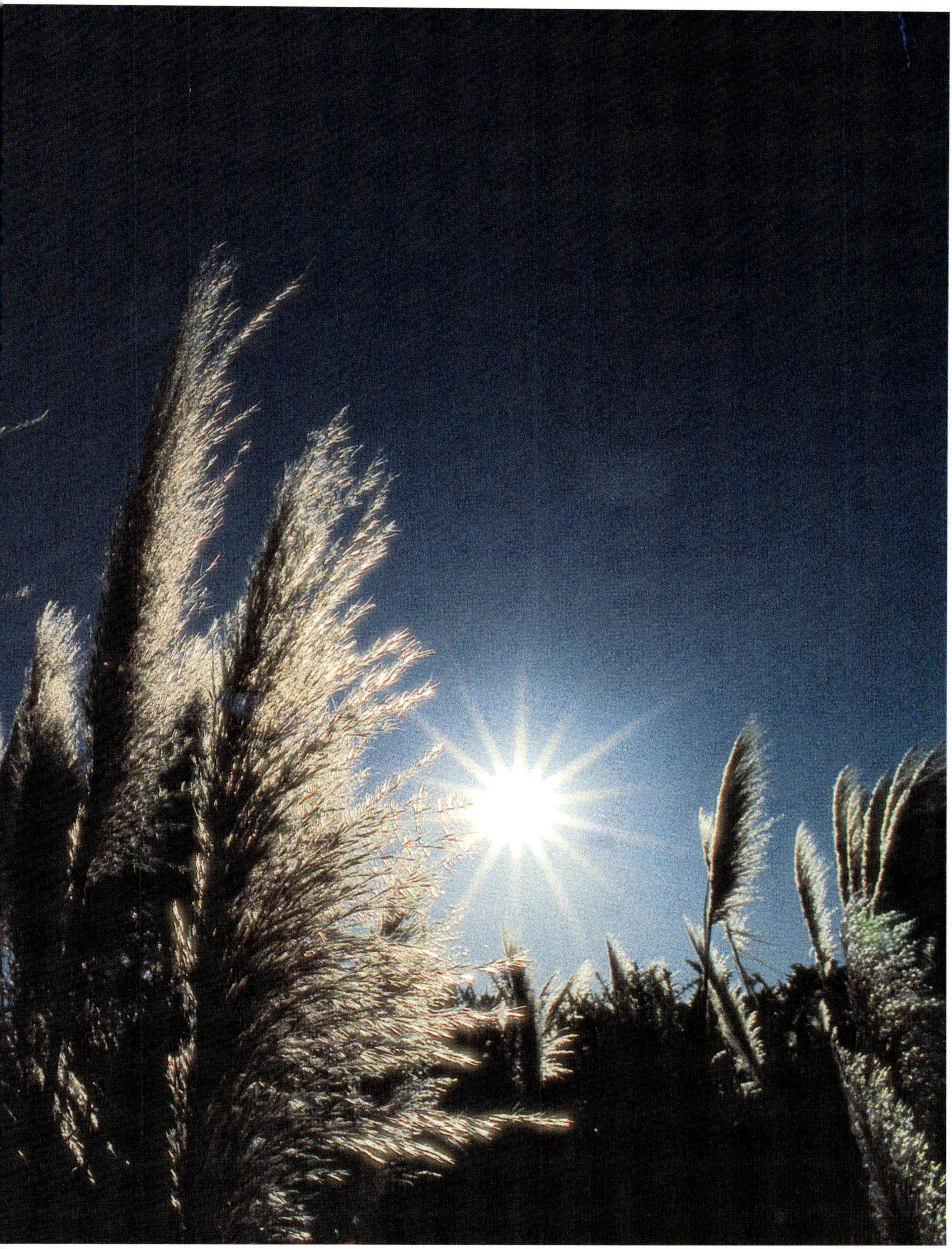

Coastline seen from the road to Cape Palliser, the southern-most point of the North Island TIM STEELE

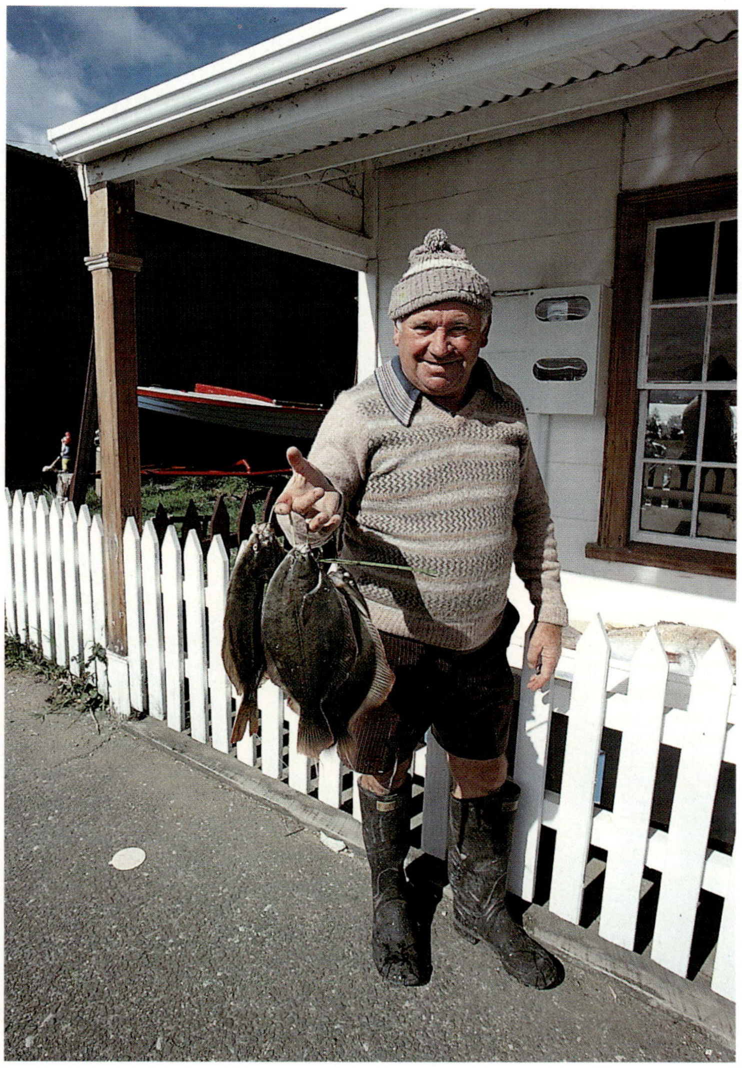

Rawene, Hokianga Harbour STEPHEN ROBINSON

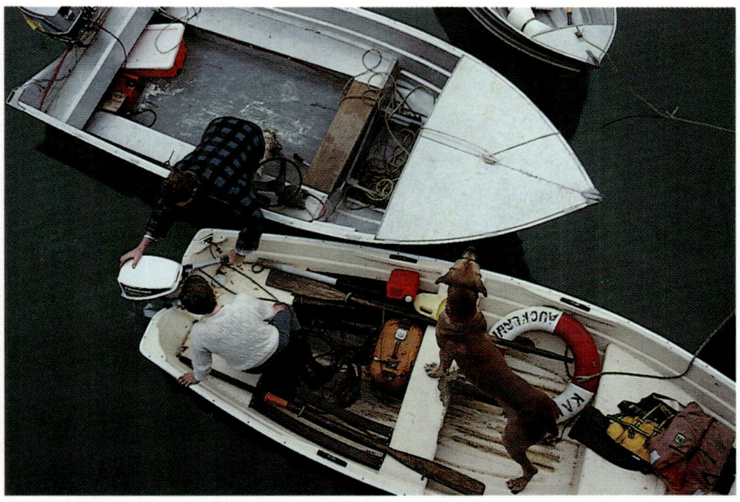

Whangaparapara Wharf, Great Barrier Island ROBIN MORRISON

EXPLORING WHO WE ARE

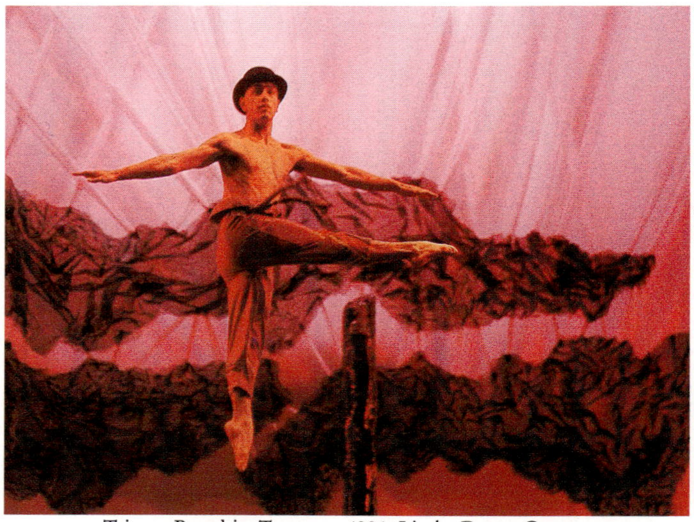

LIMBS DANCE COMPANY

Taiaroa Royal in *Tarawera*, 1986, Limbs Dance Company.

Peter Shaw

IT SEEMS THERE HAS always been an unsatisfied longing at the heart of New Zealand's European-derived culture. In the earliest period of settlement, artists looked home to England and struggled to portray their experiences in a foreign country in a manner that reflected this absent cultured background. Later, as creative people came to see themselves as New Zealanders and not colonials, the longing changed: when, they continually asked themselves, was the truly New Zealand work of art going to be produced?

Every time a new novel appeared, critics anxiously wondered whether this was the "great New Zealand novel". A new symphony was judged not so much for its own qualities but in terms of a ranking system designed to determine the work's place in the development of New Zealand's musical culture. Most people who cared saw artists as sensitive crusaders cut off from their European roots, struggling within the context of an all-pervading philistinism.

In fact a culture does not develop along a tidy continuum towards national maturity. Cultures don't suddenly come of age nor does the Great New Zealand Novel or Symphony appear to mark the event.

Our perceptions about culture in New Zealand have more recently widened. Many artists respond to a wide variety of stimuli both indigenous and international. Above all, the work produced is increasingly bicultural in emphasis as more people realise the necessity for a relationship between the imposed Pakeha culture and that of the tangata whenua.

But it was in terms of our sense of isolation that the arts first defined themselves here. It was thus only natural that the first stirrings of artistic expression should be a reflection of those admired in the old world.

John Gully's misty dynamism tells us that he felt Turner looking over his shoulder. Both Sir William Fox, the Prime Minister/painter, and the Rev. John Kinder were specialists in Claudian composition and lighting effects. J. B. C. Hoyte's careful, atmospheric views are picturesquely conceived even if the foreground classical figures of the convention are now replaced by elegantly positioned natives.

The beginnings of New Zealand literature reveal a similar pattern. Allen Curnow in his 1960 *Penguin Anthology of New Zealand Verse* puts it thus:

> *The nineteenth century colonists achieved their migration bodily but not in spirit . . . the shock of so distant a migration, and the recoil of imagination from realities, were to be transmitted through two, three or even four New Zealand generations before poets appeared who could express what it meant to be, or to have become, a New Zealander. Nationality is not in question here: only the truism that a poet must start from somewhere if he is ever to get anywhere.*

THE STORY IS MUCH THE SAME in the performing arts: musical life was dominated by brass band and choral concerts, both distinctly British imports. Maori brass bands existed too in a surprisingly large number of communities and Te Rangi Hiroa describes a thirty-strong drum and fife band

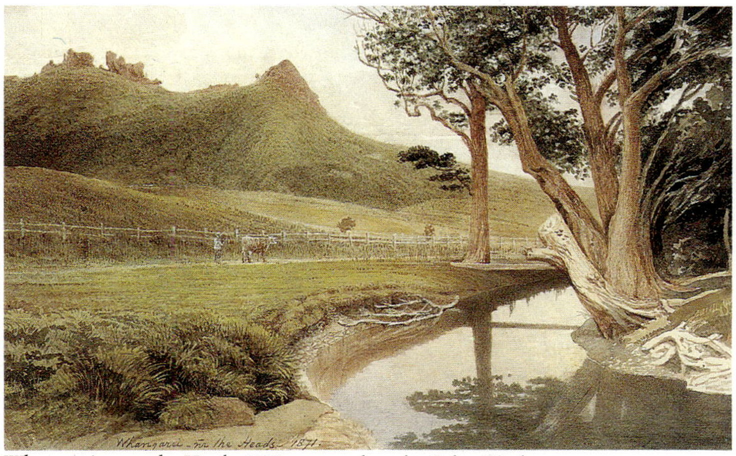

AUCKLAND CITY ART GALLERY

Whangarei, near the Heads, 1871, watercolour by John Kinder.

which escorted guests to the kainga at Parihaka, Taranaki in 1897. In the cities, choral societies and amateur orchestras flourished, all faithfully echoing the musical taste of Victorian England. The distinguished German musician and founder of the Nelson School of Music, Michael Balling, gave the country's first Wagner performances at a time when that composer's works were still struggling for European recognition.

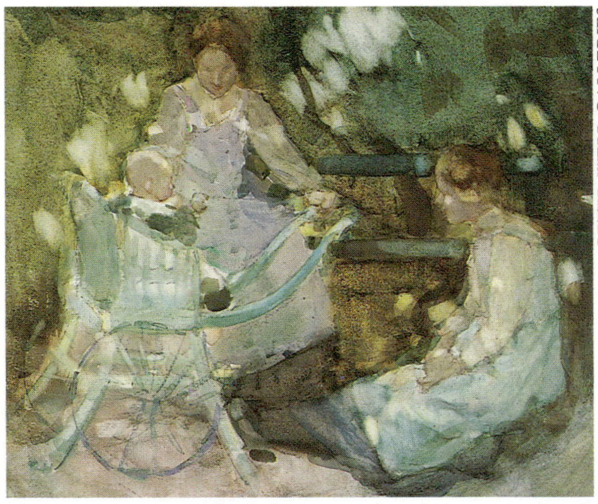

PETER WEBB GALLERIES

Two young women with a baby in a garden, 1908, watercolour by Frances Hodgkins.

Alfred Hill, the composer, although born in Melbourne, spent his formative years in Wellington where his father ran a hat shop on Lambton Quay. The talented young man studied in Leipzig, heard Richard Strauss, Bruch, Tchaikowsky and Grieg perform their own works and upon graduation in 1891 accepted the position of conductor with the Wellington Orchestral Society. Hill's 1895 work *Hinemoa*, a Maori legend for soli, chorus and orchestra, dedicated to Hone Heke, included a long plaintive melody which is believed to have come to New Zealand with a Rarotongan chief who visited King Tawhiao in 1868. This melody was absorbed by Maori listeners and changed into a hymn. *Hinemoa*'s first performance on the opening night of the Wellington Industrial Exhibition in 1896 was a triumph and was responsible for an awakening of interest in Maori traditions at a time when Maori culture was held in low regard by the colonials. Hill is still best known for the song *Waiata Poi* which had its musical origin in a poi song sung by Maggie Papakura. It later became a cornerstone of the repertoire of the singer Dame Clara Butt.

OF THE FIRST GENERATION of painters born in New Zealand, the best known is Frances Hodgkins. Her ambiguous relationship with the country of her birth is perhaps typical of them all. Born at Dunedin in 1869, she was taught by the Italian Girolamo Nerli, who encouraged her to follow her interest in portraiture and figure painting. By 1901 she was in London where she met two other New Zealand-born painters, Dorothy Kate Richmond and Margaret Olrog Stoddart. All the painters of this period, including Grace Joel, Raymond McIntyre, Rhona Haszard, Edith Collier, Mina Arndt, C. F. Goldie and Francis McCracken, felt it essential to go to Europe to study. Some, like Hodgkins, did not return to New Zealand to live but achieved considerable reputations for themselves overseas. New Zealand subject matter entirely disappeared from the work of these expatriates, though Hodgkins, like Goldie and the Bohemian born Gottfried Lindauer, did portraits of Maori subjects, not all of them entirely free from a trace of that sentimentality which is bound to creep in when, as in Goldie's case especially, they felt they were recording the last survivors of a dying race.

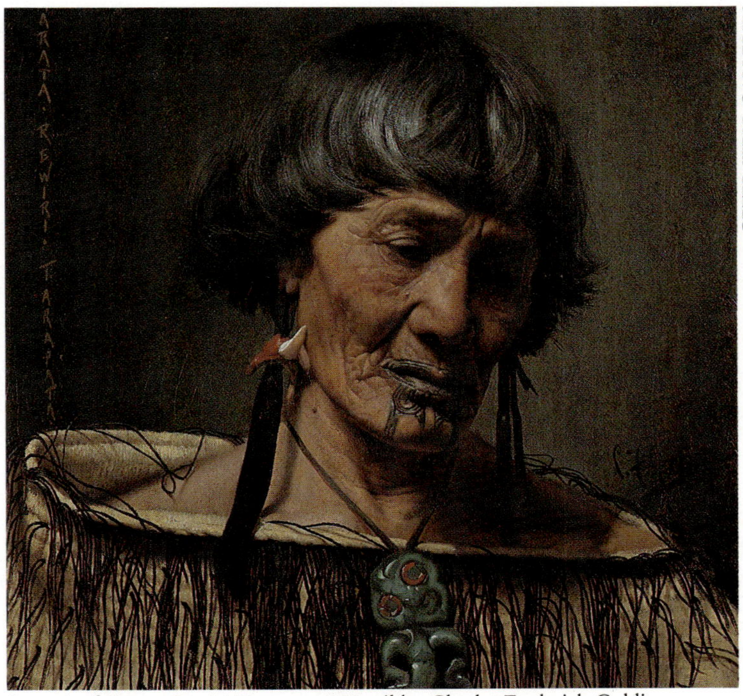

PETER WEBB GALLERIES

Portrait of Harata Rewiri Tarapata, 1902, oil by Charles Frederick Goldie.

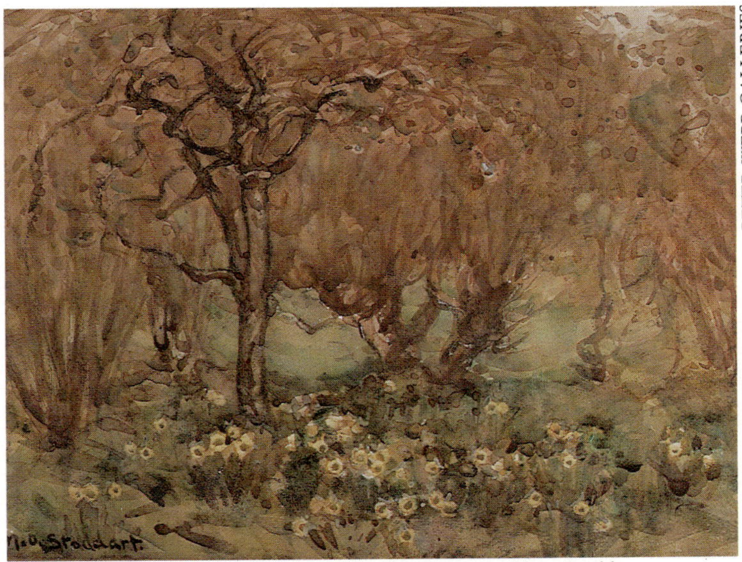

PETER WEBB GALLERIES

Autumn in the Park, undated, watercolour by Margaret Olrog Stoddart.

The Dutchman Petrus van der Velden arrived to live and teach at Christchurch in 1890. Among his most successful pupils was Sydney L. Thompson, for many years New Zealand's most popular painter.

Another painter whose work came to prominence in the late twenties and who studied at the Canterbury School was Evelyn Page (neé Polson). The freshness and vitality of her painting was to far surpass that of her teachers although, like Thompson, she continued to favour a readily accessible post-impressionistic style which has brought her considerable, if belated, recognition in the late 1980s.

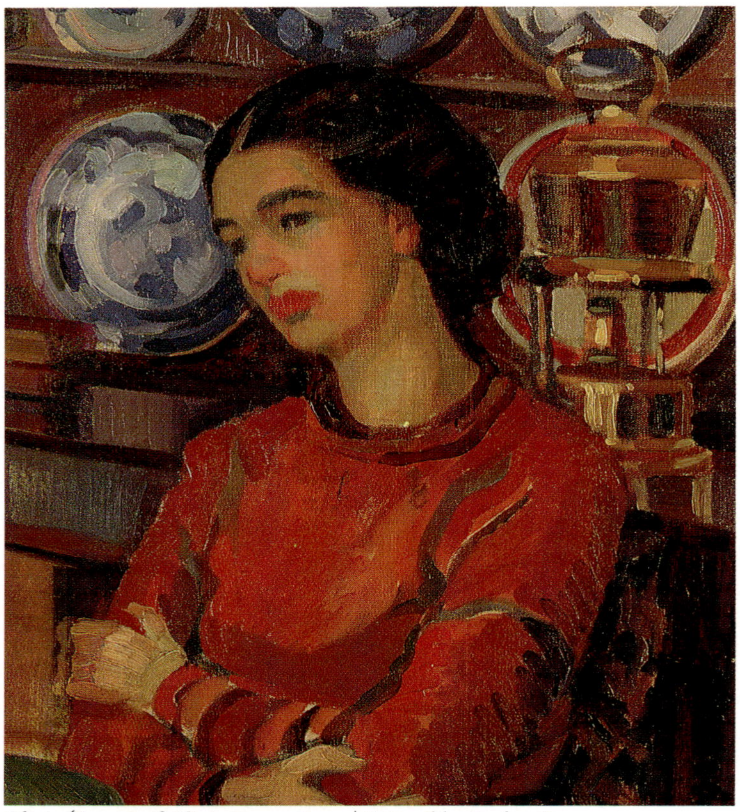

JARVIS COLLECTION, AUCKLAND

Olivia (Portrait of Olivia Spencer-Bower) 1934, oil by Evelyn Page.

Two painters whose work has excited both more fulsome praise and public bafflement in succeeding years came to the fore in the South Island during the thirties: Colin McCahon and Toss Woollaston. McCahon's early geometrical simplification of the New Zealand landscape, his placement of religious figures in the Nelson landscape, his use of symbolism, calligraphy and numbers have always challenged viewers. As McCahon said of his *Landscape: Theme and Variations*, "I hoped to throw people into an involvement with the raw land, and also with raw painting."

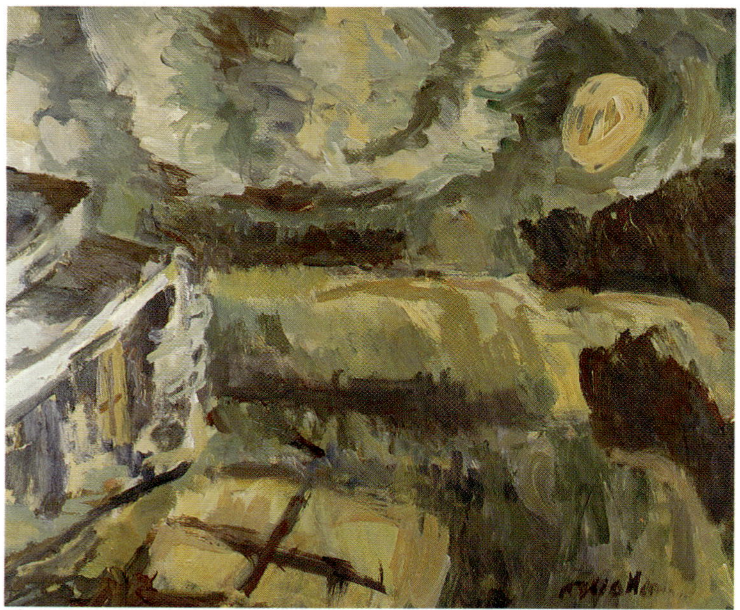

PETER WEBB GALLERIES

The Painter's House in Moonlight, 1968, oil by Sir Mountford Tosswill Woollaston.

Often murky in colour (the artist said that he wanted to paint the sunlight after it had been absorbed by the earth) and always vigorous in brushwork, Woollaston's equally uncompromising and turbulent landscapes have continued to enthrall or enrage viewers. "People still don't realise that paint is paint being exciting," he said some years ago. "It may *happen* to represent something." That he remained faithful to his own conception of painting throughout the difficult years when he supported a family on the earnings of a door-to-door salesman but is now listed in gallery catalogues as Sir Mountford Tosswill Woollaston is a commentary on the way in which artists are perceived in New Zealand society.

From the mid-1930s painting in New Zealand was to be dominated by landscapes. A general consensus seems to have been reached that a truly New Zealand culture could only be visually defined in terms of a de-populated, de-spiritualised land much like the one described in Charles Brasch's poem, *The Silent Land*:

The mountains are empty. No hermits have hallowed the caves.
Nor has the unicorn drunk from the green fountain
Whose popular shadow never heard the horn.
Lives like a vanishing night-dew drop away.

This lament betrays as much about the poet's absorption with the poems of W. H. Auden as it does about his ignorance of the relationship between the Maori and the land. For a cultivated Pakeha, the landscape is alien and works of art must register New Zealand's particular identity by depicting what the poet A. R. D. Fairburn called "the hard, clear light". Art historian Francis Pound describes "a clarified formalised naturalism" which became the approved style. It was widely believed this would lead inevitably to an art with a strong sense of national identity. In fact critics continued until recently to judge painting in terms of this arbitrary standard.

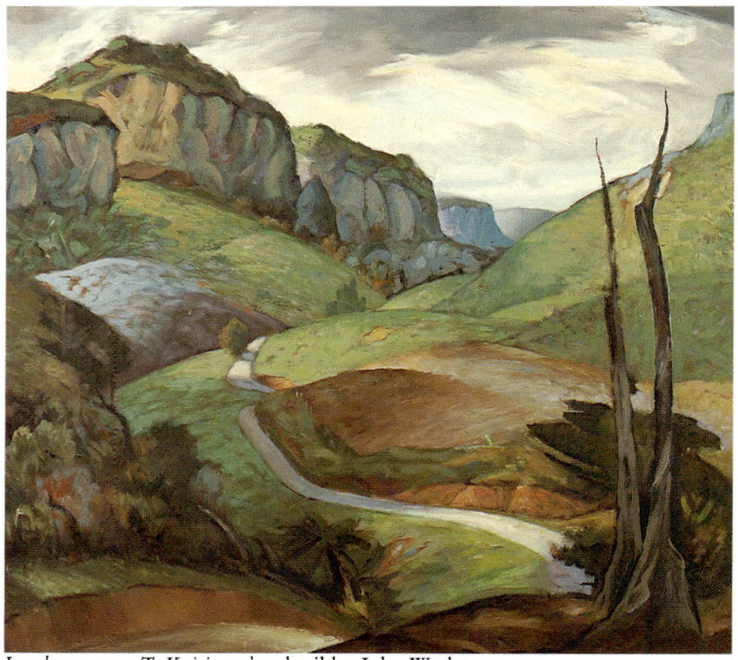

PETER WEBB GALLERIES

Landscape near Te Kuiti, undated, oil by John Weeks.

Artists were influenced by the same search; John Weeks, trained at André Lhote's Paris school, painted the limestone country around Piopio in a soft cubist style and encouraged a whole host of pupils at Auckland's Elam School of Art to do the same. In Christchurch, Rata Lovell-Smith and Rita Angus did careful bright landscapes while in Dunedin, R.N. Field encouraged McCahon, Woollaston and Doris Lusk. The English-born painter, Christopher Perkins had arrived in Wellington in 1929 and was to remain here until 1934. He saw his task as "turning the stark facts of life in this country, such as the tin dairy shed into a unit of living design" and he spoke scathingly of the "nostalgia for the softness of old England".

Perkins' *Frozen Flames*, painted in 1931, inaugurated a whole school of "slain tree" paintings, all of them depicting a landscape in which dead trees are the skeletal survivors of the bush burn-offs. Eric Lee-Johnson's *Slain Tree* (1945) is the best known but the subject also occurs in the work of Gordon Walters, Rita Angus, John Holmwood and Mervyn Taylor. In Russell Clark's painting *In the Ureweras*, a group of Maori figures moves forward out of the dead trees adding to the poignancy of the situation.

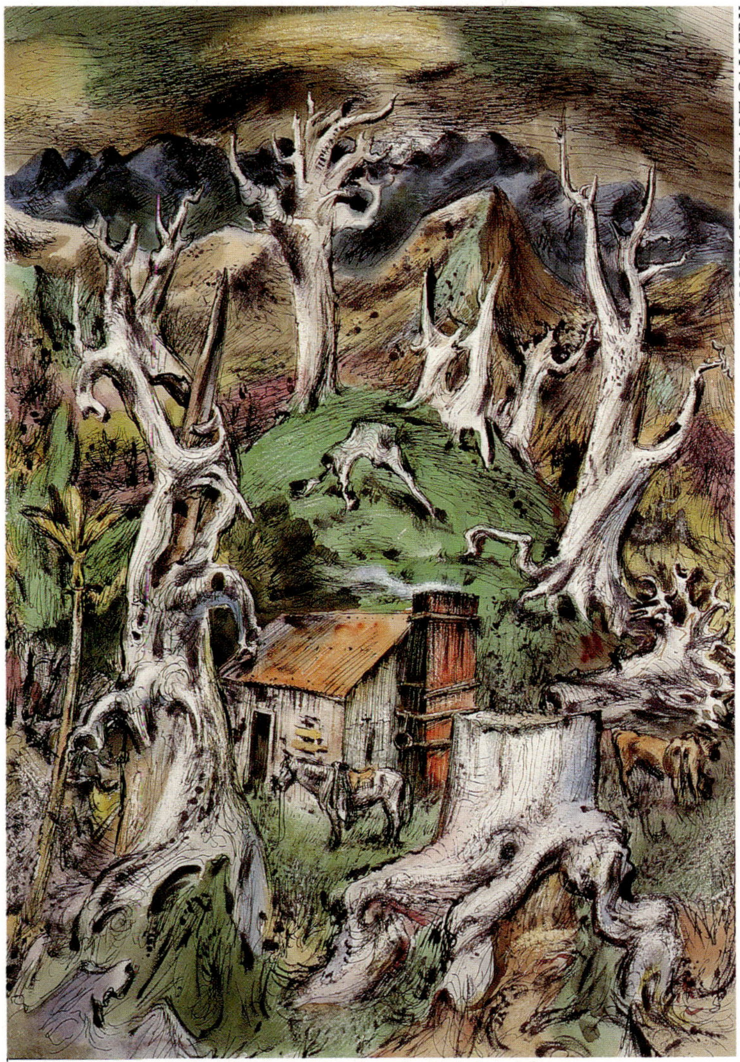

AUCKLAND CITY ART GALLERY

In the Backblocks, 1950, ink and watercolour by Eric Lee-Johnson.

Since the early 1950s, when Helen Hitchings operated New Zealand's first dealer gallery in Wellington and was quickly followed by others throughout the country, the visual arts have burgeoned. Although the demand that artists should seek to be New Zealanders first and artists second was a long time dying, today there are large numbers of painters, print-makers, sculptors and photographers all pursuing their own interests without reference to any notions of an approved way of doing things.

The magazine *Art New Zealand*, founded in 1976, provides an invaluable record of the creative energy which has characterised the arts here, particularly in the last three decades. Some figures stand out, among them Patrick Hanly, Milan Mrkusich, Gordon Walters, Ralph Hotere, Don Binney, Peter Siddell and Robert Ellis all of whom came to prominence in the 1960s; Tony Fomison, Philip Clairmont, Philip Trusttum, Gretchen Albrecht, Dick Frizzell in the 1970s; Carole Shepheard, Richard Killeen, Gavin Chilcott, Philippa Blair, Jeffrey Harris in the 1980s. The achievement of sculptors Molly Macalister, Greer Twiss, Christine Hellyar, Neil Dawson, Denis O'Connor and Terry Stringer in gaining public acceptance for their work can be seen in many public places throughout the country.

IT WAS NOT UNTIL THE 1890s that the number of New Zealand-born Europeans began to outweigh the number of immigrant Europeans in the country. Only then did the literary classics of the pioneering period such as Lady Barker's *Station Life in New Zealand* (1870) or F. E. Maning's *Old New Zealand* (1863), both of them expressive of unsettled, stateless, expatriate sentiments, give way to works like William Pember Reeves' *The Long White Cloud* (1898). But the promise of an indigenous literature was not to develop fully for another quarter of a century and, apart from Sir George Grey, few writers concerned themselves with the Maori history, tales, poems and myths handed down by oral tradition.

In the intervening years there were only scattered works of value. Blanche Baughan is one poet whose work survives, and Katherine Mansfield, working in Europe, produced her first collection of stories, *In a German Pension*, in 1911 and continued to write until her early death at the age of thirty-five. Her principal biographer is a New Zealander, Antony Alpers, and she has continued to be the subject of more critical and biographical work than any other New Zealand-born writer.

The novels the *Greenstone Door* (1914) by William Satchell and *The Story of a New Zealand River* (1920) by another expatriate, Jane Mander, are still highly readable.

If the literature of a country is a body of work continuous over a period of time and related in content, style and purpose, then New Zealand literature can be said to have begun in the late twenties with the work of such poets as R. A. K. Mason, Ursula Bethell, D'Arcy Cresswell and A. R. D. Fairburn. The decade beginning with the Depression and ending with the Second World War saw an upsurge in the number of poems and short stories printed in a variety of often short-lived periodicals. Mason was joined by Allen Curnow, Charles Brasch and Denis Glover and distinct groups of writers developed.

In the following years poetry continued strongly, much of it dominated, like the visual arts, by the natural landscape. The work of Robin Hyde, Eileen Duggan, Keith Sinclair, Kendrick Smithyman, Louis Johnson, James K. Baxter, Alistair Campbell and others is often concerned with the attempts of poets to come to terms with a land in which they feel like interlopers. M. H. Holcroft in *Discovered Isles* (1950) writes of the "need to make a home for the mind as well as the body in a land which has failed to advance beyond the status of a spiritual colony".

Social protest dominated the work of three important novelists of the Depression years: John A. Lee (*Children of the Poor*), Robin Hyde (*The Godwits Fly*) and John Mulgan (*Man Alone*). Suffering, injustice and oppression are their dominant themes. The most influential writer of fiction in the 1940s and 1950s was Frank Sargeson in whose work the conventional romanticism and fixation with "Mother England" were successfully thrown off. Sargeson's short stories made use of distinctively New Zealand speech idioms and subtly analysed New Zealand's puritanical attitudes.

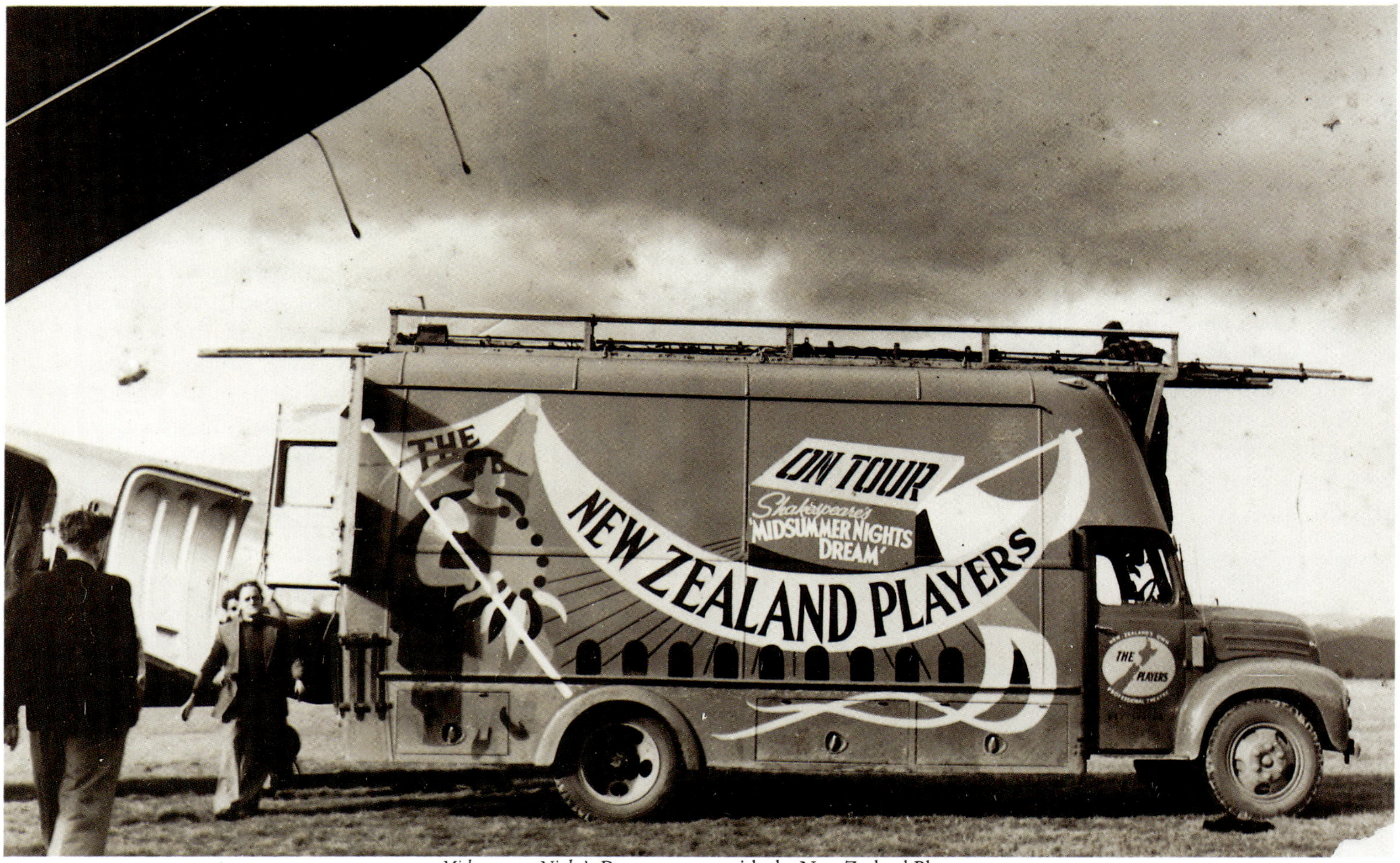

CHAS CABOT COLLECTION/ALEXANDER TURNBULL LIBRARY

Midsummer Night's Dream on tour with the New Zealand Players.

In 1957 Janet Frame, considered by many to be this country's finest novelist, produced *Owls Do Cry* and followed it with *Faces in the Water*, *The Edge of the Alphabet*, *Scented Gardens for the Blind* and other novels. In the 1980s her three-volume autobiography testified to her enduring fascination with words and her perseverance with writing despite poverty, discouragement, misunderstanding and treatment for mental illness.

The novelists Ian Cross, Sylvia Ashton-Warner, Noel Hilliard and Bill Pearson have all produced fine work although none of them has matched the achievement of Maurice Shadbolt whose *Season of the Jew* (1986), the story of Te Kooti and the early days of Gisborne, is certainly the most successful New Zealand historical novel.

In 1963 a critic writing in the *Times Literary Supplement* suggested that the full development of New Zealand fiction might require the abandonment of a "myth of the backblocks" which, it was claimed, was strait-jacketing New Zealand literature. Indeed, at that time it did appear as though the majority of novelists perceived their country in terms of small town, small-minded characters, settings and issues. Today racial, sexual, political and cultural issues are all openly dealt with in novels like Keri Hulme's *the bone people* or Witi Ihimaera's *The Matriarch* which, despite their "backblocks" settings have nothing whatsoever to do with a restricted backblocks mentality of the type complained of in the 1960s. Urban novels such as those by C. K. Stead, Maurice Gee, and Sue McCauley, feature a wide variety of articulate, sophisticated characters.

DRAMA DID NOT FLOURISH until the thirties. In 1931 the magazine *Art in New Zealand* inaugurated an annual drama competition with preference being given to plays with a New Zealand theme and location.

In 1940, however, the centennial literary competition produced no play script worthy of the prize being offered. Amateur drama societies flourished throughout the country but tended to ignore New Zealand plays. The visit of the Old Vic Company with Laurence Olivier and Vivien Leigh added to the growing pressure for the establishment of a national professional theatre.

The New Zealand Players was founded by Richard and Edith Campion in 1952 with the aim of encouraging New Zealand actors and playwrights. Despite the enormous difficulties of touring, the Players usually maintained a high standard of production and rate of attendance. By the time they ceased operations in 1960 they had presented forty plays in thirty-six towns. Four had been by New Zealand writers. A number of other New Zealand plays were workshopped, the most notable of these being Bruce Mason's *The Pohutukawa Tree*, a play destined to become a landmark in New Zealand writing because of its fearless confrontation of racial issues.

A vigorous critic and talented actor, Bruce Mason toured the length and breadth of New Zealand presenting solo performances of his own works. He edited the theatre magazine *ACT*, wrote New Zealand's first television drama, *The Evening Paper* (1965) and continued in *Awatea* and *Hongi* to place Maori concerns and Maori actors at the centre of the New Zealand stage. In the words of playwright Mervyn Thompson, "he provided more memorable evenings in the theatre than any other New Zealander."

Professional theatre remained a risky business until well into the 1970s. The nucleus audience was not large, transport costs were huge and there was a lack of suitable venues. By the 1960s theatre planners had begun to look more seriously at regional development with professional companies based in the main centres.

In the interim, actors left to study in England, among them Raymond Hawthorne, Elric Hooper, Jonathan Elsom, Bridget Armstrong, Alice Fraser and Sunny Amey. All have since returned to New Zealand as actors or directors. In 1973, Hawthorne founded Auckland's Theatre Corporate, which was initially funded by its associated theatre-in-education company. Hooper became director of the Court Theatre in Christchurch and Sunny Amey at Wellington's Downstage inaugurated a policy of producing a wide variety of plays by New Zealand playwrights.

Other theatres sprang up: Four Seasons in Wanganui (1970), Gateway Players in Tauranga (1972), Centrepoint at Palmerston North (1973) and Fortune in Dunedin (1974). Today actors and directors no longer find it so necessary to leave New Zealand in order to work in theatre.

MUCH HAS HAPPENED in the world of dance since Poul Gnatt came from Denmark in 1953 to found the New Zealand Ballet Company. When Rowena Jackson returned from Covent Garden with her husband Philip Chatfield, they were joined by choreographer Russell Kerr and Richard Campion and the four became the guiding forces behind the company and its associated school of dance until the late 1970s. By 1986 the company had a permanent staff of forty-six and was entitled to the appellation, Royal. Jon Trimmer is unquestionably the finest male dancer this country has ever produced. In Auckland the Limbs Dance Company, founded in 1977, has developed an enviable national and international reputation. Originally a part-time company of six dancers, Limbs has created an entirely new audience for modern dance in New Zealand.

NEW ZEALAND MUSIC has passed through a number of distinct phases since the first Polynesian, pre-European one. The colonial, European-dominated period lasted at least until 1940 when a still European-derived but distinctively New Zealand art music was established by Douglas Lilburn. A highly cultivated man, Lilburn had studied with Vaughan Williams in London. Returning to New Zealand, he was a close friend to many of the artists and writers in what has been called the "Landfall" generation, after the literary periodical of the same name founded in 1947 by Charles Brasch. In 1969 Lilburn gave a talk called "A Search for a Language" in which he said that "the most basic problem that we as composers are up against ... is the relationship between our human experience and our musical language." He also recalled that "Yeats and others have reminded us that if we want to be universal, we must first discover truth of experience in our own village." Lilburn addressed these two issues more seriously than any previous New Zealand composer and he founded a continuous tradition of New Zealand art music (composers Jack Body, John Rimmer, David Farquhar, Jenny McLeod, Ross Harris and others were all taught by him or closely associated with him). He achieved a professional level of composition previously unknown in New Zealand. His three symphonies, *Aotearoa Overture* and *Landfall in Unknown Seas* now regularly feature on orchestral programmes.

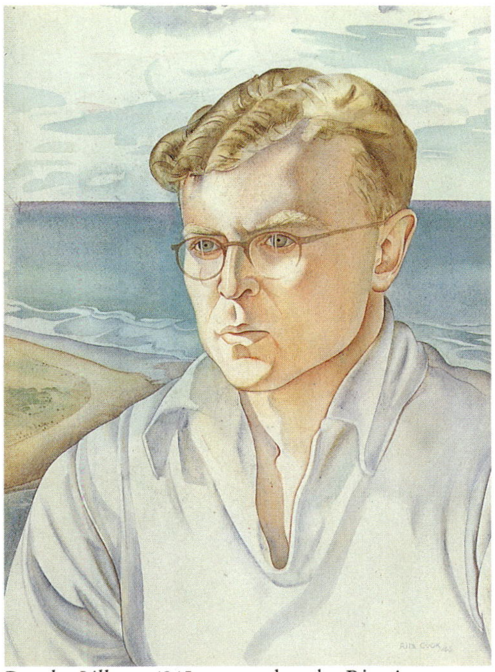

Douglas Lilburn, 1945, watercolour by Rita Angus.

In the musical performing arts there is much to be proud of. The New Zealand Symphony Orchestra celebrated its fortieth birthday in 1987 and went on to achieve extremely high standards of performance particularly under Hungarian conductor Georgy Lehel and German-born Franz-Paul Decker. The latter described the orchestra as "one of the world's best kept secrets". The Music Federation, founded in the mid-forties by Czech emigres Arthur Hilton and Fred Turnovsky, tours national and international chamber music groups throughout the country. These two men are among the group of refugees from Hitler's Europe who significantly advanced our culture. Others were the pianist Lili Kraus, architect Ernst Plischke, poet Karl Wolfskehl and philosopher Karl Popper.

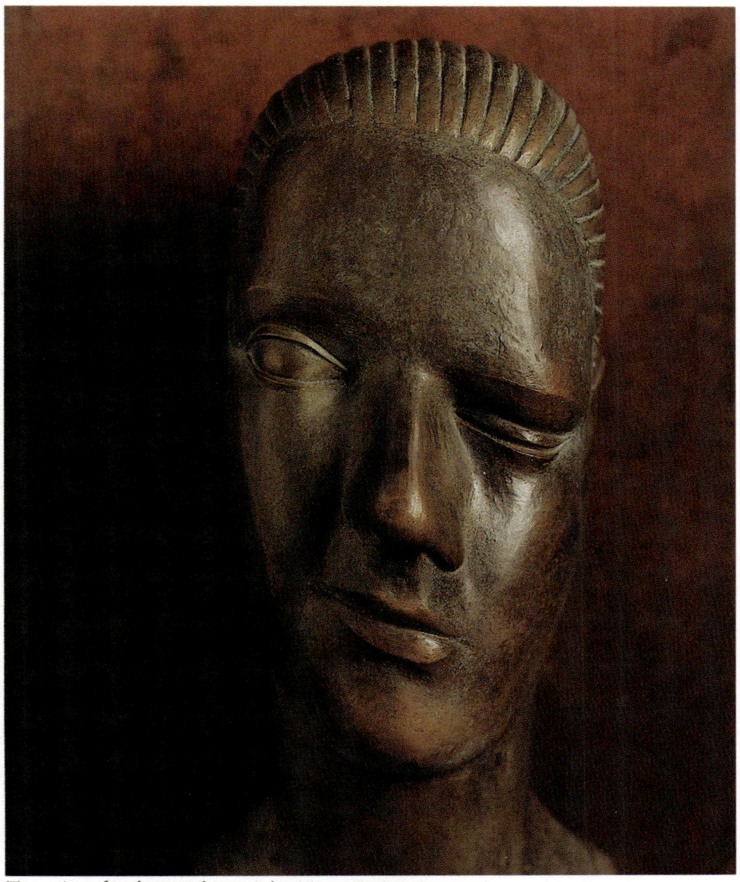

Two views head, 1988, bronze by Terry Stringer

Excellent regional orchestras have been established in the four main centres, all performing major works from the symphonic repertoire and compositions by New Zealand composers to increasingly discerning audiences. Many New Zealand singers, led by Dame Kiri Te Kanawa and Malvina Major, are principals in opera houses throughout the world while others like Wendy Dixon, Antony Benfell and Christopher Doig have busy operatic careers in both Australia and New Zealand.

IN THE CRAFTS a new professionalism is apparent, although it has its roots in the traditional handcrafts practised especially by women in both the Pakeha and Maori home. In the years after the Second World War, as the result of enlightened educational policies and the pioneering work of people like Sylvia Ashton-Warner and Alwyn Richardson, a whole generation of children was taught the creative use of materials at hand; art and craft advisers to the Department of Education travelled the country encouraging and making sure that educationalists concentrated on more than just the three "r's".

It remained difficult for people to make a living from the sale of their work or to study craft activities in depth. By the sixties the impact of Bernard Leach's English craft revival movement was being felt here, and the Japanese potter Shoji Hamada visited New Zealand and introduced high-fired stoneware and porcelain into a country which had previously only produced earthenware pottery. Len Castle, Margaret Milne and Mirek Smisek went to Japan, Peter Stichbury travelled to Abuja in Nigeria, the Quakers Harry and May Davis came from England to set up their Crewenna Pottery in Nelson. There was widespread reaction against the kind of pottery which had filled the nation's groaning china cabinets in favour of a more "back to the earth" aesthetic encouraged by Yvonne Rust, Patricia Perrin, Barry Brickell and others. By the early seventies there was hardly a married couple who did not receive at least one pottery casserole as a wedding gift. In the following decade came an understandable reaction against this approach as potters like John Parker, Warren Tippett, and Bronwynn Cornish experimented with stark shapes, bright colours and zany motifs. More and more people became interested in the work of the growing number of artists in glass so that today the work of Ann Robinson, John Croucher, Gary Nash, Peter Viesnik and Peter Raos is well known. Fibre artists of all kinds, furniture makers and jewellers produce a fascinating variety of work which is widely exhibited to an enthusiastic public fully appreciative of the blurring of the traditional distinction between the arts and the crafts.

NEW ZEALAND'S IDENTITY in the arts is characterised today by a vigorous eclecticism. It is increasingly urban, outward looking and draws on a wide variety of national and international sources. The old image of a society dominated by pursuits involving rugby, racing and beer is now hopelessly outdated. There is no longer a "them-and-us" split between the section of the population that is interested in the arts and that which is not: perhaps the best evidence of this is to be found in the much closer relationship between business and the arts, something which was almost inconceivable even twenty years ago.

The Te Maori exhibition, in bringing together a collection of Maori artifacts which previously had significance only for their tribal owners, forced Pakeha New Zealanders finally to recognise the worth and artistry of taonga which they had ignored. Ironically, it took a triumphal tour of the United States to create this awareness. The renaissance in the arts of the Maori, led by people like the weavers Rangimarie Hetet and Diggeress Te Kanawa, marks a resurgence of Maori culture and the willingness of New Zealanders to modify their previously European-oriented attitudes. For the first time Maori art has attained widely accepted prestige in its own right.

The vitality of the arts today reflects the ability of creative people here to assert themselves confidently as New Zealanders rather than as inheritors of old colonial allegiances. □

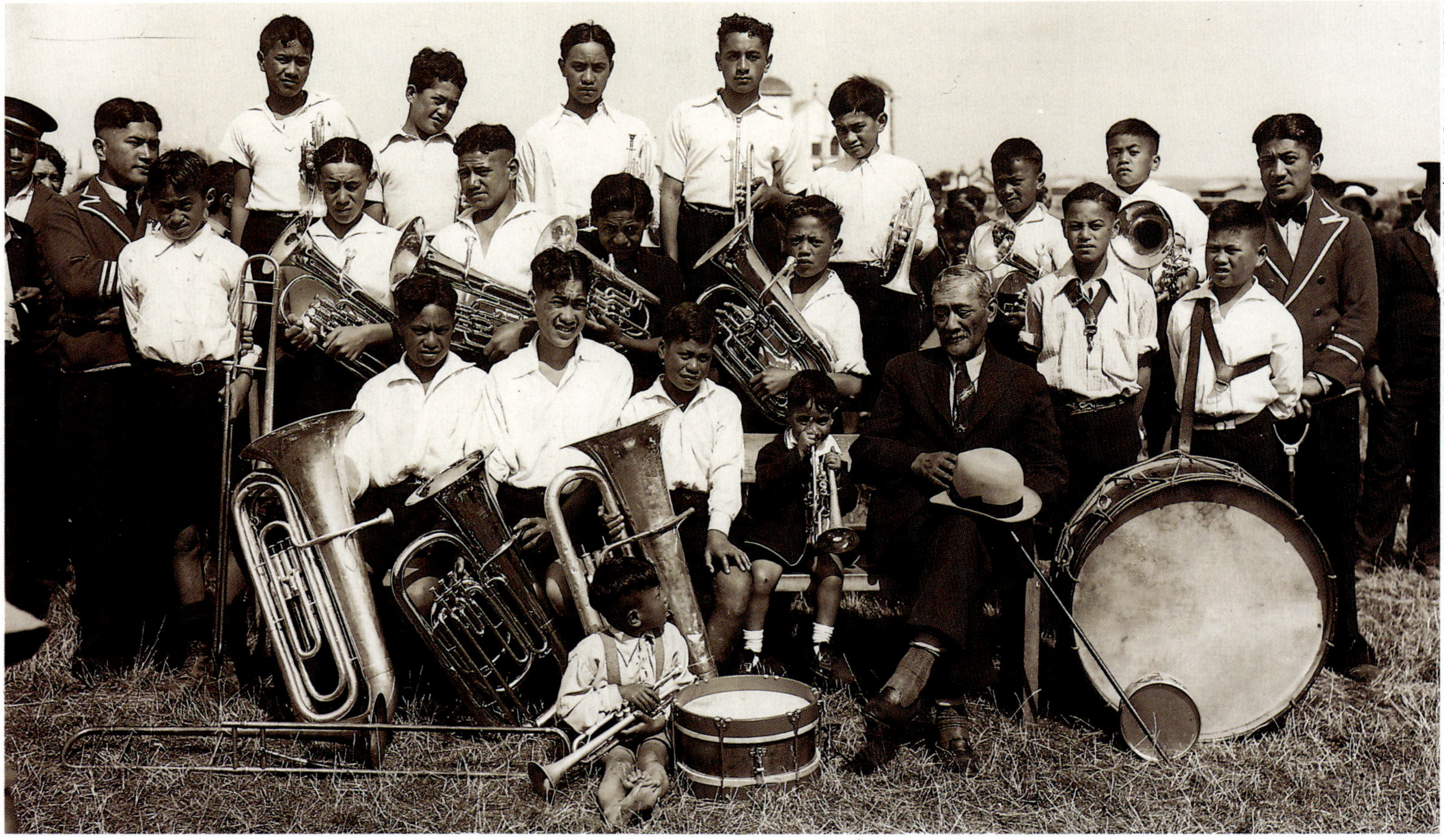

HALL RAINE COLLECTION/NATIONAL MUSEUM

Ratana brass band.

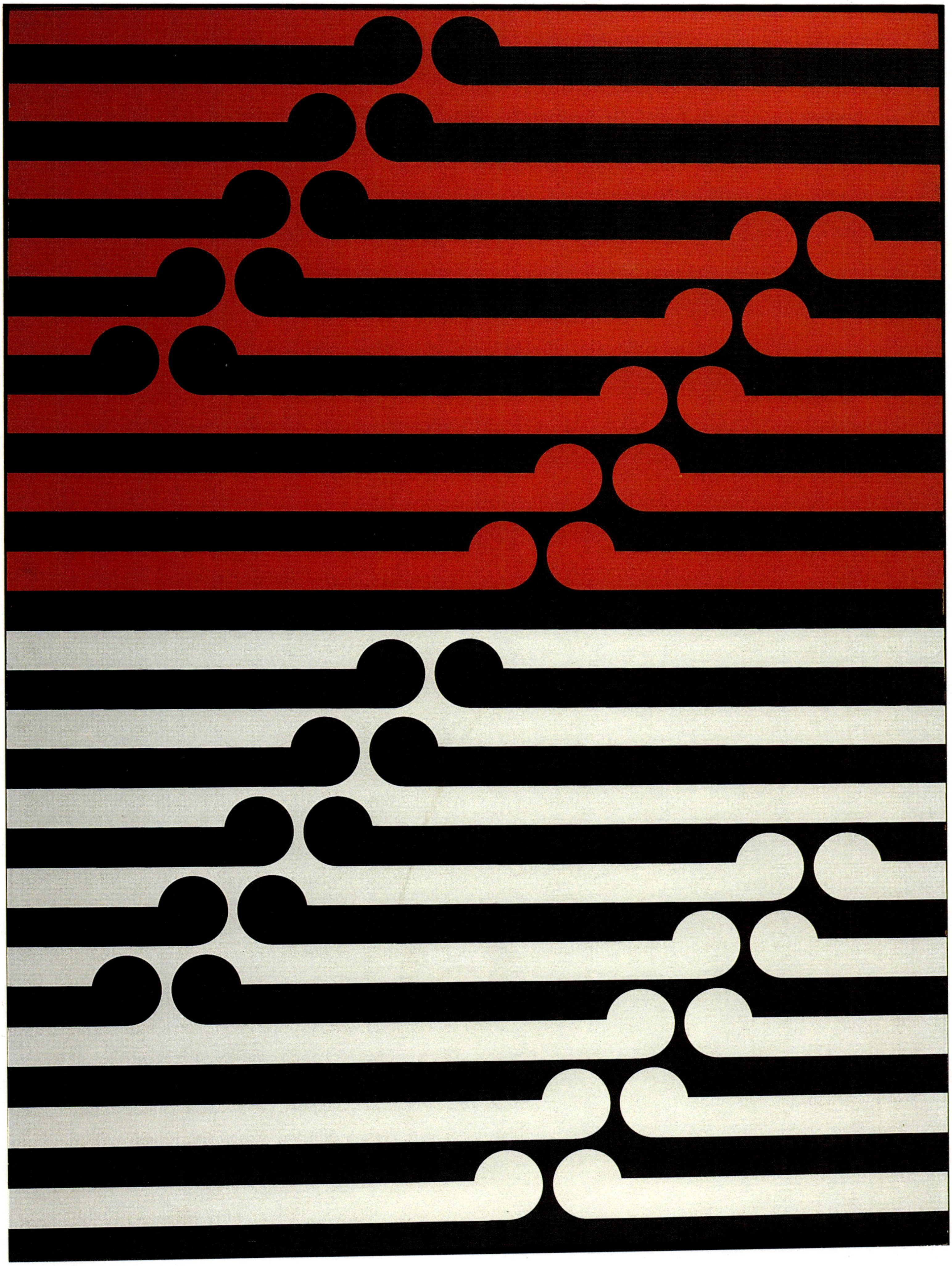

The work of painter Gordon Walters

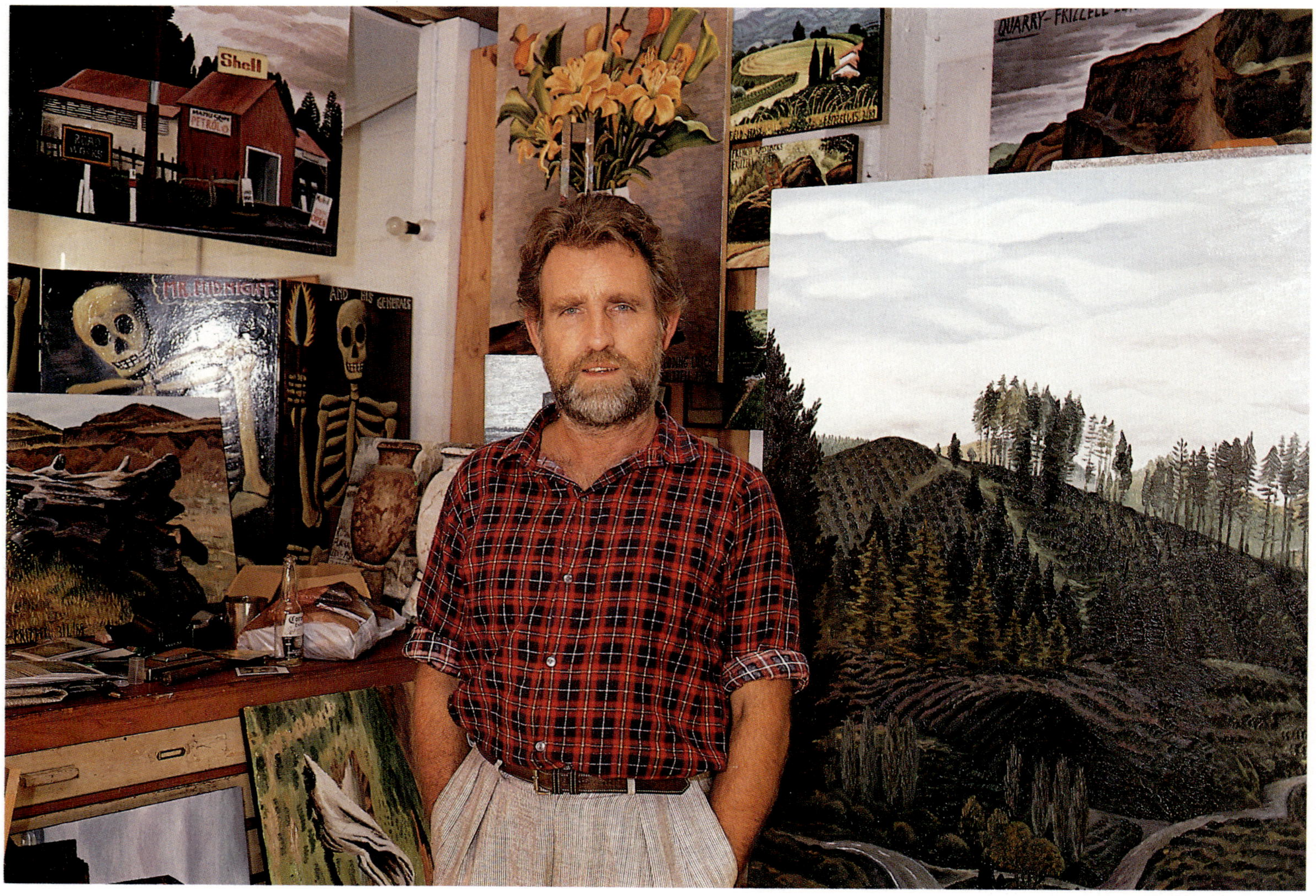

Artist Dick Frizzell

GIL HANLY

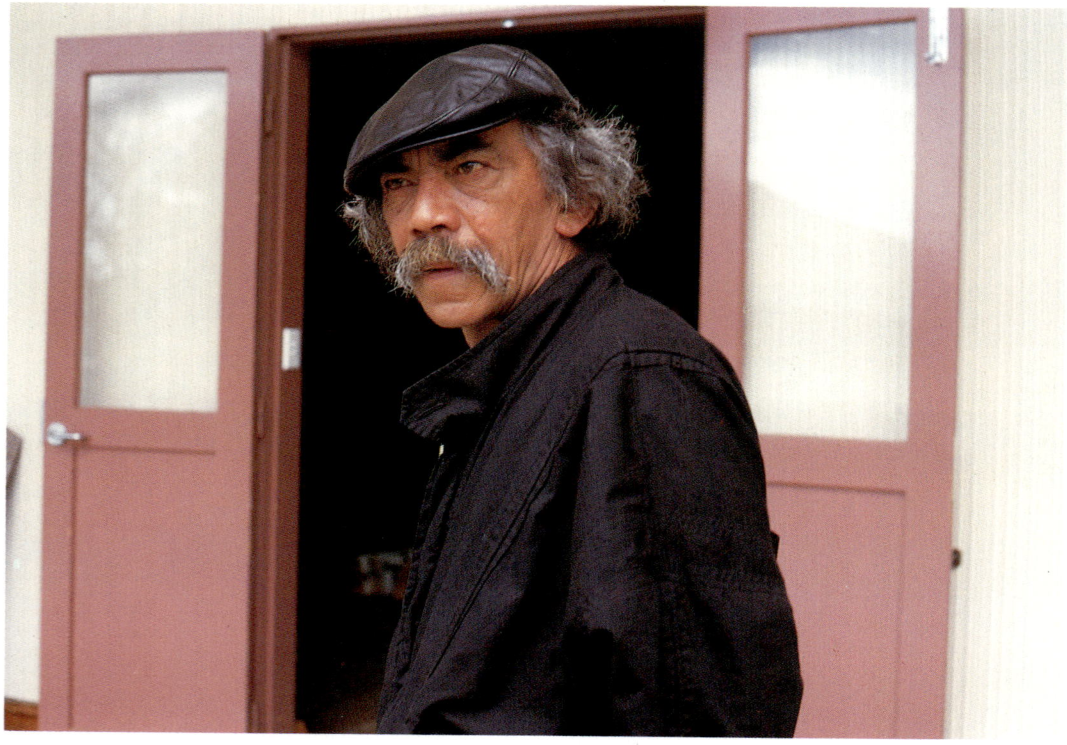

Artist Ralph Hotere

GIL HANLY

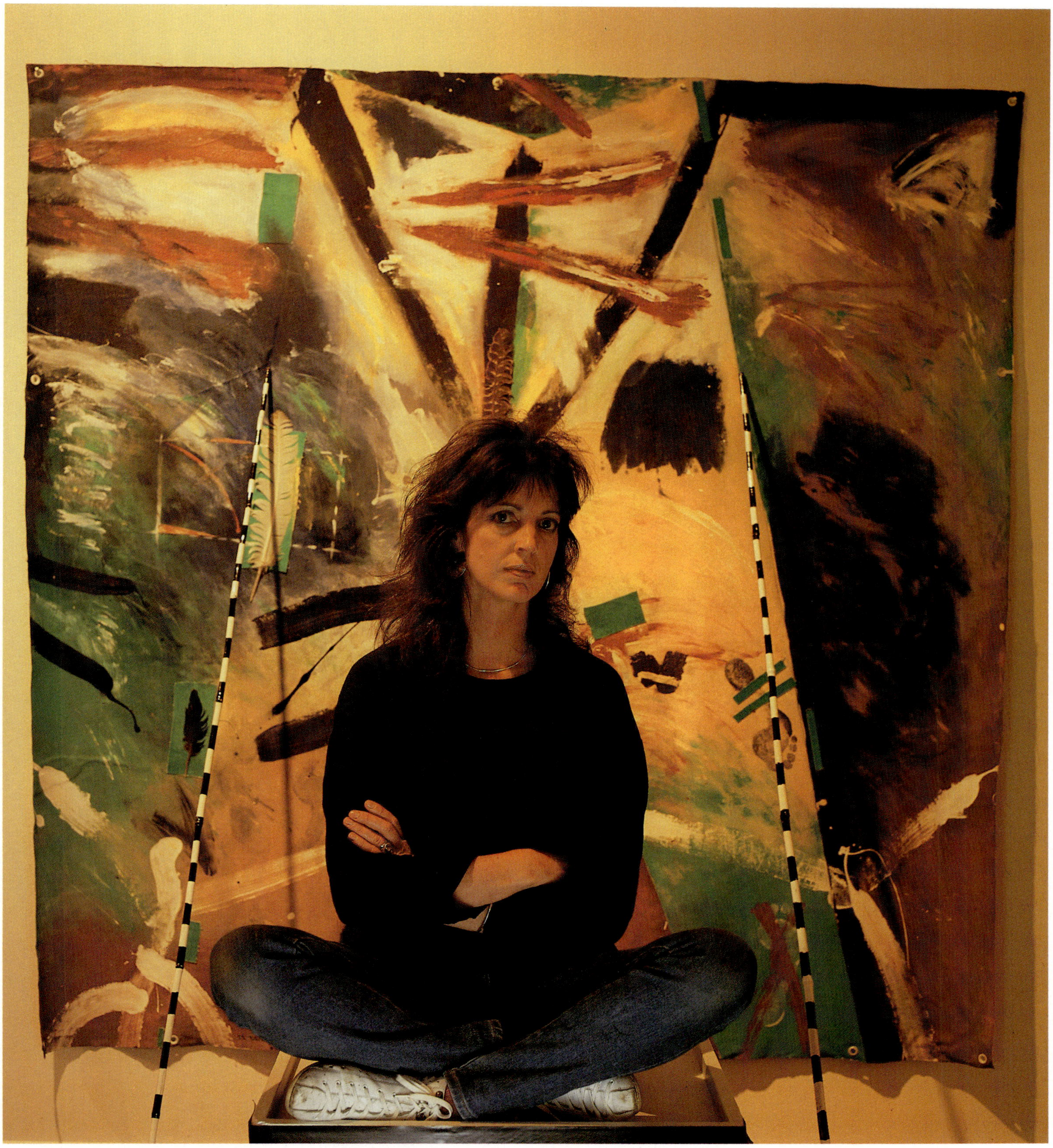

Painter Philippa Blair STEPHEN ROBINSON

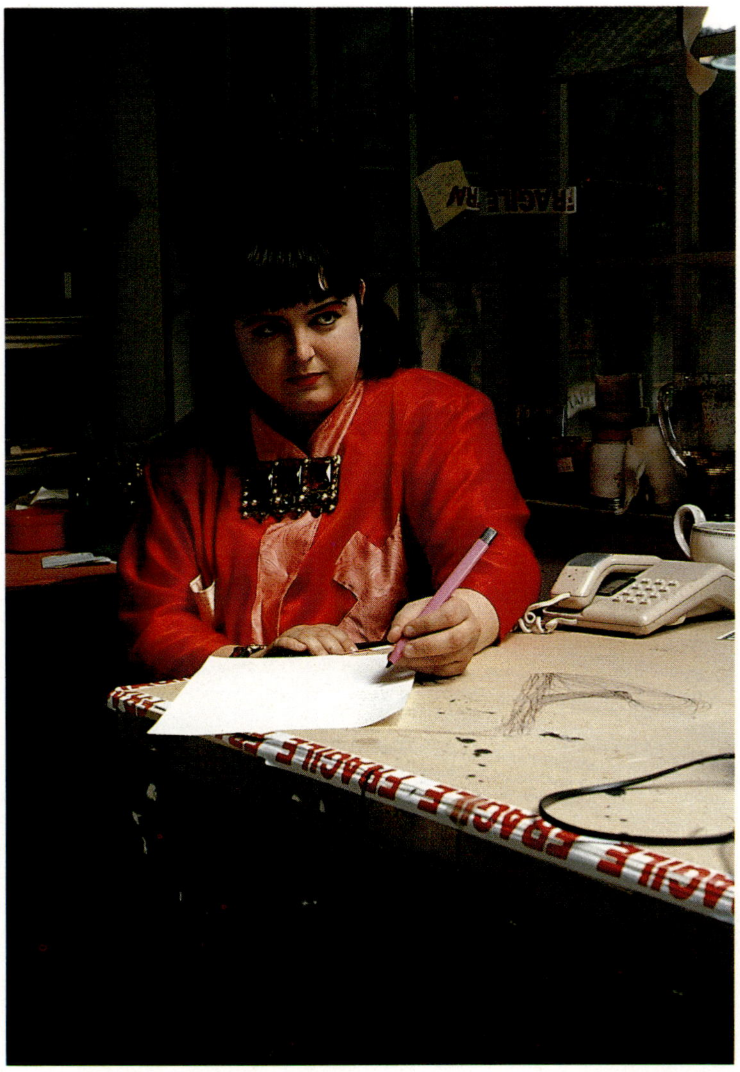

Terry Collins, wardrobe department, Mercury Theatre, Auckland STEPHEN ROBINSON

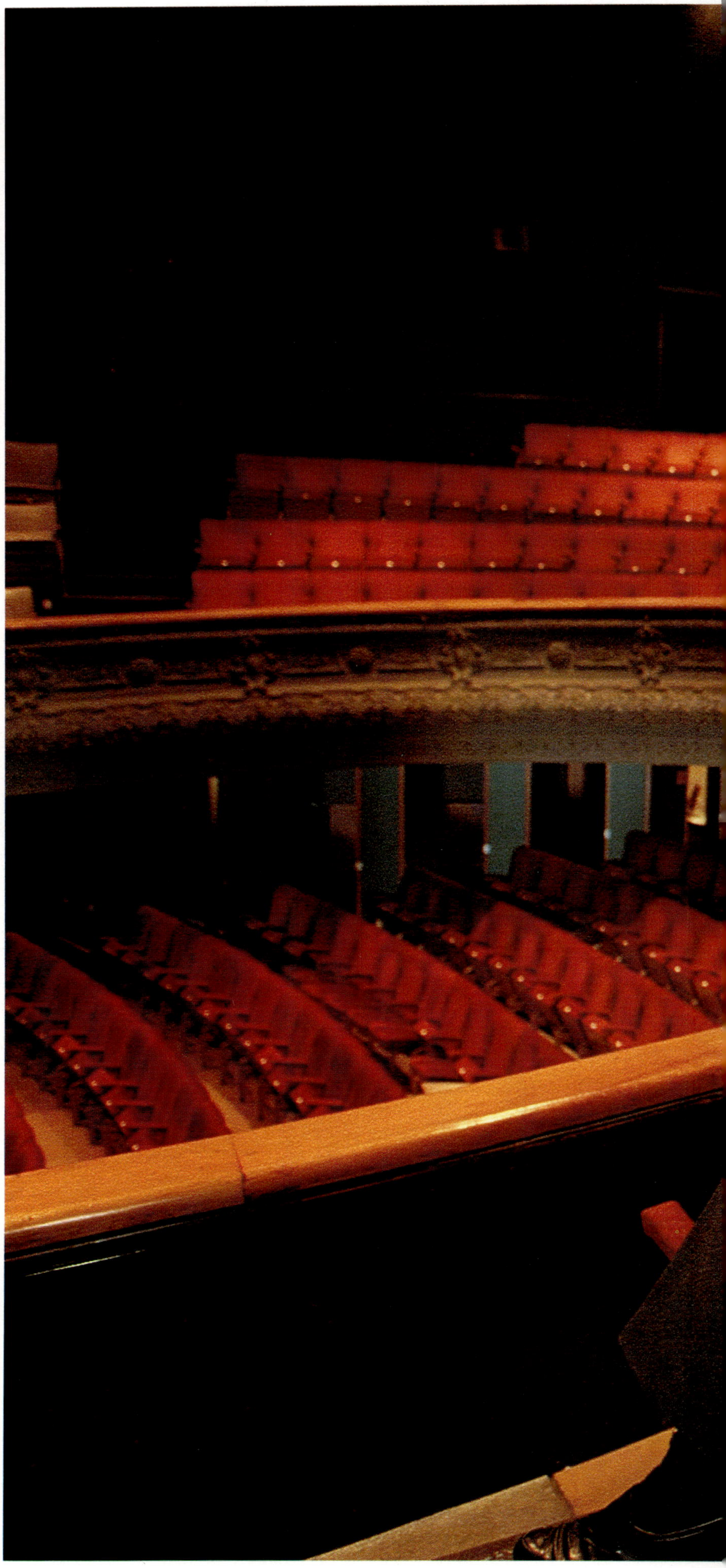

Director Raymond Hawthorne, Mercury Theatre

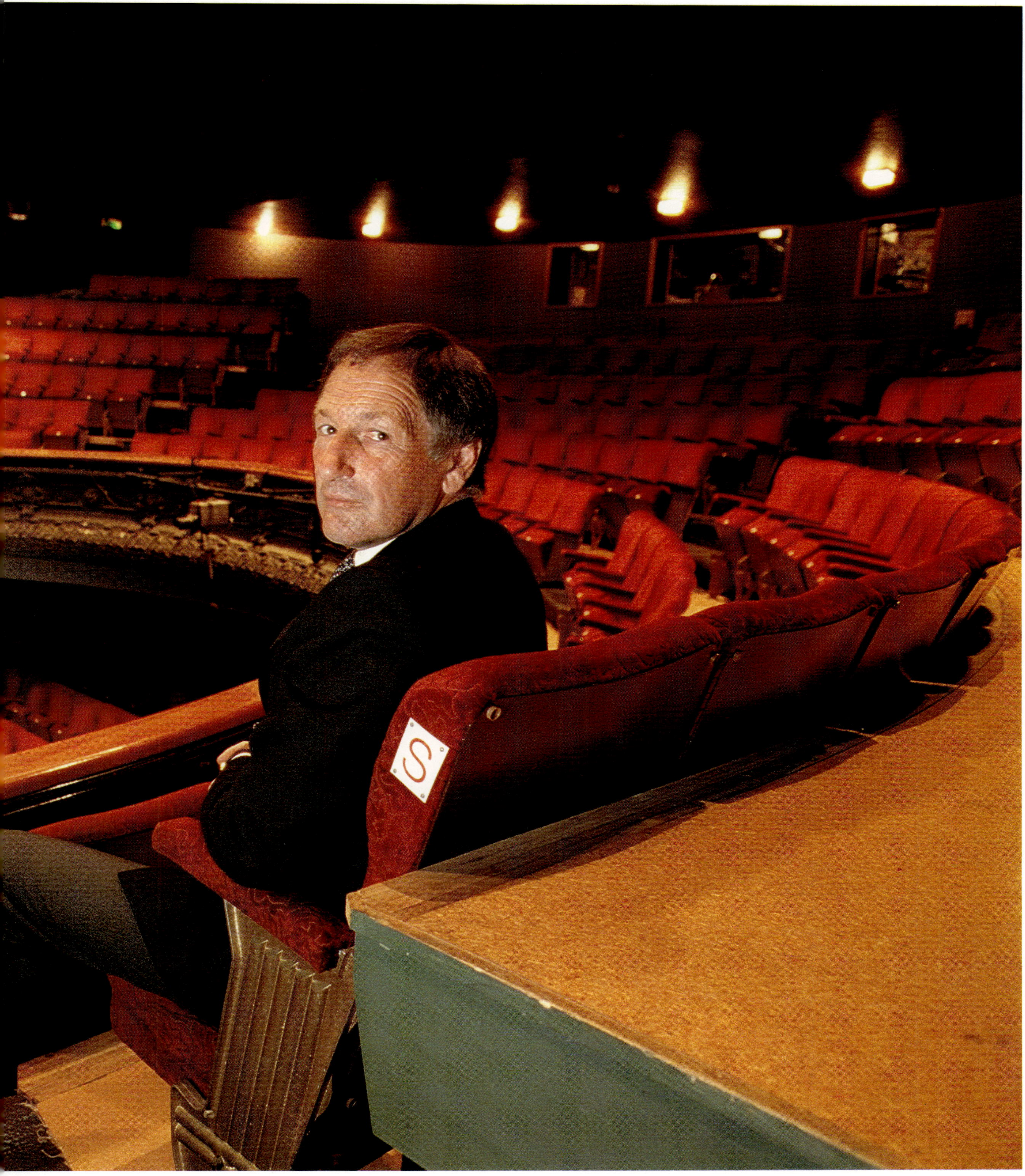

STEPHEN ROBINSON

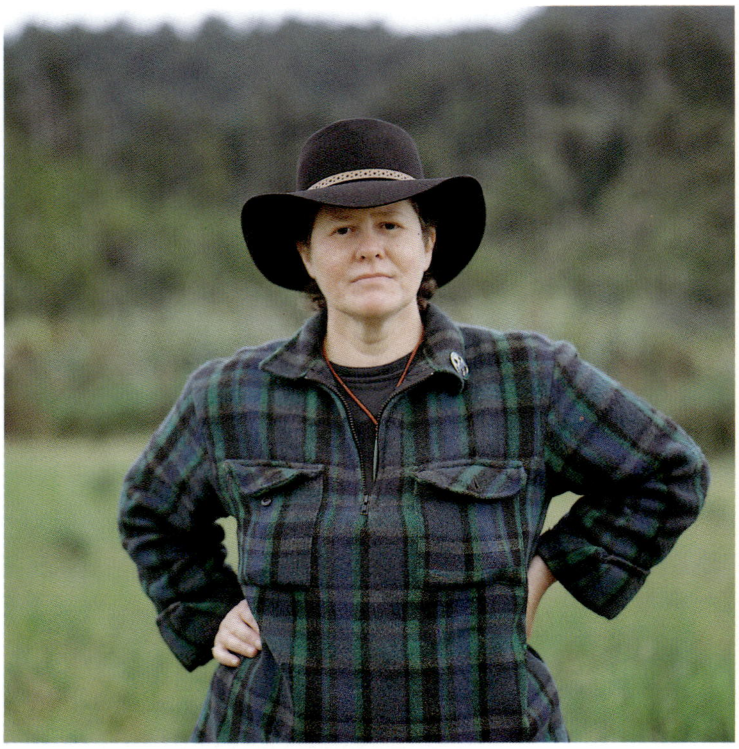

Writer Keri Hulme BRIAN ENTING

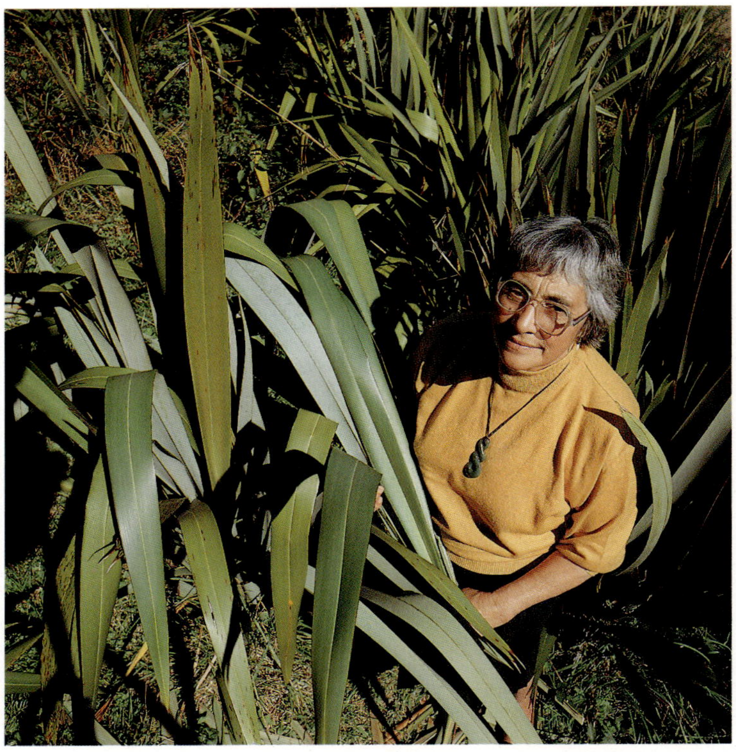

Weaver Diggeress Rangituatahi Te Kanawa with her favourite flax bush, Te Kuiti STEPHEN ROBINSON

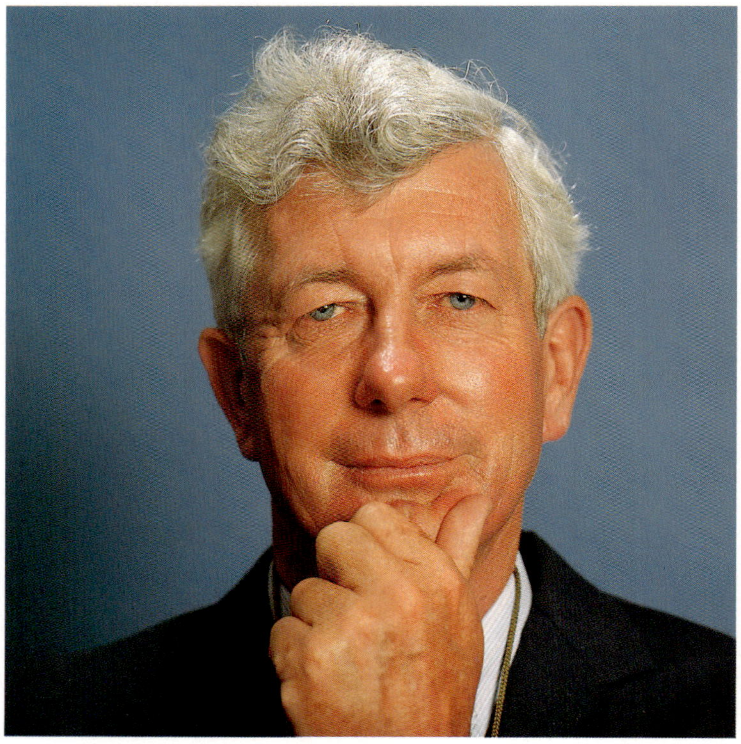

Author Ian Cross JANE USSHER

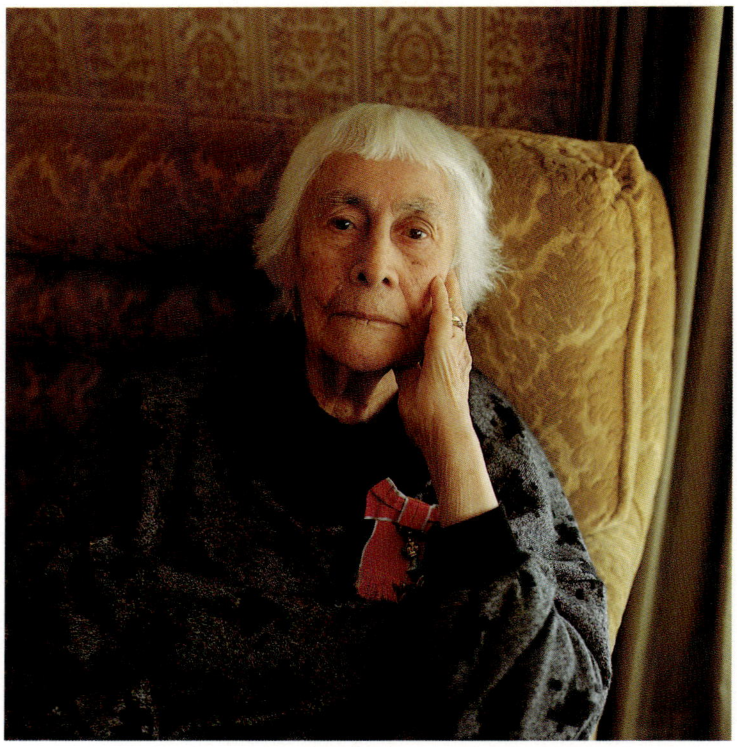

Weaver Rangimarie Hetet at Te Kuiti STEPHEN ROBINSON

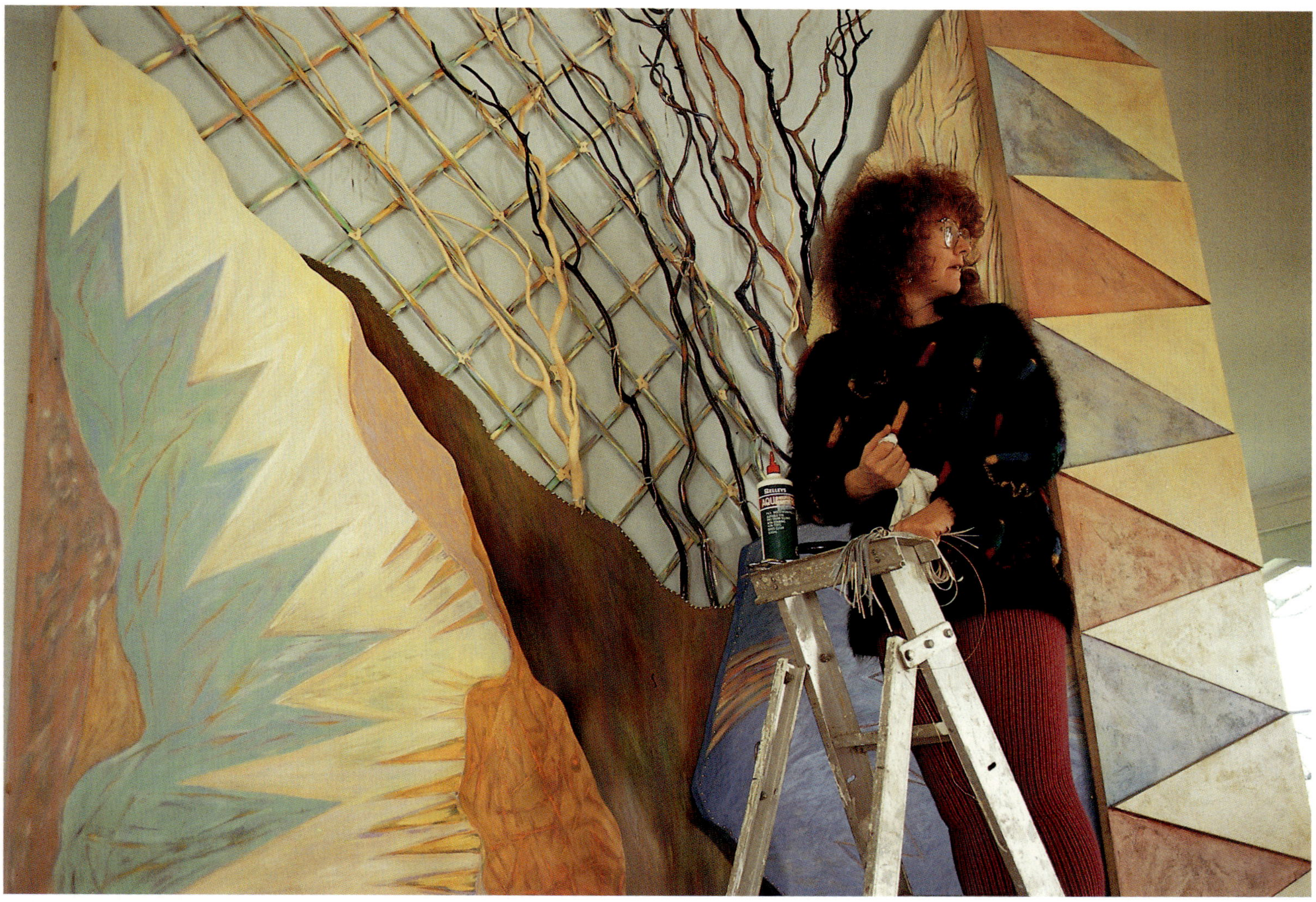

Artist Carole Shepheard GIL HANLY

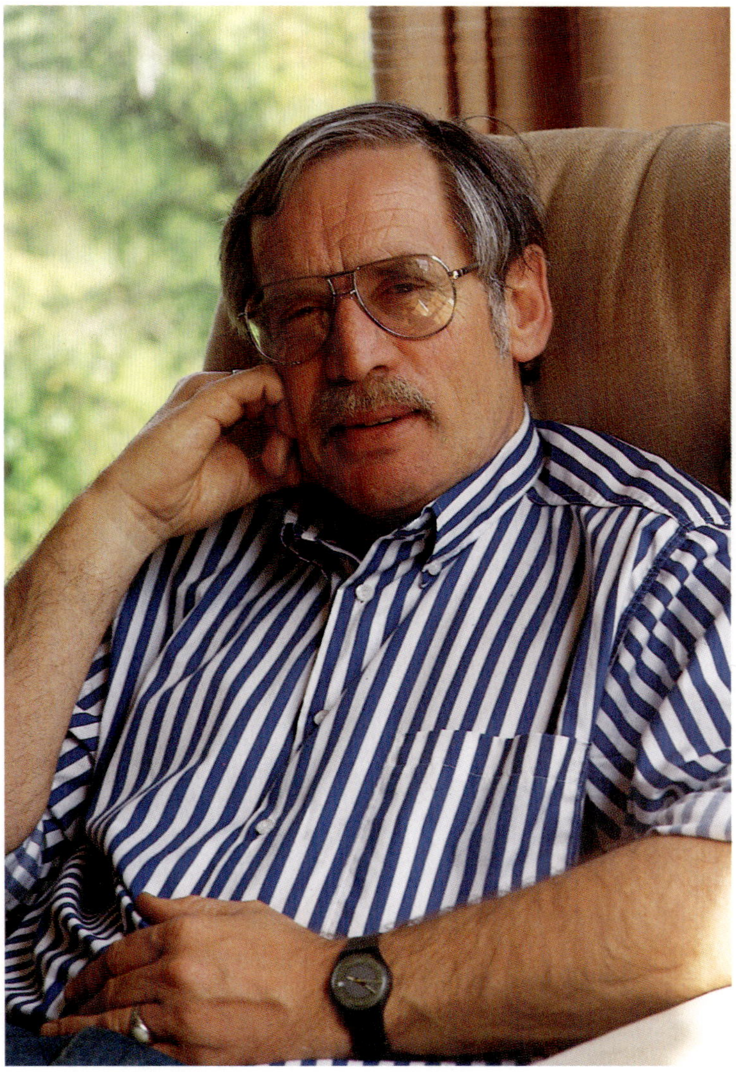

Author Maurice Shadbolt GIL HANLY

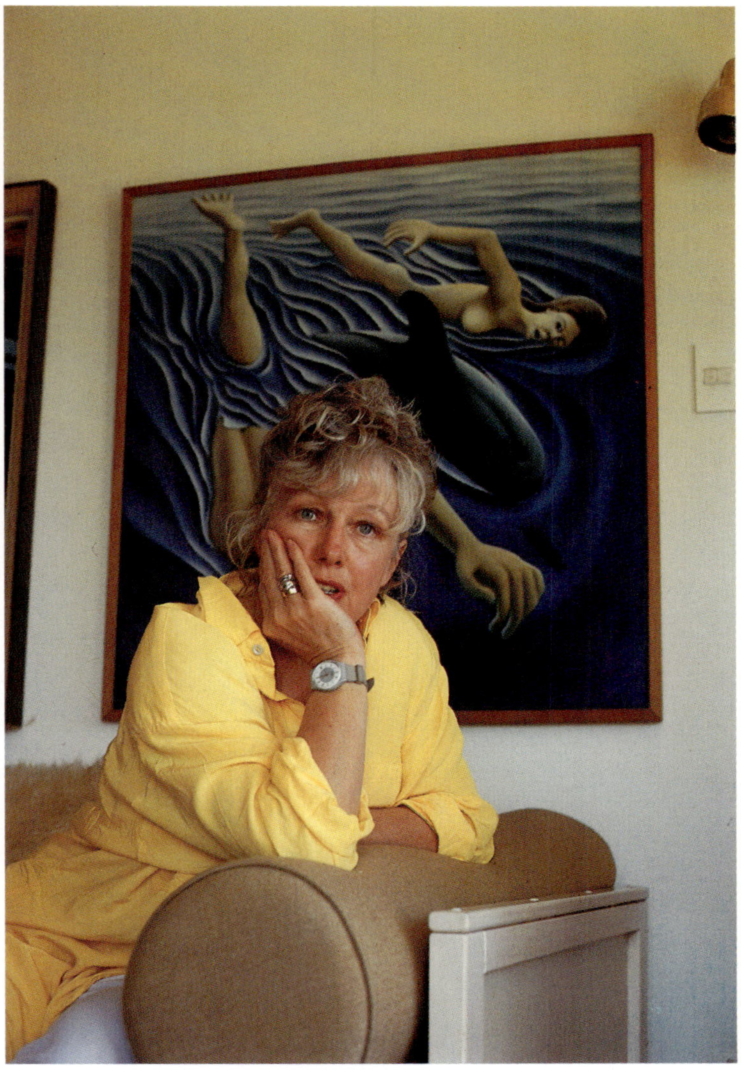

Actress Bridget Armstrong in front of Michael Smither painting GIL HANLY

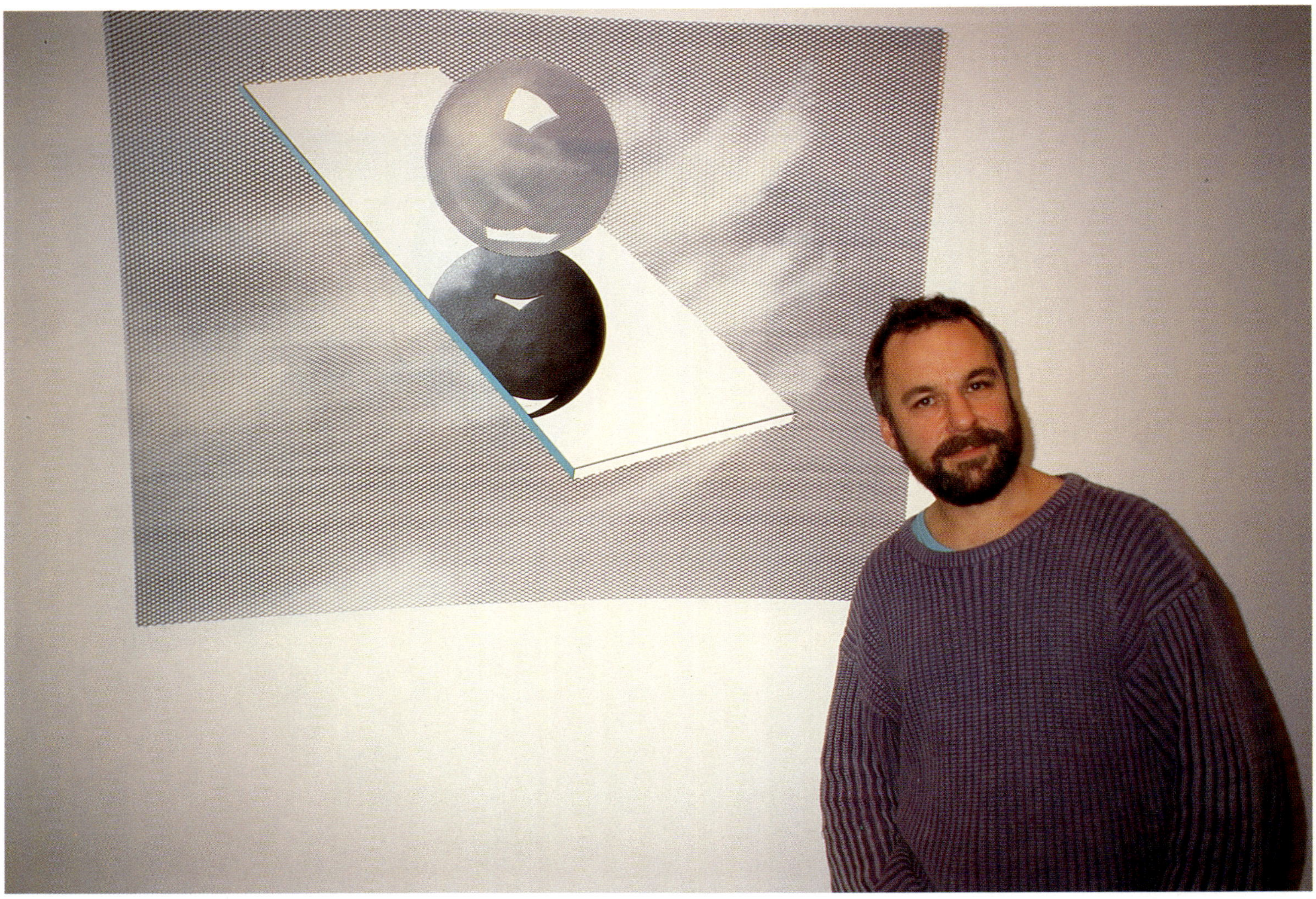

Sculptor Neil Dawson GIL HANLY

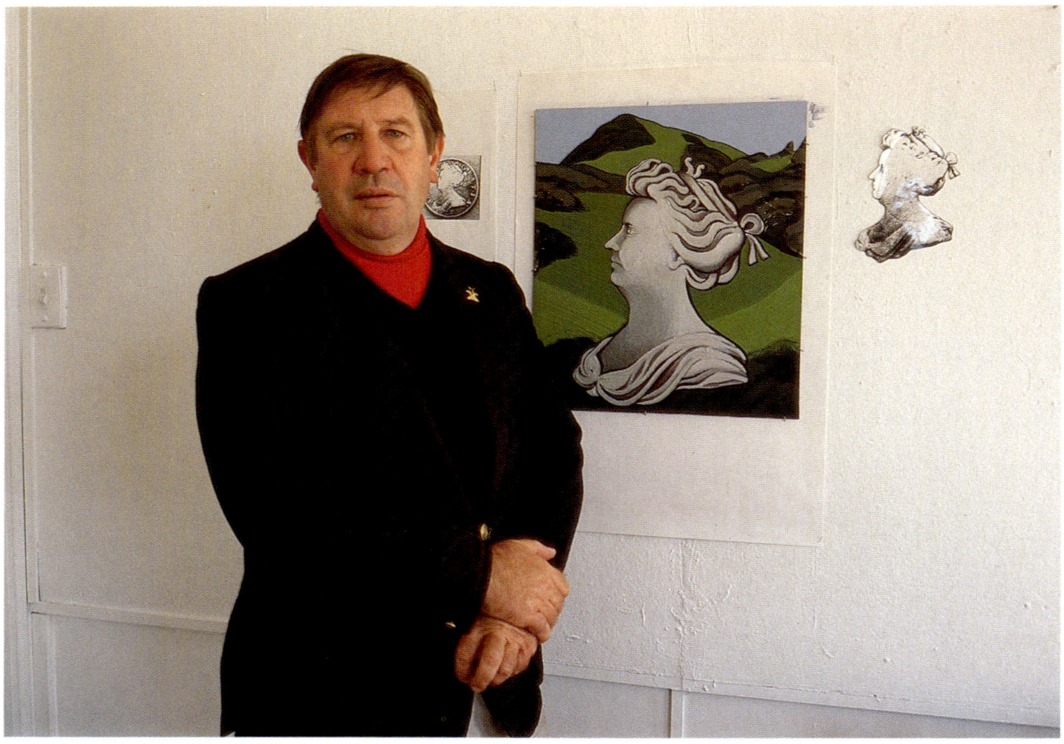

Artist Don Binney GIL HANLY

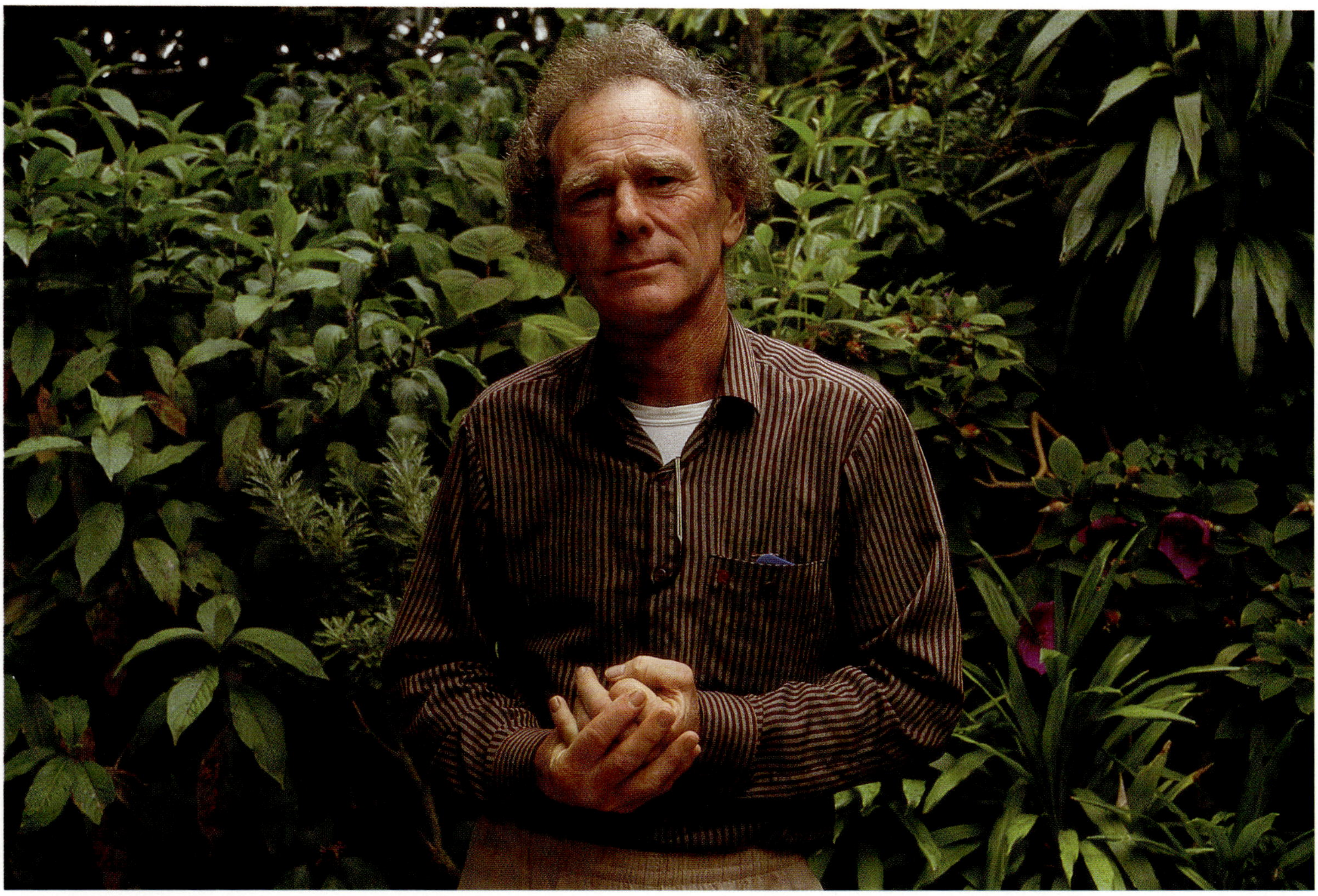

Painter Pat Hanly — GIL HANLY

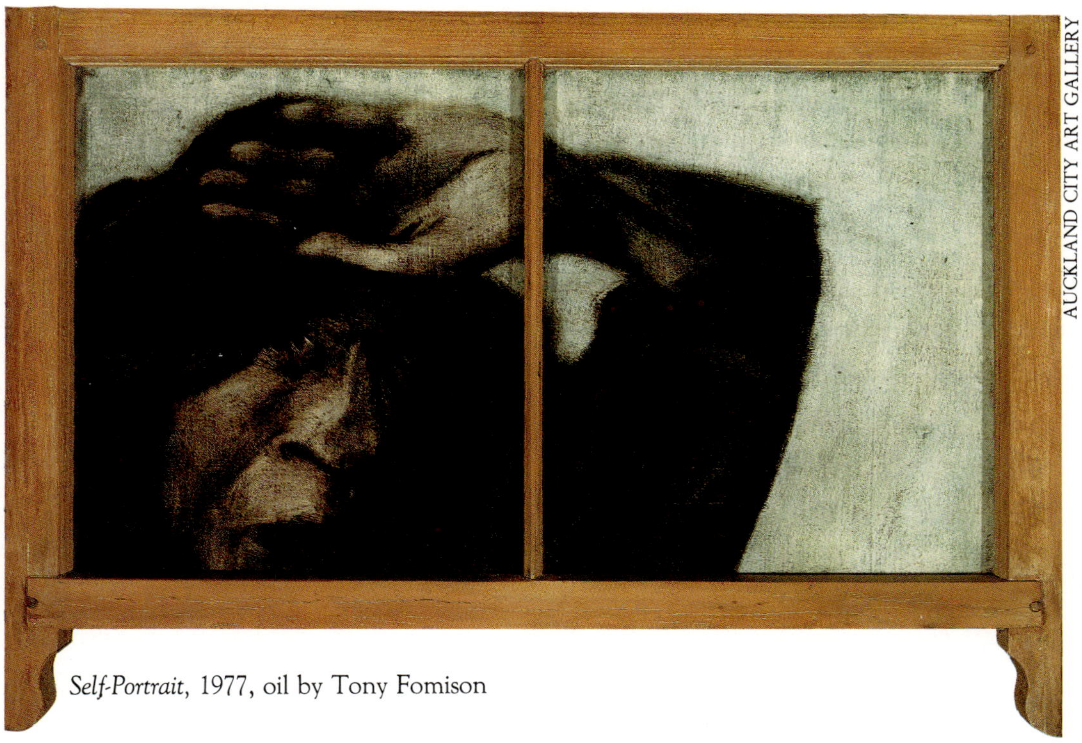

AUCKLAND CITY ART GALLERY

Self-Portrait, 1977, oil by Tony Fomison

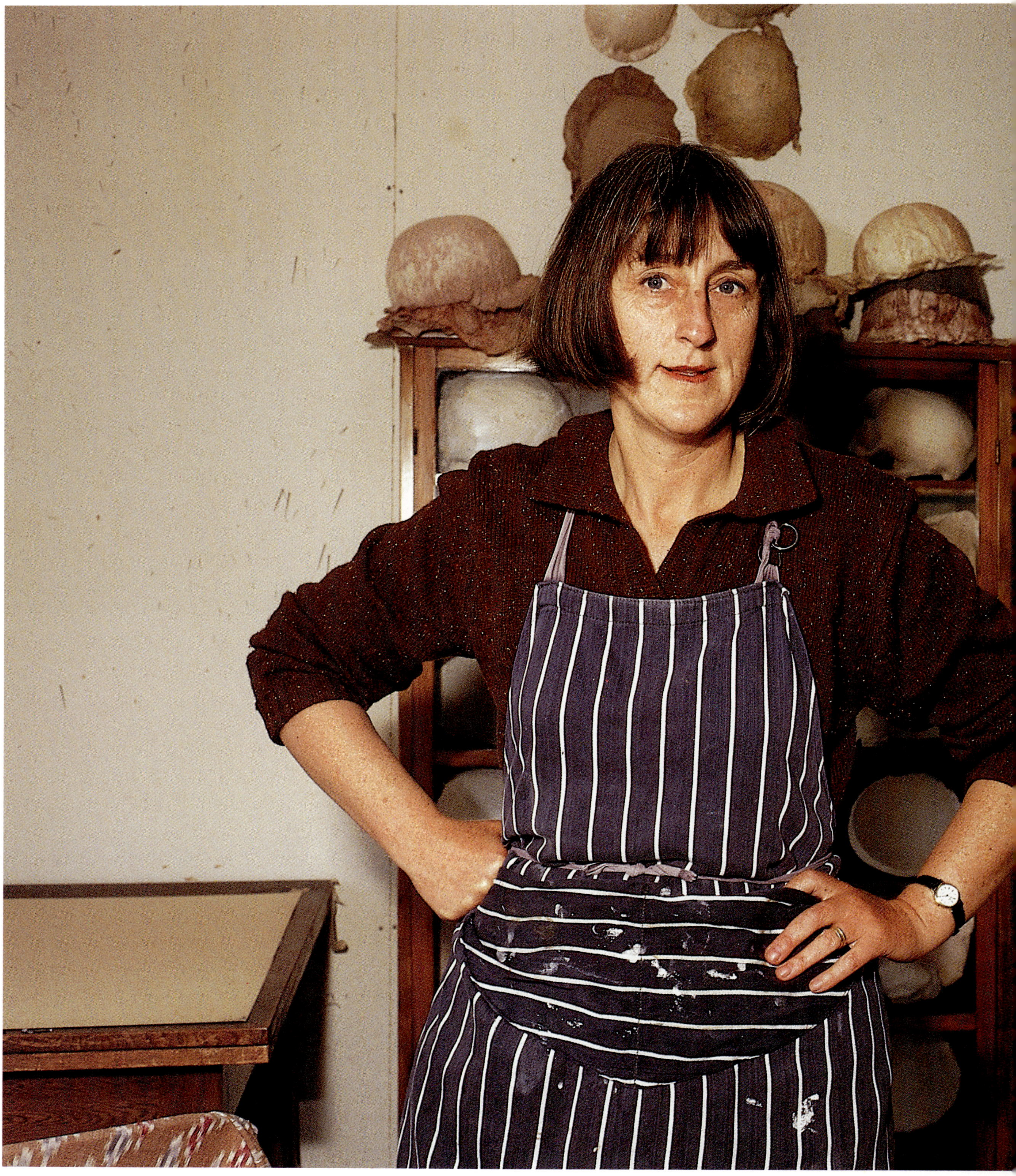

Sculptor Christine Hellyar GIL HANLY

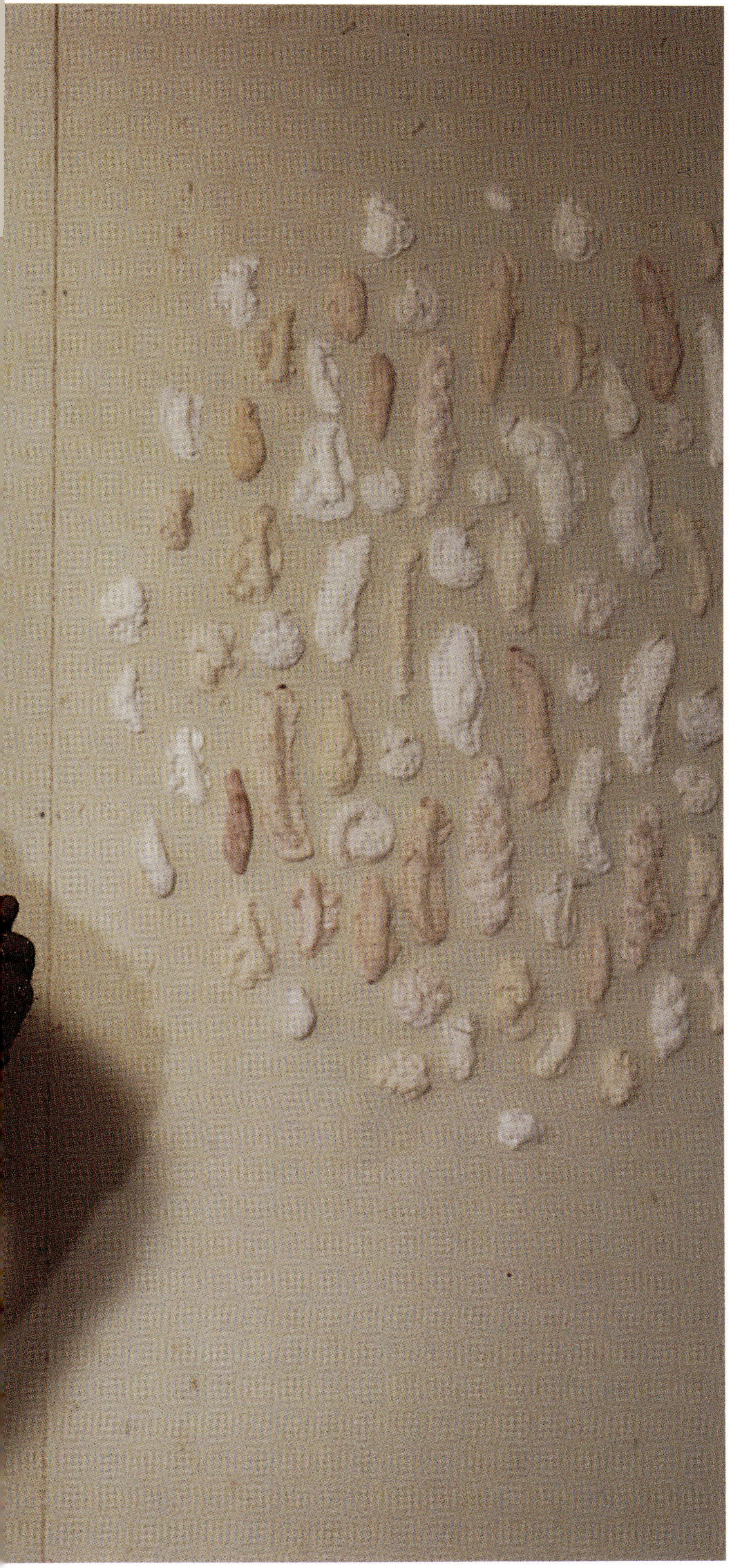

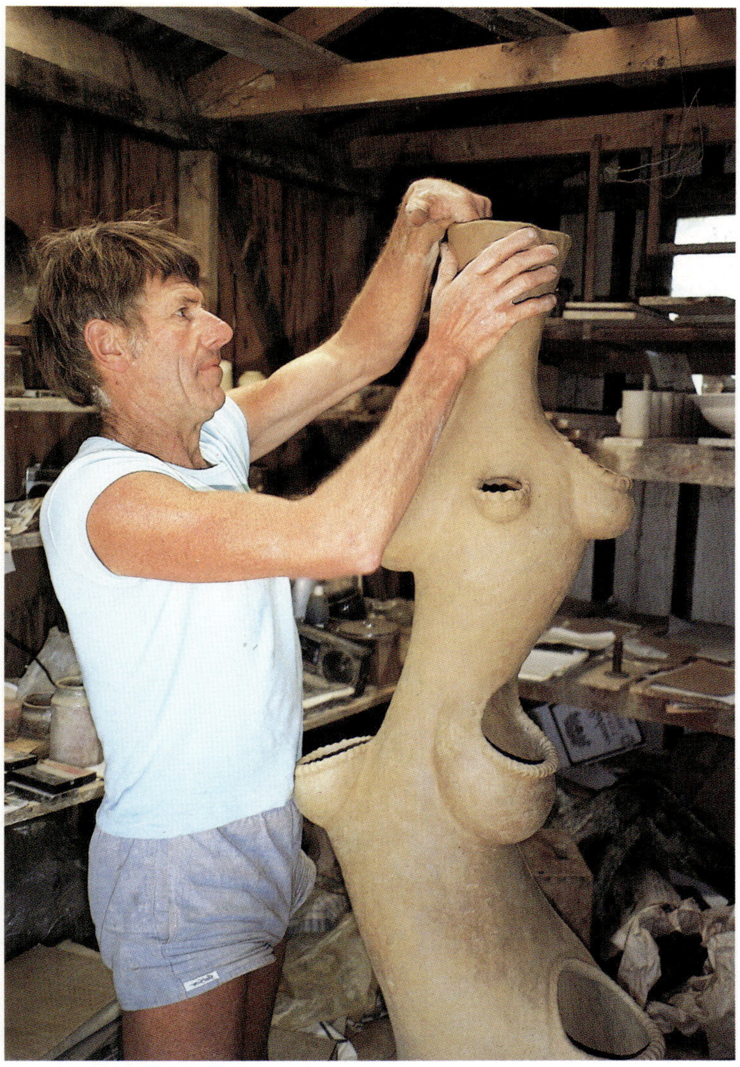

Potter Barry Brickell GIL HANLY

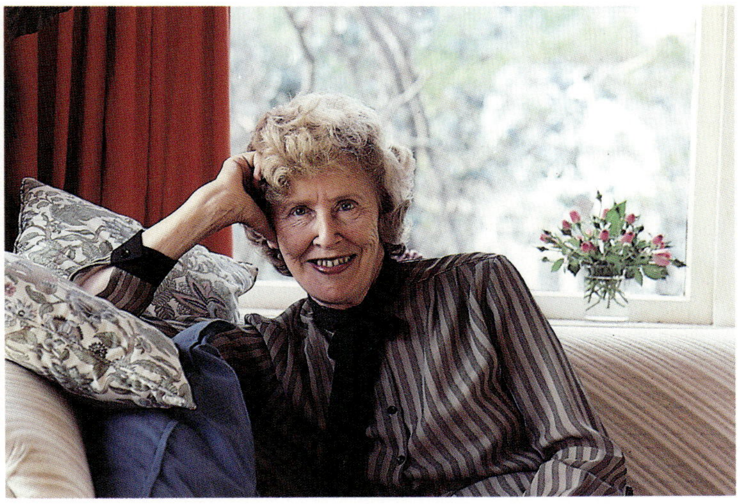

Writer Lauris Edmond TIM STEELE

THE STORY OF BUSINESS

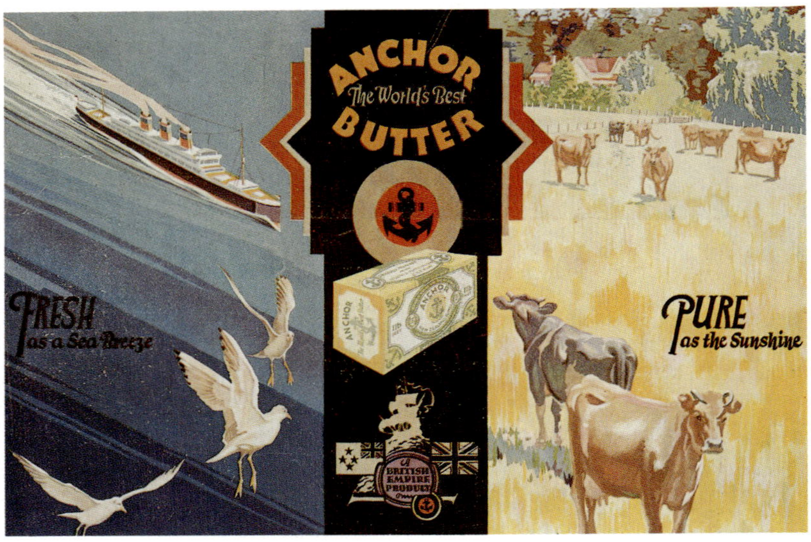

Terry Hall

PEOPLE CAME HERE for commercial reasons. The Maori because of the land and sea resources; the Europeans for valuable commodities like sealskins and whale oil. Others like the missionaries soon began acquiring land, sending the produce of their farms initially to Australia and later to Europe. The Maori were quick to seize and develop such trading opportunities with the new arrivals and the colonialists across the Tasman.

It remains fashionable to overlook the importance of business in the developing nation. The focus is usually on issues such as land wars, racial confrontation, and the social and political. This has caused many to overlook a key component in the make-up of New Zealanders. We are a vital people, and most of us are determined to improve our standard of living. New Zealand is a nation of large and small businesses. Many of our leaders have been risk takers and great traders. This has taken a country, not notably overburdened with natural resources, to a position where per head of population it is one of the greatest trading nations in the world.

New Zealand's business history didn't start 150 years ago. It was alive in pre-European times with Maori trading greenstone and other goods. They knew instinctively the art of barter. With the arrival of whalers and European explorers in the 1790s, a number of major chiefs grasped the trading opportunities this offered.

By 1827 the Maori dominated New Zealand trade and were frequent visitors to New South Wales. Some established agencies in Sydney to handle the export of timber and flax, organising the labour supply to cut and shape spars for sailing ships.

There were problems, and trade fluctuated violently. It was found the flax could not be easily used for rope, but it was widely used in New South Wales for stuffing upholstery. Early timber also got a bad name. The Maori initially sold the easily cut kahikatea, but it was too vulnerable to Australian borer and white ant. Hokianga kauri proved much more durable, and some of the earliest Australian homes boasted kauri flooring. Australian vineyards too favoured large casks of New Zealand kauri, which in Victorian times was considered far superior to French oak as it gave no 'taint' to the wine.

It was a profitable trade for both sides. A few Maori became expert sawmen, cutting planks in saw pits. The Maori insisted on handling and stowing loads on the ships, and if a captain refused to let them load, they charged higher demurrage rates. They also imposed anchorage fees. One chief, Makoare Taonui to Te Popoto, not only ran a complex sawmilling operation, but a retail store specialising in European goods. Trade covered a wide range of items, not simply, as in popular folklore, muskets and gunpowder. Heavy blankets were brought from England for the Maori tribes, while paramatta cloth, made by Sydney convicts from wool and cotton, was very popular. In 1836 there was one novel consignment of English dogs' hides, to be turned into chiefs' cloaks. The Maori entrepreneurs became famous, and shrewd negotiators "to the point of extortion".

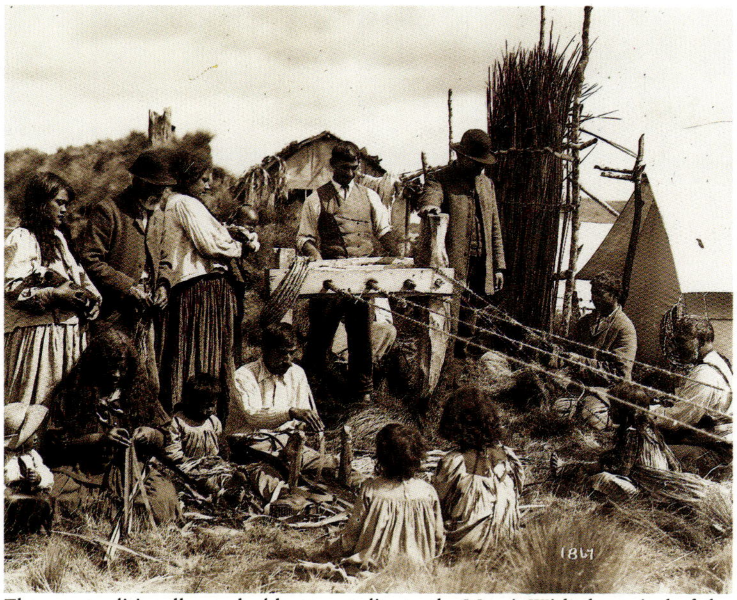

Flax was traditionally a valuable commodity to the Maori. With the arrival of the Pakeha, it was exploited commercially by both races. By the 1830s the Maori had organised the export of dressed flax to the rope makers of Britain.
NORTHWOOD COLLECTION

ALEXANDER TURNBULL LIBRARY

Whaling and sealing developed in the same period. By the 1830s there were around twenty-five shore whaling stations, many in the South Island. The Bay of Islands was the heart of this trade, with 150 ships calling a year. The local Maori and settlers grew prosperous victualling ships, growing maize and potatoes. The value of New Zealand exports to Australia reached £83,000 in 1839 and consisted of flax, black whale oil, whalebone, sealskins, dried fish, salted pork, maize, vegetables, and kauri. Much of this early kauri was shipped on to England. The value of cargoes of American ships that called at the Bay in the same year was estimated at $1,636,335, but this would have been mostly whalers from New England, Salem or Nantucket.

The adaptability of the Maori and the early Europeans laid the groundwork for what was to follow.

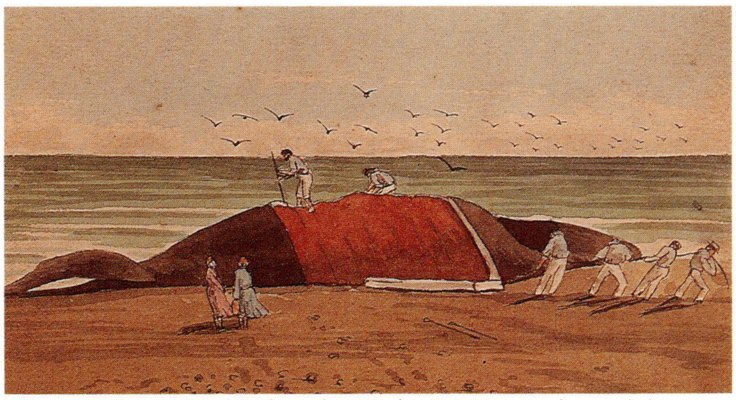

This watercolour, painted in the early 1860s by A. J. Cooper, shows whalers cutting the blubber off a whale on Mohaka Beach.

ALEXANDER TURNBULL LIBRARY

THE TURNING POINT was 1840. Politics and business are constant bedfellows. Pressured by land hungry settlers from New South Wales who arrived in almost every boat in the later 1830s, the political intrigues of Edward Gibbon Wakefield and evangelical British politicians keen to control the purchase of Maori land by Europeans, Britain acted. The first official colonists arrived in the *Tory* at Port Nicholson and the Treaty of Waitangi was signed. Land developers became increasingly active.

The words boom and bust best describe New Zealand's economic history. There have been periods of parsimony by elected leaders, business downturns, followed by self-induced booms, over-borrowing, and hasty setbacks. Throughout these some entrepreneurs flourished. In the first fifty years many of today's powerful dynasties were formed both in agriculture and industry.

There are still companies bearing names from that period: although their number is dwindling due to the process of takeover and decay. One of the earliest is L. D. Nathan and Co., although its portly founder would never recognise the mighty organisation today, following its 1988 merger with a contemporary brewing group founded by the Myers family.

Nathan was typical of the many people who were prepared to travel to the end of the world with the aim of becoming rich. He set up a general store at Kororareka in 1840, just before British sovereignty was proclaimed. He shifted to Auckland when the capital was moved there, operating both as an importer and exporter. Over the years the group mirrored the activities of most of its competitors. If there was money to be made, it would be involved. So it was active in the wine and spirit business, cordials, trading jewellery and fancy goods, tobacco, and groceries. Today it is a power in retailing: in 1980 it absorbed one of its greatest competitors, McKenzies Ltd, founded by an expatriate Australian Sir James McKenzie earlier this century.

Most of these pioneering businessmen had no intention of settling here. It was more common for young men to come to the colony with the stated aim of making as much as they could and return to buy a grand estate in the English home counties. Like their pastoral counterparts almost up to the present decade, their sons went to England for an education, preferably at a good public school followed by Oxford or Cambridge.

Some, like the members of the Harris, Sargood or Hallenstein families lived permanently in style on remittances sent from their New Zealand enterprises managed by some other member of the family. Members of the Harris family became prominent in English Liberal politics. Others, like members of the Hallenstein family, became prominent patrons of the arts.

The 1840s and 1850s were a period when the rich, with some shrewdness, could count on becoming richer. These were the times when the well educated and connected could take up a pastoral run, and make a fortune. English author Samuel Butler was one. He borrowed £4,000 from his father, developed and then sold his Erewhon property, and returned home after doubling that. He never needed to work again.

This was the period when the great agricultural service industries were born, and grew.

THE MIGRANTS BETWEEN 1840 and 1860 were more interested in land than their predecessors, most of whom were keen to exploit the riches of the sea. But by 1845 the brutal business of seal slaughter was ended when the ship *The Three Brothers* returned from the west coast with an uneconomic haul of 140 skins – compared with the 60,000 skins secured by just one ship, the *Favourite*, in 1806.

Whaling remained important. Although the early whalers had almost exterminated the white whale, they were to concentrate on sperm and humpback whales till 1964 when Trevor Norton harpooned the last to be killed by a New Zealand ship in local waters.

This was an important industry. In the early days it made fortunes. Before he was thirty, Otago's Johnny Jones controlled seven whaling stations employing 280 men from his base at Waikouaiti. Jones was a tough Sydney-sider, believed to be the son of a convict. On the spot when the Scottish settlers came to found Otago, he was able to supply them with a full range of provisions and imports brought from Sydney in his own ships.

Tall, hard-nosed and considered rough, he showed considerable financial acumen, and even started circulating his own currency in Dunedin in 1854 to stimulate trade.

His contribution to New Zealand shipping is enormous. He invested in steam vessels from the 1860s and formed the Harbour Steam Navigation Co. that was developed by James Mills into the Union Steam Ship Co.

THE INCREASING WAVE of migrants to form most of the cities and towns we know today brought other entrepreneurs. The land had to be cleared, and much unnecessary devastation occurred in huge burnoffs, especially in inland areas of the North Island where it would have been considered too costly to remove giant stands of totara and rimu before the advent of rail and reasonable roads. Most farmers for many decades regarded native trees as an expensive obstruction between them and the land.

Early foresters concentrated on the easily accessible fine stands of kauri in the Coromandel with the first water-powered mill built at Mercury Bay in 1838.

There was a shameful waste of native timber. Early mills discarded all but the heart timbers. Huge beams of fine timber were ripped down to provide arched window-frames, intricate bowed verandahs, winding staircase handrails, where up to ninety per cent of the beam would be shaved away, or the ornately carved trusses, modillions and window angle brackets that were considered so vital to decorate every Victorian home.

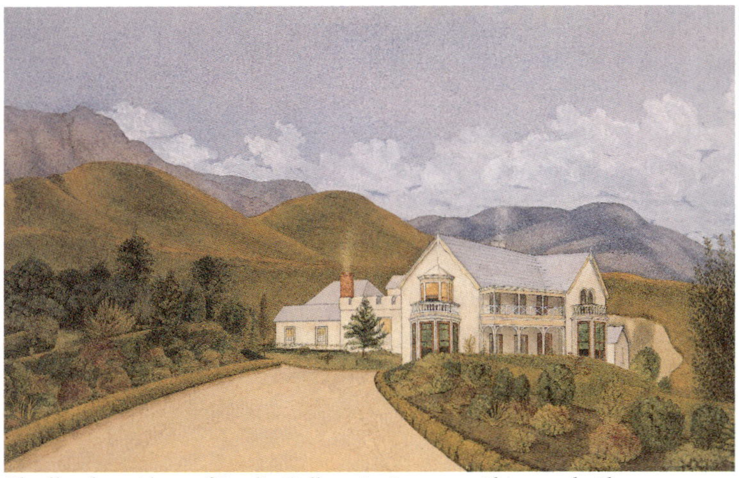

HOCKEN LIBRARY

Thurlby, the residence of Bendix Hallenstein, Speargrass Flat near the Shotover, ca 1885-1890, watercolour by Rose Cherry Morris. German-born Hallenstein set up the first flour mill in Queenstown, was a successful farmer, a Member of Parliament and German Consul, but he is best known for the New Zealand Clothing Factory, founded in Dunedin jointly with his brothers living in London.

Up to the late 1850s all this work had been done by hand. But by the 1860s builders were supplied with catalogues of fancy mouldings and architraves and the like, mass-produced on steam powered machines.

With the country's European population trebling in the 1850s, again in the 1860s, and doubling in the 1870s, these machines helped the timber industry meet an exploding demand for houses. Carpenters began building houses that were almost kitset in construction, buying not only frames and boards from sawmills, but factory produced doors, window sashes and decorative pieces.

The sawmilling industry was huge by today's standards. By 1880 there were four giant companies in the Auckland province who between them owned most of the standing kauri. When these got into difficulty they were absorbed by the giant Kauri Timber Company, largely owned by an Australian syndicate.

The demand can be gauged by one Dunedin factory alone. By 1883 Guthrie and Larnach's Dunedin Iron and Woodware Co. employed 700 men and brought two million feet of kauri from Auckland's west coast forests for their "manufactory of woodware replete with the most improved American machinery".

The ravages of the forests continued unabated. In the 1890s alone, an estimated 36,250 sq km of forests in the North Island were simply burned off. By the 1920s the authorities were forced to act to conserve dwindling native forest resources for domestic use.

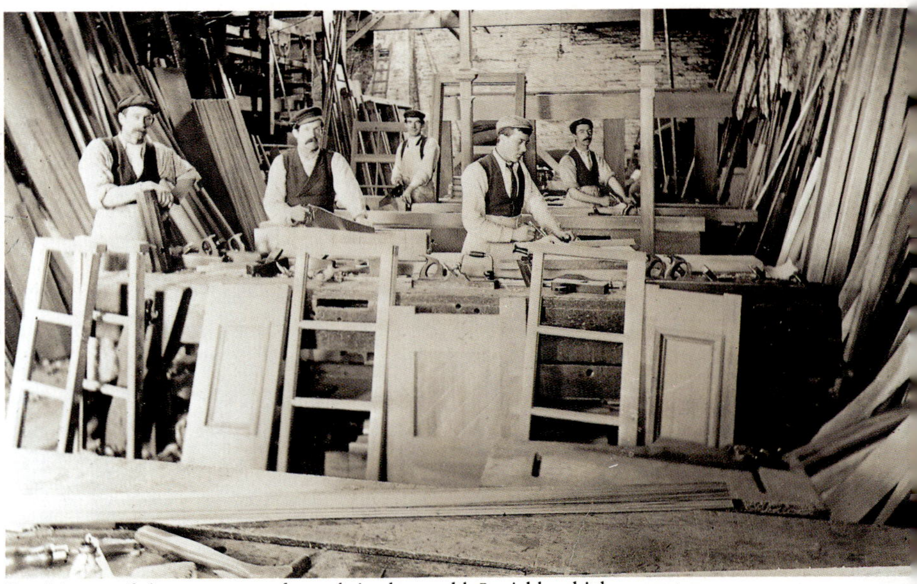

OTAGO EARLY SETTLERS MUSEUM

Kauri is one of the strongest softwoods in the world. It yields a high percentage of heartwood and defect-free timber ideal for joinery, such as the doors being made in this Otago factory. It splits easily, yet nails without splitting. A census of Auckland houses in 1861 showed that 5,236 of 6,063 recorded were made of kauri.

IN 1862 A MAJOR new resource was added to those of the sea and the land.

Early explorers had expected to find rich natural resources. But the very early years were disappointing. Frederick Tuckett made the first coal discovery at Kaitangata in 1844 and Thomas Brunner discovered the field named after him on the West Coast in 1848.

In May 1861 the Australian Gabriel Read made a discovery that was to drastically alter the fledgling country's economic prospects. His find of gold at Gabriel's Gully turned the tide of immigration from Auckland to the south. The Otago finds, later followed by others in Thames and the West Coast, helped set the South Island on its industrial feet.

Blacksmiths, brought to New Zealand to do simple agricultural tasks and shoe horses, suddenly saw the demand for their services extend to making often highly complex gold-mining equipment.

A number of foundry names are still with us today. Alexander and Thomas Burt began in Dunedin in 1862 as plumbers and gas fitters. From this small start sprang the Otago Lead Copper Brass and Engineering Works which had large shipbuilding contracts at Port Chalmers, made railway castings and hydraulic dredging equipment.

There was plenty of competition. The Otago Foundry produced gold dredges, as did the Vulcan Foundry, and the firm of R. & T. Haworth was the first maker of corrugated iron and spouting in the country in 1864.

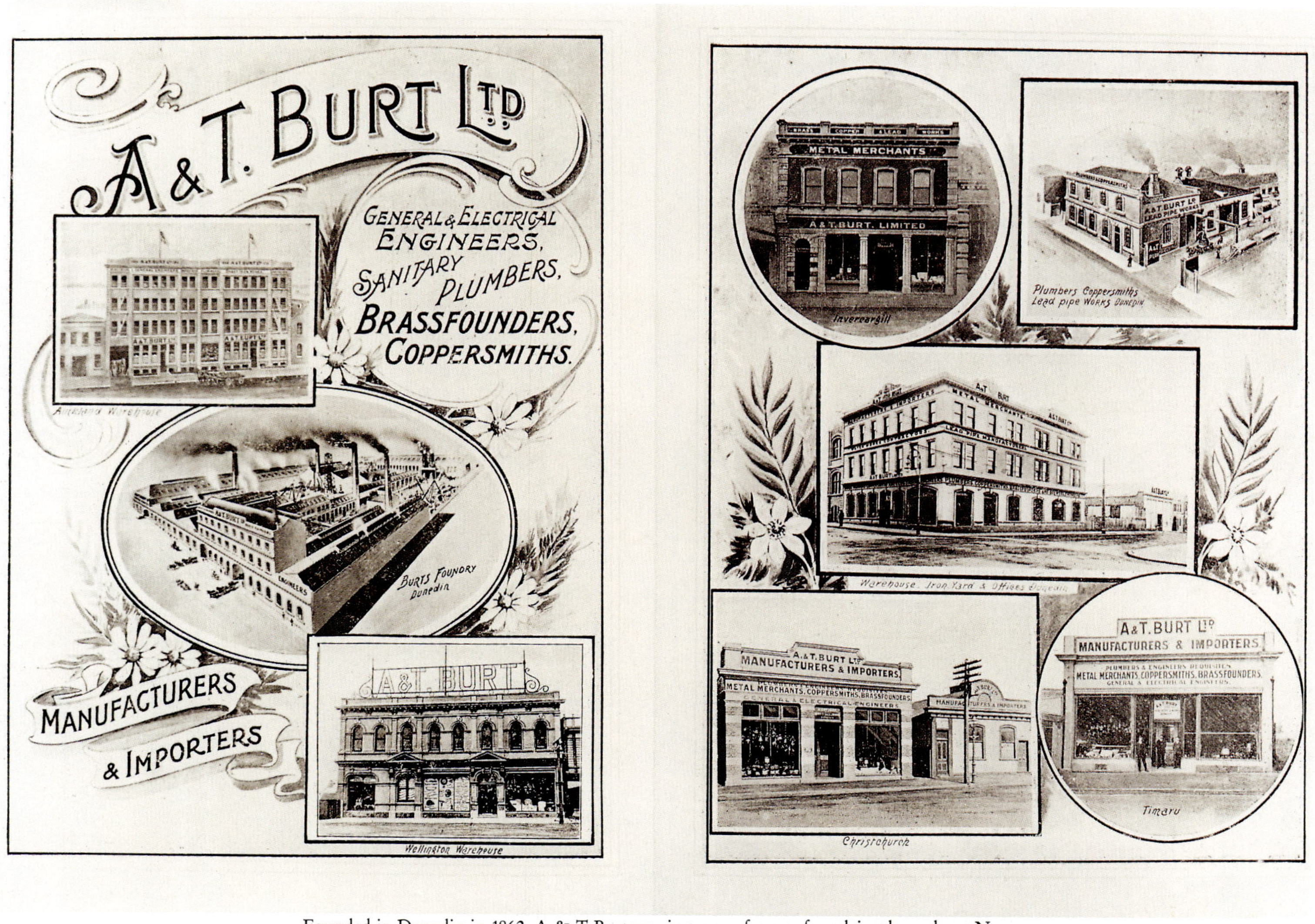

OTAGO EARLY SETTLERS MUSEUM

Founded in Dunedin in 1862, A & T Burt was just one of many foundries throughout New Zealand. In Dunedin, Henry Ely Shacklock designed and made Orion ranges. In Wellington, E. W. Mills built railway locomotives; in Auckland A & G Price invented a successful flax-milling machine.

The development of the gold-mining industry had profound ramifications. It brought a tide of immigration, including the Chinese who at one time numbered about one-seventh of Otago's population. Most went home – many in makeshift coffins. But others kept their New Zealand connections. The Sew Hoy family, who operate a significant textile business in Dunedin, kept their lifeline with China open till 1949 and the Communist takeover. The present generation is the first in nearly 130 years to regard New Zealand as their true home.

Gold sped up the process of industrialisation and saw a development of the cities. Most of the industries we regard as traditional New Zealand enterprises began then.

WHILE WOOL HAD BEEN exported in a raw state since 1835, the first was not carded till September 1871 at the Mosgiel Woollen Mill, which had previously been a dairy factory. Till then, virtually all woollen cloth had to be imported. There was a strong local demand for a particularly strong woven fabric to stand up to the heavy demands of farming, mineral prospecting and outdoor work. Men wanted woollen underwear, shirts and trousers.

The Mosgiel company had the head start, but soon there were competitors in almost every sizeable town – Bruce south of Dunedin at Milton, two other big plants at Kaikorai in Dunedin, also set up in 1871, Timaru 1885, Kaiapoi 1879, Ashburton 1885; the list is almost endless.

Most of these were to fall, some through bad management, others in times of depression, others through takeover. By 1985 the toll of rationalisation had produced just two big companies, Mosgiel and Alliance, the latter shaped from the old Oamaru mill. Alliance was to prove triumphant, with the shock failure of Mosgiel in 1980.

The ups and downs of the woollen textile industry were mirrored everywhere in the economy. As a country dependent on international trade we have always been particularly vulnerable to events overseas. Early setbacks, showing how vulnerable the economy was to such influences, were the end of the 1850s Australian gold rush followed by a fall in wool prices, and in 1860 when British confidence was affected by the onset of the North Island land wars.

The 1860s were times of great expansion thanks to the gold rushes. In 1870 Colonial Treasurer Julius Vogel proved a pre-Keynsian with the first deliberate attempt to borrow huge sums overseas for works in the public interest.

This was the period of great railway building and assisted immigration, all aided by high wool prices. Till the 1980s the most easily read barometer of the nation's health was not which political party was in power, but the price of wool. While other export earners such as mining, meat and forestry have waxed and waned, there is no doubting that New Zealand's wealth, for much of the first 150 years, was based on sheep.

In the last decade, despite the international advance of synthetics, wool prices have generally been good, touching record prices at times. But dwindling stock numbers in the last five years, despite some good returns, indicate that for the moment at least the importance of King Wool has declined as this heavily indebted country seeks new directions for its export earnings.

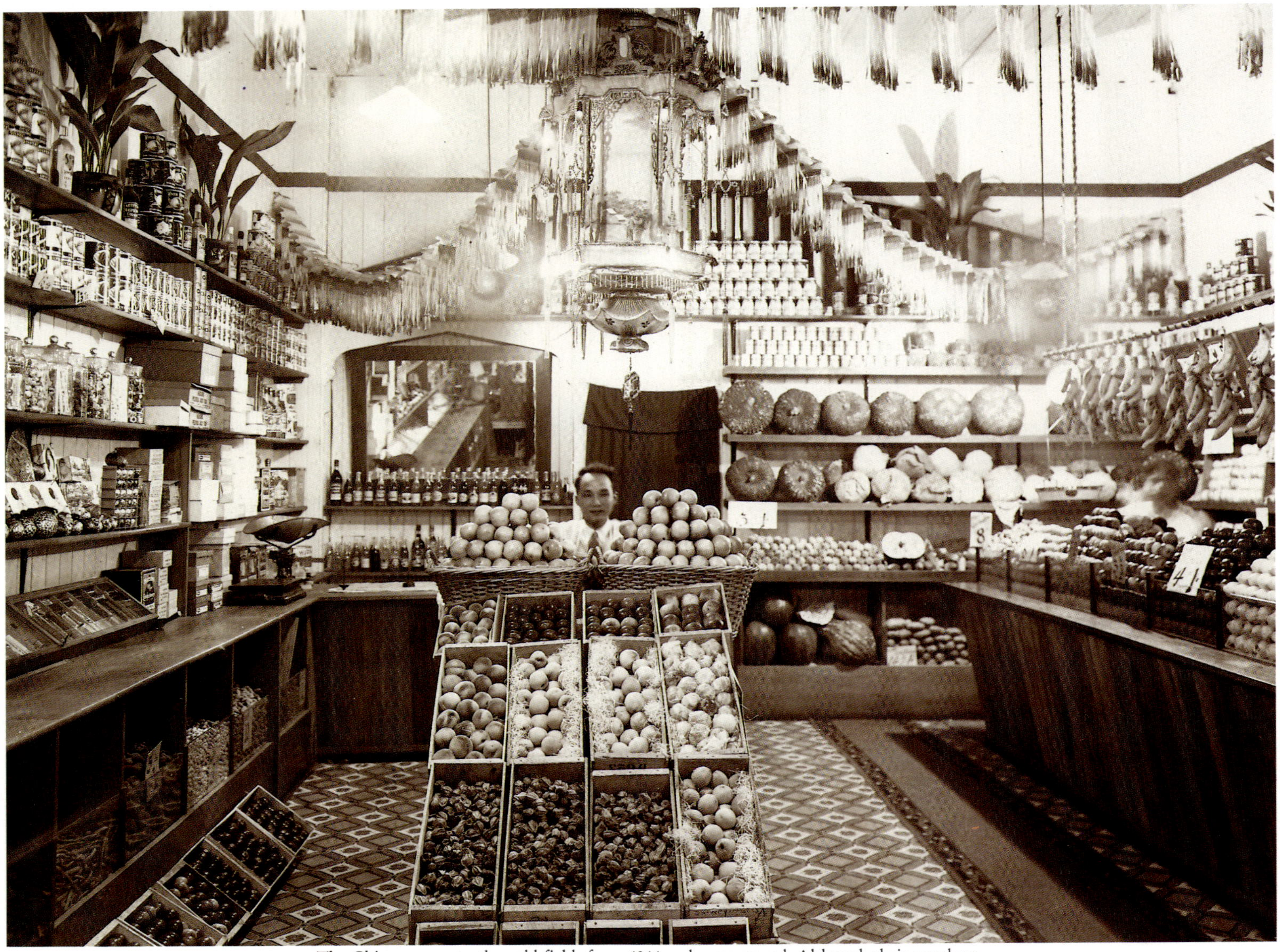

ALEXANDER TURNBULL LIBRARY

The Chinese came to the gold fields from 1866 and some stayed. Although their numbers were always few – they suffered extreme prejudice and even Acts of Parliament aimed at limiting immigration. In 1912 the residents of Sydenham in Christchurch organised a boycott of Chinese fruiterers.

THERE IS A COMMON THREAD linking all New Zealanders since the arrival of the earliest settlers; an uneasy relationship with the bank managers. They have been crucial in the country's development. Historically we have shown our confidence in this country by borrowing, often at usurious rates of interest.

Vogel is remembered for his high level of borrowing in the 1870s – he took total debt from £8 million in 1870 to £20 million by 1880. This built 1100 miles of railways, 4000 miles of telegraph lines and many public buildings, and helped finance substantial migration; the population doubled in the decade.

Vogel, however, was not the only one indulging in a frenzy of borrowing. As we saw in the 1987 sharemarket crash, the banks are also able to be carried along in a burst of expansionist lending buoyed by general optimism.

Keith Sinclair's *History of New Zealand* notes that in the 1870s some of the banks, notably the "local" Bank of New Zealand and the Colonial Bank became "quite reckless" and permitted a "frenzy of public borrowing". Between 1872 and 1879 non-government bank loans rose from £3.5 to £13.8 million. In the Long Depression, the Bank of New Zealand was only saved by an Act of Parliament and the Colonial Bank went bankrupt in 1896.

New Zealanders' love affairs with banks have seen no shortage of entrepreneurs wanting to start their own. In 1840 the first, the New Zealand Banking Co., opened at Russell. It was to fold in 1845, after it moved to Auckland.

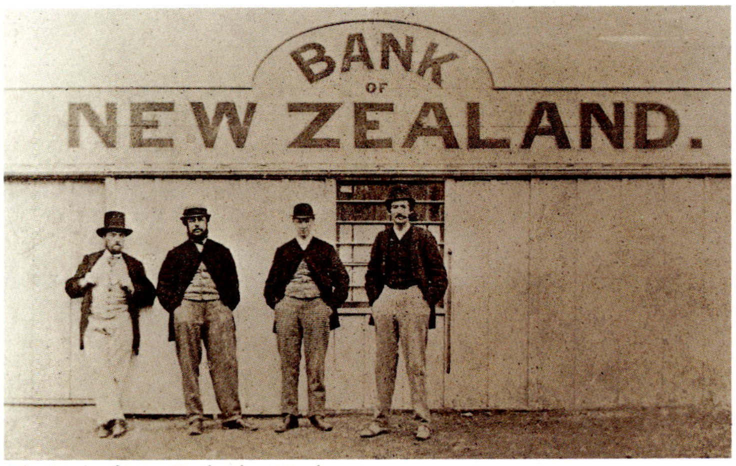

OTAGO EARLY SETTLERS MUSEUM

The Bank of New Zealand at Naseby.

In 1846 the Wellington Savings Bank was formed: it was the first of its type, and like most of its early rivals was absorbed by the Post Office Savings Bank in 1871, which for many years dominated banking for small borrowers and lenders.

New Zealand banking organisations seldom ventured overseas apart from seeing the need to keep shop windows in London.

This did not mean we were an inward-looking people in other areas. In 1859 the New Zealand Insurance Company was founded in Wellington, and quickly expanded to Australia, North America and Asia. Other insurance companies were equally aggressive abroad. Today NZI Corporation is represented in countries around the world.

With the first banks came the first newspapers. These were often strongly political, and most major towns can boast a bewildering range of titles in their history.

The men who owned the successful fledgling papers went on to become pillars of the establishment and families of wealth and prominence in their communities. The Blundell family, owners of Wellington's *Evening Post*, provided a governor-general; the Riddifords, who helped found the *Dominion* in 1907, were prominent in both farming and politics; the Hortons, who remain one of the few pioneering newspaper-owning families still in business, concentrated on the *New Zealand Herald* and from their involvement since 1876 saw it develop into a major public company.

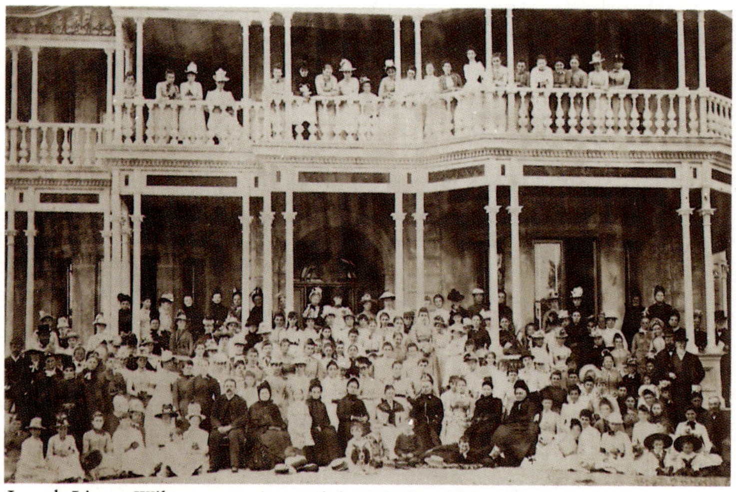
AUCKLAND YWCA

Joseph Liston Wilson, proprietor of the *NZ Herald*, lived in an Italianate mansion in Remuera in the midst of fourteen acres planted with rare trees.

AROUND THE EARLY newspaper offices and banks came all the paraphernalia of the urban dweller: bakers, butchers and general stores. Small stores, if successful, quickly grew into major department stores, and their owners became rich and prosperous. Over the years many of these stores merged; absorbing other once famous names.

The DIC, which had a troubled history in the 1980s had such a history. Founded in Dunedin in 1884, the DIC now incorporates such names as George Court and Sons of Auckland, Beaths of Christchurch, W. H. Boyes of Invercargill, and Adairs of Gisborne. The DIC itself was taken over by another venerable Dunedin firm, Arthur Barnett, in 1988.

Many of these stores were associated with yet another realm of business, the importers, who usually operated from substantial multi-storeyed blocks, just off the main street, and whose owners raced fine horses and lived in splendid style in huge homes.

Today these names are just a memory, the Sargoods, the Ewens, Ross and Glendinning. Their demise marked the switch from a country that imported almost everything till the advent of the first Labour Government, to one where many goods were manufactured.

NEW ZEALAND'S OTHER great industry, based on refrigeration, also dates from the closing stages of the first fifty years. The departure of the sailing ship *Dunedin*, which left Port Chalmers in February 1882, was an event of enormous significance. It sailed at a time of economic crisis, with wool prices plummeting. Sheep carcases were of little value and thousands of animals were being knocked on the head and slung over cliffs.

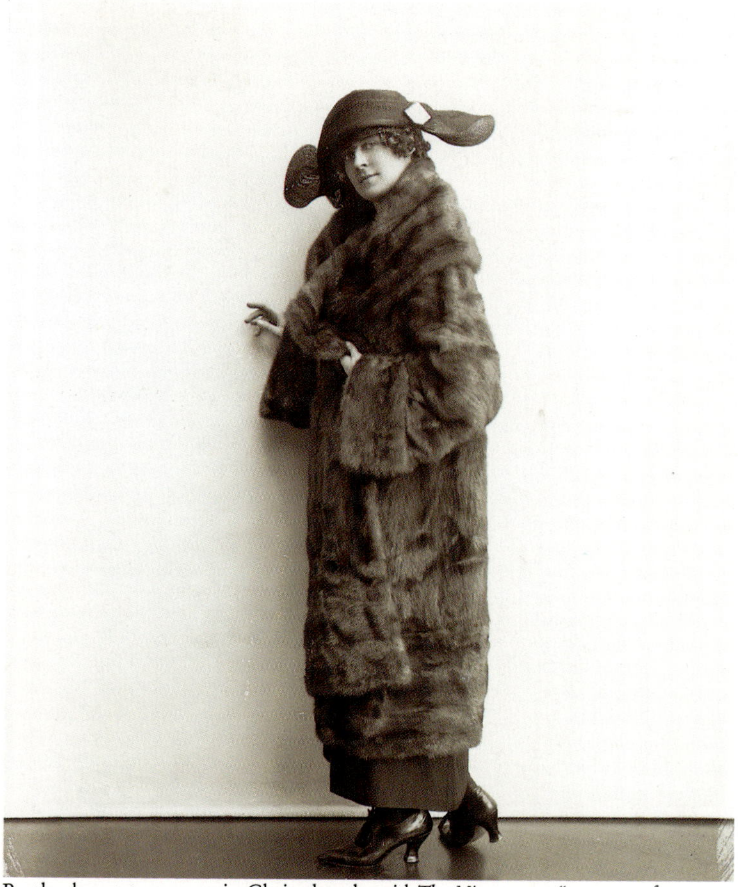
CLIFFORD COLLECTION/CANTERBURY MUSEUM

Beaths department store in Christchurch, said *The Mirror*, was "a magnet for fashionable womankind" and the "Fashion House par excellence of the Dominion". This Beaths model of 1923 wears sable mink with a lining of silk crepe imprime and a fine black crinoline straw.

The first shipments of frozen goods went from Australia to Britain in 1881, and the results were uninspiring. Of the first consignments two-thirds were either rated as "irregular" or "unsatisfactory". Against this background of economic gloom and Australian failures a group of Dunedin men founded the New Zealand Refrigerating Co. Ltd in January 1881 at Burnside, a works that is still in production.

But in the intensely competitive world that was Otago at that time they were beaten. The dynamic manager of the New Zealand and Australian Land Company, William Soltau Davidson, decided it was unwise to risk money on land and buildings for such a risky venture.

He chartered the sailing ship, *Dunedin*, and installed in it machinery to both freeze and transport the meat. He further spread his risk by including dairy products, an assortment of hare, pheasant, turkey and chicken, 4311 mutton carcases, twenty-two carcases of pork and 2226 sheep tongues. Of the consignment only one mutton carcase was condemned on arrival; the remainder sold at Smithfield at one shilling and fivepence per pound, good money in those days.

From this inauspicious start the country's great trade in sheepmeats and dairy products began. There were problems for both industries, lack of capital, shipping difficulties, anxiety too in ensuring the goods arrived in the best condition, and in the frozen meat industry in particular, frequent bitter industrial actions.

THE SECOND FIFTY YEARS began with a recession which had gradually lifted by 1895. It was a period that saw good times and steady if unspectacular progress, and ended with the slow recovery from the Great Depression of the 1930s.

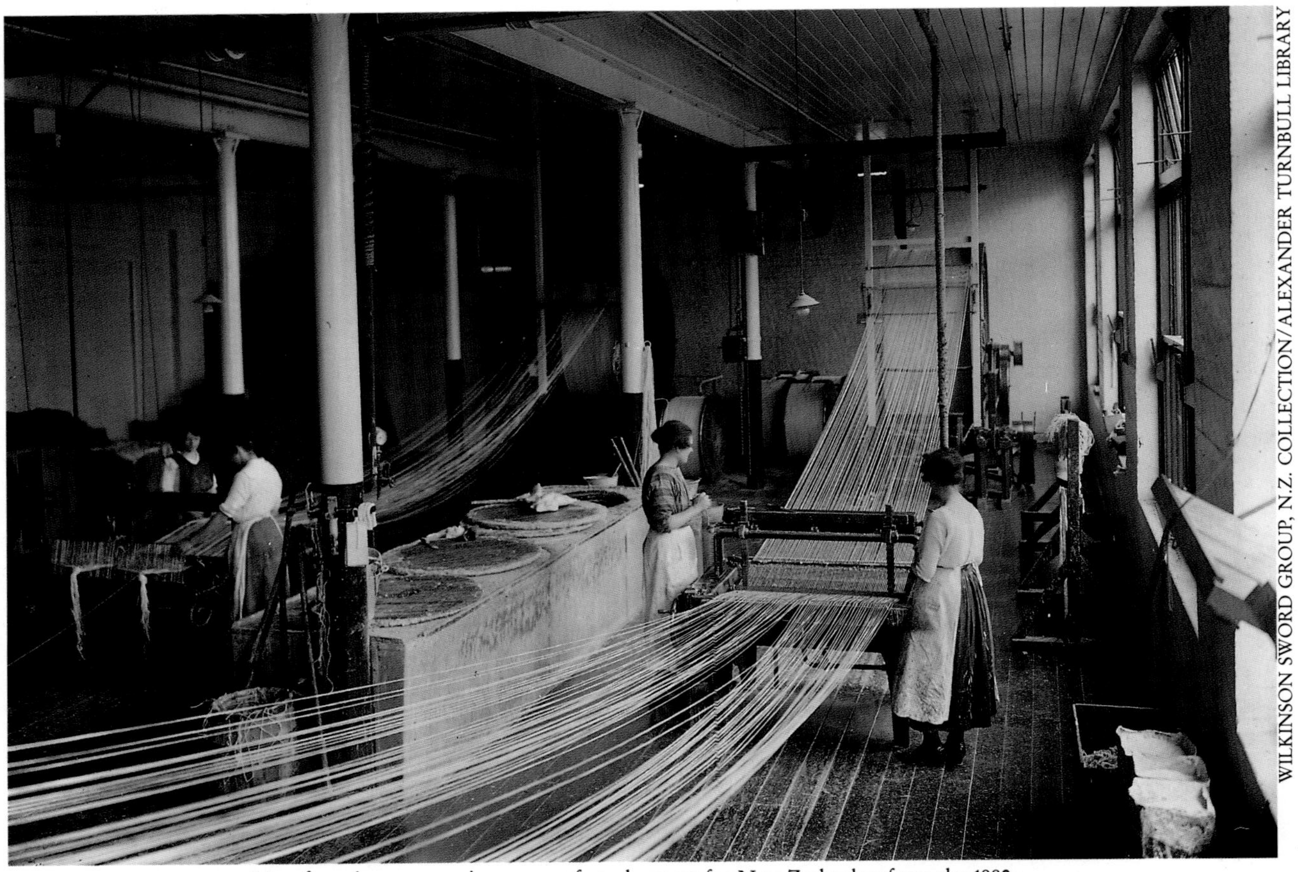

WILKINSON SWORD GROUP, N.Z. COLLECTION/ALEXANDER TURNBULL LIBRARY

Manufacturing was a major source of employment for New Zealanders from the 1880s. Constant agitation by unions led to improvements in working conditions, but the factory of 1920 was still a bleak place as shown by this photograph of women making wax tapers for matches at the Bryant & May factory in Wellington.

There was a savage loss of life in the European trenches in the First World War. Many fine young men of undoubted talent and enterprise were lost to the still-young nation.

Women were not afraid to step into the breach. The survival of the Auckland meat company R. and W. Hellaby from 1900 was solely due to the young widow Amy Maria Hellaby who for twenty years strenuously resisted all attempts to take over the company following the sudden death of both founders.

Returning soldiers put into practice ideas they had picked up serving overseas. The successful partnership of Cory-Wright and Salmon stemmed from a partnership of two army engineers and prospered supplying British-made transformers for New Zealand's rapidly developing hydro-electricity industry.

These were not idle years. Tests on *Pinus radiata* proved it could be the basis of a viable forestry industry, including the making of pulp and paper. In the 1920s Landon Smith and Douglas Wylie founded Perpetual Forests, and saw its shares hawked as far as India. This company, later to become NZ Forest Products, planted 100 million trees in the central North Island plateau.

In Hastings Sir James Wattie started a huge business canning Hawke's Bay fruit and vegetables in the kitchen of his home. In brewing, Sir Henry Kelliher, a former Otago boy, saw the opportunities of the still smallish city of Auckland and laid the foundations for a brewing empire, Dominion Breweries. In transport Sir Harry Wrigley's Mount Cook Group, and his rival Sir Jack Newman's tourist and transport group grew from modest beginnings.

By 1940 after 100 years of struggle New Zealanders felt they had come of age as a nation. The landscape was drastically changed. Cities and towns had a permanent look.

In an age dominated by the railways, major centres had huge corrugated structures, workshops where hundreds of men were engaged in every type of heavy engineering work. Locally designed steam engines, of huge size, were built and developed for the small-scale tracks. In centres like Port Chalmers large ships were built: oil-burning tugs of surprisingly large tonnages, dredges, and complex work carried out to maintain the Union Steam Ship Co.'s and Northern's huge fleet of coastal freighters and passenger liners.

ARMIES OF PEOPLE IN TOWNS worked in the textile industry, in the freezing works, or for the stock and station agents servicing a large rural community.

In each town there were people to know, such as the wealthy families involved in the local breweries. Even after New Zealand Breweries was formed and absorbed most regional companies, the local identity of its products was maintained: Speights in Dunedin, Wards in Christchurch, Red Band in Wellington. Others considered worthy of respect were the importers, wholesalers, retailers, bankers, freezing-works owners (most were still locally owned) and shopkeepers who at that time were treated with great deference: the Caugheys in Auckland, the Smiths in Wellington, the Barnetts in Dunedin.

The outbreak of the Second World War meant that for the second time in a generation, fine young men were killed overseas, many of them well educated, who would have become business leaders and men of enterprise. As in the 1920s and 1930s the loss of this talent was obvious. With no sons to inherit the business, many companies were still led by men in their eighties in the 1940s, 50s and 60s. They bred an atmosphere of great caution in business and there was relatively little innovation, and surprisingly few takeovers in a time of overall prosperity.

It was a period of business conservatism and growing wealth. People who wanted to rock the boat were not welcome. When Ron Brierley set out to shock the establishment in the early 1960s forming Brierley Investments with the declared aim to act as an asset stripper of moribund companies, he was ostracised and ridiculed as a dangerous radical. When he launched a bid for one of the most established of companies, Hallensteins, the great clobbering machine descended on the upstart. The stock exchange did all it could to handicap his company, and he was forced to fight a lengthy battle to see it listed.

BRIERLEY WAS THE HARBINGER of change. But it would have happened anyway. New younger men were fighting their way to the top.

Jim Fletcher, who like his father would eventually be called Sir James, took great risks but showed foresight in launching the Tasman Pulp and Paper Co. and continued to build in a personally low key way on the enterprise he inherited.

There were two outstanding men in the pastoral area; Sir Ron Trotter, who took Wright Stephenson to national dominance and then to international importance through the merger with Fletchers, was one. The other was Sir Rod Weir, who after proving in the early 1960s that he could set up a successful stock and station business on his own, went on to nail together almost all the independents into Dalgety Crown. This grouping was to be largely merged into FCL in 1986 due to the great pressures on the rural sector imposed by the Labour Government.

In the finance sector, Sir Francis Renouf showed brilliance lacking in most of his staid contemporaries. A self-made man from humble origins, he gained an Oxford education by sheer determination and faced up to the New Zealand broking establishment to forge Daysh Renouf and Co., and the merchant bank N.Z.U.C., companies which showed great innovation and brought fresh air to a dull area.

The 1970s and 1980s saw the emergence of people who were keen to take over from the cautious accountants who had run business from the 1920s and 1930s. Some openly admitted they were following the example of Brierley. Companies like Fay, Richwhite, Equiticorp and Chase became internationally known, coinciding with a more aggressive stance from the Bank of New Zealand.

There were brilliant originals, like Bob Jones in property. A self-made millionaire by his twenties, he found retirement boring. He was a key figure in destroying two governments, one Labour, the other a Muldoon-led National, before going on, in his forties, to take his property company to international importance.

The Goodman brothers, Pat and Peter, descendants of an old Nelson baking family, seized every opportunity available in the food business. Self-made men, in a few years of spectacular growth they forged an international alliance of major food groups, including Watties in New Zealand, Fielder Gillespie in Australia, and operations in Europe.

The 1980s were a tempestuous decade. Fortunes were made and lost on property and the sharemarket. A gamble by the government to continue the protectionist era by fostering the growth of New Zealand Steel and an array of "think big" projects, foundered, largely due to the unexpected international glut of oil.

A determined Labour Government from 1984 sought to impose new strategies to restore the country's fortunes. The process saw a drastic removal of protective barriers for manufacturers and taxpayer props for farmers.

The 1987 sharemarket crash had a profound impact on New Zealanders, even those who had little inkling of what equities were about. It provoked a crisis of confidence, and there were echoes of the financial stresses of the 1880s when a string of bankruptcies and receiverships, including Equiticorp, again focussed attention on the lending policies of the Bank of New Zealand.

The end of the decade saw renewed anxieties about the economic outlook. Serious unemployment, due to Government restructuring, became an issue for the first time since the 1930s.

What of the future?

We are entering a new and very challenging age. Economic and political events will see the relationship with Australia develop even more quickly. Although this will not be without risk, it offers prospects that should benefit both nations.

As a country we have managed the switch from a reliance on the British market with skill. Now we sell our goods everywhere. We are well placed to take advantage of the growing power of the Pacific region, led by Japan, with easy access to other increasingly powerful nations like Korea, Indonesia, and the other ASEAN countries, and the vibrant Californian economy.

New Zealand is a lucky country whose relatively small size and remoteness has bred a people who are innovative, far-sighted risk-takers.

We have every reason to face the next fifty years with confidence. □

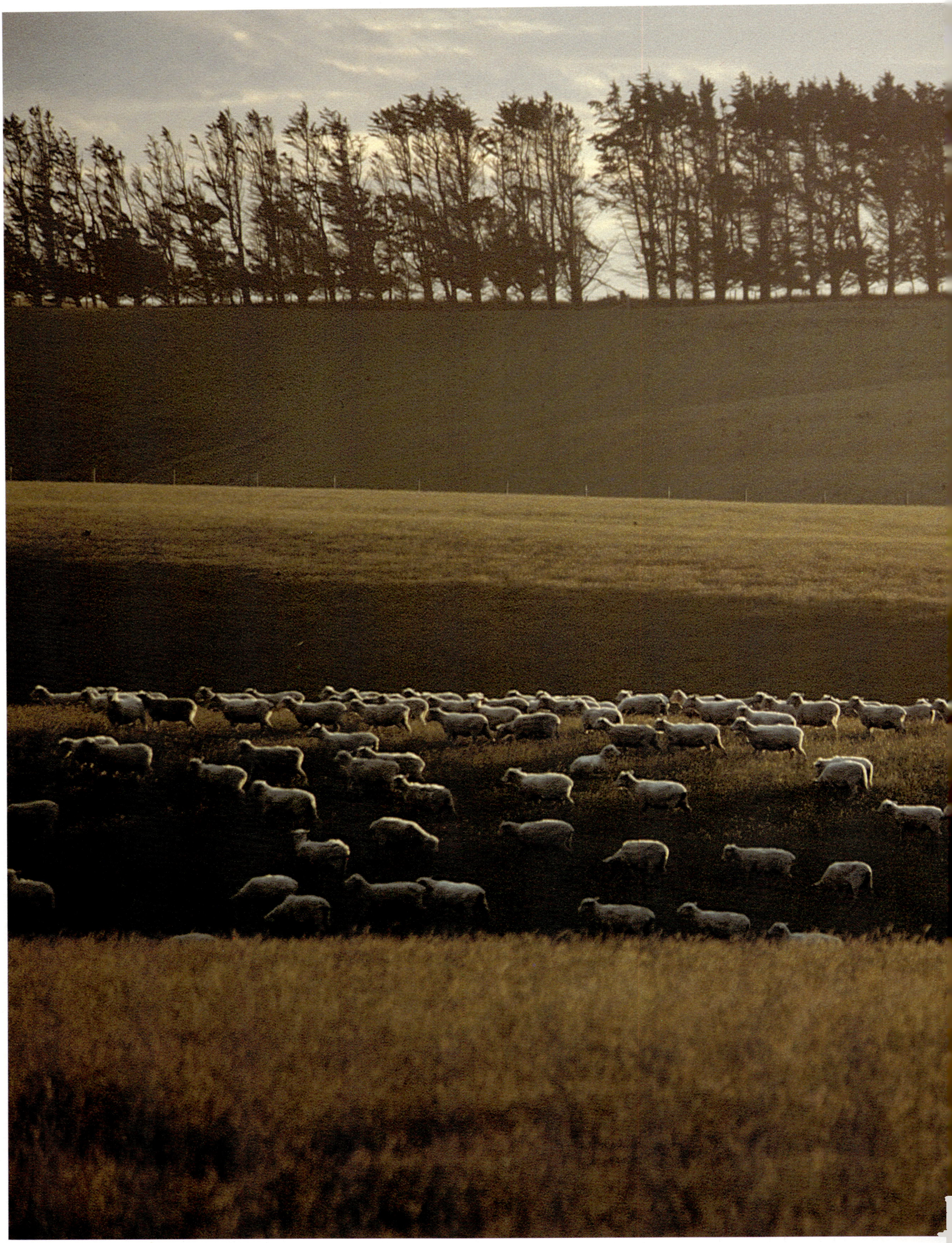

Southland sheep near Otara, east of Invercargill

GEOFF MASON

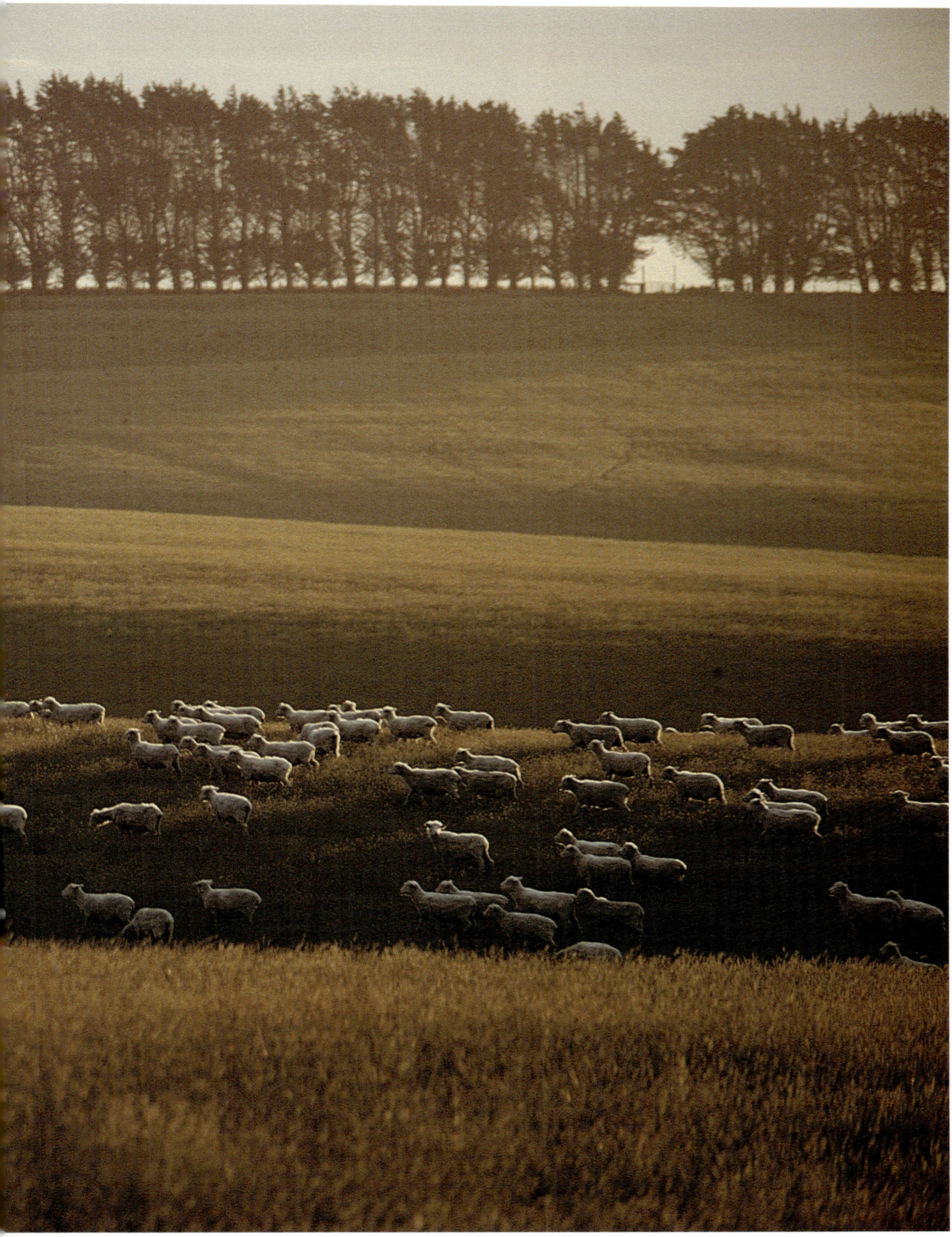

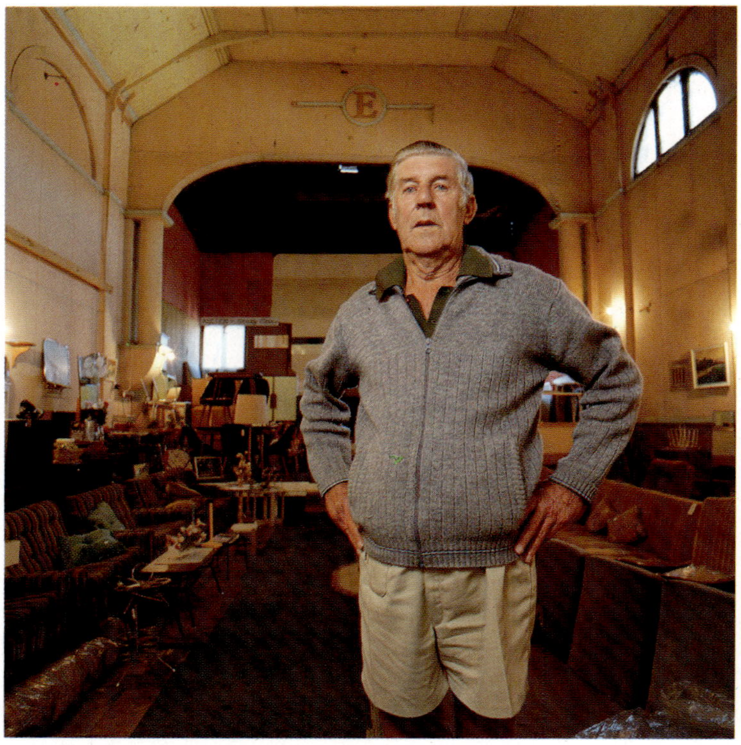

Second-hand furniture mart, Te Kuiti — STEPHEN ROBINSON

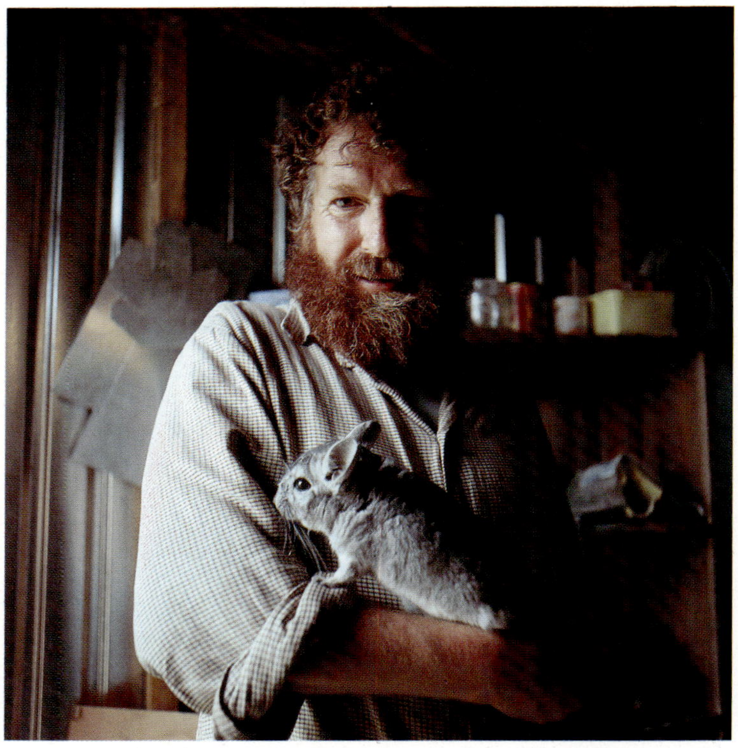

Rob Orchard, trial Chinchilla farm — BRIAN ENTING

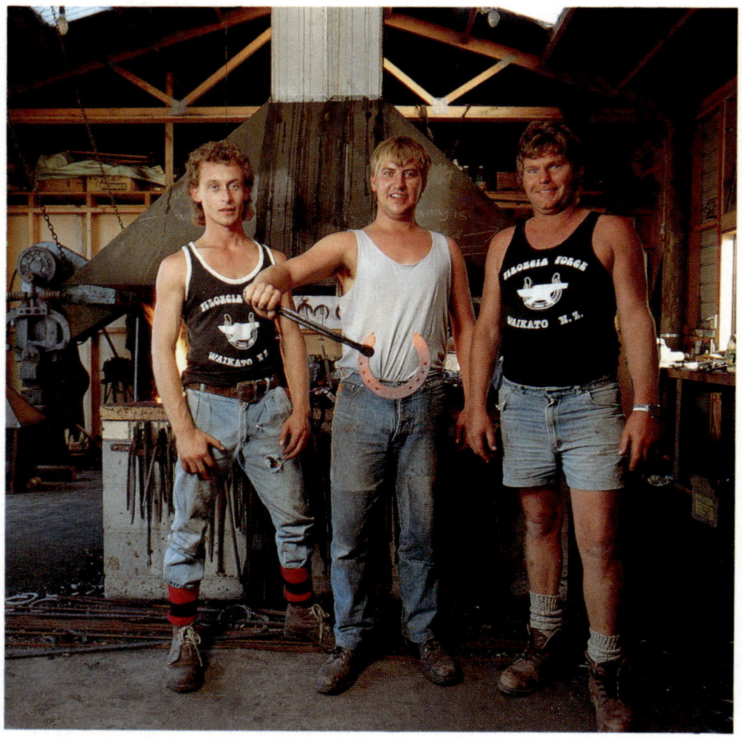

David, Richard and Jim at the Pirongia Forge, Waikato — STEPHEN ROBINSON

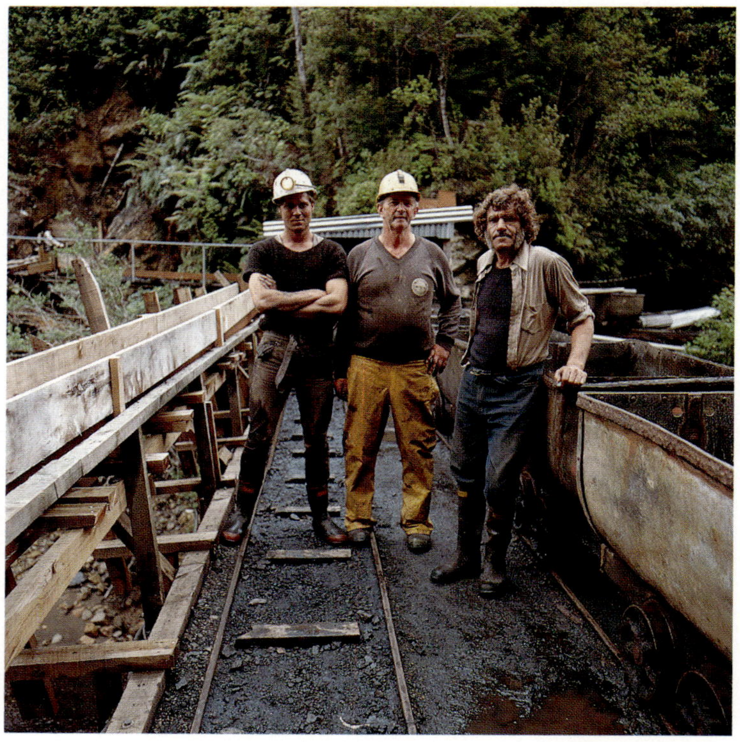

Moody-Spring Creek Mine, West Coast — BRIAN ENTING

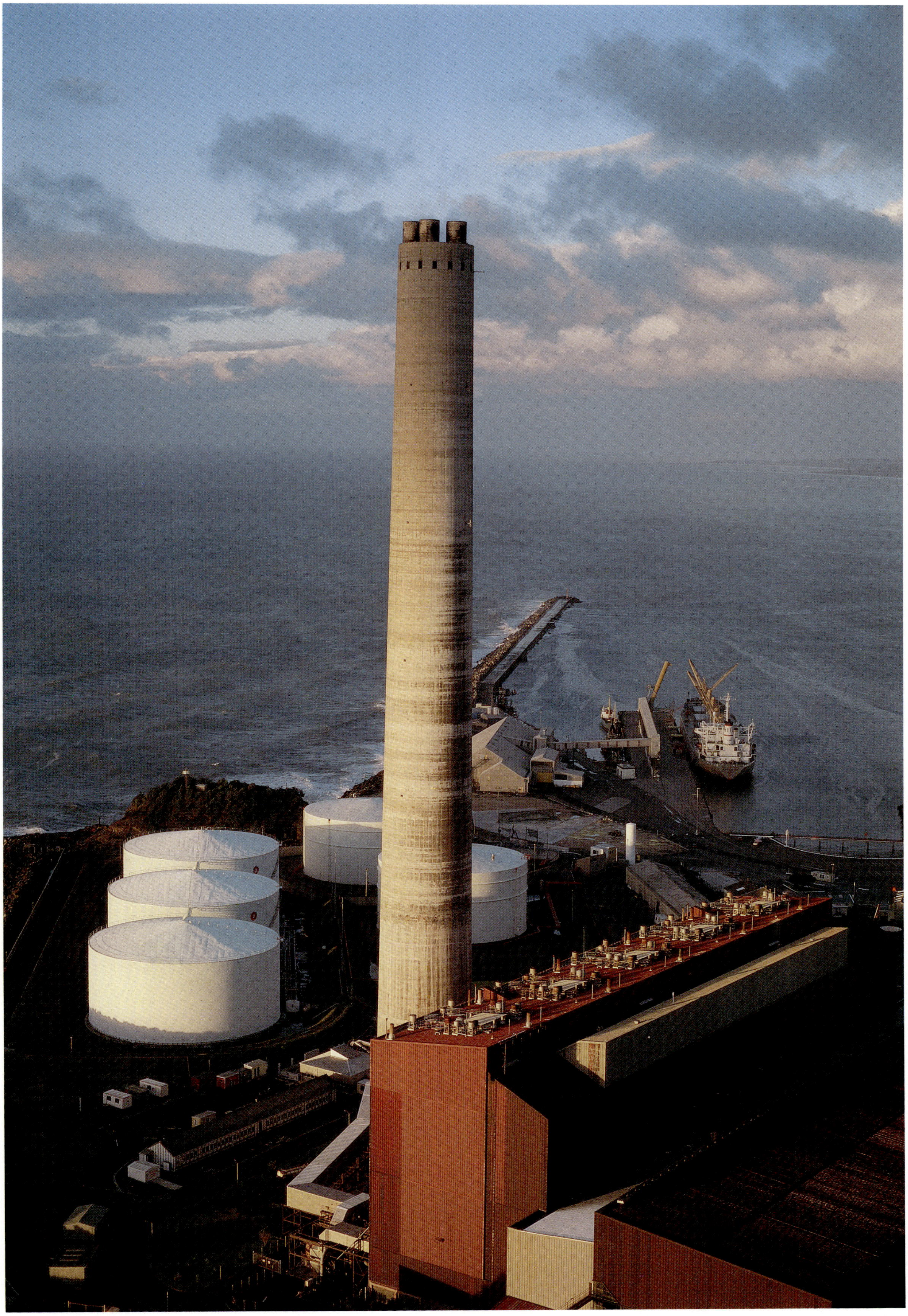

One-hundred-and-ninety-eight metre high chimney, thermal power station, New Plymouth

CRAIG POTTON

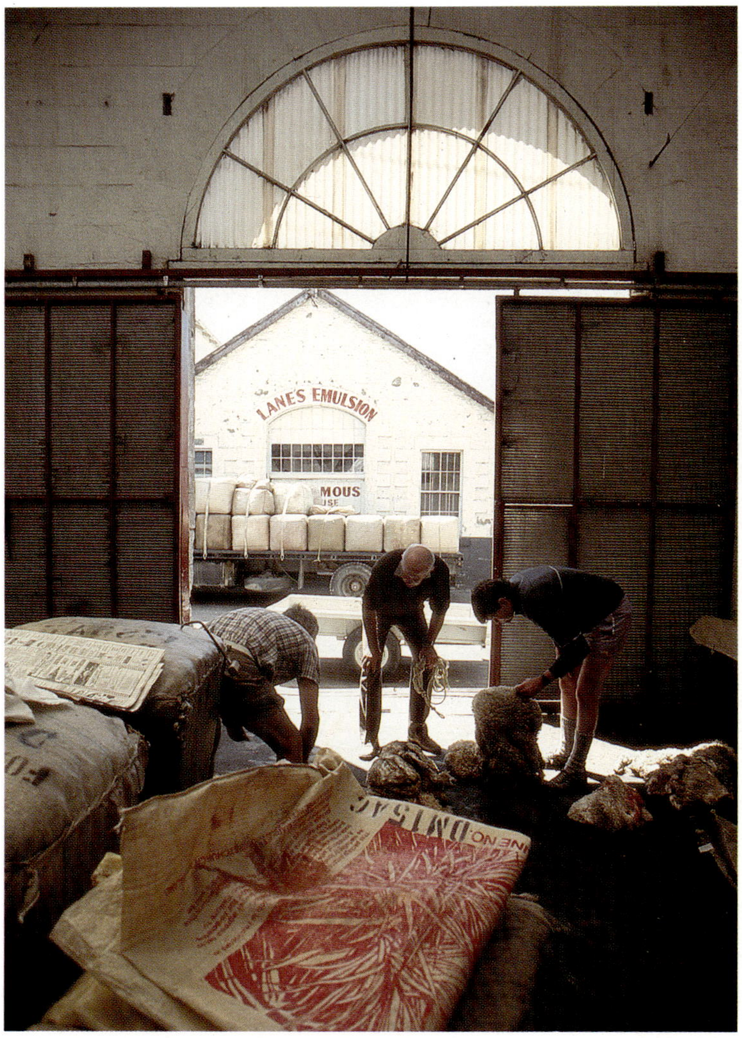

Waterfront building, Oamaru GEOFF MASON

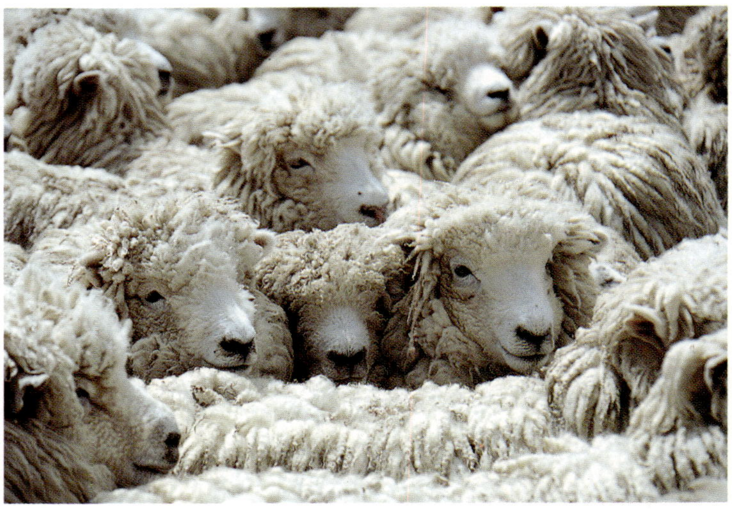

Sheep near Te Anau GEOFF MASON

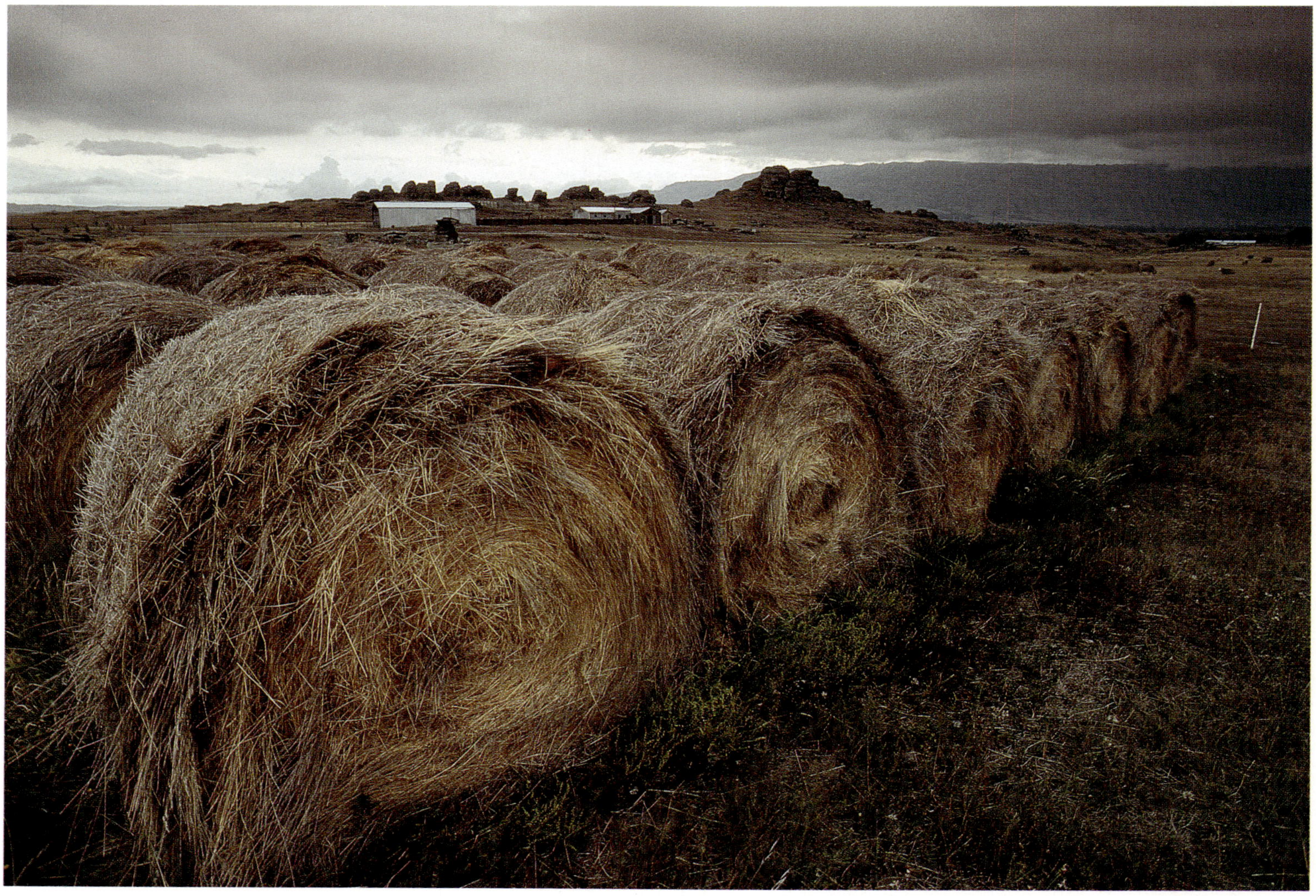

Central Otago farmscape GEOFF MASON

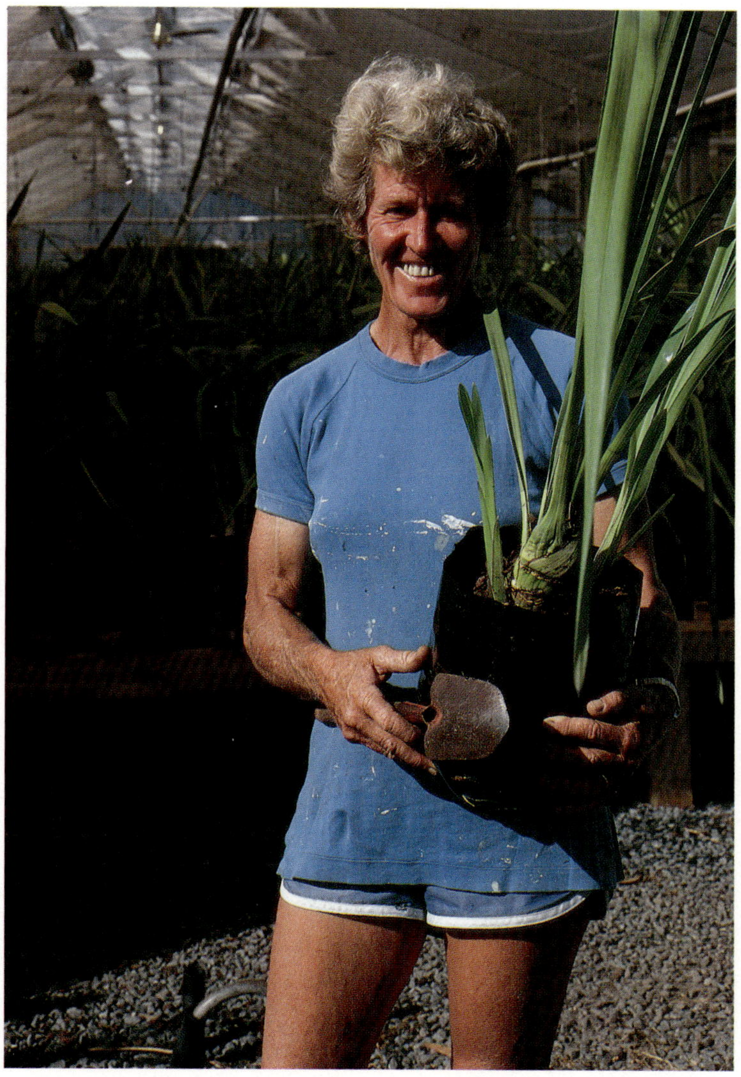
Orchid grower, California, Northland STEPHEN ROBINSON

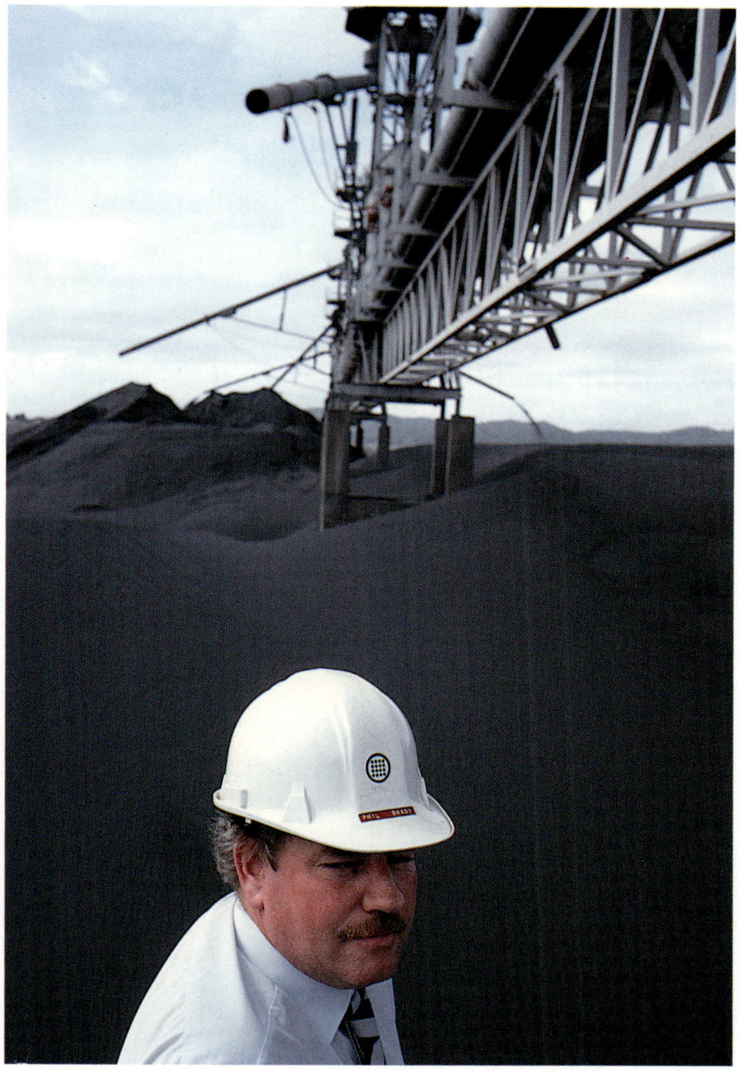
Phil Brady, New Zealand Steel, Taharoa STEPHEN ROBINSON

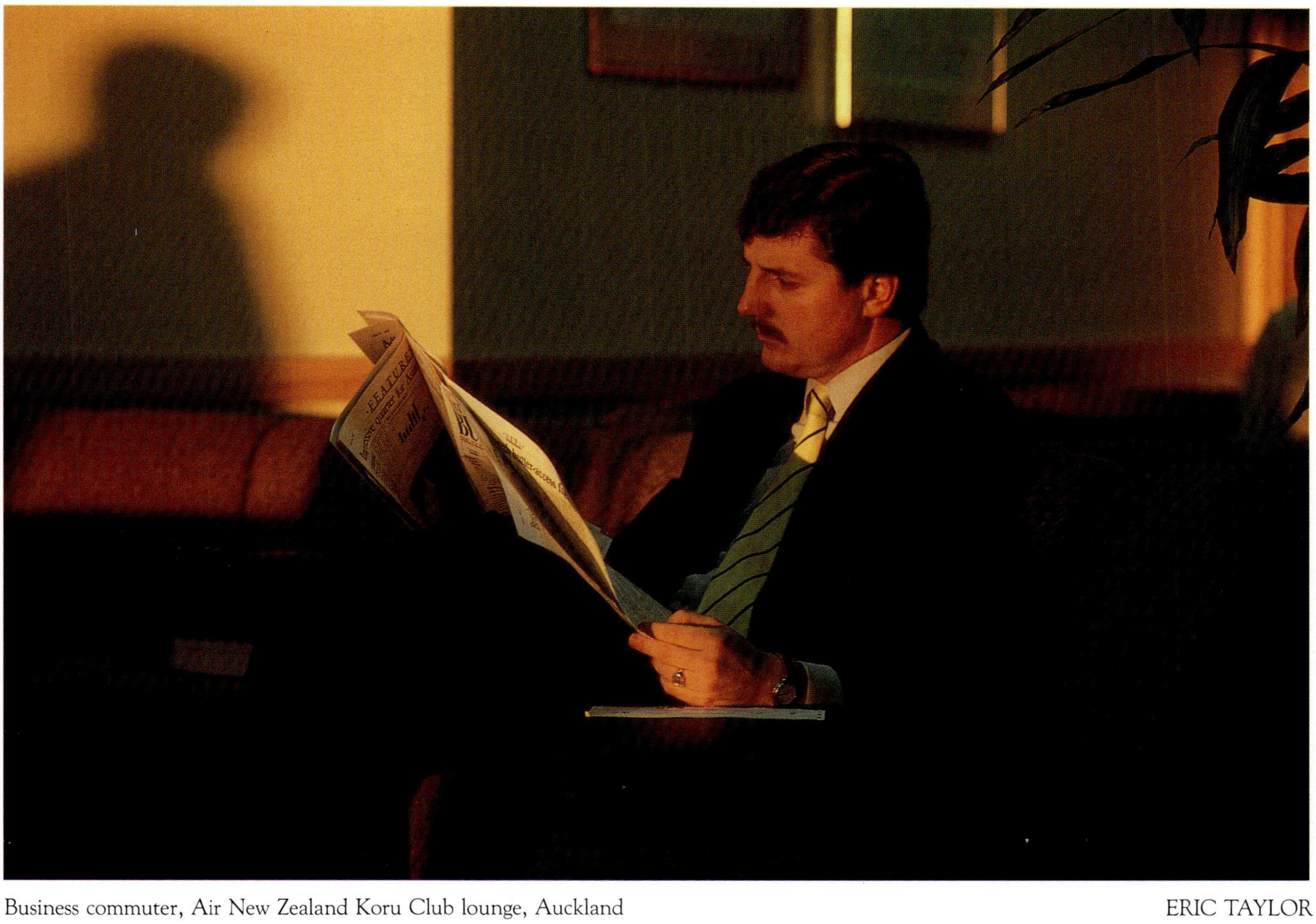
Business commuter, Air New Zealand Koru Club lounge, Auckland ERIC TAYLOR

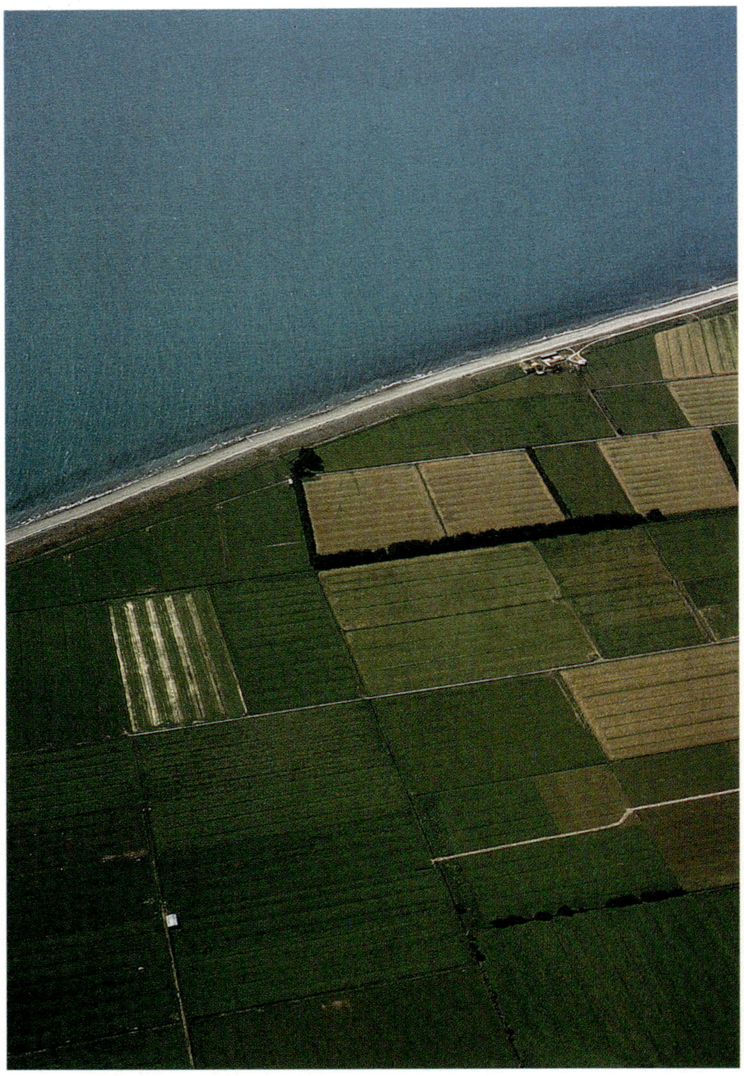

Coastal farming, Nelson BRUCE CONNEW

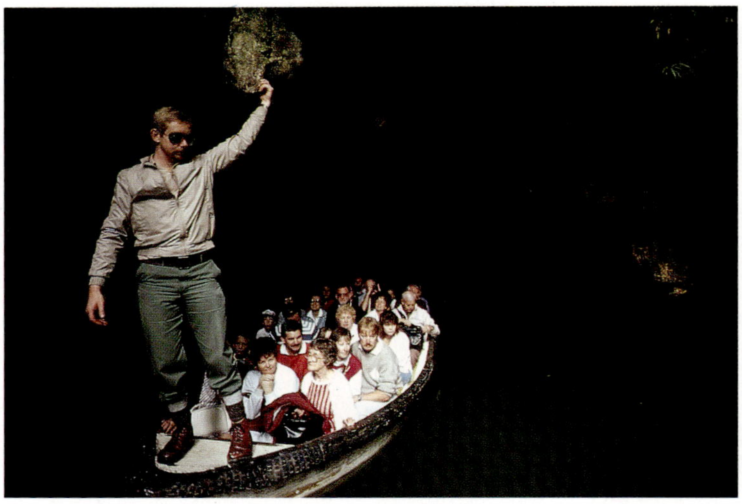

Tourists at the Waitomo Caves STEPHEN ROBINSON

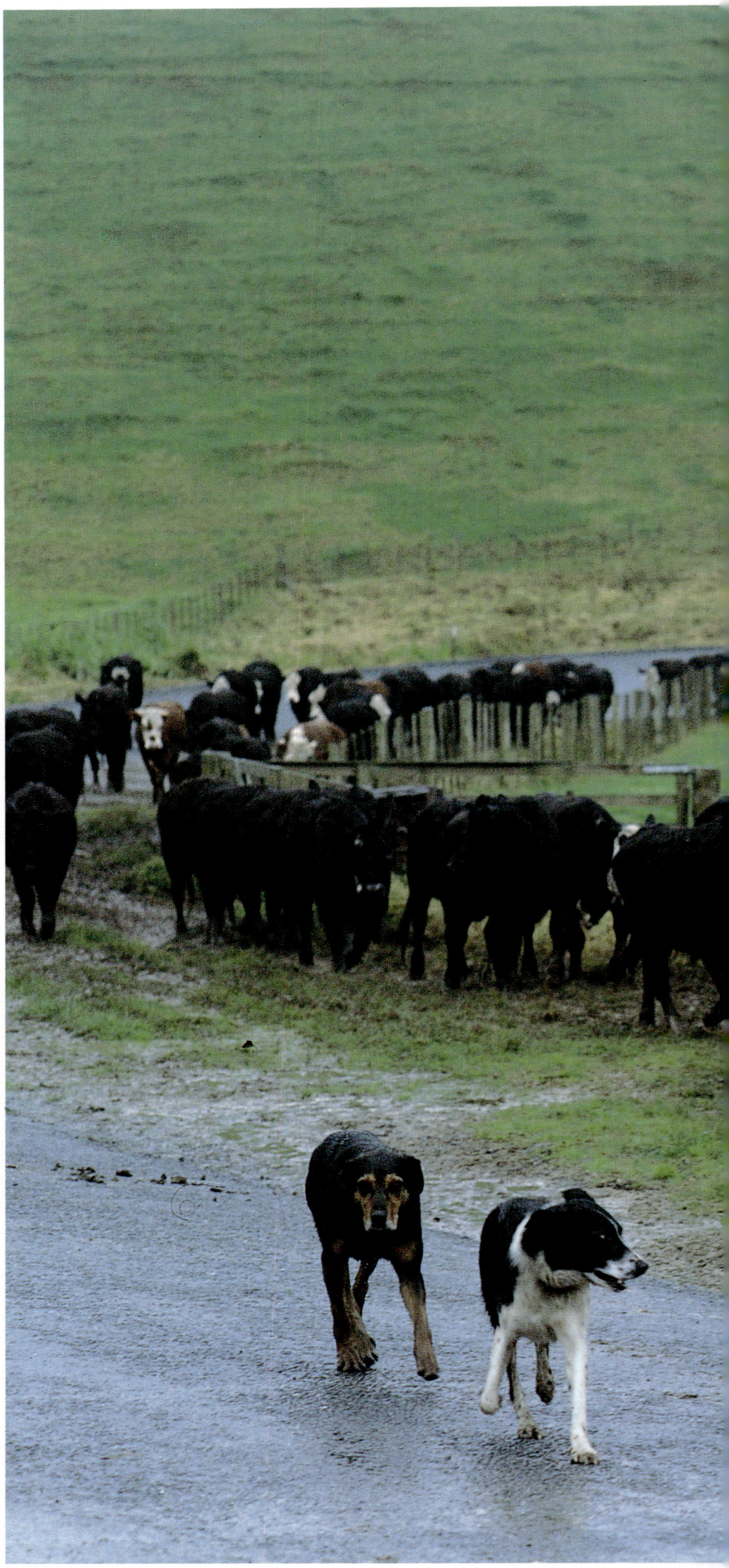

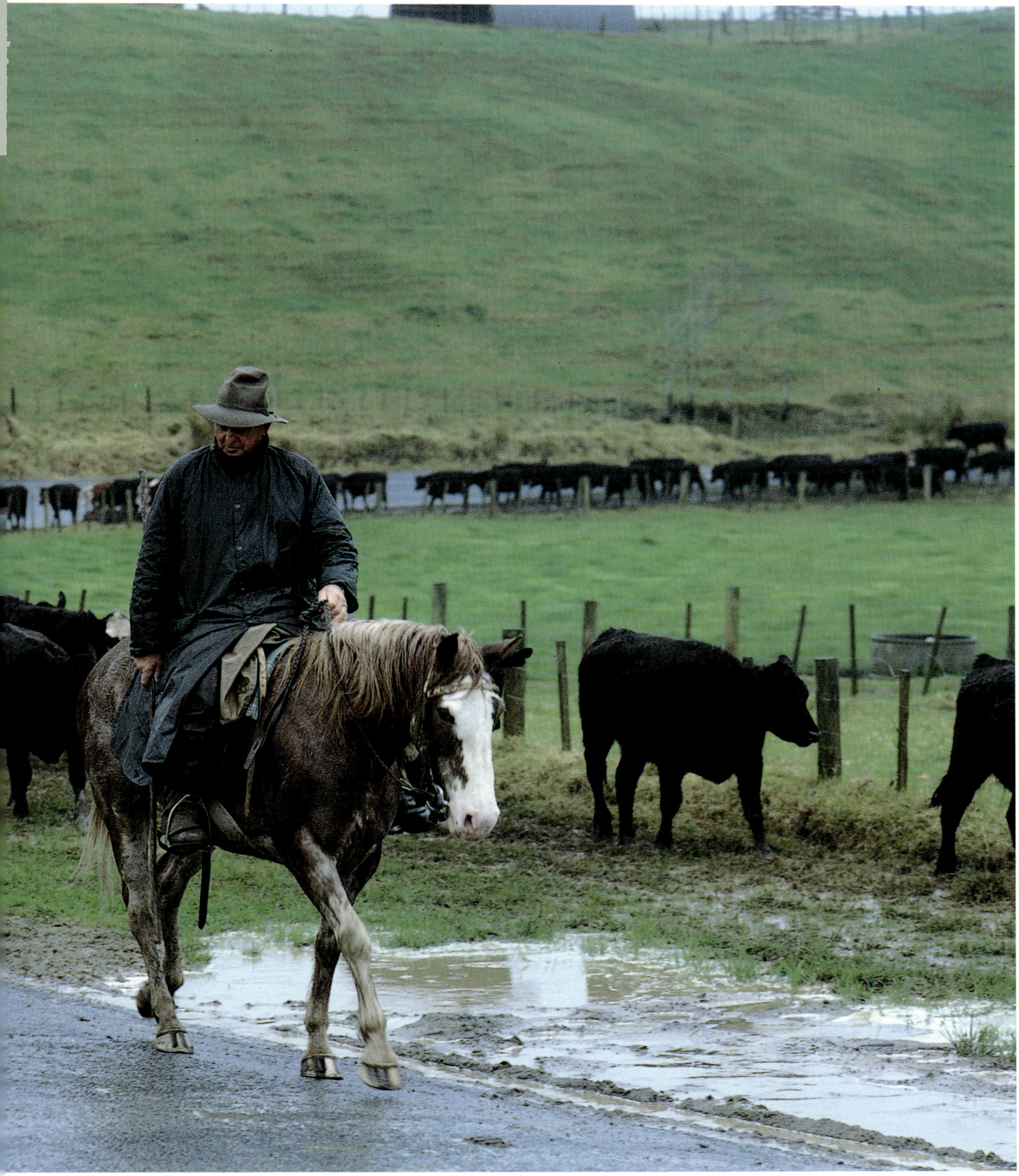

Cattle drive, Paua, Northland

ERIC TAYLOR

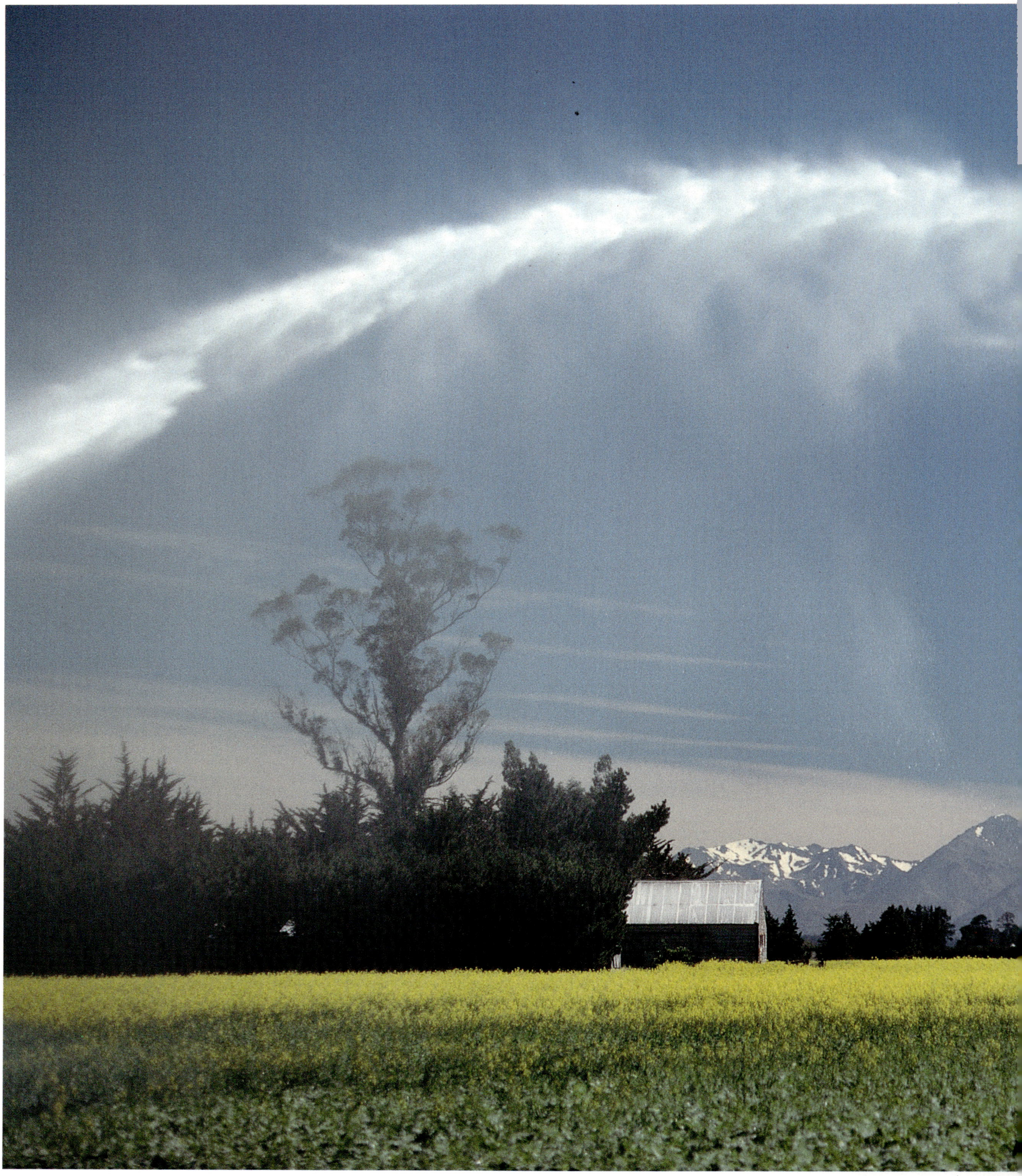

Rape field, Fairlie, South Canterbury GEOFF MASON

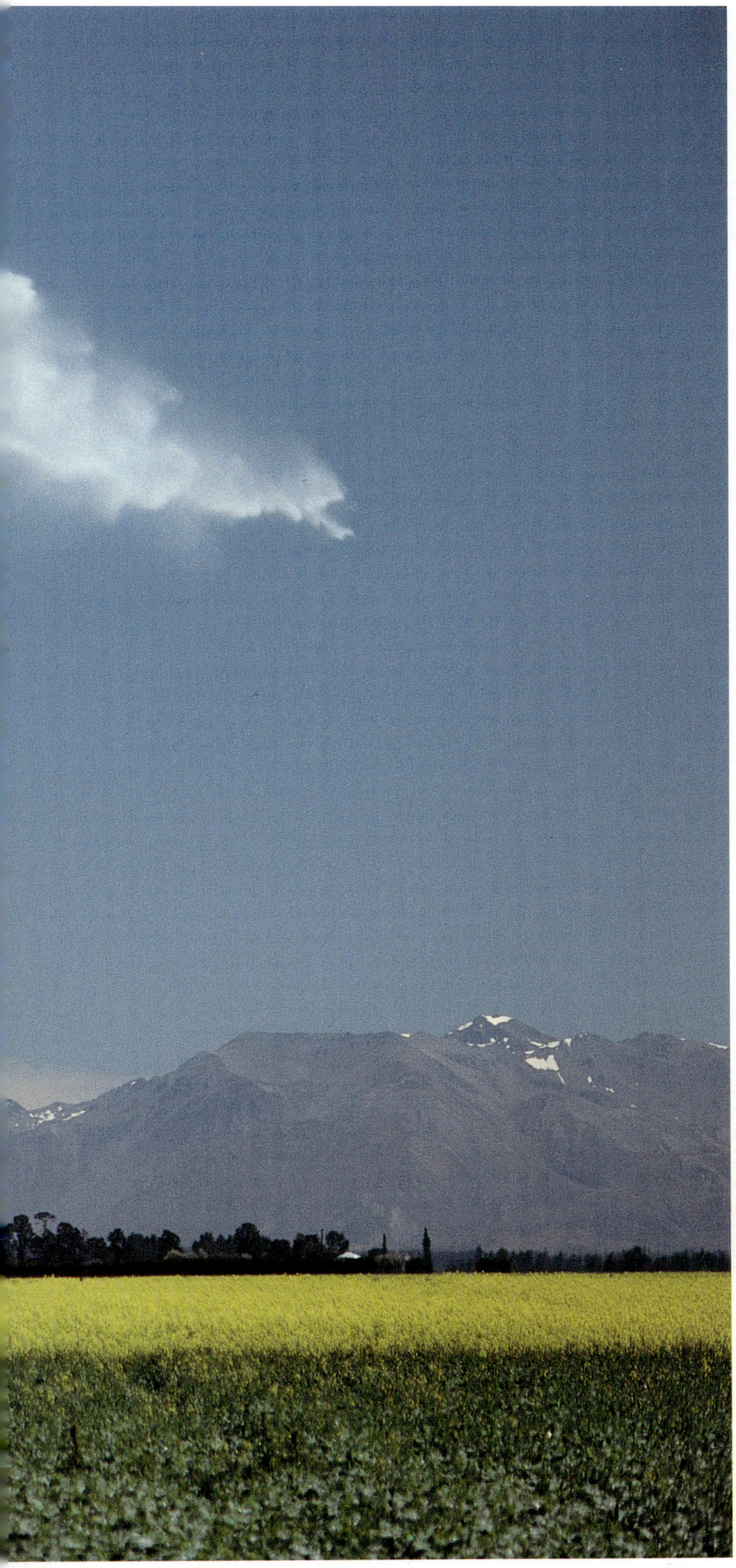

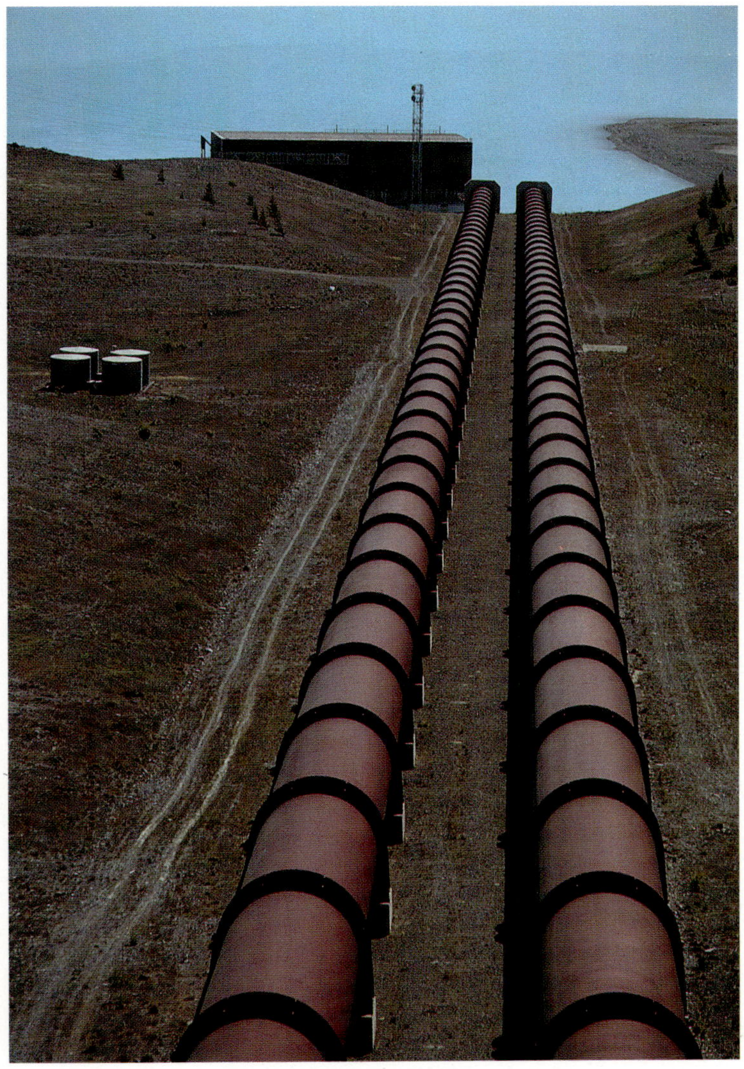

Penstocks of Tekapo B Power Station GEOFF MASON

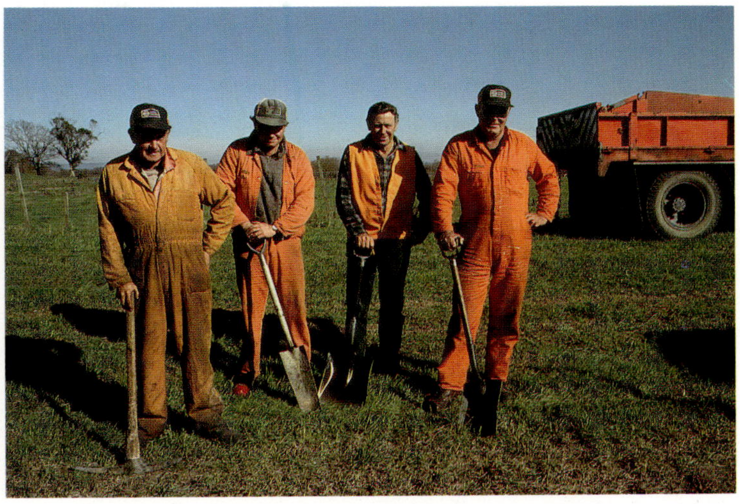

Road crew, Highway 1, Huntly STEPHEN ROBINSON

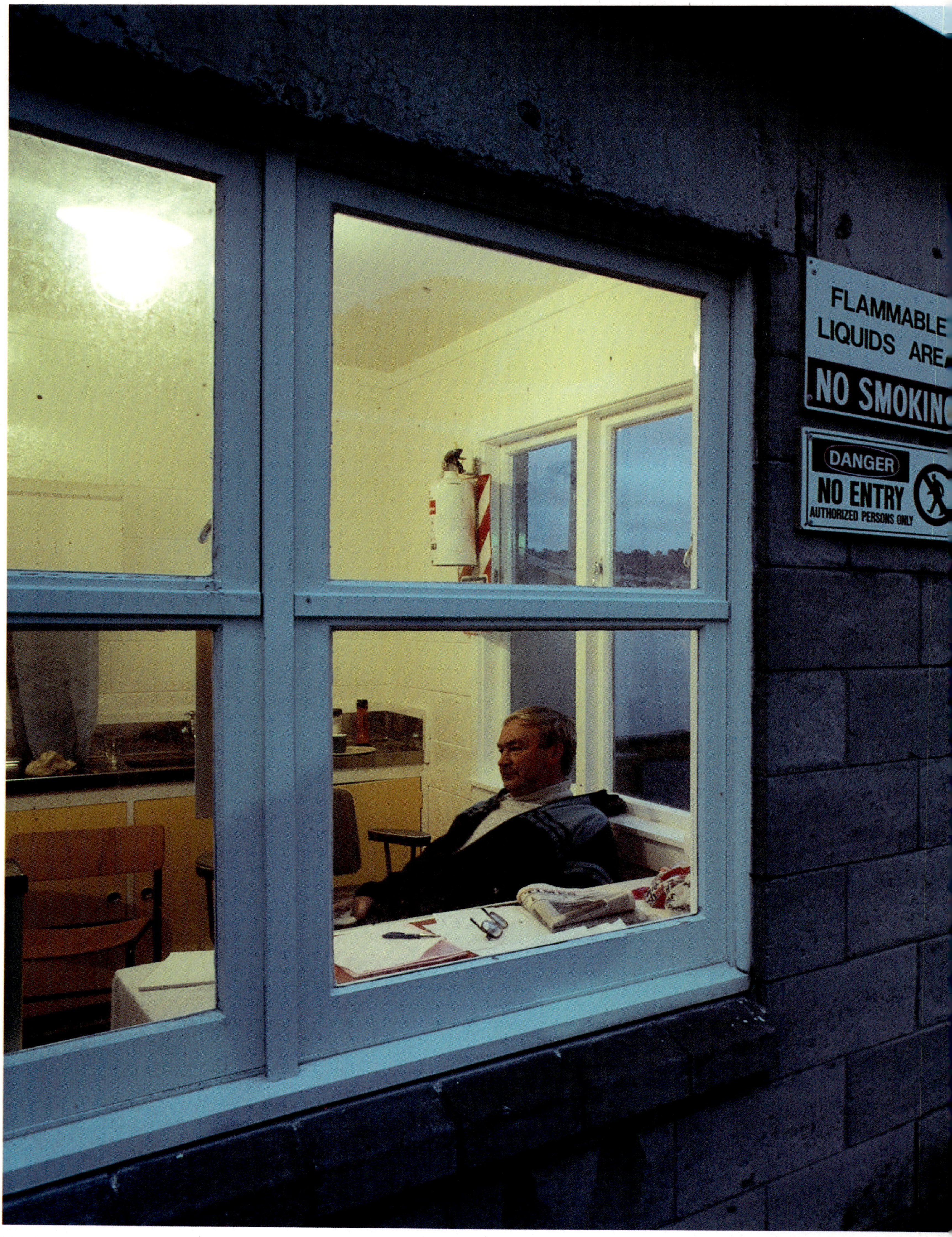

Murdo MacLeod on watch, Burnham Wharf, Wellington — TIM STEELE

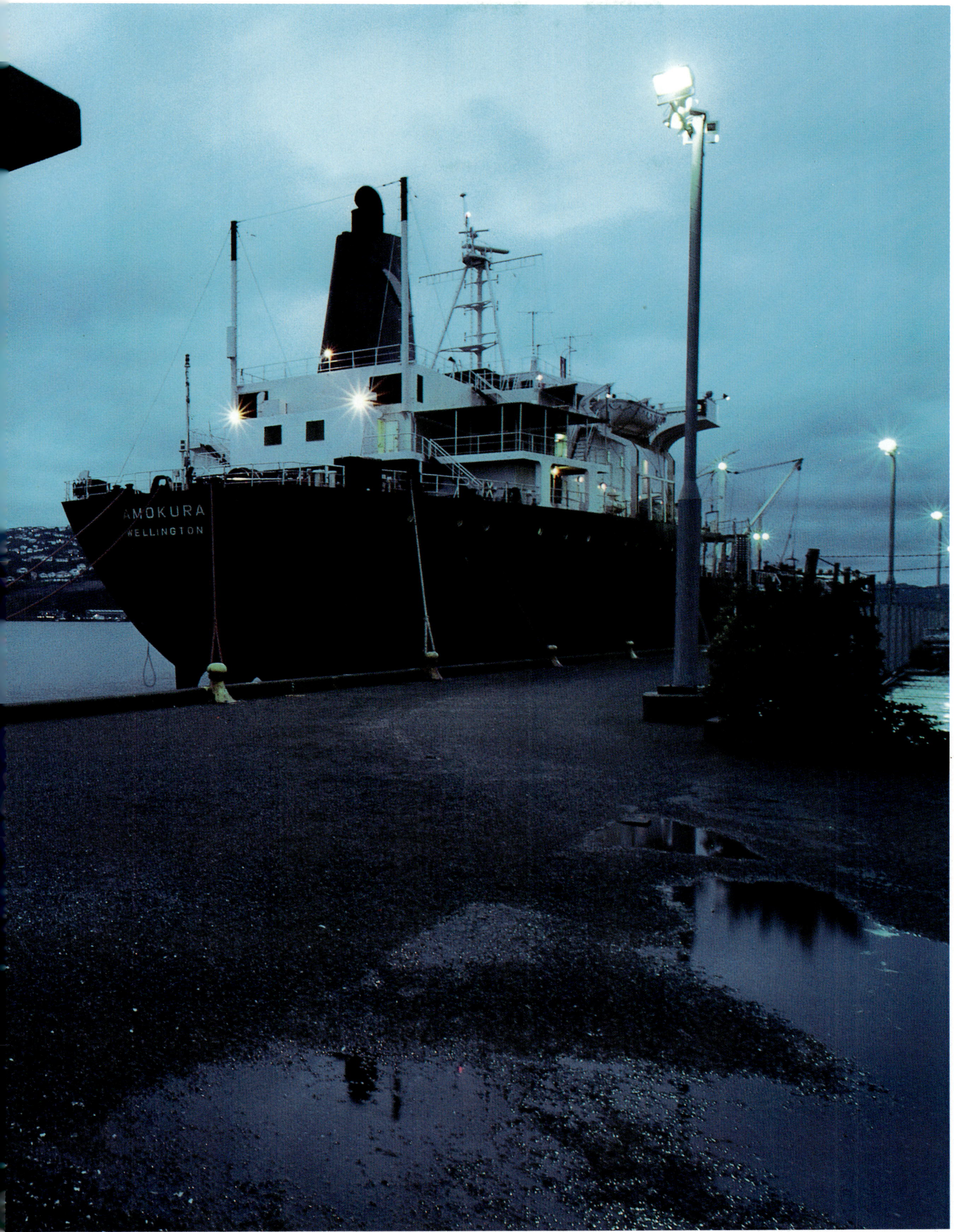
AMOKURA
WELLINGTON

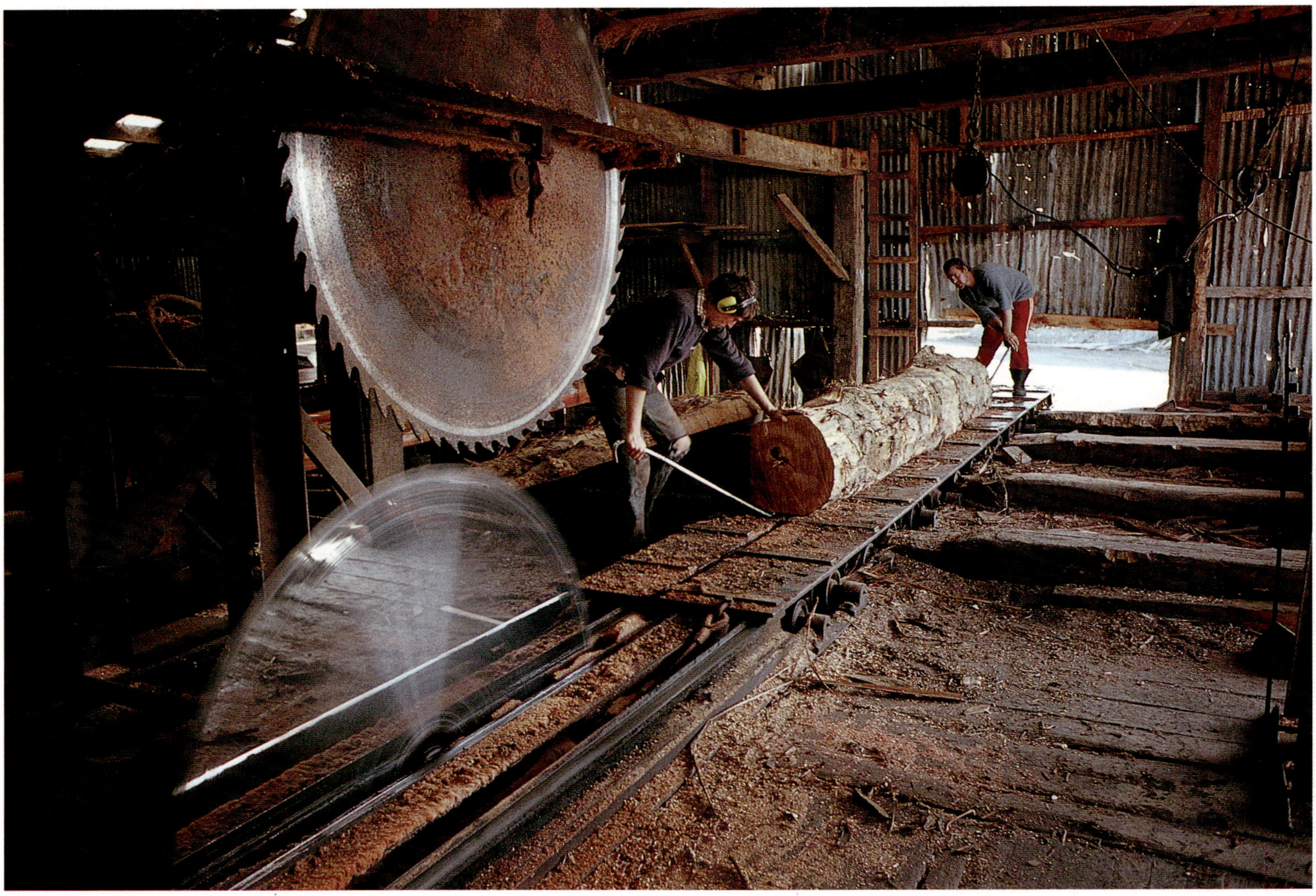

Tuatapere, Fiordland BRIAN ENTING

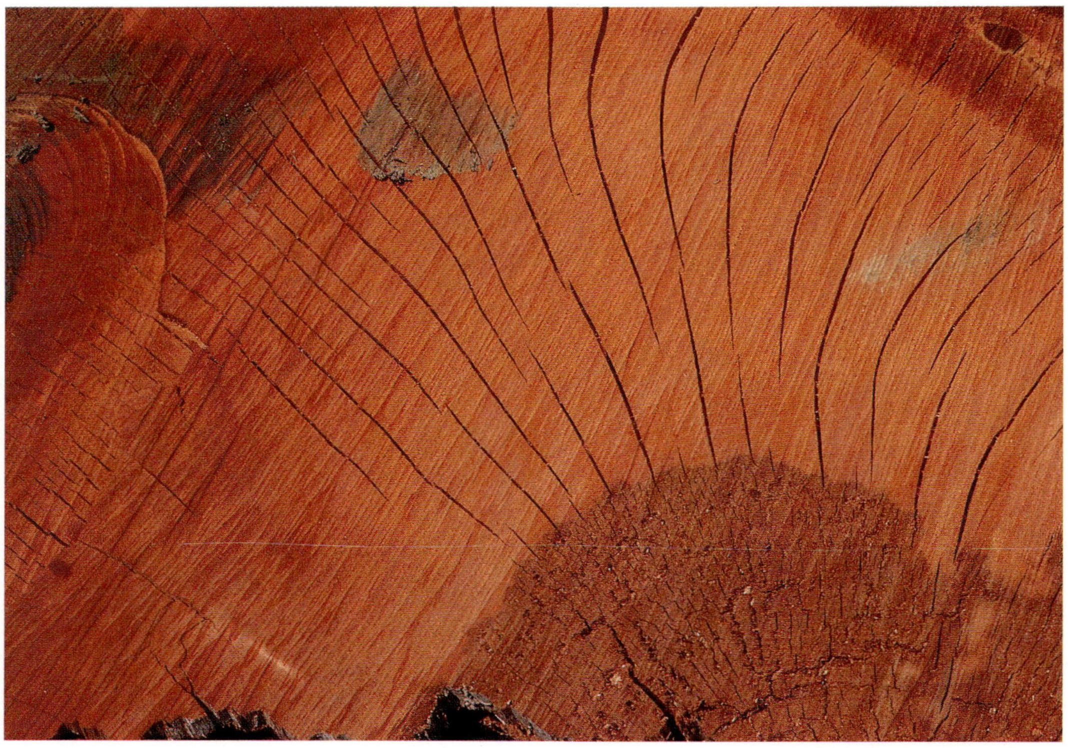

Rimu log, Tuatapere BRIAN ENTING

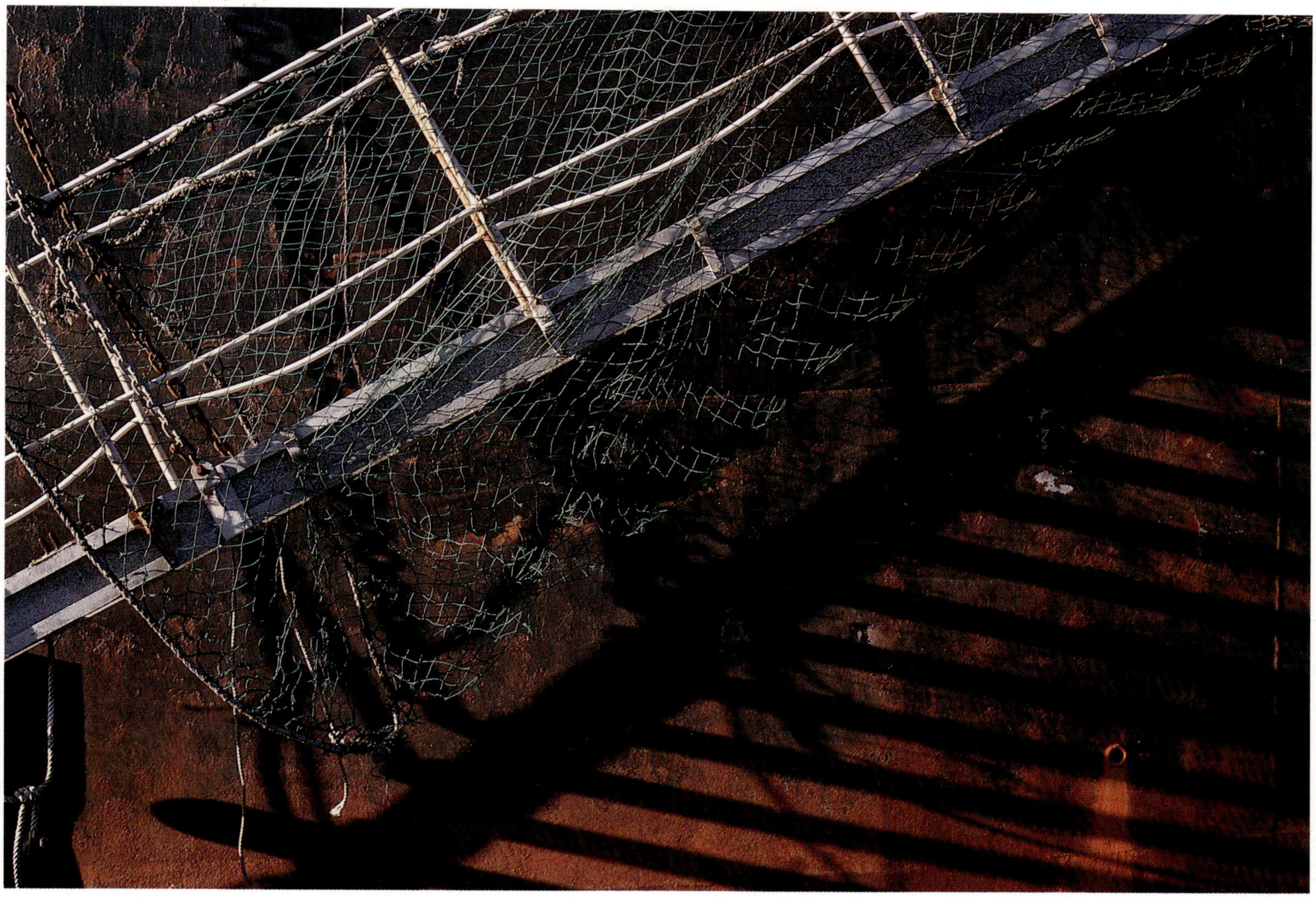

Gangway to fishing boat, Wellington TIM STEELE

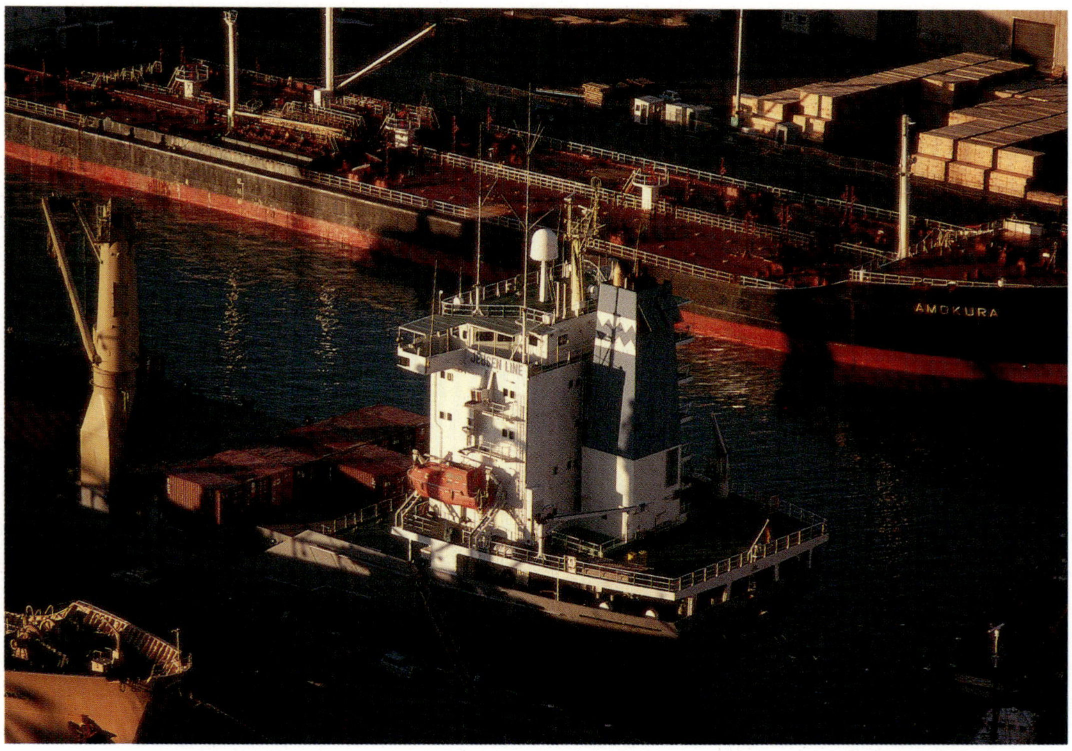

Container vessels, Napier Wharf CRAIG POTTON

HEROES AND HEROINES

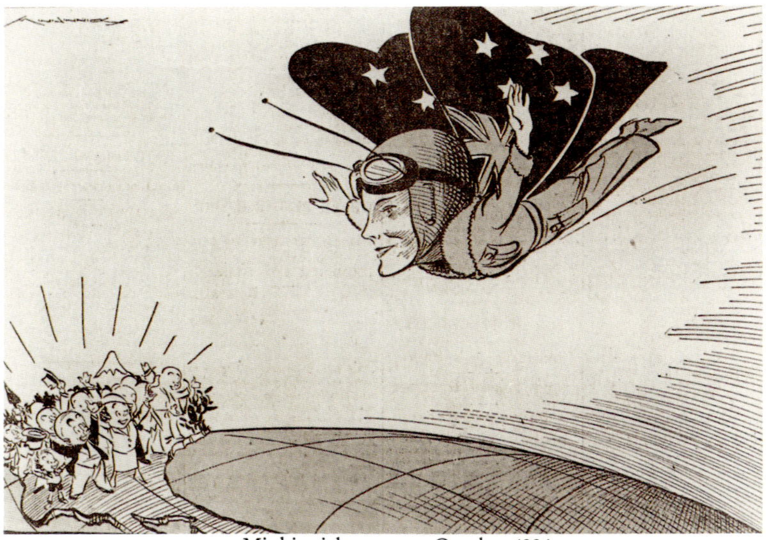

N.Z. HERALD/AUCKLAND INSTITUTE AND MUSEUM

Minhinnick cartoon, October 1936.

James McNeish

WHEN I WAS A BOY growing up in Papakura towards the end of the war, I asked my father who his heroes were. He named a few. One was an airman called "Cobber" Kain and one a soldier called Freyberg. Captain Charles Upham, VC and Bar, as I recall, was another. Women were not mentioned, naturally. I came to the conclusion that the New Zealand hero-model was entirely male and military. And all the rest, for my father went on to reminisce about a rugby idol called George Nepia, were sportsmen. I was wrong of course.

Heroes have been around for a long time. The Greeks invented them, specifying certain qualities: strength and courage in a godlike mould, usually worshipped after death. We had the fate to acquire a syllabus from England, more precisely a history book called *Our Nation's Story*, which spoonfed generations of New Zealand schoolchildren on the British model, so that we came to think the only heroes worth saluting – Gordon of Khartoum, Livingstone, Clive of India, Wolfe before the Heights of Abraham – were a kind of sub-species of Empire loyalist.

Embedded in a colonial and British militaristic tradition, it has taken us a long time to break clear and begin to discover who our heroes and heroines really are.

There are a considerable number of them. There is first the authentic kind: pre-eminently Hillary and Freyberg, but Lovelock and Michael Joseph Savage too. And then come what might be styled Others, involving an element of personal, possibly quirky choice on my part.

One or two, like the founding missionary Samuel Marsden, are collapsible. Marsden's legend as the kind and indefatigable "friend of the Maori" is marred by the image of a religious bigot who was also a flogging parson. Some are quite recent – activists like Sonja Davies and Phillida Bunkle, campaigners for women's rights and women's health; Dame Whina Cooper, the Maori land marcher; Peter Button, the helicopter rescue pilot; Rewi Alley of China, a rebel-reformer among revolutionaries. They serve to illustrate that heroes and heroines are being made all the time.

Julia Martin is now forgotten, but in 1863 as "New Zealand's Grace Darling", she entered the folklore of the time.

This young Te Ati Awa heroine risked her life to rescue the crew of the *Delaware*, an American brig trapped outside Nelson in seas not unlike those which a hundred years later would wreck the *Wahine* off Wellington.

Jean Batten, the flying "It" girl of the thirties, is just being remembered. The romance of her solo flights from England to Australia and from England to New Zealand ranks with that of Lindbergh and Amy Johnson. She flew a cranky wood-and-fabric aeroplane with one engine, capturing, besides a string of world records and a pedestal in aviation history, a place in our hearts that an enigmatic later life, one hopes, will not erode. As late

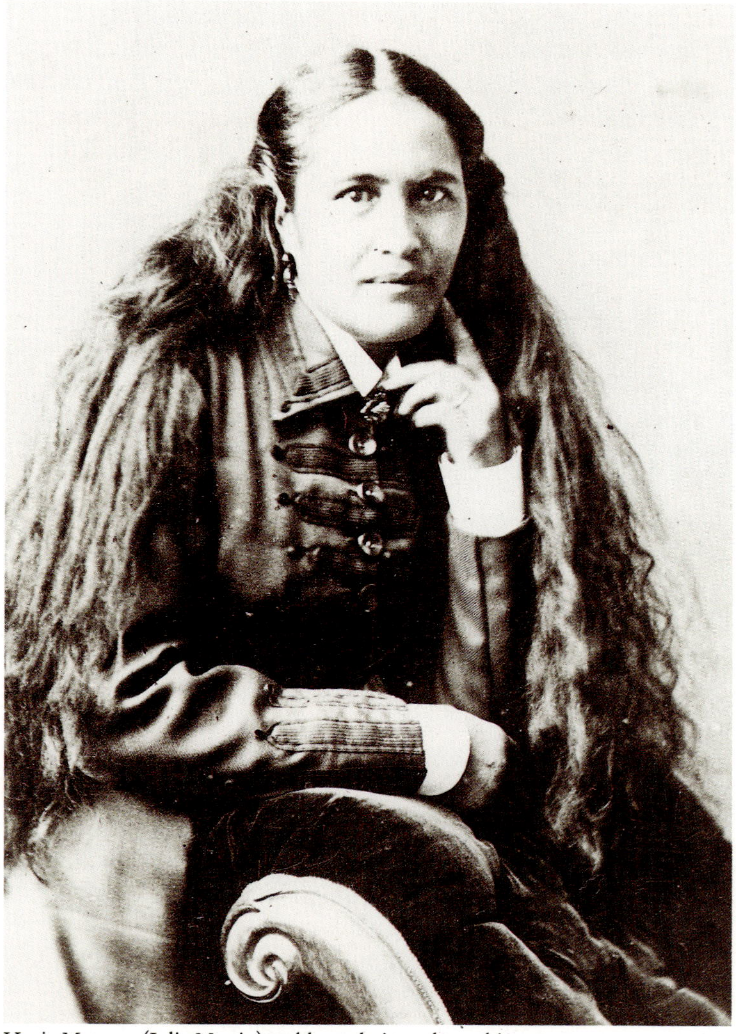

W. E. BROWN/ALEXANDER TURNBULL LIBRARY

Huria Matenga (Julia Martin) and her relatives plunged into stormy seas to rescue sailors from the *Delaware*. For this feat Matenga was presented with £50 from the Government, and a gold watch from the people of Nelson.

as 1980 her 1936 England–Australia record (five days, twenty-one hours) still held.

In 1988 the terminal at Auckland's international airport was renamed for her. Her landing at Mangere in October 1936 coincided with the arrival in Auckland by ship of her contemporary, Jack Lovelock, fresh from his Olympic triumph at the Berlin Games. They provided an unexpected "double", a bumper crop for such a tiny land. Champion flier, champion athlete, they were feted everywhere, making guest appearances as they travelled about New Zealand in separate government cars. Understandably, the country went wild.

WE HAVE TRAGIC FIGURES, animal heroes among them, Phar Lap and Opo, besides John Mulgan and Robin Hyde, all of them fated to die – three in a foreign land – at the height of their powers. Phar Lap is revealing.

When Phar Lap died, popularly believed poisoned, "done in by the Yanks", a nation mourned. Phar Lap the wonder horse (1926–32) helps us define the phenomenon of heroism – at any rate the kind of hero we in New Zealand recognise. Phar Lap was leggy and slow to mature; he achieved fame overseas (one thinks of Hillary); he became a legend in his lifetime, both model and pathfinder, the measure of later champions. A gutsy fellow too. Yet noble with it – in the words of Peter Porter, "perfect, loved like God". A kind of democratic hero. And a good sport to boot. It doesn't matter that Australia also lays claim to him or that Phar Lap, "the racing phenomenon of the century", never ran in New Zealand. He was a son of the soil, born in Timaru.

HEROES ARE MADE, NOT BORN. We may praise the act but unless society approves, sealing the act in poetry and legend, we are unlikely to offer our love or the quality of worship. Mass appeal – popularity – is the yeast that makes heroes rise, but, like yeast, it is unpredictable. Which explains in part why Savage who was a little man is an authentic hero, while Seddon who was a giant, in many ways a colossus, isn't. Despite that it was Seddon's reforms that first gained us international recognition.

The phrase we like to quote about ourselves, "New Zealand, social laboratory of the world", dates from the reforms which Seddon's government carried through – the phrase belongs to Seddon's era, not Savage's. The point is that Seddon, the nineteenth-century Liberal reformer, was merely genial. Savage was loved.

Michael Joseph Savage (1872–1940) ought to have been suspect. After all, his early career as a militant unionist put him, if not quite with the communists, virtually beyond the pale. But the gods gave him simplicity. There was a benign aura, a kindliness which appealed to the emotions of the average man. So that when, after the 1935 election victory, Savage's first Labour government began its transformation of a state into a welfare state, hardly anyone accused Michael Savage of being a socialist. "Even if," as someone has said, "you suspected Reds under his bed, you knew that at worst they'd turn out to be only a very pale pink."

Savage's photograph once hung in thousands of New Zealand homes, like an icon, and the adulation we grant him, even now, helps to explain the Mulgan phenomenon. Whether as saint or as a prophet of social change ("New Zealand in the forefront . . . "), we experience Savage today almost as a value. But not John Mulgan. Nor indeed others like him.

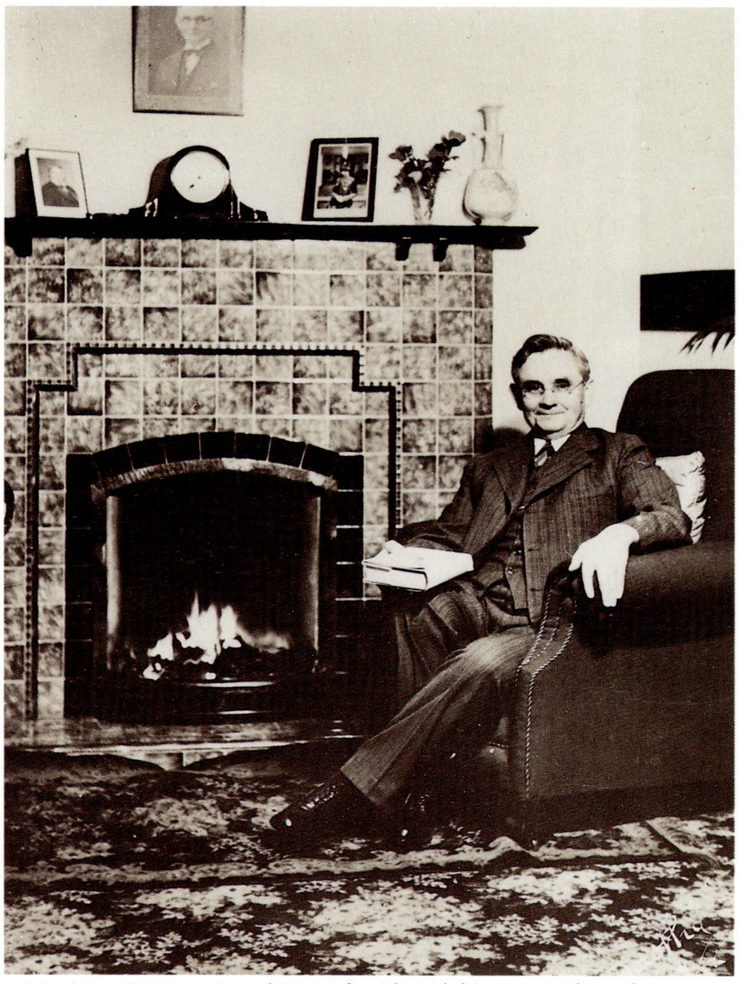

ALEXANDER TURNBULL LIBRARY

Michael Joseph Savage sits at his own fireside with his portrait above the mantlepiece, just like thousands of his fellow New Zealanders. The whole nation went into mourning on his death in 1940.

Consider for a moment Rutherford, virtually a prophet without honour in his own land. Lord Rutherford (1871–1937) split the atom. He was "the greatest physical scientist of his age." He received the Nobel Prize, the Order of Merit, innumerable other distinctions and the accolades paid upon his death were only slightly less fulsome than those Churchill got. Rutherford, unlike Savage, was born in New Zealand. In Germany he would be monumentalised, yet in the land of his birth – where are the monuments? Where is the Rutherford University in New Zealand honouring the father of nuclear physics?

Similarly with Mulgan. John Mulgan is the brilliant soldier-poet who went to Oxford in 1934 and committed suicide in Cairo at the end of the war, a matter of days before the peace. He has never been elevated to hero status. Yet, ironically, Mulgan's profile seems tailor-made – he was both brave *and* tragic, besides a man of action and an attractive personality. Moreover he died young. John Mulgan is a key figure in our history on several counts and has a following but it is not a popular one. He has in hero terms a fatal flaw – he is too intellectual. New Zealand has always mistrusted intellectual achievement. Mulgan was after all primarily a scholar and academic. Academics don't make heroes.

The irony is that it was John Mulgan who wrote the book *Man Alone*, enunciating a concept that we not only value but which has become almost a definition of heroism in the New Zealand ethos. The "loner" idea is classless, etched deep into our psyche. And not just Man Alone against the unknown, like Hillary, or against the establishment, like "Starkie" and Ettie Rout.

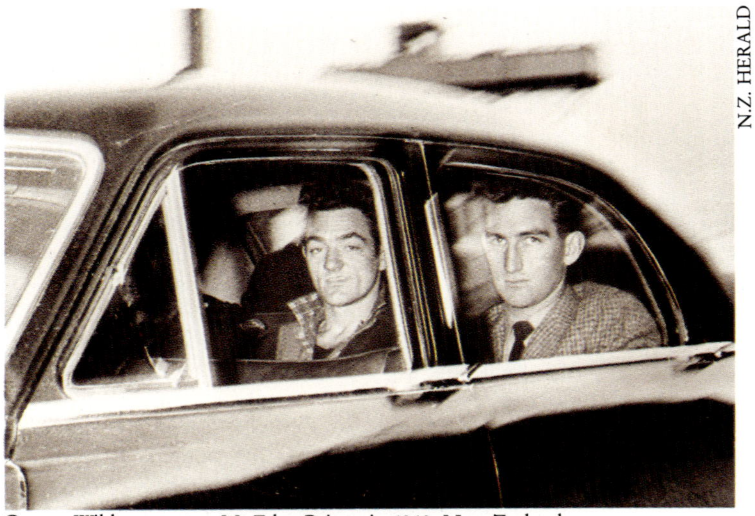

N.Z. HERALD

George Wilder re-enters Mt Eden Prison in 1963. New Zealanders were ambivalent about the fugitive Wilder, admiring his ability to outwit the forces of law and order.

There was George Wilder in the 1960s, alone on the run against the law. As the popular song of the day went:

He breaks and enters every house
To him this brings great joy ...
It seemed his one ambition was
Policemen to annoy.

Wilder was a villain, yet every time he escaped from prison he caught the public imagination, to the frustration and fury of the police who spent in all thirty-four weeks, almost nine months, tracking him down. In George Wilder is glimpsed something of the anarchy in New Zealand society. We are, in a secretive way, fascinated by lawlessness.

The legend of Wilder has a disarming side, a touch of gallantry. It credits him, rifling property as he ran, with a disarming humanity – he would tidy up afterwards and feed the cat, or leave a note for the victim apologising for the damage and any inconvenience caused. Little flourishes of gallantry that bring George Wilder closer to a gentleman-crook of English legend: an A. J. Raffles, say, rather than a Ned Kelly. Kelly shot and killed policemen. That was all very well for Ned, it wouldn't have done for George.

We like our villains more polite than they do in Australia.

CURIOUSLY, IF ONE LOOKS at Maori society, women are more visible than men. Half a century ago there was a smouldering heroine with "tohunga eyes", arguably the most influential woman in our political history, Princess Te Puea. Her successor, the Maori leader who to many incarnates the spirit of the land today, is again a woman, Dame Whina Cooper of Te Rarawa Ki Hokianga.

It is Whina Cooper's achievement, among others, to stretch a concept and clarify for many non-Maori an idea: the idea of mana. Having led, in 1975, the land march from the north in which thousands joined, she has continued to fulfil a role which has already added a dimension to the word. For better, for worse, Whina Cooper carries her mana less as a privilege or right than as a burden – as a Jew carries the burden of his race. Her personal struggle in the cause of Maori grievances highlights and embodies this idea.

Outspoken, unbowed, Whina Cooper is still, in her nineties, at the barricades.

FOR SUCH A YOUNG and such a male-oriented society we are, in historical terms, surprisingly well endowed with heroines; in contemporary life, we are almost over-endowed. Today wherever one looks in contemporary society, in almost every social issue and every fight that matters, it is women who are most involved – Sandra Coney, Margaret Sparrow, Fran Wilde, to name a few.

I have mentioned some historical figures already. Mother Aubert, of Wanganui's Jerusalem and Wellington's Home of Compassion, also suggests herself: a saintly person in her dark habit and white coif, a Mother Teresa wheeling a basket pram round the streets in the 1900s, collecting food for her orphanages. But this French-born nun is largely forgotten. More representative perhaps is Helen Wilson.

One thinks of Helen Wilson the teacher starting her pioneer farm near Levin late last century, hammering shingle nails into the roof, while her male suitor and husband-to-be arrives bearing a gift of pork, and one thinks with amusement of an early feminist? But Helen Wilson, who at the age of eighty when nearly blind wrote *My First Eighty Years*, conjures up more than that. She stands if anyone does for the anonymous Pioneer Woman of the backblocks, sustained by a meagre diet, bearing children, toiling and unsung. Heroic by any standard.

If Sir Frederick Truby King, "the man who saved the babies", had been less anti-woman, he might now be canonised. But King was vainglorious and blinkered, "the greatest obstacle," in the words of Dr Agnes Bennett, "to women's progress and emancipation that New Zealand has ever known." This is not to diminish Truby King's work and greatness. As founder of the Plunket system of caring for babies he was an innovator and a remarkable man, as Bernard Shaw went out of his way to remind us. King was a necessary hero, a man for his time, and it is not his fault if what is applauded by one age is sometimes

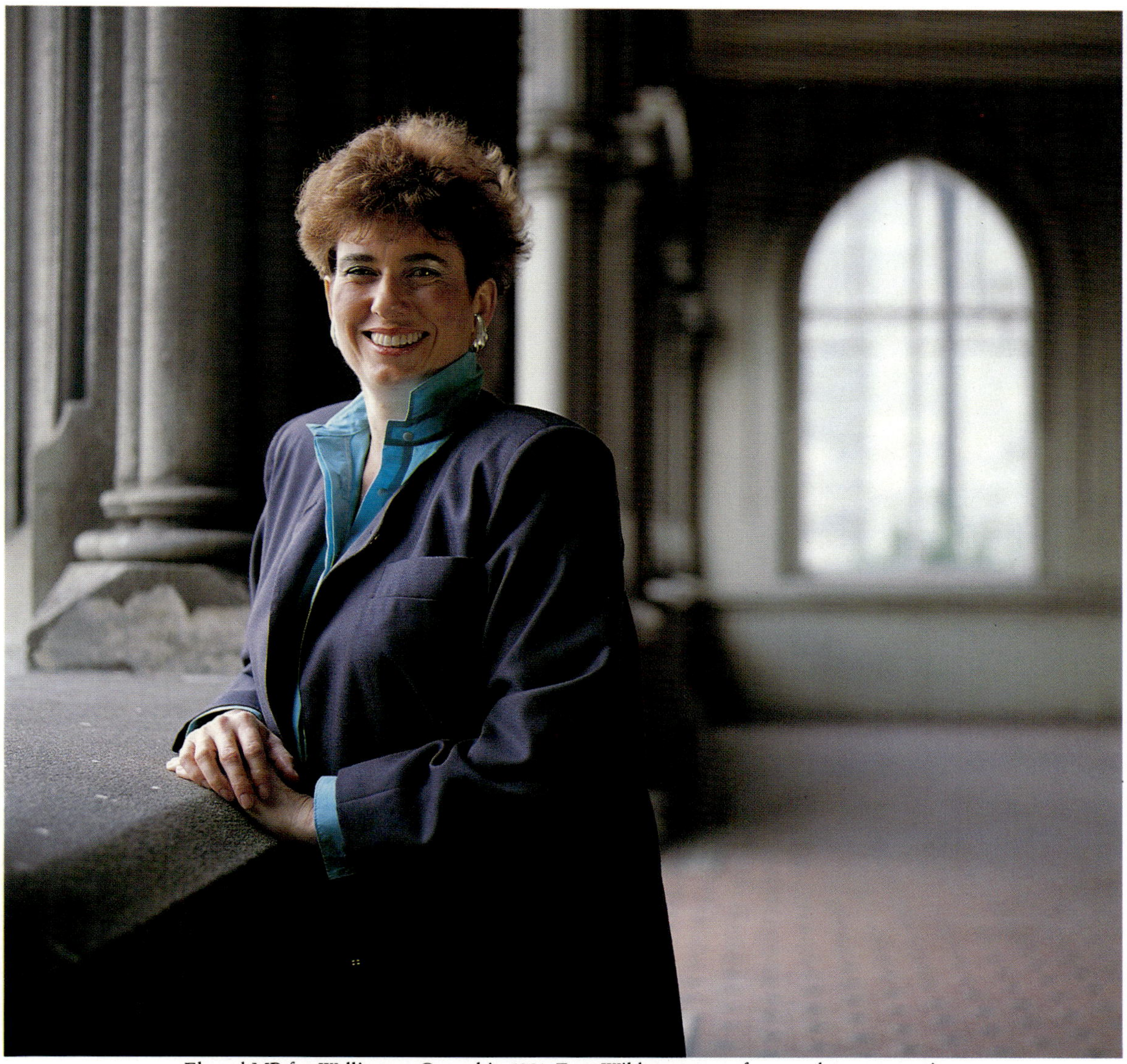

Elected MP for Wellington Central in 1981, Fran Wilde was one of a record ten women in the fourth Labour Government. Appointed Junior Whip, she was the first woman to hold this position. As a private member Wilde introduced the controversial Homosexual Law Reform Bill which become law in 1986.

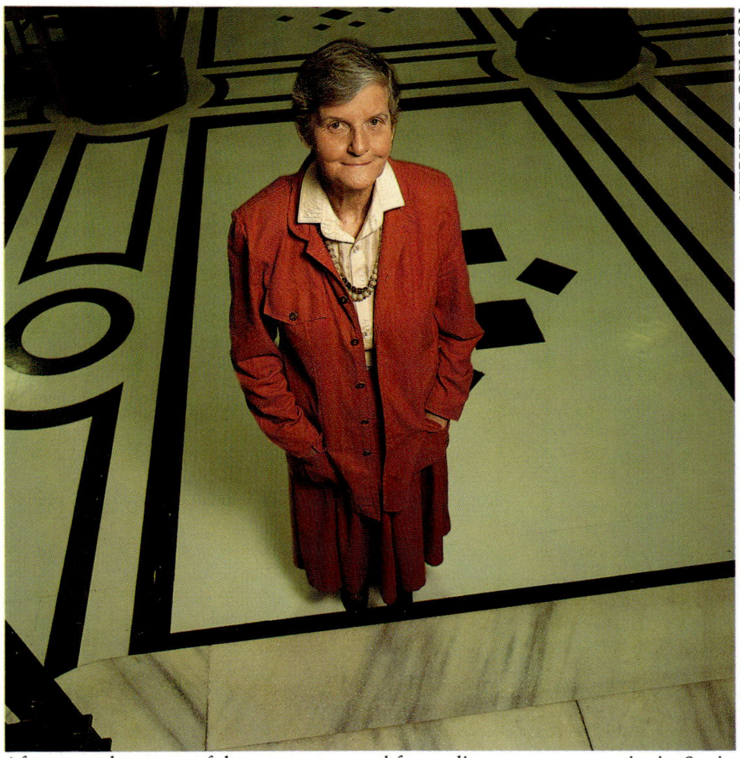

After several unsuccessful attempts to stand for parliament, veteran unionist Sonja Davies was elected to represent Pencarrow in 1987. Davies has a long history of supporting women's and workers' rights. She founded the New Zealand Child Care Association in the 1960s and was a driving force in the adoption of the Working Women's Charter by the Federation of Labour of which she was first woman vice-president.

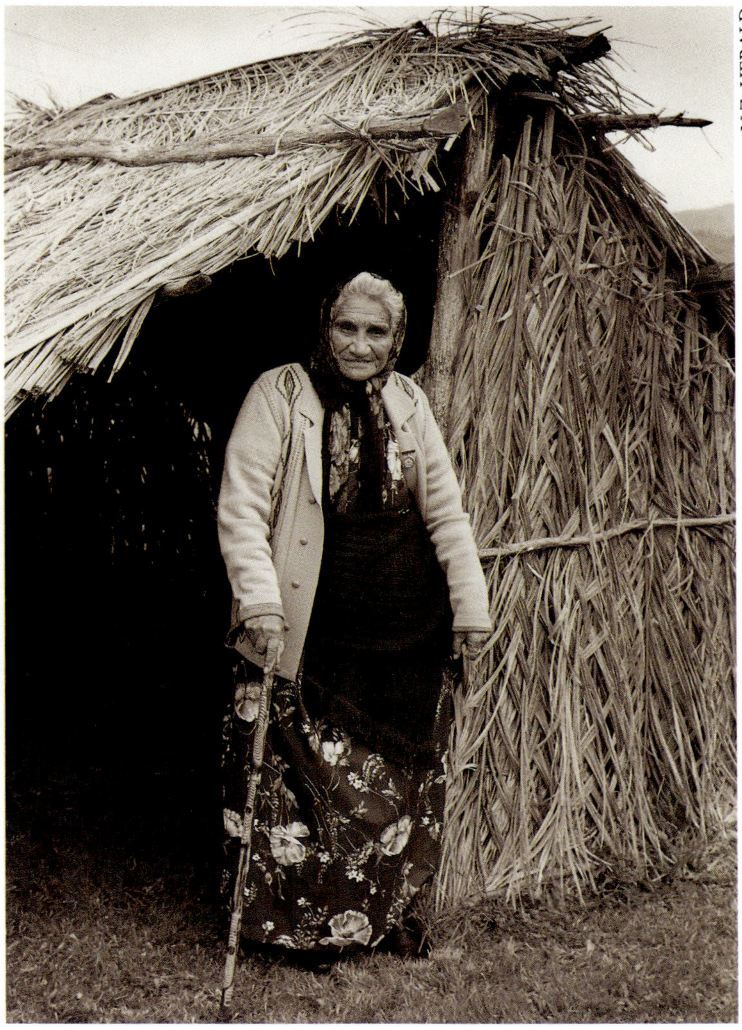

The leader of Te Roopu Ote Matakite land march, Dame Whina Cooper was the most visible Maori leader of the 1970s. This role followed earlier work as founding president of the Maori Women's Welfare League.

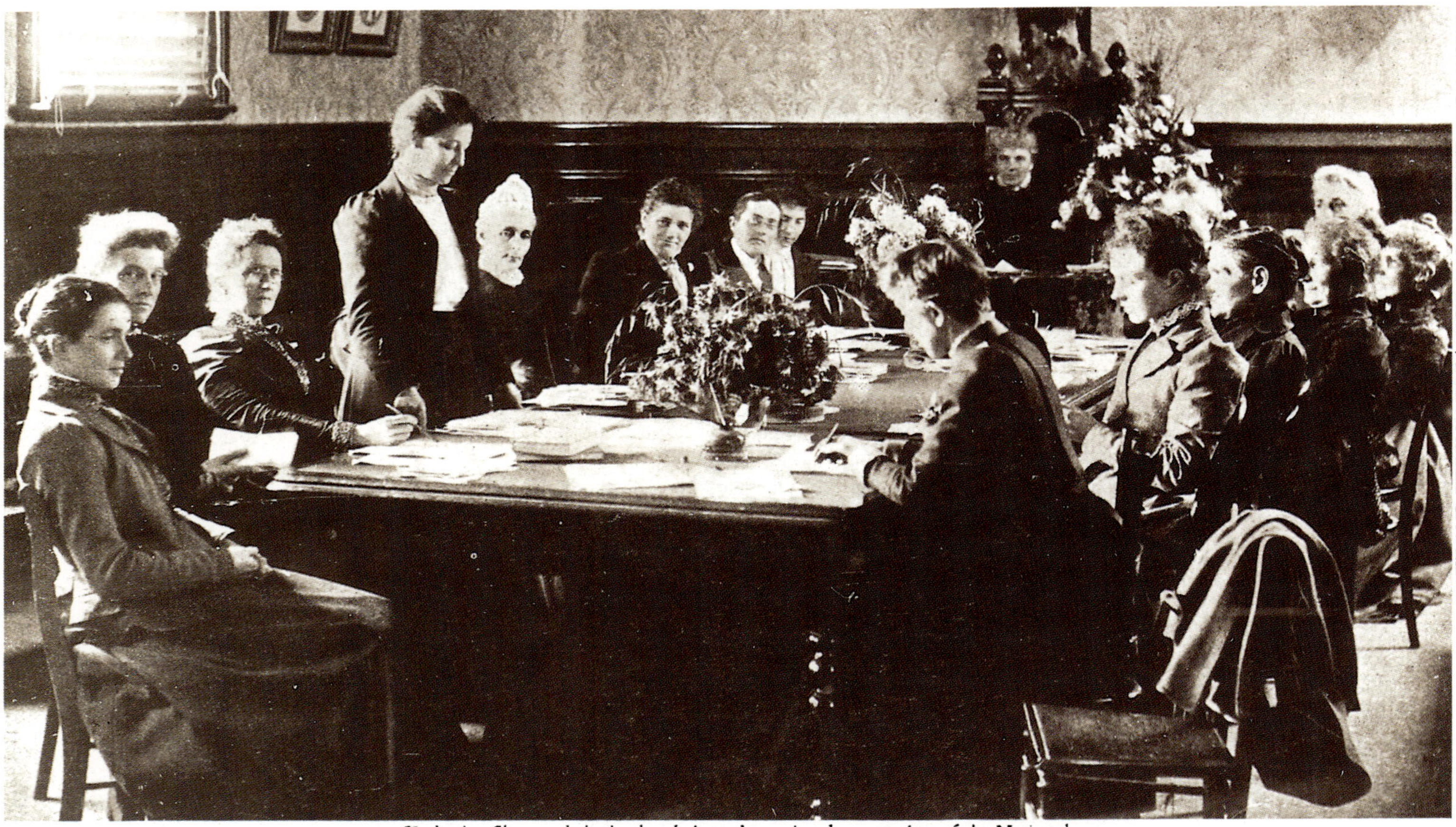

AUCKLAND WEEKLY NEWS/AUCKLAND INSTITUTE AND MUSEUM

Katherine Sheppard sits in the chair at the national convention of the National Council of Women at Wanganui in 1901. She continued her advocacy of women's rights into old age.

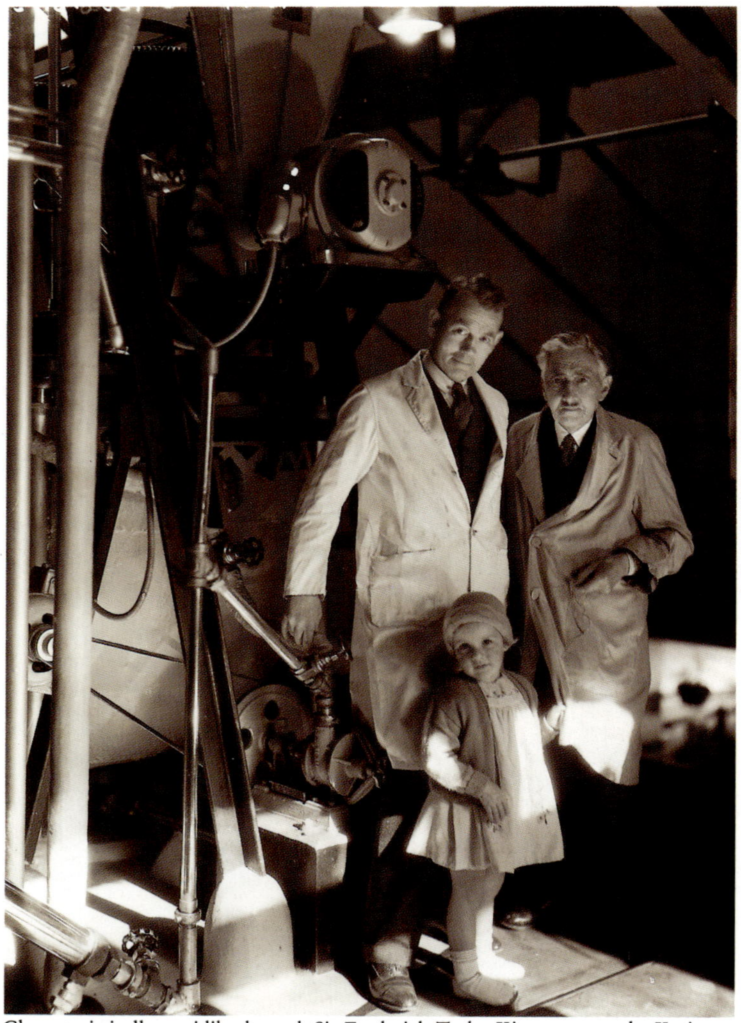

S. P. ANDREW COLLECTION/ALEXANDER TURNBULL LIBRARY

Characteristically untidily dressed, Sir Frederick Truby King poses at the Karitane Products Society, the company he established to manufacture the perfect breast milk substitutes. King's infant-feeding regimes, though rigid and authoritarian, resulted in significant reductions in infant mortality.

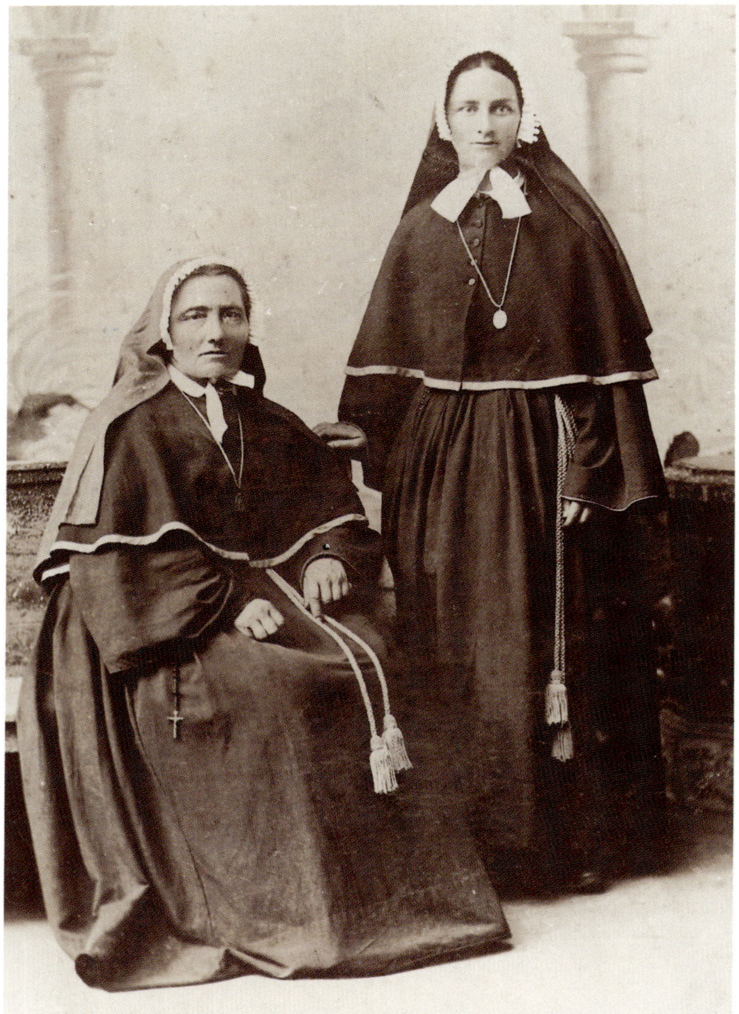

HOME OF COMPASSION

Mother Mary Aubert (left) used her nursing skills with the sick and abandoned at Jerusalem on the Wanganui River and at the Home of Compassion, Island Bay, Wellington, established in 1908. This photo, taken in 1889, also shows Sister Magdalene Savage.

condemned by the next. Like Marsden's, Truby King's reputation is collapsible.

Katherine Sheppard, the nineteenth-century suffragette from Christchurch, is not collapsible. She was not sensational – she didn't chain herself to a lamp-post like her militant counterparts in England. But Kate Sheppard dared a great deal. She fought Seddon, as well as the liquor lobby. In a sense she fought the Almighty. It was a time, you remember, when women's franchise was considered by men not just contrary to the constitution of nature, but "contrary to the ordinances of God". She never gave up. From 1888 on, she petitioned and petitioned and petitioned, and yes, well – the vote when it did eventually come may have been something of a fluke, supported as it was by prohibitionist MPs on the mistaken assumption that female voters would inevitably opt for teetotalism and help kill the liquor trade. Nevertheless Kate Sheppard's bill was passed into law. In 1893 when the franchise was finally adopted, New Zealand became the first country in the world to give women the right to vote. We are proud of it – and of her.

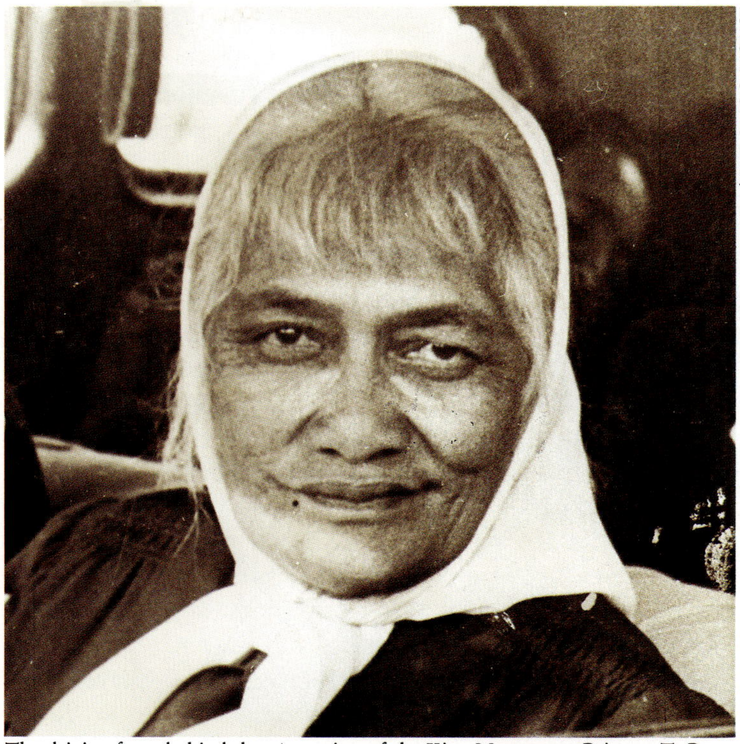
MOANA MANLEY/TURONGO HOUSE

The driving force behind the reassertion of the King Movement, Princess Te Puea Herangi directed the building of Turangawaewae Marae at Ngaruawahia as a place for the Waikato people to stand.

ALL COUNTRIES NEED HEROES. Young countries need them desperately. We had no truly national hero before Jack Lovelock.

Lovelock was the West Coast medical student who won the 1500 metres at Berlin 1936: our first ever athlete to capture an Olympic gold medal. The emotion generated by Lovelock's victory, fanned by wireless and newspaper commentary, gripped Kiwis in every walk of life. Ten years later, in 1946, when the Leni Riefenstahl film *Olympia 1936* was shown here for the first time, the response was just as immediate. As the race began, audiences packed with schoolchildren sat transfixed; then at the climax, as a thin strip of black was seen to surge and jump the field, erupted in tears and acclamation. For that moment sealed more than the winning of a medal. For me, as for so many of my generation, it was "the moment when I first realised I was a New Zealander".

We create heroes and heroines not just in our own image but because they fulfil a need – they are necessary to us. Ten years ago women activists like Sonja Davies were seen merely as stirrers. But the climate has changed. Because of their personal and political courage, they are being propelled already, so it seems, into a more durable role: inheritors of Kate Sheppard's mantle.

One woman whose durability is unchallenged is the already-mentioned Princess Te Puea of Tainui. Before Te Puea, few people, Maori included, took the idea of Maori culture seriously. By force of personality Te Puea rebuilt the Maori King movement and made Turangawaewae a household name, and it was her achievement both to give to Maori values a lustre and, simultaneously, lift them from a tribal province into a national arena. She was the first to do this, the first Maori leader to transcend tribal boundaries in a cause.

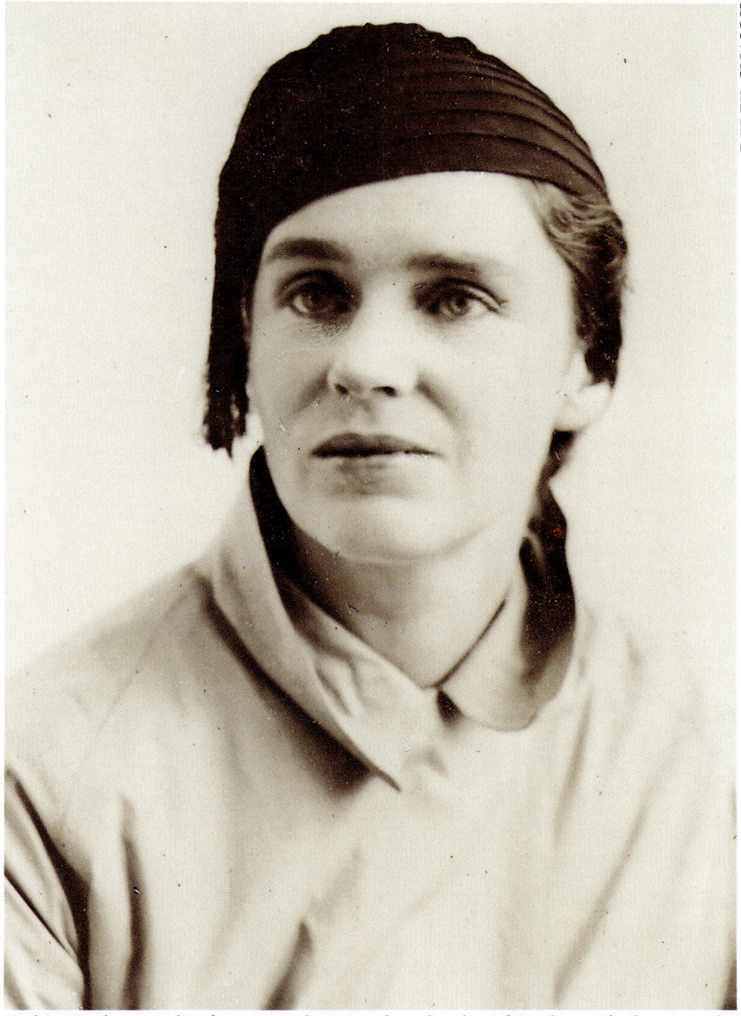
DEREK CHALLIS

Robin Hyde gave this favourite photograph to her best friend. A gifted poet and novelist, she was also a brave and forthright journalist, espousing Maori land causes when they were not popular, and travelling to the front line as a war correspondent in China.

Te Puea died in 1952 but her stature – as visionary, as conservationist – has been recognised only lately. It is her early campaign for compensation for land unjustly confiscated that anticipates the 1975 land march and today's Waitangi tribunals. Te Puea's strange turbulent story has a biblical intensity and within the scope of this essay, as a failed heroine who made good, she occupies an unusual place. During the 1914–18 war, the young Te Puea was an outcast, persecuted by the establishment for opposing conscription and leading her Waikato people

PRINCESS TE PUEA HAD a framework, almost a nationalist movement, to support her. Robin Hyde (1906–39) had no such framework, nor even a cause beyond a feeling for the underdog and a heroic resolve to write books. What is one to make of this doomed figure?

Robin Hyde has always been a cult heroine. Now in the wake of belated homage to her writing and her person she is seen as something more, something emblematic.

Robin Hyde (real name Iris Wilkinson) is the quixotic journalist who went to China and ended her life in London in a fit of depression, a matter of twenty-four hours before the arrival of a long-awaited letter that might have saved her. Discriminated against as a journalist in New Zealand, roughly handled by Japanese soldiers in China, anguished and ill, she is the pioneer independent writer who sets out on a hopeless quest to produce books and dies, expending her vital forces in the process.

She is a little extravagant for popular myth, perhaps. But she is, in the words of Prof. John Roberts, "our one example of a Scott Fitzgerald sort of character. Robin Hyde represents our Lost Generation."

Oddly enough she wrote about heroes – she is our first chronicler of heroes and still one of the few writers to have tackled the theme. Robin Hyde wrote our first important war book.

In *Passport to Hell* (1936) she wrote about a man who could both shoot a surrendering prisoner and carry a wounded digger across no-man's land "as gently as a kitten". This is "Starkie". James Stark, hero of this fictionalised biography, was a private – 5th Reinforcement, Otago Infantry Battalion, NZEF. He served on Gallipoli and in France. There is a marvellous line in the book when Starkie, drummed up for insubordination (as usual), hat off and standing to attention before the orderly officer, is asked, "Do you know what you're charged with?" Starkie replies:

"Charged with being Starkie, sir; and God knows what else."

Starkie is quintessential. A loner and a rebel, contemptuous of danger (he was recommended for the Victoria Cross), he is both the ordinary Kiwi soldier cocking a snook at authority and the man who stands against the brutality of the military machine. For a woman to produce such a book, given the climate of the day, was a kind of courage in itself.

Robin Hyde the doomed heroine and Starkie her creation, a hero despite himself, come down to us as almost inseparable, like Mackenzie and his dog.

AUSTRALIAN LITERATURE IS STUDDED with hero-mythology; by comparison ours is almost a blank. It is the artist who sets the seal, distilling and fixing the legend. For some reason our poets and writers, where they have not sentimentalised the abnormal or heroic type, have with one or two exceptions ignored it.

It was an Englishman, Samuel Butler, who signalled our first authentic folk hero: the outlaw drover James Mackenzie. "His fame," Butler wrote in 1860, five years after Mackenzie's epic drive over the pass he discovered and through the country that bears his name, "will be lasting."

Legend brands Mackenzie, the illiterate nineteenth-century Scots shepherd, a thief. The riddle of his tale – his alleged theft of 1000 sheep, his capture, trial, jail-breaks and sudden disappearance into thin air – remains fascinating. The scale of the myth suggests a wider landscape. Mackenzie has been compared to explorer-models in Australia, to American frontiersmen like Johnny Appleseed and Daniel Boone. For all that he remains, with his famous dog, a peculiarly New Zealand pathfinder.

In the literature Mackenzie is exceptional, the subject of poems, books, novels, folk songs, a major painting series by Trevor Moffitt and endless printed debate. The whole process of hero-worship and myth-making comes together in Mackenzie. In him history, legend and art are fused, though it remains a moot point whether it was the man who begat the legend or the dog.

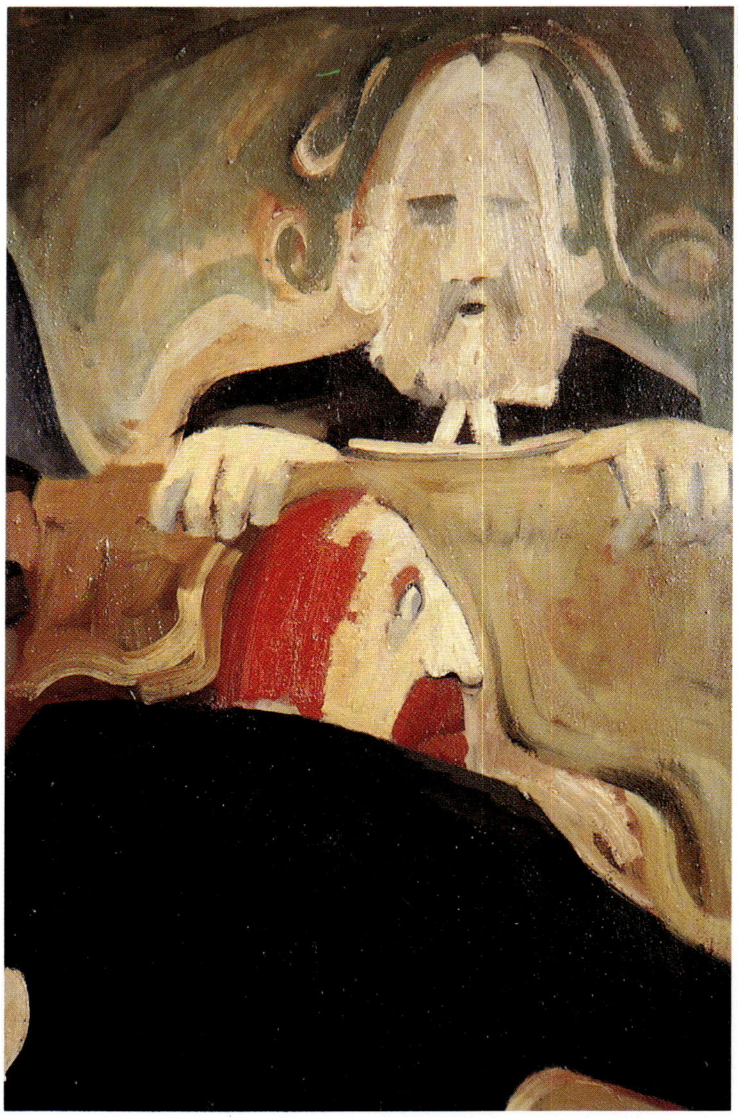
TREVOR MOFFITT

Canterbury painter Trevor Moffitt depicted James Mackenzie with red hair and a somewhat wild aspect in *Mackenzie and the Judge*, one of a series recording the exploits of the outlaw drover.

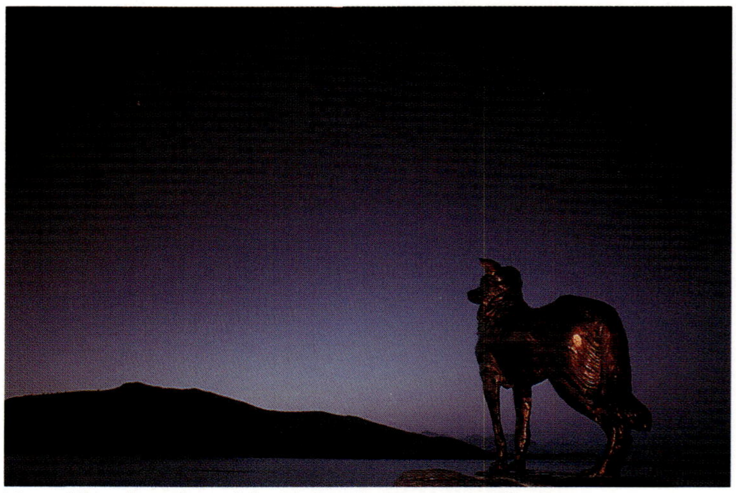
GEOFF MASON

Memorial to sheep dogs of the Mackenzie Country at Tekapo.

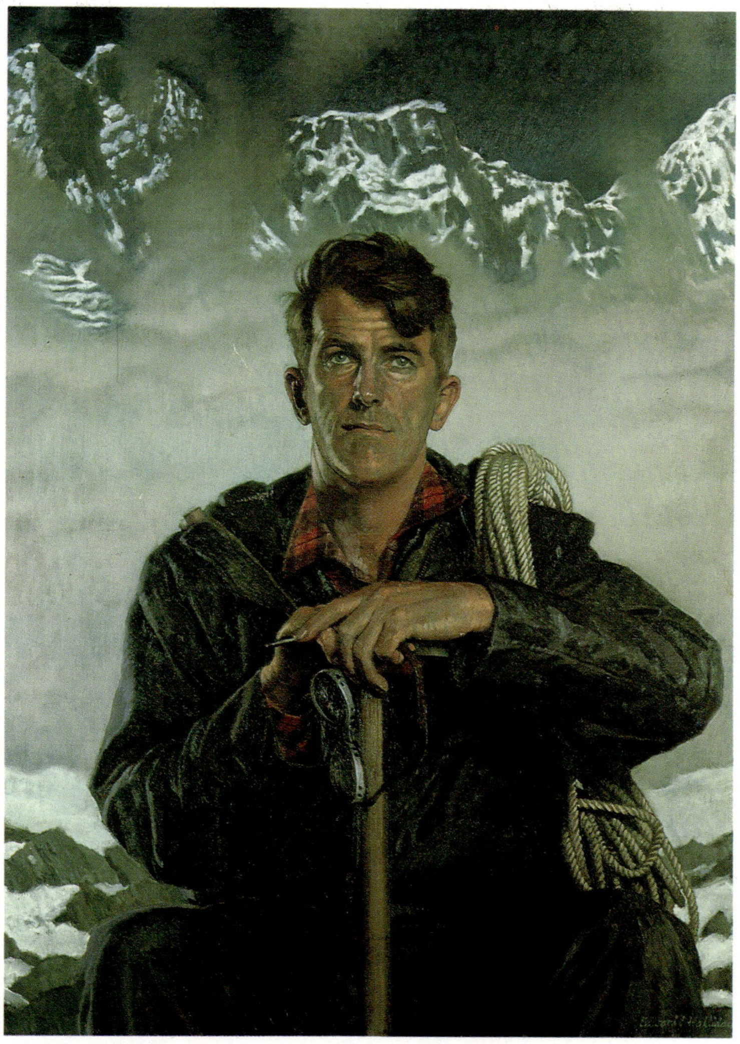

AUCKLAND INSTITUTE AND MUSEUM

Sir Edmund Hillary's ascent of Everest, coinciding with the 1953 coronation of Queen Elizabeth II, was acclaimed as "another jewel in the crown". Edward Halliday painted him in the 1950s.

MACKENZIE'S DOG WAS Hillary's great boyhood hero. Sir Edmund himself is a natural hero. We may think of heroes as abnormal people, larger than life – not Ed. He is not extraordinary. He is almost a stereotype, he even looks the part: lean, vigorous, tanned, tall, with that toothy grin. Perhaps that is why we cheer him so.

To those of us who were in England at the time, Edmund Hillary's conquest of Everest, now almost forty years old, seems like yesterday. Still today, reading and rereading the book – Hillary's description of those last few hundred feet to the top with Tenzing – one gets a lump in the throat. Yet it is not this achievement alone that makes Hillary's fame so durable, nor the later adventures, nor his lectures and books, but Hillary's more humdrum work – his Himalayan aid programmes, founding hospitals and schools for a forgotten people. Having conquered his mountain, having in his immortal phrase "knocked the bastard off", Sir Edmund has given something back to the Nepal people whose mountain it really is. This is the hero – I am quoting John Roberts again – "paying his obligation to heroism itself".

One is tempted to call Hillary the perfect hero. Thank God, he isn't. After his startling dash to the South Pole in 1958, Hillary was accused of glory hunting, of turning a British-led expedition into a race. Hillary said he just couldn't stop himself. We cheered him for that too – no longer a good sport perhaps, a good keen man all the same.

It was Emerson who said that every hero becomes a bore at last. Hillary for one proves Emerson wrong. So too does General the Lord Freyberg, "the salamander of the British Empire".

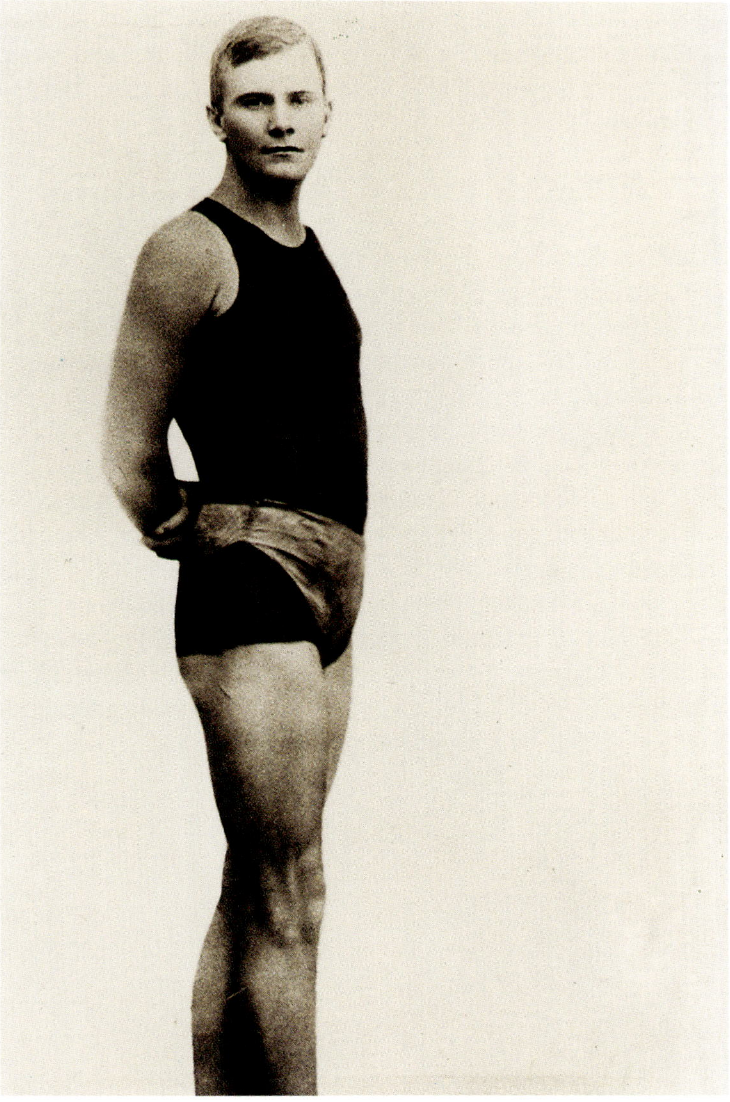

N.Z. HERALD

FREYBERG WAS NOT JUST a good keen man. As a tyro dentist in Levin in 1913, he was already training a cadet corps, simply "bursting" to find some action and win a VC.

There is something swashbuckling, almost Byronic about the early First World War Freyberg – the night swim at Gallipoli carrying decoys, naked and with body blackened; the heroism at Beaucourt where he won his VC; the way he liked to show off his wounds (Churchill counted twenty-seven scars), with "a smile that shrugs off sublime achievement". The legend that comes down to us of the soldier of two wars who Knew No Fear is not exaggerated, but it is not unrivalled either. One thinks of Dick Travis in the First World War, of Upham on Crete in 1941. Of our first Maori VC, the young Ngarimu at Tebaga Gap in 1943. Their bravery and contempt for danger were, like Freyberg's, so astonishing as to seem inhuman.

We honour "Tiny" Freyberg for something quite else, something we can still relate to – because he was a manager of men. Before the fiasco of Crete we, the New Zealand Division, were little more than a group of armed citizens in uniform; after Crete, when Freyberg reformed the division in the North African desert, we became an army. Before Crete, Freyberg committed Kiwi "detachments"; after it, he committed "New Zealand". The glow of family pride felt by "Tiny's" troops in the desert was matched by a surge of nationhood experienced back

A New Zealand freestyle swimming champion, Bernard Freyberg undertook an epic swim at Gallipoli on a mission to confuse the Turks. Coated with lampblack and grease and towing flares in a bag, Freyberg swam ashore at Bulair, north of Anzac Cove, to stage a mock landing.

home. This was new. It was largely one man's doing. As the war progressed, Freyberg's preoccupation became more and more the care and welfare of his men. Every time Freyberg made himself unpopular with his more senior allied commanders, refusing to bow to requests to commit wastefully or to fragment the division, he further strengthened the sense of national identity.

WAR HEROES MAKE strange bedfellows – Freyberg, Upham ... Archibald Baxter too. They have little in common, except they were men for their time, proof, if proof were needed, that it is time and place that make the hero. Not the other way about.

Charles Upham, born in 1908 and the only fighting man to win the Victoria Cross twice, is complex. His sustained feats of arms, first on Crete and then at Ruweisat Ridge in the Western Desert before he was captured, made him one of the more celebrated figures of the last war. Upham is both hero and anti-hero, the one who finds his niche in battle and then withdraws, unwilling or unable to talk about it. "Poor Charlie," his mother is reported as saying when news came in 1945 that he had been awarded a Bar to add to the VC won on Crete, "he's so shy. He'll probably take to the bush for a while." As indeed Upham did, retiring to a farm in the South Island and refusing all offers of gifts and further honours.

Archibald Baxter, another South Island farmer, received no decorations for his heroism in the First World War. For being a conscientious objector he was placed on board a transport for Europe, stripped naked before the troops and forcibly dressed in uniform; in Belgium, for refusing to kill, he was subjected to field punishment – "hung", as his poet-son reminds us, "from a torture post at Mud Farm" – and then exposed at the front, alone and unprotected, to bombardment by enemy shells. He suffered almost to the point of death. His autobiography, *We Will Not Cease*, a quite unbitter book, has become a classic with today's generation of New Zealanders.

Inevitably, since the father gave so much to the son, James, chiefly the courage to take a stand against popular opinion, we are bound to consider that wild literary genius too. James K. Baxter's death in 1972, the prophecy and manner of his dying at 46, touched thousands, Maori as well as Pakeha.

We shall always remember what this poet said and wrote; and if some now question his "sainthood" as phoney it is largely because, as a self-styled hero, James K. Baxter questioned it himself. Certainly the role he played at the end, as a bearded guru ministering to the dropouts and the deprived, was heroic.

Archibald Baxter remains the more authentic figure, standing, in the words of the son, "for the country pride and gentleness". He is the closest we have to a martyr.

What is left?

What is left are a man and a woman, a sportsman and a fanatic. Invincible in their way.

The man is George Nepia (1909–86), the young spoon-faced Maori who was the only fullback selected for the 1924 All Black team on its thirty-match tour of Britain and France. Nepia's skill and courage on that unbeaten tour made him a hero to the rugby world. We were not ashamed to use words like glory then. Rugby was our gospel; we led the world; and if it is true, until the image was spoiled in 1981, that most young New Zealanders identified with the All Blacks as an ideal of glory and manhood, then George Nepia is the personification of that ideal.

Even New Zealand women – we may be about to forget – succumbed to that ideal. One, who was born in 1940, says: "I was brought up like that. All my heroes were male, and it was considered *glorious* to be an All Black." Why? – "We had so few heroines. There was nothing else to put in their place."

Television in a series of biographies about outstanding New Zealand women has recently helped fill this gap. Two of these women, Kate Sheppard and Te Puea, have already been mentioned. One, who has not, was a speed typist with light wavy hair and startling blue eyes, Ettie Rout.

In the First World War she organised a task force of Volunteer Sisters and sailed to the Middle East where she became notorious – first in Cairo, later in England and in France – for a crusade to eliminate sexually transmitted diseases among Anzac troops.

In the House of Lords a bishop called her the most wicked woman in Britain. In New Zealand, where newspapers were forbidden by the Cabinet to publish her findings, the Prime Minister, Massey, said if he could he would order the public hangman to burn her writings. But H. G. Wells called her "an unforgettable heroine", the French gave her a medal and Ettie Rout seems, for a fanatic, to have been remarkably sane.

Outrage appears to have driven her. She discovered that the incidence of venereal disease among Australian and New Zealand troops in Egypt was six times greater than among their British counterparts, but this figure was so embarrassing it had to be buried in the Imperial statistics. Determined to protect Kiwis at risk, Miss Rout set up canteens and hostels and designed her own portable prophylactic kit; then, to ensure that every man going on leave had one, began to issue it herself, going among the diggers in camps and billets and intercepting them on railway platforms.

ETTIE ROUT (1877–36) WORKED a sixteen-hour day and did not, like Florence Nightingale, take to her bed. She returned to New Zealand only once, died unnoticed in Rarotonga and exemplifies – what? Perhaps that the stuff of which heroines are made is less absurd than the competence and attitude of those in authority who seek to oppose them.

Doubtless Ettie Rout and one or two others appearing in this chapter will seem eccentric choices, obscuring "worthier" claimants who have been omitted – the missionary Volkner, the explorer Brunner, the epic Te Rauparaha, the mythical heroes Maui and Kupe. They are omitted because either they seem too remote or else too narrow, too solemn, despite the cruel difficulties they faced. They belong more properly to a longer treatment, to a thesis or a book. Heroes ought to engage our affections, or at least tell us something about ourselves. □

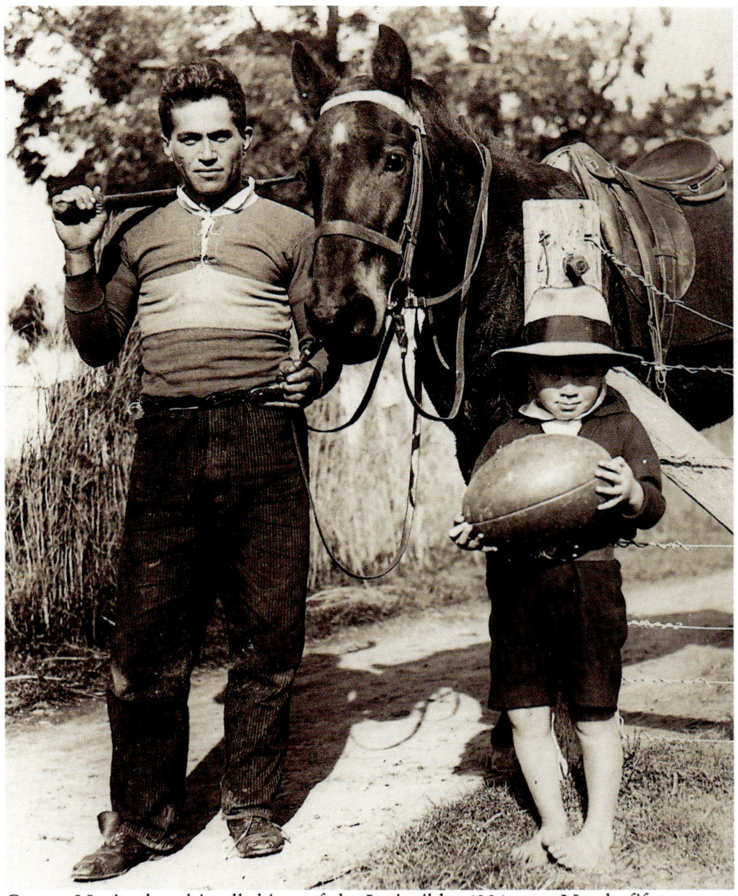

ALEXANDER TURNBULL LIBRARY

George Nepia played in all thirty of the Invincibles 1924 tour. Nearly fifty years later, Nepia received a standing ovation from a packed rugby stadium in Wales when he returned to the scene of his triumph. He is shown here at his farm in Rangitukia with his son.

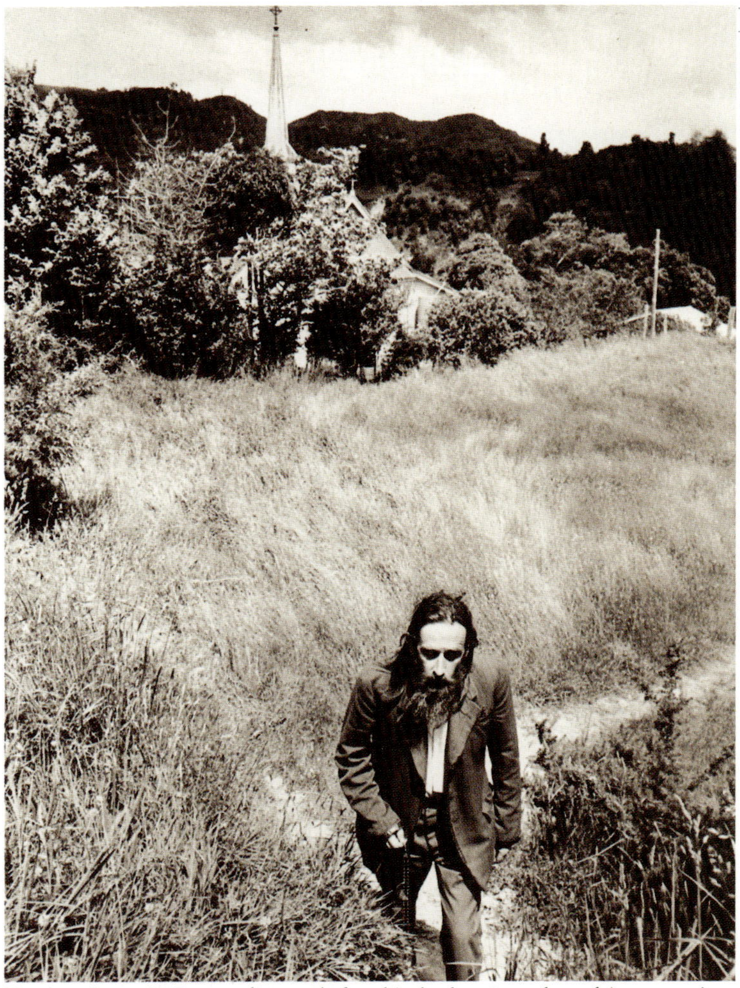

N.Z. HERALD

Hemi, or James K. Baxter, the year before his death at Jerusalem, the community for drug addicts and down-and-outs he founded on the Wanganui River.

Ettie Rout (centre) with the first contingent of the Volunteer Sisters about to leave for Egypt in October 1915.

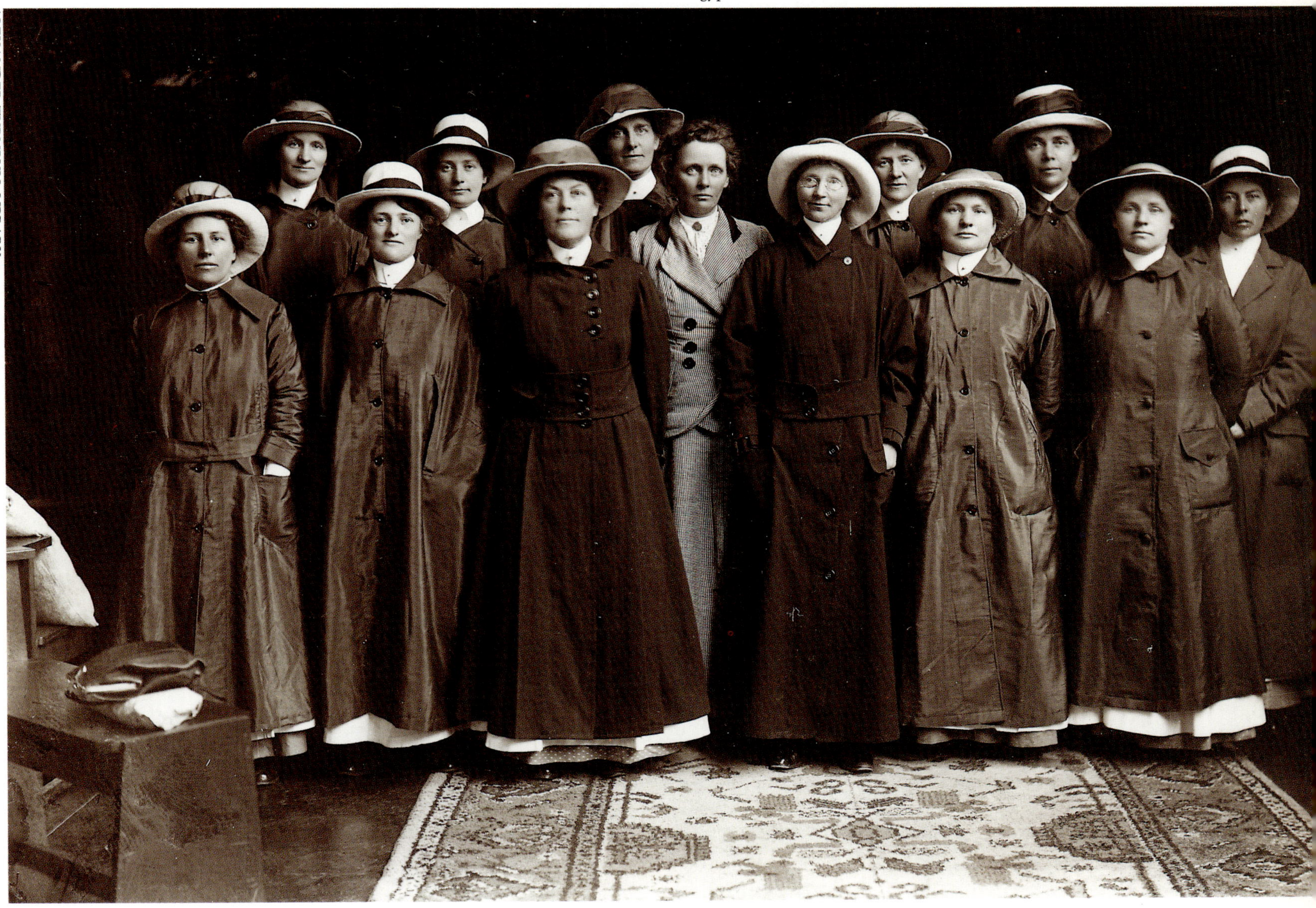

ALEXANDER TURNBULL LIBRARY

A BALLAD OF COUNTRY LIFE

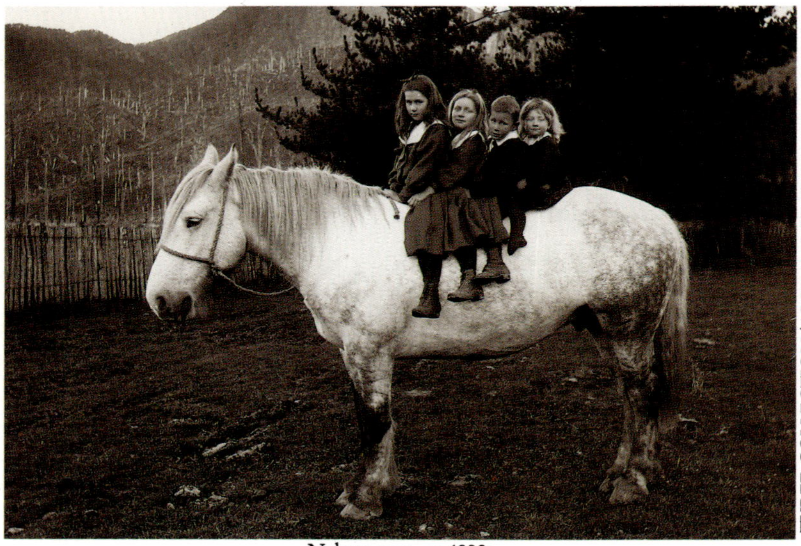

TYREE COLLECTION/ALEXANDER TURNBULL LIBRARY.

Nelson area, ca 1890s.

Gordon McLauchlan

"EVERYONE LIVED IN the country then. The towns were country towns and the cities . . . well, there were none really in the urban, metropolitan sense of the word. All the suburbs were country towns and the cities were just collections of suburbs with a bigger shopping centre in the middle."

I knew my auntie was going to break out a story. She was much more at home ransacking the imagination than ruminating on the historical or sociological meaning of the old days. And, yes, she did.

"Something ominous hangs in the New Zealand air when there is no wind, because the wind is almost always with us.

"This particular time, the April rain keeps on coming for the second day, not whirling and whipping around your head the way it does in the spring and summer, but with direct, unrelenting persistence. The strain is from not knowing when it will stop. The sky hangs low with light seeping in only at the edges, drawing a line around the tops of the western hills as the afternoon wears on. The willow trees along the creek are bedraggled with no wind to shake their heads.

"The rain is still falling in the same way the next morning as though the seamless layer of cloud has an inexhaustible supply. The word around town is the rain has been falling just as steadily up in the ranges which puts the whole valley in danger.

"The telephone is out so I get dressed up for the rain and go to look at the bridge. It is something to do to make the waiting endurable. The trouble usually starts at the bridge with branches from upstream catching in the piles, damming up the creek and sending it over the banks and round the edges on to the road. Or the weight of the water will take the bridge with it.

"I get my four-year-old dressed as well, ready in case we have to leave, but tell her to stay in the kitchen. Then, just as I walk out the gate, your Uncle George arrives on his bike, soaking wet and cold. He tells me to pack warm clothes and some blankets for all the kids, and some food. We will have to leave the house because the river is spilling over the stopbank at Oapere Bridge, five miles upstream. We have to walk up the hill to the school.

"Our oldest, Ronnie, arrives on his bike just as George is leaving to get our neighbours together: the McPhersons, the Wilsons and the Hudsons.

"We start up the hill to the school. Joan Wilson is wearing her best coat and hat with a piece of canvas draped over her like a hood and cloak. It is a wonder she doesn't have her high heels on.

"Marie Hudson and I have not talked for a year because the school nurse found nits on Colin Hudson's head and next time the nurse came my Irene and other kids had them too and had to have their heads shaved. Her kids are slovenly and dirty and so is she, and in my anger at Irene losing her beautiful yellow hair I told her that. So we are awkward for a while but gradually the

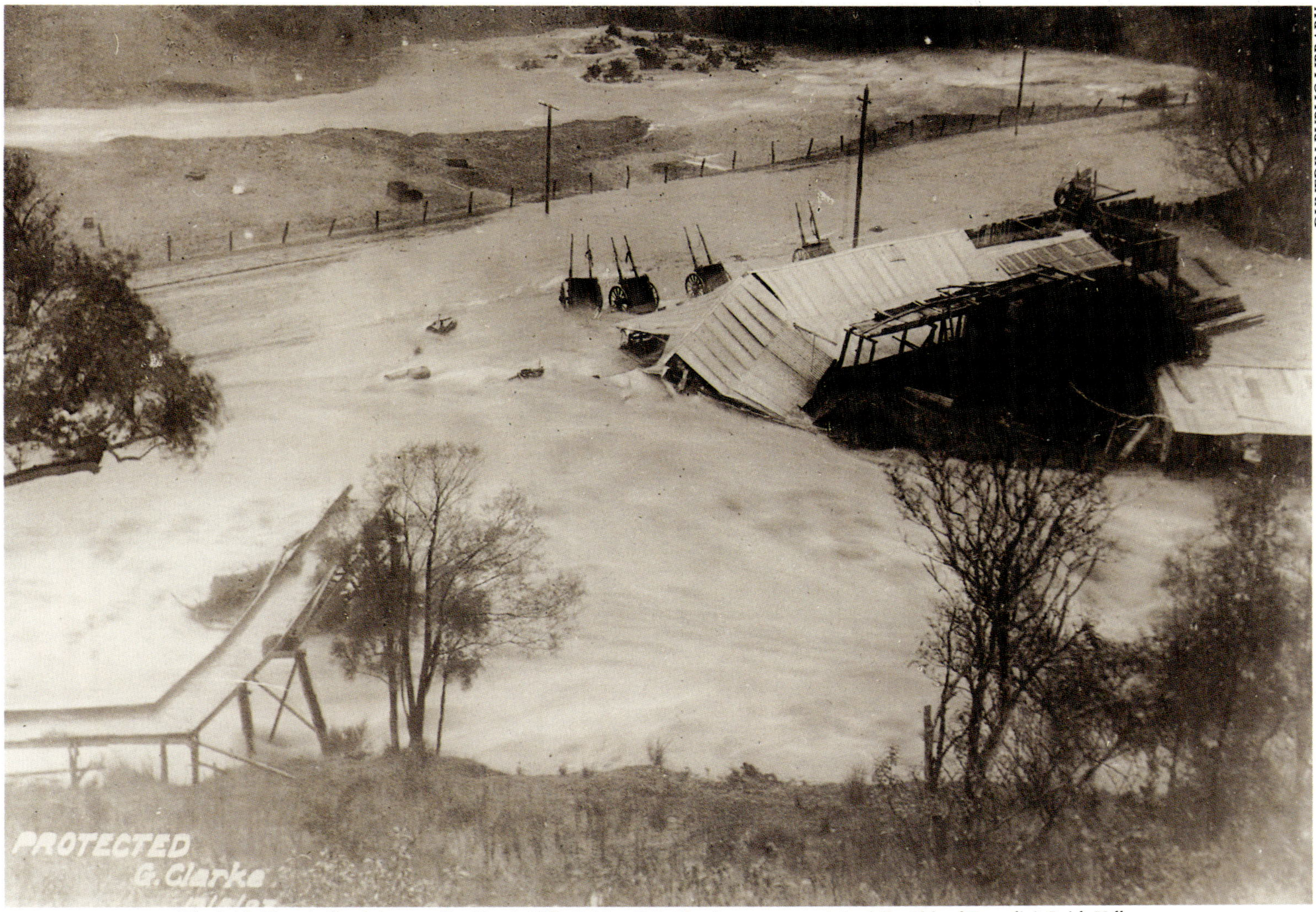

DUNEDIN PUBLIC LIBRARY

The Leith River in flood destroys Davidson's Mill, 13 May 1923. Floodwaters covered the full width of Dunedin's Leith Valley.

awkwardness goes away as we all slog up the hill. No matter what you say about Marie, she is always cheerful in a nervy way and that shrieking laugh of hers is a distraction.

"It is good to be together. Not that we feel at risk ourselves but there is the lurking anxiety that our house will be flooded. It makes such a mess and the vegetables and fowls will all be lost; and deep in the pit of your stomach you know how dangerous the flood is when the men have got their boots and their heaviest, warmest clothes on. Drowning is the New Zealand death.

"George and some of the others are building up the stopbank on each side of the bridge where the water would break through into the main part of town, packing sugarbags with river silt. The shopkeepers are in their shops lifting stock off the floor and the low shelves, stacking it on the counters.

"We've lost the power as well as the phone at the school but we've got the big fire going in the teachers' room, with two camp ovens and plenty of food to cook.

"Food is women's work so that is what we do. Whenever there is a crisis and we can't do anything directly to help, we cook and we eat and we force it on the men. It is something to do.

"The men come back when it gets too dark to work, except George, Dan Brown and Colin Harris who keep alert near the bridge. They will sound the fire brigade siren if the bank looks like giving. Ronnie and his mate, Lenny, take some sandwiches and scones and a thermos of tea down for them. Another three men will take over at midnight.

"The rain on the roof drones on and there's no break in the clouds as we settle the kids down for the night.

"I get angry about Ronnie because I'm worried. They haven't come back although I know they are probably waiting for midnight to come back with George. The rain stops at 11 o'clock and we all feel a lot better. God, I hope the weather breaks up.

"About half-past eleven, a wind has begun stirring and we are feeling more relaxed, when Dan Brown bursts in. He's been crying, I can tell by his eyes, and he comes straight to me and pulls me into the teachers' room, shuts the door and tells me that the bank broke just above the bridge, not badly, but he backed his cart up with bags and rocks in it and ran over Colin Hudson in the dark. He actually stopped the cart on Colin's back and didn't notice what had happened until he got down and found the body half-submerged in the mud.

"George and Bert Harris were taking poor Colin's body to Dr Watson's place a bit further down the hill from the school. I had to tell Marie. Me of all people. I thought she'd scream and yell, but she just sobbed and kept trying to pull her jersey over her head. She kept sobbing and pulling things over her head for days.

"That was in 1929. The creek quickly rummaged through our shed and through the McPherson's house before it ran back into its bed about a hundred yards below the breach. The fowls were all right but we had to pull the cabbages and caulis a bit before their time and gave most of them away."

MY AUNTIE TOLD ME the story in just that rambling sort of way with comments running in and out of cul-de-sacs off the main highway of the narrative, conveying, as they always do, as much about the talker as the tale.

Her knitting needles clicked away as she sat in a large chair. Her hands moved with the most marvellous confidence and dexterity at knitting, or tapestry, or just plain sewing; in contrast to the rest of her body which seemed anchored inside a shapeless bulk that made getting into or particularly out of her chair a breathless struggle.

She was our most enthusiastic teller of family stories when I was a kid, because she had the time I guess, and because she did not patronise me the way some of my uncles did by dutifully, virtuously, *telling young Gordon a story*. Hers were complete, like novels, rolling across stretches of time over old landscapes. My father and mother also enjoyed talking about things that had happened to them, their parents and grandparents, but their approach was more anecdotal, more I-remember-the-time-when-my-mother . . . but whatever the style, they were letting the past seep through into the present. That way it became my past as well as theirs. By the time I had heard one of Auntie's sagas or Dad's or Mum's anecdotes three or four times the tone was more detached, less personal. They became more like family lore.

What was common to all the stories was that people dealt with their own concerns head-on, because there was no way around them. They were not burdened by vicarious worries of abstract people in other places. Rape was what happened to Clara Johnstone when she was only thirteen and it was a personal problem that everyone had to attend to. Some people were disgusting about it, Auntie claimed, by almost blaming the poor kid because she was a cheeky brat. A lot of people were angry and nasty about it because it worried them until they caught the man and they could focus on him and sympathise with Clara. But the Johnstones left for Auckland a few months after the trial.

Enmity was personal in all these stories and sometimes deep and unforgiving, with not-speaking feuds that lasted for years. You didn't hate in limbo, conceptually, on principle, intellectually, things you only knew about second-hand from radio and television. You hated locally and people who attracted it left town like the Johnstones.

I MENTION THAT STORY of the flood because it has become significant to me. I know now how important 1929 was. It was the year something ended in New Zealand and what replaced it was more than twenty years away. The Depression of the 1930s and the Second World War were a sort of interlude. The year 1929 was the last year this country was a province with a remote, imagined London as its capital. Rural Anglo-New Zealand began to die in the trauma of the Great Depression and the war, and when this country arose in the 1950s, it was never so isolated or provincial again.

For more than a hundred years, the only New Zealanders who left to visit the metropolitan northern hemisphere were either uncharacteristically wealthy or went to fight someone else's war. The country developed a rural culture that enveloped the cities and towns. It peaked in the 1920s. While it may have oppressed the imagination and been intolerant of the extraordinary, it was a society in which people really knew each other.

BEFORE 1929 ORDINARY PEOPLE were left alone for long periods of time. It took parliamentarians days to get to parliament and an upper house and the pace of life ensured that change was slow and gentle. The slower news travels, the more ephemera falls off its edges.

And what is not always understood is that for two or three generations, New Zealanders lived in profound isolation even from one another within their own country. In 1888, Paris-educated Adela Stewart went to Auckland from Athenree, near Katikati in the Bay of Plenty, where she and her husband had settled ten years before. Her health had not been good, so she wanted to see a specialist:

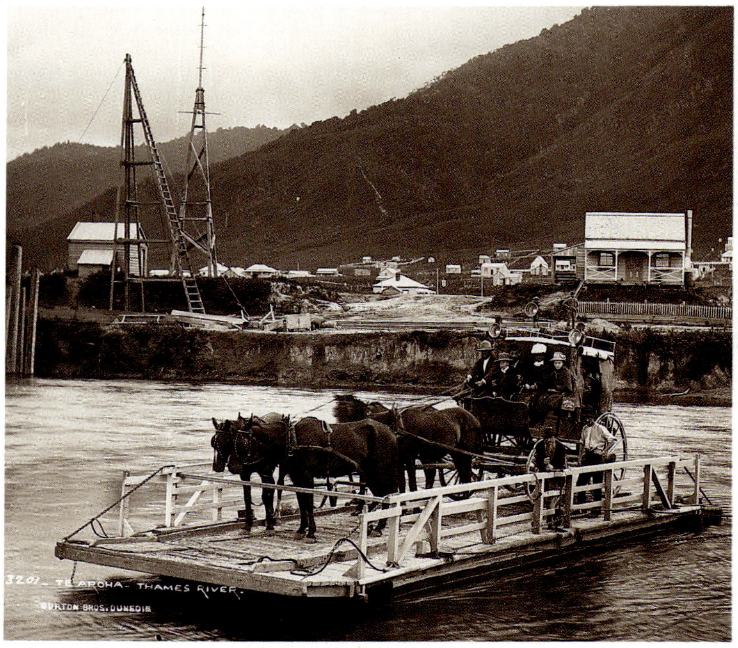

BURTON BROS/NATIONAL MUSEUM

Crossing the Thames River at Te Aroha.

> *We left home by coach and changed horses at Paeroa where there was no time for dinner. We changed again at Hikutaia, got a hurried cup of tea, one shilling each; and through awful swamps and bad roads reached the Thames, forty miles from Athenree, in seven hours. We got into a cab, rushed quarter of a mile to the wharf and saw our boat for Auckland steaming away; it had got tired of waiting for our belated coach from Tauranga. So we turned back and put up at Symington's Hotel.*
>
> *Sunday followed, a very wet day, and the once busy, but now semi-deserted, goldmining town, looked unutterably wretched . . . On Monday we left at 8am in the SS* Rotomahana *and reached Auckland at one.*

WHAT WAS IT LIKE? Those us of who haven't experienced it can never quite know the special despair or delight that went with living in that rural New Zealand culture. Washing clothes on the washboard or boiling them in the copper and wringing them by hand, or trying to dry cotton, linen, and woollen clothes through a long, wet winter. Or cooking, baking, washing, ironing and cleaning an old house for a big family through a succession of long unchanging days. Or steaming dry in front of an open fire or a kitchen stove when you've been excruciatingly cold for hours. Or getting satisfaction from doing ordinary things in a satisfying way, things we now call crafts. Or living closely with neighbours you can't easily flee from even for a few hours, your family's lives inextricably threaded through those of others. Or being truly alone, not lonely in a crowd, but truly alone. Or walking through a paddock in the spring and seeing the scrub coming through the chewed out grass and knowing you are losing and soon may have to load up and move out. Or holding on to a hand that grips like pliers in spasms of pain while you wait in hope the doctor can get there in time.

We can never quite know but we can listen hard to how some people have described it from the earliest days.

The first woman on the Waikaka Run went there in December 1858, and lived in a warrie at what was later the junction of three populous roads, and yet she was there twelve months before she saw another woman.

The same experience befell another woman a dozen years later on an out-of-the-way run in the Hokonui.

Two travellers through Otago Central in 1859 saw only one woman. When she saw them in the distance she tore down on horseback to see if, by any chance, her husband was one of them. He had ridden away to get cattle four months earlier, and she had heard nothing of him ... Next day the two run-seekers met her husband coming with the cattle. Shortly after, he was drowned crossing a river ...

"A Lonely Existence", by Herries Beattie

This was my first experience of illness in the backblocks, and I've never forgotten it. The Kawhia doctor came and said that the patient must go out to Waikato Hospital at once; that meant a long and exhausting journey through the Pekanui by waggon. Mrs Griffiths lay in a mattress in the bottom of the waggon and I rode beside her till they came to the main road, trying to look after her and cheer her ... She was in pain and I hated leaving her. When I rode soberly home, I said to my husband, 'Perhaps I'll never see her again.' He looked stricken at my miserable face and said, 'It's hard on a woman in the backblocks. It might have been you.' Then, very sadly, 'We were rash. This is no place to bring a woman.'

Days That Have Been, by Mary Scott

Work is an anaesthetic to loneliness. Inge has heard that somewhere and found it to be true. With the house clean and cosied up, she set about the backyard. She dug little ditches to drain the water from the puddles that were a permanent feature by the back door. She spread river sand on the slippery path that led to the lavatory some distance from the cottage. Looking like a sentry box but smelling odious, this necessary commodity accommodated a long seat with two round holes, one for adults and a smaller one for children – with a footstool to enable them to mount the throne. Underneath was an enormous cavern dug deep into the ground. Vera just hated going there and 'hung on' as long as she could, dancing and clamping her legs together until nature forced her to enter.

Candles and Canvas; A Danish Family in New Zealand, by Poula Langkilde Christie

In summer the bathwater tasted of the river it had come from, very nice to drink, and the larvae of aquatic insects came out of the tap with it. In winter, icicles hung off the taps in the garden, frost lay white and crunchy underfoot, and the milk in the kitchen meat-safe froze so that you could eat it like ice-cream ..

The great rains of Taranaki – once ... it rained every day for three months – pelted down at us and made a river of the driveway, wherein it was nice to paddle and where, when the water had eventually drained away through an interesting circular iron grating, drowned worms lay pink upon the gravel. On the wet, stormy night, how cosy it was to snuggle into bed and listen to the downpour on the corrugated iron roof. My father would come and play the tin whistle to me – one of his more surprising accomplishments – or with his Scottish songs soothe me to sleep. 'Bonnie laddie, Hielan' laddie' . . while the wild rain pelted down.

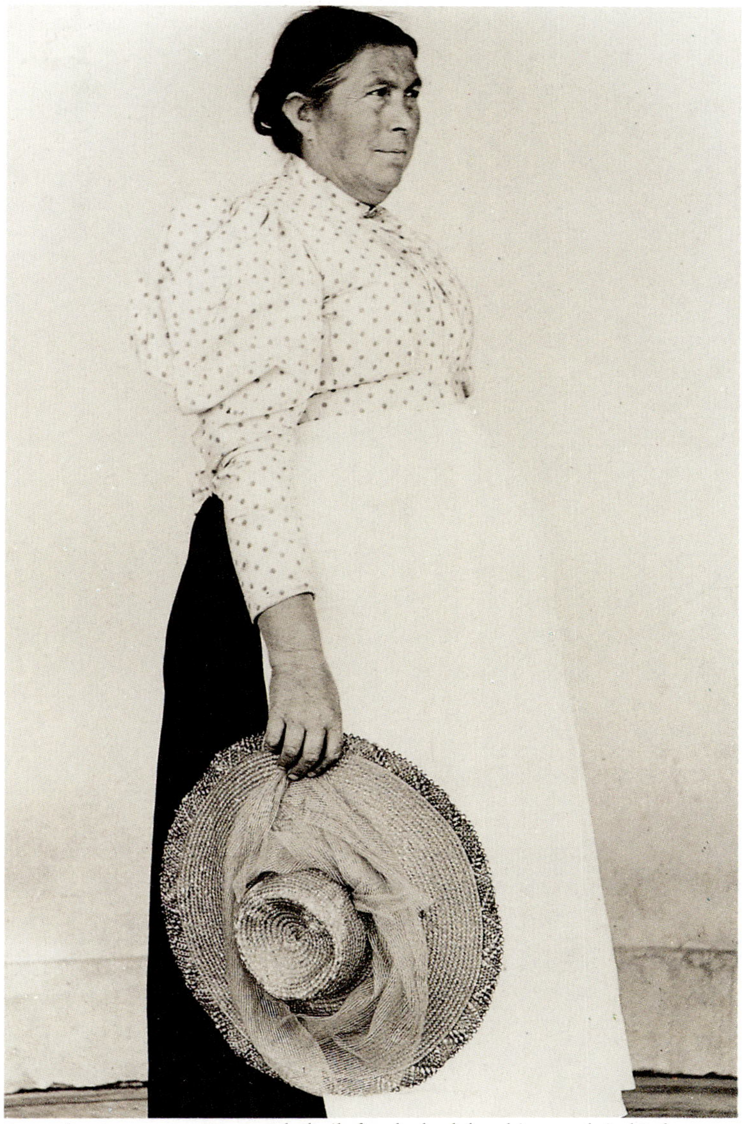

J. J. KINSEY COLLECTION/CANTERBURY MUSEUM

A sturdy pioneer woman, stoutly built for the back-breaking work in kitchen, garden and milking shed which would be her lot.

Springtime in Taranaki, by Douglas Stewart

Some years ago, ill health sent to New Zealand a highly qualified London doctor. For the past fourteen years he has lived and worked in Littledene. He has promoted in the community a positive attitude towards health, and has encouraged the people to make the best use of the many advantages of country life. It is because of his influence that Littledene has an open-air school, with its avenues of trees growing into arbor classrooms for future generations of children. The school was able to introduce a milk ration for underweight children through his influence; his interest in the farming community has popularised the testing of cows suspected of tuberculosis.

In fact, everything of value in this community can be traced, as elsewhere, to the work of one or two individuals. But the undifferentiated country community, which has so many obvious advantages, has a serious drawback; everyone is entitled to express an opinion about everything. The result is that the human tendency to resist everything that threatens one's sense of security in the old order is continually apparent. The voice of the majority is resistant to change ...

It took five years of argument to get electric light, two years of controversy to get consolidation of schools. In every discussion, people who are not even remotely connected with the issues are loudest in their disapproval. At a meeting in the old condemned schoolrooms in the days before consolidation, a wealthy farmer who owns a motorcar and a radio said, 'This schoolroom was good enough for me and it is good enough for my grandchildren.'

Littledene, by H. C. D. Somerset

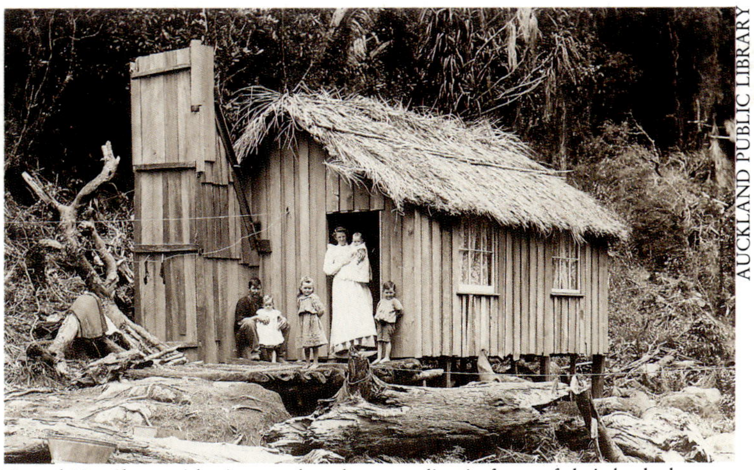
AUCKLAND PUBLIC LIBRARY

Mr and Mrs Short with nieces and nephew standing in front of their bush shanty, Kennedy Bay, Coromandel, ca 1902.

BY THE 1920s, THE NEW ZEALAND landscape had begun to have a lived-in look. The country was settled, with a peasant society, in our summer of contentment, culturally featureless, blissfully bland. If you were able to adjust to that it was an untroubled, bucolic land.

Expatriate author Hector Bolitho came back in 1927 and wrote:

Like all people who lead calm, happy lives, New Zealanders pursue culture and uplift with gauche eagerness. I do not decry second-rate art and writing and the deliberately literary coteries of colonial towns. Great thinkers and writers have too often sneered at surburban taste . . .

The Leonardos and Wagners and Shakespeares and Scotts of this world are few. Directly New Zealand puts aside the plough and takes up the pen with serious artistic aspirations, then will come a sad day for New Zealand. People are better off when they are living first-rate lives and giving their leisure to amateur pursuit of second-rate watercolour painting and inconsiderable, sincere verse-writing, than they are when they give themselves up entirely to artistic production. New Zealand was made to be one vast farm, with healthy, middle-class people working its earth, strong and serious in their grip of life, and self-deceived amateurs in their appreciation of the summits of thought and artistic creation.

Outrageously patronising though Bolitho may have been, he was writing at a time when perhaps no other country in the world could match New Zealand's basic wealth and quiet security, and I think that was what he was trying to explain.

Alas, it was not the same when he came back in 1946. He wrote in a magazine that he had left his home country after another visit with a "mixture of relief and regret".

His relief, he wrote, was "because with all its noble social experiments, the Socialist Government has made the country extremely uncomfortable for the visitor", and his regret was "because New Zealand's good pioneering liveliness was dead forever".

After twenty years of cultural bewilderment and slow transition, New Zealand began to grow into the urban country of today, for better or for worse. The returning immigrant ships in the 1950s took thousands

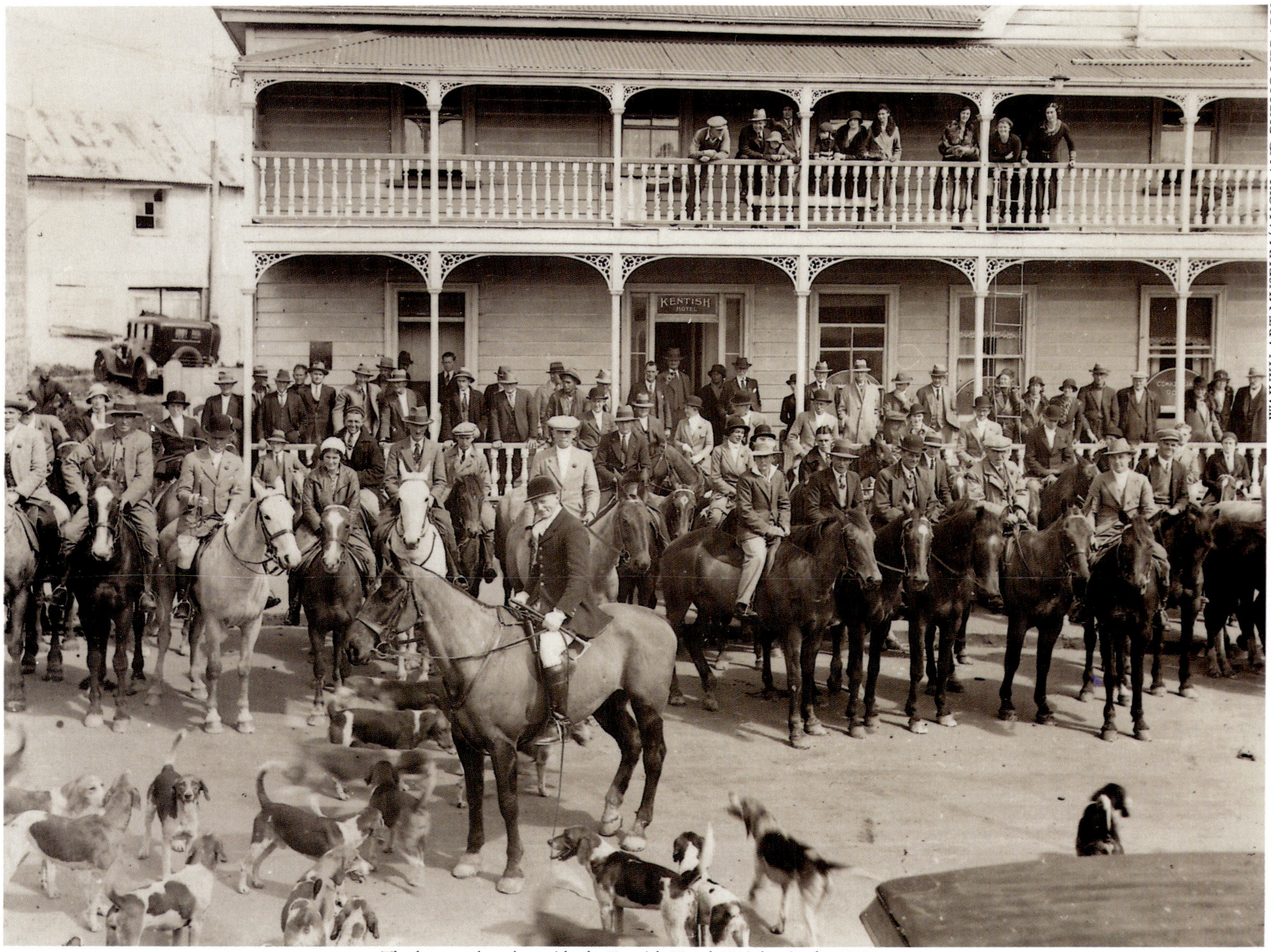

WAIKU ART MUSEUM/AUCKLAND PUBLIC LIBRARY

The hunt gathered outside the Kentish Hotel, Waiuku, in the 1920s.

of young New Zealanders to Britain on working holidays. The first generation of passenger jets arrived here in 1965. A few years later came the cavernous jumbos and they ultimately brought deregulation and low air fares. For twenty-five years now New Zealanders have been slaking a thirst for travel that built up over decades of travellers' tales.

Few people live in the country now, and that includes farmers. The most remote of them from any pocket of the country is closer by many hours to Auckland than Adela Stewart was.

A yearning remains that living in the country is somehow morally and spiritually good for you. For many years the Health Department had its mental homes in the country with plots of land for patients as part of the therapy. Thousands of people go bush for holidays, or want to live near a remote beach. Will that hold on . . . ?

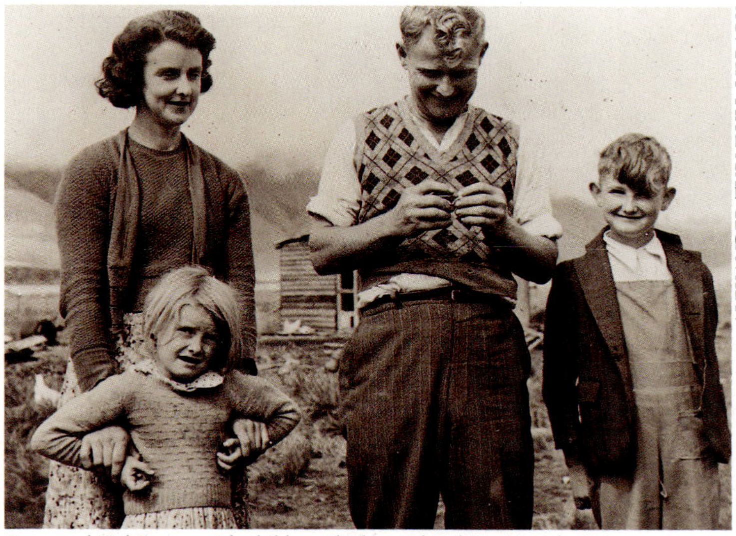

ALEXANDER TURNBULL LIBRARY

Grace and Ted Porter with children Shirley and Robert, Manuka Point Station, 1943.
PASCOE COLLECTION

There were strong negatives about the great New Zealand rural culture. Moral bullying was rife and cruel, and repressions were devastating to the imagination. We've gained much in comfort and sophistication and tolerance. But have we lost something too? I think so but we can never know for sure. I'll leave it to your imagination. Trying to go back to it is like building time machines, science fiction.

It is easy enough to see from the perspective of the 1980s that something changed in 1929, but one New Zealander, Bill Pearson, knew in 1951 that one culture here — especially the rural culture — had peaked and he looked at the future with extraordinary accuracy:

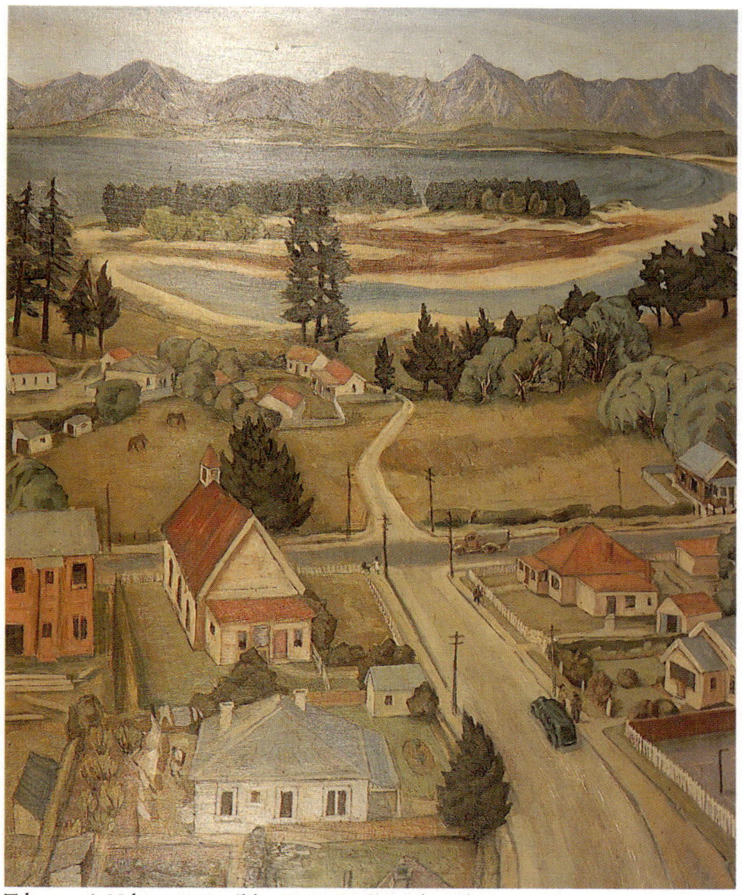

HOCKEN LIBRARY

Tahunanui, Nelson, 1947, oil by Doris Holland (Lusk)

The intellectual usually assumes that the worst enemy is puritanism: disinfect the snuffy tin-roof chapel conscience, and our way of life will flower. But this is questionable. The puritanism of Littledene is not all debit. With the concern for our neighbours' morals goes a concern for their welfare. The gossips are at least interested in other people, they help them in sickness, help with one another's ploughing and shearing and harvesting.

But when the puritan shell is cast there is nothing to replace it except perhaps a dimly expectant hedonism inspired by radio serials and films. And the intellectual has nothing to offer either except a tepid and equally prim hedonism which he calls 'the good life' – conscientious and enlightened self-indulgence.

When puritanism goes, the New Zealander is left with that ugly 'reality': he begins to look after number one and connives at his neighbour's devotion each to his own pleasure and security. Already in the North Island there are attitudes emerging which haven't yet shown in Littledene – shallow and sneering hedonism, the disavowal of responsibility to and for one's neighbour, less restraint in antipathies to minorities like Maoris, Catholics and especially Jews, priority given to the pursuit of money and pleasure – generally a slicker and more hard-boiled attitude. It is possible for a South Islander in Auckland to feel uprooted in the indifference and hostility of the people. □

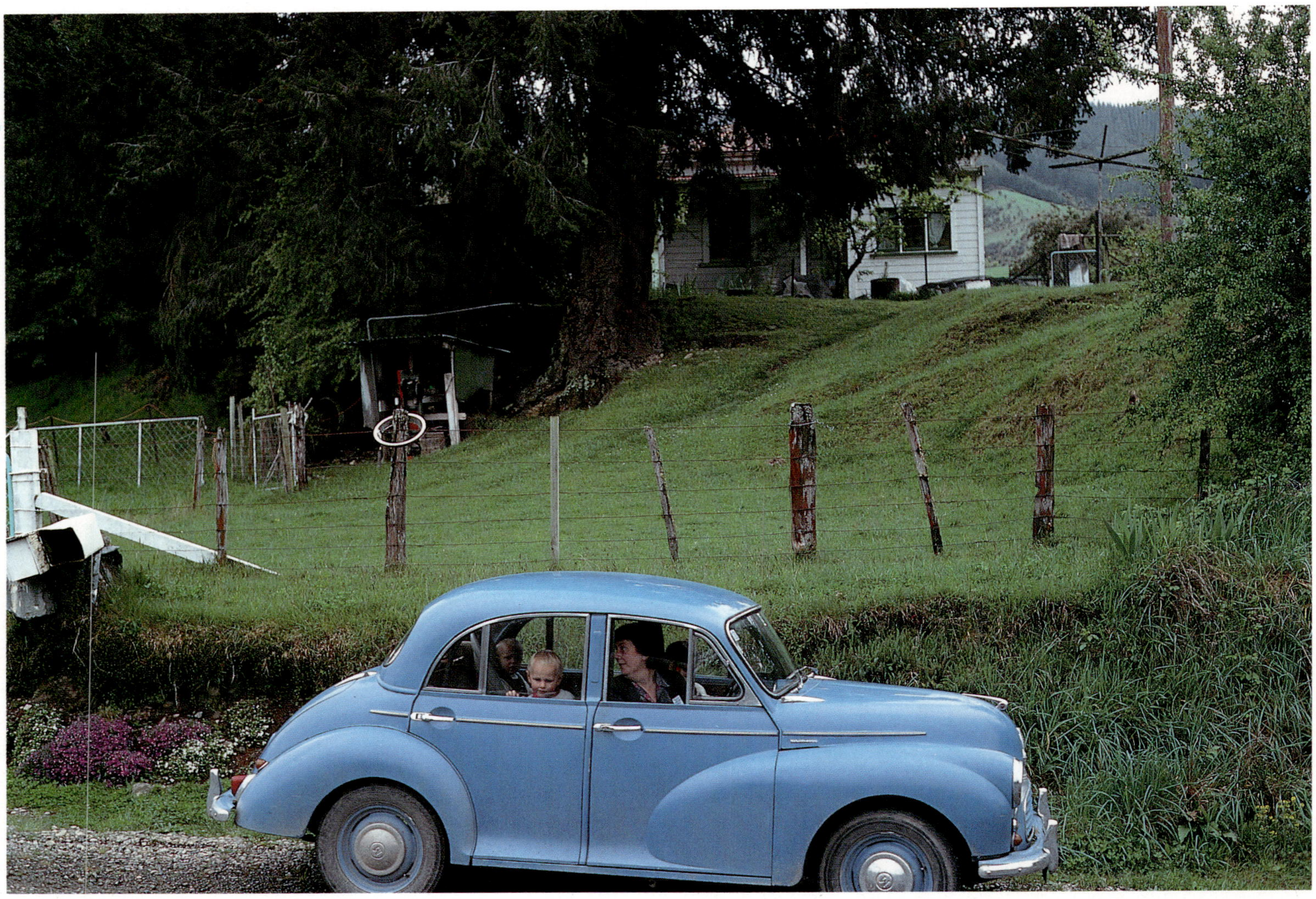

Family in Morris Minor, Motupiko, between Motueka and Murchison BRUCE CONNEW

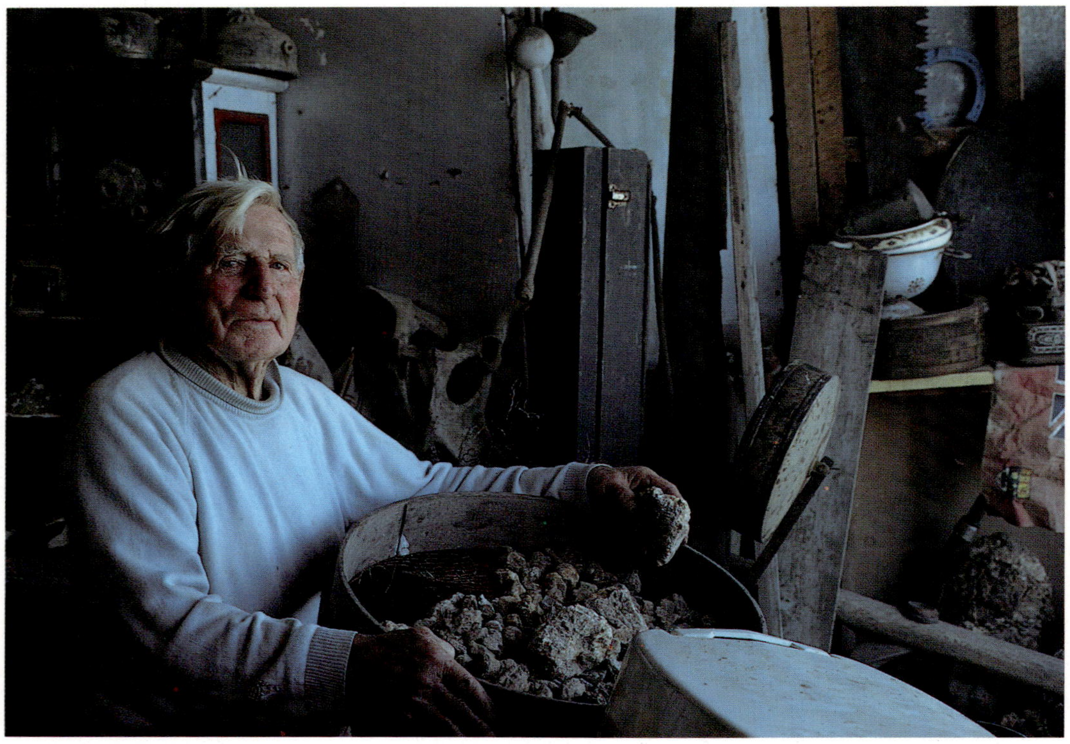

Charlie Hutley with old gum from the gum fields, Awanui, Far North STEPHEN ROBINSON

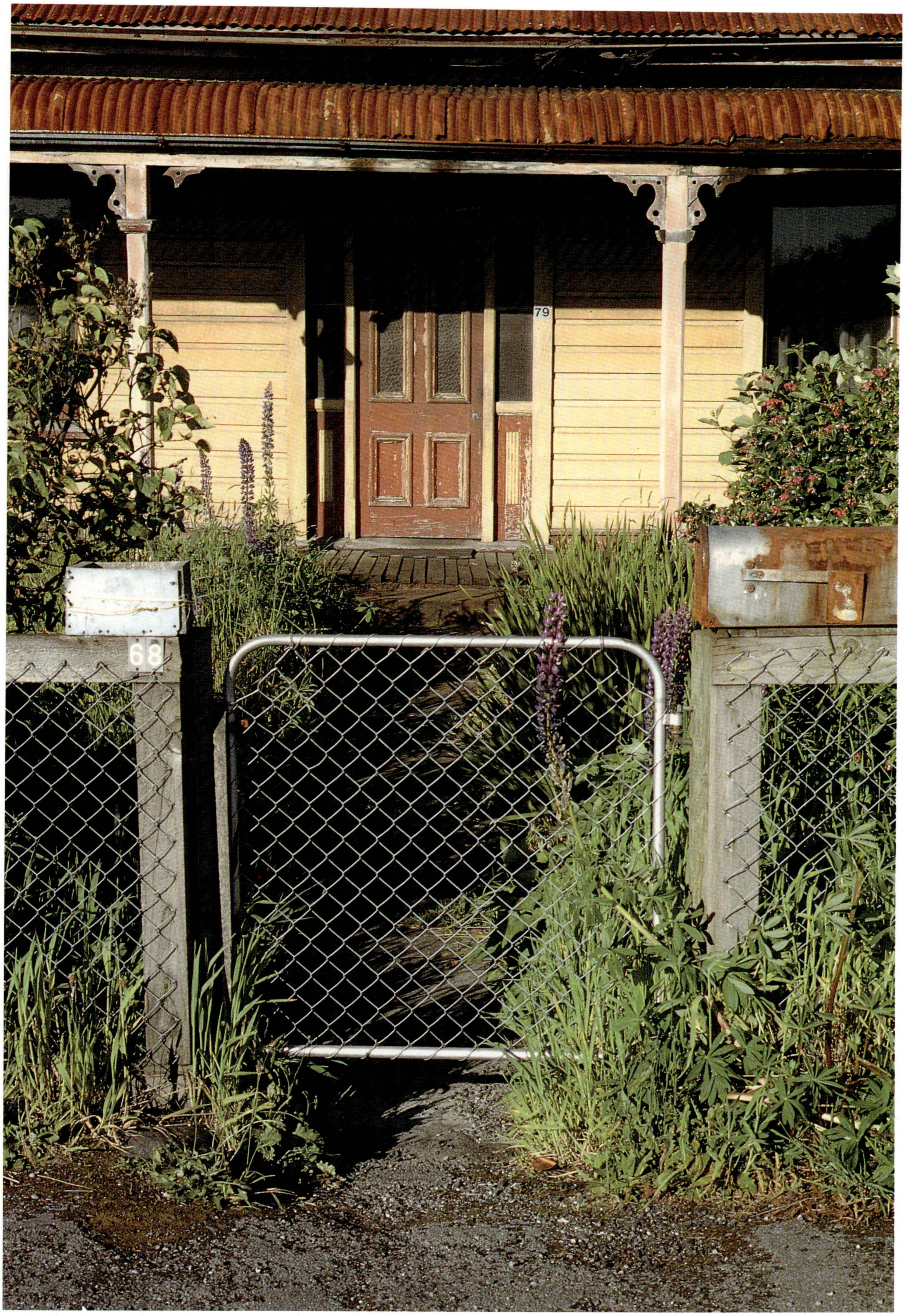

Hokitika, West Coast

BRIAN ENTING

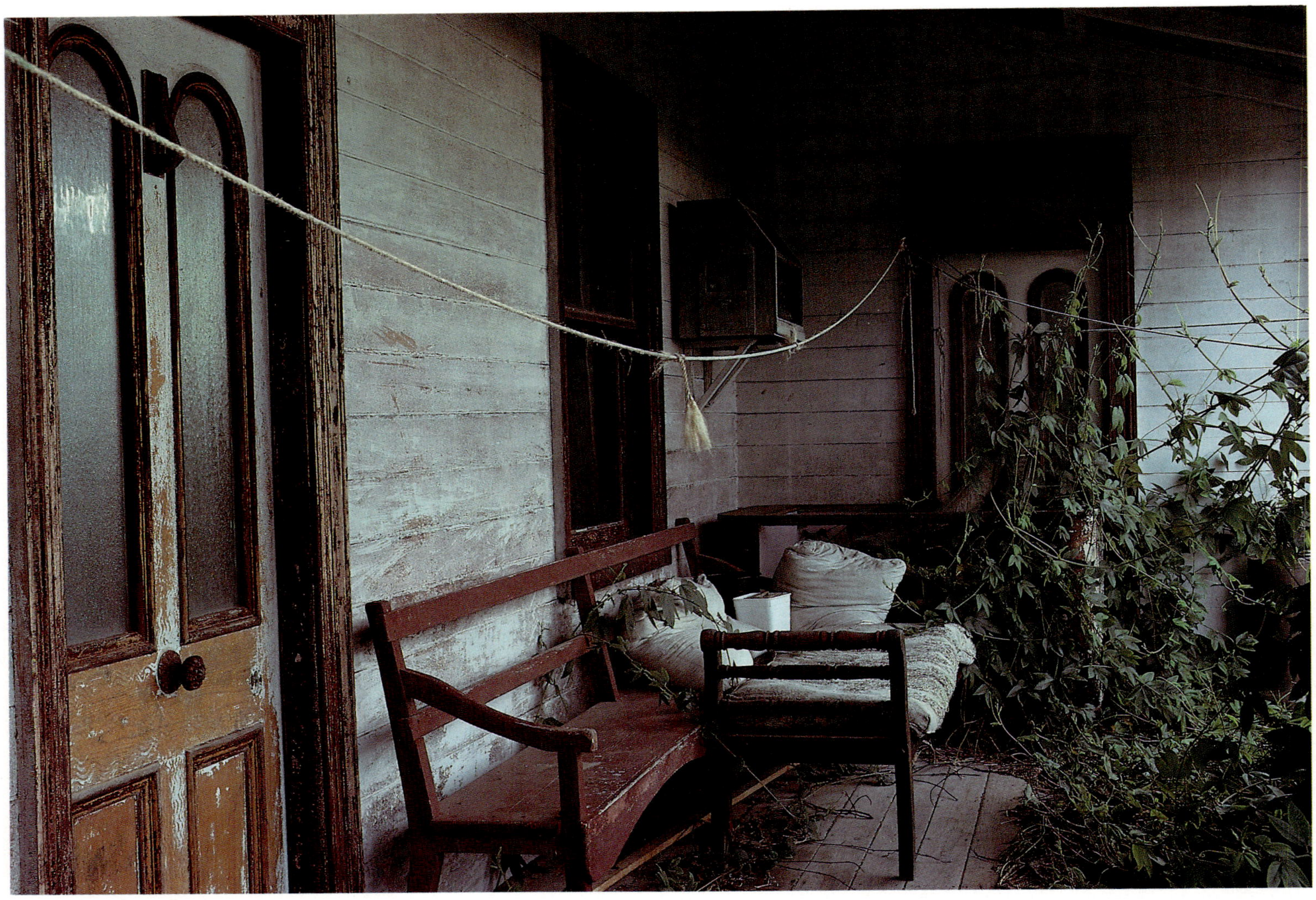

Boarding house, Stewart Island — ROBIN MORRISON

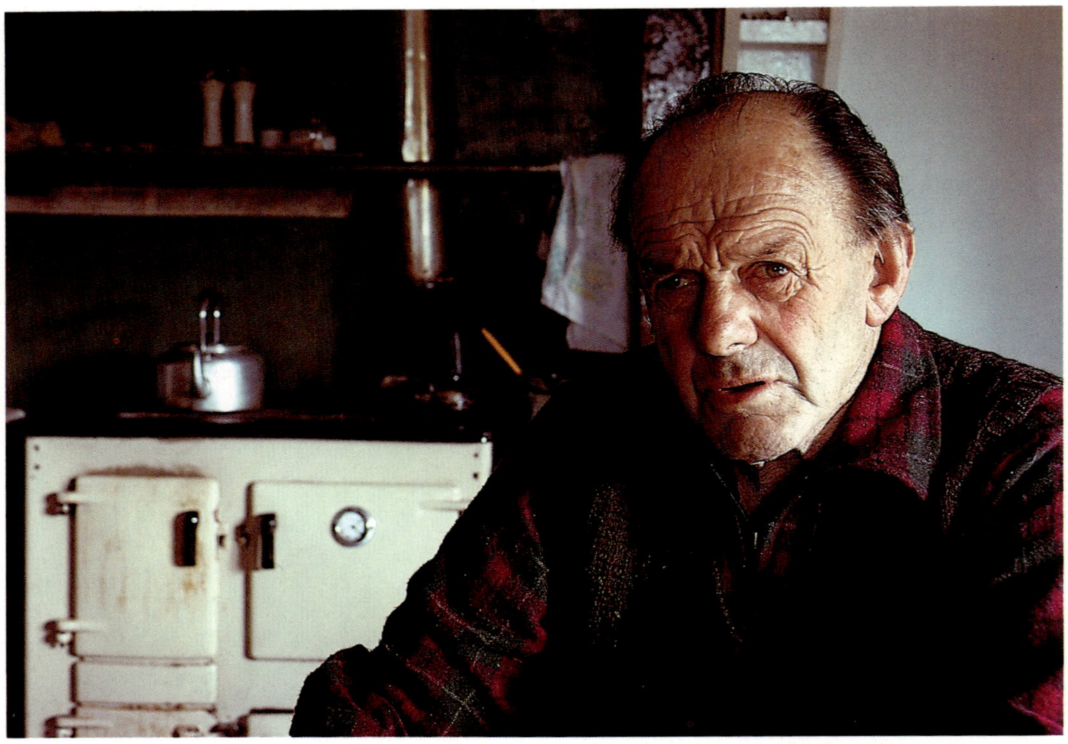

Pat Prenderville, Waitangi, Chatham Islands — ROBIN MORRISON

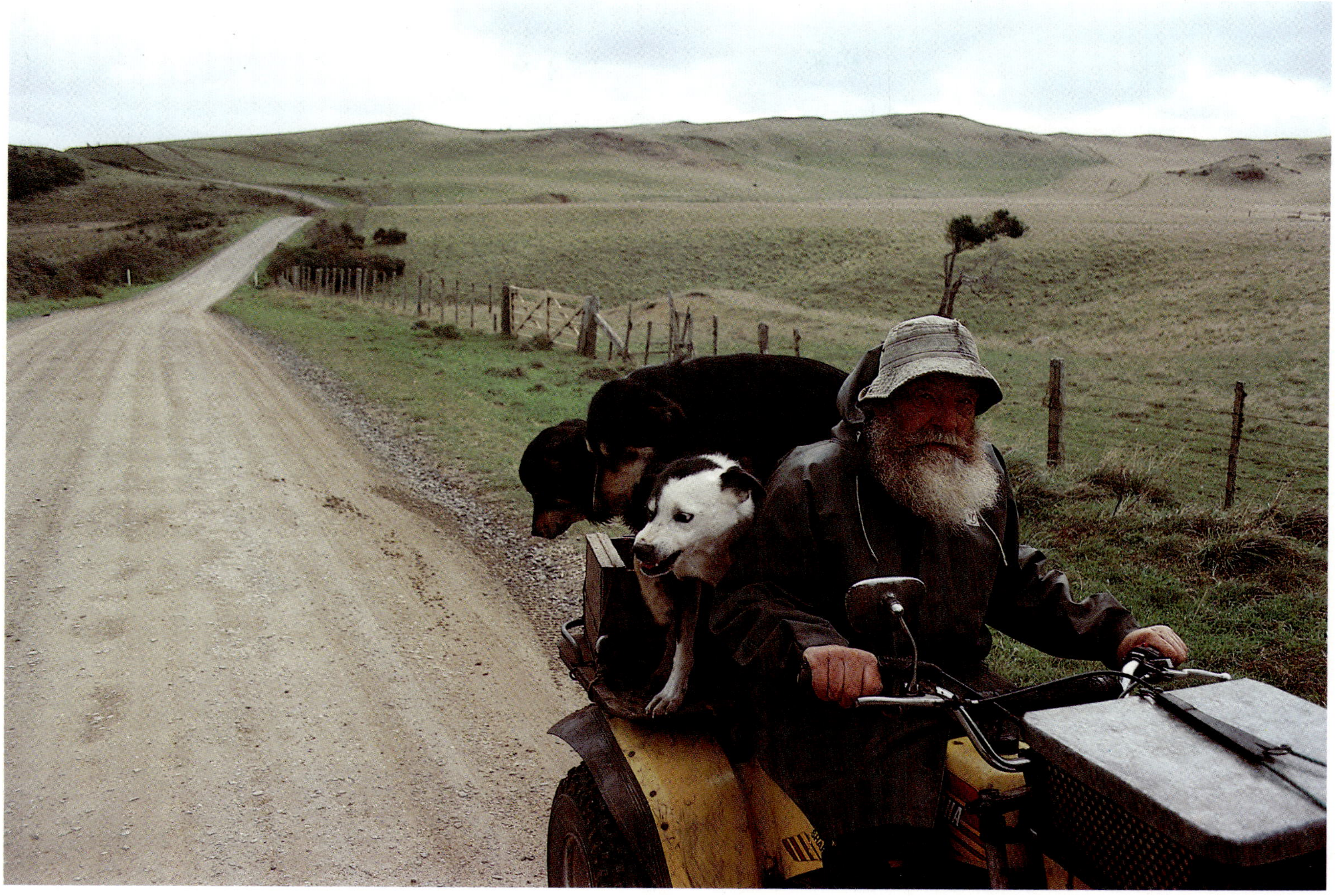

Ron Seymour, near Waitangi, Chatham Islands ROBIN MORRISON

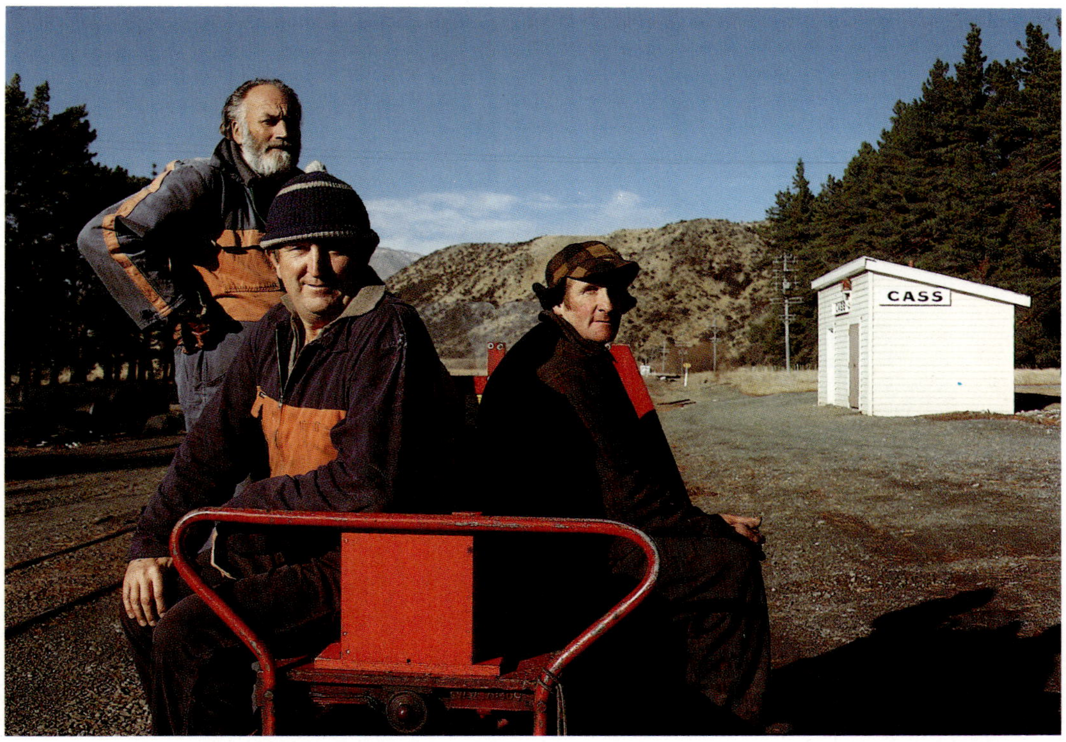

Eric Wisdom, Tex Carlyle and Barry Drummond at Cass Railway Station ROBIN MORRISON

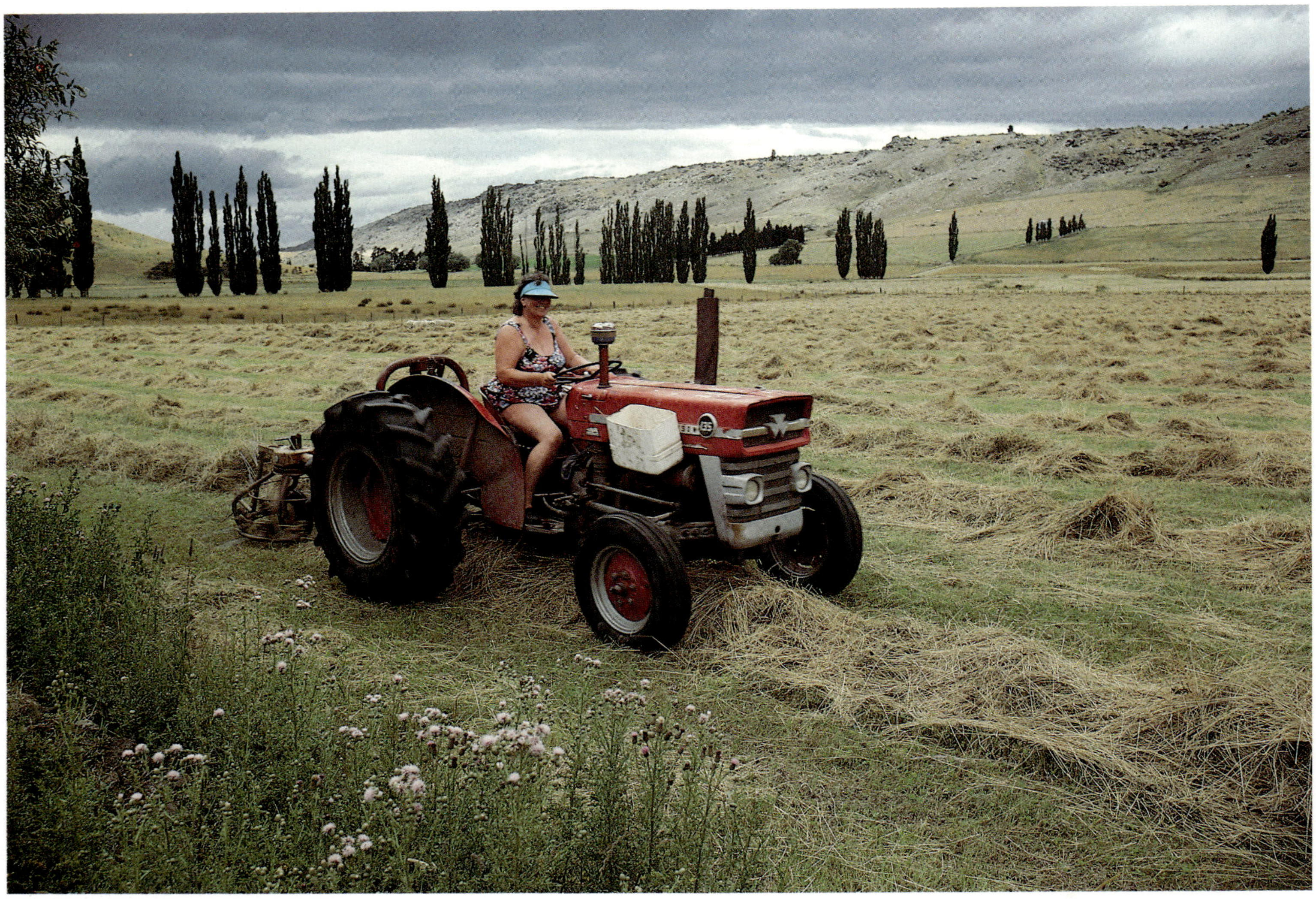

Turning hay near Roxburg GEOFF MASON

"Stanley's Motto", Macraes Flat GEOFF MASON

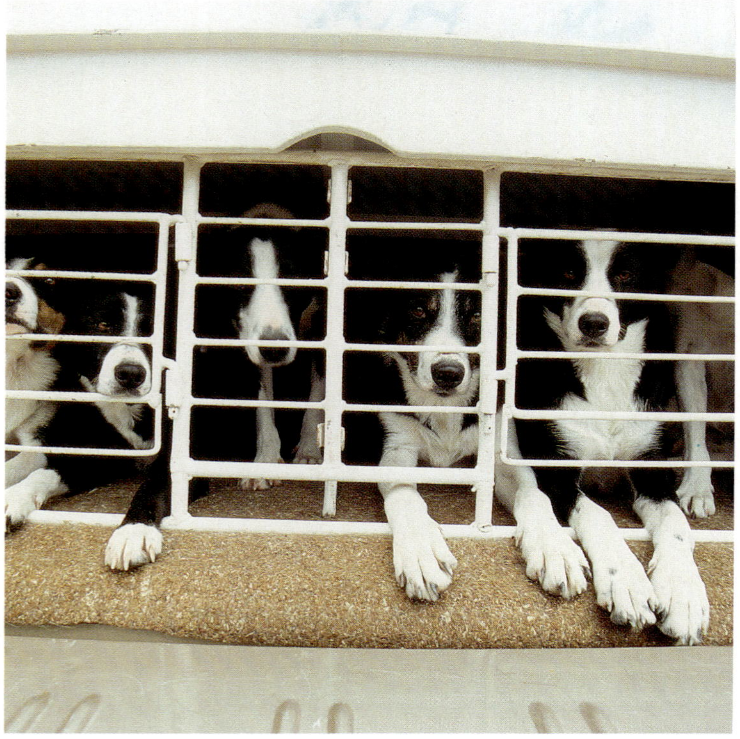

Sheep dogs waiting their turn, Lake Country A & p Show, Lake Hayes GEOFF MASON

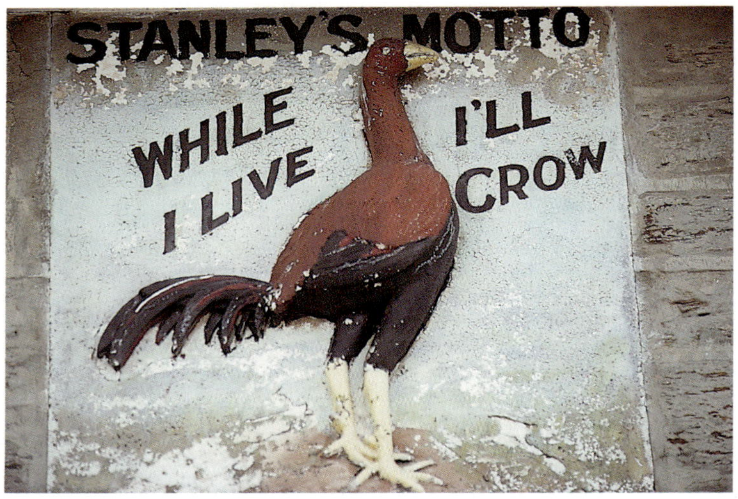

Central Otago GEOFF MASON

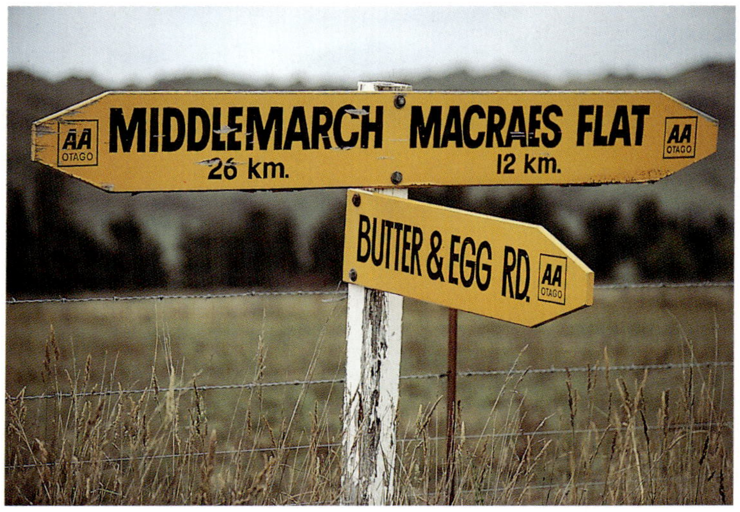

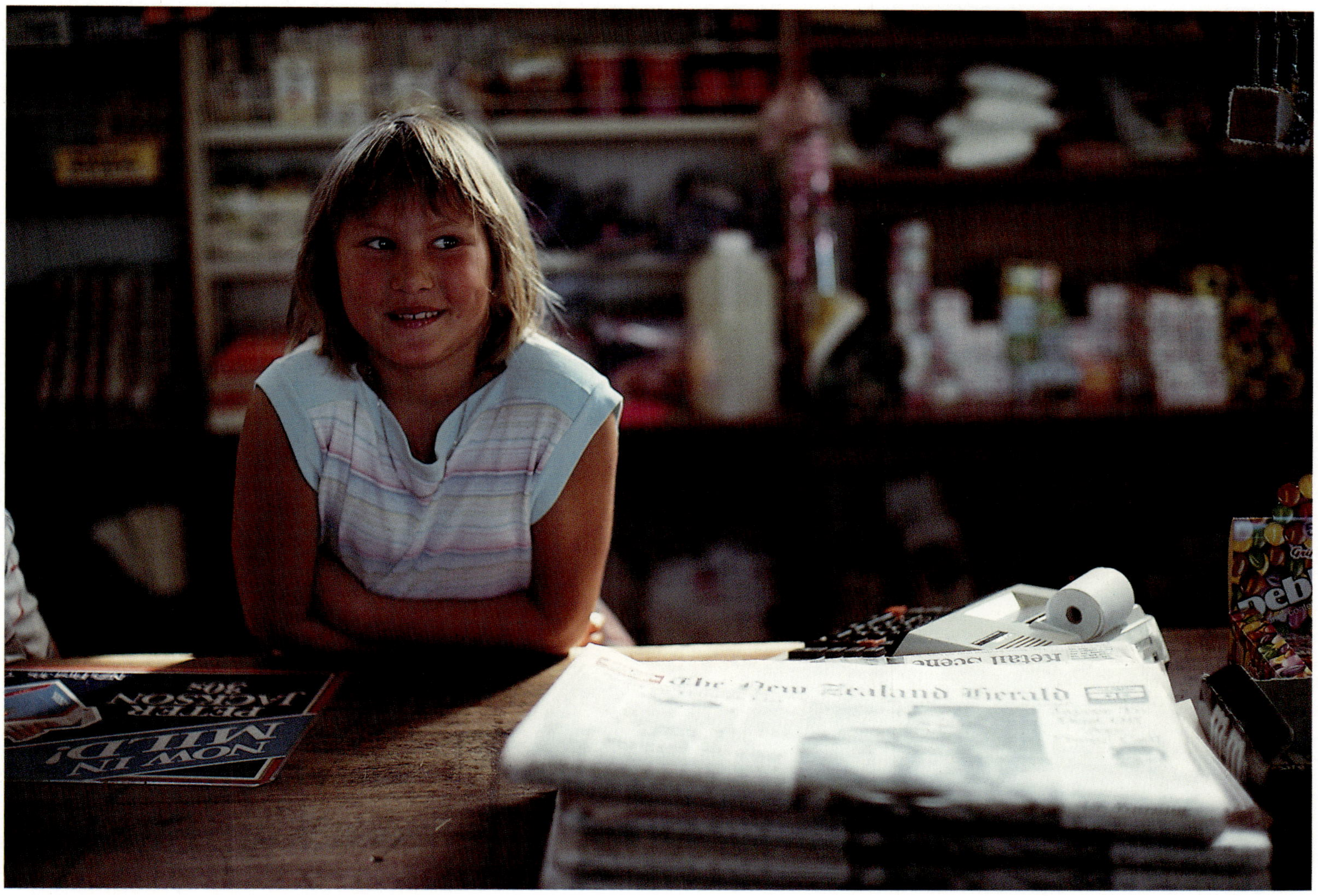

Waiharara Store, Far North — STEPHEN ROBINSON

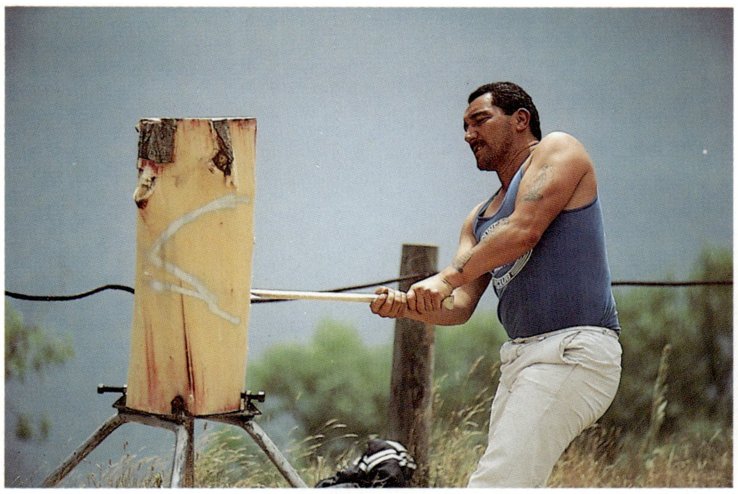

Lake County A & P Show, Lake Hayes — GEOFF MASON

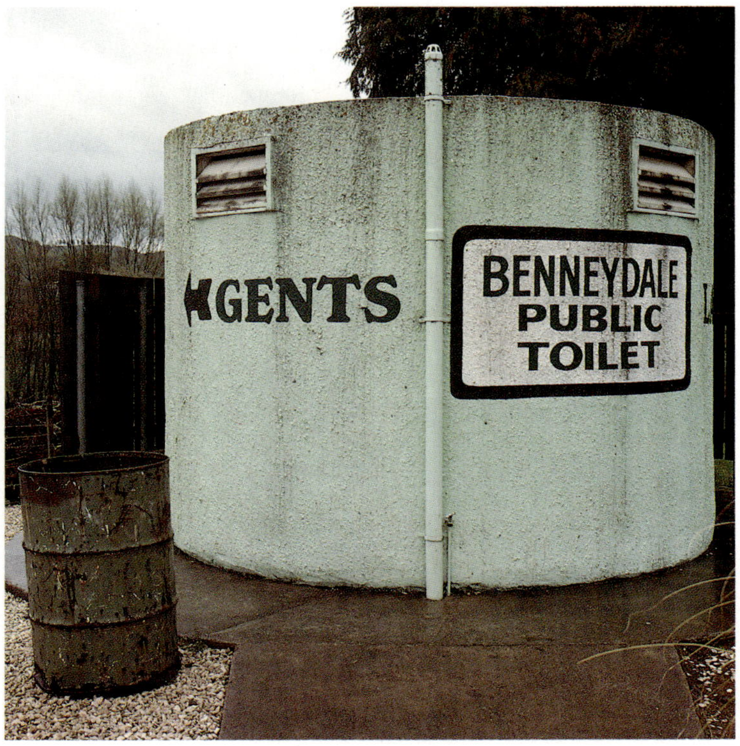

Benneydale Public Toilet — CRAIG POTTON

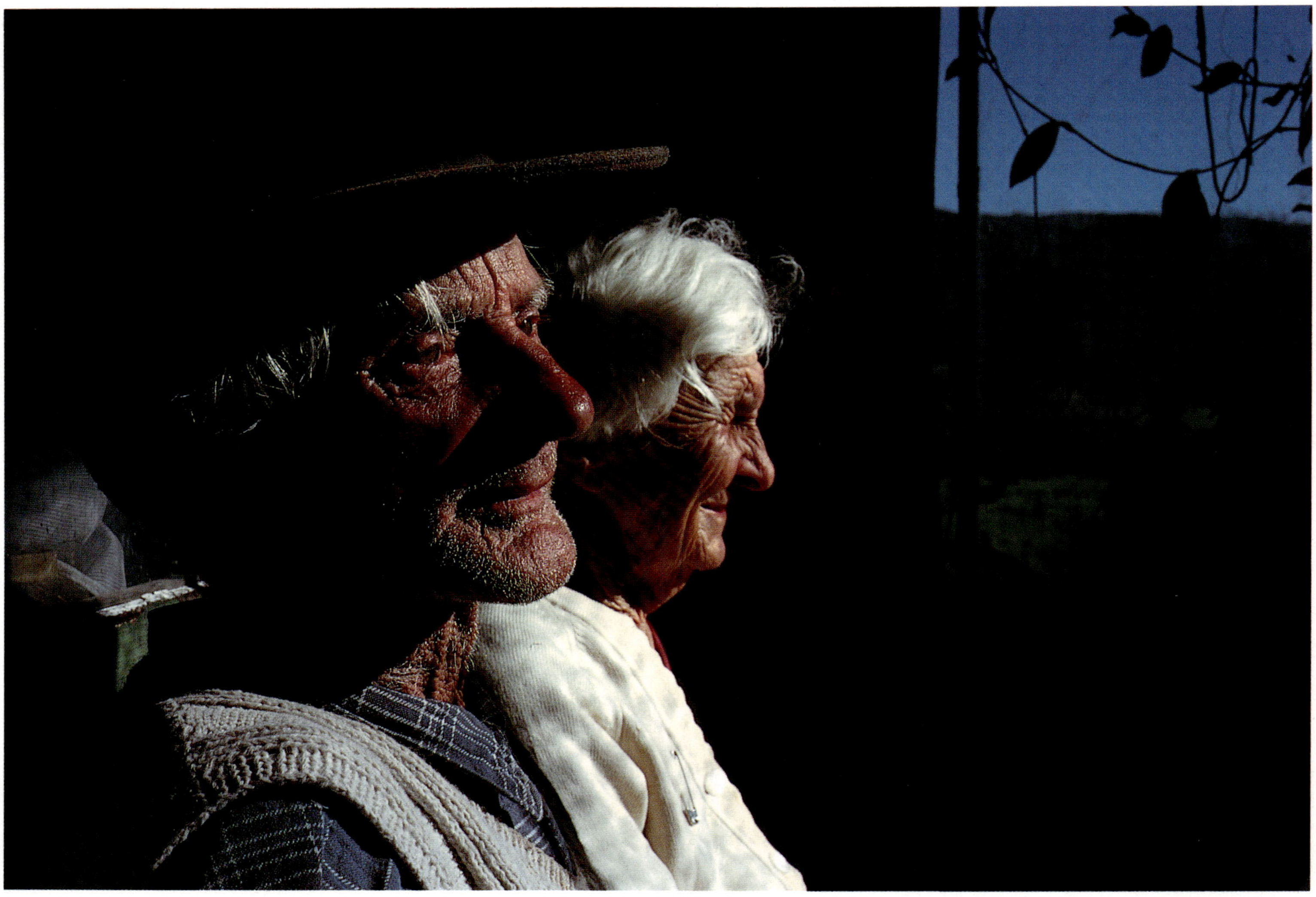

Cecil and Vida Rhodes, Pakawau, Golden Bay — BRUCE CONNEW

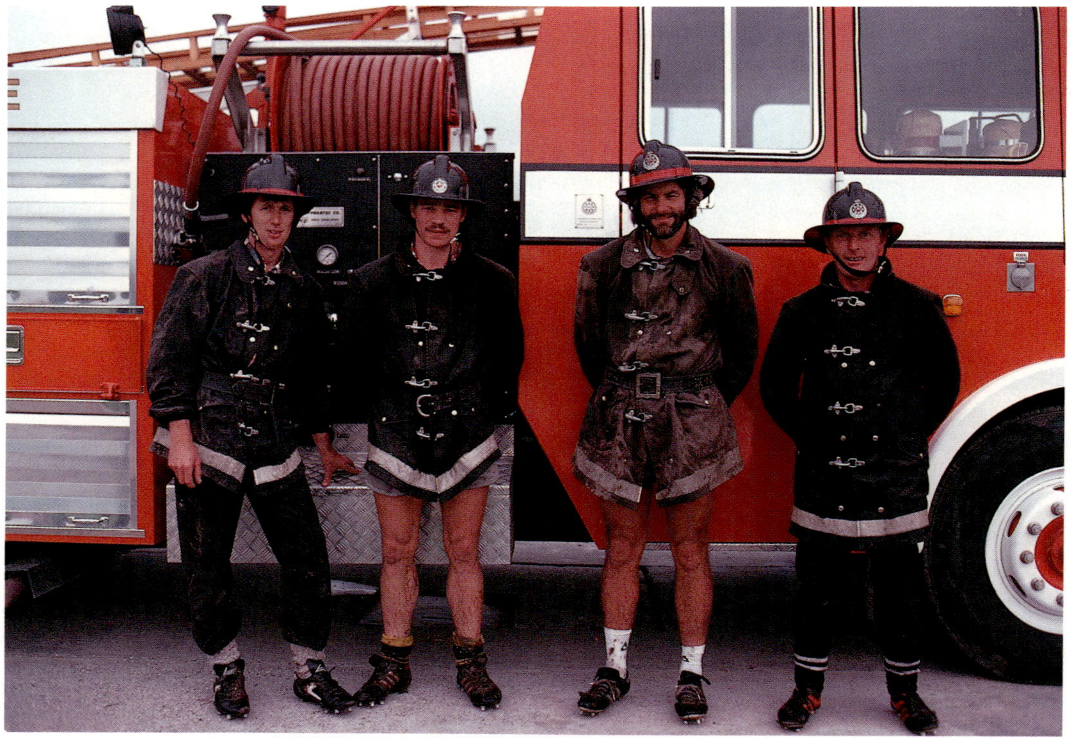

Hokitika Volunteer Fire Brigade — BRIAN ENTING

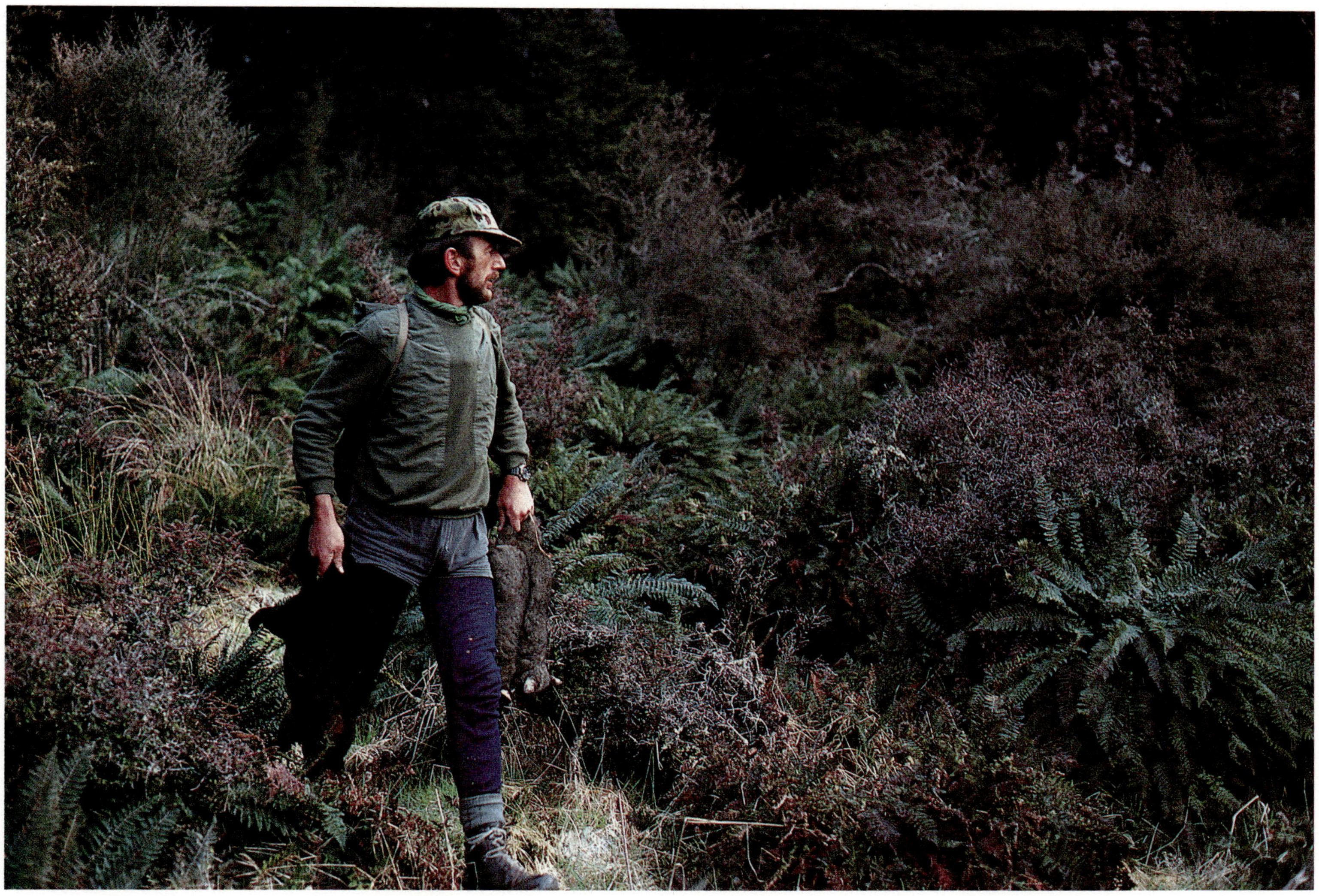

John Dearden, opossum trapper, Upper Cobb Valley, North West Nelson Forest Park BRUCE CONNEW

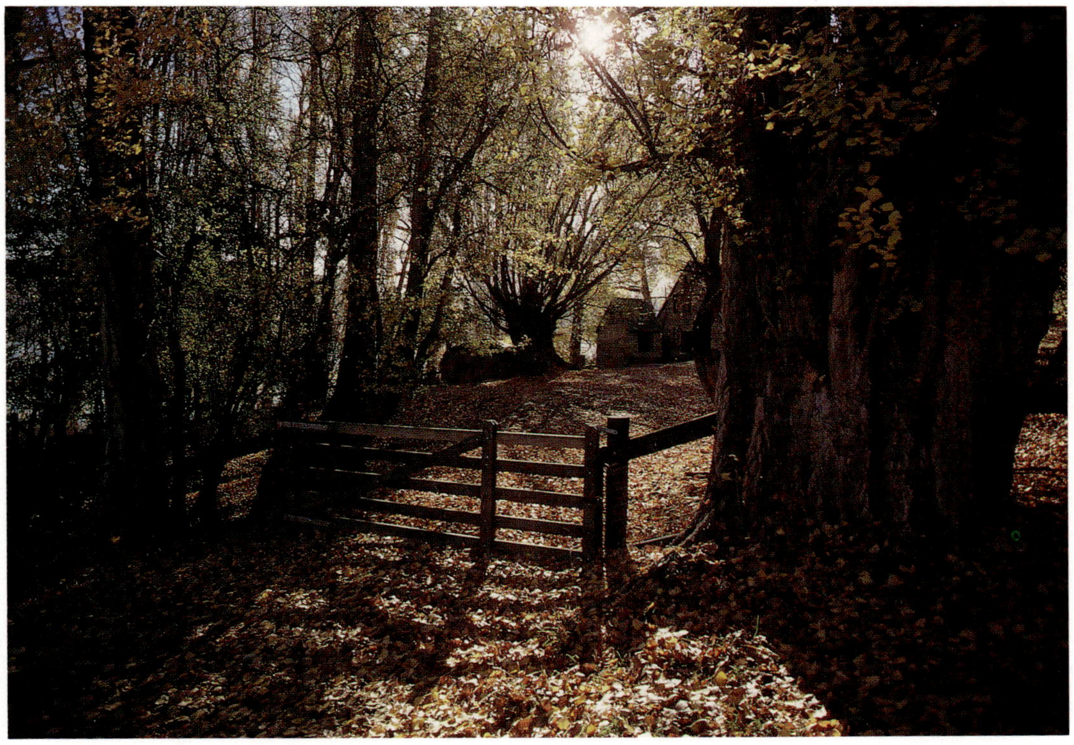

Houses, Lake Hayes, near Arrowtown GEOFF MASON

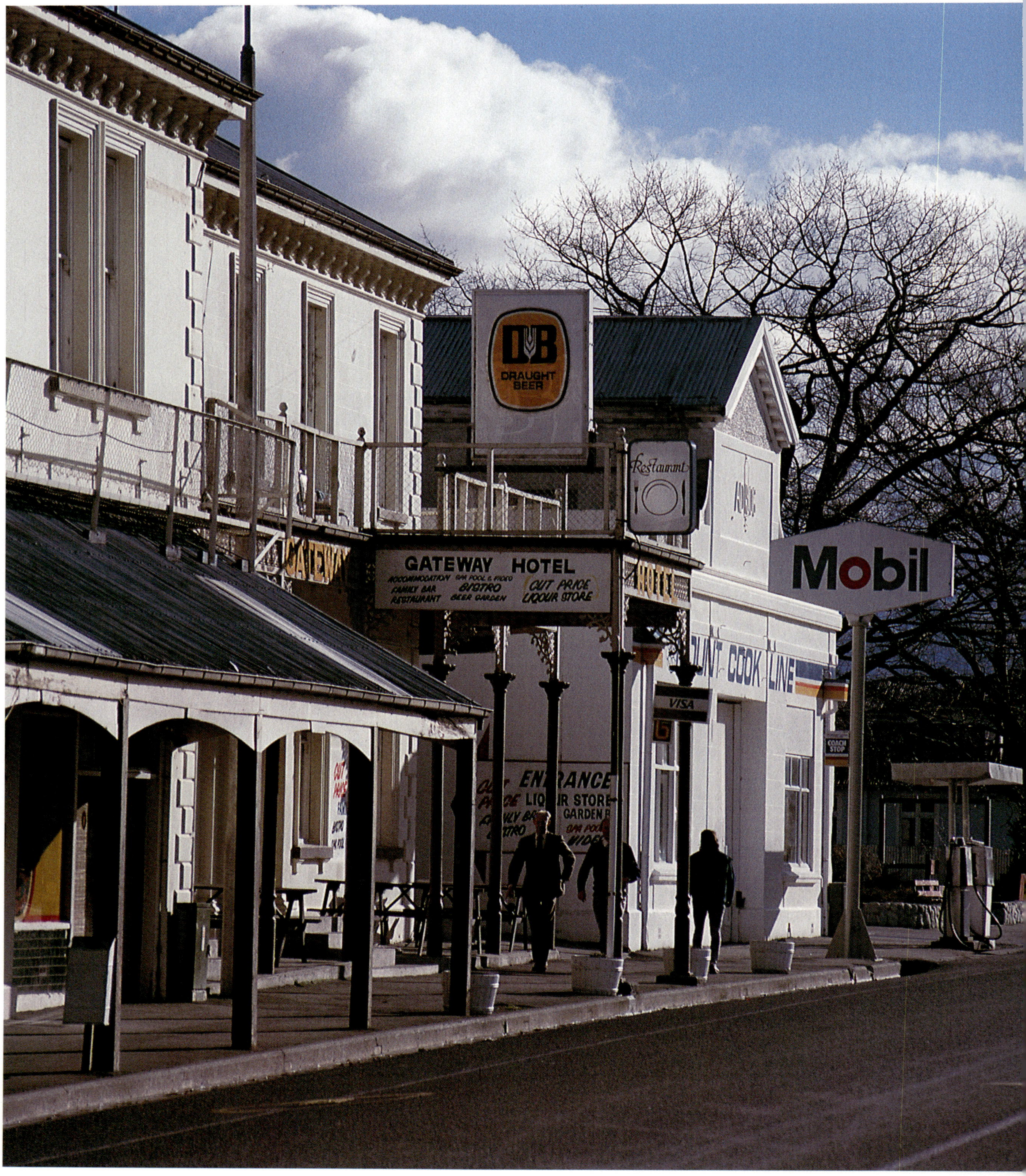

Fairlie

ROBIN MORRISON

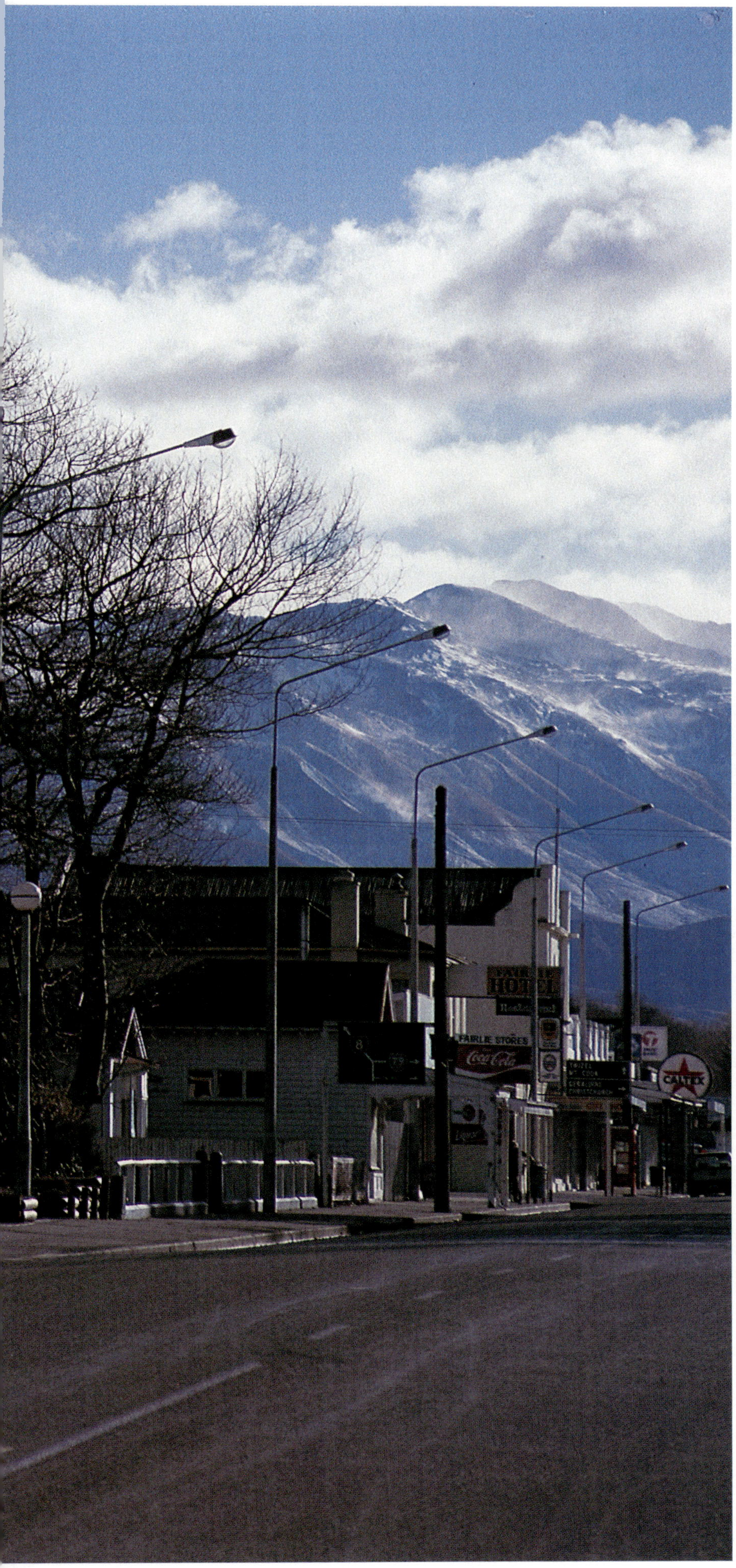

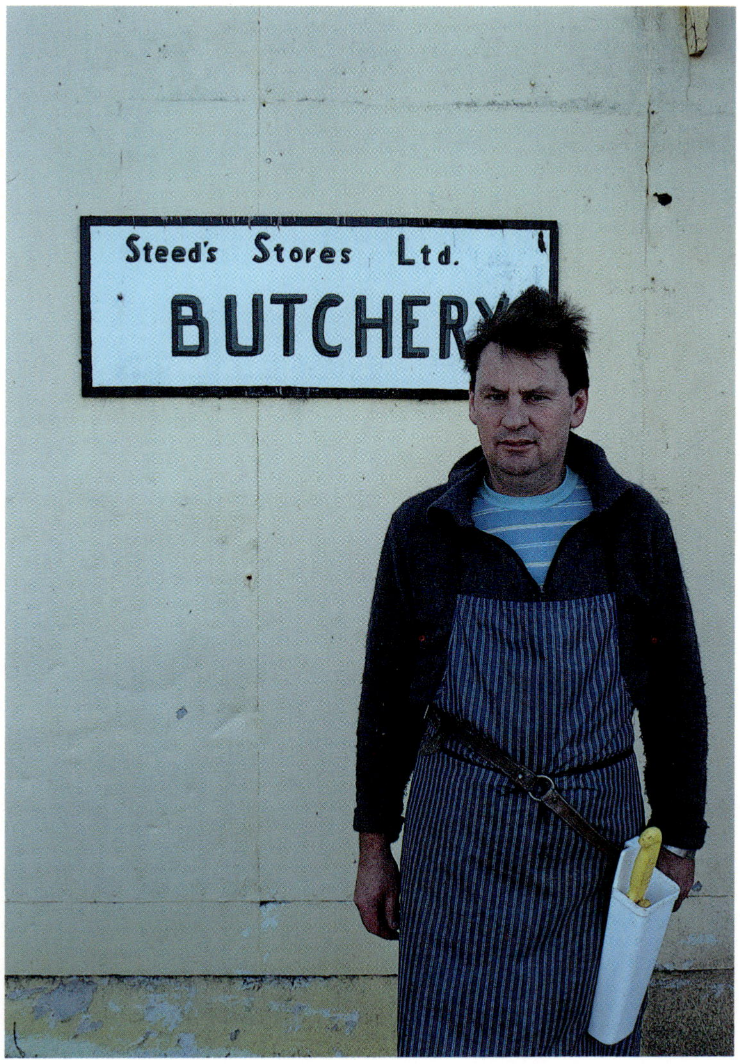

Waiharara Butchery, Far North STEPHEN ROBINSON

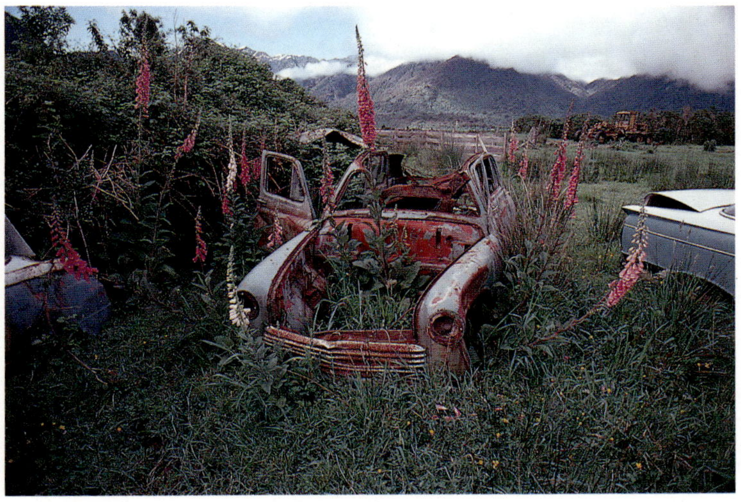

Rural West Coast, near Ross BRIAN ENTING

COMING OF AGE

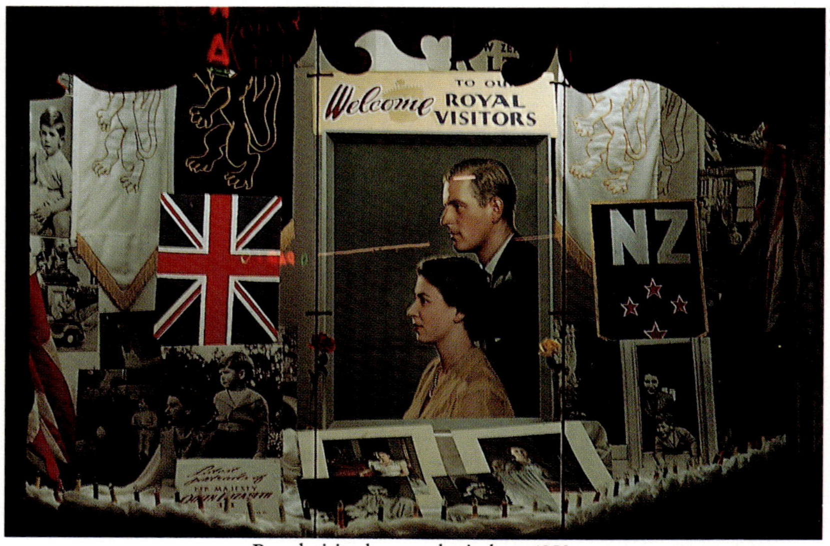

LANCE BLACKMAN

Royal visit, decorated window, 1953.

Hamish Keith

IN 1950 THE NEW ZEALAND suburban Saturday night was filled with a faint and poignant music. From church and lodge halls drifted the sounds of sloppy saxophones, out of tune pianos and plodding drums tracing out a displaced and timeless music. It was not timeless in any classical sense, but simply without relationship to any period or place. Hearing it, a traveller from some other land would be hard put to identify just where they had arrived, or in what year.

Waltzes jostled side by side with cowboy music. The ribald songs of cockney London vied with the sentimental love ballads of New York or choruses from the *Desert Song* and *The Student Prince*. The *Tennessee Waltz* gave way to the *Blue Danube* and *Buttons and Bows* to *My Old Man Said Follow the Band*.

The only New Zealand songs likely to be mixed into the medley were *Maori Battalion* and *Blue Smoke*. Few of those who sang the latter would have recognised this 1947 composition of Ruru Karaitiana for one of their own. They would certainly have recognised *Now is the Hour*, which traditionally ended New Zealand social occasions, but they may not have known that two years before, Maewa Kaihau and Clement Scott's Maori song had become a million-selling hit single for Bing Crosby.

In some parts of the country, most notably Auckland, jive as a hangover from the wartime American presence might have been added to this musical mix.

These sounds of revelry, muted before the electrification of musical fun, came from weddings or parish dances or, more often, twenty-first birthday parties, as that generation conceived in the optimism before the Great Depression reached their majority. Coming of Age was a ritual taken very seriously then. Perhaps it was by way of compensation to those whose childhood and adolescence had been spent in two of the most traumatic decades twentieth-century New Zealand had witnessed.

Inside the hall the Pakeha version of the extended family would have gathered to mark the rites of passage in a celebration as structured, within its own tradition, as any in Arnhem Land or the New Guinea Highlands.

Dress was uniformly drab. Men wore double-breasted suits if they had them and sports coats and grey flannel trousers if they did not. Jackets or suits, their colour was a consistent and nondescript monotony of greyish-browns and brownish-greys. Shirts were universally white, worn with sombre and seriously knotted ties. As the evening hotted up, jackets might be removed, ties imperceptibly loosened and shirt sleeves rolled, with the tightness of a tourniquet, as far up the upper arm as they could reach.

There was just a fraction more variety for women. A few might have been wearing a variant of the post-war Dior "New Look": a wide and full skirt with a hemline dropping to the prescribed 170 mm above the ground. Most, though, would have still worn the just-below-knee length, clumpy austerity of wartime styles.

The twenty-first birthday parties of sons were generally regarded as having more significance than those of daughters. Perhaps this was a reflection of the instinctive sexism of the times. More likely it was simply a canny economy by a family that knew it would soon face larger bills and even greater resources of social energy celebrating the daughter's wedding.

The supper tables would have been loaded with food of a monotonous whiteness relieved only by the chemical red of steaming saveloys or the yellow of pastry pies and sausage rolls. Piles of sandwiches, rolls of tinned asparagus, scones, pavlovas, cream sponges, a birthday cake decorated, perhaps, with a monstrous silver key. The refreshments were unchanged from those the poet D'Arcy Cresswell had described as "a sickly and fictitious food" a generation before.

Dotted amongst these would be tastefully grouped bottles of fizzy drink in savage oranges, reds and greens, and towering above those the tall brown elegance of bottled beer from the local, favourite brewery. At the back of the hall, located conveniently near the lavatories, a bar would sport kegs or half-gallon glass jars of draught beer and, perhaps, sweet sherry.

Off the dance floor, sexual segregation was total. Whatever family ties were being strengthened or renewed, fraternisation across the sexual barrier was limited to a brief public exchange of courtesies. Only very occasionally was this rigid protocol blurred for the aged or newly engaged, and then only slightly.

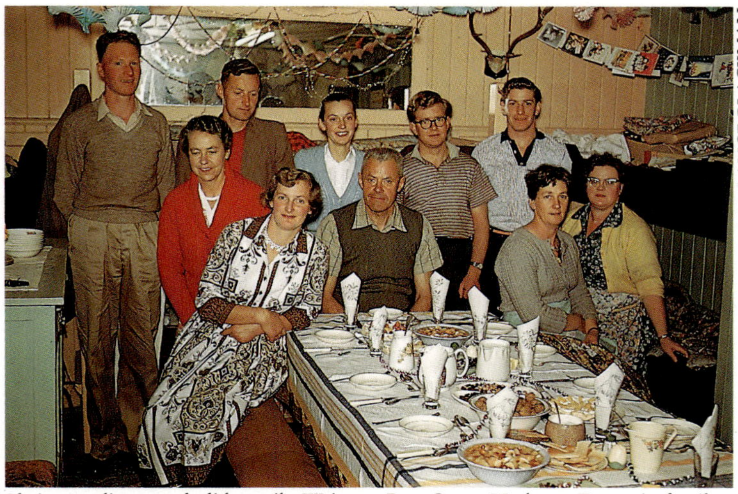

LANCE BLACKMAN

Christmas dinner at holiday crib, Waipuna Bay, Otago Harbour. Fountain family and friends, 1960.

THINGS WERE DONE DIFFERENTLY on marae. But for the vast majority of suburban New Zealand in 1950 that was foreign territory, strange and remote, if they had heard of it at all. For a restless adolescent becoming aware of the world in that year, the ritual coming of age seemed entirely without meaning. The New Zealand transition from youth to age was barely perceptible in ways other than the merely physical. Life was a continuous stream of unchallenging certainties. School, job, marriage, children – an endlessly repeating cycle. The life and lifestyle, clothes, manners and tastes of parents were there to be effortlessly replicated by their children.

Group photographs of the period have a sadness about them quite unlike those of any other. Men, particularly, look universally old and drained, gazing out at the camera like prisoners in a time capsule. It was as if they only came in one age and one model. Even photographs of sporting teams have this curious quality.

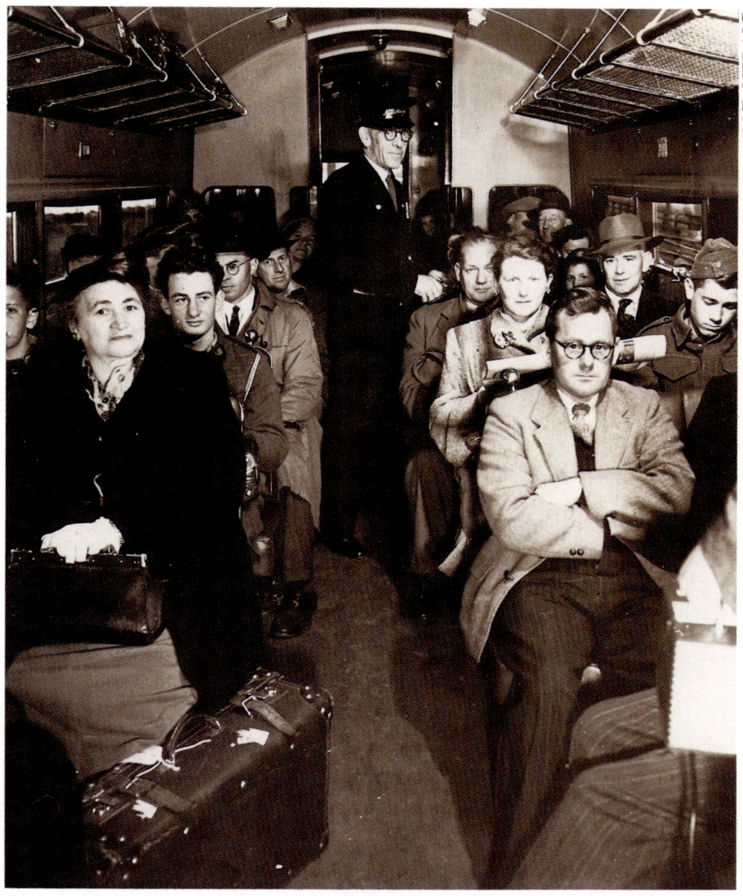

N.Z. HERALD

The sombre quality of citizens in the 1950s illustrated by the passengers in the Hutt Valley multiple unit electric train, 1953.

Grown-up New Zealand in 1950 did not want challenge or change. It had had enough of that in the previous twenty years to last several lifetimes. Pakeha New Zealanders had achieved a seamless security at last and nothing would persuade them to give that up. They would not be persuaded out of it by questions of identity and place or the troublesome burden of a history.

If the twenty-first birthday symbolised the social continuity of that year, the state house perfectly represented its aspirations of unchallenged security. The extraordinary drive from 1935 to house white working-class New Zealand had barely been halted by the war. By 1950 the vast state suburbs of Auckland and the Hutt Valley were the breathtaking achievements of social engineering on a scale hardly dreamed of before. Only a few malcontented intellectuals or poets had the temerity, or vision, to question this teeming suburban dream and see in it an anti-culture and the foundations of a millenium of mediocrity.

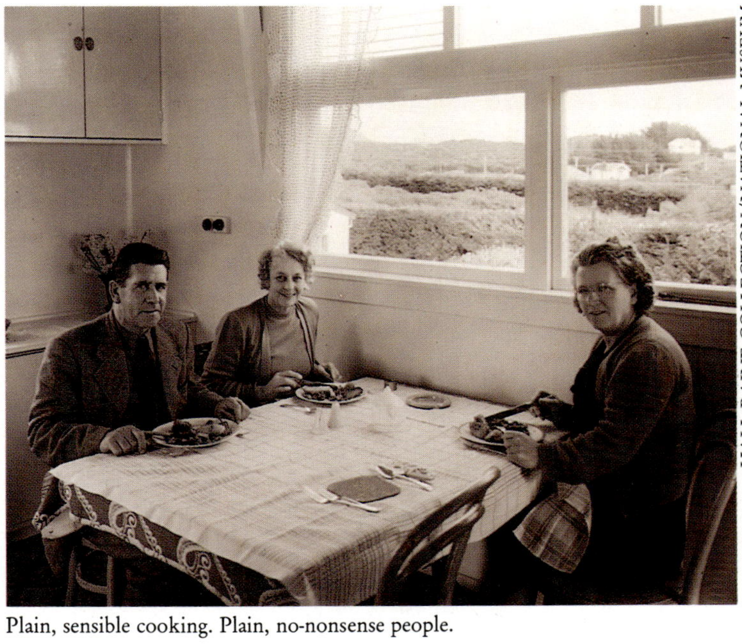

HALL RAINE COLLECTION/NATIONAL MUSEUM

Plain, sensible cooking. Plain, no-nonsense people.

Unlike Australia, New Zealand had turned its back on the urban potential of its recent past. It was as if the depression and the war had created a chasm between past and present that the general imagination of the time could simply not bridge. To a person, the nation had retreated into its tiny-windowed, tiled-roof suburban fortress and pulled down the blinds on past and future.

In his 1950s poem *Secular Litany*, M. K. Joseph perfectly captured the stagnant calm of that moment in New Zealand time:

That we may never lack two Sundays in a week
One to rest and one to play
That we may worship in the liturgical drone
Of the race-commentator and radio raconteur
That we may avoid distinction and exception
Worship the mean, cultivate the mediocre
Live in a state house, raise forcibly-educated children
Receive family benefits, and standard wages and a pension
And rest in peace in a state crematorium
Saint Allblack
Saint Monday Raceday
Saint Stabilisation
Pray for us.

From all foreigners, with their unintelligible cooking
From the vicious habit of public enjoyment
From kermesse and carnival, high day and festival
From pubs and cafes, bullfights and barbecues
From Virgil and vintages, fountains and fresco-painting
From afterthought and apperception
From tragedy, from comedy
And from the arrow of God
Saint Anniversaryday
Saint Arborday
Saint Labourday
Defend us.

When the bottles are empty
And the keg runs sour
And the cinema is shut and darkened
And the radio gone up in smoke
And the sports-ground flooded
When the tote goes broke
And the favourite scratches
And the brass bands are silenced
And the car is rusted by the roadside
Saint Fathersday
Saint Mothersday
Saint Happybirthday
Have mercy on us.

And for your petitioner, poor little Jim,
Saint Hocus
Saint Focus
Saint Bogus
And Saint Billy Bungstarter
Have mercy on him.

Little Jim's prayers were not answered for long. From the early 1950s a torrent of challenge and change gathered increasing momentum, sweeping before it all his security and certainty. With them went all the cherished illusions and myths of white suburban New Zealand. Those comforting and soporific notions of equality and racial harmony, of endless tolerance and state-subsidised wellbeing that had protected little Jim, his wife and children and mates at the pub from the real world and from all its tragedy and comedy.

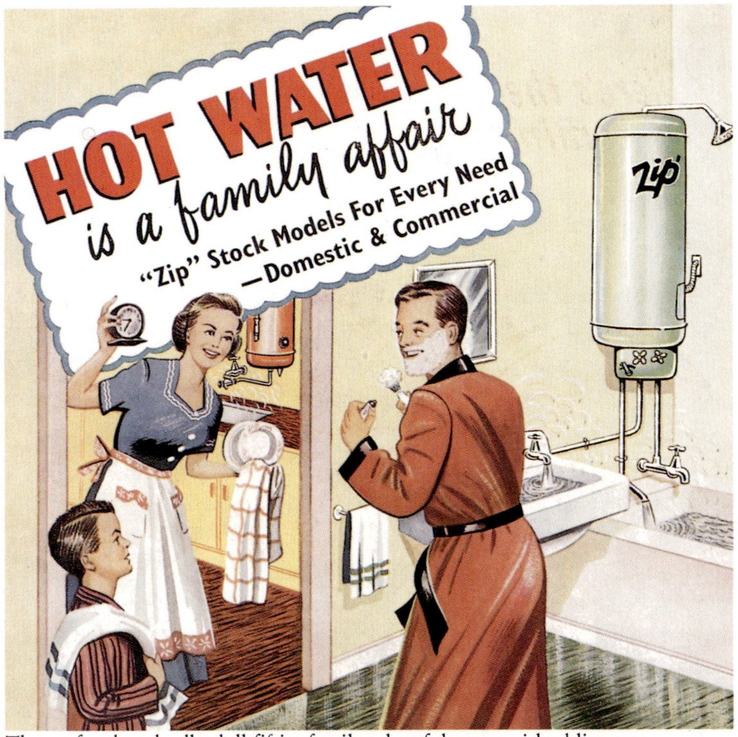

The perfect but deadly dull fifties family: cheerful mum with obligatory apron, and son, carbon-copy of the brilliantined father.

N.Z. HERALD

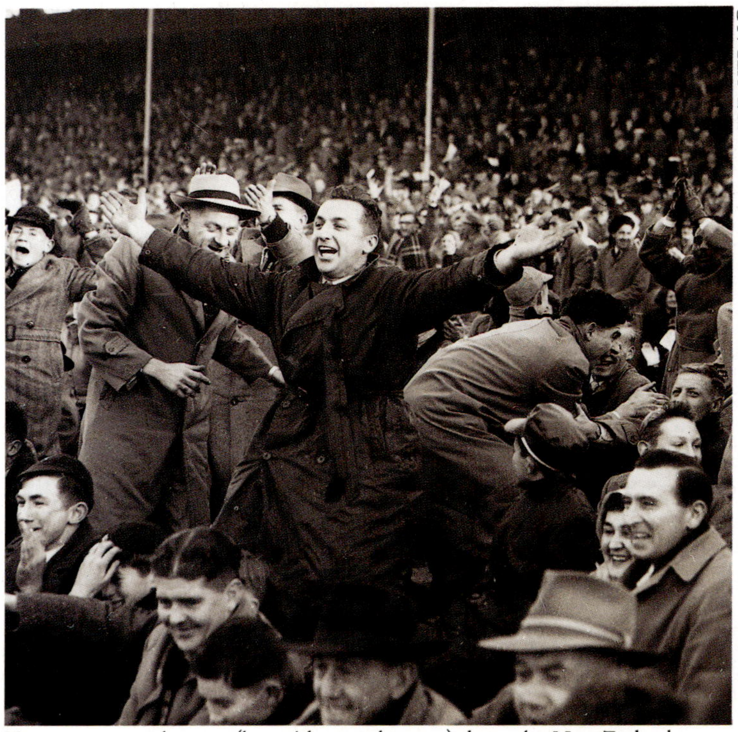
Uncustomary exuberance (but with a good reason) shown by New Zealand supporters at the first rugby test against the Springboks at Dunedin in 1956. The game was won by New Zealand 10 points to 6. The series went to New Zealand three matches to one.

LES CLEVELAND

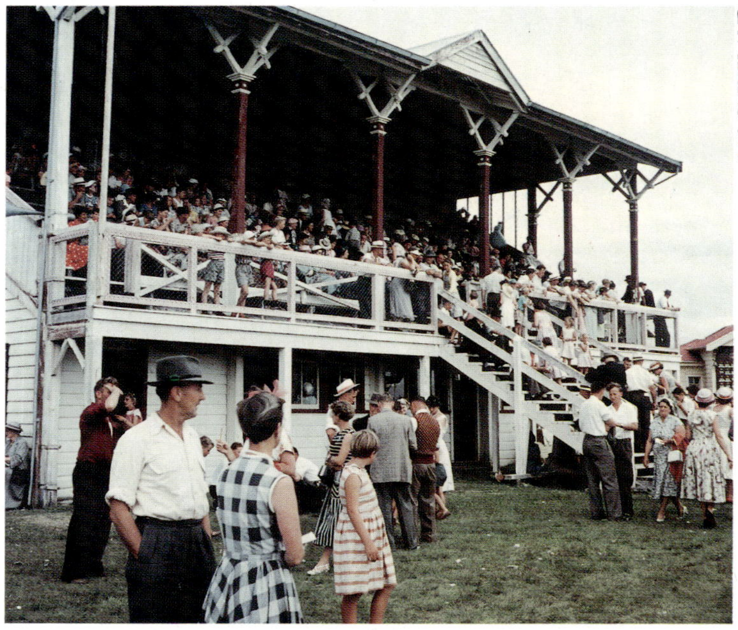
Race meeting at Kumara, South Westland, Christmas, 1959.

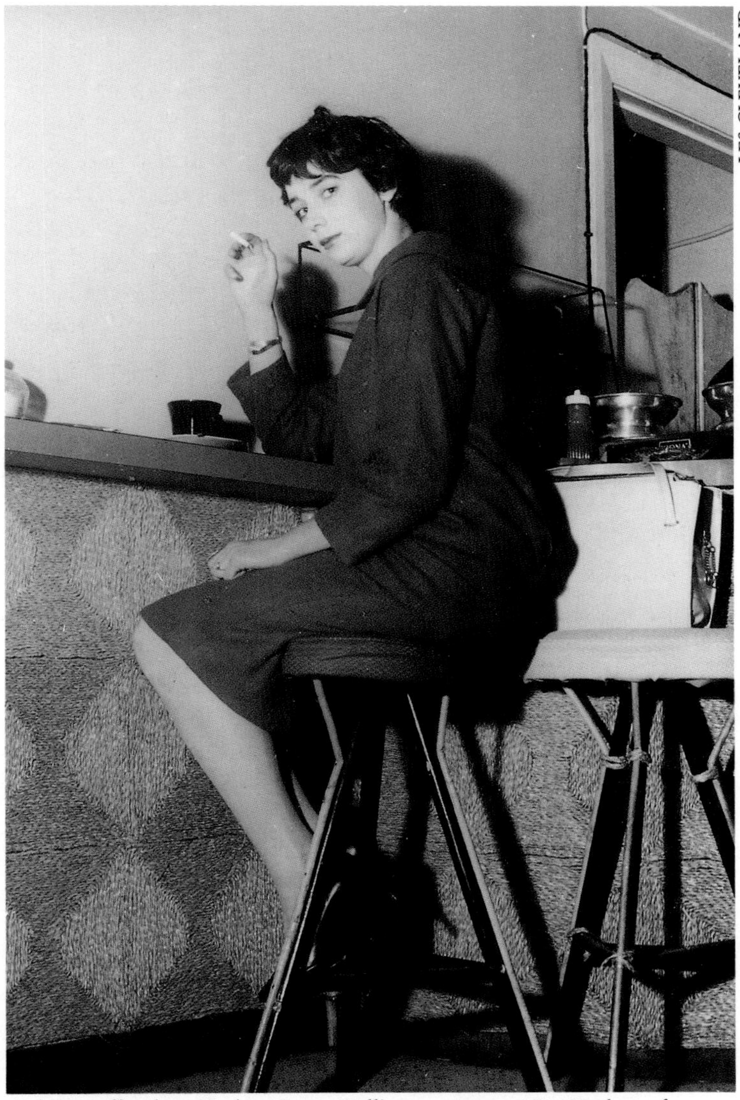

Girl in a coffee shop, Herbert Street, Wellington, August 1959. Mothers of teenaged girls saw coffee bars as suspect and warned their daughters away from them.

THE HARSH AND INVIGORATING realities of the mid-twentieth century crashed on to New Zealand like some refreshing wave changing it beyond recognition. For the majority of participants in the 1950 twenty-first birthday party, most of those changes would seem intolerable and unthinkable. For the restless adolescent disturbed by the faint sounds of their celebrations they were an inevitable awakening from what social commentator Bill Pearson in 1952 christened New Zealand's "fretful sleep".

In that awakening, art and writing became possible, as did a sense of place and history, the mapping of futures and strategies to cope with the painful top-hamper of social change. Into it foreigners came with their unintelligible cooking and there were pubs and cafes and vintages and, if not much fresco-painting, an art a new generation would have no difficulty recognising as their own. And distinction and exception, however much resisted and resented, became a condition of New Zealand life. Not the least of these was the definition of the boundaries between youth and age; and the word teenager made its way into the New Zealand language.

Inasmuch as the term means a defiantly different taste, youth culture is as obvious a part of the contemporary scene now as it became from the mid-fifties to sixties. The vigorous street styles of urban New Zealand in the 1980s are as much a reflection of the vigour of the contemporary culture in general as they are a defiant beating of its boundaries. In the 1950s that defiance was often a painful business. Far from being a component of any general culture, it ran distinctly against its grain.

The social and cultural poverties of the 1930s and 1940s were simply a dull ground bass to the children of those decades. They were troubled and challenged by the notion of change and adventure. And as the decade of their adolescence wore on, the youth culture of the United States in particular had powerful messages for them. They were no longer simply content to flow in the turgid wake of their elders. Their disquiet created moral panic after moral panic in their parents.

In 1954 the sexual experimentation of a small number of Hutt Valley teenagers became the stuff of a national scandal leading to a special government committee of inquiry into Moral Delinquency, whose report was posted to every home in the country. It came to no conclusions and offered no solutions other than dark hints that the influences of American pop songs and comics were not good.

From then on various style cults like Teddy Boys and Girls, Bodgies and Widgies, Milk Bar Cowboys, Mods and Rockers would inspire the same kind of fear and loathing in older people that ethnic gangs did a generation later. Magistrates in court would regularly order spectators, witnesses and defendants off to get a haircut and sometimes even went so far as to condone assaults on long-haired youths. Gangs of short-back-and-sides servicemen would stalk Auckland and Wellington streets looking for fashionable youths to barber forcibly.

But for all the antagonism it engendered, the youth revolution that began about 1954 – and it deserves to be called no less than that – was in the vanguard of New Zealand social change. It ran deeper than the slavish copying of American models and it was critical in stimulating questions of identity and a search for an emerging New Zealand culture.

New Zealand youth wanted their own heroes, even if they were unsure just how to go about locating them. By 1958 Johnny Devlin's version of the Elvis Presley hit *Lawdy Miss Clawdy* was outselling the original more than two to one. This was the beginning of the line that leads directly to the vigorous New Zealand popular music of the eighties. Far from regurgitating foreign sounds, bands that began in inner city pubs shaping their live music from the tastes of their New Zealand peers have moved on to an international market as influences in their own right. Groups like Split Enz, Mi Sex and Crowded House did not succeed merely by doing someone else's thing better, but by doing their own superbly well.

In the same way the clothing styles adopted from Presley's and other Rock movies in the fifties, and London's Mary Quant and Carnaby Street in the next decade, laid the base for the talented contemporary fashion industry. London and Europe still add their influences to the current fashion, but the nexus of style has shifted to Tokyo and California – another signifier of the profound social changes of the past thirty years.

Questions of place have troubled thoughtful New Zealanders throughout this century. Until the 1950s, though, they were mainly the concern of a small minority and then mostly expressed in terms of adapting a European culture or belonging to it in some meaningful way at a distance. That there might be equally significant cultures to adapt and appropriate closer to home was hardly debated.

Nor did it occur much to New Zealanders before 1950 that they would ever be anywhere but in another

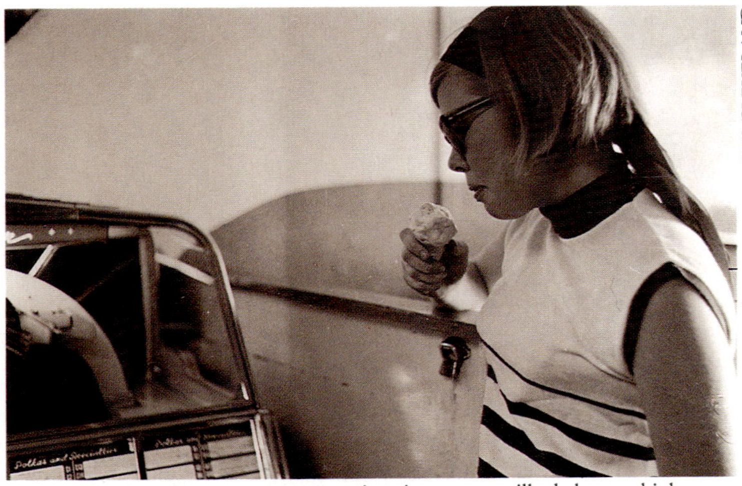
LES CLEVELAND

Girl in a milkbar, Westport, 1960. American ice cream, milk shakes, and juke boxes. New Zealand was about to lose its insularity and enter the world.

England set in a greener and more pleasant land. Their imaginations might not have been able to bridge the gaps in their own history or even consider coming to terms with the Maori culture with which they cohabited. But for some reason they could leap quite easily across half the world and three-quarters of its cultures to arrive at what they believed to be their spiritual home.

Even when physically threatened by a Pacific power in 1942 they could still commit almost their entire defence force to the European war and leave their home front to someone else to defend. But from 1950, a combination of a shift in world power politics, the abandoning of traditional trade alliances and a whole raft of other influences progressively convinced more and more New Zealanders that they lived alone in the Pacific. Not the least of these was a major change in the attitudes of a generation growing up both more open to the larger world and more sensitive to the singularity of its own.

Significantly, a whole generation of writers on art and literature have earnestly rejected notions of national identity as having any particular cultural relevance. They are right to do so, since identity in a culture is what a person assumes and in turn what the culture recognises in them. It is not something that has to be fought for or aspired to at some future time. But in 1950 no Pakeha New Zealander, however passionately they yearned to, could have seen their own culture as anything they could have assumed or that would recognise them.

There was then no popular literature, art, music, lifestyle that had them in it. That restless adolescent, disturbed by the Saturday birthday party, would have had no ready access to a literature or an art that spoke to them of their experience. When on the rare occasions they were encountered they often struck the imagination with such force as to change that young person's life.

My own encounters speak, I believe, for many. Dawdling home from school one day in 1947 I picked up from the roadside a tattered paperback book, which, to my amazement, mentioned New Zealand on almost every page. I could not put it down. I read it and re-read it late into the night, secretly huddled with a torch beneath the blankets. It was Jim Henderson's wartime autobiography, *Gunner Inglorious*. I was ten years old and for the very first time in my life I became aware that New Zealanders wrote books – something I believed in my innocence was accomplished only by foreign people.

By wonderful coincidence in that same year I was taken by my parents to an exhibition of the Christchurch Group. I saw nothing else in that gallery but the astonishing religious paintings of Colin McCahon. I knew of Christ's Passion, but it had never until that moment seemed to have had anything to do with where I lived. At ten I had been shown that where I was was somewhere after all and that those who lived there had a value all of their own. The first links that would bind me to a culture of my own had been forged.

T.S. ELIOT SAYS SOMEWHERE that before a nation has a culture it has a cuisine. It is an elegant conceit, but it carries with it more than a grain of truth. Just how much radical changes in a country's lifestyle are a reflection of cultural evolution and how much they contribute to the process is a moot point. A national pride in New Zealand food and wines is a commonplace in the 1980s. It is generally taken for granted that not only do these resources have the potential to compete, but they can and have achieved an excellence that gives them an international status. It was not always so. New Zealanders' tastes in food and drink, and their puritanical views on the public consumption of them, were once a common subject for international ridicule.

Eric Linklater, the Scottish novelist, was typical of the critics. He arrived here by flying boat early one morning in 1951 and immediately encountered the country's hostile brand of hospitality when he attempted to have a whisky and soda brought to his room. He reported on our food in his book *A Year of Space*.

The natural quality of the food is so good that it deserves both skill and reverence in the kitchen. What lordly dishes a French housewife would make of it! But the New Zealanders, like the Scots, think that baking is the better part of cookery, and spend their ingenuity, exhaust their interest, on cakes and pastries and ebullient, vast cream sponges. Soup is neglected, meat mishandled. I have seen their admirable mutton brought upon the table in such miserable shape that the hogget – so they call a sheep of uncertain age – appeared to have been killed by a bomb, and the fragments of its carcase incinerated in the resultant fire.

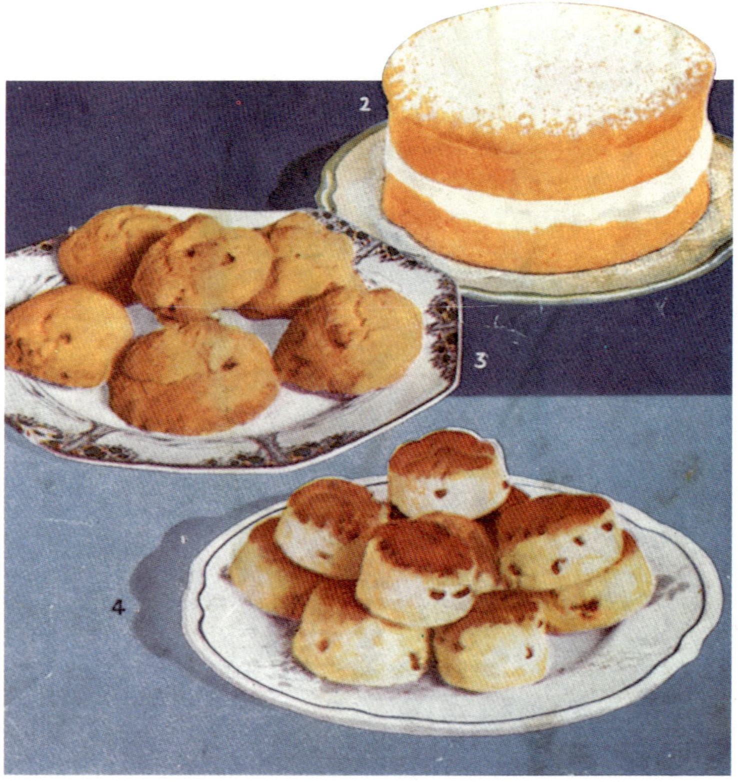

The *Edmonds Cookery Book* with its familiar rising sun motif was the dominating influence in New Zealand cooking until Graham Kerr shocked New Zealanders by talking about pâté and coq au vin instead of meat loaf and oxtail stew.

Linklater saw in New Zealand an absence of an urban culture and the curious development of suburbs on a vast scale around an urban vacuum. He put this down entirely to New Zealand attitudes where a "social legislation has decreed that social life must stop at 6 p.m.".

Civilisation needs conversation, and conversation requires some help. But in New Zealand the pubs are closed before sundown and the restaurateur is by law strangled in his infancy. There are some good hotels, and all I saw were brightly clean; but about the hour when little boys should be put to bed, life ebbs away from their public rooms, as if ashamed to linger . . . Urban life is poorly furnished . . .

Yet only a generation later, New Zealand chefs were not only transforming the eating habits of their fellow citizens but winning international awards in London and Paris and establishing splendid restaurants in Sydney and Melbourne. There is, as yet, no singular New Zealand cuisine, perhaps such a thing is not possible. But there is an innovative approach to that natural resource that Linklater thought so notable that is markedly different to the traditional cuisines ingeniously adapted to present it. There is a New Zealand flair with food that is increasingly being remarked upon and on which an increasingly sophisticated national palate is making its demands.

The growth in New Zealand restaurants is nothing less than extraordinary. In 1961, when at last the consumption of wine was restored by law to public dining in other than hotel dining rooms, provision was made by the then Licensing Control Commission for a mere ten restaurant licences for the entire country. Twenty years on, restaurant guides list several hundred.

Linklater and other contemporary visitors had nothing to say about New Zealand wine. Not surprisingly, perhaps, at a period in the country's development when wine survived only as a rough red country plonk or a sickly and dangerous sweet sherry. Yet oddly enough a visiting Frenchman in 1840 was impressed enough by one of the first vintages, which he described as a "light white wine, very sparkling and delicious", to speculate on its future as an export. And many after him remarked on the same potential.

To those who lived here, however, wine was treated with the gravest of suspicions, although perhaps not all would have gone so far as one Prime Minister, William Massey, who attempted in 1918 to persuade Parliament to outlaw New Zealand wine, describing it as a "degrading, demoralising and sometimes maddening drink to many who use it".

Things were no better in 1946 when the Royal Commission on licensing reported that "a considerable quantity of wine made in New Zealand would be classified as unfit for human consumption in other wine producing countries".

Yet exactly half a century after Prime Minister Massey attempted to have them banned, an English wine writer, Jancis Robinson, could confidently describe some New Zealand cabernets as "world class" and favourably compare the evolution of modern winemaking here to that in Italy. In the comparison, Robinson judged the New Zealand industry to have what she called "more classically based stunners" than the Italian. Wine had come a long way from the sweet sherries, sickly ports, "purple death" and "Dally plonk" which would have been all that restless adolescent would have encountered in 1950, if there had been any encounter with wine at all.

To those of a determined seriousness, popular music and entertainment, fashion, wine and food might seem trivial matters when measured against weightier cultural manifestations such as art, literature and classical music. In truth there is no hierarchy in culture, or if there is it is of an artificial and academic manufacture. When the expression of people's identity can be as easily assumed as the clothes they wear, the wine they drink, the food they eat and the entertainments they choose, then they and their culture have come of age.

New Zealand at the end of the decade of the eighties has become a country of challenge and diversity. The comfort of the mediocre and timid might be painfully challenged by these things, but it has given the land an energy and purpose it has not had before.

As the tangata whenua insist on and achieve recognition and respect for their millenial culture, so it has begun to dawn on Pakeha New Zealanders that they too have begun to achieve a culture and style of life that is to be found in no other place. The dynamic that flows between those two cultures – the one so established and so certain of its values, the other hardly yet begun – will be the power that drives a singular New Zealand, for better or for worse, into the twenty-first century. □

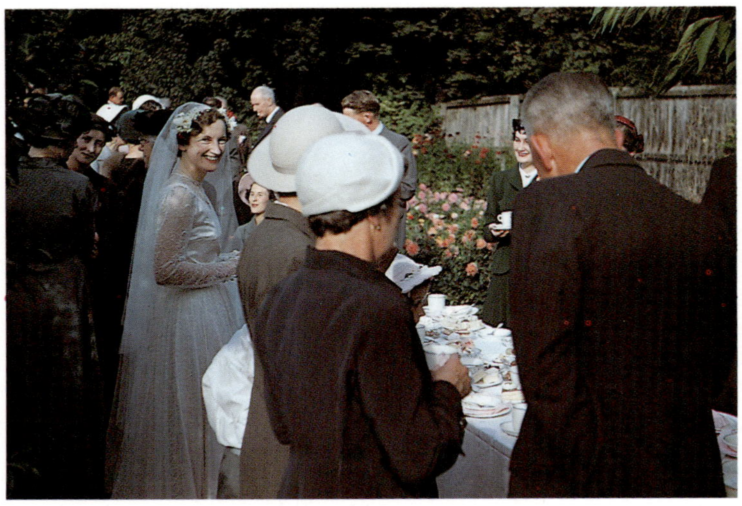

Wedding breakfast in private garden, Fendalton, Christchurch, 1955. GARY BLACKMAN

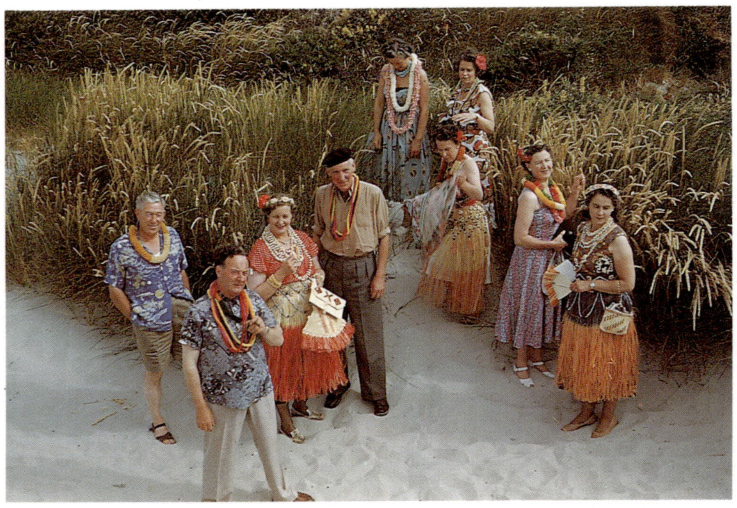

Hawaiian party at Aramoana, Otago Harbour, 1953. LANCE BLACKMAN

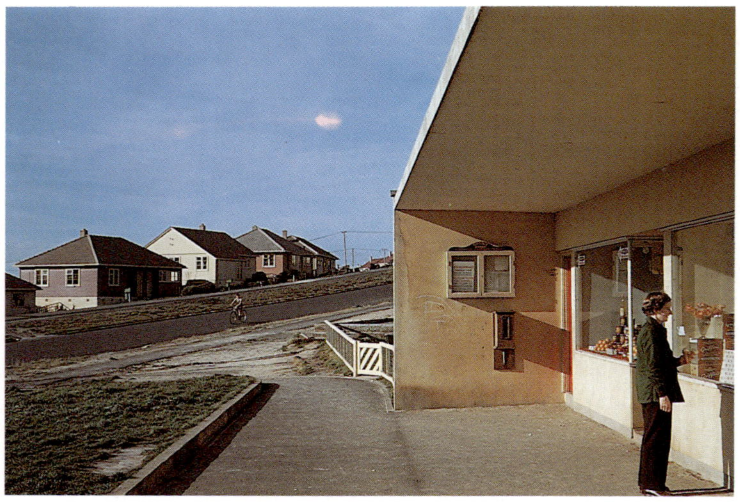

State houses and store, Corstorphine, Dunedin, 1955. GARY BLACKMAN

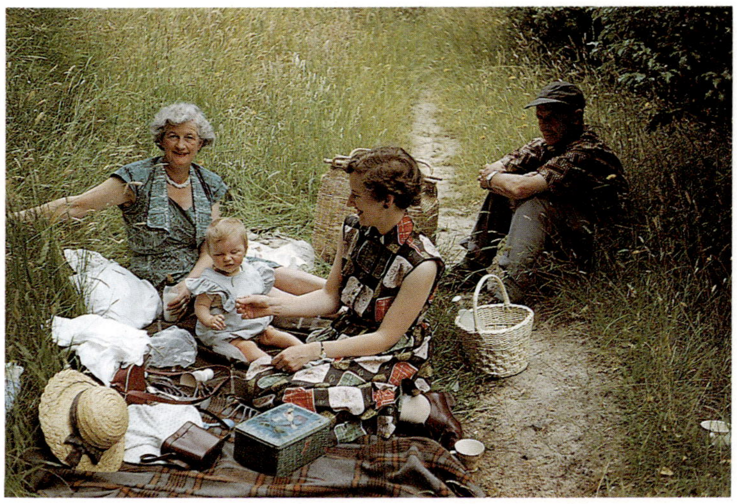

Family picnic, Victoria Park, Christchurch, 1957. GARY BLACKMAN

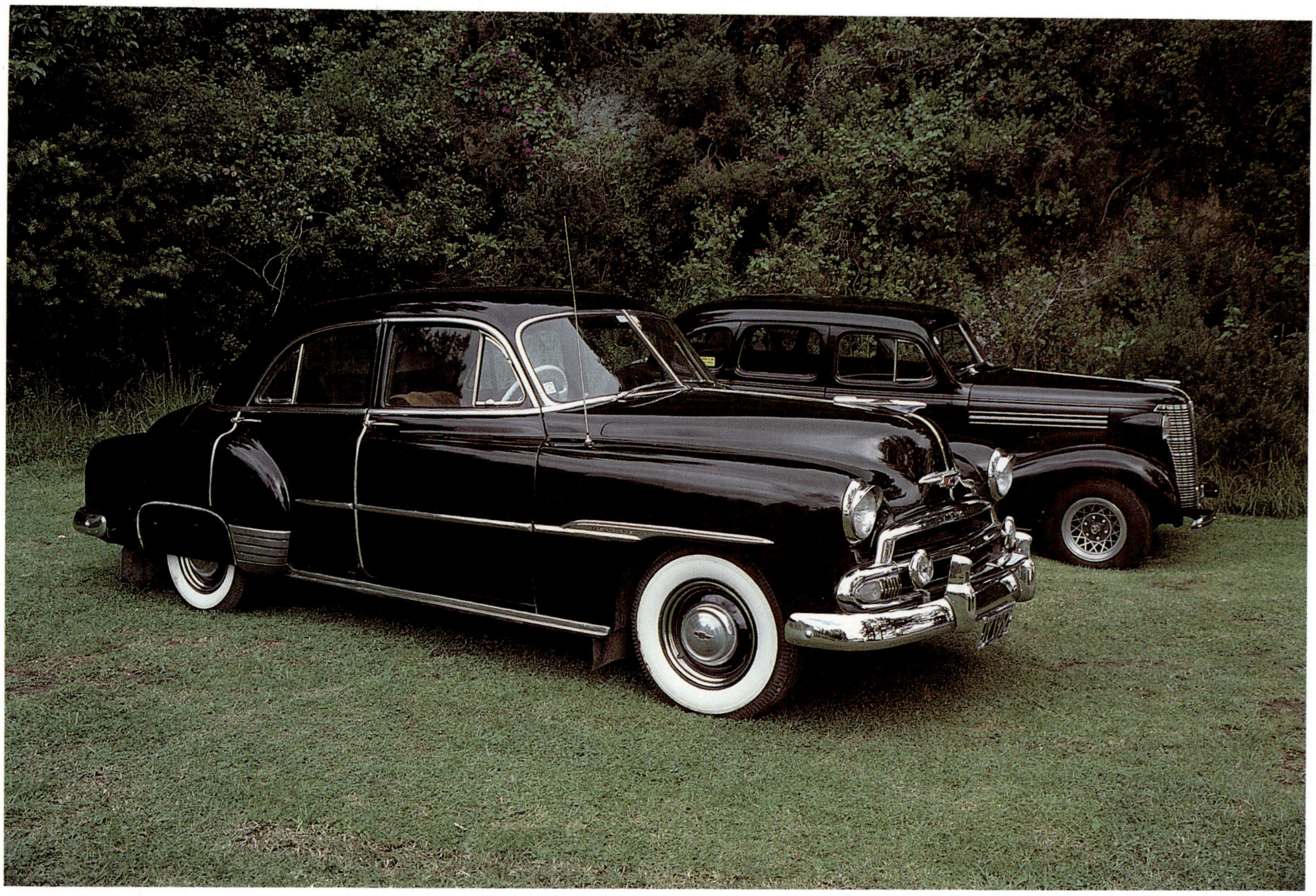

Russell

STEPHEN ROBINSON

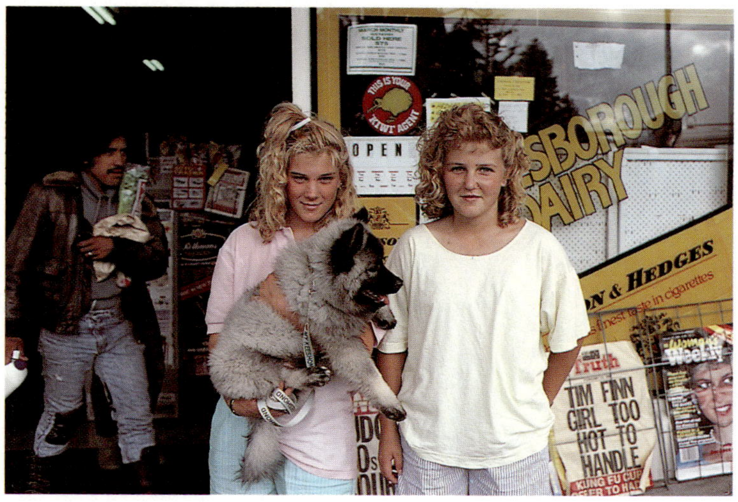

Rochelle, Charmaine and Sam the dog outside the Hillsborough Dairy, Auckland

TIM STEELE

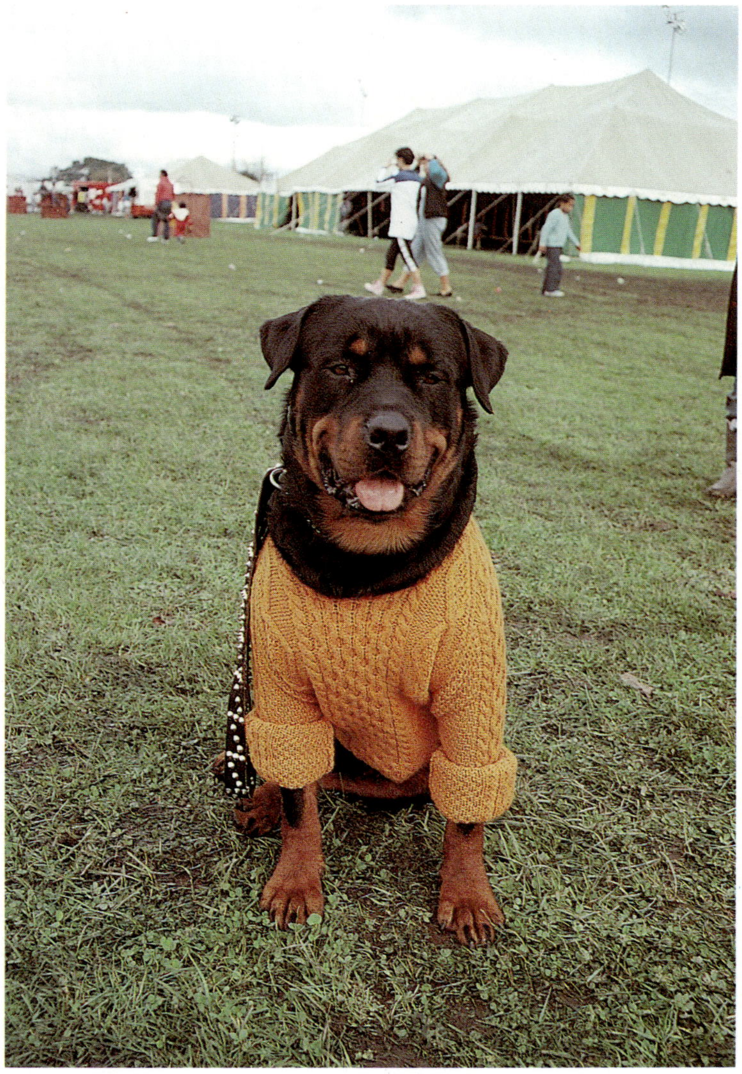

Rottweiler in jersey, Ngaruawahia

ERIC TAYLOR

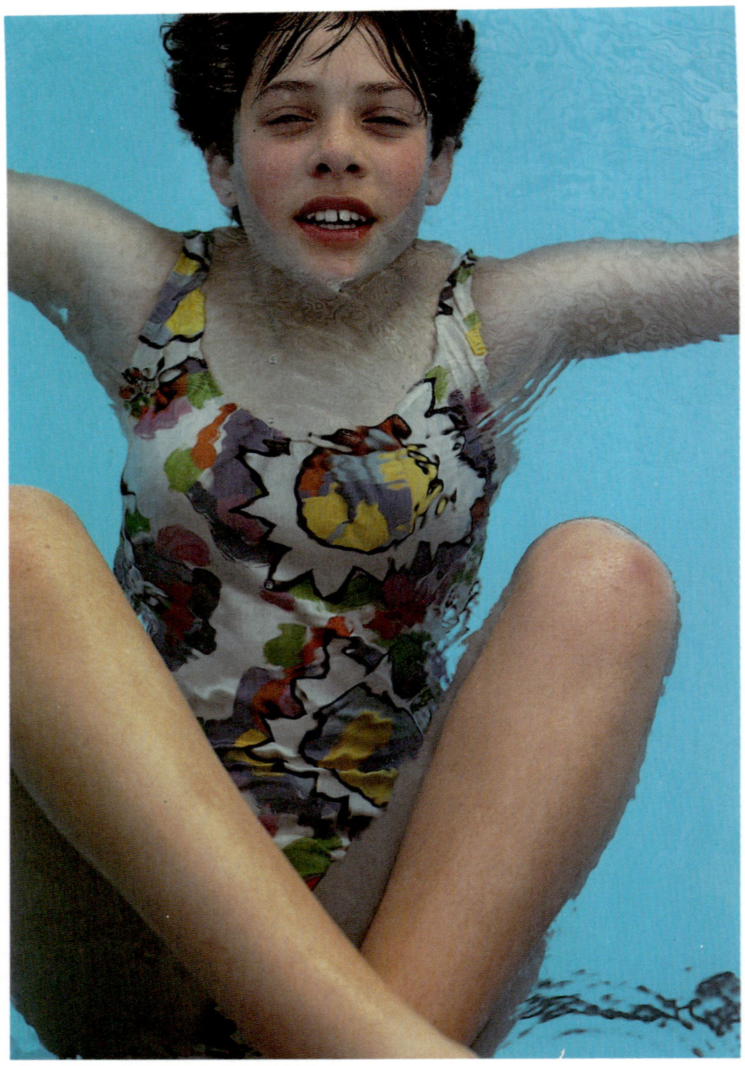

Sally Connew at Riverside Swimming Pool, Nelson — BRUCE CONNEW

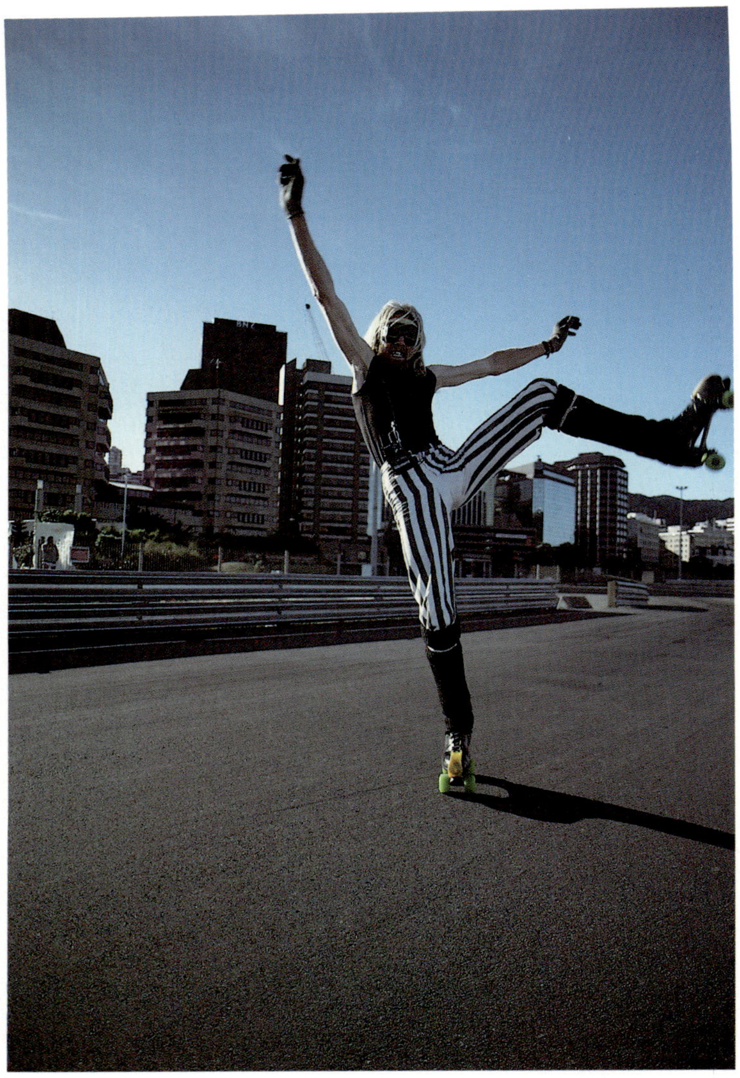

Mike Hurrell, street skater, Wellington waterfront — TIM STEELE

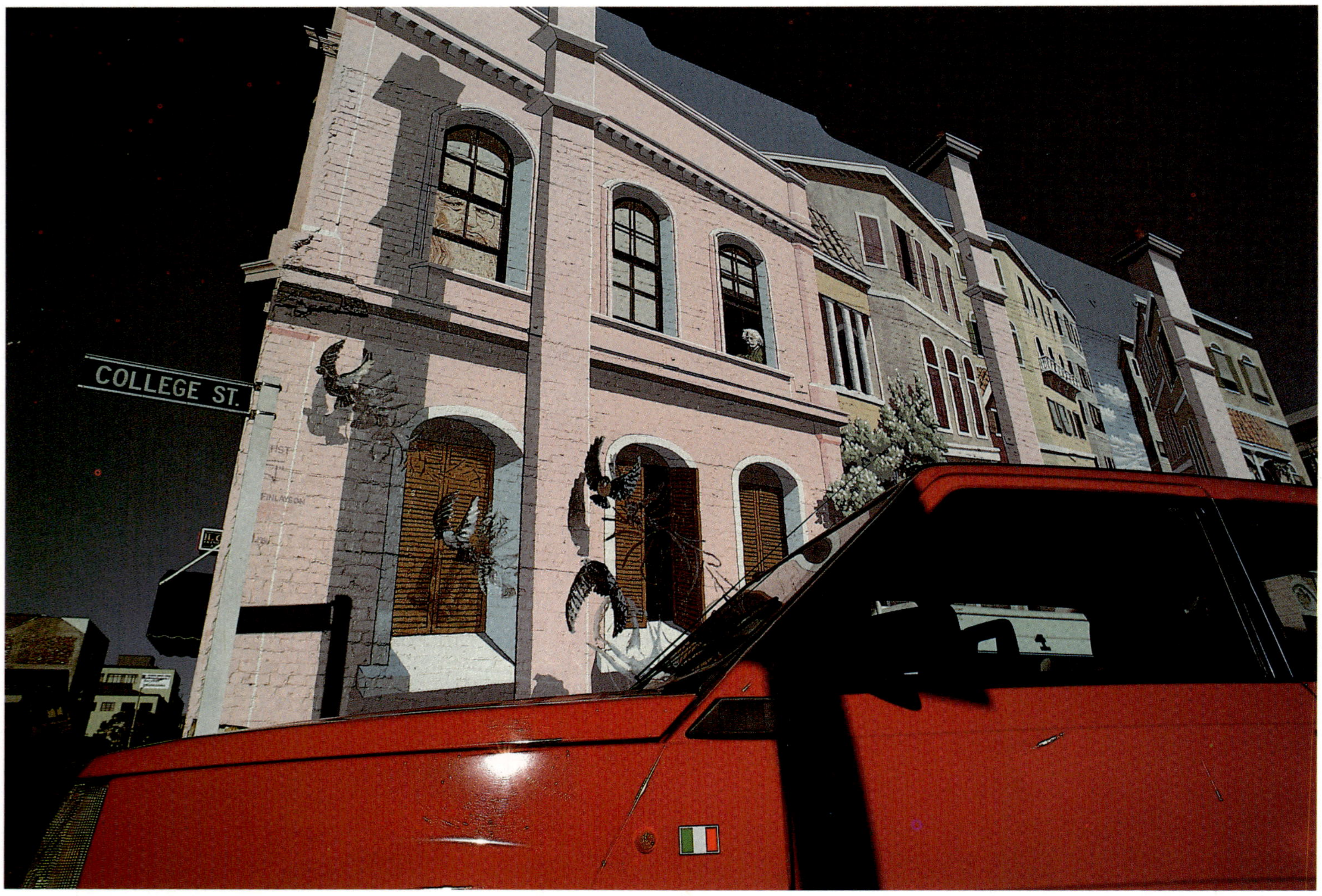

Il Casino restaurant mural, College Street, Wellington — TIM STEELE

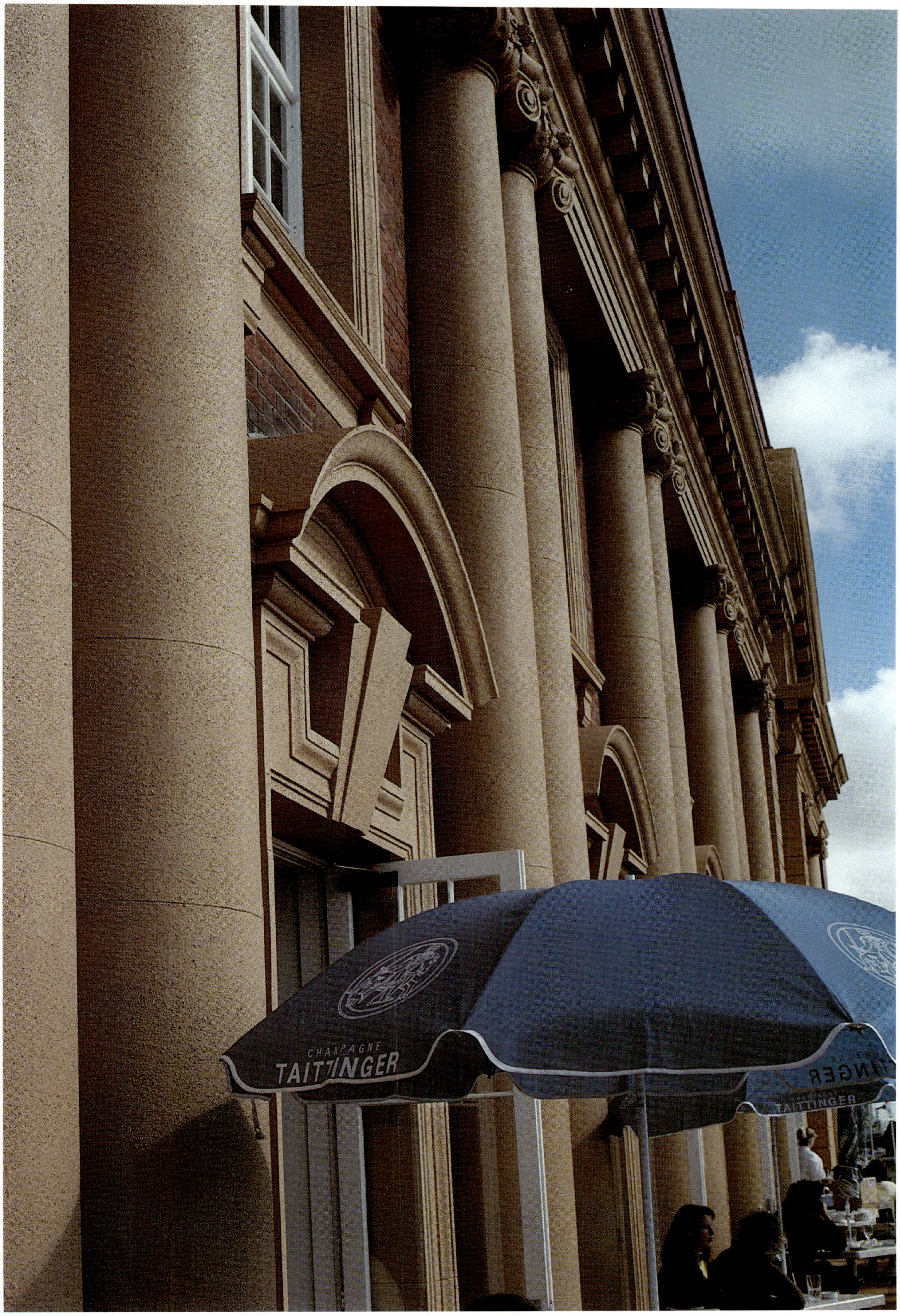

Harbourside Grill, old Ferry Buildings, Auckland

STEPHEN ROBINSON

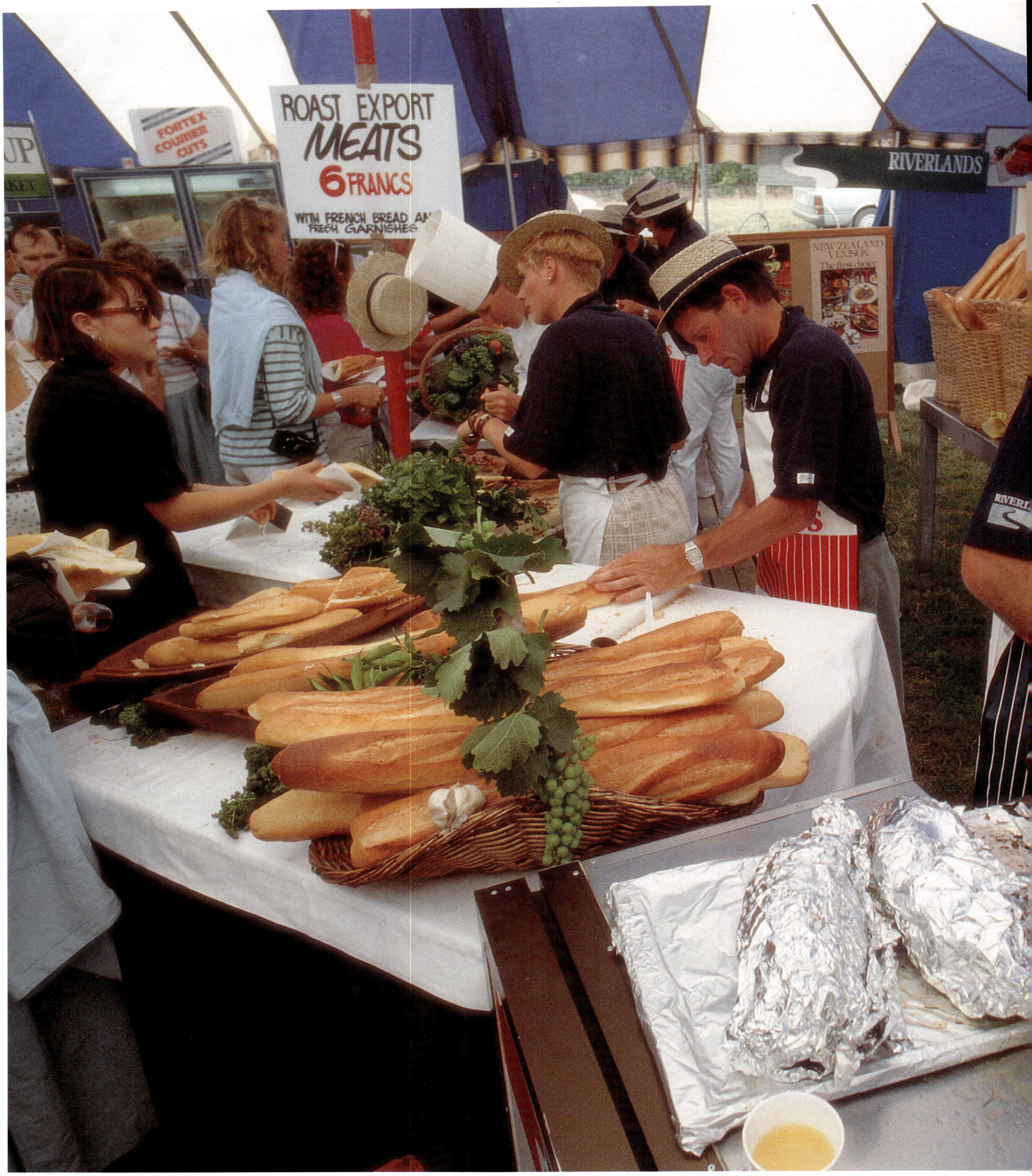

Marlborough Food and Wine Festival, 1989

STEPHEN ROBINSON

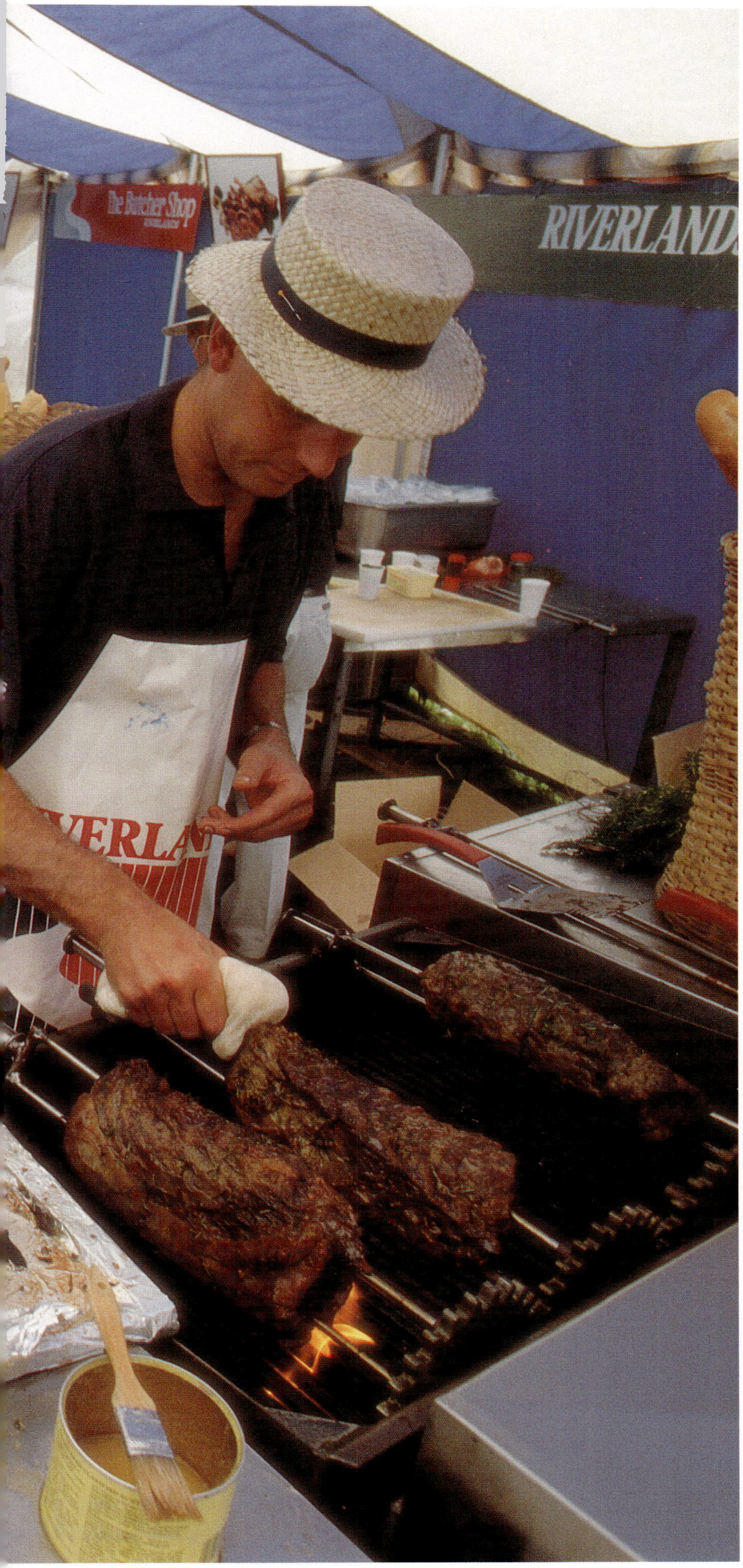

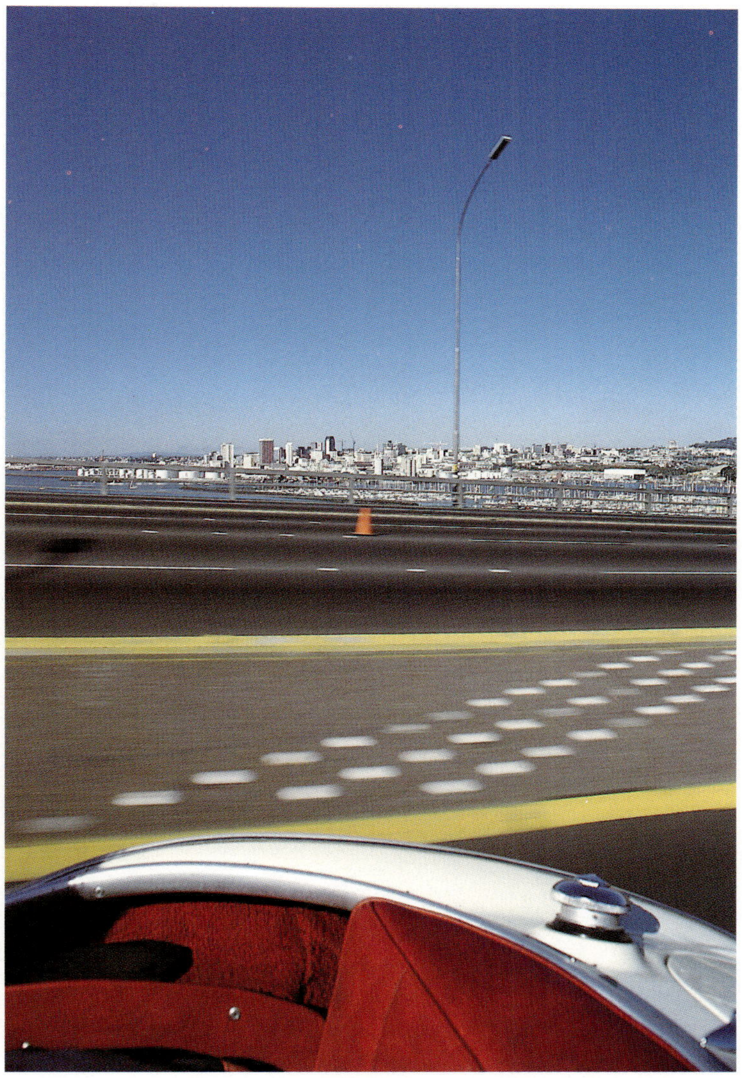

Crossing Auckland Harbour Bridge STEPHEN ROBINSON

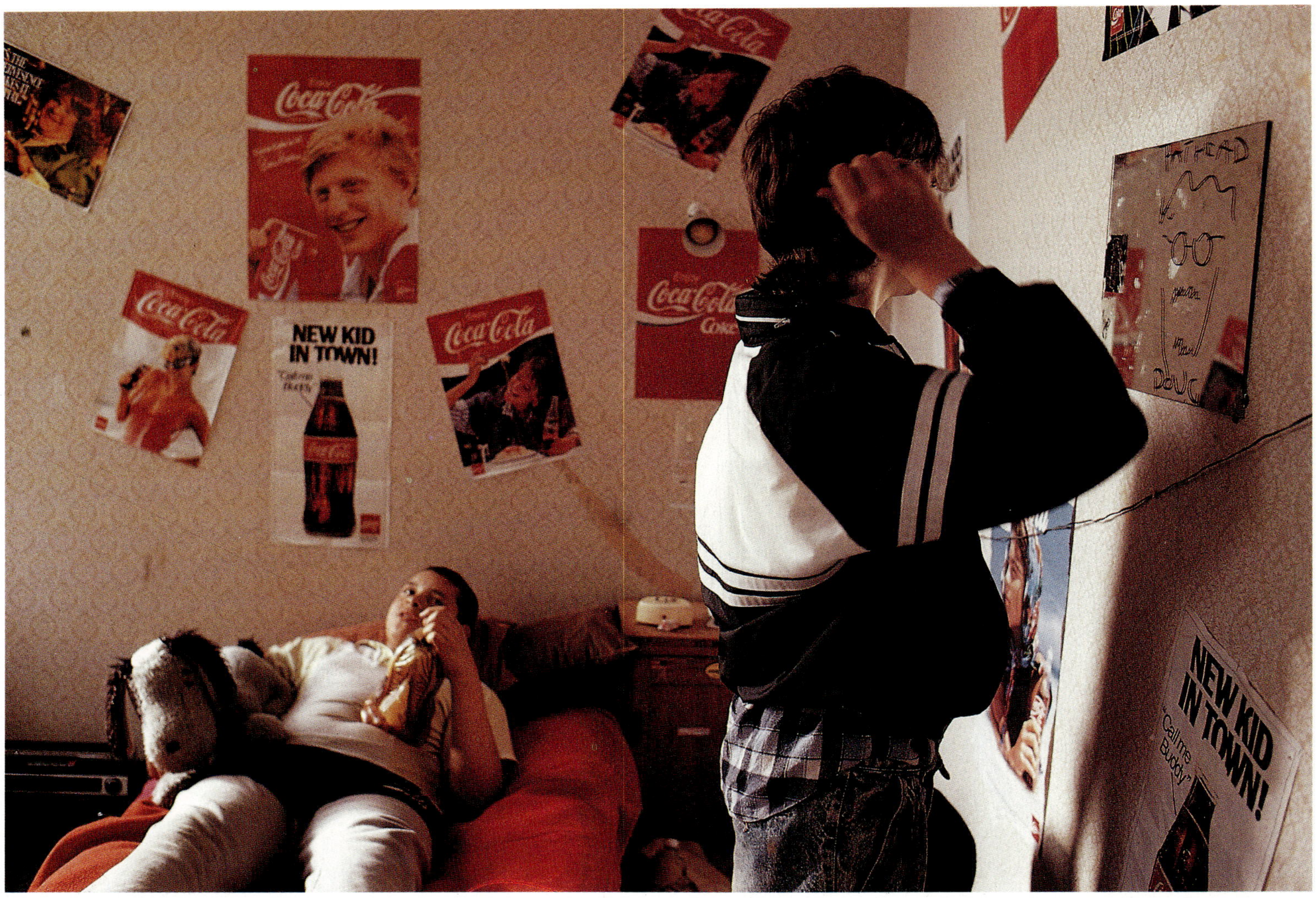

Garindale Boy's Home, Nelson, (now closed) BRUCE CONNEW

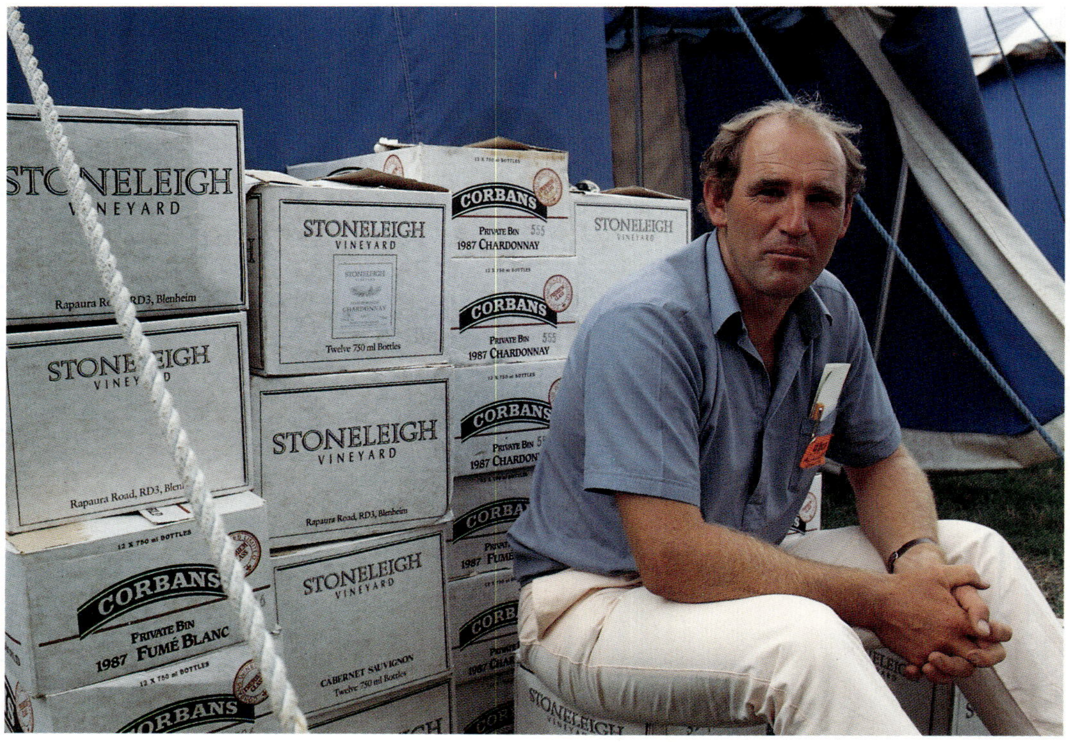

Marlborough Food and Wine Festival STEPHEN ROBINSON

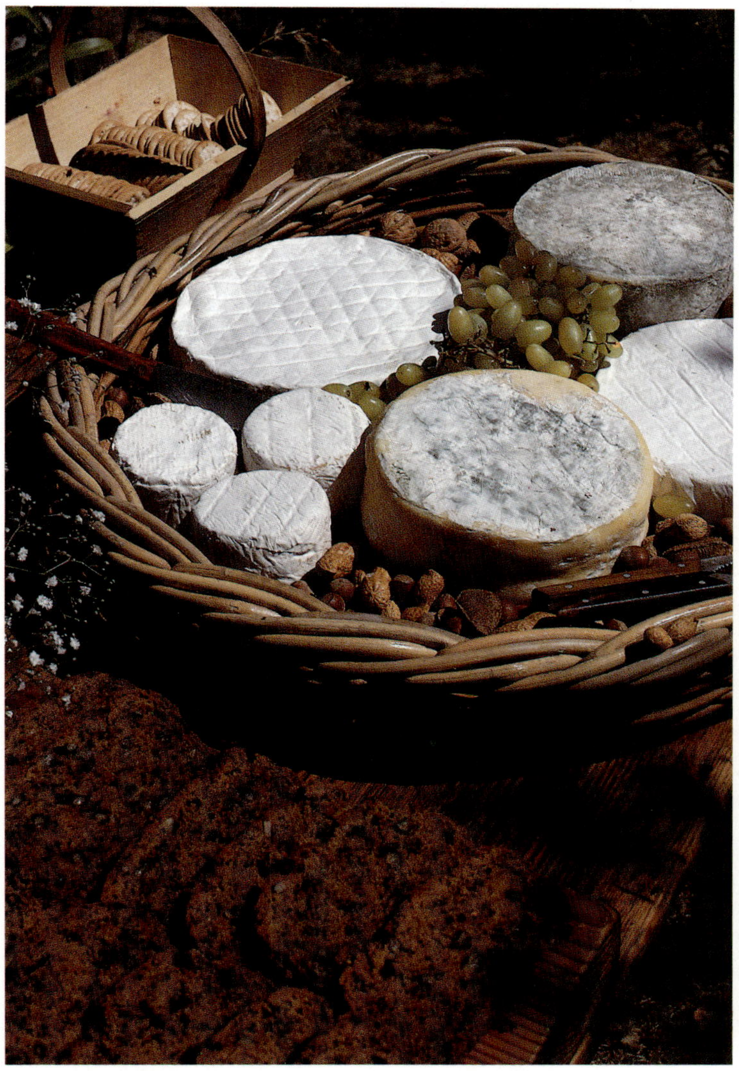

Wedding, Otaki STEPHEN ROBINSON

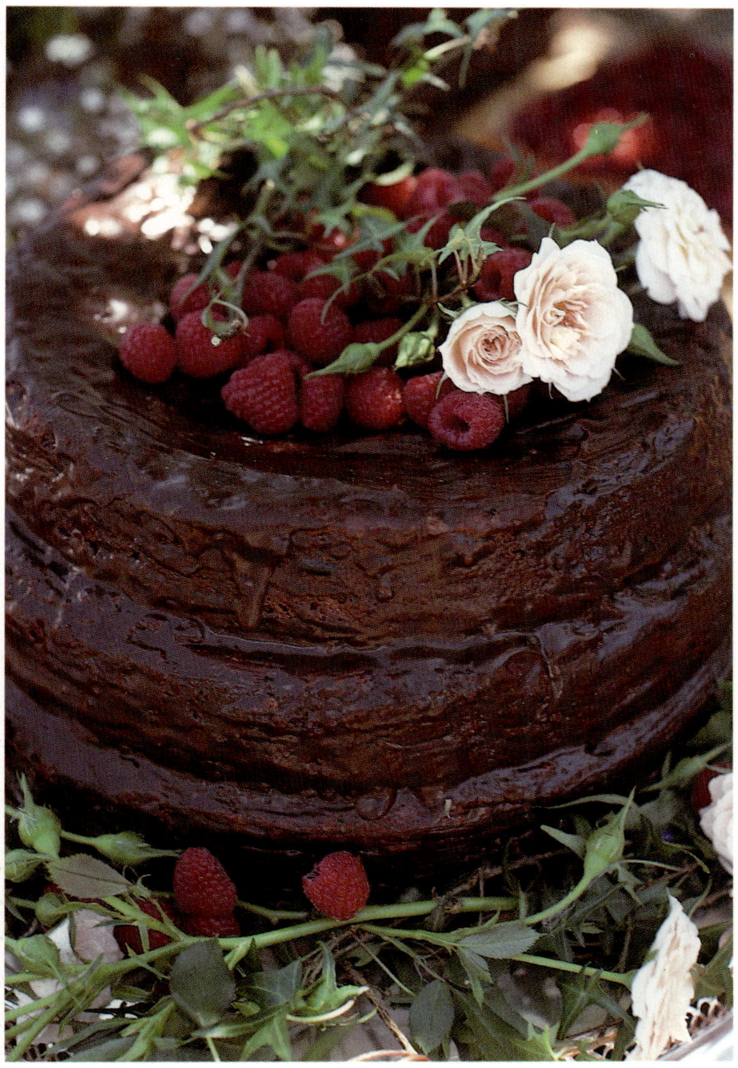

Wedding, Otaki STEPHEN ROBINSON

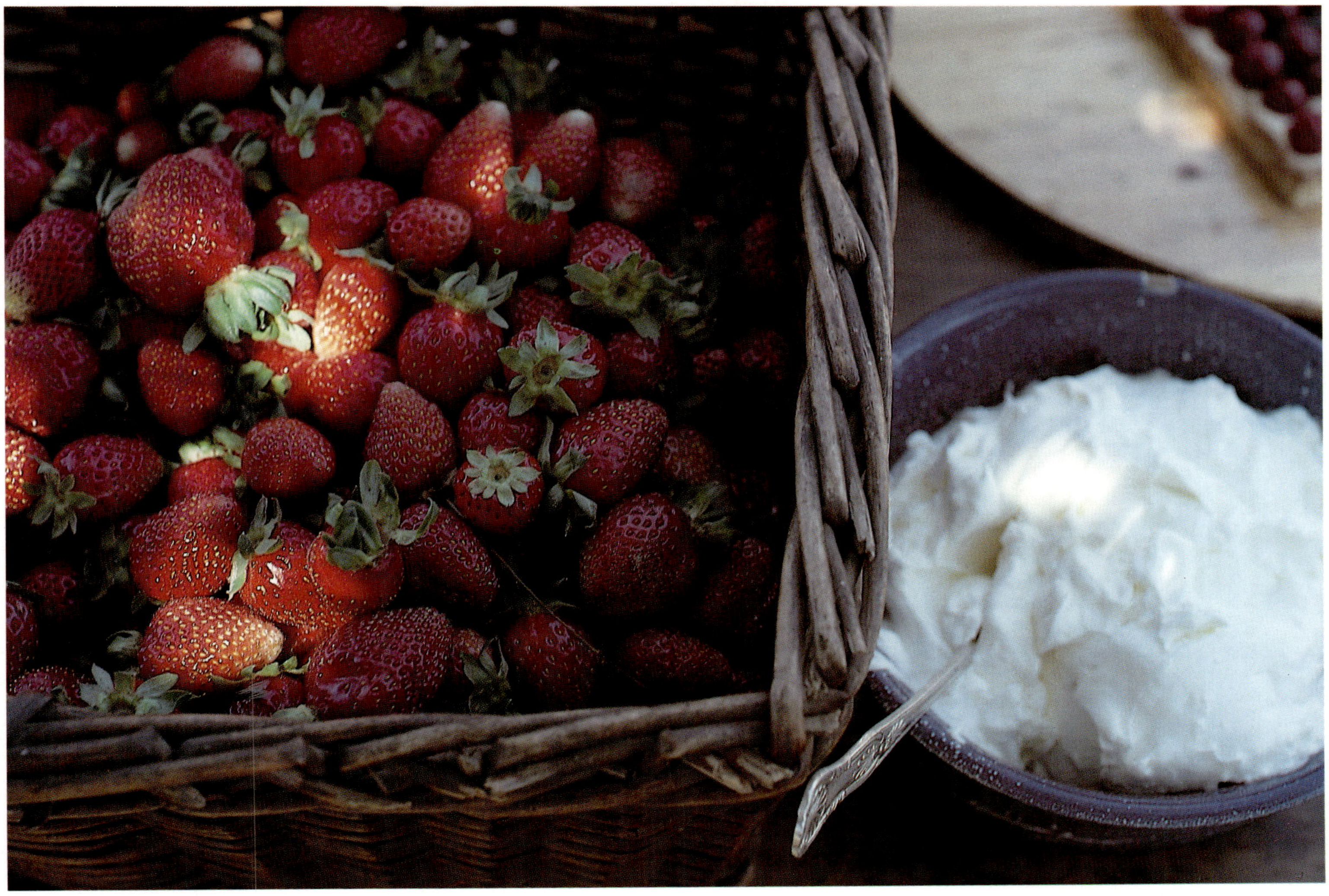

Wedding, Otaki STEPHEN ROBINSON

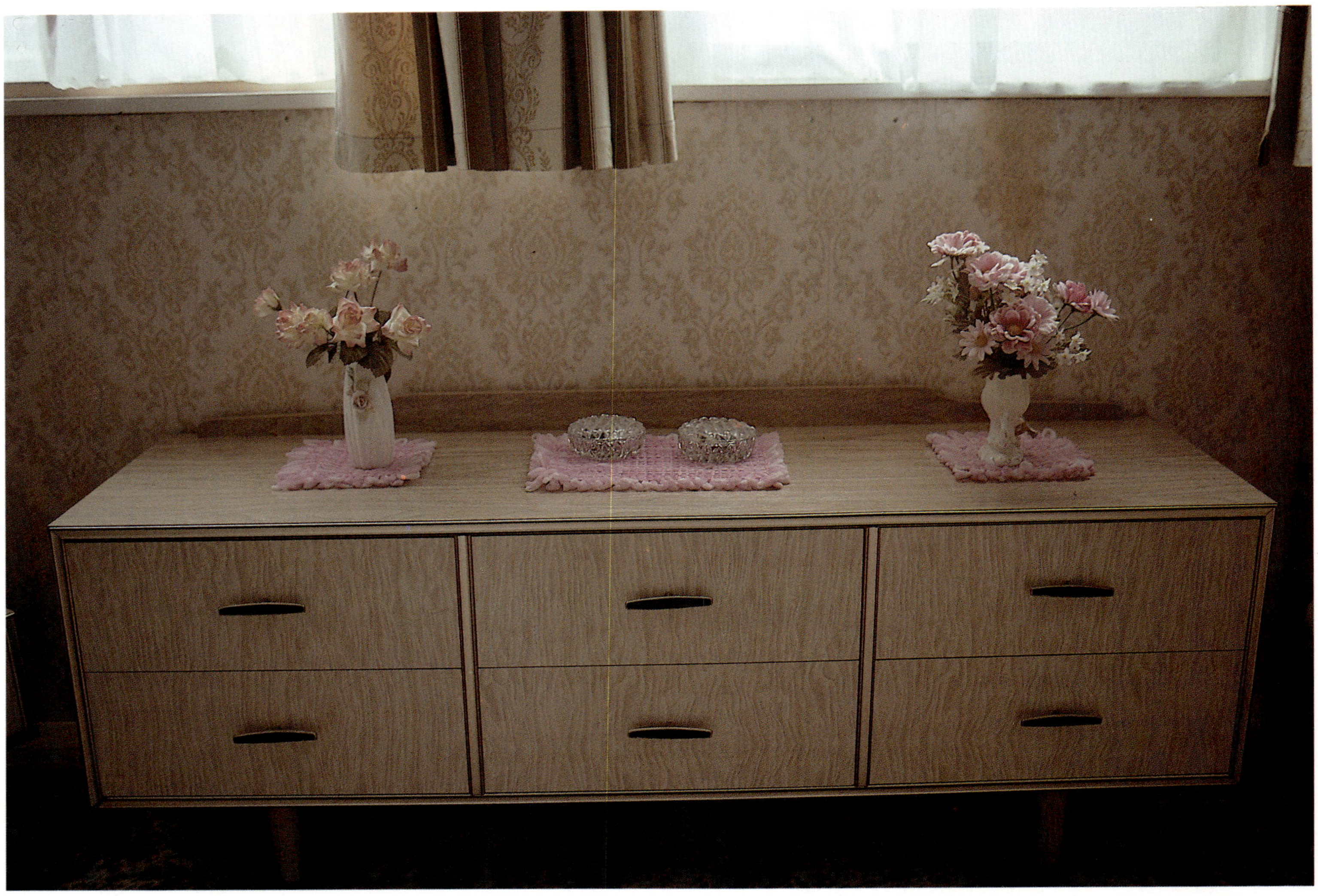

Beach house, Kina, Motueka STEPHEN ROBINSON

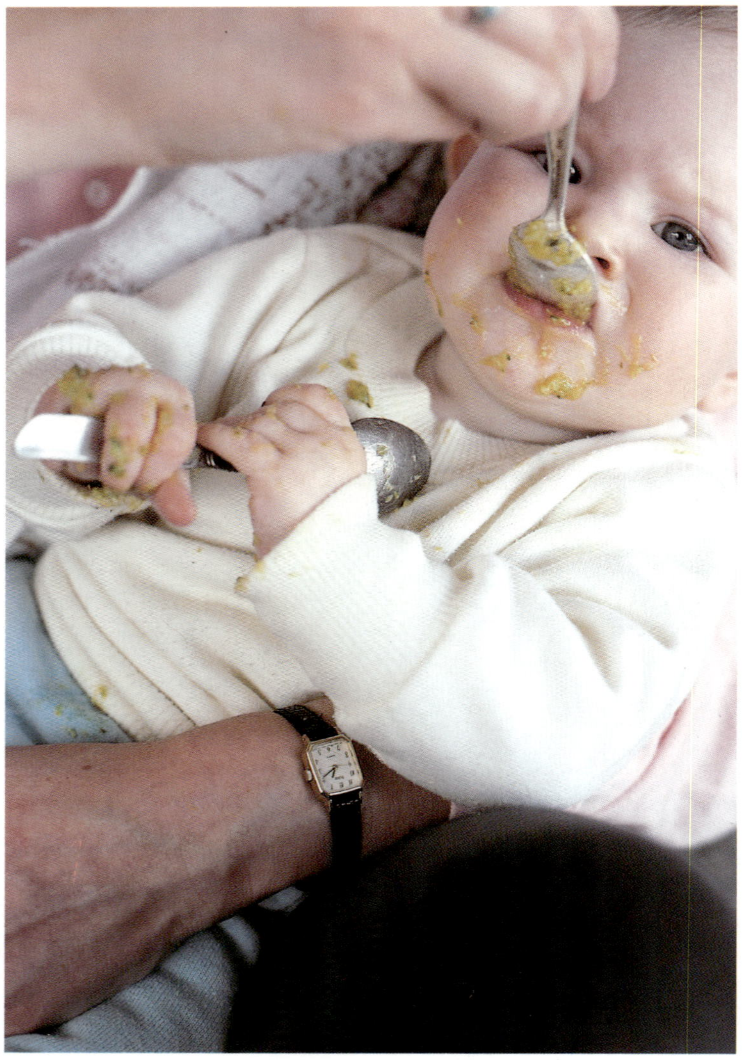

Alice Marie Thomas Connew's first solids BRUCE CONNEW

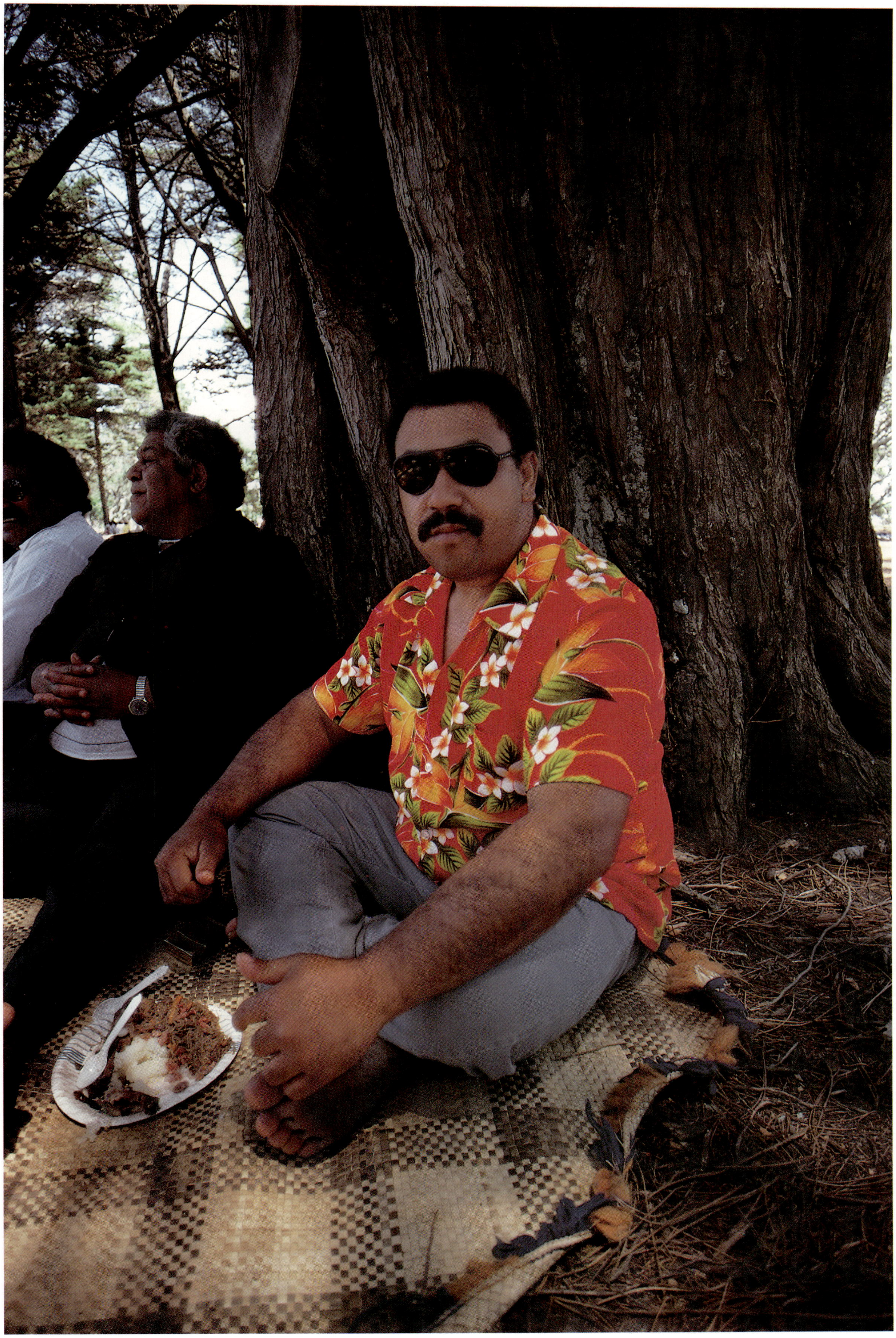

THE ADVISORY BOARD

Chairman
Sir Leonard Thornton

Christine Cole-Catley

Dame Whina Cooper

Jeremy Coney

Professor Kenneth Cumberland

Hamish Keith

Robert Mahuta

Shona McFarlane

Hon Mike Moore

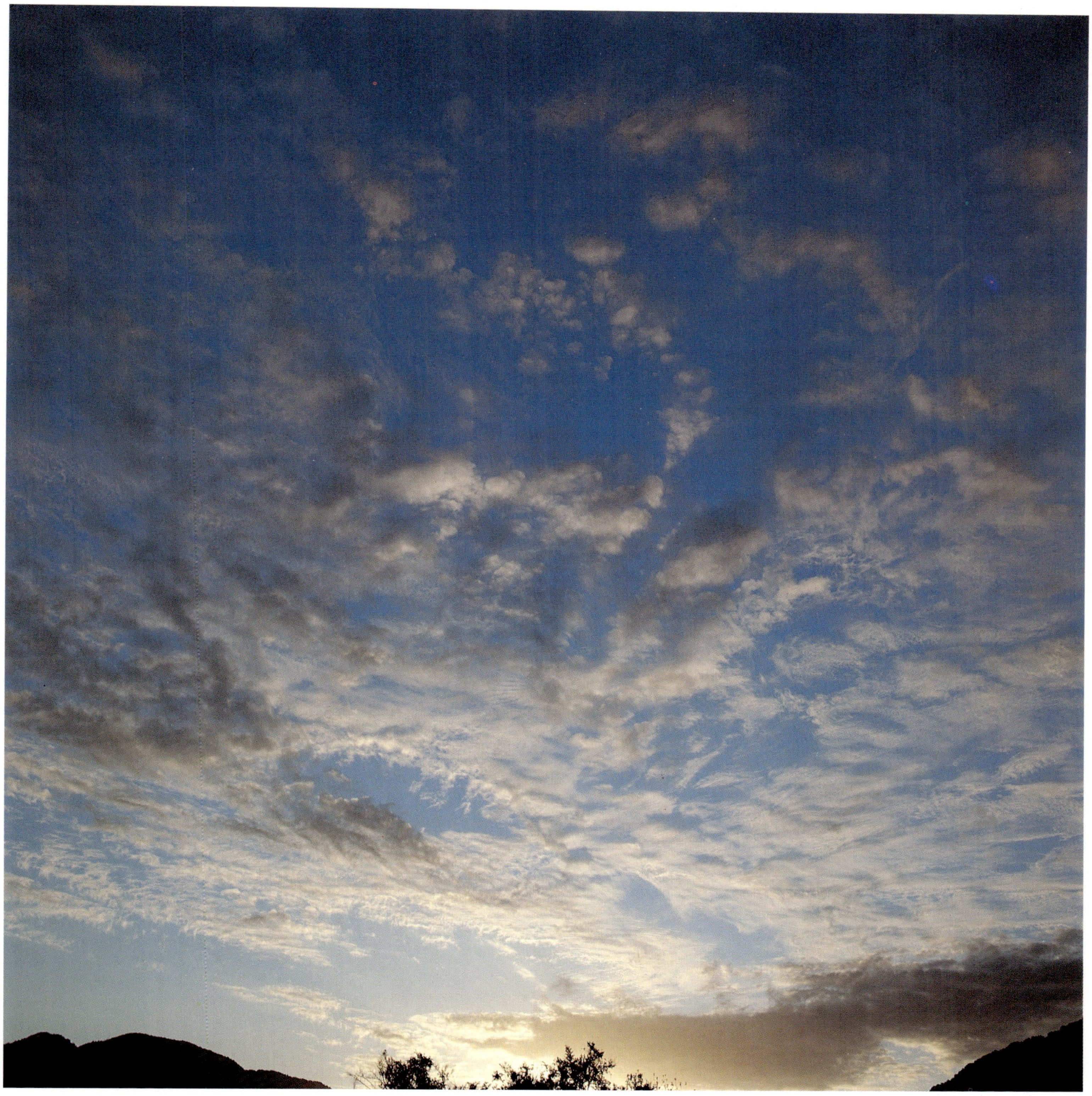

Franz Joseph West Coast BRIAN ENTING

THE PHOTOGRAPHERS

Bruce Connew learned photography in England, and in 1976 made a major documentary study of an Australian aboriginal community. Returning to New Zealand, he had much of his work published in the *Listener*, with major assignments on New Caledonia and South Africa. The latter work has been published in book form and exhibited at the National Gallery. In 1989 he went to the Burmese jungle to photograph the revolutionary struggle of the Karen ethnic minority group. He won the 1986 Beattie Award for Photographic Journalism, and now works freelance, based in Auckland.

Brian Enting is best known for his natural history photography, which has taken him to many wilderness areas in New Zealand, Australia and Africa. After more than twenty years in the advertising and photographic industry, he now operates from his Upper Hutt house. He has contributed to many local and international magazines and exhibitions, and has published three photographic books. He was one of the founding trustees for the New Zealand Centre for Photography and became its director in 1987.

Gil Hanly began to take her photography seriously after attending a Photo Forum Summer School in the late 1970s. In 1984, she left her bookshop job and began working as a freelancer, documenting issues of the day, especially those of peace and social justice. Her books include *Peace is More than the Absence of War* and *The Book of Auckland*, with text by Tessa Duder. Her forthcoming titles focus on city gardens and the Waitemata Harbour.

Geoff Mason is a freelance photographer and highly respected teacher of photography. In 1979, scholarships and grants from the New Zealand Professional Photographers Association and the Queen Elizabeth II Arts Council enabled him to study photography and photographic education in the USA, Europe and Asia. He now lives in the high country of New Zealand's South Island.

Robin Morrison taught himself photography while living in London in the late sixties. He has had many books published overseas and locally, and his work is represented in New Zealand galleries and the Metropolitan Museum of Modern Art. His *The South Island of New Zealand—From the Road*, made possible by a Queen Elizabeth II Arts Council grant, won the non-fiction section of the New Zealand Book Awards in 1982. He has since published books on historic Australian, Irish and English villages and country towns. He lives in Auckland.

Craig Potton worked for several years in the conservation movement, while also involved in local body politics in Nelson where he lives. He became a freelance author and photographer in 1981, with work being published internationally. His publications include handbooks on New Zealand's national parks. Recently, he has formed his own publishing company, the first major book being *Images from a Limestone Landscape*. He is currently working on books on an aerial perspective of New Zealand and the geothermal and volcanic region.

Stephen Robinson studied photography with Geoff Mason, becoming a freelance photographer in 1982. The following year he completed a major essay on Australian long-distance trucking, then travelled and worked in North America and Europe before returning to New Zealand in 1987. He has been involved in many group shows, has had two solo exhibitions and regularly contributes to magazines. He lives in Auckland.

Tim Steele was born in British Guiana but has made New Zealand his home since 1975. He lives in Auckland where he is a freelance photographer. He specialises in landscape and portrait photography. He has travelled and photographed widely overseas, with his most recent work published in *Focus on New Zealand*.

Eric Taylor was born at Thames, but began his photographic career while living in Perth. He returned to New Zealand in 1979 and began photographing the landscape in colour. His first book, *This Land of Light* won the New Zealand Book Award for book production in 1983. Other books are *Volcanic New Zealand* and *New Zealand*.

Jane Ussher trained in photography in Wellington where she still lives. She has worked exclusively for the *Listener* with an emphasis on large format portraiture work. She is currently Illustrations Editor of the *Listener*. In 1984, her work was featured in a book on Northland, written by Fiona Kidman.

THE AUTHORS

Laurie Barber is an Associate-Professor of History and Dean of the School of Humanities at the University of Waikato. He is the author of six books and currently teaches in military and New Zealand history. He lives in Hamilton.

Terry Hall is Business Editor of the *Dominion* newspaper, based in Wellington, and is one of the most respected business and economic journalists in the country. He has worked as Chief Sub-Editor for the BBC, specialising in international affairs, and has won major journalism awards for economic, superannuation and insurance reporting.

Keri Hulme has published poetry and short stories over a long period. Her acclaimed novel *the bone people* initially could not find a publisher. It went on to win the important British Booker Prize in 1985. Hulme is a member of the Kai Tahu tribe and has lived on the West Coast of the South Island for more than a decade.

Kevin Ireland, poet and writer of prose, recently returned to New Zealand after two decades in Britain. His *Selected Poems*, published in the Oxford Poets Series, was his tenth volume of poetry. He writes a regular column for the *Listener* called "North Shore" after the North Shore of Auckland, where he lives. In 1989 he became Literary Fellow at Auckland University and is compiling a survey of fifty-two New Zealand novels.

Colin James is a Wellington freelance journalist, specialising in politics. He is a former Editor of the *National Business Review*, and is a frequent political commentator on radio. He has written a number of books, monographs and chapters on political, social and economic issues, including *The Quiet Revolution* in 1986, a classic study of contemporary New Zealand.

Hamish Keith is one of New Zealand's leading art critics who, in 1969, co-authored the seminal work *New Zealand Painting: an Introduction*. His other books include the major social history *New Zealand's Yesterdays* and the best-selling *Becoming Single: A Resource Book for the Newly Separated*. He is a former chairman of the Queen Elizabeth II Arts Council and lives in Auckland.

Gordon McLauchlan is a versatile journalist and author, having worked in print, radio and television. His book *The Passionless People* (1976) was a best seller and the title has become part of the language. His other works include *The Farming of New Zealand* and Bateman's *New Zealand Encyclopedia*. An Aucklander, McLauchlan was for four years host of the TVNZ Sunday morning magazine programme *Weekend*.

James McNeish is a Wellington novelist and playwright of international repute with work published in several languages. His novels include *Mackenzie*, *The Glass Zoo*, *Joy* and *Lovelock*. *Penelope's Island* will appear in London in 1990.

Buddy Mikaere claims affiliations with the majority of the central North Island tribes, but regards himself as a member of Ngati Pukenga. He has made a career in industrial relations and personnel work and is currently employed as the personnel manager of New Zealand's largest cable-making company. He writes in his spare time and in 1988 his first book *Te Maiharoa and the Promised Land* was published. It is the story of the nineteenth century South Island prophet Hipa Te Maiharoa and his search for justice over land grievances.

Ron Palenski is one of the country's most experienced journalists, now specialising in sports writing for the *Dominion* and *Dominion Sunday Times* while based in Auckland. Voted Sports Journalist of the Year in 1987, he has written books on rugby, cricket and New Zealand's participation in the Olympic and Commonwealth Games.

Peter Shaw is a prominent Auckland freelance journalist, critic and author who since 1981 has written a column on the arts for Auckland's *Metro* magazine. He has a particular interest in the history of architecture, and his book *Art Deco Napier: Styles of the Thirties* was published in 1987. He is currently working on a history of New Zealand architecture to be published in 1990.

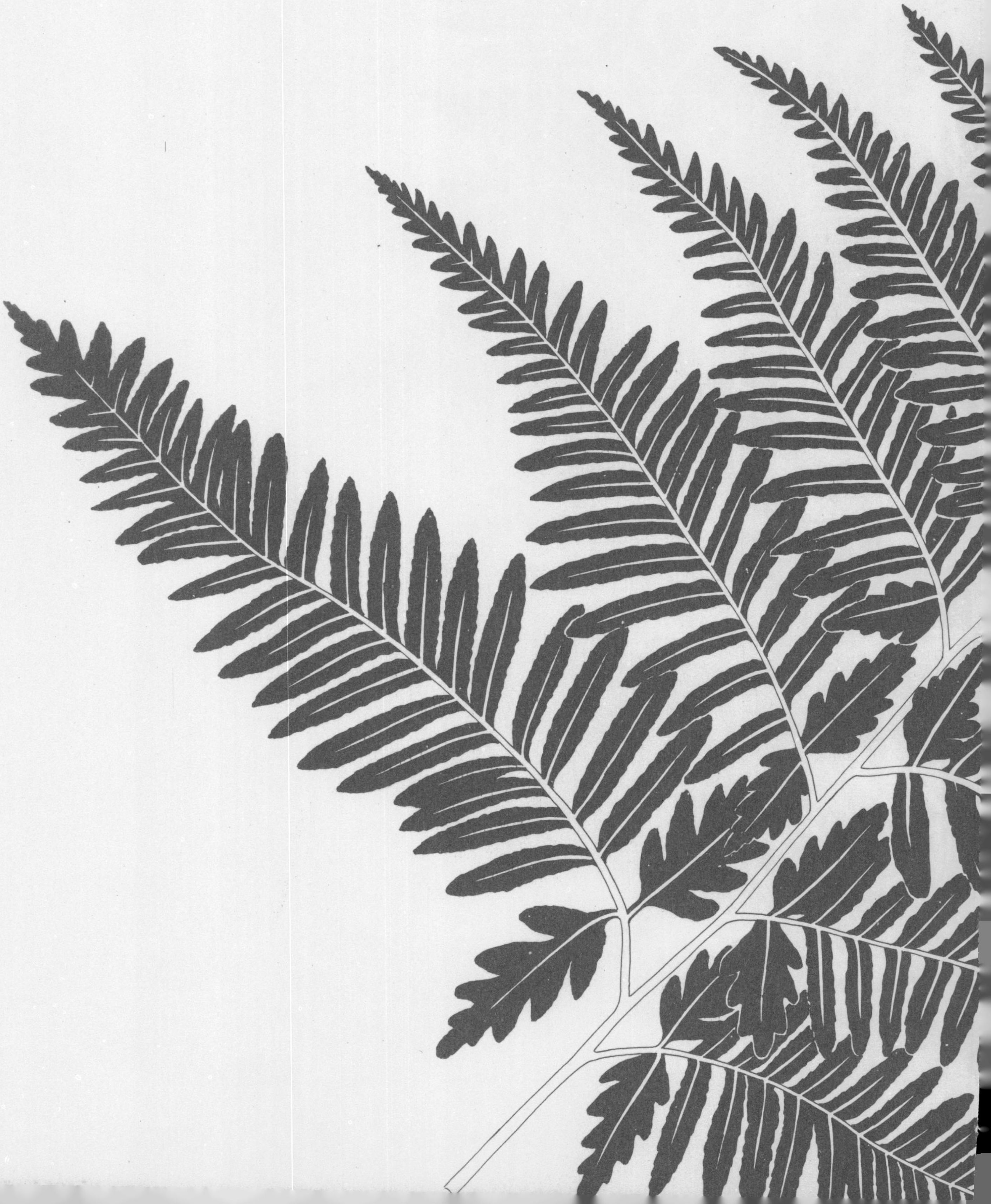